Mary P. Follett

JOAN C. TONN

Mary P. Follett

CREATING DEMOCRACY,
TRANSFORMING MANAGEMENT

Yale University Press
New Haven & London

Set in Sabon type by Keystone Typesetting, Inc.
Printed in the United States of America

Library of Congress Cataloging-in-Publication Data
Tonn, Joan C.
Mary P. Follett : creating democracy, transforming management / Joan C. Tonn.
p. cm.
Includes bibliographical references and index.
ISBN 0-300-09621-6 (hc : alk. paper)
1. Follett, Mary Parker, 1868–1933. 2. Women social reformers — United States — Biography. 3. Social reformers — United States — Biography. 4. Social structure. 5. Democracy. 6. Management. 7. Psychology, Industrial. I. Title.
HN57 .T695 2003
303.48'4'092 — dc21
2002010807

A catalogue record for this book is available from the British Library.

The paper in this book meets the guidelines for permanence and durability of the Committee on Production Guidelines for Book Longevity of the Council on Library Resources.

10 9 8 7 6 5 4 3 2 1

Frontispiece: Mary P. Follett, 1917. Reprinted from *Community Center,* June 1917, 3.

To Thomas N. Brown and JoAnn Moody
In celebration

Contents

Illustrations

Preface

The way people manage to live their lives without prior rehearsal is amazing and insufficiently wondered at. To provide such rehearsals vicariously, to extend one's range of lived experience, is one of literature's important functions, enabling us to live more fully because we have imagined more fully. That is true of biography and it is true of the novel.
— *Phyllis Rose,* Writing of Women

I was introduced to Mary Follett's work in 1969 during a graduate seminar in organizational psychology conducted by Professor Arnold Tannenbaum at the University of Michigan. As we traced the evolution of such concepts as power, control, leadership, and conflict, it became apparent that Follett had made extraordinary contributions to organizational theory and behavior. But so little was known about this early twentieth-century woman that we could only wonder how she had developed such insights into social organization and why her work seemed largely forgotten.

In 1981, as a newly tenured faculty member at the University of Massachusetts Boston, I decided to write a paper or article about some of Follett's contributions to organizational theory. I expected this to be a quite straightforward project. But I soon found myself preoccupied with questions about Follett's personal life. Who was Mary Follett? How did she develop her ideas?

And why were her views so remarkably ahead of her time? Finding it impossible to focus on my original project without at least trying to answer these questions, I decided to give myself three months to learn as much as I could about Follett. Three months turned into years.

Learning about Mary Follett was no easy matter. She had apparently destroyed most of her personal papers before moving to London in 1928, and once there she instructed her friend Dame Katherine Furse to destroy whatever papers survived her death. Follett seems to have been concerned that her papers might become the property of her brother, whom she considered unable to understand or appreciate her accomplishments. Furse, however, in a move that can be fully appreciated only by biographers, complied only partially with Follett's instructions; she allowed Lyndall Urwick, a young English admirer of Follett's work, to search the papers for material that might be suitable for publication. As a result of his intervention, several typescripts of Follett's lectures on social organization and business management were saved and published.

Over several years of investigating primary sources in the United States and the United Kingdom, I located almost 250 letters, including one set of intimate personal and professional correspondence spanning the fifteen years of Follett's most productive work. I also collected information from interviews, organizational documents, the correspondence of colleagues, genealogical histories, and medical records that explain much about Follett's life and work. Perhaps my greatest disappointment was the paucity of photographs. I was unable, for example, to find even one photograph of Isobel Briggs.

I have been fortunate throughout my work to have had the support of the Follett family. George D. Follett (now deceased) and Nancy Follett Alvord, Mary Follett's oldest nephew and niece, responded generously to my requests for help and demonstrated their confidence in countless other ways. My efforts to build a collection of papers for this biography were supported by grants from the University of Massachusetts, the Radcliffe College Research Scholars Program, the National Endowment for the Humanities Summer Stipend Program, and the Quincy (Massachusetts) Arts Council.

A wide range of private individuals, manuscript curators, and librarians have also provided essential help. Elliot M. Fox (now deceased) generously shared his own research notes. Others have been similarly forthcoming: Lincoln P. Bloomfield, Helen Blustin, Cary Carpender, James T. Dennison, Elizabeth Dunker, Edna Finn, Frank B. Gilbert, Richard Hocking, Horace Holway, Elizabeth Lindeman Leonard, Juliana C. Mulroy, Richard D. Mulroy, Ethel Page, Jeanette Peverly, Katherine B. Shurcliff, and Mrs. Charlotte Taylor.

At my own university, the staff of the Joseph P. Healey Library responded with good humor and able help. Thanks especially to Janet DiPaolo, Stephen Haas, Molly Matson, Chris Roberts, Frances Schlesinger, and Janet Stewart. At Radcliffe, Jane Knowles helped me make sense of Follett's ten-year experience as a student at the Annex and Radcliffe College and initiated me into the world of historical research with expertise and grace. The helpfulness of the staff of the Schlesinger Library and the Harvard College Archives made them especially pleasant places to work, and I am grateful to Barbara Meloni, with whose assistance I gained access to significant information about Follett's health. I also benefited from the collections of other Boston-area libraries: the Baker Library at the Harvard Business School, the Boston Athenaeum, the Boston Public Library, Brandeis University, the Harvard Law School Library, the Houghton Library at Harvard, the Massachusetts Historical Society, Simmons College, the Society for the Preservation of New England Antiquities, and Wheelock College. In Quincy, Follett's hometown, and nearby Braintree I received help from Linda Beeler, Hobart Holly, Doris Oberg, Lillian Wentworth, and Larry Yeardon. Librarians elsewhere in the United States responded graciously and ably to requests made by mail and in person. I extend particular thanks to Jerry K. Burns, Carolyn A. Davis, Elaine K. Dixon, Amy S. Doherty, Karl Kabelac, David Klaasen, Lawrence Naukam, Judith A. Schiff, and Saundra Taylor.

Numerous scholars have lent assistance at various stages: Thomas Bender, Gunther Boroschek, Constance K. Burns, Carolyn Elliott, Marlene Fine, Richard Freeland, Zelda Gamson, David Hammack, Rus Hart, Jean Humez, William R. Hutchison, Sam Jelinek, Polly Kaufmann, Monica McAlpine, Joan Moon, Ann Phillips, Mary Stevenson, David Stewart, Sharon Hartman Strom, Gillian Sutherland, Arnold Tannenbaum, and Chuck Wrege. Sara Kelly, M.D., helped me interpret medical terminology and better understand the state of Follett's health. A number of students at the College of Management participated directly in my research: Fran Amatucci, Julia Carty, Fay Lavrakas, Cathy Nadel, Anju Nagpal, Peggy Pate; thanks especially to Rebecca Marcoux.

In the United Kingdom, I was generously assisted by librarians and others, including Doreen Mortimer, Ann Phillips, Lord Asa Briggs, Sybil Oldfield, Sidney and Isabel Cabot, Robert Johnson, Thomas I. Rae, Joanna Bosanquet, Mary Ruth Tabor, and Pauline Graham. I am also grateful to Gail Thomas, the Librarian at the Henley Management College, home of the Lyndall F. Urwick Archive.

Friends were crucial. Martha and David Dill unfailingly gave the immediate and long-distance support and encouragement that are the special province of old and dear friends, and Martha read the first sixteen chapters of the manuscript. Jane and Richard Pagett listened to my frustrations, shared the excitement of unexpected discoveries, and celebrated accomplishments. Roslyn Watson helped me remember to live my own life while trying to tell the story of Mary Follett's. And, finally, I wish to thank my remarkable sister, Janice Freeman, whose acceptance and loving support form part of the foundation on which I live my life.

My dear friend and life partner, JoAnn Moody, read every word — more than once — and came to share my passion for Mary Follett. While her expert advice was priceless, JoAnn and her son, Justin, also contributed in more subtle ways — for much of this book was written, as Mary Follett might have put it, within a "total situation" of loving, trusting, and joyful family relationships.

One person more than any other was invaluable to me in the writing of this book. Thomas N. Brown, former professor of history at the University of Massachusetts Boston, offered wise counsel on matters of substance and style with intellect, enthusiasm, grace, and wit. I came to treasure each conversation.

I am grateful to Larisa Heimert of Yale University Press for the confidence she has shown in my work and for her support in bringing the manuscript to publication. Thanks also to Jenya Weinreb and to Ann Hawthorne for her superb copyediting.

Throughout this book, I refer to Mary Follett — not to Mary Parker Follett. Throughout her career, Follett referred to herself as Mary Follett, as did her friends and colleagues. In formal programs or in publications, her name was usually written as M. P. Follett or Mary P. Follett. "Parker" seems to be an affectation introduced after her death.

Introduction

More than one hundred years after the publication of her first book in 1896, Mary P. Follett (1868–1933) remains one of our preeminent thinkers about democracy and social organization. Without the benefit of modern research methods, Follett developed such original, penetrating analyses of leadership, power and authority, conflict, and group behavior that her ideas form the basis of much of our modern discourse about organizations and management. Rosabeth Moss Kanter, of the Harvard Business School, has observed that "many so-called new management ideas are previewed in Follett's work." Warren Bennis, at the University of Southern California, is even more emphatic: "Just about everything written today about leadership and organizations comes from Mary Parker Follett's writings and lectures." The continued vitality of Follett's thought is attested by the 1995 decision of the Harvard Business School Press to republish a selection of her writings, along with essays by several leading thinkers in management and organizational studies in the United States and elsewhere on the contemporary significance of Follett's writings.[1]

Follett's work has always been well known in the fields of management and public administration, but now other academic disciplines — political theory, psychology, sociology, mediation and dispute resolution, social work — are also discovering the significance of her work. Nor has Follett's influence been limited to the United States. Today her ideas are being studied in countries as diverse as Japan, Germany, Australia, Italy, France, and Peru.[2]

Despite this widespread interest, until now there has been no published biography of Follett. Thus, the question has remained unanswered: Who was this amazingly perceptive woman?

As an adult, Mary Follett was hardly captivating in physical appearance. She was tall (five feet seven or eight inches), bony, and angular. The heavy, dark brown braids of her childhood gave way in middle age to a buoyant "Gibson girl" style, but later in life she resumed her braids, woven close to her head like a tight-fitting cap. Follett paid considerable attention to her clothing, but her choice of old-fashioned styles and high-necked blouses made her appear stiff and solemn.

Yet her plainness faded as soon as she spoke. The warmth of her voice, the elegant gestures of her hands, her stylish wit, and her attentive listening were irresistible. Follett, one admirer recalled, was an "inductive worker *par excellence*." He recalled that she "would talk to anyone who cared to talk to her, and [she would] really listen. She was continuously testing her ideas against the facts brought to light as the results of these countless conversations."[3] Follett relished these exchanges because "differences of opinion, rightly welcomed and followed up, were, she believed, the food of our souls, the materials of our growth."[4] Differences, if handled collaboratively, could lead to something *new.*

A *summa cum laude* graduate of Radcliffe College, Follett continued reading history, economics, philosophy, political theory, psychology, sociology, and biology for the rest of her life. But her real passion was teasing out of these fields corresponding strands of thought that might illuminate human relationships. An erudite cross-fertilizer, she delighted in challenging distinguished academics to stretch beyond their disciplinary boundaries. At the same time, she could illuminate for any audience the most complex concepts with homely, unforgettable metaphors drawn from the minutiae of daily life.

She was hopeful and optimistic, and many who listened to Mary Follett found themselves coaxed to a larger vision of their role in society — and then inspired by her passion to a program of action. One of few not moved by her magnetism was the novelist Virginia Woolf, who met Follett at a 1932 dinner party in England. Characteristically acerbic in her diaries, Woolf described Follett as "verbose and diffuse."[5]

For thirty years Follett lived in a devoted and loving relationship with Isobel Briggs, a vibrant teacher of Shakespeare and the headmistress of a Boston private school. Two decades older than her partner, Briggs devoted herself to helping Follett flourish in her career. The two especially cherished their cottage in the mountains of Vermont, where they read books, relaxed, walked in the summer daisy fields, and shared sparkling conversation with visitors.

Follett also had "hosts of friends." She deliberately reserved time for them, and her letters were "gems of wording." Unusually for the time, "she had a gift for friendship with men at least as great as her gift for friendships with women," and she built coequal friendships with both the husband and wife, as in her relationships with Richard and Ella Cabot and Henry and Mary Dennison.[6]

Follett was a woman of "rounded culture," according to one associate, and she and Briggs were devotees of music, art, and theater in both the United States and Europe. But above all, Follett was a reader, not just of mind-stretching tomes but also of mysteries that Briggs would get for her from the Boston Athenaeum.

Patience, Follett once confided, was the only virtue she could claim. But her friends and colleagues were more likely to see her as intense, tenacious, and persistent. When a problem presented itself, she was eager to develop an action plan and was resolute about getting things accomplished. Her refusal simply to let things take their course led some to perceive her as controlling. Her penchant for analysis sometimes exasperated even her closest friends and associates. At the same time, she could be very hard on herself. One associate described her capacity for self-criticism as "infinite." In her personal life, she hardly ever gave way to impulse. If she did, one friend quipped, she felt almost sinful.[7]

A woman of great personal dignity and reserve, Follett was extremely reluctant to share with friends the fears and frustrations occasioned by a serious chronic illness that was misdiagnosed throughout her adult life. She often could tolerate only a diet of milk, potatoes, and pudding, and at times her physical suffering confined her to bed for weeks or months at a time. During one such episode, while she was writing *The New State* (1918), a doctor warned her that she might not live.

Yet live she did, until 1933. The accomplishments of her sixty-five years mark this New England thinker and doer as one of our most outstanding theorists about democracy and social organization.

Even when Follett was a young woman, it was clear to her friends and her professors that she had an extraordinary mind. With the publication of *The Speaker of the House of Representatives* (1896), her groundbreaking, controversial analysis of political power, the wider world, too, began to recognize her abilities. Reviewers compared her analysis favorably with Woodrow Wilson's

Congressional Government (1885), and Follett's book is still considered one of the most insightful and well-reasoned ever written about the U.S. Congress. Other equally brilliant works followed.

In *The New State: Group Organization, the Solution for Popular Government* (1918), Follett boldly grappled with issues of profound significance to a democratic republic whose very survival a mere half-century after the end of the Civil War was still in doubt. Democracy, Follett contended in *The New State,* should be "a genuine union of true individuals," but this sort of union had never existed in America. To attain it, Follett argued, we must "leap at once from the region of theory, of which Americans are so fond, to a practical scheme of living . . . it is not merely that we must be allowed to govern ourselves, we must learn how to govern ourselves; it is not only that we must be given 'free speech,' we must learn a speech that is free; we are not given rights, we create rights; it is not only that we must invent machinery to get a social will expressed, we must invent machinery that will get a social will created."[8] To replace a mythical democracy with the actual workings of one, the American people would have to "find a new principle of association." In elucidating that principle, Follett wrestled with issues that continue to resonate in our national life: how to create continually a common purpose or "collective will"; how to accommodate our need for collective control while preserving our individual freedoms; how to cherish our differences and, at the same time, integrate them; how to develop leaders that empower us rather than dominate us.

The New State, according to Benjamin R. Barber, is "an American classic of participatory democracy." And Jane Mansbridge praises Follett's recognition that democracy depends on *local* democratic processes and institutions, as well as her "insistence that the associations on which democracy should be based can maintain difference within unity, conflict within integration."[9]

Creative Experience (1924), Follett's last book, was written following almost two years of service on minimum wage boards in Massachusetts—an experience that whetted her appetite for further group studies. Now, more than ever, she felt certain that the future of American social, political, and economic life depended on the working out of a new kind of group process. Surveying current efforts to resolve conflict in groups, Follett found jurists and economists too enamored of an "equilibrium" of interests, political scientists too enthralled with a "balance" of power, and ethicists too committed to "compromise."[10] Follett rejected compromise because it sacrificed the integrity of the individual, and she saw little to recommend the balancing of interests and power, as these tactics merely rearranged what already exists.

A more promising route to "constructive" conflict seemed to Follett to lie in the eclectic reconceptualization of behaviorism offered by Harvard philosopher and psychologist Edwin B. Holt and the emerging research and theorizing of the German Gestaltists. Their work had demonstrated that behavior is a function of the interplay between a continually changing organism and the environment, which produces an evolving situation. Seeing our behavior and ideas as a product of this dynamic interplay, she deemed it unrealistic to expect that differences could be harmonized solely by intellectual activity. The successful resolution of conflict, instead, depends on changing behaviors — on engaging conflicting parties in activities that, over time, create a new situation in which their differences actually can be integrated. If we were to adopt this sort of nonhierarchical integrating as our primary mode of human association, it would have profound implications, Follett argued, not only for our understanding of the origin and exercise of power, but also for the dynamics of governing expressed in "the will of the people," "the consent of the governed," and "representation," and for the functions served by the legal system in a democratic society.

The New State and *Creative Experience* were informed by insights gained from twenty years of civic and professional work in Boston's immigrant neighborhoods. Through projects developed for the Boston Equal Suffrage Association for Good Government and the Women's Municipal League of Boston, Follett honed her formidable entrepreneurial, political, managerial, and fundraising skills and became an inspiring mentor to a new generation of Boston civic leaders. Dissatisfied with the efforts of the neighborhood settlements and the public schools to foster community, Follett slowly evolved a new approach to preparing Boston's newest citizens for their civic responsibilities: she created organizations in which they could govern their own activities and, thereby, prepare for participation in democratic government.

Follett's efforts, however, stirred controversy. Moving beyond the concept of the settlement (the model of reform to which many women were deeply committed) engendered suspicion and a certain amount of ill will. Urging that some of the limited resources of her suffrage organization be used in civic reform infuriated those who were single-mindedly pursuing the right to vote. Focusing on neighborhoods conflicted with the trend to centralize municipal and school government. Involving laypeople in civic education threatened the status of the new professional educators. And preparing citizens to make up their own minds about local issues undercut the power of the ward bosses. Follett, however, was at her best in complex, difficult situations; her efforts brought about the establishment of locally run community centers in virtually every neighborhood of Boston and, at the same time, contributed significantly to the organization of a national movement promoting community life.

Business leaders with whom she had worked in these civic endeavors urged her to apply her ideas about group association, leadership, power, and conflict resolution to the management of their own increasingly large and multifaceted business organizations. Follett soon became intrigued with the vast opportunities that business management presented for experimenting with more group-oriented and egalitarian forms of social relationships. She was particularly enthusiastic about the efforts of businessmen such as Edward and Lincoln Filene, Henry Dennison, and B. Seebohm Rowntree to involve their employees in new forms of organizational control. "Business, because it gives us the opportunity of trying new roads, of blazing new trails, because, in short, it is pioneer work, pioneer work in the organized relations of human beings, seems to me," Follett told one business audience, "to offer as thrilling an experience as going into a new country and building railroads over new mountains." Solving problems in business management "may help toward the solution of world problems, since the principles of organization and administration which are discovered as best for business can be applied to government or international relations. Indeed, the solution of world problems must eventually be built up from all the little bits of experience wherever people are consciously trying to solve problems of relations. And this attempt is being made more consciously and deliberately in industry than anywhere else."[11]

In these and other endeavors, Follett was not one to shrink from high-powered intellectual exchanges. At various times in her professional life, she visited or corresponded with such notable public figures as Roscoe Pound, Walter Lippmann, Harold Laski, Viscount R. B. Haldane, Bernard Bosanquet, and leaders of the English pluralist movement. Follett spoke at Harvard and Syracuse Universities, the Taylor Society (later to become the Society for the Advancement of Management), the Rowntree Conference at Oxford University, the Bureau of Personnel Administration in New York (which sponsored the country's first executive development seminars), the American Historical Association, the American Philosophical Association, the Ford Hall Forum (the renowned public lecture series in Boston), and elsewhere. In these appearances, she more than held her own with deans and faculty in business and public affairs, heads of corporations, business consultants, and intellectuals of every stripe — from the philosopher Alfred North Whitehead to the industrial psychologist Elton Mayo.

Nothing would have pleased Follett more than knowing that her ideas have helped shape the continuing search for effective ways of organizing human relations. "I hope . . . there is nothing in what I have said that sounds dogmatic," Follett said in one of her last lectures. "I am not so much urging you to admit the principles that I have put before you as suggesting that you should try them out and decide for yourselves. I am urging that we should all of us take a conscious and responsible attitude toward our experience."[12]

A Childhood That Was Rarely Happy

A few days before her death, Mary Follett read the memoir that her friend Ella Lyman Cabot had written about her own family of origin, the Lymans. The memoir was a portrait of Victorian gentility and grace, where family life was "remote from the world, where all was gentleness, low sounds, headaches, family love, prayers, little jokes, New England economies; where her father read Plato to her mother and brought midwinter violets and camellias from the Waltham greenhouse . . . where everyone loved her . . . where her little sisters planted kisses on all the empty chairs at breakfast to be ready for their occupants." Such childhood memories must have presented a sharp contrast with Mary's own. In a note written to Ella from her hospital bed, Mary confessed: "These are the people I care most for, the people of that period. I hope there is a special Victorian Heaven & that I shall go there. I am sure that is my spiritual home."[1]

Mary Follett's mother, Elizabeth Curtis Baxter, was among the seventh generation of Baxters born in America. Gregory Baxter had fled religious persecution in England in 1630 and helped found Boston. As land around the original settlement grew scarce, Boston annexed a large area a few miles to the south, where settlers were allowed to purchase four acres per family member at a favorable price. In 1639 Gregory Baxter, then a freeman of the Massachusetts Bay Colony, settled his family near a coastal inlet on Quincy Point.[2]

From the beginning the Baxter men were involved in town government, serving in posts such as town moderator, selectman, surveyor of highways, and tithingsman. The first four generations were farmers, but in the mid-1700s one of the men worked as a clothier. His sudden death from lockjaw compelled his widow to support their eight children by running a small store. One of her sons became a butcher, the trade from which his son Daniel would make his fortune.

Daniel Baxter, Mary Follett's maternal grandfather, was extolled in his obituary as "an example of what industry, common sense and care will do for any one in the battle of life."[3] Born in 1803, he attended school for only three winter terms; he spent his youth helping his father deliver meats to other South Shore communities. At age twenty-one he opened his own business, traveling almost fifteen miles to the markets in Brighton, west of Boston, to purchase cattle for butchering.

Baxter was one of a number of tradesmen and merchants who were seeking to profit from Quincy's growing population and expanding industrial base. From colonial days the town had been noted for shipbuilding and had experienced some success in fishing, but by the early 1800s the manufacture of boots and shoes had become the major factor in the local economy. Quincy was also acquiring a reputation as "the Granite City." Solomon Willard, a self-taught architect, had proposed using Quincy granite to build the Bunker Hill Monument in Charlestown and had devised several inventions that made it possible to remove from the quarries enormous blocks of rock. The granite was to be transported from the quarry site to Charlestown, almost twenty miles north, by means of a railway to the Neponset River. The "Boston granite" building style grew in popularity, and the Granite Railway became the first link in a system transporting Quincy granite to retailers all across the country. Several quarries were opened, and the population of immigrant quarrymen and stonecutters increased dramatically.[4]

During this industrial transformation, twenty-six-year-old Daniel Baxter married Abigail Curtis, who was not yet quite seventeen, and set up housekeeping in Quincy Point. The marriage was a fortunate match for Baxter: his father-in-law, Noah Curtis, owned a large factory for the making of boots and shoes and, having been regularly elected to significant offices in town and church government, was an esteemed figure in the community. The newlyweds' first child was born in 1829, less than seven months after their marriage, and twelve others followed in rapid succession. By 1841, when Elizabeth

Curtis Baxter arrived, sixth among the four boys and six girls who survived childhood, Daniel had moved his family up from Washington Street on Quincy Point to the home of his deceased father on School Street. Nearer the new center of town, this site also had land available for expansion of the Baxter store.

Throughout Lizzie's childhood and adolescence, her father's wealth and social standing grew. No longer just a butcher, Baxter advertised "English and West India goods and groceries, also, beef, pork, and provisions, of all kinds, at wholesale and retail." More significantly, Baxter invested his savings. In 1836 he became the youngest of the incorporators of the Quincy Stone Bank, the first commercial bank in town and the first in the United States to be capitalized through public subscription of its stock. Less than ten years later, Baxter was named a director of the new Quincy Savings Bank and served in that position for twenty years. In another venture, he joined other "active and substantial citizens" in organizing the Quincy Mutual Fire Insurance Company. As each of these organizations thrived, their founders' wealth grew. Baxter invested his earnings in real estate and became such a substantial land-owner that his property tax payments were overshadowed only by those of "Quincy's royalty," Charles Francis Adams and the Adams family estate.[5]

A prudent and cautious man, Baxter believed in conducting public affairs as he would his own business, "owing no man anything."[6] Local citizens respected this conservative philosophy and repeatedly elected or appointed him to positions of honor and trust in the community. He served on the Board of Selectmen for fourteen years and was chairman over half the time; he also served at various times as assessor, school committee member, surveyor of highways, and overseer of the poor. In 1858, when Lizzie was seventeen and the family's last child was born, Daniel Baxter — in a rare public display of his wealth — moved his father's house off the School Street site and built in its place a handsome Greek Revival house.

George Follett, Mary's paternal grandfather, failed to match Daniel Baxter in financial success and social respectability. Follett, the son of a Worcester, Massachusetts, farm laborer, was one of numerous blacksmiths who came to Quincy in the early 1800s to do iron and metals work for local industries.[7] By 1825, a year after Daniel Baxter opened his own business, George Follett was doing well enough to marry Betsey Hobart, a daughter of a respected local boot manufacturer. However, unlike Baxter, who transformed himself from a butcher into a merchant, financier, and landowner, George Follett remained a blacksmith all his life. The tools in his small blacksmith shop were his only personal property until he inherited the house of his wife's parents. At his death in 1877, Follett's estate amounted to only $1,400, in contrast to Baxter's $350,000.

The Folletts had three daughters and three sons who survived to adulthood. George Dexter and William Hayward, the older boys, worked as painters, a fairly secure trade given Quincy's building boom. Charles Allen, who would become Mary Follett's father, was born in 1841. He worked for a time as a machinist, no doubt drawing on what he had learned in his father's blacksmith shop. But Charles Allen Follett's life would be irrevocably changed by the onset of the Civil War.

The dramatic impact of the early days of the war on the inhabitants of Quincy was recorded by Charles Francis Adams. Thirty young men answered the first call for volunteers in April 1861, forming a unit called the Hancock Light Guard; less than two months later, one of them, Frederick Souther, was mortally wounded in the unit's first engagement of the war.[8] In mid-June, almost immediately after the news of Souther's death reached Quincy, Charles Follett, then barely nineteen, rushed to join the cause, enlisting in the 12th Massachusetts Regiment, which was forming at Fort Warren in Boston Harbor. A few days later, perhaps learning that his experience as a machinist was needed in the artillery, he received a discharge so that he could enlist in the First Battery of the Light Artillery of the Massachusetts Volunteer Militia. Charles and his twenty-five-year-old brother, William, signed on for three months, a term that most observers, in those early optimistic days of the war, believed would be sufficient to quell the southern rebellion. But the stunning defeat in late July by the Confederates at Bull Run dispelled any notions of an early victory. As a result, when the Follett brothers' original enlistments expired in September, they signed on for three years, this time in the Third Battery, a unit raised and initially commanded by their cousin, Dexter H. Follett, of Boston. In recognition of their prior service, William was appointed to the rank of sergeant, and Charles was named a corporal.[9]

Though finely equipped and dressed in uniforms made to order, the officers and men of the Third Battery required several months of training before being placed in service in the spring of 1862 as part of the Northern Virginia Peninsular Campaign, an effort to win Richmond. The campaign failed, and the army withdrew after a month's siege against Yorktown, a tactic that one soldier described as "throwing away life needlessly . . . about as foolish as throwing a handful of beans at the side of a brick house, expecting to demolish it." The Third Battery lost five men. Six weeks later, on May 27, it suffered additional casualties at the Hanover Court House in a battle that would come to have special significance for Charles Follett. During the battle, his unit abandoned its guns; and four days later, presumably because he had failed to demonstrate the kind of leadership the situation demanded, Charles's rank was reduced from corporal to private.[10]

Throughout the summer the Third Battery periodically participated in serious engagements, and closed the year at Fredericksburg, the battle called by some the "most useless slaughter of the Civil War." Here the Union infantry, in full view of the battery, made six frontal assaults across a bare plain on the entrenched Confederate artillery and infantry; hurled back each time, the Union forces lost almost 13,000 men.[11] Throughout these campaigns William Follett displayed "soldierly bearing and bravery," gaining a commission as second lieutenant and, early in 1863, an assignment to brigade headquarters; in June 1863, perhaps through William's influence, Charles was assigned there, too, just in time to witness the furious but unsuccessful Confederate assaults against the massed Union artillery defenses at Gettysburg. The brigade was inactive for the remainder of the year, but in late November William, while on detached duty with an ordnance train, was captured by Confederate cavalry. Taken first to the infamous Libby Prison and moved several times during his eighteen-month imprisonment, his health was irreparably damaged.[12]

News of William's capture arrived at almost the same time as the government's offer of a bonus for men who would reenlist in the field. Charles extended his commitment through the end of 1866 and performed well enough to merit promotion to corporal. In May 1864 he returned to the front lines and a month later replaced the battery's mortally wounded best gunner. He assumed his new role just as the battery was beginning two months of incessant cannonading of the Confederate fortress at Petersburg and preparing a defense of the Weldon Railroad. Throughout this period Charles kept a diary, in which he reported the weather and casualties with equal dispassion. Cryptic and prosaic, Follett's diary contains no grand reflections on either his own future or the future of the nation; it is simply a record of one young man's effort to persevere in his fourth year of war.[13]

By the time Charles was mustered out in June 1865, his brother had already returned to Quincy. Soon thereafter the town mobilized to honor all its young volunteers. Daniel Baxter, whose nineteen-year-old son had been one of the earliest volunteers, chaired a committee to prepare a proposal for building a soldiers' monument and, a year later, served on a five-man committee charged with overseeing the expenditure of funds. Mrs. Baxter and her daughters, Lizzie and Mary, contributed money to "The Lincoln Fund" for the assassinated president's widow.[14]

The Follett brothers' war records were hardly unusual: nearly a thousand Quincy men had served in the Union forces, and more than a hundred had lost their lives. However, the fact that the Folletts not only had volunteered but had done so at the beginning of the conflict contrasted sharply with the machinations of those who had paid bounties in order to avoid military service. Since strength of character was far more important to a self-made man like Daniel Baxter than property or social standing, the Follett brothers' display of will and determination must have had a positive effect on his decision to allow his daughter Lizzie to marry Charles. In addition, Baxter was probably encouraged by William's successful readjustment to civilian life. He had married a popular local schoolteacher, Lydia Averill (who years later would be a positive role model for Mary Follett), fathered a son, and found a good job in Boston. Finally, Baxter surely was conscious of Lizzie's age; already twenty-six and the oldest daughter still at home, she soon would no longer be "marriageable." And so, on December 4, 1867, in the Unitarian First Parish Church of the Presidents, where the influential Daniel Baxter owned two pews, Elizabeth Curtis Baxter married Charles Allen Follett.

At first their future looked bright. Quincy's economy was booming; only sixty-six farms remained in this rapidly growing town of 6,700. Ten working granite quarries and twenty-two other industries created numerous opportunities for Charles to return to his prewar job as a machinist, but instead he ventured a step up the social ladder, opening a small "news depot" in a shop next to the post office. From this location in Quincy Square, he delivered newspapers and magazines, sold books and stationery, and ran a small circulating library. Later that year the town selectmen demonstrated their confidence in his prospects by appointing him one of ten local police officers. But Charles soon began having difficulty adjusting to his new responsibilities. In August 1868 the "proprietor of the periodical room," was reported to have dislocated his elbow while wrestling with one of the young merchants in the square. Nine months later, when Charles sold his interest in the store to E. B. Souther, the editor of the local newspaper wrote that the community would be "gratified to learn" of the sale, implying that the new owner would be an improvement over the old.[15]

Charles Follett was a tall, slight, handsome young man, his light blue eyes complemented by a sandy complexion and his brown hair tinged with red. In a photograph of him in his war uniform, however, his eyes are opaque and his gaze indirect, creating an impression of languidness or even melancholy — a state possibly induced by extended war service. The troops on both sides of the conflict were hardly more than boys when the war began, and many were away from home for the first time. Conditions were deplorable: the average soldier was sick enough from typhoid, dysentery, "fevers," or tuberculosis to require hospitalization in primitive and unsanitary facilities two or even three times a year; in hospitals such as these, more than twice as many men died from disease as were killed in action. Many men could tolerate this continual threat of illness, the exhausting "mud marches," the extremes of heat and cold, and the long periods of tedium broken by horror and fear only if they dulled their senses with whiskey. The army allowed the soldiers one ration of whiskey per day and the officers any quantity, as long as they paid for it; but the hoped-for relief was elusive. The commissary officer for the Third Battery observed that "those who made free use of [whiskey] were much oftener in the hospital, and on the sick-list, than those who did not drink." In addition, the soldiers' drinking created new problems, including brawls occasionally serious enough to be labeled "whiskey riots."[16]

When Charles returned home, he found whiskey even more available than it had been in the army. Quincy had numerous licensed and unlicensed purveyors of liquor. Some of the local Yankees contended that the town's intemperance was a result of the influx of foreign immigrants, but wiser folk knew that Quincy had had a reputation as a "rum town" as early as John Adams' day. By the end of the war, the liquor interests had grown so strong that Quincy had become their "liquor-selling centre"; the dealers bought the support of Democratic politicians, who could deliver the votes of Quincy's Irish immigrants on licensing questions.[17]

It is impossible to be certain whether drinking was the sole or even primary cause of Charles Follett's business failure; after all, he was a man of modest education and was totally inexperienced as a merchant. He might have responded to the failure of his periodical business by reverting to his original trade as a machinist had not his older brother come to his aid. Since the end of the war, William had been working in Boston as a clerk in a metals importing and wire manufacturing firm owned by Dexter H. Follett, the cousin whose artillery battery the brothers had joined during the war; soon Charles had a job as a clerk at Farrar, Follett & Company, too, and commuted there each day with William via the Old Colony Railway.

During these early years of their marriage, Charles and Lizzie lived in houses owned by Lizzie's father. The first was located beyond the Baxters' house on School Street near the main road to the quarries, about a fifteen-minute walk from Quincy Square. This small frame house was probably where Mary Parker Follett, their first child, was born on September 3, 1868.[18] Shortly thereafter the family moved to a larger house on Quincy Avenue, the southern residential extension of the main business thoroughfare. But Charles did not stay there long. By the spring of 1870, the tuberculosis that William Follett had contracted in the Confederate prison camps forced him to stop working; within a year he was dead. The impact on Charles was profound: not only did he leave his job at Farrar & Follett, he also left his wife and three-year-old daughter, moving alone into Boston. William's death almost certainly contributed to Charles's drinking, and liquor was easily available on his commute to Boston. Another man described the dangers: "In Boston you get out at the Old Colony depot and you see nothing but rum-shops. I used to pass by them and refuse one or two invitations, but the third would fetch me sure . . . Rum has made a beggar of me, gentlemen, just as true as you're born."[19]

Having grown up in a home where the father was not only successful but also predictable and dependable, Lizzie could not have been emotionally prepared for her husband's lack of direction and inability to hold a job. Nor was she prepared to provide for herself. Women of Lizzie's social class, influenced by the popular magazines and newspapers that preached a gospel of "true womanhood," aspired to the life of "piety, purity and domesticity" characteristic of ladies of leisure rather than to formal education. Although her father was willing and able to come to her rescue, her increasingly desperate situation must have been deeply embarrassing; her older sisters' husbands had become successful businessmen and esteemed citizens while Lizzie's was becoming a caricature of a drunken Irishman. Nevertheless, as "a true woman," Lizzie was expected to submit to fortune: "Always conciliate" and "Do not expect too much" were the prescribed "Rules for Conjugal and Domestic Happiness."[20]

After leaving his family, Charles took a job as a painter, the occupation that his oldest brother, George Dexter, had pursued for many years before moving to Boston after the war to open a restaurant.[21] By 1872, however, George, who was thirteen years older than Charles, had stopped working altogether, probably as a result of the combination of heart disease and mental illness that would later lead to his death. Charles replaced George in the restaurant and gradually regained his equilibrium. After an absence of almost a year, he rejoined his wife and daughter in the house on Quincy Avenue, and soon thereafter, the Follett's second daughter, Annie Wood, was born. She lived only four months, dying abruptly of cholera.[22] As an adult, Mary was enormously reticent about her feelings and reluctant to discuss either her family or childhood, but many years later she may have referred obliquely to Annie's death as she tried to console friends who were fearful about their daughter's slow recovery from an illness: "Please tell Mrs. L. how deeply I sympathize with her . . . One of the saddest experiences of my life was distress and anxiety over a child's illness."[23]

At the time of Annie's death, Mary was too young to fully comprehend the loss, and she probably responded by seeking reassurance from her parents. Sadly, just at this time Mary was again abandoned by her father. Perhaps Charles blamed himself for Annie's death. Although physicians generally accepted the idea that cholera was the result of "having imbibed some quantity of a specific poison," and they knew that cholera could strike the wealthy as well as the poor, most people thought much along the lines of a contemporary article in the *New York Times:* "It is the curse of the dirty, the intemperate, and the degraded." And Annie's father not only had been "intemperate" but also had exposed the family to the filth and diseases of the city by continuing to work in Boston.[24]

When Charles left his family this time, George Follett was so disturbed by his thirty-four-year-old son's increasingly unseemly behavior that late in 1875 he had his will drawn so that the money Charles was to receive would be placed in a trust rather than being awarded to him outright; only the interest and one-quarter of the principal could be drawn each year until the fund was exhausted.[25] The following year, just at this lowest ebb in Charles's reputation, Dr. Henry A. Reynolds, a "reformed inebriate" from Maine, appeared in Quincy to deliver a temperance lecture at the Town Hall. No one could have anticipated the outcome. Quincy's liquor interests had easily weathered every reform effort, including those mounted by a local resident, Henry H. Faxon, a wealthy, voluble, and determined foe and the best-known temperance leader in the state.[26] The citizens of Quincy were a difficult audience for temperance orators to impress. This time, however, those crowded into the hall gave the speaker their attention.

In a style reminiscent of the methods of Alcoholics Anonymous, Reynolds abjured the temptation to preach to his audience, instead confiding in them by "telling what he had suffered, and how near he had come to the drunkard's grave." Begging the addicted to accept his help, Reynolds said that "he pitied those who had fallen victims to the cup, and called them his brothers; and offered to do anything he could to aid and assist them in removing the demon from them." In closing, he invited those addicted to drink "to come up and sign the pledge." The response was astonishing; before the evening was over, more than a hundred men had signed a pledge admitting that they had "drunk intoxicating liquors to excess" and vowing never to drink again. The exhilaration of that evening persisted the next day. An afternoon session "for men only" culminated in the establishment of a Reform Club, and the new members' zeal was so inspiring that hundreds trying to get into the town hall for Dr. Reynolds' evening lecture spilled over into a second session in the nearby Orthodox church. That evening, two hundred men were moved to sign the pledge, and by the end of the week, when the names of all the signers were printed in the local newspaper, Charles Follett's name was among them.[27]

3

"An Eager, Fearless Mind"

Virtually all of Mary Follett's friends learned about her early years from the few fragments of experience she chose to share — incidents that must have evoked images of a somber, lonely childhood, since they came to believe that she "missed much that other children had." The villain of the piece was not her father, who was described as deeply religious and devoted to his daughter, but her mother, who was seen as incompetent, demanding, and "alien" to Mary's interests.[1] Mary seems to have reacted to the unpredictability of her father's behavior as children of alcoholics often do: she was forced to grow up quickly and had little contact with other children until adolescence. She also displayed an early resolve to take control of her own life by excelling in the forum most accessible to her — her own education.[2]

Mary might ordinarily have begun her education in Quincy's public school system, but just at the time she was old enough to attend, the schools were under intense scrutiny. The size of the system had increased dramatically under the pressure of the growing immigrant population, and "the annual cost to the town of educating each child . . . had increased during [the previous decade] from six to fifteen dollars." Most people believed that the quality of the children's education over the same period had shown no "perceptible improvement." Frustrated, the Quincy school committee, whose members in these years included both John Quincy Adams and his brother, Charles Francis Adams, decided in 1873 to test the quality of instruction by conducting the yearly examinations of students themselves. The results were shocking: students could recite from memory sophisticated rules of grammar but could not write even an ordinary letter; they could give wonderfully dramatic readings from pieces with which they were familiar, but were simply bewildered when asked to read material that was new. Convinced that the old pedagogies of memorization and recitation were inadequate, the committee "went to work to remedy matters," but, as Charles Francis Adams admitted, "they succeeded only in destroying the old system, without developing a new one."[3]

Fortunately, Quincy's private schools provided a ready alternative to the archaic and chaotic public system. The Adams Academy, established in 1872 according to terms set in John Adams' bequest to the town, was designed to prepare boys thirteen years and older for the "best American colleges." Another school established that year, by contrast, had as its mission providing girls and boys of any age with a "practical" education. This Greenleaf Street School was supervised by the beloved and esteemed minister of the Baxter family's church. In announcing the opening of the school, the Reverend John D. Wells assured parents that "whatever undoubted advantage is to be gained from the study of Latin, the Higher Mathematics, and other branches ordinarily pursued in Latin and High Schools, I deem it of the utmost importance to lay a sure foundation in the elementary practical studies . . . Such a training alone is no mean preparation for many of the active pursuits of life." The Greenleaf School, therefore, offered instruction in subjects entirely appropriate to a young girl of Mary's social station: "Reading, Writing, Spelling, Arithmetic, Geography, Drawing, Grammar, French, History, Singing, Composition, General Science, Sewing."[4] It almost certainly was here that four-year-old Mary Follett began her education.

The intelligence that Mary demonstrated early in her education "was a great source of pride to her father," who, as Mary later recalled, "show[ed] her off to his friends by making her do mental arithmetic." Charles's abstinence brought greater stability to the household, but a certain amount of damage had already been done. Her father's unpredictable behavior coupled with the abrupt death of her infant sister had made it difficult for Mary to trust, and that distrust would later manifest itself in a deep ambivalence about intimacy and a need to control personal relationships. And now, with her father's return following so closely on her first scholastic achievements, any childhood fantasies Mary might have had that her own earlier deficiencies or misbehavior had caused him to leave may have been reinforced. If she felt loved for what she did rather than for herself, the pressure to perform would have been unremitting.[5]

For almost three years after Charles rejoined his family in 1876, the Folletts took in boarders at their house on Quincy Avenue — apparently an idea that had evolved through Charles's work at his brother's Boston restaurant and then at an inn near the mental hospital where George was probably taken before he died. The presence of three male boarders in her home must have been a trying experience for Lizzie. Not only was she required to do a kind of domestic work for which she surely felt unsuited, but the boarders also posed a threat to the family's already precarious social standing. By the 1880s family boarding had become "identified exclusively (if erroneously) as a lower-class practice" and had lost "its middle-class respectability."[6]

Matters were made worse by the fact that family boarding didn't pay very well. Charles was forced to seek a job with regular wages and found himself back in the boot and shoe industry, where he had worked before the war. Still, he was lucky to have the job. Just about this time, the Quincy boot and shoe industry was beginning its decline, and Charles probably acquired his position only because the factory was owned by Lizzie's relatives. Hired as a boot cutter, Charles's annual wages must have been about six hundred dollars; since the Folletts had only one child, Charles's wages surely covered their basic expenses, but the "numerous other little things" were easier to secure with the supplementary income from the boarders. In return, the family had to endure a loss of privacy and, after the birth of Mary's brother, George Dexter, late in 1877, cramped living conditions. Relief finally appeared in 1879 when Lizzie's mother died, leaving seventy-six-year-old Daniel Baxter with only a son and a soon-to-be-married daughter living at home. Needing a woman to run the household, Baxter invited Lizzie and her family to join him in the big School Street house.[7]

School Street was one of the most impressive in Quincy. The south side had been considerably spruced up by the removal of the few remaining boot shops and the addition of an ornate iron fence to the grounds of the stately Catholic church. And the open highland area adjacent to the north side was dotted with grand homes all the way from Hancock to Franklin Street, where the Baxter house stood. The graceful curving lines of the Edwards house, perhaps the most splendid on the street, featured a gambrel roof that ended in flaring Flemish eaves, while Dr. Stetson's house next door featured many details typical of Greek Revival "cottages" of the period. The Patrick McDonnell house, an imposing three-story structure that belonged to an Irish immigrant who had built his fortune in Quincy's granite business, was situated next to the seven-acre Baxter estate. Daniel Baxter's house, also built in the popular Greek Revival style, was considerably grander than Dr. Stetson's cottage up the street. The three-story center section was oriented to the street like the traditional American gable house, allowing a wing to be appended on the left and a subsidiary servants' wing at the rear. The house gained much of its dignity and grandeur from the four stately Ionic columns that rose to the top of the two-story front portico.[8]

At one time, the house and grounds had been cared for by servants and hired hands, but in the 1880s family members did the work, presumably as a way of "paying for their keep." The Folletts may not have found life in the Baxter house luxurious, but it surely was more comfortable than their house on Quincy Street. The move seems to have been particularly good for Mary's father. Charles became increasingly active in the Paul Revere Post of the Grand Army of the Republic and helped to found the Granite Temple of Honor, a local branch of a temperance organization; he was elected to positions of leadership in both organizations and used these offices to coordinate charitable events for families of Civil War veterans and to speak publicly on behalf of temperance. In his comrades' eyes, he was "always cheerful, always ready to respond to the call for assistance . . . [having] sympathy for every sorrowing heart, and alms for every needy soldier."[9]

Almost immediately after the Folletts moved to the School Street house, Mary took the next step in her education. A new private academy had recently opened a few miles southwest of Quincy. The benefactor of the Thayer Academy, General Sylvanus Thayer, had been superintendent of the United States Military Academy at West Point for sixteen years before taking command of the Army Corps of Engineers; as chief engineer in charge of constructing fortifications on the eastern coast of the United States, he handled large sums of money and was in a position to benefit from "the custom which allowed army officers a commission on all disbursements." Although Thayer did not approve of this practice and refused all commissions due him, he learned that the funds would "become a part of his estate regardless of his acceptance." Since he had already provided his alma mater, Dartmouth College, with the Thayer School of Engineering, General Thayer decided to use the disbursement commissions to found an academy that would improve secondary education in his hometown. He instructed the executors of his will to admit free of charge any qualified student who was a resident of Old Braintree, a designation that included the town of Quincy, but left the academy trustees free to decide whether to accept girls as well as boys. Fortunately for Mary Follett, the trustees decided in favor of the girls.[10]

From the beginning, Thayer Academy offered both a college preparatory course and a general course, the latter being intended "to lay substantial foundations for business pursuits for young men, and prepare young women for the preliminary and first advanced Examinations for Women at Harvard University." While the college course emphasized classical studies, the four-year general course divided students' recitation hours almost evenly among seven areas of study: English literature, history (Roman and English), Latin, modern languages (French and German), mathematics (algebra, geometry, and plane trigonometry), the sciences (physics, botany, astronomy, geology, chemistry), and a category of miscellaneous subjects that included mental science, rhetoric, theory and practice of accounts, drawing, and vocal music. After only six years, the two courses of study were deemed so successful that Thayer administrators could boast that "the Academy has sent [young men] to Yale, Harvard, Amherst, Williams, and Bowdoin . . . [and] several young women have successfully passed the examination for admission to Harvard." There was no need to mention that these young women could not actually attend Harvard classes; the merely symbolic nature of the Harvard examination for women was well understood. The Academy seemed to acknowledge the limited collegiate opportunities available to women in 1883 when it began an explicit effort to recruit those women who had less grandiose aspirations; according to its revised statement of purpose, the general course was to provide a "good English education such as . . . a woman fitted both for intelligent society and the duties of a refined home would require."[11]

Both the general and college courses, however, were expressly designed to be more advanced than those generally found in high schools in eastern Massachusetts. Academy officials therefore advised potential students to spend a year or two in their local high schools before seeking admission. The demanding nature of the curriculum also led the trustees to specify that "candidates for admission must not be under the age of thirteen years," a policy they apparently adhered to, since students entering in the first four classes were, on average, more than fifteen years of age. In June 1880, however, eleven-year-old Mary Follett appeared with forty-three other candidates to be examined for admission to the academy. She performed well enough in "reading, writing, spelling, English grammar, arithmetic, geography, and history of the United States" to be one of the twenty candidates admitted. The new students would find the curriculum as difficult as advertised: of the twenty-one pupils enrolling in September 1880, only eight completed their full course of study and graduated.[12]

Mary quickly sensed that she had to approach this opportunity as though her whole future depended on it. One indication of her seriousness of purpose appears in an incident concerning her name, or more precisely, her childhood nickname, "Minnie." In those days many young girls were given nicknames, and the editor of the local newspaper was troubled by the girls' increasing reluctance to relinquish these names as they grew older. Scanning the list of names of young women who had recently been examined for admission to the teachers' college, the editor was appalled to find names more appropriate "to mere household pets rather than to young women who are approaching maturity and who are engaged in serious work" and published a front-page article condemning the practice. "Minnie" was one of the diminutives singled out for attention, and the editor urged those using this particular nickname to return to "Mary," a name "much more euphonious and dignified" and more appropriate for a time "when women are contending for higher consideration as rational beings, and when the range of their occupation outside of the domestic circle is constantly widening and growing in importance." A few months before this article appeared, the names of the candidates successfully completing the June 1880 examinations for Thayer Academy were added to the Admissions Book; Mary's name appears there as "Minnie Parker Follett." However, after the publication of the editor's admonition, Mary apparently regretted having used her nickname at the exam: her entry was changed, and thereafter Minnie Parker Follett was known by the "more euphonious and dignified" appellation Mary.[13]

Mary's seriousness about her education paid dividends. She completed the course of study almost exactly as it had been prescribed, falling behind only in the first term of her third year, when "weak eyes" made it necessary for her to drop English literature and then German; but by the spring term she had made up so much work that the headmaster allowed her to substitute Latin for German and thereby stay in step for graduation with her class. "Little Follett," as her classmates called her, received very high marks: her lowest yearly average, a sparkling "97.6 of 100," occurred in her second year; she did even better in her first and third years and finished with a flourish, capturing a 99 in her senior year. Although these scores were several points above the class average, another young woman truly excelled. Harriet Cammett French, the class valedictorian, was the daughter of Judge Asa French, a prominent Braintree attorney and the trustee most responsible for bringing the academy into being.[14] Harriet's older brother and sister already had graduated from Thayer, and another sister, Mary Sophia (Sophie), would soon enroll. Harriet and Sophie French became Mary Follett's first real friends.

Harriet remembered spending "many happy hours" in the Baxter house. "I can easily think myself back into that big white house," she recalled, "when we read all sorts of things together and talked about everything in life, I believe, as girl friends will." Only one aspect of Mary's character puzzled her new friend. "She seemed almost alarmingly devout to me," Harriet recalled, "rather a different Mary from the challenging little spirit I knew in every day life." Mary's intense religious devotion may have emanated from a desire to please her father. Charles and Lizzie had originally joined the Baxter family's

Unitarian church and had had Mary baptized there; but when Charles returned to the family in 1876, he began to worship at Christ Church, the Episcopal church where his parents had been members and he had been baptized. Charles's return to the church of his childhood, apparently born of his renunciation of alcohol, resulted in a commitment to the faith sufficiently noticeable for Harriet to remember him as a "profoundly religious man." In 1878, a few months after the Folletts' son, George, was born, Charles seemed to assert himself, perhaps for the first time, as the head of the family: the baby was christened at Charles's church, and on the same day nine-year-old Mary was rebaptized there too.[15]

Even though Mary was two years younger than Harriet, she created such a vivid impression that Harriet found it easy to describe her fifty years later. Mary was "rather tall and slight," Harriet recalled, with "heavy brown braids" falling down her back, "dazzling teeth," and "deep blue eyes" that reflected such "childish candour" one might have been inclined to underestimate her. But Harriet and others at the academy quickly learned that this young girl possessed more than an innocent and undissembling nature—she had "an eager, fearless mind."[16]

When this "challenging little spirit" arrived at Thayer, the core faculty consisted of a classics scholar, a scientist, and a former principal of a school for girls. The classics scholar, Professor Jotham Sewall, was an ordained minister and former professor of ancient languages at Bowdoin College. Headmaster of the academy, this venerable figure was remembered by Harriet's older brother as "a gracious presence, irradiating cheerfulness and calm courage, happiness and peace, the joy of goodness and virtue, the beauty of simplicity." Besides teaching Greek in the college course, Sewall also taught classes in rhetoric and mental science, allowing general course students such as Mary an opportunity to study with him during their senior year. The second member of the teaching group was Charles Pitkin, a graduate of Harvard College and an instructor in chemistry at the U.S. Torpedo Station in Newport. Pitkin's curriculum in math and physics made such skillful use of laboratory work that students thought this "debonair" young man "extremely brilliant" and were convinced that he "knew the text books of his day like A,B,C." Pitkin enhanced his skills by completing his doctorate and then teaching chemistry at two medical schools in Boston, but he was faithful to Thayer Academy and remained a member of the faculty for forty years.[17]

The third member of this group, Anna Boynton Thompson, would be the only woman appointed a master teacher at Thayer Academy for more than twenty years. Although she was only twenty-nine when the academy opened in 1877, Thompson had already experienced more than many women her age.

Anna Boynton Thompson, 1890. Archives, Thayer Academy, Braintree, Mass.

Her father, a young, untested clergyman assigned to missionary work on the midwestern prairies, drowned in 1852 when Anna was only four. Her mother struggled for several years to make ends meet, but finally took the radical step of leaving Anna and her younger sister in the care of friends so that she could return to Boston to study medicine. Eventually, however, she decided that the girls' education was more important than her own and brought them to Boston when Anna was fourteen years old so that they could study at the Girls' High School. To make her daughters' education possible and, later, to pay for their two years of study and travel in Europe, Mrs. Thompson restricted her own activities to operating a large boardinghouse; only summertime visits to England and the Mediterranean were salvaged from among her personal dreams. Acutely conscious of what her mother had had to forgo, Thompson would struggle all her life to be worthy of the sacrifice.[18]

By the time Anna Boynton Thompson was invited to join the Thayer faculty, she had already established a reputation as a dynamic teacher, first in Everett, Massachusetts, and then as the principal at the Bird School, an experimental school for girls in South Boston. Thayer Academy, however, offered new challenges: she would be responsible for designing the curriculum in history and English literature and would have an opportunity to work with students preparing to seek college degrees. Relishing the challenges and welcoming the hard work, Thompson accepted the offer and stayed for forty-four years.[19]

Thompson was small in stature, but in every other way her students found her an awesome figure. Her habit of wearing black drew her students' attention to her face, and her black hair was pulled back so severely that not a single strand interrupted the gaze of her "black piercing eyes." Passionately committed to the life of the mind, Thompson tried to foster something of the same intensity in her students, but found that "they are poor, and hard-working, and therefore utilitarian in their views . . . they all want to cram history and literature in a term or a year." If she was to be of genuine help to them, she knew that she must persuade her pupils that "history is of practical use, something they will need and that will be of service to them in daily life."[20]

Nothing irritated Thompson more than the idea that learning history was the accumulation of "a hodgepodge of unassimilated, unrelated facts." "What the pupil of a free republic needs," she argued, was not more facts but "training in the ability to reach his own premises for his own times." The method of training on which Thompson relied was the "topical analysis"; it required students to read widely on a particular subject and then, using inductive methods of reasoning, to construct a logical analytical framework from which "provisional major premises" could be discerned. She did not stop there. Insisting that students take responsibility for their own thinking, she required each to present his or her completed analysis in class. A young woman of those early years recalled the system: "We studied our topic, put an analysis on the board, stood out in front there beside it, and gave our 'lecture.' Miss Thompson could not be bluffed, and if anyone did not know the topic, she was extremely quick to find it out." Each presentation was followed by a discussion period during which the other pupils were encouraged to analyze critically the premises that had been offered and to decide which, if any, should be eliminated.[21]

Thompson nurtured Mary Follett's analytical skills, insisting that she learn both how to defend a thesis and how to analyze the reasoning of others. Mary also profited from being encouraged by the Thayer faculty to express her ideas in public. Professor Sewall's rhetoric course provided the necessary training, and the annual Founder's Day and Graduation ceremonies provided the occasions. Girls as well as boys took advantage of these opportunities and delivered numerous declamations and original essays. And on the occasion of Mary's graduation, "the young ladies of the class" were said to have "excelled the young gentlemen."[22]

Both the faculty's enlightened approach to education and her own intellectual mettle are evident in Mary's choice of subject for her first public presentation, an essay delivered at the 1883 Founder's Day celebration. Mary eschewed the common practice of drawing her topic from textbooks or other "authoritative" sources. Instead, she apparently based "The Schoolmate as an Educator" directly on her own experience, namely, the interactions that had taken place among students as they engaged in Thompson's "topical analysis." The proposition implicit in the essay title — that the pupil as well as the teacher could be an educator — must have seemed radical to Mary's late nineteenth-century audience. Even audiences of the 1920s would find it difficult to accept Follett's contention that formal authority is neither a necessary nor a sufficient condition of leadership.[23]

This 1883 Founder's Day essay has not been located, but two others that Mary wrote during her years at Thayer have survived almost intact. The first, an analysis of the work of the late eighteenth-century English poet William Cowper allows some insight into the values she had been learning from Thompson and others. Mary's distinct preference for order and proportion is evident in her criticism of Cowper for failing to join his "charming" natural pictures "into one harmonious whole" and for allowing his "melancholy nature" to erupt too often into "wild sorrow." The simplicity of Cowper's vividly "cheerful" pictures of nature, however, redeemed him, marking him "a gentleman, high minded, and refined." Although Mary admired Cowper's decision, inspired by the French Revolution, to make the downtrodden English peasants his poetic subjects, she criticized him for showing no "heroic spirit" in righting the great wrongs he had seen. Apparently, the socially conscious Thayer faculty had persuaded her that genuine social reform required not only "lofty ideals" but also "useful achievements."[24]

The final essay that Mary delivered at Thayer suggests an early fascination with psychology. Intrigued by mesmerism, mind cure, spiritualism, and other mind-body phenomena discussed in the text used in Sewall's senior-year mental science course, Mary wrote her commencement essay, which she titled "Expectant Attention," about forms of mind control. Relying almost solely on the course textbook for information, Mary maintained that the apparent ability of the mind to control the body could be "explained as resulting from expectant attention" — an unconscious state in which "the mind becoming possessed with the idea that certain sights, sounds, and feelings are to be experienced" gave that idea "a dominant power, so that various sensations which have no place in the world of fact, will by the all powerful agency of the mind . . . be created." For a young woman who was bent on controlling her own life and determined never to be quite so vulnerable again, the idea that her own unconscious might be a source of heretofore-unexplored mental powers was a compelling revelation.[25] Mary's decision to deliver a speech on mind-body phenomena to an audience that included her parents is especially significant when considered in light of her father's struggle with alcoholism. Convinced of the power of the mind to control the body, she surely admired her father's apparently successful pledge of abstinence, but the fact that it had been so long in coming was a source of deep remorse.

One other member of the 1884 Thayer graduation audience surely listened to Mary's presentation with rapt attention. For years, Anna Boynton Thompson had suffered, virtually in silence, a mental and physical anguish so excruciating that it had left her almost in despair; but now, hearing from one of her pupils about the healing potential of mind control, Thompson once again dared to hope for a cure. She enthusiastically embraced the tenets of "the mind cure" and thereby eventually altered the course of her own life and Mary Follett's as well.[26]

4

"What Shall We Do with Our Girls?"

"I had been ailing so long," Anna Boynton Thompson confided in an 1891 letter to her friend Alice Mary Longfellow, "that I had gotten into a morbid condition. My whole attention was fixed upon my self. I watched my feelings with all the energy and faithfulness I possess, and each new one filled me with the greatest alarm. I lived in constant panic, expecting apoplexy, and paralysis, and softening of the brain, and what not, every moment. And the more I watched my sensations, the more strange and alarming they grew. It seems to me that I have run through every possible queer, frightful feeling that a human being can have. I was afraid I should die every morning, and afraid I should not, every afternoon my suffring [sic] was so extreme."[1]

In her struggle to regain her health, Thompson would face a dilemma central to the lives of many nineteenth-century women — and one that would bedevil her pupil Mary Follett in later years. Desperate for help, Thompson placed herself in the care of physicians whose methods were much like those of Dr. S. Weir Mitchell, the leading nineteenth-century American expert on female nervous conditions. In Mitchell's view, the "hysteric" females treated in his Philadelphia clinic "had wrecked their own nervous systems through emotional self-indulgence" and the "taxing pressures of 'inappropriate' ambition"; such women seemed "inappropriately aggressive, dominating, even predatory" to their male physicians. If these women were to be returned to health, the paternalistic physician believed that he would have to counteract these undesirable tendencies. Mitchell's method of asserting control over the patient was the famous "rest cure," in which the patient had "complete bed rest, daily massages, plenty of food, and no outside stimulation — no books, no conversations with friends, only consultations with staff and doctors." Using this regimen, Mitchell hoped to "teach" his recalcitrant female patients to be "more passive and warm and thus more 'feminine.' "[2]

Among the treatment options available to Thompson in the Boston area was the Adams Nervine Asylum, a facility specializing in the treatment of "nervous people who were not insane." Established in 1880 by Boston brahmins in the suburb of Jamaica Plain, the facility had room for thirty patients, all of them women. In its first three years of operation, 14 percent of the patients admitted to the Adams Nervine were teachers — women suffering from the "care of dependent and invalid relatives, overwork outside the schoolroom, and anxiety attendant upon an indifference to and lack of attachment for their work."[3]

Thompson certainly was not indifferent to her work, but she must have felt seriously constrained by it. Bound up in the often mundane activities of secondary school teaching, she had had little opportunity to utilize the intellect nurtured by her mother's sacrifices and was now displaying all the classic symptoms of depression and hysteria. Subjected to the treatment that had successfully "cured" many women hysterics, an incensed Thompson later wrote: "The doctors only increased my evils. The [sic] put me abed, and fed me every two hours. The most terrible indigestion was the result. I suffred [sic] all that a sluggard and a glutton can suffer, and wasted my time, and my strength, and my life."[4] Seeking relief from this degrading treatment, Thompson found a genuine alternative in "the mind cure."

Thompson was one of numerous middle-class, native-born men and women who were "anxious, harried, often unwell, and . . . no one seemed to know why." Nineteenth-century physicians were truly baffled by the way their patients converted their fears and phobias into physical symptoms, and few had any idea about "how to reverse the process." Eventually, as patients began to realize that orthodox medical practice could not cure their ills, they turned in increasing numbers to forms of mental healing.[5]

Today the most widely known form of mental healing is undoubtedly Christian Science, but in the last decades of the nineteenth century, the Christian Science church had considerable competition. The *Boston Post* reported "at least four schools of mental healing in Boston" in 1885, and the next few years saw the establishment of several more. Most of these groups, writes Stephen

Gottschalk in his scholarly study of Christian Science, "were led either by defectors from the Christian Science movement or by practitioners of modes of faith healing and mesmerism that antedated Christian Science." Mary Baker Eddy therefore took great pains to "distinguish Christian Science as clearly as possible from the mushrooming 'mind-cure' movements."[6]

One of the major distinctions between Christian Science and New Thought —the most formidable of Mrs. Eddy's mind-cure competitors—concerned their "differing relationships with Calvinism." Christian Science teachings hold that man is in desperate need of redemption, "that 'mortal mind' has within itself no resources on the basis of which to work out this salvation, and that men are thus wholly reliant upon divine revelation for an understanding of the way that leads to salvation." In New Thought teachings, however, "one finds a conscious and almost total repudiation of Calvinism," Gottschalk contends. To New Thought adherents, man was not evil and did not require redemption; instead, the "unfinished" human creature would eventually reach perfection merely by turning the "beneficent power of human thought" toward "right" thinking. By 1910, 85,000 men and women were self-professed adherents of New Thought (as many as those of Christian Science), and "twice as many again," attracted by the movement's commitment to both self-help and self-abandon, "regularly read the copious literature of mind cure without leaving the standard denominational folds."[7]

The "treatments" advocated by the mind cure movement were a self-administered series of mental exercises that Thompson could learn either by attending lectures or, more likely, by reading the mind curists' books and pamphlets in the privacy of her home. The mind curists advocated optimism and a large dose of humor—calling to mind Norman Cousins' claims for the beneficial effects to be gained from watching the Marx brothers' films. "Mirth is heaven's medicine," wrote one mind curist. "Everyone ought to bathe in it. Grim care, moroseness, anxiety, all the rust of life, ought to be scoured off by the oil of mirth."[8]

If Thompson could believe what she had heard in Mary Follett's essay— that "the contemplation of fancied ailments often results in a real malady due to no other cause, than a change in the circulation produced by the fixation of the attention upon the body"—there was a chance that she could cure herself simply by redirecting her mind from illness to health. Furthermore, mind curists contended that their methods might even be capable of relieving illnesses arising from other than "mental" causes. "The confident expectation of a cure," Follett had maintained, "is the most efficacious means of producing it, even although the disease involves some inorganic change, and the remedy possess no more medicinal power than hot water." In other words, in both prevention and treatment of illness, the mind cure gave Thompson a chance to regain control of her own body.[9]

The numerous publications through which mind curists shared their methods borrowed freely from a variety of sources, including Swedenborg, Emerson, and William James, but two metaphors were pervasive: "the Everlasting Arms," and the reservoir, or "All-Supply." The passive quality of these metaphors might at one time have made them repugnant to New Englanders, noted for their individualism and self-reliance; but the demands and opportunities of late nineteenth-century society had driven many to doubt the adequacy of their personal energy and talents and persuaded them that efforts to sublimate their fears had failed. Longing "at least for a few medicinal moments" to be free of the cares, obligations, and contradictions of their lives, the suffering sought shelter in "the Everlasting Arms." But the mind curists sought only temporary shelter and created "schedules and mental exercises" that would allow them to "let go" safely. "They did not want to have anything to do with experiences that came unbidden, and might never go away," explains Gail Thain Parker in her study of mind cure. However much the mind curists needed a respite from their anxieties, they also felt compelled to return to the fray, renewed by the reservoir of the All-Supply.[10]

Anna Boynton Thompson found her shelter and strength, at least initially, in a religious conception that had once been dominant in New England, namely, that faith naturally empowers the individual to do good works. Soon, however, Thompson came to rely less on religion and more on philosophy. "Religion and Philosophy seem to teach the same lesson," Thompson wrote a friend in 1892, "to get out of self, and lose one's self in a higher nature. Christ, and Spinoza's Substance, and the Transcendental Ego are means of escape, and I suppose it is the temperament that chooses between them." But this strong-willed woman did not find it easy to be passively receptive to the workings of the "higher nature." Next year, she continued, "I hope to be wise, and put in practice what I believe. I am going to do nothing myself, but be simply an instrument of the Power behind . . . So every day I shall try simply to be passive, to receive the strength as it is poured into me, and to be sensitive to the guidance that is always about us. From the little breathing space of a summer holiday, life looks very simple, for the task is set us, and the power given, all we have to do is to be receptive, and sensitive, and obedient. But in the rush and struggle of workdays, I forget, and think it is I who am doing, and who must do. It seems to me that this forgetting is the Mother of all Sin—this separation from the sum total of being, and fancying that I am an individual, one, and alone, instead of a branch of the Vine, fed by its sap, and one with all the other branches."[11]

Perhaps Thompson struggled so because for her, as for Charlotte Perkins Gilman, another mind cure adherent, letting go was "the fatal sign of feminine weakness." All of Gilman's enthusiasm for the tenets of New Thought came to nothing in the end because abandonment of self-control, even if it were to a "higher nature," threatened "everything that she loved best about herself, her 'hand-made character.' " Gilman's eventual disavowals of the mind cure movement, Gail Thain Parker contends, "throw into bold relief the achievements of those strenuous women who were able to get what they needed from New Thought." "Letting go" helped them endure rather than despair in the face of the numerous restrictions society placed upon women, but at the same time it required of them a genuine "act of courage."[12]

The optimism and serenity that Thompson found in mind cure was greatly facilitated by her discovery, that same month, of the existence of the Harvard Annex, where women could take courses taught by Harvard professors under the auspices of the Society for the Collegiate Instruction of Women. "I made up my mind instantly that I did not care whether it killed me or not," Thompson wrote in 1891; "I would go to the Annex. I commenced work immediately [1884] and have grown stronger every year, till today it seems to me as if my strength were infinite."[13]

Anna Boynton Thompson was being nourished by the intellectual excitement of her studies at the Annex, but the emotional stability of her young protégé Mary Follett was about to be severely tested. On the first day of 1885 Mary's grandfather Daniel Baxter died, and just seven weeks later her forty-three-year-old father abandoned her for the last time, dying suddenly of pneumonia. Charles Follett's G.A.R. colleagues, stunned by his death, found the preambles and resolutions customarily issued on such occasions "too formal to express a loss like ours"; still, they expressed their grief to Lizzie and her children, recognizing "the shadow of the greater loss and darker sorrow that fall upon the hearts of [Charles's] own loved family." Lizzie Follett was so overwhelmed by these events that even eighteen months later friends were hoping that a summer with her children and a few friends on the Maine coast would reawaken her "good health and spirits."[14]

During this period, more than ever before, Mary needed her mother's emotional support, but Lizzie Follett had difficulty reassuring her children. No doubt feeling deserted both by her husband and by the father on whom she had repeatedly relied, it was not easy for Lizzie to face the future. The problem wasn't money, at least not directly. Daniel Baxter had provided equally for each of his eight living children, and the executor's initial inventory suggested that Lizzie stood to receive more than $40,000.[15] Still, the situation must have been fearfully intimidating. Would her family be able to stay in the School Street house, or would the house have to be sold in order to divide the estate? Would she receive her portion of the estate in the form of property? And if so, where was she to get the cash to pay for the family's living expenses? Underlying all these immediate questions, Lizzie, who was only forty-three and still had a family to raise, surely worried about whether the money would last a lifetime.

Mary, apparently sensing her mother's inability to cope, quickly "took over the whole responsibility of her brother George." Perhaps she was convinced that this was what her father would have wanted. In any case, the determined effort of this sixteen-year-old woman to become "the man of the family," though surely unsettling for everyone, did not surprise her friend Harriet French. "It was like her that even at that early age when girls are often absorbed in their own affairs she realized that George must not be left [solely] with [his] mother's guidance."[16]

Nineteenth-century social convention reinforced Mary's effort to carry on in her father's place. A young woman was expected to devote herself to the needs of her family, Joyce Antler writes in her study of the claims that nineteenth-century families made on their daughters; a proper daughter, even if she had acquired a college education and was suitably prepared to assume other work, remained at home if her family needed her.[17] Mary might have tried to defy these conventions, but she would quickly have learned that she had no real alternative to remaining with her family. An early marriage might have provided a way out for some girls, but Mary, several years younger than her Thayer classmates and an intellectual "child prodigy," was unlikely to have had a bevy of suitors waiting impatiently in the wings. Her youth also effectively prevented her from embarking on a career. No matter how much the sixteen-year-old might have hungered for new experiences and growth, her mother surely would have considered her too young either to train for work as a teacher or to go off to college.

On the surface, Mary may have seemed to suffer her fate willingly, but underneath she was considerably less sanguine. Years later Mary would tell a close friend that she "was never allowed to play with other children" and "often regretted this," the friend recalled, "telling me that she used to watch her school companions going off swimming or skating while she had to hurry home to take care of her mother or her younger brother." The lingering bitterness may have caused Mary to exaggerate some of the stories about her mother's demands, for at least one friend was led incorrectly to believe that Mary's mother became a lifelong invalid immediately after her husband's death.[18]

Almost from the moment that her father died, Mary Follett would be free of this web of family obligations only during the hours she spent on lessons sent to her by the Society to Encourage Studies at Home, an organization that one observer saw as "furnishing an excellent answer to the question so often asked in families, 'What shall we do with our girls?' " Founded in 1873, five years before the more famous Chautauqua Literary and Scientific Circles, the society was the idea of Anna Eliot Ticknor, George Ticknor's privileged daughter. Ticknor had learned of the existence of an English Society for the Encouragement of Home Study, in which well-educated ladies offered other women of their class a means of continuing their studies without exposing themselves to the "dangers" inherent in collegiate education. Intrigued, she proposed an American society "to meet the wants of great numbers of our countrywomen who have very limited social or educational opportunities," coming to them "as a generous and sympathetic friend" who would provide a respite from the "tireless and thankless drudgery" of their lives. She did not doubt that the women her society would serve were "anxious to reach out to studies which enlarge or enrich one's life" and would do so if only the necessary "books and teachers, and time and sympathy" were available.[19]

The format that Ticknor and her friends designed for their society differed in several respects from the English model. The English society confined its work to helping women of the upper classes, but Ticknor was determined to aid women of all classes, particularly those who had been denied the opportunities available to their more fortunate sisters. The English society assisted its students primarily by providing prescribed plans of coursework, expecting the students to complete them without further assistance. Ticknor, by contrast, saw that the uneven educational preparation and difficult personal circumstances of the American students would require individually planned courses and close, continuing communication between student and teacher. Finally, the English society required students to present themselves in London for a competitive examination at the end of their work, but Ticknor doubted that competitive examinations had any place in her more individualized system. In any case, examinations were impractical in a country where the distances to be traveled were vast and many students would be women of modest financial means.[20]

Ticknor's sensitivity to the special needs of the women she hoped to serve, unusual for one of her social class, helped to ensure the society's success. In the first six years, enrollment expanded from 45 students in 7 states to 785 students residing "in 38 States, 1 Territory and Canada," a growth so remark-able that one respected observer saw it as "worthy of a modern university." The project's success was all the more astonishing because it occurred in the context of Ticknor's assiduous efforts to avoid publicity. "We have kept very quiet about our work hitherto," Ticknor said, "but presently, when our circu-lar is handed about, it can no longer be a secret. We hope, however, never to get into the newspapers."[21]

One article concerning the society's work, however, so pleased the members that even Ticknor was moved to note its publication. Herbert B. Adams, an eminent historian at Johns Hopkins, reproduced for *The Independent* a talk he had given about the society's history curriculum to a recent meeting of the American Historical Association, an organization founded the preceding year for the "promotion of historical studies in the country at large." Adams had found the society's work so impressive that he credited Ticknor and her origi-nal correspondents with "an intellectual revolution" achieved "as efficiently as Sam Adams and the Boston town fathers once accomplished a political revolution."[22]

However flattering this comparison may have seemed to Ticknor, it also was reason for concern. The last thing that she and her associates wanted was to be seen as revolutionaries, at least not on the subject of women's roles. "We desire always," Ticknor wrote, "to use our influence in showing women that intellec-tual pursuits may be, and should be, associated with the practice of household duties, and with the growth of heart-kindliness in all domestic and social relations." Ticknor elaborated on this theme in a letter written to a long-time student who had grown restless at home. "Some wise person has said, 'To be content with limitations is freedom; to desire beyond those limitations is bondage.' This does not mean that we may not have aspirations, but that we must not allow them to tyrannize over us, or to go beyond reason. The intellect is a high and noble part of us, but it needs to be balanced by the affections and all the duties and responsibilities that flow from them . . . You are acting on this principle at this moment in staying at home to help your parents and to teach your brother and sister, and you will find your reward very soon, I believe, in recovering the right balance and proportion of your wishes."[23]

For this young woman, study with the society no longer seemed adequate recompense for her devotion to her family, but for Mary Follett home study was a promising new adventure. In September 1885, almost immediately after her seventeenth birthday made her eligible for the society's courses, Mary and her friend Harriet French applied for permission to enroll.[24] They received a "programme of studies" describing the twenty-four subjects within the soci-ety's six departments (English literature, history, art, French, German, and, re-

markably for the time, science) and instructions for choosing a desired subject for the next eight-month term. To be eligible for any and all courses in
her chosen subject, Mary had only to identify her choice and pay a three-
dollar fee.

History was one of the society's most popular departments and probably
was the area in which Follett did her work. Follett's first contact with the
department would have been the standard letter of welcome in which the
department head, Mary C. Peabody, told each new student that the society
was willing either to purchase books for her at a reduced rate or to lend books
to her at the rate of one-half cent a day from the society's sizable lending
library. The letter also asked for information, including the amount of time
available to her for study, the extent to which she had studied history already,
and the books that were easily available to her. Follett's responses to these
questions would have been used to guide Peabody's selection of a suitable
correspondent. The quality of the correspondents was impressive. Reviewing
their credentials, Herbert B. Adams asserted that work with these women "in
many cases . . . amounts to a graduate course for young women already fairly
trained in our schools or colleges."[25]

The history curriculum had four subject areas: the traditional triad of ancient, medieval, and modern European history, and American history, a subject less often taught. Follett already had gained considerable familiarity with
the traditional subjects from her work with Anna Boynton Thompson, but she
had not studied American history since grammar school. Well aware of how
poorly educated American students were about their own country's history,
Herbert B. Adams found it "especially gratifying to see so much attention
bestowed by this Society for Home Study upon the history of their own country . . . It is all important that American girls, as well as American boys, should
learn that . . . toward true freedom for man and woman, history tends, and
finds its fairest expression in America." Because few American history textbooks had yet been written, simple ones, such as Higginson's *Young Folk's
History of the United States,* were supplemented with a variety of atlases
and maps, encyclopedias, "biographies, historical romances, poems, plays and
magazine articles"; syntheses of these diverse materials, it was hoped, not only
would illumine topics concerning America's past, but also would enlighten
discussions of contemporary political questions.[26]

In 1886 the history department formally added a fifth subject, political
economy, to the curriculum. The recent publication of two advanced textbooks had made it relatively easy to teach high school and college students
about the production, distribution, and consumption of wealth and the numerous applications of political economy principles. The society used these

texts in its courses but, at least in the early years, seemed to focus almost exclusively on "the theory and history of charity," "recent developments in philanthropic work," and "the best methods for the prevention and cure of pauperism." Apparently "charity" was one of the few applications of the principles of political economy that Ticknor and Peabody felt it suitable for young women to study.[27]

The society's pedagogy, refined over the years by Ticknor and her associates, was based on a design originating in the history department, where "the method is that of research in various works, rather than adherence to a single text-book." Each month Follett was asked to read several items from the course bibliography and then, from memory, to organize and summarize the material in concise written notes. After checking her "memory notes" against the text, she made any necessary corrections and, on request, submitted the product to her correspondent for comment. Since each correspondent had only a few students, Follett's submissions would have received considerable critical attention. In addition to preparing the notes, Mary had to write a four-page topical analysis each month, using a method similar to the one that she had learned from Anna Boynton Thompson: she read a variety of sources on an aspect of the subject being studied, compared and contrasted the sources read, and then formulated her own conclusions. Students unfamiliar with the method could find it extremely taxing. "At school," one young woman confided, "I have only to memorize and recite," but she rarely found the work for her correspondent so easy. Here, the young woman exclaimed, "I am compelled to think, which is very troublesome!" Students progressing through the lessons at the "regular" rate also took monthly examinations, responding "on honor" to questions sent by the correspondents. Reviewing some of these examinations, Herbert B. Adams was pleased to find that high standards had been set. "Such papers passed successfully by all candidates for the degree of bachelor of arts," he asserted, "would be a test at once honorable and gratifying to any classical department of an American college, whether for men or women."[28]

The success of the society's pedagogy was highly dependent on the individual student's motivation and discipline and on what the society called "the peculiar personal relation between one woman and another." When these relationships "worked," and they seemed to more often than not, students gained more than knowledge of particular subjects and careful habits of study and reflection. Some women felt that their studies had saved them from personal disaster, and they struggled to express the depth of their gratitude without being indiscreet. "[My correspondents] have aided me," one woman wrote, "when they could not have any conception how much it was to me, or how it helped to displace, or prevented other things." Others, whose personal situations were not so desperate but whose talents had nonetheless been suppressed by family claims, also were helped by their studies. Embedded in the educational philosophy that Ticknor and her correspondents articulated was a rationale for studying that seemed to assuage the students' guilt and placate their families. We study, the students learned to declare, not because we are selfish and uncaring, but because we are obligated to a higher being. One woman expressed it this way: "I feel a lack of that knowledge which seems so essential to the women of our time who would be all they are capable of being; who would render unto the Giver of the blessed privilege of living in this beautiful world a broad, well-developed life."[29]

Even though Anna Ticknor was fond of saying that "it is the home we are working for" and she surely did not intentionally encourage young women to leave their homes in search of collegiate education, the experiences that Ticknor helped to create sometimes had exactly that effect. Mary Follett's three-year involvement with this "separate" female social institution brought her not only respite from the pressures of family obligations, but also challenging goals and the pleasure of hard intellectual work — and it legitimated her desire to continue her education.[30] Buoyed by her experiences, Follett eagerly sought a new challenge, and by the autumn of 1888 she had found one in the Harvard Annex for Women.

5

"Very Unusual Privileges"

Mary Follett's decision to seek a college education was unusual. In the 1880s, less than 2 percent of women aged eighteen to twenty-one enrolled in college, and few of those who graduated were thought to be "agreeable to the fancy of either sex."[1] The public's generally disdainful image of college women is captured in this vivid 1883 portrait by a writer for *The Nation.* "[The college graduate is] a woman who is undomestic in her habits and unfeminine in her tastes, who takes the initiative in conversation, is perpetually agitating for some 'cause,' or 'reform,' is ill-dressed and untidy, in fact regards dress as a unimportant matter, and the desire to attract the attention and interest of men as 'frivolous.' To make the picture more hideous, she is generally thought of as wearing spectacles and carrying an umbrella, and as having a family of neglected children and a miserably uncomfortable husband at home."[2]

In fact a college graduate was as likely to have no husband as an "uncomfortable" one, particularly if she was one of the first two generations of graduates, among whom the proportion never marrying hovered around 50 percent. Even those graduates who chose to marry tended to do so later in life and to have fewer children than their counterparts in the general population — hardly behavior that would endear them to their native-born kin, who were fearful of being outnumbered by immigrants.[3]

If a young college aspirant managed to persevere despite such pervasive animosity, she still had to overcome fears that pursuit of a college education might destroy her health. Dr. Edward Clarke's 1873 assertion that women "could not [study and learn] and retain uninjured health and a future secure from neuralgia, uterine disease, hysteria, and other derangements of the nervous system" caused considerable alarm. His book, *Sex in Education,* went through seventeen reprints, and it took well over a decade of research and public debate before supporters of women's education managed to refute Clarke's assertions.

Mary Follett's health had been troublesome even while she was a student at Thayer: "eye strain" had forced a temporary postponement of her studies, and her menses were almost always painful. Even more serious was a case of typhoid three years after her Thayer graduation that left her feeling never "quite as strong again."[4] These health problems might have shaken Mary's confidence in her ability to withstand the rigors of collegiate study had she not known that the Harvard Annex was having only salutary effects on Anna Boynton Thompson. Furthermore, the health pamphlet that the Society to Encourage Studies at Home distributed to all its students assured her that studying would not impair a young woman's health as long as she pursued her studies with balance and moderation. Insufficient intellectual stimulation could lead to depression or even insanity, but the opposite extreme, the society warned, also held dangers. Very active women — "delighting in the use of their intellects, intensely alive to all kinds of responsibility, desirous to crowd every waking moment with interest and action" — too often sought enjoyment in the place of what was "right and wholesome." A student's good health could be maintained only if intellectual interests were "well regulated, and not encroaching on home duties . . . brain work must alternate with muscle work."[5]

A young woman could overcome public skepticism about her physiological capacity for advanced study and antagonism about her apparent rejection of the traditional feminine role only if she possessed an intense personal will. But in the 1880s women were taught to be "deficiency-motivated," Allen F. Davis writes in his biography of Jane Addams, to be "dependent, other-directed, and sensitive to other people's approval, affection and good will; to become, in other words, the very model of the genteel female." Nevertheless, a few young women managed to move "against the current of their times," having been insulated from society's expectations by "some condition in their lives . . . that gave them a source of energy, even a sense of destiny, which would not permit them to accept the conventional female role." This condition, according to Carolyn Heilbrun and others, was the feeling of being an "outsider."[6]

Mary Follett had been an outsider almost from birth. Her father's alcoholism and early abandonments of the family had labeled the Folletts as different from the families of her peers and may have precipitated the complex family dynamics that resulted in Mary's alienation from her mother. Follett enjoyed some relief from her isolation while she was a student at Thayer, but when her father died only a few months after her graduation, Mary's isolation deepened. Craving a sense of belonging—what she later would describe as a need to be a part of "a larger consciousness than that of the individual"—Follett was driven to free herself from the sterility of her mother's family claim.[7]

The frustrations and loneliness of Follett's adolescent years were still apparent years later in her description of the adolescents she had come to know in her social and civic work. How curious it was, Follett mused, that the ages of fourteen to twenty—the years during which "the occupation for one's whole life is chosen"—should be the most neglected ones. Adults failed, as she saw it, in their obligation to nurture young people's "growing feeling of sensitive independence" and "craving for self-direction," instead assuming that a young person's "place in the community" could simply be prescribed. Such prescriptions were bound to fail, Follett argued, because the "psychology of the situation" virtually guaranteed adolescent rebellion. Few other prominent women reformers were as confident as Follett that this "craving for self-direction" was as alive in young women as in men; instead, many of them continued to prescribe domestic roles—albeit enhanced ones—for other women while boldly carving out new ventures for themselves.[8]

Among the first generations of women who pursued a college education, many were fortunate to have the active support of at least one parent.[9] But any hopes that Mary Follett might have had for parental encouragement were dashed when her father died. Follett's mother, fond of "dress and society," showed little appreciation for nontraditional aspirations; and she undoubtedly looked to her son rather than her daughter for financial security and a restoration of the family's tarnished social image.[10] Furthermore, Lizzie had little reason to be sanguine about her daughter's future. Mary was insecure about the traditional feminine social graces and "self-conscious" about her appearance. Even as an adult, she showed little flair for dress and style; "she obviously spent much care and trouble over her clothes," remarked one male admirer of her later years, but "they never quite 'came off.' "[11]

Mary's mother might have exerted more pressure on Mary to conform to the traditional feminine role had she not learned from her own roller-coaster life how vulnerable a woman could be when she was totally dependent on a man. If nothing else, a college education would afford her daughter the opportunity for employment, protecting her from the vicissitudes of a married woman's life. Paying for this education, however, was another matter. According to Barbara Solomon, coping with the high costs of a college education "took extensive planning except for the most affluent. On the average in 1890, teachers earned $250 per year, ministers $900, physicians $1,200. Male college professors earned $1,200–1,500 in 1905. To any of these, the $350 (tuition, room, and board) required annually to send a girl to Wellesley College was hardly affordable . . . most families cut costs by sending their children to schools near home or in the same state, eliminating or at least reducing expenses for room, board, and transportation."[12]

If Mary were to forgo the residential colleges and enroll in the Harvard Annex as Anna Boynton Thompson had done, the savings would be considerable. Tuition for two-year-long courses would cost only $150, and Mary could commute to class. The train from Quincy to Boston provided reliable service and cost a mere ten cents per trip; but commuting also meant that Mary endured slow trips between Boston and Cambridge in poorly lit horsecars, which, despite their straw-strewn floors and smelly oil stoves, often were terribly cold in winter.[13]

The relatively low cost of attending the Annex was probably not the only reason that Mary preferred it to colleges such as Mount Holyoke, Smith, Wellesley, and Boston University. Each of these institutions was seen by the educational and literary elite of Boston as having serious deficiencies. Mount Holyoke was considered "a preparatory school for the colleges, and an ineffective one at that, for it did not offer the classical training required for college admission." Wellesley College and Boston University set higher standards and thereby gained a certain amount of respect, but the evangelical predilections of their founders still made them seem "provincial, narrow, and sectarian" to the "liberal, enlightened, and urbane" Unitarians. The best college of the lot, according to the liberal reformer Thomas Wentworth Higginson, was Smith College in Northampton. But Higginson, an early supporter of women's higher education, was one of many who anxiously awaited the day when Harvard College would "open its doors to women." To persons of his class, "the only institution of higher education that counted" was Harvard.[14]

Anna Boynton Thompson, "intellectual to her fingertips," was also convinced of Harvard's academic superiority, and she wanted her most promising students to have access to the Harvard College professors — even if it could be only through the Annex. Thompson had no hesitation about trying to influence a student's college choice. On one occasion, after learning that a talented student might choose one of the residential colleges over Radcliffe (as the Harvard Annex came to be known), Thompson complained directly to the young woman's mother. In her characteristically blunt style, she announced that Radcliffe was the only college where this young woman would "amount to something." Anywhere else, she was sure to "become an ordinary wife and mother."[15]

Despite Harvard's position as the preeminent college in the region, the new Harvard president, Charles William Eliot, knew that major reforms had to be undertaken if Harvard was to compete successfully with newer institutions such as the heavily endowed Johns Hopkins University.[16] Under Eliot's leadership, the 1870s became a time of change at Harvard. The woefully inept Law and Medical Schools were "reorganized and given new standards of excellence and efficiency." The Graduate School of Arts and Sciences was founded, and men of the stature of Henry Adams, Josiah Royce, William James, Charles F. Dunbar, and George Lyman Kittredge were appointed. And since a number of these new scholars had been educated at German universities, they eagerly supported Eliot's effort to recast Harvard as a university — a place where specialized, "scientific" scholars could devote themselves to the unrestricted pursuit of truth.

These were formidable accomplishments, but the reform with which Eliot is most widely associated today was the institution of the elective system. Harvard's decision to substitute "a broadly elective course of study for the old prescribed classical curriculum" was widely copied around the nation; it was instrumental in the dramatic expansion of undergraduate and graduate course offerings, the identification of new areas of scholarship, and the formation of new academic departments. The elective system also fostered pedagogical reform; forced to compete for students, Harvard professors had little choice but to replace dull class recitations with the more dynamic pedagogies of the German university — seminars, experimental laboratories, and scholarly lectures.[17]

Despite his willingness to sponsor other controversial Harvard reforms, Eliot vigorously opposed the idea of enrolling women. In his view, women were incapable of producing the scientific scholarship that was to be the hallmark of the "new Harvard"; even as late as 1908, this otherwise remarkable reformer was arguing that educated women could best serve as "splendid assistants" to their husbands. Eliot's persistent opposition to their cause persuaded many supporters of women's higher education that women could be educated at Harvard only if a method could be found that "stirs no prejudices, excites no opposition, involves no change of policy for the University." Such a method finally was found in the scheme by which the women's colleges were established at Cambridge University in England. The founders of Girton and Newnham hoped eventually to have their institutions accepted into the university system, and they knew that this could be accomplished only if their standards were essentially equivalent to those for men. To secure appropriate instruction and evaluation of the students' academic performance, the founders were forced to rely on informal university ties. Professors who supported the cause of women's higher education came to the colleges to give instruction, and many even permitted women to attend their university lectures; the services of the regular examiners also were secured, albeit "unofficially" and at a time and place different from the examinations for the men. The women of Girton and Newnham performed so well in the exams that the university was persuaded in 1881 to establish its first formal connection with the colleges. The university agreed to open the Tripos (degree) examinations to women; successful candidates would be awarded a certificate and their names would be published in a class list, "though separate from the men." The university was not prepared, however, to accept official responsibility for their instruction and would not even consider making women candidates for University degrees.[18]

The men and women who sought to translate the Cambridge University model to Cambridge, Massachusetts, were "a community of friends — long established, stable, and enduring." They also were experienced in educational matters. The women of the group were veterans of both the Harvard Examinations for Women and the Society to Encourage Studies at Home, and the men included a number of Harvard faculty. This small but influential group persuaded Eliot to allow a survey of Harvard faculty to determine which of them would be willing to give private instruction to women. Forty-one of the fifty-four faculty surveyed, including many distinguished professors, expressed interest for the year 1879–80. The magnitude of the response suggested that Harvard faculty might be enticed to give courses if they were offered sufficient compensation. Assured of adequate faculty support, the Society for the Collegiate Instruction of Women was ready to seek prospective students; but the founders, ever solicitous of Harvard, distributed their circular only after its language had been approved by President Eliot. The announcement described the society's courses as "private" — to reduce the likelihood that the public would see the Annex as formally connected with Harvard — and carefully avoided any promise of a degree.[19]

Over the years, the lengths to which Harvard officials would go to avoid any perception of a formal connection with the women of the Annex created some comic moments. One of the most memorable concerned the Bowdoin Prize competition of 1888, an event that took place only a few months before Mary Follett enrolled at the Annex. Harvard annually made awards up to $100 to students whose English dissertations were judged worthy; Annex students were excluded. Seeking to rectify this situation, "a friend of the young ladies" offered "smaller prizes for dissertations by them, with precisely the same range of subjects" and then arranged to have the evaluations conducted by "precisely the same judges." The segregated competition worked flawlessly the first year, but in the second, the Harvard faculty judges were mistakenly sent both sets of papers with "nothing to distinguish their sources." The judges awarded first prize and the "rather unusual award of the full sum ($100)" to a paper written by E. B. Pearson. Only later did they discover that Pearson was a student at the Annex. The embarrassed judges — all Harvard professors — quickly revoked Pearson's $100 prize and instead gave her "the humbler Annex prize of $30." Their reconsideration forced Pearson, in the words of one Boston scribe, to pay "$70 outright for the privilege of being a woman." Naturally, Pearson's Annex classmates were indignant about the injustice she had suffered, but they also took great delight in the judges' discomfort. It seems that one of the judges had disapproved of the Annex from the beginning and had been quoted as saying "that neither the brains nor the bodies of women were quite equal to severe study."[20]

The Pearson incident exemplifies how inferior the Annex women were made to feel, and how careful they had to be so as not to jeopardize the Annex experiment. In student reminiscences of these early years, the word *inconspicuous* appears with haunting regularity. "It was always impressed upon us that we must be inconspicuous," one student of the 1890s recalled, "and must never cross the Harvard Yard, unless we were attending some special lecture or reading . . . It was borne in upon us very frequently that the University as a whole scorned us, and only the broad-minded professors were really interested in our success." "We quite understood," another student recalled, "that we were to be entirely inconspicuous at Harvard at all times. We were cautioned not to walk through the Harvard yard, and this was not entirely a matter of Victorian etiquette. Twice when I was doing research work in the stack at Gore Hall I was hustled out of sight by an attendant while President Eliot went through with a party of visitors."[21]

Acutely aware that their presence at Harvard was "very much on suffrance," Annex students came to demonstrate unusual pride in themselves and their college. "We who have been here long, cannot help caring a great deal about our college, queer and scrappy as it must seem to a Wellesley girl," Eleanor Pearson wrote in an 1889 "letter" to the Wellesley College community. "We acknowledge that we shall never get a degree, that we are wholly dependent on what time and strength the instructors have left from their college courses, and that we run a risk of leading lives isolated from our fellow-students; but to us the spirit of the place outweighs it all. To us the life in Cambridge, with all the advantages which it and Boston offer, the chance to study with men who stand among the ablest in America, the companionship of a picked set of girls representing the best culture of New England, and above all, the utter freedom . . . the freedom to study what we choose and when, to live with whom we like, in short, to order our lives for ourselves in all those outside matters which are such a help or a hindrance to the inner, — all this is what the Annex means to us."[22]

The discrimination that Annex students suffered was profound. A full-time Harvard College student, for example, could count on fifteen or sixteen hours per week with his instructors, but full-time students at the Annex were granted only eight to ten. Despite the intensity with which many Annex students approached their studies, it would be misleading, Sally Schwager writes in her thesis on the founding of Radcliffe College, "to conclude that the Annex woman received the same instructional advantages of her Harvard peer."[23]

Mary Follett's first visit to Fay House, the home of the Harvard Annex, surely was something of a shock. Thompson had probably warned her to expect neither dormitories nor college grounds, but Fay House was even more "inconspicuous" than the Annex students. The Society for the Collegiate Instruction of Women had originally rented space in a private home on Appian Way; but by 1883 these quarters were no longer sufficient, and Fay House was purchased. This Federal-style house — located west of Harvard Square, across from the Cambridge Common — had little to distinguish it from other Cambridge homes, but it did have the advantage of having both old Harvard associations (being the place where "Fair Harvard" was written) and ample space for the secretary's office, a pleasant third-floor library, a science laboratory, and a number of lecture and recitation rooms.[24]

From its inception, the Annex enrolled a large proportion of "special students," mostly women who had been teachers or were intending to teach; in 1888, the year that Follett enrolled, almost three-quarters of the Annex's 115 students were specials.[25] Older and absorbed in their own responsibilities, the specials seemed hardly to notice the absence of dormitories and other trappings of extracurricular life at the Annex, and some were delighted to be able to avoid the "distractions" that "college life" posed.

The specials included a number of women who had long desired a college education but whose families could not or would not pay for it; teaching gave these women a means of acquiring the income and independence necessary to attend college. Although these part-time students often did not graduate until their late twenties or thirties, they were rewarded for their persistence with job security in the "burgeoning high schools"; money-conscious school boards were anxious to hire women rather than their more expensive male counterparts. Teaching eventually became so popular among female college graduates that a 1917 study by the Association of Collegiate Alumnae revealed that almost three-quarters of the thirty-five hundred women who had graduated from college between 1869 and 1898 taught at one time.[26]

Because Mary Follett entered the Annex as a special rather than as a matriculating student, she could take any course provided she was able to secure the instructor's permission. Among the professors who repeated their Harvard College courses for Annex students were two young men who had recently been appointed professors of American history. One of them, Albert Bushnell Hart, would have a profound influence on Follett's collegiate experience. Few American colleges had any teacher of history — much less American history — on their faculties in the 1880s, so the availability of Hart and Edward Channing on the same faculty was a most unusual opportunity for Follett. Hart, a midwesterner who had studied with Hermann von Holst at Freiburg, was assigned to teach the coveted general American history course, while Channing, a talented product of Yankee and Harvard culture, initially had to serve as the department "handyman." Soon, however, Channing created a research course modeled after the Johns Hopkins historical seminar and allowed his rival, Hart, to share in teaching it.[27]

Historians who have compared the work of these two pioneers of American history usually judge Channing to have been the better scholar, but Hart undoubtedly made the more impressive contributions to the organization of the profession. Perhaps more than any other single person, Hart was responsible for producing the textbooks on which the teaching of American history came to be based. At the time of Hart's appointment to the Harvard faculty, Samuel Eliot Morison tells us, "the only available histories of the United States since the Revolution" were those by Richard Hildreth and von Holst. Given his interest in pedagogy, Hart was acutely aware of the need for new materials and responded by writing and editing several textbooks of his own and by collaborating with Channing in their famous *Guide to the Study of American History*.[28]

This prolific professor's contributions to the profession, however, ranged far beyond the production of textbooks. He was one of the founders of the august *American Historical Review* and served on the editorial board for twelve years. He participated in the setting of professional standards by serving as a member of two influential national committees charged with investigating history teaching in colleges and secondary schools. And he helped to popularize American history by contributing his "superb presence" and "sonorous voice" to innumerable historic and civic occasions. In recognition of these and numerous other professional accomplishments, Hart was elected president of the American Historical Association in 1909.[29]

Albert Bushnell Hart, 1890. Courtesy of the Harvard University Archives.

During the first year of his Harvard appointment, Hart wrote the lead essay in G. Stanley Hall's *Methods of Teaching History,* a book whose list of contributors reads like a "Who's Who" of the profession. Hart's conviction that history is best taught through the investigation of original sources was a central theme of his essay, and Anna Boynton Thompson may have been drawn to his 1887–88 research seminar by a desire to experience this young professor's pedagogy firsthand. Impressed with what she found, Thompson thereafter sent her best history students to Hart; and he, in turn, came to admire her "genius" at inspiring students to a "vivid intellectual life." Given their mutual admiration, Thompson's protégé Mary Follett must have found it a simple matter to gain access to Hart's courses.[30]

Follett's decision to study history in preparation for a career as a teacher was one of the few occupational choices considered appropriate for a young woman of her social class. Her choice was undoubtedly influenced by Anna Boynton Thompson and very likely as well by her aunt, Lydia Averill Follett. William Follett's widow had been deeply involved in the 1870s public school reforms that came to be known nationally as the "Quincy System."[31] The careers of Follett and Thompson demonstrated to Mary that teaching could offer both security and a vocation. They thus served as models for the kind of independence that Barbara Solomon tells us inspired many young women to seek a college education.[32]

Thompson might have moved into the background once she had helped Follett gain admission to the Annex, but this was hardly her style. Thompson took a continuing interest in her students, encouraging them and, when she believed it necessary, rebuking them. In letters written to Blanche Hazard, a talented Thayer graduate who was a student at the Annex from 1892 to 1894, Thompson repeatedly advised resting "all you can" and sleeping "nine hours a night as I do"; only in this way, Thompson thought, would this "small and weak" young woman achieve "as marked success as Miss Follett." Thompson also advised persistence. To succeed, Thompson wrote Hazard in her remarkably frank style, "you must stay years at the Annex that your intelligence may grow and that your wit may make up for your weakness. Otherwise you will not accomplish much in this world."[33]

Young women were often cautioned not to expect too much of themselves, but Thompson encouraged high aspirations. "I expect a brilliant future for you," Thompson told Hazard. "Look far ahead and make broad plans. Ask yourself now what is the very highest thing you can do for yourself in the next ten years, lay the plan carefully, and then question yourself every day, if you have taken one step towards." Thompson knew that it would be extremely difficult for these young women to make a mark in the world. Sometimes her advice was cautionary, as in her use of the maxim "Be sure you are equal to the occasion." But she also made concrete suggestions, sometimes about projects that might be undertaken. "Dr. Hart continually asks me to write articles for publication upon my ideas of teaching History," she wrote young Blanche Hazard, "but I have no time. When you take Sophomore themes you can do it for me, and publish in Educational Journals, and become famous, and get a fine position." At other times Thompson encouraged Hazard to work at making a favorable impression on men who might aid her career. "Do as well as you can in both [professors'] departments," Thompson urged, "and if they recommend you strongly someone will help you." In another letter Thompson was both subtle and shrewd in the tactics she advised: "All you can do to repay [this professor]," Thompson wrote, "is to help increase his reputation, by speaking of his generous friendship, when you have opportunity."[34]

At least some of the professors who taught Annex courses treated Thompson as a colleague, especially in their willingness to confide in her about the progress of her former students. Thompson made judicious use of these comments in motivating the young women. In her campaign to convince Hazard to study at the Annex a second year, Thompson told her that "Professor Ashley [Harvard professor of economics] spoke in high terms of you . . . He said that it was very desirable that you should study with him another year." Thompson also used the professors' comments to chide her former pupils. "You have done all I expected you to do," Thompson wrote to Hazard, "in spite of pretty dresses and short stature. Is it not odd that Professor Ashley thought you 'frivolous'!! because you wear such pretty dresses?"[35]

Thompson certainly had no cause to worry that Mary Follett might be seen as frivolous. Like many other specials, Mary took little part in Annex social life, apparently joining only the Debating Club. She even resisted the Idler, the most popular of the Annex clubs, where activities ranged from "afternoon teas and musicales . . . to donkey-parties, private theatricals, and fancy dances"; the object of the Idler, Eleanor Pearson candidly observed, was not "improvement, mental or moral, but amusement." Mary Follett would probably have felt out of place in this frolicsome scene, feeling as she did a "great debt for very unusual privileges." Instead, Follett focused on her studies and quickly gained a reputation as "a quiet, serious girl and a deep student."[36]

During Follett's first year at the Annex, 1888–89, she enrolled in just one "half-course" each term. In the fall term Follett (and Harriet French, her friend from Thayer Academy) took the introductory course in political economy, in which they read John Stuart Mill's *Principles of Political Economy* and Charles Dunbar's works on banking.[37] In the second term Follett enrolled in Albert Bushnell Hart's "Constitutional and Political History of the United

States, 1783–1865." Conceiving the course as a forum for showing "how and why the Union grew," Hart endeavored to do more than simply describe the Constitution, the federal system, and the branches of government. His lectures took up the "great Constitutional questions" and analyzed them in the context of historical events. The question of the rights of the citizen, for example, was considered in the context of the Sedition Act; the question of the removal of Indians from their native lands under a review of Jackson's administration; and states' rights under secession. "Unsettled questions in our history" were the subject of a series of required "special reports" by students.

To keep these novice investigators "from too close a dependence on a few books" and "to train them in the use of authorities," Hart required the use of numerous sources included in his detailed topical outline. At least one Annex student thought that four required papers and "a little constitutional treatise each week" was "piling it on rather thick!" And many students even found Hart's lectures a challenge. He spoke "as fast as tongue can wag," one recalled, "while we poor wretches sweat along with our pencils and try to note down a word here and there." Even Hart came to believe that there was "no line of courses in college in which, on the average, more is required" of the students; but his courses were among the most popular in the college.[38] Follett responded enthusiastically to Hart's challenging pedagogy and received a grade of A+ for the term.[39]

The following autumn Follett returned to the Annex and elected a heavy load of three full courses. The least inspiring was undoubtedly "European History from the Middle of the Eighteenth Century," taught by Silas M. Macvane, McLean Professor of Ancient and Modern History. Those who studied personally with Macvane, writes Samuel Eliot Morison, profited enormously from his "cool wisdom," but the average undergraduate found him "one of the dullest lecturers that ever addressed a class. His dismal monotonous delivery, broken by periods of prayer-like silence with closed eyes, took all the life out of his students."[40]

Barrett Wendell, Follett's "Advanced Composition" instructor, was anything but monotonous; many Annex students found his criticisms of their work "sarcastic" or even "unkind." On the one hand, Wendell's behavior toward the Annex students merely typified his general "contrariness and eccentricity," but it also reflected a fundamental antipathy toward the Annex. In an 1899 article in the *Harvard Monthly*, Wendell finally wrote openly of his views, trying to awaken the Harvard community to the dangers posed by the Annex. Any professor who had "taught both men and women," Wendell asserted, "must be aware of the comparative lack of mental resistance which he finds in a class composed wholly or chiefly of the latter." A man who "likes to teach women," Wendell warned, was "in real danger of infatuation" and was placing in jeopardy the "pure virility of Harvard tradition."[41]

Despite Wendell's disparagement of the Annex students' capabilities, some were able to learn from him; to these students, he was a "needed goad" and a source of "lasting help." In the Annex version of Wendell's course, students wrote two kinds of themes: brief "daily themes," which cultivated "ease of expression and regular habits of work," and the longer, fortnightly themes, which focused on "correctness and vigor of expression." During the second half-year of the course, the student's fortnightly papers could be written on a topic of her choice — thus enabling the Annex student to connect her training in composition with studies in her favorite subject area.[42]

Follett's fortnightly papers may well have been written in connection with her third course, Albert Bushnell Hart's "Topics in American History and Modern Constitutional History." Follett was one of five women in the research seminar who were preparing an "elaborate thesis based on the study of original sources." Of the topics under investigation, three concerned slavery — a subject which Hart's abolitionist father and his professor at Freiburg, von Holst, saw as central to the American experience. Two other topics, including the one Follett had chosen, concerned a matter of considerable contemporary interest: the appropriate relation of the legislative and executive branches of government.[43]

Whatever intrinsic interest Follett had in her topic — the evolution of the power of the modern Speaker of the House of Representatives — it seems almost certain that her decision to write a book about it was inspired by the confidence that Albert Bushnell Hart showed in the talents of his female students. Hart was so pleased with the quality of their research that he developed a new monograph series so that their "permanent contributions to the literature of American History" might be published. Woodrow Wilson, by contrast, then a disgruntled teacher of political science at Bryn Mawr, wrote in his 1887 diary that "lecturing to young women of the present generation on the history and principles of politics is about as appropriate and profitable as would be lecturing to stone masons on the evolution of fashion in dress."[44]

Hart met weekly with each seminar student, listening to progress reports, discussing difficulties, and suggesting work for the next week. One of Mary's classmates fondly recalled how Hart used to "complain" about the seminar students. "I give those girls enough work to last for a month, and think they are off my mind," he would say, "but in a week they are back asking for more." The quality of the seminar students' investigations so impressed Hart that he appended an unusual message to his grade report. "I wish to bear testimony," Hart wrote, "to the extraordinary faithfulness and interest of the class and to their quickness of discernment and ability to use their knowledge wisely."[45]

The combination of Hart's interest and Follett's hard work paid dividends; by the end of the academic year, "several chapters" of her investigation of the Speaker of the House of Representatives had been written. Hart was so impressed with Follett's "careful research" and "high powers of analysis" that the *Boston Evening Transcript* quoted him as saying that her work would become "the acknowledged authority on the subject." Hart also expressed his confidence in private conversations with Anna Boynton Thompson, telling her that Follett might "look forward to a Ph.D." Despite Hart's enthusiasm about her work, it was difficult for Mary Follett to envision herself as a scholar. That image of her future would emerge from yet another "very unusual privilege" — an inspiring year at Newnham College in Cambridge, England.[46]

6

"The Great Milepost and Turning Point"

Anna Boynton Thompson was responsible for Mary Follett's year at Newnham, Harriet French recalled — perhaps "not financially" but surely "in every other way." In the summer of 1890, Thompson made one of her regular summer pilgrimages abroad to study, but this time, instead of sailing alone from New York, she took Follett along. When Thompson returned to America at the end of the summer, Mary decided to stay.[1]

Follett surely was more fortunate than many other women in obtaining opportunities to develop her talents; but first at the Annex and now at Newnham, she could see how the accomplishments of women were belittled by those who wished to keep women in their place. When Mary arrived at Newnham in July 1890, the college was buzzing with pride over a Newnham student's stunning achievement in Part I of the mathematical Tripos examination; at the end of the Easter term, Philippa Fawcett had been placed "above the Senior Wrangler," scoring higher than the top-ranking male student. Some tried to detract from her achievement, spreading rumors that Fawcett had "ruined her health by overwork," but nothing could diminish the pride felt by supporters of women's higher education. Fawcett's victory was "much more than a personal event," recalled one knowledgeable observer, "for it was a triumphant vindication of the women's colleges, and one of those startling sensational things which travel all over the world, and do more than years of unanswerable argument to promote a good cause."[2]

On the evening of Fawcett's triumph, the college dinner was "the occasion for very heartfelt toasts and speeches, and the bonfire which followed in the garden was a great relief to young ladies who could no longer go on being ladylike. They chaired Philippa all over the place, and the undergraduates from Selwyn came in and joined them in making a really satisfactory noise . . . It was simply the most perfect thing that had ever happened . . . The next day, of course, the news had got out to the world. *The Times* and many other papers had leading articles . . . Telegrams came to [the Fawcett home] 'like snowflakes in a storm,' until even the telegraph boy was driven to ask what was going on in the house, and suggested that it might be a wedding. 'Oh no!' was the housekeeper's answer; 'it's a great deal better than that.' "[3]

Even as Fawcett's victory proclaimed that women were capable of significant work in mathematics — a subject that had long been thought to be beyond their intellectual capabilities — the students of the Newnham Political Club were demonstrating women's aptitude for politics and government. The nature of Follett's participation is unknown, but it seems almost certain that her interest in "actual government" would have drawn her to this "most flourishing of all the [Newnham] societies."[4] Begun in 1884, the Political Club functioned as a Parliament with a Speaker, government and opposition, and constituencies. Contemporary political questions were the focus of the students' debates, and in the clash of views they "learnt to be familiar with parliamentary procedure, and . . . learnt a good deal about public questions." The club was an "immediate success" and quickly became "the absorbing interest of all the competent" students. The students made every effort to be current in their deliberations, even making arrangements "for any special news to be telegraphed direct to the college, so that the students might not have to wait until the morning papers came in." The telegrams often caused "a good deal of excitement."[5] News of the scandalous Parnell divorce case — an event that for a time ended Gladstone's campaign for Irish Home Rule — probably arrived in one of these urgent telegrams during Follett's year in the club.[6]

Being limited to "playing" at politics might have been a bit frustrating for Follett, who was "ambitious to the end," according to one Newnham friend. But Mary's delight in her newfound freedoms and recognition of the tenuousness of her privileged existence served to keep her frustrations from deepening into bitterness or militancy. Rather, Follett came to see the year at Newnham as her "happiest days," a time when she felt "free from New England restrictions."[7]

The restrictions experienced by young women in this era usually were the most pronounced when they were living at home. John Seeley, a Cambridge University historian, maintained "that while it often happened that boys had 'too little home,' girls had 'too much.'" But few shared Seeley's views. At an 1870s conference where proposals for women's colleges were considered, "*the objection had been that girls would be taken away from home.*" Fears about what would happen to young women if they were removed from the protection of their parents grew so intense that Millicent Garrett Fawcett, one of the Newnham founders and the mother of Philippa, the mathematics marvel, came to feel that "wishing to establish a college for women in Cambridge was like wishing to establish it on Saturn." Because public opinion would not allow a real "lady" to take private lodgings in town to attend the lectures that the Fawcetts and Henry Sidgwick were organizing, Sidgwick furnished a Cambridge house at his own expense and employed an older woman to preside there. Sidgwick's determination paid dividends. "There is a good deal of zeal here for women's education," Sidgwick reported to his mother when the lecture series finally began, "not much fanaticism and not much serious opposition." But the absence of vocal opposition did not deceive Sidgwick; the calm, he wryly observed, was probably due to the fact that "*all the jokes have been made.*" Sidgwick's suspicions seem to have been well founded. Before long, in addition to the traditional "passive hostility and sniggers," women coming up to Newnham also had to suffer disparaging comments about their intellectual capabilities and femininity.[8]

Despite the overt hostility directed at the women students, Newnham's residential concept proved a success. To accommodate the growing number of students who wished to enroll, eight and a half acres of land were acquired beyond "the Backs" of the men's colleges. The first of Newnham's red-brick Elizabethan buildings was built in 1875, and by 1890 two others had been added to the site. "The whole place is on a small scale," Alice Mary Longfellow wrote her sister, "delightful, & picturesque as one could desire." The Newnham grounds, while not as stately as the courts of the men's colleges, had their own charm. "On a fine summer's day," an American visitor in the early 1890s reported, students "may be seen basking full length on the lawn watching the tennis players, or curled up under the trees with a book, wandering arm in arm up and down a shady avenue, or forming cozy little tea parties in sheltered nooks."[9] Plantings of ivy, clematis, and other vines climbed the walls and wound their way around the ornamental brickwork above the white-trimmed doors and windows. All this created an aura of substance and permanence — something sadly lacking at the Harvard Annex.

In the early years of the college, the whole experiment might have been jeopardized by a few students determined to test the limits of their freedoms;

but Henry Sidgwick was reluctant to impose numerous restrictions. "My own feeling," Sidgwick wrote to a colleague, "is that we ought to run all risks that Liberty brings with it . . . Restraint of Liberty is our rock ahead, I foresee." There were rules, of course, but college life offered these young women much greater freedom than they had enjoyed while living at home. The doors to the residence halls were open until eight during the summer terms, six during the winter; and students were allowed out till eleven if they signed out and in. Students were expected "not to absent themselves" from lectures, but it was "quite optional" whether the afternoon and evening "work hours" were used for study. They also were quite "free to go where they will," including the grounds of the men's colleges. This practice contrasted sharply with Follett's experience at Harvard, where Annex students were actively discouraged from passing through Harvard Yard. Newnham students could attend dances and the theater, take boats onto the Cam, and even spend an afternoon at a "kettle-drum" tea of one of the Cambridge dons provided they were accompanied by a chaperone. Nor did Newnham impose special rules "as to the way Sunday should be kept," although parents would probably have welcomed such regulations. The absence of such a requirement, ironically, seems to have had the effect of encouraging church attendance; many students chose the Sunday services at King's College Chapel, which was "kindly thrown open to the women students." The students responded to their new liberties with considerable maturity and rarely abused their privileges. "What strikes one as most characteristic of Newnham," wrote an American visitor in 1890, "is the ease with which the students turn from work to play, from play to work, and the energy they throw into both. At one moment the halls are alive with sound of music and laughter; the next moment a dead silence reigns."[10]

Perhaps more than any other feature of residential life, Newnham students valued having their own rooms. "To find oneself given a room of one's own," Sybil Oldfield writes in her biography of Newnhamites Flora Mayor and Mary Sheepshanks, "with a fire, bookshelves, a table for working at and armchairs for friends, was to discover a perfect combination of privacy and warmth, of intellectual stimulus and emotional support." The college provided the basic furnishings — a bed, chairs, and a desk — but in most other aspects of decoration students were encouraged to express their individuality. Consequently, maidenhair ferns and pots of primulas could be found next to photographs and curios brought from home; beds were transformed into daytime divans with yards of bright Indian cotton purchased in London; and rugs were spread on the floor to give both warmth and color. One of the joys of having one's own room was the opportunity to invite "guests" in for late evening "cocoas." Shortly before ten o'clock, when the bells of the neighboring colleges rang, there was "a general closing of books." Each "hostess" served cocoa and cakes to the young women she had invited, and the rooms came alive with games, songs, and sparkling conversation.[11]

A "cocoa" became a genuine social event when an invitation was received from someone as popular as Melian Stawell, the young classics scholar who became Follett's friend. Stawell was "the most striking personality at Newnham at that time," Mary Sheepshanks recalled, a person of "outstanding ability, striking physical beauty and grace."[12] Endowed with "every gift," this brilliant young woman even had the athletic skills of a tennis champion.[13] When Stawell invited Flora Mayor, then a first-year student, "to dance with her and afterwards to come and see her," Mayor proudly wrote her sister, "you don't know what an honour that is, but she is absolutely the Queen of the College." The men of Cambridge were also attracted to this talented Australian beauty. On one occasion, her entry into a room full of people prompted a man to exclaim, "At last the gods have come down to earth in the likeness of a woman!" And another, a fellow classics student, thought Stawell was "a lovely person." "I think she's very superior indeed," Edward Marsh wrote to Bertrand Russell after their first meeting, "she seems to have quite a rare feeling for beauty in art, I hope we shall see more of her."[14]

As Stawell recalled it, she and Mary Follett "made friends at once," for Stawell had been "struck by [Follett's] ardour" even before she realized her "brilliance." Being befriended by the "Queen of the College" surely was a thrill for Mary, who had been shy and withdrawn during her first years as a college student.[15] Stawell could empathize with Follett, being a foreigner in England herself, and probably used her savvy as a second-year student to help Mary adjust. This was not, however, to be a fleeting college friendship. Stawell, like Follett, had felt isolated and unloved in her family and had known the "bitter experiences of childhood quarrels" and "the loneliness of trouble." Perhaps the sharing of these painful childhood experiences helped forge a bond of friendship that was to endure a lifetime.[16]

As important as Stawell's friendship was in encouraging Follett to be more outgoing with her peers, the interest and encouragement of the Cambridge faculty were equally significant in Follett's development. As a Harvard Annex student, Mary had been accustomed to receiving instruction from Harvard professors who repeated their courses at the Annex. At Newnham College, however, several forms of instruction were available. In some subjects, students were taught by female tutors of the college; in others, Cambridge lecturers repeated their lectures at Newnham; and sometimes Newnham students were permitted, at the lecturer's discretion, to attend regular university and college lectures. The last form of instruction, while a distinct opportunity, was also somewhat intimidating. Alice Mary Longfellow, who studied at Newnham in the mid-1880s, wrote in her diary about how relieved she was to discover that the "ordeal" of attending a lecture with young men was not *"very formidable . . .* as there are only about a dozen of them & nine of us."[17]

Among the Cambridge instructors who admitted women to their lectures during Follett's year at Newnham were four historians: John Seeley, Regius Professor of Modern History; Mandell Creighton, Dixie Professor of Ecclesiastical History; and two younger men, William Cunningham, university lecturer in economic history, and George W. Prothero, the history tutor at King's College. Political philosophy lectures were offered by Henry Sidgwick, Knightsbridge Professor and the primary force behind the establishment of Newnham College.[18] This group of men was responsible for virtually all the major reforms in the study and teaching of history at Cambridge. And these were the men with whom Follett would study as she continued to work on her analysis of the role of the Speaker of the House of Representatives.

When John Seeley was appointed to the faculty in 1869, he was "very much aware of the poor regard in which History was held at Cambridge." The absence of clearly articulated methods of investigation or even an acceptable scheme for organizing historical "facts" caused many observers to doubt that the study of history would ever be more than a gentleman's literary hobby. Historical study at Cambridge was held in such low esteem, Peter Slee tells us in his Cambridge doctoral thesis, that the field was in serious danger of being banished from the curriculum. Responding to this threat, Seeley set for himself the task of justifying the study of modern history as an academic discipline. It was largely through his political savvy and persistence that history survived at Cambridge and secured sufficient support for the creation of an independent history Tripos examination. Along with Henry Sidgwick, Seeley believed that every well-organized subject provided the necessary means to achieve a sound mental training; the particular worth of studying history, therefore, hinged on its "permanent value, or utility." Seeley was less interested in having students learn either historical facts or methods than in finding ways to teach them to "reason upon the historical process in contemporary terms."[19]

Just as Sidgwick, John Stuart Mill, and Henry Fawcett had argued that political economy could be utilized in the cause of social welfare, Seeley proposed creating a "science of politics" as a means to "effecting truly progressive and peaceful political change" in an era when the authority of the church was in decline. "In common with a school of social critics from Carlyle to Chesterton," writes Deborah Wormell, "Seeley diagnosed a severe and persistent threat to social stability from the material and cultural gulf between classes in England. His desire to avert revolution was at the root of all his social theories.

Success, in his view, depended on the willingness of the elite to close the gap by means of education, and of the mass to be thus moulded and enlightened."[20]

Believing that everyone "who studies political institutions, whether in the past or in the present, studies history," Seeley wanted his fledgling historians to concern themselves with the growth of states in the modern world, investigating relevant political facts and providing instruction for future political leaders in a new "school of statesmanship." Although Seeley did little to make his "science of politics" a reality, it achieved such wide acceptance as the rationale for teaching history that Seeley's views dominated the Cambridge history curriculum for the next ten years.[21]

Despite Seeley's contributions to the reform of the history curriculum, he soon found his ideas under attack. In the early 1880s, at almost the same time that Hart and Channing were initiating major changes in the Harvard history curriculum, newer members of the Cambridge faculty also began to agitate for change. Having had to learn the historian's craft while teaching, these younger men were especially sensitive to the failure of the Cambridge curriculum to teach methods of writing history. In their eyes, the fact that a first class honors degree in history could be obtained without knowledge of original sources was simply "scandalous." It was time, they argued, to make the ability "to sift and to compare historical evidence" an essential requirement for the degree.[22] The first public spokesman for the reformers' position emerged when Mandell Creighton delivered his January 1885 inaugural lecture as Dixie Professor of Ecclesiastical History.

Creighton disputed both the aims and the methods of historical study that Seeley had fostered. Seeley had persuaded the Cambridge faculty to accept the study of history as an academic discipline insofar as it served as a "school for statesmanship." Creighton found this rationale too narrow; the quality of judgment engendered by studying history, Creighton argued, could be useful to "many different classes of minds." Creighton was especially critical of the failure of the Cambridge curriculum to teach history through a process of "critical reflection on original sources." This issue also deeply troubled George W. Prothero, one of the younger historians who was virtually self-taught in the area of medieval history. The history Tripos, Prothero argued, should qualify a student "as a teacher of the subject, or as a further investigator of some branch of the same." To accomplish this reform, he proposed reducing the number of required examination papers in subjects such as politics and law and substituting for them studies of historical method and investigations of the original sources of a particular historical period.[23]

Seeley did not deny the validity of the reformers' criticisms. Even though his personal experience had been that his most original ideas came not from extensive study of primary sources, but from "reflection on what was already known," Seeley believed that the study of original sources was a important part of an historical education. It had been omitted from the Cambridge curriculum, Seeley explained, largely because of the difficulty in ascertaining a student's knowledge of method and sources under the Tripos examination system. A dissertation could be required of advanced students, but this was not practical for the vast number of history students. Seeley therefore thought it better to have lecturers introduce original sources "in their own time and their own way." Mandell Creighton was already doing so, and Seeley himself had begun to promote discussion of original sources in his "conversation class."[24]

In spite of the fact that there was no ready solution to the evaluation problem that Seeley posed, the Cambridge faculty revised the curriculum later that year. Under the new scheme, the training of future historians was accorded the same importance as the training of political leaders and statesmen, and the student's knowledge of the original sources of a particular period was made "a more prominent feature of the Tripos." To provide time for instruction in methods, a compromise was forged: the study of political institutions, Seeley's first love, was retained as a requirement, but the other requirements in politics, law, and economics were eliminated; and students, for the first time, were allowed to choose their advanced studies either from "cognate sciences" such as politics, law, and economics or from purely "historical" subjects.[25]

Follett's studies with Albert Bushnell Hart had prepared her well for the revised Cambridge curriculum, and she took immediate advantage of the opportunities available to her. One December evening, after attending Mandell Creighton's evening lecture in the Emmanuel College dining hall, Follett was introduced by Creighton to Justin Winsor, the historian and Harvard College librarian, who was visiting Cambridge. Follett spoke approvingly, Winsor later reported, of the "labors of Seeley and Prothero . . . among the Newnham girls" and "the inspiring character of Creighton's talks in the class-room at Newnham, where his kindly yet searching questions forced his pupils to their best endeavors." At the same time, however, Winsor recalled, "she was not unmindful of the warm efforts by which the history-students of the Harvard Annex are so admirably nurtured under Prof. Hart."[26] No wonder. The scientific study of the power of the American Speaker that Follett had begun under Hart's direction was exactly the kind of historical investigation that would have merited the approbation of all parties to the Cambridge curriculum controversy.

A successful presentation of a portion of her work on the Speakership to the Newnham Historical Society helped to build Follett's confidence in her abilities as a scholar. The exact topic on which she spoke is not known, but her friend, the talented classics scholar Melian Stawell, remembered that Mary "was concerned . . . about the too great gap between the Executive and the Legislative functions in America, and she believed that the work of the American Speaker might be developed so as to bridge it." This occasion gave Stawell a new appreciation of Follett's desire to excel. " 'Oh, it isn't good enough,' she broke out to [Stawell] as she shook the unread paper in her room before the meeting, 'and I did so want to do something good for my America.' " Follett's passion for perfection, born out of the experiences of her childhood, was reinforced in this particular situation by the tendency of Americans from Cambridge, Massachusetts, to view Cambridge University as "Mecca." Because the Annex had tried to emulate Newnham and John Harvard had graduated from Emmanuel, here more than anywhere Follett was anxious to give a good account of herself and her college. She apparently succeeded. It was my "first glimpse of her power," Stawell later recalled. "Of all the brilliant discourses I have heard since by young University members, masculine and feminine, this was one of the most brilliant."[27]

Follett would later call her year at Newnham "the great milepost and turning point in her life." Her Harvard Annex education had been validated by the distinguished Cambridge University faculty, and Follett, as a result, felt "free and hopeful" and "looked forward eagerly to life as a scholar." Henry Sidgwick, in particular, seems to have "opened the door to living for her." Sidgwick's blend of utilitarianism and commonsense intuitionism were not the "reigning views of the England of his time"; that distinction went to the Oxford idealists. Perhaps as a result, Sidgwick's legacy to Follett was less concerned with a particular set of philosophical ideas than with her choice of analytical style. Sidgwick's work, in Brand Blanshard's view, "stands as a permanent implicit criticism . . . of too facile a system-building on the one hand and of too ready surrender to 'reasons of the heart' on the other." He sought always "to rethink older positions into full clarity, to show with inexhaustible patience where, how and how much the actual facts required their amendment, and to bring conflicting positions into harmony by credible compromise."[28]

Unlike Thomas H. Green, Sidgwick's contemporary at Oxford, the Cambridge philosopher rarely had students clamoring to get into his classes; but certain talented individuals — the historian Frederic W. Maitland, the classical scholar Lowes Dickinson, the economist Maynard Keynes, and the statesman Arthur Balfour — found themselves deeply influenced by what Sidgwick gave them. Sidgwick's influence, according to Blanshard and others, "was attained less by his conclusions than by the manner of man he was — by his ways of thinking, writing, and teaching, and perhaps above all by the atmosphere of impartial reasonableness that pervaded his thought and his action." Arthur

Balfour, one of Sidgwick's earliest students, who also was his brother-in-law and lifelong friend, said of Sidgwick: "Of all the men I have known he was the readiest to consider every controversy and every controversialist on their merits. He never claimed authority; he never sought to impose his views; he never argued for victory; he never evaded an issue. Whether these are the qualities that best fit their possessor to found a 'school' may be doubted. But there can be no doubt whatever that they contrived to give Sidgwick the most potent and memorable influence, not so much over the opinions as over the intellectual development of anyone who had the good fortune to be associated with him whether as pupil or as friend."[29]

An eccentric figure, Sidgwick in appearance and mannerisms seemed almost a caricature of a nineteenth-century university professor. He was "small in stature," with a "full ambrosial silken-textured beard [that] set off the large brow and clear-cut nose." Notoriously indifferent to dress, Sidgwick was so absent-minded and exhibited such an abstract, absorbed manner while lecturing that he sometimes seemed to pass into a state of "ecstasy." Although Sidgwick was burdened with a pronounced stammer, many took great pleasure in his talk, which "like a mountain stream, [was] full and sparkling, pouring along regardless of the nature of its banks." In discussion and debate, James Bryce found Sidgwick both engaging and adept, "seeing in a moment the point of an argument, seizing on distinctions which others had failed to perceive, suggesting new aspects from which a question might be regarded, and enlivening every topic by a keen yet sweet and kindly wit."[30]

A man of such superior intellect might have seemed a formidable and unapproachable figure, but Sidgwick's fine sense of humor helped to give him more human dimensions. A Newnham student who was visiting his house for a dinner party recalled with amusement that after all the guests had gone, "Sidgwick leaned against the mantel and, balancing himself on one foot upon the coping about the hearth, kept his wife and me intent as he discussed the maladjustment of the universe as evidenced by the fact that when your dress shoes begin to be comfortable they cease to be presentable." This gentle wit and "constant and almost excessive self-criticism" kept Sidgwick from intellectual arrogance.[31]

Sidgwick's instrument for stimulating the minds of his pupils to "independent intellectual action" was the Socratic method; for the truly capable students, these dialogues were exhilarating. "However small the class might be," Frederic W. Maitland recalled, "Sidgwick always gave us his very best, not what might be good enough for undergraduates, or what might serve for temporary purposes, but the complex truth, just as he saw it, with all those reservations and qualifications, exceptions and distinctions which suggested themselves to a mind that was indeed marvelously subtle, but was showing us its wonderful power simply because even in a lecture-room it could be content with nothing less than the maximum of attainable and communicable truth."[32]

Students less gifted or less motivated than Maitland, however, did not always appreciate Sidgwick's subtlety. Alice Mary Longfellow confided to her diary that she was frustrated by Sidgwick's inclination to be "so hair splitting & microscopic in his criticisms, & so remote & incoherent in his manner"; furthermore, she was provoked "that he should have spent half the course over Hobbes, & now crowd Bentham & Mill into such small space." A session with Sidgwick all too often left Longfellow feeling "like the most weak minded of 'plain men.' "[33]

Mary Follett, by contrast, seems to have felt only "affection and admiration" for Sidgwick. In the May term, she was one of only two students enrolled in Sidgwick's lectures on the "History of Political Theory"; when the other student withdrew, Sidgwick continued the lectures for her alone.[34] Private coaching from Henry Sidgwick, another Newnham student attested, was a memorable experience.

> Surrounded by walls composed entirely of books, [Sidgwick] would sit with my paper before him, and point to a cross he had made in the margin; then, lifting his mild blue eyes to my face, he would ask, "What exactly did you m-m-mean by that, Miss Sickert?" Leaning back, gently touching the tips of the fingers of one hand with the finger-tips of the other, he would continue to gaze at me as if I were very far away . . . Then he would say something of this sort: "I want you to begin at the beginning, as if you were explaining to somebody who knew nothing about it" . . . And, in a series of Socratic questionings, he would proceed to clear away the rubbish and open up the line of thought . . . It seems strange that I should have been so excessively afraid of him. Partly that was due to his remote and abstracted manner, but partly also, I think because he presented me with a very difficult standard of intellectual integrity: to observe, to record, to deduce with no aim but the truth, as nearly as one could hit it. No stress of after years could shake the result of this discipline. No easy path to difficult conclusions could satisfy. Truth is not simple.[35]

A few months after leaving England, Follett wrote Sidgwick a letter. "I gained much inspiration from Cambridge," Follett told him, "particularly from your lectures in political science & political philosophy. For the history student a year at Cambridge seems to me an era in his life." Struggling for a way to express the full extent of her gratitude, Follett closed her letter with a pledge: "Perhaps . . . the best way in which a pupil can thank her teacher is in trying to give to others something of what she herself has received. And this I shall try to do."[36]

Despite her delight over her Newnham experiences, Mary came home at the end of the year. A friend of later years thought that she had been "called home to take care of her mother," but this seems unlikely. Although Mrs. Follett naturally would have been anxious for her daughter to return, there is no evidence of a family crisis.[37] Mary stayed on at Newnham until the May term lectures had ended, and Mrs. Follett vacationed as usual — in New Hampshire in the weeks preceding Mary's return and afterward on Cape Cod.[38] Another sign that all was well at home was the grand party that Mrs. Follett gave on the morning of Mary's return, transforming the spacious parlour of the School Street house "into a beautiful flower garden" and filling the dining room with "choice hot-house and domestic plants." In this lush setting, a "large number of prominent society people, including many distinguished personages from Boston and Braintree," welcomed Mary home.[39]

It was an auspicious return. Within a few weeks, Follett was invited to give lectures in political science at a private school in Boston. This school was almost certainly the one founded a decade earlier by Boston's innovative educational philanthropist, Pauline Agassiz Shaw. Shaw was the Swiss-born daughter of the Harvard naturalist Louis Agassiz and the stepdaughter of Elizabeth Cary Agassiz, president of the society that supervised the Harvard Annex. The Agassiz family was experienced in the running of private schools. In an effort to meet household expenses, Mrs. Agassiz had established a private school for girls aged fifteen to eighteen in their home and operated it for eight years.[40]

When she was only nineteen, Pauline Agassiz became the wife of Quincy Adams Shaw, a thirty-five-year-old descendent of the Parkmans and the Shaws, two distinguished Yankee families. Shaw would soon become one of New England's wealthiest men, successfully opening the Calumet and Hecla copper mines of Michigan with the help of his wife's brother, Alexander. In 1880, in an effort to provide a better education for her own children and those of her friends, Mrs. Shaw opened a large private day school in the Back Bay of Boston. Of the 236 students enrolled in 1891, only one-quarter were older than fifteen; many of the older boys left to attend the elite college preparatory academies.[41] Still, the Yankee surnames of many of Shaw's students — Adams, Eliot, Greenough, Hallowell, Homans, Morison, Nichols, Perkins, Saltonstall, Shattuck, Wigglesworth — represent a formidable slice of Boston's social register.[42]

Mrs. Shaw's School was widely recognized as the most progressive in Boston. It was coeducational through all the grades — then almost unheard of in

Pauline Agassiz Shaw, ca. 1868. The Schlesinger Library, Radcliffe Institute, Harvard University.

Boston — and was a leader in innovative curricula and methods.[43] A full range of traditional subjects was taught: composition, rhetoric, literature, history, mathematics, sciences, classical and modern languages. But the school also offered a number of unusual courses, especially favoring those that encouraged "hands-on" learning. In "inventional geometry," for example, students were taught to make complex geometric constructions from a single piece of cardboard. A clay-modeling class encouraged students to design and create figures that could be baked and taken home. "Sloyd," a Swedish system of manual training, taught students to use woodcarving tools to reproduce a variety of plaster-cast objects in a series of "carefully graded and systematically constructed exercises." Shaw had seen the sloyd system during a trip to Europe and apparently was intrigued with its "synthesis of physical labor, respect for work, self-reliance, and habits of order, accuracy and neatness."[44]

It was in this innovative climate that Follett was invited to give her lectures on political science to "girls between 17 & 20." "It is an experiment," Follett excitedly informed Henry Sidgwick. "If it is successful it may go far towards changing the methods of studying history here. History teaching in America is at present in a transition stage. In most of our preparatory schools (schools just below the colleges) history teaching consists almost entirely of stuffing the pupils with the facts of narrative history. Nothing is known of political science and political philosophy. I do not mean that those subjects are not taught; that could not be expected; but the teachers themselves know nothing of them. It seems to me that a teacher who knew something of political science & political philosophy could infiltrate much into her pupils and make history much more valuable to them than it could ever be by learning a string of facts."[45]

The reforms that Follett hoped to make in history teaching were only beginning to be recognized as necessary by the nation's educators. Albert Bushnell Hart opened the report of his 1887 survey of history teaching in American secondary schools by remarking that "it is not many years since the question, how is history taught in the United States? could be answered in only one of two brief ways; it was not taught at all; or it was taught perfunctorily from single text-books." The teaching of American history, according to Hart, was in a particularly sad state. It was "omitted entirely in half the schools, and, where taught, occupies less than half the time allotted to history [or less than three hours a week for the equivalent of one school year]." Because of their poor historical education, secondary school teachers rarely gave lectures or engaged their students in discussion; "by far the most frequent" method of instruction was to have students study from a textbook and then to give them examinations on the historical "facts." Unfortunately, there was little likelihood of rapid reform of these methods, since the preparation of secondary school teachers was woefully inadequate. As late as 1884, Harvard president Charles W. Eliot "declared without fear of contradiction that the great majority of American colleges had no teacher of history — much less of American history — on their faculties, and that even 'in so excellent an institution as Princeton there is only one professor of history against three of Greek.' "[46]

In addition to collecting information from principals and teachers in the secondary schools, Hart surveyed a number of college students about their precollege experiences. Only one-sixth of them reported that reading beyond the text had been required in their history classes, and nearly a third seemed to Hart "to have read, or a least to have remembered, absolutely nothing outside of their text-books." To improve this dismal picture, Hart recommended a more complex role for the secondary school teacher. "He must teach facts; and for that purpose the text-book and recitation system is best adapted. He must show the relations between them; and lectures and talks will bring out those relations. He must accustom the pupil to assemble material for himself and to test it; the topical method affords the necessary training. He must lead the student to think and judge a little for himself; and the preparation of topics and outside reading will induce some degree of such independent thought."[47]

Hart's recommendations and a similar set of guidelines promulgated by the 1893 Madison Conference on History, Civil Government, and Political Economy seem to have had a positive effect. By 1899, when the American Historical Association's distinguished "Committee of Seven" published its report on history teaching at the secondary level, it was possible to announce that "the old rote system is going by the board. Practically every school now reports the use of material outside the text-book, and recognizes that a library is necessary for efficient work; and nearly all teachers assign topics for investigation by the pupil, or give written recitations, or adopt like means of arousing the pupil's interest and of leading him to think and work in some measure independently, in order that he may acquire power as well as information."[48]

Further achievements in historical education, however, would be not possible, the committee warned, unless history was allotted more time in the secondary school curriculum. A four-year requirement was recommended: ancient history, medieval and modern European history, English history, and, in the student's last year, American history and civil government. The committee also thought it important to encourage a more "scientific spirit" in the teaching of history; the report urged teachers to assign collateral reading from multiple sources, to involve students in original investigations, and to require the preparation of more written work.[49]

Finally, this 1899 report recommended that history be taught in the context of political science — the very thing that Follett had been experimenting with earlier in the decade at Mrs. Shaw's School. Students, the committee observed, "should be led to see that society is in movement, that what one sees about him is not the eternal but the transient, and that in the processes of change virtue must be militant if it is to be triumphant." Joint instruction in civil government and the history of American institutions could provide "practical preparation for social adaptation and for forceful participation in civic activities"; some members of the committee also surely hoped that it might socialize the numerous Irish, Italian, and eastern European immigrants to reject the ward boss and political machine in favor of candidates espousing traditional Yankee values.[50]

This new emphasis on government and political science troubled some historians. They were especially worried that the political scientists' incursions into the traditional domain of history threatened to relegate historians to "fact-finding." Cognizant of the historians' concerns, the committee tried to assure their primacy by asserting that "civil government can best be studied as a part of history. What we desire to recommend is simply this, that in any school where there is not time for sound, substantial courses in both civil government and history, the history be taught in such a way that the pupil will gain a knowledge of the essentials of the political system which is the product of that history; and that, where there is time for separate courses, they be taught, not as isolated, but as interrelated and interdependent subjects."[51]

The controversy between historians and political scientists must have seemed familiar to Mary Follett. During her year in England, she had seen how Cambridge encouraged students to learn history in the context of political science, law, and economics while Oxford, under the leadership of Bishop William Stubbs, championed the study of history "for its own sake." That Follett was more inclined to the Cambridge view of this controversy is clear from her letter to Henry Sidgwick. "As a patriotic American," she wrote, "I am anxious my country should not be behind" in the adoption of these new methods of teaching history. "I feel also as if I owed a duty to England to make some practical use of what I had learned there." Anxious to add her "little" to the effort "in the right way," Mary sought her former professor's advice. Known as a man of "tireless patience . . . which nothing but pretentiousness could disturb," Sidgwick undoubtedly gave Follett some words of encouragement.[52]

The lectures apparently were a success. Follett was offered a regular teaching position at Mrs. Shaw's School and taught there for almost four years. Throughout this period, however, most of Follett's energy was devoted to completing her book on the Speakership.[53]

The Speaker of the House of Representatives

Follett's decision to study the Speakership can be attributed largely to the influence of Albert Bushnell Hart.[1] Students in Hart's research seminars were reminded repeatedly that governmental institutions are "a growth, not a creation" and were required to study the actual functioning of American institutions of government rather than simply acquainting themselves with the intentions of the framers of the Constitution. Each semester Hart provided his classes with a list of appropriate research topics, more than half of which typically concerned "some phase of modern government."[2] In addition, he challenged his most talented students to undertake investigations that he deemed worthy of their talents. The American biographer and historian Samuel Eliot Morison, for example, recalls being urged to write a biography of Harrison Gray Otis — an idea that "was as astonishing to me, a junior in college, as if he had suggested that I should design a cathedral or run for the presidency."[3] In the late 1880s, when Mary Follett began her studies at the Harvard Annex, one of the most pressing problems of American government was the chaotic functioning of the House of Representatives. As such, it periodically appeared on Hart's list of recommended research topics, and Hart may well have encouraged Follett to focus on some of the difficulties of the House for her research seminar investigations.

Members of the minority party in the House of Representatives had grown increasingly bold in the 1880s in their efforts to obstruct legislative business and had come to see filibustering and other delaying tactics as their right. During debate on one bill, "no fewer than eighty-six roll calls were taken, each consuming about half an hour." On another occasion a single member "kept the House engaged in roll-calls for eight days in his attempt to secure consideration of the bill organizing the Territory of Oklahoma."[4] Calls for reform finally began to appear, including one in September 1889 from a young Massachusetts representative who was appalled by what he had seen. "The American House of Representatives today," wrote Henry Cabot Lodge, "is a complete travesty upon representative government, upon popular government, and upon government by the majority."[5]

Albert Bushnell Hart tried to make his students aware of the increasing impotence of the House. Two of the several topics that Hart assigned for class discussion and debate during the 1887–88 academic year, for example, concerned the House of Representatives: the first asked whether it was appropriate for minority members of the House to use filibustering as a tactic to defeat the majority's legislative proposals; the second asked whether having the president's cabinet sit as members of the House would foster creation of a coherent legislative program.[6] Understanding the full range of problems facing the House of Representatives was beyond the capabilities of most students, but Mary Follett's excellent academic preparation and her superior work in Hart's earlier constitutional history course boded well for the enterprise she was about to undertake.

As a result of her historical studies with Thompson and Hart, Follett knew that the era in which the modern House of Representatives was conducting its business was characterized by rapid economic, social, and political change. The thirty-year period following the Civil War was a time of unprecedented economic growth. By the end of the century, railroad expansion, new industrial technologies, and the introduction of capital markets had allowed America to join Great Britain and Germany in the ranks of the world's leading industrial powers. The economy also experienced three major recessions, fed by unregulated financial markets and the integrated character of the massive cartels and trusts. Owners slashed wages, forcing their workers to bear much of the economic burden of the recessions; and the workers retaliated, forming unions and engaging in disruptive work stoppages and strikes. Even American farmers temporarily abandoned their characteristic independence, organizing to protest the high interest rates and falling prices. Economic instability was only one element of the complex environment of the 1870s and 1880s. Settlers continued to surge into the American West and brutally forced American

Indians from their native lands. European immigrants flooded into the cities of the East and Midwest in such numbers that by 1880 over a quarter of the nation's population lived in urban areas. The needs of these new citizens for jobs and other services proved to be fertile ground for the emergence of ward bosses and machine politics.

The complexity of this economic, social, and political environment created an ever-increasing volume of congressional business. During the Congresses of the 1870s, around 37,000 public and private bills were introduced; by the mid-1880s this number had doubled.[7] The key legislative controversies of the period concerned tariffs and the currency, and both issues were complicated by the growing tension between the requirements of a national economy and the desires of local and special economic interests. As early as 1865, it was clear to many that the high tariffs on imports, enacted to protect American industries during the Civil War, should be reduced. But every attempt to do so ended with special interests frustrating the reformers' efforts or, even worse, raising rather than lowering the tariffs. The high tariffs produced such embarrassingly large treasury surpluses that even pork-barrel projects and patronage failed to eliminate them. Currency questions also became a battleground. During the thirty years following the Civil War, there had been continuing controversy between those who wished to keep the inflated wartime money supply and those who would contract it by returning to hard currency. During these turbulent years, the only pieces of legislation that emerged from the Congress with anything like unanimous support were the Interstate Commerce Commission (1887) and the Sherman Anti-Trust Act (1890). But even these were undermined by ambiguous wording, lax enforcement, and adverse judicial decisions.[8]

Among the factors inhibiting the passage of important national legislation was a persistent pattern of divided government. Only once during the seven Congresses between 1875 and 1889 did a single party control the presidency as well as both houses of Congress.[9] This pattern of divided government, James M. Burns writes, was further complicated by the fact that in the Congress, the "political pendulum oscillated wildly. In the most volatile part of the country — the more heavily urban areas stretching from Wisconsin and Illinois through New England — the Republicans won 115 congressional seats to the Democrats' 54 in 1888, lost to the Democrats 63 to 106 two years later, split 88 to 89 in 1892, and overwhelmed their foes 168 to 9 two years later. The Democrats lost a total of 113 seats in the 1894 congressional elections, the largest pendulum sweep since the Civil War."[10] The stunning electoral shifts of the 1880s sent so many new members to the Congress that one in three was newly elected. The resulting lack of continuity so exacerbated the disorder caused by party factionalism that it was almost impossible to move legislation through the Congress.

In earlier years, the president might have been able to bring order to the congressional chaos, but postwar battles over Reconstruction had seriously weakened the presidency. Congressional Republicans had bitterly opposed the conciliatory programs proposed by Presidents Lincoln and Johnson. Determined to reassert legislative control of the government, the Republicans clashed repeatedly with Johnson and finally impeached him. Johnson was eventually acquitted in his 1868 Senate trial, but the Radicals' campaign against him successfully stripped the presidency of much of its authority.[11] The Republican presidents who followed Andrew Johnson into office — Grant, Hayes, Garfield, Arthur, and Harrison — conspicuously lacked political and personal skills, and several of their administrations were wracked by corruption and scandal. The political instability that resulted is evident in the presidential contests of the 1880s. In these three elections, the victor "edged out his closest opponent by less than 1 percent"; and the 1888 winner in electoral votes, the Republican Benjamin Harrison, actually received fewer popular votes than did his opponent, Grover Cleveland. Even Cleveland, perhaps the most active of the Gilded Age presidents, depended on a volatile partnership with the fiercely independent "Mugwumps." As a result, he had little latitude for exercising leadership in his first-term dealings with the Congress. His failure to fashion new federal policies and programs, however, was equally a product of Cleveland's conviction that the federal government should have only a "limited mission."[12]

What little leadership did exist during this turbulent era seemed to be located in the Congress. Thaddeus Stevens, the powerful Pennsylvania representative who had led the impeachment fight against Johnson, tightened legislative control over appropriations from his position as chair of the newly created House Committee on Appropriations. Senator John Sherman from Ohio was responsible for the successful compromise legislation on the currency. House Speaker James G. Blaine used his appointment prerogatives to create committees that would serve the aims of his party. William McKinley used his position as chairman of the House Committee on Ways and Means to secure passage of the 1890 McKinley Tariff. And Thomas B. Reed, whose imposing presence and formidable skills as a parliamentarian and a debater made him the unquestioned Republican leader in the House for almost twenty years, persistently advocated reform of the House rules.[13]

Writing about the Congress in his 1888 masterpiece *The American Commonwealth*, James Bryce, the highly respected English observer of the American scene, asserted that the Congress "has succeeded in occupying nearly all the ground which the Constitution left debatable between the President and itself." At the same time, however, Bryce concluded that the Congress was "no more respected or loved by the people now than it was seventy years ago," and had developed "no higher capacity for promoting the best interests of the State."[14] A curious paradox is reflected in these remarks. The Congress — a body that many thought had grown too strong vis-à-vis the executive branch — was nevertheless unable to transact the nation's business.

By 1890 there was widespread agreement that the element of the legislative process most in need of revision was the committee system. The committees had originally been created as a means of coping with the increasing flow of congressional business. But by 1885 they had come to have such importance in the passage of legislation that Woodrow Wilson (then a new professor of history and politics at Bryn Mawr) had disparagingly called ours "a government by the Standing Committees of Congress." Wilson's sentiments were echoed ten years later by Mary Follett when she said that "the Congress no longer exercises its lawful function of law-making; that has gone to the committees, as completely as in England it has passed to the Cabinet." The problems that accompanied such heavy reliance on the committee system were most apparent in the House of Representatives, where the diffusion of power and competitive jealousies among committee chairmen made it impossible to produce a national program of legislation. In *Congressional Government,* Wilson charged that the committee system was incapable of fostering either opportunities for legislative leadership or better coordination between the legislative and executive branches of government. The system, as he saw it, had produced a federal government that "lacks strength because its powers are divided, lacks promptness because its authorities are multiplied, lacks wieldiness because its processes are roundabout, lacks efficiency because its responsibility is indistinct and its action without competent direction."[15]

A certain amount of coordination and control was provided by the Speaker of the House — enough so that Wilson recognized the Speakership to be "a constitutional phenomenon of the first importance, deserving a very thorough and critical examination." James Bryce went even further, describing the Speaker's power as "so far-reaching" that it was "no exaggeration to call him the second, if not the first political figure in the United States." But neither Wilson nor Bryce believed that the Speaker of the House of Representatives could bridge the gap between legislative and executive functions of government, and Wilson was firmly opposed to the idea of concentrating more power in the Speakership.[16]

According to Wilson, nothing less than a radical change would resolve

America's governmental problems. In his 1879 article, "Cabinet Government in the United States," Wilson proposed giving "to the heads of the Executive departments — the members of the Cabinet — seats in Congress, with the privilege of the initiative in legislation and some part of the unbounded privileges now commanded by the Standing Committees." These cabinet ministers, according to Wilson, would see the "practical impossibility of holding their seats, and continuing to represent the Administration, after they had found themselves unable to gain the consent of a majority to their policy," and, on such occasions, would resign.[17]

The idea of instituting cabinet government in America was not new. As early as 1873 Gamaliel Bradford, a Boston banker and congressional critic, had given "much publicity" to a plan for cabinet government in a series of essays in *The Nation*. Bradford's articles were used so extensively by Woodrow Wilson in his 1879 paper on the subject that Wilson's biographer Henry Bragdon thought Wilson's complaints about Congress had done "little more than paraphrase Bradford's articles." Wilson did depart from Bradford's analysis, however, in his conviction that a parliamentary system would attract better men to public office and develop stronger political leadership. For Bradford this was incidental, but for Wilson it was central.[18]

Bragdon surmised that Wilson's early ambition to be an orator and parliamentary leader in the tradition of William Gladstone attracted him to the idea of cabinet government — and may have clouded Wilson's judgment about the feasibility of instituting a parliamentary system in America. An admirer of English institutions, Wilson saw cabinet government as promising what he saw as the virtues of the British parliamentary system: "open debate informing and eliciting the opinion of the nation, careful scrutiny of legislation, party discipline based on coherent programs, and government by a trained and responsible elite." Wilson was not opposed to the centralization of legislative power. He objected to a system that placed a premium on informal power, such as personal charm, bargaining by political interests, and skillful manipulation of the rules.[19]

By replacing what he viewed as a covert and despotic committee structure with a system of cabinet government, Wilson hoped to promote grand parliamentary contests between political parties — "jousts" in which a member's skill in oratory and debate would give him "an opportunity for placing himself, by able argument, in a position to command a place in any future Cabinet that may be formed from the ranks of his own party."[20] Wilson apparently did not feel threatened by centralized power as long as his particular intellectual and rhetorical prowess was given full rein and he had ample opportunity to win a place among the leadership elite.

A few years after publication of his essay on cabinet government, Wilson wrote *Congressional Government* (1885). This time he did not explicitly recommend the institution of cabinet government, and some analysts have cited this as an indication of a fundamental change in Wilson's position. But Henry Bragdon argues that "Wilson was just as intent as ever on persuading Americans to take over cabinet government." According to Bragdon, Wilson "thought it good tactics merely to display the vice of the American system alongside the virtues of the British and to trust his readers to transform the invidious comparison into the inexorable conclusion."[21]

The publication of *Congressional Government* brought Wilson immediate acclaim, but his cabinet government proposal also had detractors. Mary Follett's studies at the Annex placed her squarely in the midst of the nation's most vocal opposition. A. Lawrence Lowell, then a Harvard instructor of government, had made one of the first concerted attacks on Wilson's book, taking the aristocratic view that "the introduction of ministerial responsibility in the United States might make the popular will so powerful that the temporary whims of the majority would overwhelm minority interests." A few years later another Harvard man, Freeman Snow, echoed Lowell's objections; in a paper delivered at the 1889 American Historical Association meeting, Snow contended that the chance of gaining more able political leadership through a cabinet system did not outweigh the dangers that would arise from abolishing the safeguards embodied in the constitutional checks and balances.[22]

In March 1891, while Mary Follett was at Newnham, the protest against cabinet government was joined, albeit on quite different grounds, by Albert Bushnell Hart. Hart had been acquainted with Wilson for several years and had been sufficiently impressed with his "ability to make new generalizations and to induce others to see them" that he had invited Wilson to write the last of the three-book series, "Epochs of American History."[23] Wilson accepted the offer and was still working on this volume when Hart's article, "The Speaker as Premier," appeared in *The Nation*. Hart agreed with many of Wilson's complaints about the Congress, but he felt certain that Wilson was underestimating the Speaker's capacity for legislative leadership. Hart's conviction that the Speakership was a politically powerful position surely evolved, at least in part, from reading the results of Mary Follett's initial investigations; but his views were also influenced by the success with which the new Republican Speaker, Thomas Brackett Reed of Maine, had recently acted to restore order to the deliberations of the House.

Thomas B. Reed was elected Speaker in December 1889, after the Republicans regained the majority in the House. Two months earlier, Reed had written an article in the *North American Review* charging that the existing rules of the House "only delay and frustrate action." He promised that an effort would be made in the next Congress "to change the rules so that business can be done and the scandals of the last Congress avoided."[24] His word was made good. Despite having been elected Speaker by a mere two-vote margin, Reed immediately moved to block the adoption of the rules of the preceding House and succeeded in having the matter referred to the Rules Committee — a group that Reed chaired and controlled with a three-to-two majority. Ten weeks passed before the new rules were brought to the floor. In the interim, an incident occurred that caused immediate consternation in the House.

The Republicans, having only a 170 to 160 voting edge, had considerable difficulty maintaining a 165-member quorum on the floor. The Democrats were quick to take advantage of the Republicans' slim majority; simply by sitting in silence rather than casting their votes, they could cause a quorum to "disappear" and thereby could dissolve the House. This obstructionist tactic, which effectively blocked Republican legislative initiatives, had been employed by minorities on both sides of the aisle for more than fifty years. But when the quorum "disappeared" on January 29, 1890, the move elicited an unprecedented response from the Speaker.

> A West Virginia election case had been called up, only to be challenged by the Democratic leader, Charles Crisp of Georgia. On an ensuing roll call the Democrats declined to vote, dissolving the quorum. Reed calmly intervened: "The Chair directs the Clerk to record the following names of members present and refusing to vote." He then proceeded to call out the names of 38 members he spied on the floor. Pandemonium broke loose, and for three days the House debated the ruling. The Democrats, led by Crisp and ex-Speaker Carlisle, defended the traditional House practices, stressing the minority's need for protection from arbitrary majority rule. The chief Republican spokesmen, Joseph Cannon of Illinois and William McKinley of Ohio, argued that the majority must be given the power to govern. Reed's ruling was finally upheld by a party-line vote.

Because Reed's swift and decisive response in this incident was seen as outrageous and dictatorial by many, he was denounced on the floor of the House as a "tyrant, despot, czar." "Never before had the House of Representatives witnessed such a scene," Mary Follett later wrote, "its presiding officer condemned, and subjected to the most violent abuse, on account of a parliamentary decision."[25]

The furor over the Speaker's ruling had not yet subsided when, only a few days later, Reed's new rules proposal emerged from committee. The proposal sparked "protracted discussion" even in the Republican caucus; but the rules were "reported to the floor, debated heatedly for four days, and finally adopted, 161 to 144." The "Reed rules," Roger Davidson and Walter Oleszek tell us, "revolutionized House procedure . . . by completely revising the order of business, outlawing dilatory motions, reducing the quorum in Committee of the Whole to 100, authorizing that committee to close debate on any section or paragraph of a bill under consideration, and permitting every member present in the chamber to be counted in determining whether a quorum was present."[26]

Reed's firm hand in the quorum controversy and his success in instituting new House rules revealed for the first time to the general public the magnitude of the Speaker's power. Reed's detractors were deeply troubled by these revelations and attributed the growth of that power to Reed's personal ambition. Albert Bushnell Hart, on the other hand, attributed the growth of the modern Speaker's power largely to the ascendancy of the Congress during the years following the Civil War. The Speaker's powers as "moderator, as party chief, as the appointer of committees, and as the dispenser of the right of taking part in debate," Hart wrote in his 1891 article in *The Nation,* had developed gradually; and as these powers increased, the Speaker's role was becoming "more and more important, and more and more desired." The Speaker's standing would rise even further, Hart predicted, now that he could appoint the committee that decided the order of business in the House. As the dominant member of the Rules Committee, the Speaker had finally become the "recognized political chief, formulator of the policy of the party, legislative Premier."[27]

Two months after the publication of Hart's article, Wilson sent Hart a letter in which he took exception to Hart's conclusions. "No officer who belongs wholly to the legislature," Wilson wrote, "can ever reproduce for us the functions of the English Prime Minister." Furthermore, Wilson, who in these early years was quite distrustful of popular government, believed that cabinet government was preferable to a strong Speakership. "The guidance of a body of men in some sort at least constituting an *outside* body with *other* responsibilities besides the merely legislative, seems to me," Wilson cautioned, "a safe body to exercise leadership; while the leadership of one man supreme within the legislature, with no responsibility for administration, seems to me an unsafe leadership."[28]

Mary Follett joined this apparently amicable dispute between Hart and Wilson when, only a few months after her return from Newnham, she delivered a paper on Henry Clay's speakership to the annual meeting of the American Historical Association in Washington, D.C. Her paper had been submitted by Hart, along with a paper written by another of his students, W. E. B. DuBois, after Speaker Reed's controversial rulings gave new significance to

Follett's analysis of how skillfully Clay had wielded the Speaker's political power.[29] When students and faculty at the Annex learned about the acceptance of Follett's submission by Herbert B. Adams, then secretary of the association, the news caused "almost as much excitement and pride as had Eleanor Pearson's earlier triumph over Harvard with her Bowdoin Prize dissertation."[30]

At the time of the founding of the American Historical Association in 1884, the *Boston Herald* wrote that "too much cannot be made of such an institution. It registers the rise of a new generation of Americans and the growth of a better method in the study of history." By the end of its first full year of operation, the new association had enrolled 228 members, and within six years the membership rolls had grown to more than 640. The association's annual meetings, which drew as many as a hundred registrants during these years, gave the new generation of professional historians opportunities to share the results of their research.[31]

The association had been founded to provide a national forum for "the exchange of ideas and the widening of acquaintance, [for] the discussion of methods and original papers." Yet women were marginal figures in this new scholarly venture. Despite the existence of fairly liberal membership regulations in the early years, only about 5 percent of the members were women. The program for the national meeting rarely included more than one or two women; and when the gentlemen members of the association gathered "after every evening session . . . in the pleasant rooms of the Cosmos Club," women, of course, were excluded.[32]

Mary Follett was one of only two women on the program of the December 1891 annual meeting. When she rose to speak on the morning of the second day of the conference, the lecture hall of the National Museum was filled — but apparently not for a fully scholarly purpose. W. E. B. DuBois, patronizingly described by the *Washington Post* as "a young colored man who speaks the purest English without a tinge of racial accent," was the "feature of the morning session which attracted most attention." Follett's presentation nevertheless received extensive coverage in the *Post* and was the lead item in the *New York Times's* report of the day's events.[33]

Follett told her audience that she had tried to replace the "reminiscences and hearsay" so long associated with Henry Clay's Speakership with new conclusions based on a careful analysis of "the records." This analysis, Follett argued, demonstrated that Clay was actually "the first political Speaker," and thereby disproved the assumption "that the political development of the Speaker's power dates from recent times." Much of the interest that the press displayed in her remarks stemmed from this provocative assertion that Henry Clay, not Thomas Reed, was the first truly political Speaker.[34]

No other Speaker, Follett told her audience, "so combined the functions of a moderator, a member, and a leader" as did Clay. Whether casting his vote, speaking from the floor, stating the question, or rendering parliamentary judgments, Clay used his position "so as to influence the mind of the House." Furthermore, he was straightforward about his intentions, doing "what he did confessedly as leader of his party, to push through the measures he had at heart." According to Follett, Clay's Speakership was not, as some had contended, a time of harmony in the House; but the members were surprisingly willing to acquiesce in Clay's conception of the Speakership. She thought it "a fact of the greatest significance that the cries of tyrant and despot, so often raised of late years against Speakers less domineering, were not then heard."[35] How, she wondered, was this to be explained?

Follett approached this question with "an eager curiosity," and her answer — a description of Clay's personal qualities — reveals a fascination with the personal sources of power. "[Clay] displayed in the first place a remarkable tact . . . Few Speakers have known so well as Henry Clay how to measure their power so as to obtain the utmost possible, and yet not go beyond that unwritten standard of 'fairness' . . . to observe the subtle yet essential difference between 'political' and 'partisan' action . . . Still more was his success due to that wonderful personal fascination which few could withstand . . . All testify to the marvelous charm of his voice and manner, which attracted attention, awakened sympathy, and compelled obedience." Clay's personal style contrasted sharply with that of the controversial Thomas Reed, whose "glacial manner and rapier-like wit" could annihilate an opponent. To a congressman who was complaining that Reed had "made light of his remarks," Reed offered a typical retort, "I will say to the gentleman that if I ever 'made light' of his remarks it is more than he ever made of them himself."[36]

Clay and Reed each had an "imperious will," but Clay's "personal magnetism" gave him "easy leadership of the House" together with "complete ascendancy over his own party." Clay's "qualities of brilliant and creative leadership," Albert Bushnell Hart later wrote, "have much attracted [Follett]."[37] Follett saw in Clay's style of leadership a possible alternative to coercion and other forms of formal authority. Clay's strength of character, personal charm, and consideration for his colleagues had allowed him to exercise pervasive influence despite the apparent limitations of his office.

Clay's appealing personal qualities might have led Follett to adopt a one-dimensional, "great-man" view of the Speakership, but she avoided this temptation and explored the darker side of Clay's character. Nor did she limit her analysis of the development of the Speaker's power to the personal qualities of the men who have held the office. "The development of the Speakership," she astutely observed, "has depended in part upon political ideas current when the Government was founded, in part on the men who have filled the office and given form to unwritten laws, in part on the rise of new conditions which require a new system."[38] Although Follett considered these complex factors only briefly in her paper on Clay, they would become the focus of an intense, four-year investigation that would culminate in the publication of *The Speaker of the House of Representatives.*

Follett's manuscript on the Speakership eventually grew too large to be published in the Radcliffe monograph series. Seeking an alternative, she applied through Albert Bushnell Hart to Longmans, Green and Company, the prestigious English house that had published some of Hart's own work. She succeeded. Longmans offered Follett a contract in September 1895 and published *The Speaker of the House of Representatives* early the following year.[39]

In the opening sentence of the preface to her book, Follett boldly asserted: "The power of the Speaker of the House of Representatives, unknown to political theory, is the central feature of our actual system of government.[40] Follett reached her conclusion after painstakingly examining the rules and the records of debates in the House of Representatives and the House of Commons; reading numerous accounts of political events in newspapers and journals; and searching volumes of correspondence, diaries and memoirs for items bearing on the development of the Speaker's power.[41] Having been taught first by Albert Bushnell Hart and then by the historians at Newnham to be skeptical about "ideal" formulations of government, Follett had instead meticulously studied its "actual" functioning.[42] "For a just appreciation of an office depending so much upon unwritten practice," Follett observed in her preface, "this work should have been the labor of some member of the House of Representatives long experienced in public life. Since none such has come forward, I have ventured the task, and have tried by patient study of the records and by inquiry from men in public life at least to prepare the way for a proper study of the Speaker."[43]

While Woodrow Wilson could rely almost exclusively on personal impressions and secondary sources in writing *Congressional Government,* Follett knew that a woman did not have the luxury of offering undocumented observations and arguments. If her work were to have any credibility, it would have to be seen as scientific in its analysis. Indeed, Albert Bushnell Hart tried hard in his introduction to Follett's book to establish the scientific character of her conclusions: "Miss Follett appears to have worked in a impartial and scientific spirit to solve a knotty problem in history and practical government . . . Though [her] conclusions are distinctly opposed to the teachings of many writers, they are evidently not put forward for the sake of contradicting others, but simply to state generalizations which seem to the author's mind best to interpret the mass of facts. The author is compelled to her belief by her own collection and analysis of the evidence. That evidence is voluminous, carefully sifted, and lies before the reader, or is made accessible by generous footnotes."[44]

To compensate further for her lack of personal experience in institutions of government, Follett conducted interviews with men who had participated in the affairs of the House; included among them were two former Speakers, Nathaniel P. Banks and Robert C. Winthrop of Massachusetts.[45] Follett may have got the idea for these interviews, then an unusual form of social investigation, from Bryce's *American Commonwealth* (1888): in preparation for his book, Bryce had traveled around the United States to speak with numerous scholars and political figures. It was one thing, however, for Bryce — Regius Professor of Civil Law at Oxford and a respected member of Parliament — to solicit interviews. It was quite another for Mary Follett — a student, a woman, and a person lacking distinguished family connections — to have the courage to do so. The confidence that Follett needed to approach people in positions of political power was undoubtedly bolstered by her year at Newnham. Newnham faculty and staff had always had close ties to prominent political figures, and faculty dinners and teas gave the students valuable opportunities to meet and converse with them. Even the Newnham students, through their family relations, opened doors to important political figures. All this surely would have helped Follett overcome her natural fears about interviewing prominent public figures. According to one lifelong American friend, the richness of Follett's experiences at Newnham caused her to blossom "as in a forcing house," because "the rather inexperienced girl came back [to America] far more formed and assured."[46]

Follett's use of interviews and other inductive methods of investigation in her study of the Speakership is one of the characteristics that mark her as a member of a pivotal intellectual movement of the late nineteenth and early twentieth centuries — a movement that Morton White has called the "revolt against formalism." Formalist thought — "fixed and static in its formulation" and comprised of "timeless verities, stated in a very generalized form" — dominated American intellectual life throughout much of the nineteenth century.[47] Writers such as Oliver Wendell Holmes, Thorstein Veblen, John Dewey, and Charles Beard argued that formalist thought was too little concerned with the concrete realities of modern American life and far too moralistic.[48] These rebels urged the adoption of a new approach to scholarship, one that would replace all forms of *a priori* reasoning with "scientific" methods based on the intensive investigation of experience. The truly scientific scholar would begin by thoroughly ascertaining the facts and then would reason inductively from these facts about causes and consequences.[49]

Several of these antiformalist thinkers were also committed to understanding the cultural aspects of human behavior. Charles Beard, for example, urged his fellow historians to study political actions in their larger social context and exhorted his colleagues to break down the boundaries artificially separating history from other disciplines.[50] Here, too, Follett anticipated the formalists' methods by demonstrating an early commitment to interdisciplinary historical research. Not only had she been exposed to Cambridge University's highly interdisciplinary history curriculum, but she also had been taught the value of employing multiple disciplinary perspectives in historical research by her Harvard Annex professors. "History," Albert Bushnell Hart told his fellow historians, "should teach more than the political events and activities surrounding great leaders." Hart urged students to investigate "diaries, travels, autobiographies, letters, and speeches" because he found them "more real and more human." To facilitate such investigations, Hart produced numerous source books for students containing illustrations of "social, political, and occasionally economic conditions, to show how ordinary people lived."[51]

The economist William James Ashley, with whom Follett had begun to study at Radcliffe College (formerly the Harvard Annex) in 1895, urged economic historians to employ a variety of perspectives in the conduct of their research. "Economic considerations," Ashley told his audience in his inaugural lecture, "are not the only ones of which we must take account in judging of social phenomena . . . economic forces are not the only forces which move men." Although Follett's study of the Speakership did not fulfill all the methodological prescriptions of Beard and other Progressive historians, her Namier-like analysis did succeed in introducing her readers to the complex constellation of forces that, at various times, had had some part in shaping the Speakership. Indeed, Follett's willingness to look at her subject from a variety of perspectives would come to distinguish her work on social organization.[52]

The industriousness and intelligence displayed in Follett's analysis would pay dividends with her reviewers. "While some member [of Congress]," noted the reviewer for the *New York Times*, "might have made a book more attractive to the partisan and more entertaining from the popular point of view, we should not expect from any Representative either the industry or the impartiality which are exhibited by this author who modestly says that she has sought 'to prepare the way for a proper study' of her subject." The reviewer for *The Times of London* wrote approvingly of Follett's "diligence of research, accuracy of statement, independence of appreciation, and originality of treatment." And the reviewer for the *Political Science Quarterly*, history professor Anson D. Morse of Amherst College, pronounced her book a treatment of "rare excellence." Morse continued: "In few recent works belonging to the field of politics and history do we find so much evidence of the conditions which are essential to the making of a good book — a well-chosen theme, grasp of subject, mastery of material, patient, long-continued, wisely directed labor, good sense and good taste." C. H. Smith, who taught American History at Yale, was even more effusive, calling Follett's book "the most important contribution to our knowledge of the working of our governmental machinery since Woodrow Wilson's *Congressional Government*."[53]

Follett's book begins with an exploration of the genesis of the Speaker's power: she analyzes precedents in the English House of Commons, the various American colonial assemblies, and the Continental Congress. She then turns to the principles and politics governing the choice of a Speaker and provides a brief account of each speakership from 1789 to 1895. Finally, following a detailed examination of the evolution of the Speaker's parliamentary duties and powers, Follett examines the political power accruing to the Speaker as a result of his position as the leader of his party.

According to Woodrow Wilson, the highly political character of the late nineteenth-century Speakership represented a distortion of the intentions of the framers of the Constitution. In making this claim, Wilson was simply reiterating the widely held view that the Speakership had been modeled on the impartial moderator of the House of Commons.[54] Follett, however, refused to accept this *a priori* argument and insisted that the intentions of the writers of the Constitution could be known only through a careful study of the historical record.

As the first step in her study of the actual experience of the Speakership, Follett investigated the supposed impartiality of the English Speaker. Quoting extensively from sources on English parliamentary history, she demonstrated that before the eighteenth century the Speaker was rarely impartial; instead, he acted either as the servant of the Crown in Parliament or, on occasion, as Parliament's advocate to the Crown. It was not until the nineteenth century, according to Follett's reading of the documents, that the English Speaker became a consistently impartial moderator. On the basis of this analysis, Follett argued that those who were seeking "the customs and institutions" brought by the American colonists from England would do better to look to the partisan English Speakership of the sixteenth and seventeenth centuries.

Turning to the workings of the colonial assemblies and the Continental Congress, Follett considered how the colonists' English traditions might have been modified by new conditions in America. In preparing this portion of her investigation, Follett probably sought the advice of the Harvard historian Edward Channing, whose "History and Origins of American Institutions" was one of the courses in which Follett enrolled immediately after her return from Newnham.[55]

Follett's investigation of these colonial legislative bodies persuaded her that "new conditions" in America did indeed have a marked influence on the character of the Speakership. As the colonists' dissatisfaction with the Crown and its royal governors grew, resistance came to be embodied in the colonists' primary elected official — the Speaker. After the formation of the republic, the Speakership continued to represent a check on executive power, but this time the executive being checked was the new nation's president. Another of the "new" conditions that Follett saw as affecting the character of the Speakership was the vastness and isolation of many of the American congressional districts. In England, where each member of Parliament was considered to represent the whole country, having the Speaker act as an impartial moderator caused no loss of representation for his district. In America, however, the widely differing needs of geographically disparate districts made such a scheme unworkable. If the American Speaker had restricted himself to the role of an impartial moderator, he would in effect have disfranchised his own congressional district.[56]

Follett's analysis of these and other conditions led her to reason in the following way about the intentions of the framers of the U.S. Constitution:

> What they intended must be inferred from that with which they were familiar: they knew a Speaker in the colonial assemblies who was at the same time a political leader; they knew a presiding officer of Congress who was both a political leader and the official head of the state with important administrative functions; they knew a president of the Constitutional Convention who to his power as chairman added all the influence to be expected of one acknowledged as the foremost man of the nation. Few of their number had ever been in England, and there is no reason for believing, as has been frequently asserted, that they provided for a Speaker similar to the [currently impartial] presiding officer of the House of Commons. It is reasonable to assert that they expected the Speaker to be a political leader.[57]

Follett probed deeper. To know whether the Speaker's current power was, as Hart put it, "a natural, normal, and inevitable development of our system of government," Follett thought it necessary to turn to the organization of the House of Representatives, "which had the right by its rule and practice to define the actual status, powers, and duties of the Speaker: thus alone can we learn whether a new kind of office was created in 1789 or whether the precedents of a hundred and fifty years were to be followed; whether the Speaker was intended to be simply a moderator or whether he was to be a great party leader."[58]

Issues arising over the selection of the Speaker in the years before the Civil War suggested to Follett that the Speakership had already become an office of considerable significance. Four prewar elections were hotly contested. Political parties, realizing the advantages to be gained from having "one of their own" in the office, anxiously sought control of the Speakership; but the parties were forced to compete with other interests for party members' votes. According to Follett, private individuals and corporations, regional interests, and supporters of particular political positions were all active in influencing the votes of individual House members. Then, too, she saw that House members were influenced by purely personal concerns: a preference for a likable candidate or for a man of good character, a desire to be on the side of the eventual winner, or a desire to have the committee appointment that might result from the election of a particular candidate for Speaker.[59]

After the Civil War, tremendous economic growth created extraordinary demands for new national legislation — demands that Follett believed the House had been unable to meet because of party factionalism and the absence of presidential leadership. Only by giving more control to the Speaker could the nation's business proceed. Follett also argued that the power of the Speakership had been enhanced by the tendency of recent Speakers to promote their own policies — to lead, rather than merely to serve their political parties. She found it especially intriguing that "each of the three most recent Speakers has gained his chief power in a different way." Follett continued: "If Carlisle had asserted a power, Reed had insisted upon the same, and Crisp had continued it, the inevitableness of the development of the Speakership would be more apparent. Yet it is really a much more suggestive fact that when popular opinion takes from the Speaker one method of control he immediately finds another. If no Speaker has yet seized upon the sum of all the gains made by his predecessors, nearly every one since the Civil War has continued by some device to assert his mastery. The drift of power to the Speakership is as clear as the fact that strong and forcible Speakers have greatly affected the development of that power." The combined effect of all these developments, as Follett saw it, was a House of Representatives that was no longer the holder of legislative power. "It is but the maker of the real maker [of such power], the Speaker of the House of Representatives."[60]

Having offered a persuasive, "scientific" explanation of how the Speaker's power had evolved, Follett might have concluded her book and left to others the debate about the appropriateness of the Speaker's power, but she boldly continued: "The power of the Speaker seems not only inevitable but, under our present congressional system, desirable." Few of the men who were reviewing her book agreed with this conclusion. "These views may be sound for today and tomorrow—for this Congress and the next," wrote *The Nation*'s reviewer, "but they are assuredly short-sighted." Furthermore, the sophistication of Follett's argument worried him. "Our author reasons with such strength and clearness, and fortifies her position with so many illustrative facts, that a large part of her readers will accept her statements as the whole of the case and her conclusions as the end of the whole matter . . . Moreover, the ability with which they are presented serves to veil the dangers and evils of the system from the growing intelligence of the country."[61]

What this reviewer found most objectionable was Follett's audacious weighing in on the dispute over the quorum—a place where, as he put it, she "deflects from her plain historic road and takes part in what must still be regarded as an unsettled and recurring political controversy." The reviewer curtly dismissed "her view and opinions and reasons" as "but a reflex of those of Speaker Reed." The reviewer for the *New York Times,* also put off by Follett's involvement in these discussions, asserted that "the historical and analytical parts of her work are more satisfactory than those in which she turns to suggestions and argument."[62]

Albert Bushnell Hart apparently anticipated this sort of reaction and tried to defuse the criticism in his introductory remarks to the book. If the author speaks on a contemporary political question, Hart seems to say, she does so not to rationalize an existing political position but to harvest the fruits of scholarship. "Miss Follett has made her own discoveries, arranged her own material, and expressed her own results in her own words, subject only to criticism and suggestion . . . Upon this basis of carefully ascertained fact the author has based her deductions, which are also her own. She has started out with no thesis to prove, and has had no political bias to overcome . . . [Furthermore,] the author would be the last to protest at any candid attempt to controvert her evidence or to gainsay her conclusions. For the purpose of this book is not to sustain a thesis, but to lead to the discovery of the truth."[63]

Despite several attacks on her conclusions by American reviewers, reviewers for both *The Times of London* and *The Spectator* were persuaded that the American House of Representatives could not do without a strong Speaker. Even though such a Speaker would have lost the attribute of impartiality by which, the reviewer in *The Times* claimed, "we in England rightly set so much store," the American Speaker nevertheless would have acquired "in its place the special powers and functions which are needed to preserve the House of

Representatives from anarchy."[64] Since critics usually argued that the House of Commons' Speaker was the model America should emulate, Follett would have enjoyed the English reviewers' remarks. The English seemed to appreciate that the conditions of government in America were different and that, as a result, the forms of leadership should also be different.

The only American reviewer who seemed genuinely delighted by Follett's conclusions was Theodore Roosevelt, then an ambitious police commissioner in New York City bent on reform. Roosevelt had made no secret of his admiration for Speaker Reed. "Not for many years," Roosevelt exclaimed in a December 1895 article in *The Forum,* "has there been a man in our public life to whom the American people owe as great a debt as they do to Speaker Thomas B. Reed." The "magnificent courage and superior power" that Reed had displayed during the Fifty-first Congress were, in Roosevelt's judgment, "of vital consequence to the future well-being of republican institutions." Seeing that Follett shared his own estimate of Reed's significance, Roosevelt was quick to praise Follett's astuteness. Unlike Wilson and some others, Roosevelt maintained that "she has faced facts as they are; and has not been blinded by seeming analogies between our own and the English system. A large proportion of the academic reformers always treat the fact that the speaker is no longer a mere moderator, as a misfortune to be deeply deplored. In reality, as Miss Follett shows . . . it is in the interest of good government that [the Speaker] should wisely, firmly, and boldly exercise the powers, and accept the great responsibilities, which have come to be associated with an office which can now only be successfully filled by a man who is both a great statesman and a great party leader." Roosevelt's laudatory review may well have been written at the urging of Albert Bushnell Hart. Roosevelt had been Hart's friend since their years as classmates at Harvard and had joined Hart as a founding editor of the *American Historical Review.* Hart perhaps suggested that a review of Follett's book would provide a perfect forum for commenting on Wilson's cabinet government proposal. Seizing the opportunity, Roosevelt devoted one-third of his review to an attack on Wilson's ideas.[65]

Follett was more evenhanded than Roosevelt had been in her treatment of Wilson's ideas. She readily acknowledged that the two great defects of government identified by Wilson in *Congressional Government* still remained. Until a system could be found that would develop stronger political leadership and foster better connections between the executive and legislative branches of government, the legislative process would continue to suffer. Nevertheless, Follett saw little merit in Wilson's cabinet government ideas and warned her readers not to accept them. The advocates of a cabinet system, she cautioned, "sometimes forget the vast changes which would thus be necessitated, if not in the written Constitution, at least in our practical, working Constitution." The practical problems of implementing cabinet government persuaded Follett that "if it be possible to reach the same ends by means already accepted in Congress, it is plainly desirable."[66]

Follett's conviction that cabinet government would not solve America's current legislative problems arose in part from her analysis of the obstructionist controversies of the 1880s in the House of Commons. The Irish members of Parliament had "found in [obstruction] an effective and not unconstitutional means of calling attention to their contention that the British Parliament was unfitted to deal with Irish questions." As a result, the House of Commons, just like the American House of Representatives, had suffered disruptions so severe and persistent that it was prevented from doing its business. The Commons responded to obstruction by enacting for the first time a closure regulation and by empowering the Speaker to veto a closure motion if he believed it unfairly cut off debate. This new veto power posed a threat to the traditionally impartial character of the Speakership. James Bryce, writing in the October 1890 *North American Review,* warned that "English ministers and majorities may in the future desire to have a partisan in the chair, seeing how helpful he may be to them." Nevertheless, Bryce did not wish to turn back. Convinced that the House of Commons could not do without a closure rule, he saw that substantial discretionary power must reside in the Speakership; otherwise, the majority party almost certainly would abuse its power and limit debate.[67]

Follett likewise believed that the difficulties facing the American House of Representatives could be resolved only by giving the Speaker greater power. She would "throw upon the Speaker the responsibility of compelling the adjustment of [legislative] measures to one another, for he alone can do it," and she would lay on him "the duty of bringing forward legislation needed by the country, and of pressing it to a vote." This kind of power, Follett argued, "is safely exercised by the Premier in England, and could not be dangerous in America." Follett saw the Rules Committee as a "natural development" through which the Speaker would exercise those new responsibilities. Working together, the Speaker and the Rules Committee would constitute a "legislative commission" of the kind once proposed by John Stuart Mill.[68]

Follett's reviewers, however, adamantly resisted the idea that further centralization of the Speaker's power was both inevitable and desirable. "Even if it be granted," wrote the reviewer for the *New York Times,* "that the Speaker's power has been increased by natural drift, that the exercise of it as it now exists is required for that direction of legislation for which provision is made in no other way, it does not follow that the further and rapid increase of it should be promoted by special effort." The writer for *The Nation,* who was even more strongly opposed to any increase in the Speaker's power, warned his readers that the office already was "Premiership run mad."[69]

While Follett had asserted in her book that "it would certainly be advantageous to secure efficiency without concentration [of power] were it possible," she was convinced that conditions did not allow a return to the "old congressional system." "The old way," she firmly declared, "has ceased to exist. Certain difficulties attendant on the methods of procedure in the House have been overcome by giving certain powers to the Speaker. If these are denied to him, the difficulties recur and must be overcome in some other way. The country does not stand still."[70]

Follett's ready acceptance of institutional change reflected yet another of the characteristics that she shared with the antiformalist intellectuals: study of the past did not mean "veneration of the past."[71] Follett's attitude toward institutional change may well have been influenced by her studies with the Harvard economist William James Ashley. Another of Ashley's students, Mary K. Simkhovitch, recalled that one could not go away from his courses without a sense of "the vast sweep of change implicit in history" and a conviction that "change is inevitable and is always taking place."[72] Follett's receptiveness to institutional change was most apparent in the latter chapters of her book. There she argued that if the legislative process could be improved by modifying the House rules or by amending the Constitution, then such reforms should not be delayed.

> Some one has said that a written constitution seems to exert a certain spell on the human mind, and we think of it not only as something absolutely fixed, but as absolutely right, as if there were a peculiar sacredness about it. It is necessary to recall . . . that [the Constitution] was not laid down positively and arbitrarily as the only right form of government, or the best form of government, but adopted with great fear and foreboding as a possible solution of a difficult problem; that it rests upon a substratum of previous law and practice; and that its framers proceeded to add to it a body of statutes and practice which represent experience . . . The question is not that of the best form of government abstractly, but of the form best for us at the present moment, in harmony with the actual working of our institutions.[73]

What change was Follett calling for? Greater accountability of the Speaker. "The one thing in the present position of the Speaker which is much to be regretted, and which will always tend to produce evil results until remedied," Follett warned, "is the possession of such important prerogatives without definite responsibility." Her words now seem prophetic. From 1903 to 1911, Joseph Cannon of Illinois stretched the Speaker's powers to the fullest. In the absence of any system for holding the Speaker accountable to his party or the people, Cannon became a "virtual dictator." It took a herculean effort by Democrats and a group of progressive Republican "Insurgents" to wrest from Cannon his place on the Rules Committee and his power to appoint that committee's members — thereby effectively ending the era of the strong Speakership.[74]

Unfortunately, Follett's ideas about how to make the Speaker more accountable form the weakest part of the book. Restricted to studying the political process through documents, memoirs, and a few interviews, Follett was seriously handicapped in her efforts to create a realistic proposal for reform. She focused only on the "first step" of a remedy, arguing that there could be no accountability until the "great weight of the office is thoroughly understood" by the public at large. Once her readers looked the Speaker's power "squarely in the face," Follett felt confident that "there should be no delay in uniting power and responsibility."[75]

Follett's failure to present concrete recommendations for ensuring the Speaker's accountability did not, in the eyes of her reviewers, detract from her extraordinary accomplishment. During this era, "respectable" women rarely dared to express an opinion on any sort of political issue other than suffrage and social welfare. Surely this was on the mind of the writer for *The Nation* as he composed his review. He was simply astonished that such a perceptive political analysis had been written by a woman: "Many people will admit that this is a remarkable book for a young author: many more people will admit that it is a remarkable book for a young lady; but when we read what may be called the practical part of the book . . . and view in it, clearly, the complexities of that tumultuous parliamentary body which we know sometimes as the 'bear garden' and sometimes as the House of Representatives, we are tempted to go farther and say that it is a remarkable book to have been written by any other person than a member of Congress — by a member having much experience, studious habits, commendable industry, and endowed with unusual powers of analysis and generalization." Struggling to explain how a woman had achieved such remarkable insights, the reviewer told his readers that the author "is a daughter of 'good old New England stock,' a graduate of Radcliffe and a student of history in other institutions." But he apparently found this reference to Follett's background gratuitous, for the reviewer quickly added that he would "speak of the book precisely as if it had been written by any other person."[76]

Much of the brilliance of Follett's analysis is due precisely to the fact that the author was a woman, because it was Follett's position as a woman in late nineteenth-century society that forced her into the role of "political outsider."

Because she did not have easy access to the political scene, Follett had to shape her ideas about the Speakership out of widely disparate experiences. She supplemented her reading of a wide range of primary and secondary sources with interviews; she drew analogies with changes that were taking place at other levels of government; and she used her own experience as a woman in late nineteenth-century middle-class society to understand the value of informal sources of power and the potential benefits of radical institutional change. In order to integrate such diverse material, Follett also found it necessary to theorize — to think creatively about possible relationships and patterns in the evidence.[77] And in this theorizing, her outsider's position seems to have worked to her advantage. For while Follett had had to compensate for the disadvantages of being an outsider by devoting extraordinary talent and energy to the process of empirical research, once she had done so, she was quite free to theorize about the possible virtues of the Speaker's political power. Indeed, it was her skillful theorizing about the complexity of the Speaker's role that enabled her to imagine benefits that might accrue from the Speaker's growing political power while most insiders, committed to preserving old political ideals, could only deplore that power.[78] The result of her theoretical and empirical labors was a book that modern writers have called "one of the most remarkable and perceptive books ever written about Congress."[79] Equally important for us, it is a harbinger of virtually all Follett's mature ideas about power and control.

Americans have traditionally feared concentrations of power. Thus it is remarkable that Woodrow Wilson and Mary Follett, perhaps the most notable writers on the Congress during the late nineteenth century, agreed that the problems of American government could be resolved only by a greater centralization of power. The means by which Wilson and Follett proposed to accomplish this centralization, however, were strikingly different. Wilson considered the informal machinations of the committee system totally unsuited to his own values and aspirations and proposed instead a formal, adversarial system — cabinet government. In a cabinet system, the individual member, rather than finding "his activity repressed, and himself suppressed," could employ intellect and rhetorical skills to make an "influential mark" on legislation and join the leadership elite.[80]

Mary Follett, by contrast, advocated a form of centralization based on the very thing that Wilson deplored — informal power. Follett did not deny the importance of the formal authority inhering in the Speaker's position, but her investigation of the Speakers' use of their prerogatives convinced her that formal power alone did not guarantee the Speaker's ability to govern. Seeming to anticipate her later work on "the illusion of final authority," Follett argued that Speakers were most effective not when they engaged in dramatic rhetorical contests over party principles but when they used their informal power to make complex and troublesome decisions palatable to the members of the House. She illustrated this phenomenon in her discussion of the controversial committee appointment process. The Speaker knows that his appointment power cannot "be exercised with entire freedom. The construction of the committees is a duty requiring the utmost caution and deliberation . . . What this officer does attempt to do is so to balance the various considerations as to accomplish his own aims, please his party, satisfy individuals, meet the reasonable expectations of the minority, and appear respectable to the country — a laborious task greatly increased by the large number of new men and the importunity of members for particular places."[81]

Furthermore, Follett recognized that a Speaker was most successful in gaining acceptance of his decisions when he combined personal qualities of leadership with power derived from his position. In the egalitarian culture of the House of Representatives, Follett saw that "promptness, energy, firmness, courtesy, and great tact" could often succeed where purely positional or hierarchical power was sure to fail. She also was sensitive to the volatility of power, arguing that the Speaker's power must be seen as dynamic, rising and falling according to the members' sense that it was being exercised fairly and in the pursuit of mutually desired ends.[82] These and other insights about the nature of the Speaker's power predated by more than forty years Chester Barnard's influential discussion of "informal organization and the subjective aspect of authority" in *The Functions of the Executive* (1938).

Finally, and perhaps most central to her emerging notions about power and control, Follett was not as ready as Wilson to assume that the Speaker's power had been achieved at the expense of the rights and freedom of other members of the House. Rather than being controlled by the Speaker, the members of the House were obeying what she would later call the "law of the situation." "Occasionally," Follett wrote, "when a Carlisle or a Reed sits in the chair and boldly removes the veil which ordinary usage throws over it, we hear outcries against 'a political moderator,' and the House is censured for submitting to such arrogation of authority. But it must not be supposed that the House is too weak to control its presiding officer, or too ignorant and short-sighted to understand what he is doing. It feels, consciously or unconsciously, that to some one must be given the right of leadership. The Speaker has acquired it, first, because tradition did not exclude a political chairman; secondly, because our Speakers have been, on the whole, men ready to assume guidance; but above all, because under the congressional system which has existed ever since 1789, this power drifted most naturally to the presiding officer. The committee system has made necessary some unifying influence in legislation; and in this necessity lies really the whole secret of the Speaker's position."[83]

In these remarks, Follett hinted at a proposition that would be central to her later work, namely, that obedience to a collective will that the individual participates in making need not mean either the subordination of the individual or the domination of the individual by others. "It has been perhaps unfortunate," Follett wrote near the end of her book on the Speaker, "that giving power to the leaders has always meant with us taking it away from the individual members at the cost of jealousy and hard feeling. In the House of Commons the Premier has more authority than any of our leaders, but it coexists with greater power also on the part of the individual member."[84]

Years later, in *The New State* (1918), Follett would take up this matter again. Calling the idea of the "independent" individual a myth, she would attribute to its prominence much of the difficulty of achieving community in America. But for now, the abstractions of "individual" and "community" would take a more concrete form. Having completed her book on the Speakership, Follett began searching for a vocation in which she could make use of her enormous personal talents and, at the same time, satisfy an increasingly active social conscience.

8

"To I. L. B."

Follett had long thought that she would have a vocation as a teacher of American history, but her years at Mrs. Shaw's School during the early 1890s raised serious doubts about her commitment to teaching. Once Follett had completed her political science lectures and joined the regular teaching staff, she no longer had the luxury of instructing only advanced students; now she had to deal with students who were barely in their teens. This new role surely caused her some insecurity, and Follett responded, as new teachers often do, by running a highly regimented classroom. One of her young students, Margaret Nichols, found this approach less than inspiring. Her primary recollection of Follett's class was that "we were not allowed to open our desks during class without permission. Between classes we received orders: 'Open desks, take out your topic books and Buckley's pencil and eraser. Close desk.' This was partly to prevent any possibility of peeking at convenient papers inside the desk during recitations."[1]

For someone of Follett's intellect and training, listening to the mundane classroom recitations of novices must have been difficult to endure. Nevertheless, it is not surprising that Follett at least tried a career in secondary school teaching. She had entered college to qualify for work as a teacher, and her aspirations were reinforced both at the Annex and at Newnham. More than half of the students who left Newnham between 1871 and 1893 were employed as teachers, and virtually all of them taught at the elementary or secondary levels; less than 10 percent were employed in other occupations, most in secretarial work. At the Annex, the push toward teaching was even more intense. More than two-thirds of the students who graduated before 1915 were gainfully employed as teachers at some point after their graduation; this figure rises to over 80 percent when those who were never employed are excluded from the calculation. Of course, few other jobs were available to middle-class women. A college education "was not an opening up of wider opportunities as it so often seemed to the pioneers or to the young," Martha Vicinus writes in her study of independent women of the late nineteenth century, "but a narrow staircase leading to more education as an ill-paid — but respected — teacher."[2]

About a year before Mary began teaching at Mrs. Shaw's School, her childhood friend and Annex classmate Harriet French married and moved to another part of the country. If Mary had still been the painfully shy and withdrawn girl who had first appeared at the Annex, Harriet's departure might have left her feeling terribly alone; but with the confidence she had gained at Newnham, she was able to make several new friends.[3] One who would remain close over the years was Elizabeth Balch.

Balch was one of four sisters of Emily Greene Balch, the talented economist and social reformer who won the 1946 Nobel Peace Prize. Instead of following her sister's example and taking a degree at Bryn Mawr, Elizabeth chose to study history at the Harvard Annex and remain at home. Follett and Balch were classmates for the first time when Mary came back from Newnham, taking Edward Channing's course on political theory and American institutions and Albert Bushnell Hart's research seminar. Balch had little appreciation for the rigorous primary sources research that Hart demanded of his students; Hart's only aim, as Balch saw it, was "information and facts massed and marshalled." Her sympathies were with Edward Channing, who was fond of quoting Henry Adams: "For facts as facts I have an utter contempt." Balch's liberal Unitarian, Yankee background seems to have influenced her preference for Channing. She pictured Hart as "a rather crude Middle Westerner, his mind lacking in charm and versatility," while Channing, on the other hand, was a fellow "New Englander of old family, critical and cultivated."[4]

Balch's youthful snobbery also may have affected her evaluation of Mary Follett's family. The Folletts, Balch later wrote, were of "good New England stock" but had "few if any members of outstanding ability, wide social affiliations or experience." Mary herself seemed only "a delightful companion" until, like Melian Stawell before her, Balch heard Mary speak. Follett's commanding performance marked her, in Balch's mind, as a person of "unusual ability." She recalled "how in stage fright [Mary] walked with me up and down the hall" before making her presentation about Newnham to the Annex Graduate Club, "yet when she began to speak she was composed and unselfconscious and every word was well chosen and the whole address finished and full of zest and interest."[5]

One of the forms that the friendship between Follett and Balch took was a shared love of literature. At Newnham, Melian Stawell had been an avid reader of Meredith, Ibsen, and Browning, and now Follett took great pleasure in reading these authors with Balch and other Annex friends. In this period, only Browning had anything resembling a wide audience, and all these writers were considered "obscure" and "difficult." Follett, however, was not deterred. "Always," Balch recalled, "her mind went ranging ahead with most catholic taste and her own force and vigor." She devoured *Peer Gynt* and Ibsen's intense psychological portraits, especially *The Lady from the Sea*. She also was intrigued by the novels of George Meredith, reading *Sandra Belloni* "over and over again." The "girlish enthusiasm" that Follett and Balch had for Meredith extended to the works of Robert Browning. "Pompilia," the deathbed monologue of the young woman whose tragic life is the subject of *The Ring and the Book*, always "meant much" to Mary.[6]

Follett's fascination with these particular works of literature no doubt lay in their portrayals of women who dared to act outside traditional women's roles. Perhaps more than any other Victorian author, George Meredith explicitly exposed "the situation of women as the key to a critique of society." Meredith's contention that marriage was "an instrument of restraint," Jenni Calder writes in her analysis of Victorian fiction, made him a special favorite of contemporary feminists. In his novels, marriage "stifled women, limited men, reinforced class barriers, and inhibited freedom of thought and action."[7] Ibsen's works likewise were noted for exposing the destructive quality of traditional marriages. In *The Lady from the Sea*, Dr. Wangle is made to relinquish his conviction that marriage gives him the right to direct and control Ellida's life before either of them can be happy or fulfilled. Attacks on marriage, domesticity, and "proper" society resonated strongly with Follett. She probably identified these conventions with her mother and was determined to avoid them. Although none of the fictional women created by these Victorian authors really succeeds in assuming responsibility for her own life, each of them struggles for control over her own destiny and sometimes even slays her own dragons. In the experiences of these women, Follett could catch at least a glimpse of a life in which, in Carolyn Heilbrun's words, "a woman, without clothing herself in the character of a man, yet goes forth, full of hope and purpose, into a world that men have always dominated."[8]

"Going forth" had become Follett's central problem. She could do little more to shape her destiny as long as she remained in Quincy with her mother. "Little sympathy" existed between Mrs. Follett and Mary; and this was all the more troublesome because Mrs. Follett, in Harriet French's eyes, was "a dominating sort of person who rarely failed to make you conscious of her presence." Elizabeth Balch, too, found Mrs. Follett's temperament and demeanor disturbing. She recalled spending a lovely day with Mary reading aloud Hardy's newly published *Tess of the D'Urbervilles* when their idyll was broken by Mrs. Follett's appearance. She was "tall, pallid, peevish and artificial," and Balch found her "very alien to all our interests."⁹ Mary's difficulties with her mother led her to appreciate George Bernard Shaw's description of family life as all too often being a state "cut off equally from the blessings of society and the blessings of solitude."¹⁰

Follett undoubtedly put up with this tense, uncongenial home environment, despite being twenty-four years old, largely out of a sense of obligation to her younger brother. Possessing neither the intellectual gifts nor the drive of his older sister, George, who in 1892 was just beginning his education at Thayer Academy, quickly fell behind in his studies. At first Mary intervened on his behalf and persuaded the headmaster to allow George to drop English so that he might "give his whole attention to Latin and Mathematics." But George, who already was fifteen, "wasn't very amenable" to his sister's interference and rebelled by failing his Latin examinations. When the headmaster refused to let him move on with his class, George's motivation plummeted even further. He accomplished so little during the next academic year that the headmaster decided to hold him back once again. In the summer of 1894, George left school for good.¹¹

Her brother's abortive academic career surely aroused ambivalent feelings in Mary. She had assumed a special responsibility for George after their father's death, so his academic failure, in some sense, was hers; but she probably also felt relieved that she was no longer quite so compelled to live at home. Ending a two-year hiatus in her own coursework, Follett took her first explicit steps toward obtaining a college degree when she passed required examinations in English and algebra at Radcliffe College. Harvard Annex supporters had known for some time that their graduates were at a disadvantage in obtaining teaching positions because the Annex did not offer a degree; but they had delayed in seeking a charter, hoping to persuade Harvard to award its A.B. degree. Finally, in 1894, Elizabeth Cary Agassiz negotiated a compromise. Radcliffe was chartered as an independent corporation, awarding its own degrees. The degrees were cosigned by the president of Radcliffe and the president of Harvard, signifying equivalence with the Harvard degree. In addition, the president and fellows agreed to serve as visitors of Radcliffe. A majority of Annex alumnae and many feminists were outraged by the compromise; they had urged Mrs. Agassiz to hold out for the Harvard degree. But the Annex students seem to have been more accepting and, like Follett, went about the business of completing the requirements for the new degree.[12]

The difficulty of commuting to Cambridge and Boston daily so that she could teach as well as study finally gave Follett a reason to leave home. Later that same year, shortly before her twenty-sixth birthday, she took up residence in the Back Bay building that housed Mrs. Shaw's School.[13] Sharing the accommodations with Follett at Eight Marlborough Street was the woman who would eventually be her life companion — the school's forty-six-year-old principal, Isobel Briggs.

Isabella (Isobel) Louisa Briggs was born in November 1848 to William and Isabella Bunnett Briggs of Great Yarmouth, Norfolk, on the east coast of England. Briggs's father, a forty-eight year-old Yorkshire nonconformist, was a coal merchant and a ship owner in this busy working seaport. Briggs's mother, already thirty-seven at the time of Isobel's birth, was William Briggs's second wife. Three daughters from Briggs's previous marriage, aged sixteen, nineteen, and twenty-one, shared the family home on Yarmouth's South Quay along with William and Isabella's young sons, aged seven and one. Young Isobel quickly became a middle child in this "second" family when her birth was followed by two more children. Given the large size of the household, the Briggses were fortunate in being able to afford the help of a cook, housemaid, nursemaid, and governess.[14]

Like Mary Follett, Briggs suffered serious losses early in life. Her mother developed breast cancer and died before Isobel's seventh birthday. Her father quickly remarried, no doubt seeking help in raising the younger children; but he, too, was soon dead, a victim of gangrene poisoning following a minor accident.[15] Fifteen-year-old Isobel, her sister, and her three brothers then had to make their own way in the world.

Middle-class fathers in mid-nineteenth-century England were "repeatedly warned," Martha Vicinus tells us in *Independent Women,* "to make plans for their daughters after their deaths." Otherwise their daughters were in danger of joining a group that was a source of endless fascination and horror to journalists of the period: overworked and destitute gentlewomen who were "eaking out an existence . . . on the edge of respectable social circles." William Briggs seems to have heeded these warnings. Realizing that his estate would not be sufficient to support all his children, Briggs saw to it that both Isobel and her younger sister, Alice Bertha, received a decent education.[16] Isobel's formal schooling began well before her father's death, perhaps as early as age twelve. Precisely which school Isobel attended is not known, but her father would have had few options. As one headmistress of the time observed, "There were many schools for girls and there were good schools, but the many were not good and the good were not many."[17]

Anxious to prove that women students were as capable as young men, the women who ran the better institutions began to campaign for the opportunity to enter their students as candidates for the Oxbridge examinations. The Cambridge examiners were the first to agree but did so only on condition that candidates' names and results for local and higher local examinations not be published. The examiners were worried that women would not be able to withstand public scrutiny of their examination results. The absence of published results makes it virtually impossible to verify the report in Briggs's obituary that Briggs, though she was about the right age to be a candidate, was "the first to take the university examinations that were open to her sex in England."[18]

Young women who completed their secondary school education in the years before the opening of the Oxbridge women's colleges often stayed on in their schools to become teachers. Most teachers earned less than a pound a week — enough to assure a middle-class woman the basic necessities of life, but not enough to "maintain her social status, according to her peers."[19] Even worse, teachers often were pressured to retire by their mid-fifties, despite the fact that few schools provided pensions and teachers rarely could afford to save for retirement. Whatever financial stability Briggs managed to secure during these years was a result of an inheritance from her father. When Isobel was only nine, William Briggs had written a will instructing his trustees to "maintain, educate and bring up my children being sons until they shall reasonably be able to provide for themselves and being daughters until their marriage." He further stipulated that after the death or marriage of his widow, his assets were to be sold and "equally divided between such of my children as being sons shall attain the age of twenty one years or being daughters shall attain that age or marry." As a result of these generous provisions, Isobel may have received as much as 800 pounds from his estate.[20]

This inheritance, though not sufficient to support her for a lifetime, did allow Isobel to take what would otherwise have been an extraordinary risk. In 1880 at the age of thirty-two, apparently without either relatives or a position awaiting her, Briggs left England for the United States. In her research on independent Englishwomen of this era, Martha Vicinus writes that any professional woman whose "promotion did not come by the age of thirty-five . . . could expect to earn no more and gain no better position than she held."

Briggs apparently had not yet secured a position as a headmistress and may well have decided that she had little to lose in trying her fortunes elsewhere.[21] Then, too, perhaps having absorbed her nonconformist father's willingness to challenge social conventions, Briggs may have hoped that America would provide a climate more amenable to educational reform.[22] Sentiments such as these were expressed to a friend and fellow teacher by another young English-woman of the late nineteenth century — a woman who eventually led the re-form of English teacher training colleges: "wouldn't you like to go to America, Canada, or the great wide west? where perhaps there might be more chance of finding out what manner of being you were? — where there is more room, more freedom, and one is not so hide-bound by conventions — where you could get nearer the soil, and as I said before, not be stifled by artificialities and habits and conventions, your own and other people's. Oh wouldn't you like it, wouldn't you? wouldn't you?"[23]

If Briggs came to America hoping for a chance to experiment with new educational curricula and methods, she was remarkably successful. After her arrival in Boston, Briggs somehow "got in close touch" with Pauline Agassiz Shaw and was selected to be the head of Shaw's new school.[24] As in all of Shaw's enterprises, it is difficult to determine how much of the school's innova-tive character was attributable to Shaw and how much to the person she hired to run the organization. But there is no question that Briggs was there from the beginning, helping to develop this progressive, coeducational school and ap-parently managing it with expertise and energy.

Administering an organization of the size and complexity of Mrs. Shaw's School was a major responsibility, and Briggs sometimes imposed "strict disci-pline." One student recalled an incident in which she thought Briggs "rather inflexible and severe": "One had to attend school the first day and the last day and there were no exceptions. I remember the case of Mrs. Wigglesworth, who lived next door but wished to remain in the country until a few weeks after the opening of school. She promised to have her daughter Anna tutored during her absence from school. Miss Briggs was adamant. 'If your daughter is not pres-ent the first day of school she cannot attend at all.' And she didn't."[25] Of course, what this teenager saw as Briggs's "inflexibility" was probably seen quite differently by members of the teaching staff. To them, it probably seemed an admirable effort by their principal to persuade parents to place a high priority on education — even when the child in question happened to be a girl.

Much about Isobel Briggs remains a mystery, including her physical appear-ance. One of Mary's nephews remembers being impressed with Isobel's "spar-kling eyes" and her style of dress, which was noticeably more modern than the "very severe" clothing worn by his aunt. He also remembers Isobel as being "shorter and rounder" than Mary.[26] Because Briggs was the principal of the school and twenty years older than Follett, these two women might never have become intimately acquainted had Briggs not made a most unusual request; she apparently asked Follett to give her "some instruction" in political philosophy. Briggs was a woman of considerable education and had "quite a reputation for teaching Shakespeare and the English classics"; but political philosophy and political science were new to her, only recently having become subjects of serious study in English universities. Follett wrote Henry Sidgwick about the request, telling him that this "lady of long experience as a teacher . . . knows that [political philosophy] is taught in England & knowing that I have been there takes it for granted that I know something about it." Follett apparently wished to accede to the request, for she anxiously inquired of Sidgwick what he considered "the best way to teach political philosophy."[27] Surely one attraction of giving these "lessons" to Briggs was the opportunity to share stories about Newnham and the people she had met there; friends would later recall that Follett "never tired of analyzing the shades of difference between English and American points of view and characteristics."[28] Then, too, Briggs's interest came at a fortunate time for Follett. She had returned from Newnham to find her mentor, Anna Boynton Thompson, absorbed in a new intellectual passion — the study of philosophy — and enthralled by her Annex colleague Alice Mary Longfellow.[29] For daily support and encouragement in Follett's scholarly ventures, Thompson was no longer the most reliable source.

During the years that Follett taught at Mrs. Shaw's School, much of her energy was devoted to finishing her book on the Speakership. The normal frustrations of scholarly investigation and writing were made all the more difficult for Follett by her "passion for the most minute detail," an analytical style that her studies with Henry Sidgwick undoubtedly reinforced. Follett's "hair-splitting" so frustrated most of her friends that they were incapable of providing real help; only Briggs "always provided a patient attention and sympathy." Isobel's contribution to Mary's writing, at least as Elizabeth Balch saw it, could "hardly be overstated. [It] was discussed with [Briggs] phrase by phrase, and sentence by sentence and often modified and remodified in accordance with her suggestions. Every thought was worked out in the clash of discussion between them. Hour after hour of absolute devotion being given by Miss Briggs to this intellectual task which took infinite patience."[30]

Briggs's influence on Follett was at once steadying and stimulating. It was common for older teachers of this era to urge young colleagues "to seize the new opportunities opening up for women." M. Carey Thomas's favorite teacher often told her: "Minnie, I wish I had the chance you girls have — it is too late for me to begin to study now — all I can do is to give you what

thoughts I have and help you all I can and then send you out to do what I might
have done." For a young female academic to feel respected and encouraged by
an older colleague — especially one who was thought to be "equally endowed
with gifts of the intellect" — was a moving experience; and the younger woman
often responded, not surprisingly, "with gratitude and love."[31] Follett quickly
made Briggs the central figure in her life. In September 1895, when Follett
went to New York to sign her Longmans contract, it was Briggs who accompanied her. And soon thereafter, when the manuscript was completed, Follett
dedicated it not to Thompson, Hart, or Sidgwick, but "To I. L. B."[32]

The increasingly intimate relationship between Briggs and Follett received
its first real test with the planned closing of Mrs. Shaw's School in 1896.
Shaw's children, for whom the school had been established, had completed
their education; and Briggs, who over the years had become Shaw's close
friend, was in her late forties, nearing the age at which English headmistresses
typically retired. In November 1895, apparently wishing to spend at least part
of every year in the country, Briggs purchased fifteen acres of land for $500 in
the foothills of the Green Mountains of Vermont. There, on West Hill outside
Putney, she and Mary planned to build a house.[33] The summer that the house
was being constructed, Follett (and presumably also Briggs) vacationed in the
Adirondacks, a trip that Briggs's long and intimate association with Pauline
Agassiz Shaw no doubt made possible. Shaw individually owned more than
650 acres in the vicinity of the rapids that join Upper Saranac Lake to Round
Lake and was a member of the Saranac Club, a group that owned land in the
upper Adirondacks which was "used as a private club for them and their
friends."[34]

The "deep new friendship" that Briggs and Follett shared sometimes left
others feeling "shut out." Many years later Elizabeth Balch admitted that she
had been surprised and hurt by her exclusion, feeling that she and Mary "were
already so intimate." At the same time, however, Balch acknowledged that she
had not been capable of the emotional support that Briggs seemed so able to
provide.[35] Mrs. Follett, too, may well have felt left out. Mary and her mother
had never been close, but Mary, with her sense of daughterly obligation, had
always maintained some semblance of family ties. Now even this tenuous
connection was in danger of being broken — and by a woman whose age placed
her almost in direct competition with Mrs. Follett for Mary's affections.

In her investigations of independent women of the nineteenth century, Martha Vicinus found that in the latter part of the century, families whose daughters rejected marriage for a permanent relationship with another woman often
attacked the friendship, seeing it as "a subversive outlet for ambitions and
hopes that went beyond familiar domestic subjects." Even in loving families,

Carroll Smith-Rosenberg tells us, the struggles of these "New Women" for autonomy "often led to estrangement from their own mothers and female kin, who remained within the old female world and who feared the attraction the new world held for their daughters." In many cases "resentful words" were exchanged, and the daughters suffered "lingering guilt."[36] During the period that Mary Follett was teaching at Mrs. Shaw's School, her decision to live in Boston had seemed justified by the multiplicity of demands on her time; but with the closing of the school, few of these demands remained. Continuing to live in Boston when her obligations consisted only of a single class at Radcliffe would have seemed an unequivocal rejection of her mother—and this, Mary apparently was not prepared to do. At the end of the summer, she left Isobel and returned to her mother in Quincy.[37]

Follett's reluctance either to establish a permanent home with Briggs or to rely on her for financial support was only partly a result of Follett's personal character and family circumstances. The 1890s mark a turning point in societal views about relationships between women.[38] Briggs, who was twenty years older than Follett, was a product of the era of romantic friendships. Born in 1848, she grew to adulthood during an era in which the "distinctly male and female spheres" of the nineteenth century made intense and sometimes sensual female love both a "plausible and socially accepted form of human interaction." Martha Vicinus, Carroll Smith-Rosenberg, and Lillian Faderman have convincingly described this world in their studies of the first generation of "New Women" in England and America. Middle-class women lived within a "secure and empathetic world" of sisters, first cousins, aunts, and nieces—a world that had its own separate customs and rituals. At the heart of this female world lay "an intimate mother-daughter relationship" and an apprenticeship system in which "mothers and other older women carefully trained daughters in the arts of housewifery and motherhood."[39]

The first opportunity that a young middle-class girl had to develop relationships of her own occurred when she went off to boarding school. There, Barbara Miller Solomon tells us, "it was natural and desirable for a girl to have an intimate friend and to form with one or two others a 'bunch' or 'coterie,' the little crowd of peers who knew each other's deepest thoughts and feelings. The members of the clique gave each other respect and affection akin to love, as well as encouragement in their new adventure." Briggs, who had lost her own mother so early in life, probably came to cherish the "surrogate mother" tradition of the girls' boarding schools. "Older girls," writes historian Carroll Smith-Rosenberg, " 'adopted' younger ones, who called them 'Mother.' Dear friends might indeed continue this pattern of adoption and mothering throughout their lives: one woman might routinely assume the nurturing role of pseudomother, the other the dependency role of daughter. The pseudo-mother performed for the other woman all the services which we normally associate with mothers; she went to absurd lengths to purchase items her 'daughter' could have obtained from other sources, gave advice and functioned as an idealized figure in her 'daughter's imagination."[40]

Women could participate in tender, even sensual friendships because, as Nancy F. Cott tells us, both women and men accepted a nineteenth-century ideology of women's "passionlessness."[41] Indeed, the openness that prevailed in letters and diaries about these romantic friendships reflects the then widespread belief that these relationships were a natural part of growing up. Since "closeness, freedom of emotional expression, and uninhibited physical contact" were discouraged between women and men, relationships between women were seen as an acceptable, even desirable, training ground for the roles of wife and mother. "The point is not that these young women were hostile to young men," Smith-Rosenberg writes. "Far from it; they sought marriage and domesticity. Yet in these letters and diaries men appear as an other or out group, segregated into different schools, supported by their own male network of friends and kin, socialized to different behavior, and coached to a proper formality in courtship behavior. As a consequence, relations between young women and men frequently lacked the spontaneity and emotional intimacy that characterized the young girls' ties to each other."[42]

Under the circumstances, it is hardly surprising that some of these New Women came to love each other. "It was the friendship with other girls that I think of," one Newnham student recalled as she wrote of her college experiences. "The slow exploration of another human being, the discovery of shared perplexities and interests, the delight in our new companions' gifts and, maybe, beauty (for beauty was not wanting in those years) — these were excitements." Most of the "eager emotional responses" of the Newnham women "were little more than passing 'crushes,' called *Grandes Passions* (or 'GPs' in Newnhamese)."[43] In at least some college friendships, however, a "need for closeness and support merged with more intense demands for a love which was at the same time both emotional and sensual." Some even grew into "primary sexual relationships."[44]

A few years before Mary Follett enrolled in college, the social acceptability of romantic friendships between women first began to be questioned. A phenomenon called the "smash" was thought to be having deleterious effects on the health of college women. A committee of the Association of Collegiate Alumnae (now the American Association of University Women) took up this issue in the 1880s as a part of its overall investigation and defense of the health of college women. Although the committee's final report does not mention the "smash," an 1882 letter written by Alice Stone Blackwell, a member of the committee who had graduated the previous year from Boston University, makes clear the committee's concern. "The committee gave it as their strong opinion that one thing which damaged the health of the girls seriously was 'smashes' — an extraordinary habit which they have of falling violently in love with each other, and suffering all the pangs of unrequited attachment, desperate jealousy etc etc, with as much energy as if one of them were a man . . . If the 'smash' is mutual, they monopolize each other & 'spoon' continually, & sleep together & lie awake all night talking instead of going to sleep; & if it isn't mutual the unrequited one cries herself sick & endures pangs unspeakable." Since they "had very little of that sort of thing at B.U.," Blackwell thought that the problem could be attributed to the "massing hundreds of nervous young girls together, & shutting them up from the outside world," such as happened in the women's residential colleges.[45]

Despite the emotional upset that a "smash" could cause, romantic friendships between women still were not seriously questioned until they were seen as offering large numbers of women an alternative to marriage. Before 1870, a woman who wished to "flee the world with a special friend" had little hope of doing so; "familial responsibilities and economic dependence" made such arrangements impossible. But by the last two decades of the nineteenth century, better education and opportunities for employment allowed at least some women to live together outside their families. In New England permanent relationships between women became so common that they were known as "Boston marriages." College-educated women were especially likely to reject marriage, inspired by "dreams of autonomy and power" and, as M. Carey Thomas put it, "hopeful of doing something splendid after all."[46] The general public first became aware of the tendency of college women not to marry when an 1895 survey reported that "more than half the graduates of women's colleges remained spinsters" — a figure that compared with "only 10 percent of all American women." The result, Lillian Faderman tells us, was "a great public outcry. There had been at that time a general agreement that every married couple in American needed to produce at least three children for the Republic to survive, and higher education for women (and all who were connected with it) was now held accountable for these women's escape from their patriotic duty."[47]

Follett was still susceptible to pressures to marry. She was only twenty-seven at the time this study was published — barely a year older than her mother when she had married. Only a decade earlier, a woman of Follett's social class might have resisted such pressures by establishing a permanent relationship with another woman. But now, doing so meant that she would risk being branded as selfish and something of a threat to society.[48] The work of historians such as Nancy Sahli and Lillian Faderman makes it clear that by the 1890s "the innocent female world of loving friendship . . . was crumbling." The decade of the 1890s was " 'a crucial transitional period in the conceptualization and social experience of homosexual relations' in both America and Great Britain. Whereas earlier in the century women's friendships were consistent with their dependent status, the affection between women who were in a number of different ways declaring their equality — or, even more unsettling, their similarity — to men threatened the social, moral, and sexual order."[49]

There is no evidence that Follett had to contend with accusations that she was a lesbian. Even in medical circles, lesbianism would receive little discussion until late in the decade, and it was not until the 1920s that public charges of lesbianism were leveled as a means of attacking women's intimate friendships. Still, some college women of the 1890s were beginning to worry about whether intense attachments to other women might be seen by society as "sexually deviant." One young woman who was sensitive to signs that same-sex friendships might be seen as "unnatural" was Willa Cather, then a student at the University of Nebraska. Cather was angered by this judgment, calling it "unfair," but she "reveals her acceptance of conventional wisdom," Sharon O'Brien surmises in her study of Cather, "by agreeing, however reluctantly, with its accuracy."[50]

The emotional turmoil that followed in the wake of Follett's decision to leave Briggs was surely a trial for both of them, but Mary, especially, must have struggled. For like other women in the generation of the "unsentimental nineties," she was reluctant to give in to her emotions. Women had for so long been considered incapable of reason that "self-respect and power" seemed to hinge on "greater self-control, greater distance from others." The emotional restraint exhibited by Follett in dedicating her book "To I. L. B." contrasts sharply with the florid dedication made by Anna Boynton Thompson in her book on Fichte less than a year earlier. Thompson was a woman of Briggs's generation rather than Follett's, and the expansiveness of her dedication reflects this generational difference. "To Alice Mary Longfellow," Thompson wrote, "I dedicate this work as an expression of the affection and gratitude I bear her for friendship, for unfailing sympathy, for profound help in thought and life."[51]

Follett's determined effort to control her emotions received a severe test when, at one point during the separation, Briggs sent her a letter "suggesting breaking off the friendship . . . feeling that to Mary it was not as deep and serious as to her." Already entangled in a complex web of emotional obligations to her mother, Mary was understandably wary of the intensity of Isobel's needs. Elizabeth Balch happened to be visiting when the letter arrived and remembered seeing Mary "disturbed to her depths, not excited or sentimental but with the profound emotion which only a really big person can feel."[52] Follett undoubtedly felt torn. On the one hand, Isobel surely was the embodiment of Mary's fantasies — someone who appreciated her drive and intellect, yet was capable of love and support. But Follett's troubled childhood had made her extremely cautious about trusting and had forged, instead, a fierce self-reliance. However unnerving it was to contemplate an end to her friendship with Isobel, Follett apparently felt that it was wiser to remain in Quincy.

Follett dealt with the confusion and pain elicited by the separation from Briggs by immersing herself in her studies at Radcliffe. The previous year she had taken political economy courses from William James Ashley, including Ashley's graduate research seminar, where she had begun a comparison of the works of Adam Smith, the eighteenth-century Scottish social philosopher and political economist, and A. R. J. Turgot, the eighteenth-century French economist and financial reformer. Follett resumed this investigation in earnest after her 1896 return to Quincy.[53] Ashley was the editor of a series of "Economics Classics" for Macmillan and had planned a reprint of Turgot's *Réflexions sur la formation et la distribution des richesses* for this series. But when he became aware of the poor quality of the existing English translation, Ashley decided that simply reprinting it was "out of the question." He then "ventured on a new translation" — most likely with considerable help from Follett. In the summer of 1896, Ashley wrote the Harvard College circulation librarian that Follett "is now engaged with me in a work on Turgot." She was in need of certain books and journals concerning the project, and Ashley asked that these be sent to her at the Saranac Club.[54] Virtually all the materials were written in French, but that posed no problem for Follett. Sometime after her return from Newnham, Follett apparently decided that fluency in other languages was essential to her scholarly pursuits. To increase her competence, she brushed up on her Latin and then took advanced courses in French literature (1894–95) and German literature (1895–96) — classes that required reading without translation.[55]

When Macmillan published Ashley's new volume on Turgot in 1898, readers received more than a new translation. In a brief introductory essay, the editor took up the academic controversy about the extent of Turgot's influence on Adam Smith, arguing "that there are not inconsiderable portions of Adam Smith's treatise of a distinctly Physiocratic character." The editor also included in the volume a few excerpts from Turgot's correspondence because they helped establish the ways in which Turgot could be considered a true physiocrat (a promoter of free trade and laissez-faire economics). Since the relationship between Turgot and Adam Smith was the very issue that Follett had been investigating in the graduate seminar, it is worth noting that Ashley failed to acknowledge the presumably substantial contributions that Follett made both to the introductory essay and to the compilation of excerpts from Turgot's correspondence.[56]

Follett's reaction to Ashley's perfidy was probably tempered by several factors. Follett had received mixed reviews of her book on the Speakership, and several writers had sharply disagreed with her about the appropriateness of the Speaker's power. A person less sensitive or less demanding of herself than Follett might have been able to shrug off the reviewers' criticisms, but Follett probably took each comment to heart.[57] Given the unpleasantness of that experience, she may well have thought it foolish to involve herself in academic controversies about Turgot when she had no further plans for that sort of scholarly work. She no doubt also realized that a translation of Turgot promised little in the way of either money or prestige. Follett's book on the Speakership, a topic of considerably greater contemporary interest, had generated numerous reviews but disappointingly slow sales. Only after the turn of the century, when the controversial tenure of "Uncle Joe" Cannon of Illinois precipitated a battle in the House over the power of the Speakership, did Longmans issue a series of three reprintings. By contrast, Wilson's *Congressional Government* was reprinted twice during its first year of publication and fifteen times by 1900.[58]

Still, Follett probably felt at least some resentment over Ashley's deception, and this may have contributed to her growing uncertainty about whether she really wanted to pursue an academic career. Only half of the women receiving doctoral degrees before 1900 completed their doctoral work in less than eight years; and almost all women doctoral students had to work as teachers in order to meet expenses.[59] Follett, who was already twenty-nine in 1897, may well have wondered whether such a substantial investment of time at her age was wise. Then too, Follett lacked a clear scholarly purpose. Perhaps if Albert Bushnell Hart had developed a central theme within which his students could fashion their research — such as Turner's "frontier thesis" or Beard's "economic determinants of American political behavior" — Follett might have found a comfortable scholarly niche. Or, alternately, Follett might have found a hospitable line of research if William James Ashley had been allowed to focus less on medieval studies and more on contemporary economic problems during his tenure at Harvard.[60]

But even if Follett had been able to approach graduate study with a clear scholarly purpose, there still were numerous other obstacles to overcome. Harvard would not confer its Ph.D. degree on women, despite the fact that, beginning in 1894, women could enroll in graduate courses, take oral examinations, and prepare a doctoral thesis. By 1900, four women who had completed all requirements for the Harvard Ph.D. were deprived of the degree in this way.[61] Even Radcliffe did not offer the Ph.D. until 1902, having repeatedly voted to wait in the hope that Harvard would relent and grant women its degree. Anna Boynton Thompson, long Mary's mentor in academic matters, received a Radcliffe A.M. in 1899 but apparently did not even try for a Harvard Ph.D.[62] Johns Hopkins University, then the other top-flight history program in the nation, was also closed to women; there, women were not even admitted to graduate courses until 1907.

Of course, there were other, less prestigious programs that offered doctorates in history and political science to women before 1900. Among them were the University of Chicago, Cornell, Syracuse, Yale, and Bryn Mawr. But if Follett were to attend one of these institutions to obtain her Ph.D., the education available to her at that time almost certainly would have been inferior to what she had already known at Radcliffe and Newnham, and the financial burden on her would have been substantial. Still, a degree from any of these institutions would have virtually guaranteed Follett a faculty position at a good women's college. Demand was increasing for courses in Follett's areas of specialization, and there were few doctorally qualified women available to fill teaching positions. Only 18 of the 229 doctoral degrees conferred on women before 1900 were in the field of history; even fewer, 5 each, were conferred in political science and economics.[63] Then, too, "to have been [Albert Bushnell Hart's] pupil was enough recommendation for a young scholar to a university post," Samuel Eliot Morison later would write — at least if that scholar was a man. Unfortunately, Follett's experience at Mrs. Shaw's School seems to have quenched any desire she had had to be a teacher. In October 1897, when Hart and Thompson took the lead in forming the New England History Teachers' Association, Follett did not join.[64]

Follett took no more classes at Radcliffe after the 1896–97 academic year; instead, she fulfilled the requirements for her degree by passing examinations in elementary Greek, elementary geometry, and physics. Finally, in June 1898, Mary Follett graduated from Radcliffe with an A.B. degree; of the forty-six graduates, she was one of only four women whose degrees were conferred *summa cum laude*. Graduating with Follett in the class of 1898 were Anna Boynton Thompson (also *summa cum laude*); Maud May Wood, who would soon become Follett's colleague in the Boston Equal Suffrage Association; and Gertrude Stein.[65]

A few months after her graduation, Follett celebrated her thirtieth birthday. Mary probably felt more relief than trauma over having reached this

Radcliffe College Class of 1898. Mary Follett is seated immediately below left railing, second from left. Radcliffe Archives, Radcliffe Institute, Harvard University.

milestone, since at age thirty, single women like Follett "could put aside any pretense of being marriageable and concentrate upon their own interests." The troublesome aspect of this period of Follett's life was her uncertainty about what to do with her education and talents. Martha Vicinus reminds us that "Jane Addams is only the most famous example" of many young women who, "after successfully breaking away and going to college, went through a period of debilitating illness before they could acknowledge their own needs and fight for their realization."[66]

Another who struggled for a decade before she found satisfying work was Alice Hamilton (1869–1970), a physician and the "foremost practitioner" in the field of industrial toxicology in the early years of the twentieth century. According to Barbara Sicherman, Alice Hamilton "defined her dilemma as an inability to integrate her scientific work with the Hull House ideal of service; not only did they seem to be hopelessly incompatible ideals, but she found it difficult to define her relationship to either. Neither domain, science or service, satisfied her fully. The laboratory, a world of men, gave her an opportunity to develop a special competence and, she hoped, to prove her worth as an individual. But in the end she found it rather sterile and removed from life."[67]

Mary Follett, too, was dissatisfied with the isolation of historical scholarship. Conscious of having had "very unusual privileges," she ardently hoped to "make some practical significance of what she had learned."[68] Male contemporaries, such as Theodore Roosevelt and Woodrow Wilson, could do so by taking their scholarly ideas into the political arena, but it was not at all clear how Follett might put her expertise to use once she had chosen not to teach.

In this time of uncertainty and confusion about her future, Follett was probably tempted to turn to Isobel Briggs for emotional support. But like the many talented women studied by Martha Vicinus, the pressures Follett felt "to do and be so much" made personal relationships both "more important and more problematic." For now, she would continue to cope with her fears alone, but she made this choice with great ambivalence. "Our happiness, our sense of living at all," Follett would write in later years, "is directly dependent on our joining with others. We are lost, exiled, imprisoned until we feel the joy of union."[69]

9

Self-Realization and Service

In 1897, the year before her graduation from Radcliffe, Follett took a position as a clerk in the office of J. Otis Wardwell, a prominent Boston attorney. Surely one attraction of working for Wardwell was that it again offered Follett sufficient reason for leaving her mother and moving into Boston. The first year, she took a room on Worcester Street in the upper part of the South End; the next, she moved to Five Haviland Street, beyond the fashionable Back Bay near the Fenway. Living in furnished lodgings could not have been a very desirable arrangement for Follett, since it meant "a loss of status" for a woman of her class, but she had little choice.[1] Only hospitals, schools, and charities made a practice of providing their women employees room and board as part of the salary; and since Follett probably earned little more than a thousand dollars per year, spending a substantial portion of her salary on an apartment no doubt seemed foolish.[2] After a year of roominghouse life, Mary probably would have much preferred living with Isobel, but by then Briggs had taken up residence in the new house in Vermont.

Follett's new employer had had a brief but impressive career in Massachusetts Republican politics. He had served five consecutive terms in the Massachusetts House (1887–1891) and, by the beginning of his second year, was "recognized as the Republican leader on the floor."[3] After being narrowly defeated in his second attempt to become House Speaker, Wardwell left the legislature. He moved his law practice to Boston and became associated with Samuel Walker McCall, the newly elected U.S. representative for the Eighth Congressional District.[4] McCall was known as "one of the most scholarly men in American public life" and was a great admirer of Thomas B. Reed.[5] McCall's likely appreciation of Follett's analysis of the evolution of the Speaker's power, along with Wardwell's personal interest in the functioning of the Massachusetts Speakership, may explain how Follett was invited to take a position in Wardwell's office; but her introduction to these men most likely came by way of Albert Bushnell Hart, a Republican who was active in local and national politics.[6]

Working for Wardwell would have given Follett a chance to use the research skills she had developed through her study of history and economics, and she was probably quite pleased to be associated with two such highly regarded Republicans. Her father had not been involved in party politics, but her grandfather, Daniel Baxter, had been an "ardent" Republican and a Mugwump; when Grover Cleveland defeated James G. Blaine in the 1884 presidential election, Baxter reportedly "threw open his entire house and lit all the gas jets" in celebration.[7]

J. Otis Wardwell's specialty was corporation law. He already had a number of important clients, including the Edison Electric Illuminating Company and the Boston Elevated Railway.[8] Wardwell's involvement with public service corporations dated from 1890, when he chaired a special committee to investigate charges of corruption "in the incorporation of certain elevated railways in the city of Boston."[9] In the three-year period before Mary Follett went to work for Wardwell in 1897, the city of Boston was abuzz with controversy over the award of public franchises for an elevated railway and construction of a subway under Tremont Street, a major downtown thoroughfare.[10] Transit leases in Massachusetts had traditionally been limited franchises that could be revoked after a year or two if the company charged exorbitant fares or provided poor service. Indeed, corporations of all kinds had traditionally been more tightly controlled in Massachusetts than in other states. Incorporation had long been treated "as a device by which groups of private entrepreneurs served as agencies of the state toward a public purpose." Many in the Massachusetts business community continued to hold this view and were suspicious of "modern" financiers who regarded the corporation primarily as a private money-making enterprise. Disturbed by the possibility that the city might lose control of its transportation system if the West End Company's proposed fifty-year lease for the subway was approved, a few businessmen decided to stand in opposition.[11]

Edward A. Filene, the thirty-six-year-old department store magnate who was becoming one of the most progressive businessmen in the nation, took the lead in this battle and searched for a lawyer to help him make his case to the legislature. At first it seemed no one was interested, but then Filene discussed the matter with Louis D. Brandeis, a successful Boston corporation attorney who had done other business for Filene's firm. Brandeis had seen the problems a monopoly could create and eagerly agreed to oppose the railway interests. The arguments made by Filene, Brandeis, and others in the fall of 1896 persuaded the legislature to reduce the subway lease from fifty to twenty years and to require the West End Company to pay the city a substantial annual rental fee.[12]

Even before the subway issue was resolved, there was activity on another front. Early in 1896, in order to gain the necessary capital to build an elevated system for Boston and its suburbs, the Boston Elevated was sold to J. Pierpont Morgan. To manage their efforts to gain legislative approval for the new elevated plan, the "Pierpont Morgan-West End interests" engaged J. Otis Wardwell as their legislative counsel. It was during this legislative campaign that Mary Follett worked in Wardwell's office. The *New York Times* predicted that Wardwell would be managing "one of the most bitter legislative contests that has been waged in recent years."[13] There is no way of knowing exactly what sort of work Follett did for Wardwell, but her expertise as a researcher and writer would surely have been useful in preparing the numerous documents necessary for legislative hearings.

The charter amendments that the Elevated was seeking from the legislature were designed to benefit the company by maintaining a five-cent fare (in an era of generally declining transit fares) and limiting annual payments to the city. In addition, the Elevated sought permission to complete its system by leasing the Tremont Street subway from the West End Company. Brandeis and the advocates of public control learned about the proposed charter amendments fairly late in the legislative process and vigorously opposed them though letters to the *Boston Evening Transcript* and in legislative hearings. Their efforts came too late.[14] In June 1897 the charter amendments were passed and signed by the governor.

There is a tendency today to construe the battle between Brandeis and the Boston Elevated syndicate as a sharply drawn contest between representatives of the public interest and financiers bent on personal financial gain. In truth, however, the Elevated syndicate had widespread support in Boston, both within the business community and among the general public. Compared with the transit systems of New York or Chicago, Boston's system was "most woefully deficient." The Elevated seemed just the organization to fix it and, in the process, create badly needed jobs for men from the city's immigrant neighborhoods. A *New York Times* article of 1897 reported that there "is scarcely a [Boston] citizen who is not discussing and worrying over the miserable transportation facilities existing here." The culprit, as the *Times* saw it, was a faction in the West End Company that had refused, despite the complaints of Boston citizens, to make changes in an obviously deteriorating system. By comparison, the Elevated seemed a remarkably progressive corporation. It was prepared to invest the capital necessary to improve the system and had even convinced the recalcitrant West End Company to allow the Elevated to lease the subway. When the bill allowing the Boston Elevated to proceed with its plans was enacted in June 1897, the *Times* confidently predicted that the system "will not only be a financial success, but a public boon."[15]

The first inkling that the "boon" might turn into a public scandal appeared later that year, when the terms of the Elevated's proposal to lease the West End Company's facilities were made public. The length of the lease (ninety-nine years) caused immediate suspicion, since it was four times as long as any previously approved in the Commonwealth. Before the subway lease could be implemented, it had to be approved by the Railroad Commission. Brandeis and other opponents took this opportunity to argue vigorously against the plan, calling it a "fraud upon the public." The Railroad Commission responded by refusing to approve the proposed lease; but a few days later the Elevated brought forward a compromise plan in which it offered to reduce the rental fees paid to the West End Company and to shorten the lease. This time the commissioners gave their approval.[16]

Mary Follett worked in J. Otis Wardwell's office for almost two years, leaving late in 1898 or early 1899, just as opposition to the Elevated was beginning to build.[17] Follett's decision to leave her job may well have been influenced by the arguments that Brandeis had made about the importance of public control of the city's transit system.[18] Her education had given her a sophisticated appreciation of the idea of the public interest and aroused a genuine sense of civic duty; she could hardly help but be troubled by working for an attorney whose client was accused of perpetrating "a fraud upon the public."[19] Although Follett did not know Louis D. Brandeis personally during this period, in the next decade she would become a family friend. Follett and Alice Brandeis would work together in social and civic projects, and Mary and Isobel would become neighbors of the Brandeises in Otis Place in Boston.

The two years in Wardwell's office were an important formative experience for Follett. As Wardwell's employee, she had been privy to at least some aspects of the building of a public franchise monopoly — an exceedingly rare experience for a woman — and had seen at close range the crosscutting interests of financiers, stockholders, retailers, neighborhood bosses, commuters, and reformers. Only a few years earlier, Follett's research on the Speakership had revealed similar complexities in the political relations of the House of Representatives. It seemed that at local as well as national levels of government, political parties were losing their influence. Lobbying by special interests on single issues would soon become the dominant factor in American political life.[20]

After leaving the job with Wardwell, Follett was more deeply confused about her future than ever. The social prescriptions for a woman of her class had been clear: she was to marry or, failing that, to devote herself to her daughterly obligations. Follett had done neither, venturing instead into the public arena. On the face of it, she had succeeded there: she had graduated *summa cum laude,* published a masterly piece of research, and acquired a good job. But Follett probably felt that she had failed, for she had found it impossible to keep important personal vows. After her father's death, Mary had assumed responsibility for the welfare of her younger brother; but George had rejected her help and failed miserably in his academic pursuits. Follett had then vowed to become a teacher, seeing it as a way to repay the intellectual debts she owed to those who had encouraged her in her own education; but her disillusionment with teaching had deprived her of this satisfaction. For a time, a life of scholarship promised a viable alternative to teaching, but that vision, too, had been clouded by institutional obstacles and the lack of a clear scholarly purpose. And now the work with Wardwell, which Follett had probably hoped would be a way to "make some practical significance" of what she had learned, had ended — perhaps as a result of Follett's disillusionment with her employer's values. In the past when Follett had needed encouragement or guidance, she had been able to turn to her teachers for help, but this time Mary had to face "hard words" from them for having abandoned her writing. Desperately needing the sympathetic ear of a friend and time to think things through, thirty-year-old Mary Follett finally took refuge with fifty-year-old Isobel Briggs in Vermont.[21]

For almost two years, Briggs and Follett "lived quietly together . . . preoccupied by the interests and demands of their country life." In the "quiet beauty" of this "far-away hill top, surrounded by upland pastures & woods, rolling country, wide spaces, & with the lovely hills in the distance," Follett found an "atmosphere of peace" that she would never know anywhere else. Mary and Isobel christened their country house "Overhills." The name was apt, for whether sitting on the long front porch or looking out the enormous living-room window, one could look east across the hills all the way to Mt. Monadnock in New Hampshire. Briggs's architect, A. Wadsworth Longfellow, who worked in the tradition of H. H. Richardson and Frederick Law Olmsted, carefully sited buildings in relation to the landscape.[22] Even the interior of the three-story house had a distinct country flavor; in the living room an open-beam ceiling and rustic stone fireplace evoked the outdoors, and the wall covering was chosen because its texture and color "like redwood bark" provided "a restful contrast to the green all around them."[23]

Since the property had neither running water nor electricity, Briggs was fortunate that she could afford "live-in help." A young couple from the Carolinas, who were among the few blacks in Windham County, were hired as servants. Summer days at Overhills were filled with walks in the hills, long drives, and picnic lunches; winter brought sleigh rides into nearby Brattleboro and long hours of reading from the living room's well-stocked bookshelves. No matter what the season, however, their "greatest pleasure" was talk — "merry, often witty, always stimulating" talk. It was a "very active and vitalizing" life, Elizabeth Balch remembered, but "so far as creative work went — fallow."[24] Where work was concerned, Follett was deeply discouraged.

For an unmarried woman, a job could provide needed financial security, and a career could offer a sense of competence and accomplishment; but neither would truly satisfy Follett's desire to "make something of herself." This she could have only through a vocation or "calling," in which "work constitutes a practical ideal of activity and character that makes a person's work morally inseparable from his or her life." To modern ears, the concept of vocation sounds sentimental — even a bit foolish; only in the "professions," Robert N. Bellah and his colleagues tell us in their book, *Habits of the Heart,* do Americans of today retain vestiges of the traditional ideal of a "calling": "[A calling] subsumes the self into a community of disciplined practice and sound judgment whose activity has meaning and value in itself, not just in the output or profit that results from it. But the calling not only links a person to his or her fellow workers. A calling links a person to the larger community, a whole in which the calling of each is a contribution to the good of all . . . The calling is a crucial link between the individual and the public world." America's republican traditions legitimated a man's search for a calling, but women were customarily excluded from the public sphere. In 1850 de Tocqueville wrote that Americans, despite their commitment to democratic principles, "do not think that man and woman have the duty or the right to do the same things." Indeed, "inexorable public opinion carefully keeps woman within the little sphere of domestic interests and duties and will not let her go beyond them."[25]

Mary Follett, having failed in her search for a calling despite her most determined efforts, resolved during this period at Overhills to open her life to the workings of a larger will. In doing so, a passage from Dante's *Paradiso* came to have special meaning for her. Traveling through the heavens, Dante's Wayfarer pauses in the sphere of the "inconstant" ones — those who failed, despite "right-directed" wills, to keep personal vows or who "were in some way ineffectual in their pursuit of their goals on earth."[26] The Wayfarer inquires of Piccarda whether these "pale spirits" are satisfied in the lowest sphere of paradise or "have any wish to rise to higher station/to see more, or to make yourselves more dear." Smiling, Piccarda responds:

> Brother, the power of love, which is our bliss,
> calms all our will. What we desire, we have.
> There is in us no other thirst than this.
>
> Were we to wish for any higher sphere,
> then our desires would not be in accord
> with the high will of Him who wills us here;
>
> and if love is our whole being, and if you weigh
> love's nature well, then you will see that discord
> can have no place among these circles. Nay,
>
> the essence of this blessed state of being,
> is to hold all our will within His will,
> whereby our wills are one and all-agreeing.
>
> And so the posts we stand from sill to sill
> throughout this realm, please all the realm as much
> as they please Him who wills us to His will.
>
> In His will is our peace. It is that sea
> to which all moves, all that Itself creates
> and Nature bears through all Eternity.[27]

Mary placed above her bed a line from this passage as a personal motto: "*In la sua voluntade e nostra pace*" — In His will is our peace.[28]

Follett's desire to be passively receptive to the workings of a larger will calls to mind Anna Boynton Thompson's response to her own health crisis fifteen years earlier. Brilliant and ambitious at a time when there was little opportunity in society for women to use their talents, Thompson felt her accomplishments agonizingly small compared with her dreams and desires. It was through her study of the nineteenth century Idealist philosophers that she regained her spirit — coming to view her life as an essential element, however limited, of the divine Will. The inspiration that Thompson received from the tenets of Idealist philosophy may well have encouraged Follett to look for help there, too.[29] "The poverty of individual life," Thompson argued in an 1899 *Educational Review* article, "can at no moment of time suffice the one absolute will: in the beginning and forever it appears as a mighty, multitudinous self, whose infinite number and variety of members compensate for the limitations of each." Exhorting her readers to action, she continued: "We must each, singly and individually, hold ourselves ready for this higher revelation . . . by holding daily and hourly the whole being open to God, waiting for the inflowing of divine wisdom, the clear sight of the perfect ideal which he would have us work out . . . that we may learn to know whither it urges . . . and may learn to say and to prove 'Lo I, even I, am come to do thy will.' "[30]

Sentiments such as these were attractive to educated men and women of the late nineteenth century, troubled as many of them were by the specter of a Darwinian universe in which divine will and human purpose played little, if any, role. Feeling themselves "forced to choose between faith and reason," many found a comfortable synthesis in the writings of the German Idealist philosophers. The Idealists clearly valued reason over faith, but their "emphasis on the spiritual character of ultimate reality and on the relation between the finite spirit and infinite Spirit" seemed to place them, at the same time, "firmly on the side of religion."[31]

Others during this skeptical era were less concerned with salvaging their religious beliefs than with bringing meaning and purpose to their lives. Many of these middle-class men and women turned to the writings of the Oxford Idealists.[32] Thomas Hill Green's philosophy, in particular, seemed to give back to his adherents "the language of self-sacrifice" and taught them how they "belonged to one another in the one life of organic humanity." Indeed, Green's ideas helped to fuel virtually all the late nineteenth- and early twentieth-century efforts by the English middle class to better the lot of the lower classes.[33] In the words of one follower, "[Green] filled us again with the breath of high idealism."[34]

The heart of Green's philosophy is a belief in "an immanent God gradually realising Himself in the world through the ideal of human perfection." Green believed that "God is the idea of one's self as it might be." God "realises himself in the world," Green argued, not only in the efforts of individuals to make actual their vision of a "better" or "higher" self, but also "by making real his spirit in human institutions, customs and laws." As a result, Green saw human history as the "progressive development of man in society made possible by God."[35]

To modern readers, Green's "calm confidence in progress and human reason" seems naively optimistic; but it accurately reflects the mid-nineteenth-century, middle-class faith in the basic goodness of human nature. To Green's way of thinking, not even the existence of London's East End slums justified denouncing "asceticism and the official Christian values of charity and justice as sham." These values had validity for Green, despite his refusal to recognize churches as authorities in religious matters. He encouraged reformers to demonstrate "the clear discrepancy between [Christianity's] avowed ideals and its actual performance" and to use the guilt they aroused to motivate social change.[36]

Not surprisingly, Green's impact was particularly strong on those who came from evangelical backgrounds, as did Follett's friend Isobel Briggs. Evangelical homes, Melvin Richter writes in his biography of Green, "had a way of instilling . . . an emotional dynamic, a dedication to cause and a calling to self-sacrifice. These traits and values often survived the loss of faith in their parental creed." Green's philosophy served as a kind of "surrogate faith," encouraging the late nineteenth-century sons and daughters of evangelicals to turn their attention "away from the means of personal salvation in the next world to improving the condition of this one."[37]

Toynbee Hall, the pioneer settlement house in the East End of London, is only the most prominent example of the many social and public service institutions that were developed or sustained by a generation of Green's students. Another of the organizations that grew out of the work of Green's students "in and about Toynbee Hall" was the agnostic London Ethical Society. Even Follett's teacher at Newnham, Henry Sidgwick, who had philosophical differences with the Oxford Idealists, was "perfectly willing to collaborate in the [Ethical Society's] effort 'to set moral, social and religious problems in the light of philosophical principles'" so long as the "language of Idealist metaphysics were [sic] not used."[38]

Idealism was brought to Cambridge, Massachusetts, in 1882 by Josiah Royce, who had read Kant and the post-Kantian German philosophers while a student in Germany.[39] In his study of Harvard philosophers, *The Rise of American Philosophy,* Bruce Kuklick contends that Royce's ideas were "the paradigmatic Harvard attempt at resolving the dispute between evolution and theology" through the mid-1890s. Anna Boynton Thompson studied with Royce during the height of his career and wrote her book on Johann Gottlieb Fichte, the post-Kantian Idealist, under Royce's supervision.[40] Follett, however, gained her understanding of German philosophy and Idealist thought not by enrolling in courses but, as she put it, "by wireless" — a Boston/Cambridge atmosphere electric with these ideas.[41]

Generally speaking, the Idealist philosophers emphasized the ethic of "self-realization" — the notion that "goodness lay in the increasing growth of the individual's real self." Even Royce, who concentrated on a theory of the absolute early in his writing, began in the mid-1890s to focus on the idea of the individual. In part, this was a response to critics such as his Harvard colleague

William James, who claimed that Royce's absolute idealism deprived the finite self of its own will and freedom. Endeavoring to meet this criticism, Royce developed the concept of individuation and delivered his first paper on the subject at an 1896 meeting of the Radcliffe Philosophy Club. In a letter to Gertrude Stein, the organizer of a series of talks for the club, Royce explained that he thought the paper appropriate for that venue, since the subject was of "practical interest to people who desire to call their souls their own."[42]

Royce "sought to preserve the ideal of individualism in a world in which the individual was an atom in a complex and closely knit society," and thus, Ralph H. Gabriel argues in *American Democratic Thought,* Royce was the first American thinker to confront squarely the problem of "reconciling liberty and authority." In Royce's philosophy, it is the act of voluntarily willing the transcendence of one's own "selfish desires in an effort to achieve the general good" that makes the individual free. This notion resonates strongly with republican ideas of civic duty and concern for the public interest that are essential elements of the American political tradition.[43]

Royce assumed that in addition to "the world made known by sense perceptions"—the province of science—there exists the realm of the Ideal. In this second world, the individual self is a fragment of a divine purpose—a consciously embodied "Meaning" rather than a "Thing." And here, Royce argued, the individual is free. Although Royce admitted that there is a sense in which it is true to say that the divine spirit compels us, it is only "in the sense that it compels you to be an individual, and to be free." The freedom of the self is derived from the fact that the individual is "a *unique* expression of the divine will."[44]

Royce believed that the finite self, by its very nature, desires "to unite its will ever more closely with the divine will." This union is accomplished through a process of fulfilling a unique ideal or life plan.[45] Thus Royce enjoined the individual who would be free to "harmonise thy will with the world's Will. Express thyself through obedience. Win thy victory by accepting thy task." The individual comes to know his "certain unique vocation," Royce believed, by "interpreting himself to himself." But this self-interpretation cannot be done in isolation; it requires continual interaction with others.[46]

The influence of these Roycean notions on Mary Follett was strong. As a young woman of twenty-two, she was already puzzling over the relationship of the individual to society—although she would eventually reject the idea that individuals should subordinate themselves to the whole. Melian Stawell, Follett's friend at Newnham, remembered an evening in 1891 when she and Mary "walked up and down under the stars and discussed our democratic faith. We both confessed that we did not really know why we were such passionate believers in democracy and that we wanted above all to find out. Then May [*sic*] said, 'Do you know I feel that real democracy has as much to do with the representation of minorities as of majorities?' I . . . am sure her thought lit a light for both of us, since . . . I know she meant a great deal more than any ballot-box device of 'proportional representation.' What she felt was that real democracy must be based on the concern for the development of individual personalities everywhere and on the belief that no one personality could develop properly without this."[47]

As the 1890s unfolded, college-educated women such as Mary Follett who were bent on their own personal development began to view settlement work as a cause to which they might properly devote themselves. Jane Addams perceptively analyzed the motivations of the early settlement workers, remarking that "moving to the ghetto was . . .'more for the benefit of the people who do it than for the other class.' "[48] Women from the Oxbridge colleges were first involved in settlement work in significant numbers in 1887, when a former Newnham student promoted the idea of a Women's University Settlement in London's Southwark district.[49] Living among the poor would give these young women a chance for "public leadership and professional yet womanly work." All four Oxbridge women's colleges joined the sponsoring committee, but from the beginning Newnham and Lady Margaret Hall were the most active.[50] During Follett's year at Newnham, the head worker and others periodically visited the college to give "detailed accounts of the work carried on," and student volunteers supplemented the work of the seven women residents by going to Southwark "regularly once or twice in the week."[51]

Inspired by the example of the English settlements, college-educated men and women in the United States also began to found settlements in the poorer, immigrant neighborhoods of American cities. In his comprehensive study of the American settlement phenomenon, Allen F. Davis identifies several ways in which these settlements, which numbered more than a hundred by 1900, differed from their English counterparts.[52] With the exception of Toynbee Hall and a few others, the English settlements had close church affiliations; but in America, the settlements were largely nonsectarian, assiduously avoiding "anything that might give the impression of proselytizing." Another important difference was the American settlement workers' rejection of the "idea that reform must begin with the individual."[53] During the nineteenth century, charity organizations had concentrated almost totally on providing relief to "deserving" individuals, but settlement house residents, particularly in America, were less concerned with charity than with reforming society.

Municipal governments had traditionally provided few services to urban residents, and most of them simply did not have the administrative capacity to respond to both rapid population increases and twentieth-century demands for "pure water, adequate transportation, and good schools." Ward bosses had stepped into this vacuum, using their influence to see that immigrant neighborhoods received city services. Middle- and upper-class urbanites, however, "usually regarded this as a corrupt system, not as a means of enabling the poor to survive." The young, well-educated men and women from "old-stock" American families who populated the settlements hoped that their work in the neighborhoods would generate an alternative to the ward bosses. They were determined to investigate social conditions and to use their new knowledge to promote social change.[54]

Although several of the early American settlements were founded by men, Barbara Miller Solomon argues that the "enduring impact of the movement came from college women." As early as 1900, Jane Addams, "the creative leader of the movement," was making "some fundamental criticisms of American society." Addams argued that radical change was needed in practically "every social and political institution in America . . . if immigrants and workers were to participate in political decisions and receive the benefits of the American industrial economy to the same degree that native Americans did." Addams and many other women reformers of her generation were convinced, Jill K. Conway writes, that "women were the only people in America capable of bringing about the new order in which democracy would find social as well as political expression. As an organized force in politics, they would moralize and socialize a state which Jane Addams recognized was at present organized to protect and promote the interest of businessmen. Of even greater importance, women would be able to solve the problems of city government because the efficient management of urban affairs involved generalizing the skills of housekeeping which were exclusively feminine skills."[55]

This turn-of-the-century "celebration of women as makers of the future democratic society" seems to have had a greater impact on Isobel Briggs than on Mary Follett, perhaps because Briggs came from a strong evangelical family and her ideas about women's roles had been shaped in an earlier generation. On one occasion while Follett and Briggs were still at Overhills, Isobel reportedly asked Elizabeth Balch if she did not think that Mary "really ought to use her great abilities in some sort of larger service." Balch later speculated that Follett's reluctance to do so might have come from an unconscious realization of the "tremendous demands any such work would entail," but this seems unlikely given the fearless determination Follett repeatedly displayed. More likely, Follett was reluctant to commit herself to such a "housekeeping" venture because she doubted that she was suited for settlement work. Follett's contemporary, Alice Hamilton, found "something about the claims of the settlement that reminded her of the self-sacrificing nature of most women's lives, a pattern she was determined to avoid."[56] Follett, too, had worked hard to break out of traditional women's roles and may well have feared being caught up in those constraints again.

Follett's fears were well founded, for the settlements constrained women even as they gave them new opportunities. Women workers in English settlements rarely used their education in their settlement work, instead carving out an area of service that focused on girls' clubs, child centers, and prenatal care — work that Vicinus calls "explicitly antitheoretical and proinstinctual." This strategy had the unfortunate effect, Vicinus argues, of continuing "notions about women's special domestic sphere." In later years when women tried to establish a professional identity in social work, "this early disjunction between men's work and women's work meant that their expertise was limited to 'women's issues.' "[57] Conway suggests that in America the conviction of Addams and her generation about the moral superiority of women locked them into "the traditional stereotype of the female temperament." As a result, "they could not see themselves as they really were, notably aggressive, hard-working, independent, pragmatic and rational in every good cause but that of feminism."[58] Because Mary Follett would not accept the idea that women were the makers of a new moral order, she was denied the one ready outlet for a late nineteenth-century woman's ambitions — a full-fledged commitment to settlement life. Nevertheless, she would continue her search for a vocation, buoyed by the Idealist conviction that every individual has a unique vocation and that hers would eventually emerge through continual interaction with others.

After nearly two years of being cloistered in Vermont, Follett again felt drawn to the variety and complexity of the urban environment. She returned to Boston late in 1900 and with Isobel Briggs took up residence in their former home, the building at Eight Marlborough Street owned by Pauline Agassiz Shaw.[59] Shaw's continuing support, a product of her longtime friendship with Briggs, would prove to be crucial for Follett. On more than one occasion, working in an organization sponsored by Shaw would enable Follett to take the next step in her personal development.[60]

Long before the founding of Boston's first full-fledged settlements in the early 1890s, Pauline Agassiz Shaw was supporting settlement activities in the poorer neighborhoods of Boston.[61] She had been introduced to neighborhood work in the late 1870s when she assumed responsibility for funding a small kindergarten program that had been discontinued by the Boston School Committee. Shaw became so committed to the kindergarten idea that by 1883 she was operating thirty-one in the greater Boston area, many in the poorer neighborhoods of the city. Perhaps because Shaw had emigrated from Switzerland as a child, she was more sensitive than most upper-class Bostonians to the plight of the city's immigrants. She organized a chain of day nurseries for children of working parents and encouraged working mothers to gather in the evenings to discuss personal and family problems, participate in clubs and classes, and enjoy a brief respite from the hardships and drudgery of their lives. By 1902, eight of the kindergarten-nurseries that Shaw supported in the poorer districts of the city had evolved "into flourishing neighborhood settlement houses."[62]

It was at one of Shaw's settlements, Children's House in Roxbury, that Mary Follett began her social and civic work. Children's House was founded by Shaw in 1878, and she had been its sole support until it was incorporated in 1905. As in her other neighborhood houses, the kindergarten and day nursery provided the "entering wedge," but numerous clubs and classes soon followed.[63] Follett's project was distinctive in that it was one of few activities that Children's House would sponsor for young men.[64]

Finding ways to attract men to neighborhood settlement activities had long been a problem for the settlement movement. William I. Cole, a worker at Boston's South End House, wrote that "not a few settlements carry on a work almost exclusively among women and children, coming in contact with men chiefly on special occasions where husband and fathers appear as guests. Among none of these nationalities [the Irish, Italians, and Jews] is it customary for the men to be seen much with the women. Husbands and wives seldom go together even to church . . . Thus when a man identifies himself with a settlement, it means for him, in many cases, the surrendering of racial tradition, and the overcoming of a reluctance which has been brought about through custom and training." Seeing how many men preferred to meet in saloons and political clubs rather than in the settlements, Cole was forced to admit that the problem of "how to reach the men is one . . . which as yet the settlement has only partially solved."[65]

In some ways it seems curious that Follett chose to tackle this particular problem; after all, an educated, middle-class woman could expect to meet even greater resistance from working-class men than had her male settlement counterparts. Follett, however, had always relished a challenge. Having grown to adulthood uncertain of her parents' love and having borne unusually heavy responsibilities as a child, she was accustomed to seeking love through personal accomplishment. Melian Stawell once remarked that Mary's "keenest delight" was awakened by "the power of putting things through in spite of, no, that is too weak, *because of* difficulty and danger."⁶⁶ Unconsciously, of course, Follett may have hoped that her work with the young men of Roxbury would atone for her failure to secure her brother's future or even compensate somehow for the paralyzing ennui that had gripped her father; but more consciously, Follett was probably seeking merely to make explicit use of her education while engaging with her "fellow man."

Follett's decision to establish the Highland Union, a club in which young men could debate contemporary political issues, surely benefited from the example set by her Harvard professor, Albert Bushnell Hart.⁶⁷ Never an ivory-tower scholar, Hart lectured to lay audiences on contemporary issues and wrote nearly a thousand articles — many of which were directed to the general public rather than the academic community; he even served for several years during the mid-1890s as a member of the Cambridge School Committee. Hart continually reminded his history students that historians must be involved with the public in order to teach the skills of good judgment that are the practical foundation of citizenship in a democracy.⁶⁸

As a student of Western political philosophy, Follett knew that one of the hallmarks of citizenship has traditionally been the effective use of language in a public forum. The society of ancient Greece was divided into a public world of politics and a private world of familial and economic relations; only in the public forum, the exclusive preserve of free male citizens, could one speak influentially on political issues of the day.⁶⁹ In nineteenth-century America, skillful public speaking still was highly valued by men who aspired to positions of leadership in the public world of politics. Woodrow Wilson's father, for example, was "greatly pleased to know that extemporaneous speaking is [young Woodrow's] forte." "By all means cultivate the gift," the elder Wilson wrote his son. "It is the *diamond* among those accomplishments which ensure the future of a public man." As the home of the town meeting, New England had always had a particularly strong tradition of public oratory, with Daniel Webster, Edward Everett, and Robert C. Winthrop heading a long list of accomplished Yankee political orators; and in the upper reaches of Boston's Irish community, John Boyle O'Reilley and former congressman Patrick Collins were likewise acclaimed for their rhetorical skills. Thus it seemed quite natural for second- and third-generation Americans aspiring to careers in public life to try to emulate the great public orators.⁷⁰

By creating a setting in which Roxbury's young Irishmen could hone their skills of judgment and powers of expression on matters such as public ownership of street railways, the election of U.S. senators by popular vote, and freedom for Ireland, Mary Follett was empowering them and helping them find an effective public voice. James T. Mulroy, one of the young men who joined Follett's debating club, recalled that Follett was especially concerned that Roxbury's young Irishmen learn sound analytical skills.[71] "One important art you must learn and cultivate if you are to participate in the deliberations of men in civic life," Follett urged Mulroy, "is to think and talk in the perpendicular." Remarkably "logical and convincing herself," Follett had a "rare gift" for "inculcating straight thinking" in anyone who would "listen and heed her instructions." According to Mulroy, several young men who eventually became accomplished public speakers owed their "readiness of address and ability to 'think on their feet' " to Follett's tutelage.[72] Theodore A. Glynn, the club's first president and a man who would hold several public offices before running unsuccessfully for mayor of Boston in 1925, recalled that the debating club "meant a lot to us boys. It's a fact that the members have since become doctors, lawyers, priests, and at least one of them a high government official in the Treasury Department."[73] No matter how much promise these young men demonstrated during the debating club's early years, Mary Follett knew that she must expand the scope of her efforts if she were to help them deal successfully with the complex problems of urban life.

Many of Follett's contemporaries believed that immigration and the corruption of city government posed serious threats to democracy. During the 1880s numerous clubs and societies were formed whose sole purpose was to clean up city government through educating the masses. Early in his career at Harvard, Albert Bushnell Hart joined one such club, the Massachusetts Society for Promoting Good Citizenship, and soon thereafter became an active member of its Committee on Studies; this group hoped "by proper indoctrination of foreign-born parents and children . . . to counteract the violence injected into American life by immigrants, unacquainted with the Anglo-Saxon respect for law and for 'the republic of the founding fathers.' " As the years passed, Barbara Miller Solomon tells us, many Massachusetts Society members lost faith in education as a means of cleaning up the cities and turned their attention to immigration restriction. Hart, however, remained a staunch defender of assimilation. He "believed ardently in the Jeffersonian heritage," Samuel Eliot Morison writes in his memoir of Hart. "He once said to me, 'America will continue in the Jeffersonian tradition, or she will no longer be America.' "[74]

Hart had been convinced by his historical investigations of American city government that the immigrant was not the cause of the problems of municipal government. "To suppose," Hart wrote in his 1907 book, *National Ideals Historically Traced*, "that [the immigrant] is altogether ignorant, and incapable of understanding the American governmental system, or looks on government as simply a source of personal advantage is contradicted by the experience of a century." Citing numerous examples of foreigners who had achieved greatness in America, Hart predicted that many others would also make positive contributions, once the "race elements are welded into a composite" by intermarriage and education. Underlying this prediction were two convictions: first, that the immigrant was "a natural democrat, who enjoys the thought of a share in his own government and is quickly influenced by the opinions and standards which he finds ready to hand"; and second, that certain preferred national characteristics were sure to predominate in Hart's new composite American. "Whatever the social mixtures of the future," Hart confidently asserted, "one thing is certain: the standards, aspirations, and moral and political ideals of the original English settlers not only dominate their own descendants, but permeate the body of immigrants of other races — the Puritans have furnished 'the little leaven that leavens the whole lump.' "[75]

During the decade before she established her debating club in Roxbury, Follett repeatedly heard Professor Hart urge his fellow historians to leave their ivory towers and unite with the public, presumably to the public's benefit. Historians, Hart argued, must teach whatever lessons were to be learned from the past, helping the public understand the meaning of historical development and, whenever necessary, relinquish outmoded forms of government. To this end, Hart and two successive committees of the American Historical Association pleaded during the 1890s that more attention be given to the teaching of American history — both inside schools and out — for historical education was an essential ingredient of the process of preparing for citizenship.[76]

Mary Follett's patron, Pauline Agassiz Shaw, sponsored one of Boston's earliest and most extensive efforts to educate immigrants for citizenship. Words such as *foreigner* and *alien* were "repugnant to Shaw's democratic instincts," and she was determined to find ways to bring the city's newest immigrants into "the body politic." To enhance the "constructive citizenship of adult immigrant wage earners," Shaw, with the help of a young Harvard-educated immigrant, Meyer Bloomfield, founded the Civic Service House in Boston's North End. Opened in 1901, Civic Service House was to be a place where adults could study and serve the community rather than simply entertain themselves in social activities as they did in most neighborhood organizations.[77]

At about the same time, Shaw decided to establish a similar project in Roxbury's Ward 17. She asked Henry Bruere, a nineteen-year-old student at Harvard Law School, if he would be willing to work with the young Irishmen of the district.[78] Bruere agreed and started his project in 1902, most likely at Shaw's Children's House — the home of Mary Follett's debating club. According to Bruere, who later became the director of the Bureau of Municipal Research in New York, Shaw was convinced that Roxbury was "growing in political importance" and was hopeful that educating these young men in "American Colonial and early post-independence history" would "offset their confusion of civic life with easy job getting."[79] Bruere left Roxbury for Chicago after only a year, but Mary Follett quickly took up the slack. She founded the Highland Union, an organization dedicated to the educational goals espoused by Shaw and Hart, and made her debating club a part of this new association.[80] Mary Follett would serve the republic and help to ensure the future of democracy by fostering the constructive citizenship of Roxbury's urban immigrants.

Follett was anxious to help her "fellow man" prepare for self-government, but she was bent at the same time on developing herself. Better educated than the Highland Union's young Irishmen and in many ways more knowledgeable about the public questions they debated, Follett nevertheless had little opportunity to express her views. Indeed, Mary Follett could not even vote, for women were denied suffrage except for the election of local school committees.

Up to this point Follett had not participated in the women's suffrage movement.[81] At Radcliffe the administrative staff had always been "solidly opposed to suffrage for women," perhaps fearing that support for such a "radical" cause would jeopardize their educational experiment. The students were no more adventurous. Maud Wood Park, who graduated with Follett in the class of 1898, recalled an occasion when her English instructor required his Radcliffe and Harvard students to write a daily theme on the "proposed enfranchisement of women." Of about seventy students, only Park and one other student wrote in favor of the proposition; from that day forward, Park recalled, she "was jokingly pointed out in college as an advocate of woman's rights."[82]

Follett's lack of participation in the women's suffrage movement may also have been influenced by the moribund state of the movement in Massachusetts. After an 1895 proposal to extend municipal suffrage to women was soundly defeated in a mock public referendum, the members of the Massachusetts Woman Suffrage Association (MWSA) were so demoralized that many of the younger members left the organization. The MWSA had traditionally courted the support of upper-class Republicans, suggesting, at least implicitly, that allowing women to vote in municipal elections "could clean up urban politics, combat boss rule, and restore the municipal order upset by industrialization and immigration." This elitist strategy proved disastrous in the 1895 referendum campaign, "eliciting the strongest anti-suffrage movement in the country." Learning from this debacle, Mary Hutcheson Page, one of the few women who did not flee the MWSA after the defeat, was convinced that the organization could be revived with "vigorous new recruitment activities." The key, the historian Sharon Hartman Strom writes, was a determined effort to broaden the MWSA's constituency.[83]

Page worked hard to revitalize the venerable MWSA, but she also was convinced that new organizations must be established if the Massachusetts suffrage movement was to be revived. Accordingly, in February 1901 she put her legendary persuasive powers to use in an effort to convince Pauline Agassiz Shaw, the wealthy Bostonian and friend of Isobel Briggs, to accept the position of president of a new Boston Equal Suffrage Association for Good Government.[84] Although Shaw was a relative newcomer to the suffrage movement, she accepted the presidency, apparently attracted by the opportunity to influence this new organization's mandate. It was Shaw who insisted on the "good government" appellation and the BESAGG's uniquely dual purpose: combining "efforts to secure suffrage for women with direct activities for civic betterment."[85] "Women are only just beginning to live & to do their own work," Shaw confided to her friend, Richard Clarke Cabot. "We cannot do men's work nor they ours — but oh how much there is for us to do together, besides what each must do for himself and by himself alone."[86] The organization's formal statement of purpose was printed in the first BESAGG annual report: "the great concerns of our public life are left in the hands of men chosen by the votes cast on election day; and intelligence and right mindedness, in order to be counted in that choice, must be registered on a ballot. It is for this reason that an Association which seeks to increase wise public opinion and action in civic affairs must also seek for its members the most direct opportunity for the expression of intelligent citizenship. There is no inconsistency in the two aims. They belong together."[87]

Nothing in this statement seems particularly novel, but a 1902 letter that Shaw wrote for the Massachusetts legislative hearings on equal suffrage espouses ideas that are considerably more radical in their domestic and societal implications. "Public and private life," Shaw told the legislators, "react on each other to such an extent that they are not as separate and distinct as is often thought; and here lies, it seems to me, one great reason for giving women the ballot."

> It is that she may share the responsibilities which man has so long taken exclusively upon himself, never suspecting how near at hand was the natural coworker who could lessen his arduous task by adding her effort to the force of public workers, by bringing new thought and action to bear in public matters. By this cooperation he becomes more free to give a larger proportion of his time to the home and family, thereby lessening her cares and responsibilities, which are really as much his as hers . . . I do not know which to

emphasize most — that men should enter more into the home life, which they can do, at any moment when they approve and choose; or that women should widen their scope of activity and usefulness by taking full part in public life, which, however, they cannot do, unfortunately, until men approve and choose . . . Men and women are trying to find a way that shall lead to the greatest welfare of both. How can that be done without mutual cooperation and mutual service, in public matters as well as private? Gentlemen, we need more of man's service in the home, and we need the ballot for woman to complete public service, for all private service in the end must lead to public service, or the service of mankind.[88]

These were truly remarkable ideas. Most suffragists of this era accepted, or at least did not directly attack, the separation of public and private spheres of activity central to nineteenth-century liberalism. Furthermore, most suffragists accepted the confinement of women to the private sphere; they would be the guardians of morality and culture while men wrestled with the issues that arose in the self-interested, corrupt public sphere. Once women were given the vote, these suffragists argued, the public sphere would be purified, for women would bring private virtues to bear on public questions through the vote; the private sphere, of course, would remain unchanged.[89]

Shaw, by contrast, rejected the notion of separate public and private spheres of human activity and opposed the partitioning of women into a private sphere and men into the public. Since these spheres were intimately related, Shaw argued, each was in need of the "thought and action" of all human beings — men and women. Shaw reserved her most perceptive remarks, however, for another issue. Recognizing that the position of women in society was not solely a creation of the law, Shaw apparently did not expect, as did many suffragists of her era, that winning the right to vote would itself transform the condition of women in society. Shaw had a more complex view. Not until men became more involved in the private sphere, Shaw argued, would women be able to take "full part in public life." The fact that men had not sought greater involvement in the private sphere, even though they could "at any moment when they approve and choose," seemed to Shaw to suggest that the secondary status of women was deeply etched, not only in the law, but also in economic and social institutions.

Holding such ideas, Shaw naturally was determined to make the BESAGG more than a suffrage organization. Wherever possible, this "suffrage organization for good government" would offer both men and women opportunities for "mutual cooperation and mutual service, in public matters as well as private." A number of distinguished older women lent their names to the new enterprise, but the real work was to be done by the heads of the various committees. Eight committees were planned, each being responsible for a subject of special interest to the membership: Public Schools, Civil Service Reform, Care of the Young, the Poor and the Defective, Clean Streets and Other Civic Sanitation, Question of the Saloon, Prison Reform, Non-Legalization of all Forms of Vice, and Peace and Arbitration. Seven committees were established during the association's first year, and five women and two men were recruited to head them. One of those appointed was Mary Follett. It would be through her Question of the Saloon Committee that Follett would make her first contributions to the school and community centers movement in Boston.[90]

Mary Follett would eventually succeed in shaping the vocation she so desperately sought, but the process would be an emotionally wrenching one. She could hardly fail to notice that in 1901, while she was working almost anonymously in a neighborhood debating club and a suffrage committee on the "Question of the Saloon," contemporaries such as Woodrow Wilson and Theodore Roosevelt, whose talents had been shown to be no greater than her own, were already acquiring positions of national prominence and genuine social responsibility — Roosevelt as president of the United States (1901) and Wilson as president of Princeton University (1903). When Follett met Melian Stawell, her old college friend, on a trip to England a year or so after beginning her social work, she found it difficult to conceal her frustration. Stawell asked Follett whether she felt her decision to give up her writing to work "at boy's clubs" was not "rather a sacrifice." But at this, Stawell recalled, Follett "flamed out," even then disliking intensely "any talk of sacrifice." Trying, as always, to control her emotions, Mary proclaimed to Stawell that "sensible work for anyone else was simply work for oneself, and that was 'all there was to it.'"[91] In reality, of course, there was nothing simple about it. In order to feel that she had "made something of herself," Follett would have to fulfill her determined desire for self-realization and at the same time meet the obligations imposed by a profoundly felt ethic of service. Indeed, her need to resolve the tension created by these apparently conflicting objectives would come to motivate much of Follett's working life.

10

Ward 17

In 1902, just as Mary Follett opened her Highland Union debating club for young male Irish immigrants, the air was full of urgent warnings and gloomy prognostications from notable political commentators about the problems of city government. Both Lincoln Steffens's muckraking investigations in *McClure's Magazine* and the more theoretical treatises of the European scholar Moisei Ostrogorski echoed convictions expressed fifteen years earlier in James Bryce's second volume of *The American Commonwealth* (1888). All these writers, the historian John M. Allswang tells us, were convinced that "the machine politician was corrupt, immoral, and entirely self-serving. Moreover, his power derived from an alliance with the most untrustworthy and disreputable elements in the urban society, thus posing the threat not only of bad government but also of social danger. It was a contemporary evil requiring excision."[1]

Even though Steffens and other muckrakers exposed the complicity of big business and political parties in urban corruption, the public continued to focus its concern on the susceptibility of immigrant masses to political manipulation. An excerpt from Ostrogorski's *Democracy and the Organization of Political Parties* (1902) illustrates the period's frenzied, almost hysterical tone: "The rapid growth of the cities, inevitably accompanied by the rise of a poverty-stricken and semi-criminal class, the arrival of wretched emigrants from Europe, and the extension of the suffrage to the besotted Negroes, had, in their turn, swelled the venal contingents. The appearance, on the political stage, of the rich corporations, and, in general, of the big industrial and financial concerns . . . helped to supply the funds for buying voters . . . The electors who deliberately sell themselves belong, in the cities, mostly to the dregs of the population." A few popular writers such as Jacob Riis sympathized with the immigrants' plight, but the solutions these observers proposed either had little to do with politics or simply seconded the top-down reforms being promoted by the emerging good government associations.[2]

Albert Bushnell Hart, Follett's mentor and former teacher, offered prescriptions for governmental reform that, by contrast, demonstrate an unusual degree of confidence in the potential of the average citizen. Writing just as Follett was beginning her civic work, Hart argued in *Actual Government* (1903) that in the long run "a sentiment of civic pride" was the only effective remedy for the problems of city government: "there can be no hope of good government if people do not care that their city is dirty, unhealthy, has bad water, and is plundered by private corporations; if the well-to-do people in a city do not care that their poorer neighbors suffer."[3]

Hart hoped to arouse "civic pride" in the well-to-do, but he did not support the notion that the so-called "better citizens" or "good men" of the city should govern in the immigrants' stead. "It is a great mistake," Hart cautioned his readers, "to suppose that as a rule foreign-born citizens are less interested in good city government than natives." Indeed, Hart's historical analysis of the development of American municipal government had convinced him that "the most turbulent period of city government, the greatest dominion of mobs and the greatest lawlessness in American communities came in the thirties and forties, before the foreign elements had become dominant."[4]

Even in cities where corruption reigned, Hart refused to characterize the majority of the voters as "simply tools" of the political machine. Instead, he believed that "they are kept to their party adherence by a conviction that adherence brings them something worth having: first of all and most important, the chance of being elected or appointed to an office carrying with it dignity, power, and salary; in the second place, aid and protection in business, lawful or unlawful; in the third place, positive and unceasing relief to the wants of poor people. Thousands are the tons of coal and the barrels of flour furnished to the poor and suffering by political leaders, who often feel a genuine friendship and interest in their people; and it is not in human nature for the recipients of such favors to vote against their benefactor."[5]

The willingness of immigrant groups to accept the direction of a political boss troubled most reformers, including Hart; but he did not object, as many did, to the concentration of so much power in a single man. This phenomenon, Hart argued, "is as old as popular government; it everywhere appears in the midst of free institutions." Centers and concentrations of power were essential if the cities were to have any hope of coping with continuing population increases and the complex responsibilities of modern city government. What concerned Hart was that the party boss "makes out of politics, which is a means of serving public interest, a private and almost a commercial enterprise; and that thereby he is demoralizing the public service." The "well-to-do" could protect themselves, but Hart worried about "the poor people, the friendless people, who lose most and suffer most from his sordid rule."[6]

In spite of these difficulties, Hart was confident that twentieth-century municipal governments could succeed if knowledgeable persons could find ways to cultivate in the general public a "respect for trained expert opinion." This was bound to be a troublesome task in a democratic republic, but Hart relished the challenge. America "has the greatest mission that was ever put into the hands of human beings," Hart once wrote, "to demonstrate that a great Democracy can well and properly govern itself."[7]

Mary Follett, too, was apprehensive about the future of democratic government in America — in large part because of the role played by political parties. Trained in her historical studies to be sensitive to differences between theory and the actual practice of government, Follett astutely saw during her research on the Speakership that America had "a system of party organization and political practice which subverts all our theories. Theoretically the people have the power, but really the government is the primaries, the conventions, the caucuses." And just as she had seen the necessity of making the Speakership more accountable, she concluded here that "party politics became corrupt because party government was irresponsible government. The insidious power of the machine is due to its irresponsibility."[8] Like her former professor, Follett was convinced that party-based political machines were exacerbating the already considerable problems faced by municipal governments.

As Follett saw it, the "extra-official system" of political parties had been adopted out of the need to develop "a vast, untouched continent." This was a task that called for strong, unified political leadership, but as Follett well knew from her study of the Speakership, "American democracy has always been afraid of leadership. Our constitutions of the eighteenth century provided no one department to lead, no one man in the legislature to lead. Therefore, as we must have leadership, there has been much undefined, irresponsible leadership. This has often meant corruption and abuse, bad enough, but worse still it has meant the creation of machinery for the perpetuation of corruption, the encouragement of abuse."[9]

Although the party system had been adopted to give "the government a chance to carry out definite policies, to provide some kind of a unifying power," Follett doubted that the system was functioning as its founders had hoped. "Under machine politics we choose for our leaders the men who are most popular for the moment or who have worked out the most thorough system of patronage, or rather of course we do not choose at all. We have two kinds of leaders under our party system, both the wrong kind: we have our actual leaders, the bosses, and our official leaders who have tended to be men who could be managed by the party."[10]

If the benefits of the party system for the government as a whole were not what the founders had hoped, the consequences for the individual seemed even less salutary. "The domination of the party," Follett observed, "gives no real opportunity to the individual: originality is crushed; the aim of all party organization is to turn out a well-running voting machine. The party is not interested in men but in voters . . . The basic weakness of party organization is that the individual gets his significance only through majorities. Any method which looks to the fulfillment of the individual through the domination of majorities is necessarily not only partial but false."[11]

Follett, by contrast, put her faith in the average citizen. She agreed with Hart that a sense of personal responsibility for government and an informed, independent judgment on political issues could be developed through education. After all, she and other educated women proved that people who had long been denied their political rights could become valuable contributors to the life of the community if only they were given a chance. "Men follow party dictates," Follett wrote in her 1918 reflections on her social and civic work, "not because of any worship of party but simply because they have not yet any will of their own. Until they have, they will be used and manipulated and artificially stimulated by those who can command sufficient money to engage leaders for that purpose. Hypnosis will be our normal state until we are roused to claim our own creative power . . . Fighting abuses is not our role . . . The abuses in themselves amount to nothing. Our role is to . . . build up our own life with our power of creative citizenship."[12]

Remembering Hart's dictum that the history of American government consists of "people attempting to solve real problems," Follett knew that she could achieve a genuine understanding of the functioning of "actual government" in Roxbury only by studying its workings from the bottom up. Furthermore, she recognized that even a rudimentary grasp of how city government was perceived in Roxbury demanded a sophisticated appreciation of the social, political, and economic conditions faced by its citizens. As a result, Follett spent much of her time during her first two years in Ward 17 walking around the district, "stopping here and there to talk with shop keepers, factory super-intendents and the like." She did not rely, as did many writers on urban politics before the 1930s, on information supplied by "leading citizens" of the community. Instead, she learned about the educational and social needs of the neighborhood by employing a method popular among settlement workers — she learned from the residents themselves.[13]

Making the daily commute from her home in Boston's Back Bay to Children's House in Roxbury, Follett could hardly have failed to notice that the residential areas of the city were marked by sharp class differences. Surrounding the downtown commercial section were the tenement slums of the West, North, and South Ends — home to the newest and most destitute of Boston's immigrants. Southwest of downtown and separated from it by the green expanses of the Boston Common and Public Garden were the fashionable residential areas of Boston's elite — the Back Bay and Beacon Hill. And ringing this core city were several lower-middle-class and working-class cities and towns: South Boston, inner Dorchester, Roxbury, inner Cambridge, Charlestown, and East Boston. These "zone of emergence" communities were home to first- and second-generation immigrant families whose improved prospects had allowed them to escape the slums of the inner city.[14]

At the turn of the century, Roxbury was divided among three of Boston's city wards. One of these, Ward 17, took in much of Lower Roxbury and a small portion of the upland area. It was here, in the midst of industrial plants, several crowded tenement districts, and one small middle-class residential area, that Pauline Agassiz Shaw founded Children's House, the home of Mary Follett's debating club. Most of the lower-middle-class and working-class families who moved to Roxbury resided in the Lower Roxbury area. They came in two waves: the Irish and a few Germans in the 1870s and 1880s, Canadians and Jews in the 1890s. According to the Massachusetts census, the ward still had a largely immigrant population in 1905; only 29 percent of the residents were "American-born," and they were mostly of Irish ancestry. The Irish also formed the largest group of foreign-born residents, accounting for 58 percent of the total; but the ward also had fairly large numbers of immigrants from Canada (18 percent) and from England and Scotland (7 percent), as well as a sprinkling of Germans, Russians, Swedes, and Italians.[15]

Since Lower Roxbury's new residents had little money to spend on housing, multiple-family dwellings quickly became the norm. In some cases, new arrivals purchased existing single-family cottages and converted them to multiple-family use; in other cases, new dwellings were built: three-deckers, two-families, and row houses. These new residences, described in some detail in Sam Bass Warner's *Streetcar Suburbs,* had few amenities and little ornamentation; but they were nonetheless appealing to people who had just escaped the dismal tenements of the core city.[16]

During the mid-nineteenth century, the residents of Roxbury had enjoyed a range of employment possibilities, including many skilled positions. But during the fifteen-year period following 1892, ten of the "high grade factories" employing "nearly fifteen hundred operatives" were discontinued. In 1900, just as Mary Follett was beginning her work in Ward 17, the New England Piano Company was closed. This, according to a contemporary observer, was a particularly "bitter blow" to the neighborhood: "In the summer the older school boys found jobs in its processes and prepared themselves for regular work. Many young men started their industrial careers in the factory, and were paying for their homes on the strength of the future. When the blow came many lost all their savings and had to seek work of another character. A proportion of the forepeople and skilled workers went to pieces morally and never recovered."[17]

The remaining foundries, factories, and machine shops employed more than a thousand men; the woodworking establishments, about two hundred and fifty. But the mix of available jobs had undergone a permanent change. Now, distributors were the largest local employers, and most of them needed only unskilled laborers and teamsters. Albert J. Kennedy, who investigated Ward 17 for a study that he coedited with the prominent Boston social worker Robert A. Woods, found the lower portion of Roxbury hauntingly like "a man who has lost confidence in himself."[18]

It was Follett's new awareness of the economic and social problems faced by residents of Ward 17 that prompted her to found the Highland Union, a "social, athletic and educational club" for young men over the age of nineteen. The aim of the union was "to promote fellowship, civic co-operation, and to stimulate an intelligent interest in local economic questions." To house the activities of the new organization, she leased a dwelling at 147 Mt. Pleasant Avenue from Arthur H. Nichols, a prominent Boston physician whose daughters had attended Mrs. Shaw's School. The union's clubhouse was open to members weekday evenings and Sunday afternoons, giving them access to "a living room, reading room, games room, class room, study, gymnasium and bath room."[19] The house was situated on the southeast edge of Lower Roxbury just across the road from St. Patrick's Church and the neighborhood police station. Follett no doubt hoped that the proximity of these institutions, and the newly built residence for an order of cloistered Carmelite nuns a bit farther up Mt. Pleasant Avenue, would give volunteer workers more confidence about venturing into the area at night. According to Elizabeth Balch, this section of Roxbury "had so bad a name that policemen always went into it in pairs."[20]

In organizing a debating club specifically for the young men of the district, Follett chose a form of social work that would make explicit use of her own education. She also, however, may have consciously tried to emulate the already well-publicized work of Jane Addams and Graham Taylor in Chicago. The Hull House Men's Club, founded in 1893, held lectures and discussions on matters of political interest and became the locus of political opposition to the boss of Chicago's nineteenth ward, Johnny Powers. Also in Chicago, Graham Taylor and others at the Chicago Commons organized the Seventeenth Ward Civic Federation. The federation, like the Hull House Men's Club, was a place for community residents to hear lectures on contemporary political and economic problems and to conduct investigations of political corruption.[21]

Follett's decision to focus the activities of the Highland Union exclusively on the young men of the neighborhood was one of the few ways in which her organization differed from most of Boston's turn-of-the-century social settlement efforts. Indeed, the Highland Union subscribed to typical settlement values: it was publicized as being "under no sectarian influence and . . . in every way non-partisan"; and members were expected to demonstrate a commitment to *"right living,"* which meant, among other things, refraining from smoking in the clubhouse and from "boisterous conduct likely in any way to disturb the proper practices of other members or to injure the reputation of the Club." Elizabeth Balch recalled an occasion when "some of the young men locked themselves into the bathroom with liquor and refused to come out." Although Follett and Briggs were alone in the building at the time, Follett reportedly told the delinquents "that she would get a ladder and come in at the window if necessary whereupon they sheepishly filed out."[22]

To help control disruptive behavior such as this and to provide the young men with a suitable role model, Follett installed "a stalwart young graduate student" from Harvard as manager.[23] Follett first met Howard Woolston in 1902 when he was hired by a group of South End churches to begin "some settlement work" in the far northeast corner of Ward 17. When the churches decided to disband the project early in 1903, William I. Cole of South End House asked Follett if she "would not include in [her Roxbury activities] this piece of Settlement work, so well established, but which was not extensive enough to require the whole services of a head-worker."[24]

Follett agreed and thereby got her first experience managing a neighborhood organization that served a full range of residents: children, older girls and boys, men and women. Seeking appropriate space for the project, Follett contacted John C. Cobb, a prominent real estate speculator who owned several large tenement houses in the neighborhood. A public-minded citizen who had advised Mayor Josiah Quincy as a member of the Merchants Municipal Committee, Cobb allowed the BESAGG rent-free use of "two large connecting rooms" in one of his houses on Massachusetts Avenue. Follett next persuaded Lucy Wheelock, a prominent local educator, to provide kindergarten teachers and found other volunteers to lead the project's clubs and classes.[25]

At Follett's request, Howard Woolston took up residence in the neighborhood. "It is the aim of our Committee," Follett told the Boston Equal Suffrage Association, "to have this work conducted on Settlement principles and in the Settlement spirit, and to have the relation of the head worker to the neighborhood both a more intimate and a more vital one than is possible when he regards his relation to certain groups of boys as his only connection with the neighborhood."[26] Nevertheless, despite Woolston's position as the resident worker, Follett was "the dominant figure in the conduct of the club," a former club member recalled, "even on the disciplinary side, when needed. Miss Follett's unusual mental courage amply compensated for her physical frailty . . . Miss Follett, when at the club, spent most of her time in a small room coaching and instructing groups and individuals in debating, etc. At such times a little 'horse-play' would start in the social room adjoining. Rather than waste time by calling the manager from another part of the house, Miss Follett herself would handle the situation. Unhesitatingly and fearlessly, in a few quick steps, she would get right to the scene of action. A few well-chosen words of rebuke from her and quiet would be restored in short order. A 'call-down' from Miss Follett seemed to hurt more than possible rougher treatment and expulsion by the man in charge."[27]

During these early years, Follett gave much of her time to the union, guiding members "in their social, dramatic, debating and athletic endeavors." Debate and public speaking, not surprisingly, were her "pet" subjects, but she probably also helped to teach classes in economics and American history. Union members could attend lectures "on the history of the American Republic, dealing with the great questions, men and events of the period between 1750 and 1865," and on contemporary national problems such as the Monroe Doctrine and the tariff. The union also offered lectures on economic questions: some concerned "the history of the working man in England and the United States"; others involved presentations by labor leaders on "the present status, tendencies and needs of working people."[28]

Issues of social class were undoubtedly discussed in these Highland Union lectures, for Follett's studies with William James Ashley had made her aware of the significance of social-class variables in economic questions. The duty of the economist, Ashley told his students, "was to determine matters of welfare and to suggest means for the implementation of reform" — not by espousing the outmoded individualism of the nineteenth century, but by investigating "what has been the institutional framework of society at the several periods, what has been the constitution of the various social classes, and their relation to one another." A socialist of the Fabian variety, Ashley thought it "as certain as the rising of to-morrow's sun" that "the principal branches of production and exchange will ultimately be organized socially." Despite Follett's exposure to Ashley's socialist views, there is no evidence that she promoted socialism among the young men of the Highland Union. Some of Follett's social work contemporaries such as Emily Balch and Vida Scudder were avowed socialists, but Follett apparently kept her focus on preparing local residents for self-government.[29]

The educational activities of the Highland Union did not consist solely of lectures on politics and economics; many members had been forced to discontinue their formal education after grammar school to work full-time, and Follett surely recognized that many would find vocational classes more valuable than academic lectures. Theodore (Teddy) Glynn, for example, had lost both of his parents early in life and had left school at age thirteen to help support the other children.[30] Glynn later expressed his gratitude for the chance the union had given him to take "evening classes in law and various business subjects," fully aware that these opportunities had been available only because Follett and her colleagues "vouched for our having serious aims." Follett's confidence in the young men of the union also impressed James Mulroy, who recalled that she "had a knack of stirring one's ambitions. More than a few Roxbury young men got their first stimulus to 'amount to something,' as she used to say, from Miss Follett."[31]

In most ways the Highland Union was a typical social settlement project, but it soon developed a special character because of the intense interest shown by the seventy-five original members in municipal and state politics.[32] At least some union members were veterans of Follett's debating club and, as a result, had become knowledgeable about local and national political questions. The debating club members also "were great followers of political rallies." They took particular delight in the early campaigns of twenty-eight-year-old James Curley, a young man "on the edge of [the Highland Union] group" whose rise to political power in Boston would hold many lessons for Follett about the place of the ward boss in political life.[33] Several years older than Teddy Glynn, Curley was already fully engaged in ward politics, but he was acquainted with the union through his participation in the dramatic club. Glynn recalled with particular fondness a production of Dion Boucicault's *The Shaughraun* at the

Dudley Street Opera House in which Glynn was cast as a villain while James Curley took the role of the dashing Englishman, Captain Molineaux.[34]

Curley, like many young men of Lower Roxbury, had had a difficult childhood. When he was only ten years old, the death of his immigrant father, an ordinary day laborer, left his mother with responsibility for raising two young sons. Since the family derived its only income from her work as a scrubwoman, young James and his brother had to help support the family. At first James worked part-time, but after graduating from the Dearborn Grammar School at age fifteen, he quit to take a full-time job at the New England Piano Company. In his autobiography, *I'd Do It Again,* Curley described the piano factory's sweatshop conditions: "We slaved away in overalls and undershirts in the blistering temperatures required in those days in the manufacture of pianos . . . During the nine months I worked here, my weight dropped from 134 pounds to eighty." Curley fared better in his next position, a "boy of all work" for a local grocer, and spent eight years there; but the job offered little beyond a steady wage and an opportunity for the gregarious young Irishman to extend his local contacts. By 1897 Curley had concluded that he could escape the stagnation of his environment only by emulating numerous other Irish Bostonians who had built careers in municipal politics.[35] During his successful terms as alderman and, later, as mayor of Boston, Curley would be a key contributor to the final breakup of the Yankee Democrat–Irish political alliance that had controlled Boston politics throughout much of the last half of the nineteenth century.

For decades, aspiring Irish politicians had allied themselves with conservative Yankee Democrats in a partnership that allowed the Democratic party to control the mayor's office during twenty of the last thirty years of the century. One of the most prominent of the early Irish leaders was Patrick J. Maguire. The Democratic kingpin of Boston for almost two decades, it was said of Maguire that he "ruled the Democratic City Committee which in turn ran Boston." Maguire successfully deferred to Yankee egos, trading the prestige of public office for hefty shares of patronage whenever a Yankee Democrat occupied city hall.[36]

By the mid-1890s, however, the national and local political climate was making this long-standing alliance increasingly difficult to maintain.[37] A new generation of Irish political leaders, seeing that the "politics of deference" practiced by their elders had failed to break the Yankee grip on the economic and political life of Boston, were adopting a more aggressive political style.[38] This transformation, which created considerable apprehension among Boston's Yankees, is reflected in remarks printed in the Brahmin *Boston Evening Transcript* upon Patrick Maguire's death in 1896. The *Transcript* had opposed

Maguire throughout his career, but the paper now eulogized him. He was "a man of many admirable qualities . . . and the danger now is that his successor, whoever he may be," worried the *Transcript*'s editors, "will not use the same questionable power with equal moderation, honesty, and regard for the public service."[39]

In the apprehensive and contentious political climate of 1897, only one man seemed capable of unifying the city's wards and reconstructing the Irish-Yankee alliance. That man was Josiah Quincy. Elected in 1886 to the General Court from his native Quincy with the support of the Knights of Labor, Josiah Quincy quickly became the legislative leader of the Democratic party. His role in reforming Massachusetts' outdated labor laws won him the support of trade unionists, social workers, and the unemployed; and he endeared himself to both ward bosses and working-class men and women in his role as President Cleveland's dispenser of local patronage. Quincy also benefited from his refusal to become enmeshed in internal party disputes over William Jennings Bryan's presidential candidacy. As a result, "by every criterion except ethnicity," Geoffrey Blodgett writes, Josiah Quincy "was better prepared to try to manage the city than any man in town."[40]

Even though Bostonians recognized Quincy's qualifications for office, they were astonished when his first term as mayor placed Boston's city government at "the cutting edge of urban reform in America." Quincy believed that "everything which promotes the well-being of a large part of the population benefits all," and he made full use of city departments to provide the citizens of Boston an unprecedented range of services. In so doing, he eagerly sought the support of Boston's "best" people — enlisting them in a seemingly endless progression of new city departments, commissions and ad hoc committees.[41]

Mary Follett was undoubtedly drawn to Josiah Quincy's vision of the city and his conception of city government. Quincy's faith in the future of American cities spoke at once to her patriotism and to her desire for a vocation of service to the republic; and the plethora of commissions and committees established during his administration provided ample opportunity for citizens having appropriate expertise to participate in city government. Follett, furthermore, was rarely daunted by the magnitude of any task and would have appreciated the quiet resolve with which Quincy called Boston's citizens to action.[42]

But when Quincy remarked in *The Arena* that there was much to admire in municipal governments in Europe that were "for the people if not of the people," he revealed a paternalism similar to that of the ward bosses who helped themselves to the city treasury supposedly because, according to them, it helped their people.[43] Quincy's elitism was the one feature of his administration that Follett surely found objectionable — for as early as her year at Newnham, Mary Follett was a passionate believer in democracy, committed to the idea that citizens should govern themselves. "Every man sharing in the creative process *is* democracy," Follett would later write, "this is our politics and our religion." She illustrated her personal convictions with an anecdote: "A man said to me once, 'I am very democratic, I thoroughly enjoy a good talk with a working-man.' What in the world has that to do with democracy? Democracy is faith in humanity, not faith in 'poor' people or 'ignorant' people, but faith in every living soul. Democracy does not enthrone the working-man, it has nothing to do with sympathy for the 'lower classes'; the champions of democracy are not looking down to raise any one up, they recognize that all men must face each other squarely with the knowledge that the give-and-take between them is to be equal." Certain that every person was capable of effective participation in government if only a sense of responsibility could be aroused and opportunities provided for exercising it, Follett sought to cultivate an informed, independent electorate in Roxbury. Instead of restricting and regulating the behavior of Boston's new citizens, she would use her expertise to prepare them for self-government.[44]

Roxbury's Ward 17 provided Follett especially fertile ground for experimenting with her educational ideas, for in 1900 no boss or political machine controlled the ward's politics. Furthermore, the citywide Yankee Democrat–Irish alliance was beginning to crumble. When Josiah Quincy withdrew from the 1899 mayoral contest, the Democrats were unable to agree on a candidate. Most of the warring factions wanted Patrick Collins, "the sage of Irish Democracy," whose tenure as a Massachusetts congressman and national party leader had won him a reputation as an orator and statesman; but Martin Lomasney, the boss of Boston's West End, objected to the plan to bring Collins out of retirement and led the opposition to his candidacy. When even Collins could not unite the Irish ward bosses, it finally was clear how seriously fragmented political power in Boston had become. The Yankee Democrat–Irish alliance gained a four-year reprieve when Collins was elected in 1901 and served almost two full terms as an enormously popular mayor; but his sudden death in 1905 began a new round of competition among the leaders of Irish Boston.[45]

In Roxbury in the waning years of the century, two established factions vied for control: one led by Timothy E. McCarthy, the other by John F. Dever and Charles Ignatius Quirk. As in the other Irish wards of the city, the struggle was for control of the ward committee, because this was the mechanism for distributing patronage and controlling the annual caucus in which municipal nominations were contested. "Those were rough days in the political arena," one participant later recalled, "and the gloves were off in every fight. Politi-cal rallies often degenerated into gang fights in which the guided missiles were sticks, stones, bricks and brass spittoons. Clubs were brandished as tempers flared and unholy epithets were exchanged between rival factions." The Quirk-Dever faction was dominant in the caucus of 1899, but power shifted to the McCarthy group the following year. Indeed, it was seldom clear from year to year who would be in power. This instability created repeated dilemmas for young men aspiring to political careers in the ward, for, as one Roxbury politician later remarked, "it was no cinch to win an election if the party bosses took a dim view of you."[46]

It was during this period that James Curley made his early bids for political office, seeking one of the three Democratic nominations from the ward for the Boston Common Council.[47] His rise to power began in 1899, the same year that Josiah Quincy left the mayor's office and about a year before Mary Follett began her debating club in Ward 17. In 1902 Curley made an effort to gain political control of the ward, placing all of his energies in the fledgling Tam-many Club—a political organization that Curley founded in the hope that it might someday achieve the power of New York's Tammany Hall. In his efforts to dislodge the McCarthy faction, he received some unexpected help from a sudden surge of popular support for the Socialist party.

Political discontent was rising throughout Massachusetts: strikes and work stoppages had become common among teamsters, brewery workers, and workers in the coal distributing industry; and the prospect of national tar-iff reform created similar unrest in the boot and shoe and the leather indus-tries. One of the consequences of this widespread discontent was a sharp increase in support for socialist candidates. The 1902 socialist gubernatorial vote (10 percent of the total) was significant because many Democratic voters who crossed over to support the socialists for governor also cast their votes for socialist candidates in local contests. In Ward 17 the socialist vote helped to defeat McCarthy, and he rapidly "declined as a potent personality in Ward Seventeen's politics." This important albeit indirect victory for Curley was accompanied by other Tammany Club successes in the 1902 elections. Curley easily won reelection to the lower house of the General Court, and the Tam-many slate for ward committee defeated an alliance of the McCarthy and Quirk factions.[48]

In the battle for the Common Council nominations, the Tammany candi-dates faced a new challenge—a candidate from Follett's Highland Union. At first the members of the debating club had been satisfied to watch others running for political office, but before long they "began to have ambitions to run a campaign of their own."[49] Their candidate was Teddy Glynn, reportedly "the most popular lad in the crowd." Glynn wouldn't be twenty-one until just before election day, but his compatriots nevertheless "insisted" that he run for councilor. Glynn's victory over James J. Conboy, a Tammany Club candidate, indicates that Curley had not yet achieved complete political control of the ward.[50]

Curley served two terms on the Common Council, where he worked hard for his constituents and led campaigns for several types of social reform: enforcement of an eight-hour law, improvements in public school sanitation, adoption of a Saturday half-holiday for city employees, and construction of a hospital for consumptives. He cast other votes that were pleasing to municipal government reformers: he favored the annual publication of a list of city employees to expose padding in the city payrolls and opposed a financially unsound loan bill. Curley continued to press for reforms even after his 1901 move from the Common Council to the lower house of the Massachusetts General Court. He supported a bill for municipal ownership of gas and electric plants, introduced and gained passage of a twelve-hour law for firemen, voted for giving preference in hiring to Spanish-American War veterans, and helped to secure passage of a law providing for the release of truants in the event of illness or death of either parent. Curley also supported legislation that would make certain structural reforms in government. Prominent among these reforms was the Luce Bill, a set of provisions replacing the old boss-dominated caucuses with a precinct-based primary election system conducted by officials of the Board of Election Commissioners.[51]

In 1903, however, Curley's promising political career almost came to an abrupt end. Curley and his political associate Thomas F. Curley were accused of civil service fraud: they were said to have impersonated two of their constituents at a letter carriers' examination, taking the exam in their place. Many of the city's Yankees were appalled by the Curleys' behavior. The brahmin press was filled with such moral indignation that when Curley announced his candidacy for alderman later that year, the newly organized Good Government Association did not even oppose him. A creature as despicable as Curley, the GGA members apparently reasoned, surely had no chance of winning. Curley was also abandoned by the city's Democratic leadership: Mayor Patrick Collins, Martin Lomasney, and John F. Fitzgerald all refused Curley their support.[52]

Nevertheless, when the votes were totaled in the November 1903 primary election, a majority of the Democratic voters sided with Curley. Even though the Curleys had by then been convicted of the charges against them, the voters nominated James Curley for alderman in the first citywide primary ever held in Boston. Other Tammany Club candidates also fared well. Among the independents who were overwhelmed by this outpouring of popular support for

Curley were three Highland Union members: Teddy Glynn lost his bid for another Common Council nomination, and two others were defeated in their try for ward committee.[53]

The voters gave Curley such a stunning victory, Charles W. Trout contends, because they believed that "informal, personal government, one that operated outside the constitutional structure, was more to be trusted than the state." An anonymous writer to the *Post* found the voters' preference for these informal methods perfectly understandable given what "the poorer class of people" had to confront: "Why, practically everything is against them. If they seek a position in some factory, the union is against them; if they seek a position in the government, the civil service law bars them; if they want to open up a little store, the trust is against them. The only person whom they can approach is the politician."[54]

A few hardy souls among the good government advocates were not put off by the charges against Curley, largely because they remained impressed by his determined efforts to serve the needy people of his ward. A few days after Curley was nominated for alderman, Henry S. Pritchett, president of the Institute of Technology, addressed the Twentieth Century Club, a reform group that prided itself on being willing to "come into touch with the man who dwells on the other side of the sectarian fence, whose work is utterly unlike ours, whose point of view is different."[55] Pritchett opened his remarks with the provocative assertion that "goodness is only one of the essential characteristics of politics": "when we speak of men of high ideals and character, I wish to mention one who is a leader that it would be well worthy of every leader in the city to follow . . . James Curley. He has had more to do with clean politics than any other politician in the municipality. He will succeed because he is a young man, a local leader who knows his own business and minds it all the time, who is a man of his word. He has studied the political problem thoroughly and does all in this power to help everyone in his ward. It would be well for every young aspirant for political position to study the methods of James Curley and follow in his footsteps."[56]

Curley had grown accustomed to having to teach outsiders about the social service aspect of the Tammany Club's work. The ward is "flooded with unemployed men," Curley told a *Boston Post* reporter in December 1903, and only the Tammany Club "has helped all who applied to it." In two short years, according to Curley's count, they had "secured and provided employment for over 700 men . . . The common supposition is that our field is confined to city patronage. It is the smallest portion. We have tramped Atlantic avenue and the water front, appealing for work. Men who made pianos have become longshoremen. Watchmakers have taken to driving trucks. So it goes on. We assisted in securing employment in New Hampshire for 50 men. Then there are the destitute, who need shelter and food. For these we do our utmost. If our own pocketbooks cannot afford the necessary money, we find someone who can. Our headquarters is open the year round. There is always heat and comfort for the homeless man . . . Summing it all up, we do our very best to help everyone."[57]

Curley's method of providing help was intensely personal. He once wrote that he "did not appoint captains or lieutenants, since this practice might have promoted jealousy"; but he probably also favored this "hands-on" approach to providing assistance because recipients would then know that their help had come from James Curley. The social work done under the banner of the Tammany Club paid good political dividends. Curley did well in the regular election, placing fifth among the candidates for alderman despite the fact that the Good Government Association now was actively opposing him.[58]

Unfortunately for Curley, his success at the polls was not duplicated in court. In November 1904, near the end of his first term as alderman, Curley exhausted all his appeals and was sentenced to sixty days in jail. The night before he left for prison, his Ward 17 supporters gave Curley a remarkable send-off: "Curleyites stood shoulder to shoulder at Tammany headquarters, many of them crammed in so tight they could 'applaud' only 'with husky voices.' Meanwhile a massive crowd outside the hall 'ripped the night air with their voices.' Speakers denounced the civil service law as 'insidious,' 'iniquitous,' 'corrupt,' and 'imperfect' . . . The window panes rattled with 'the series of cheers and tigers' accorded [Curley], and, as he left the hall, scores of followers accompanied him to his home, cheering him as he walked."[59]

With such rabid support, Curley easily won renomination and election even while in jail, finishing third in a field of twenty-six candidates. As Curley saw it, his conviction on charges of civil service fraud was yet another instance of how working-class men and women were repeatedly made to suffer at the hands of formal institutions of government. One had to have a good education — something denied most of his constituents — to do well on civil service tests; but the education needed to pass the test, Curley argued, rarely was required to do the job. Unfortunately, few Yankees found Curley's line of reasoning persuasive, and those who did could not condone breaking the law.[60]

Curley's excesses made it easy for good government reformers to solidify their perception of the Yankee-Irish ethnic struggle as a "contest between reform and machine" and to equate local Republicanism — "the domain of the 'good people' of Boston" — with nonpartisanship. Mary Follett was among the few who did not accept this characterization of Boston's problems. Follett's misgivings about the party system made her equally suspicious of Republicans and Democrats, and, unlike many of her social class, she harbored no prejudices about the Irish. Gamaliel Bradford, a prominent Mugwump, had privately confessed to feelings of "terror" upon being brought into contact with the "low-browed, dirty, hard-handed animal sons of toil" from Ireland, and the Harvard art historian Charles Eliot Norton had wondered whether "a race so foreign to our own" ever could be assimilated. Some native Bostonians displayed their arrogance openly in signs that said "No Irish Need Apply," but most regarded the Irish with a haughty indifference; they were merely "Bridgets and Paddys; micks and harps; pot-wallopers, biddies, and kitchen canaries; greenhorns and clodhoppers — muckers all."[61]

Mary Follett did not share these views. During her youth, the accomplishments of the Baxter's next-door neighbor, a Quincy granite dealer, had shown her how successful the Irish could become if given a chance; and her father's struggles with alcoholism had taught her that Yankee ethnicity was no guarantee of moral superiority. Then, too, Follett's evenhanded view of the Irish surely was influenced by the hours she spent in the company of Roxbury's young Irishmen, for Follett and Briggs apparently succeeded in establishing a "quite unusual" relationship with the members of the Highland Union.[62] On one occasion, a club member who had learned that Briggs would be unable to attend a union dance "condoled with Miss F. on the disappointment which Miss Briggs must feel at being unable to attend." Later, when Briggs was told about this remark, she was thoroughly delighted, feeling "that she must have gained the relationship she desired to have them so convinced that it was her own pleasure which brought her there." The young men of the union also grew confident of Follett's affection and concern for their welfare, even though she was less emotionally demonstrative than Briggs. "Miss Follett's keen intellect was clearly apparent in everything she said or did," James Mulroy recalled. "Her kindness of heart, she tried to conceal, but try as she might, she was not always successful. Her kind deeds became known eventually. More than one member of the Highland Union in time of sickness or need was the recipient of Miss Follett's sympathy and kindliness. Once Miss Follett learned of unemployment on the part of a worthy member, she found a quiet way of steering him into a job."[63]

Mary Follett's intimate exposure to the needs of the residents of Roxbury left her better able than many outsiders to understand how crucial the Tammany Club's social service functions had become. James Mulroy's family was one of many who reportedly benefited from intercessions on their behalf by Curley's Tammany Club. When James was only twelve years old, his father died, leaving his mother with sole responsibility for raising six children; James's older brother, John, was able to help for a time, but he soon developed tuberculosis and was forced to quit his job. Just when it seemed that the family would have to be split up and the children parceled out to various relatives, Jim Curley reportedly saved the day. He found John a healthier job outdoors washing streetcars and later found work for the two oldest girls. As a result of Curley's efforts, young James Mulroy was able to continue his education and eventually to graduate from Boston College.[64] Seeing firsthand how Curley won the loyalty and affection of the residents of Ward 17 would prove significant in Mary Follett's later work.

The chance to observe political relations in Ward 17 reinforced in Follett a notion originally conceived during her investigation of the Speakership, namely, that formal authority alone does not guarantee the ability to govern; authority can be effectively exercised only when it is accepted. Convinced that the civil service system was seriously biased against them, many residents of Boston's disadvantaged wards did not hesitate to rally around Curley after his indictment on civil service fraud. They apparently found it easier to accept Curley's impropriety than to grant legitimacy to the examination system.[65] Curley and his constituents, Charles W. Trout writes, did not want "*bad* government, as the GGA implied. Rather, Curley was at many points talking about a wholly *different* government — one that would spend; one that would not be slavishly devoted to balanced budgets, especially during slumps in the economy; one that would protect the worker; one that would provide municipal services in all areas of the city rather than in the silk-stocking wards alone; one that would be active, energetic, elastic, and by all means personal."[66]

Many of Mary Follett's contemporaries labeled Curley a "venal spoilsman, a practitioner of a loutish, brutal, opportunistic, offensive political style," but Follett no doubt remembered how shouts of "tyrant" and "dictator" once had been directed at the former House Speaker Thomas B. Reed. Follett's investigation of the Speakership had convinced her of the unfairness of the accusations leveled against Reed; as she saw it, the former Speaker had simply been doing what the situation demanded. The conditions under which Reed was forced to conduct the business of the House — an increasingly complex economic and political environment and seriously fragmented political power — were strikingly similar to conditions existing in turn-of-the-century Boston. Charismatic leaders such as Reed and Curley acquired power in such circumstances, Follett argued, not because they were especially evil or their constituents immoral, but because someone had to exercise informal power on behalf of those in need when formal mechanisms of government failed.[67]

It was not until the 1930s investigations conducted by the "Chicago school" of academic political scientists, John M. Allswang contends in *Bosses, Machines and Urban Voters,* that the widely shared public perception of the ward boss as a venal political spoilsman was seriously challenged. But in reaching this conclusion, Allswang fails to take into account Mary Follett's second book, an exceedingly popular work that was reprinted four times in the United States alone before 1926.[68] In *The New State* (1918), Follett anticipated several conclusions about the role and significance of urban boss that Allswang attributes to the Chicago political scientists.

The political scientists' rigorous investigations paint a complex picture of the social context in which the urban bosses operated and the functions they served. Led by Charles E. Merriam and Harold F. Gosnell, the Chicago scholars "compiled great quantities of statistics, attended many ethnic and political meetings at the lowest level, and interviewed racial and political activists and participators." They were not apologists for the machine, characterizing it as an "inefficient and dishonorable form of government," but their grassroots investigations "suggested that the urban masses were not by any means entirely 'controlled' by the politicians but, rather, tended on the whole to make rational — if not always ideal — choices among the options open to them." Gosnell's analyses are particularly noteworthy, Allswang writes, because they recognize the error of "focusing on economic motives to the exclusion of cultural ones." Gosnell "was highly aware of the force of ethnicity — national, racial, and religious — and all of its force in politics."[69]

Mary Follett, however, anticipated much of what Gosnell argues, contending in *The New State* that it was a need for "leaders of some sort" at the local as well as the national level that had prompted the rise of "the irresponsible party boss system"; in the absence of viable city government, urban residents had "accepted party dictatorship rather than anarchy." Like the Chicago scholars, Follett adamantly opposed the perpetuation of the boss-dominated political system; but her opposition did not blind her to certain virtues in the bosses' methods of governing. "Tammany," Follett observed, "is built up on the most intimate local work: no family, no child, is unknown to its organization. And it is founded on the long view: votes are not crudely bought — always; the boy is found a job, the father is helped through his illness, the worn-out mother is sent for a holiday to the country."[70]

Allswang praises two other scholarly studies of this era, Harold Zink's *City Bosses in the United States* (1930) and J. T. Salter's *Boss Rule* (1933), for their detailed depictions of urban bosses and their methods of serving constituents. These investigations revealed that the political boss tended to share the values of his constituents — acceptance of hierarchy, loyalty to friends and the organization, generosity to the poor, reciprocity, practicality, and good personal morals; the boss, as a result, had little difficulty acting as "an intermediary between the citizen and the state." He achieved his greatest control, of course, where there was the greatest need — "the most unemployment, most conflict with the law, most difficulty in paying rent." Salter was one of the first, Allswang contends, to see that the continuing dependence fostered in its constituents by the machine might be ended by social legislation. New Deal programs would allow people to "receive services from the government as a right rather than from political organizations as a favor."[71]

But this insight, too, was anticipated by Follett, who saw powerful anti-machine forces at work in Progressive Era legislation. "As politics comes to mean state employment bureaus, sickness and accident insurance, mothers' pensions," Follett argued, "Tammany is being shorn of much of its power. The introduction of social programs into party platforms means that a powerful influence is at work to change American politics from a machine to a living thing. When the political questions were chiefly the tariff, the trust, the currency, closely as these questions affected the lives of people, there was so little general knowledge in regard to them that most of us could contribute little to their solution." By contrast, the new public agenda, which had come to include subjects such as crime, poverty, and disease, was making politics into something "which we all know a great deal about." It was Follett's fervent hope that when citizens "see clearly that the affairs of city and state are our affairs, we shall no longer be apathetic or indifferent in regard to politics . . . When our daily needs become the basis of politics, then party will no longer be left in control because politics bore us, because we feel that they have nothing to do with us."[72]

Follett did not limit her hopes for the emergence of an active citizenry to men and women of her own ethnic background and social class. In this respect her views differed dramatically from those of most contemporary reformers and the academic political scientists who followed.[73] "We can never reform American politics from above," Follett would insist in *The New State*. Fiercely opposed to any unthinking allegiances, Follett saw "little difference [in] whether we follow the boss or follow the good government associations, this is all herd life." And she found particularly wrong-headed the reform associations' preoccupation with "the nomination of 'good' men to office, and exhortation to induce 'the people' to elect them." Follett's commitment to educating immigrant Americans for self-government was enhanced rather than diminished by her experiences in Ward 17. "It is only by a genuine appreciation of the individual, of every single individual, that there can be any reform movement with strength and constructive power," Follett would write in 1918. "The widespread fallacy that good officials make a good city is one which lies at the root of much of our thinking and insidiously works to ruin our best plans, our most serious efforts."[74]

Succinctly compressing her assessment of the early twentieth-century reform associations, Follett maintained that "the motive was excellent; the
method poor."[75] Her alternative, which she would describe in *The New State,*
was partially grounded in a lesson she had learned in Ward 17, namely, the
legitimacy of formal mechanisms of government cannot simply be assumed;
legitimacy is won, or "grown" as Follett often put it, through intimate and
informal political relations. Although this conviction was formed rather early
in Follett's social and civic career, the details of her alternative method of
democracy did not emerge until Follett was well into her fifteen-year experience as a pioneering leader of the national movement for school and community centers. It was the opportunity to see community being created in these
neighborhood centers that led Follett to place her democratic faith in the
method of *The New State*'s enigmatic subtitle: "Group Organization, the Solution to Popular Government."

Substitutes for the Saloon, Schools, and Suffrage

Mary Follett's part in what eventually became a national movement for school and community centers began ironically enough in a project sponsored by her suffrage committee on the "Question of the Saloon." Virtually all the late nineteenth-century temperance organizations were intent on eliminating the saloon, but Follett adopted a different approach to the drinking problem. She had seen how important a sense of purpose and a feeling of kinship with others had been to her father in his fight against alcoholism, and she had available to her several turn-of-the-century studies of the meaning of the saloon in working-class life. Vowing to make the work of her group "constructive rather than restrictive," Mary renamed her project the Committee on Substitutes for the Saloon.[1]

Follett's committee probably took its name from a major study of the "drink problem" published in June 1901 under the auspices of the Committee of Fifty. This national committee, composed largely of academics, clergymen, and other professionals, was organized in 1893 to study the subject, hoping that the "truth" that emerged from their thorough, impartial, and "scientific" investigations would "be a guide to the formation of public opinion and to possible legislation."[2]

The committee's investigators discovered that saloons were the setting for an astonishing variety of activities. According to Raymond Calkins, author of the study, saloons offered married men and bachelors a way to escape cramped tenements and boardinghouses for convivial evenings of gambling, playing pool, singing, and talking politics. Indeed, not until the advent of organized athletics, films, the automobile, and the radio in the 1920s would other leisuretime institutions surpass the saloon in popularity among men. Saloons were attractive for other reasons as well. Free lunches were common, though the offerings were likely to be meager bowls of crackers and pickles rather than genuine hot lunches with meat. And saloons provided a number of services that working-class people would otherwise have had difficulty finding: watering troughs for the horses of teamsters, public toilets, free newspapers, check cashing, moneylending, and even a place to collect mail.[3]

Although Calkins was convinced of the importance of the social functions served by the saloon, William I. Cole and Kellogg Durland, Bostonians who had prepared a report on the city's saloons for Calkins, were not so sure. They found little sociability. In establishments of the lowest grade, which the authors called mere "drinking stands," the social element seemed "inconspicuous"; the next grade of saloon, "ordinary bar-rooms," likewise seemed "drinking places first and last," with customers remaining "but little longer than the time necessary for consuming their beer or other drink." Only in the German saloons, where proprietors commonly furnished tables and chairs for their customers and sought special police concessions for pool tables, pianos, and other entertainments, could working-class people enjoy the society typical of a gentleman's club.[4]

Elsewhere in their report, Cole and Durland contrasted what they saw as the saloons' impoverished social climate with the sociability of Boston's many "substitutes for the saloon" — settlements, the YMCA, boys' and men's clubs, the public library and free reading rooms, restaurants, coffeehouses, public parks and gymnasiums, bathhouses and swimming pools. But despite their sociability, these "substitutes" seemed to Cole and Durland to have little drawing power among habitués of the saloon. This observation led them to conclude that "the secret of the saloon's power . . . does not consist, as a superficial observer might suppose, in the social and recreative opportunities of the saloon." Instead, it lay "in the opportunity which it affords for procuring alcoholic drink." It would take more than "substitutes," Cole and Durland pessimistically argued, to drive saloons from a community; it would take "the working together of restrictive and substitutionary agencies, the former stripping [the saloon] of all incidental enticements, and the later drawing out, encouraging, and giving support to all tendencies that lead away from strong drink."[5]

Despite their efforts to be rigorously "scientific" in their investigations of the saloon, the methods employed by Calkins, Cole, and Durland seemed to give them only a limited understanding of one of the saloon's most important functions — to serve, as one turn-of-the-century observer put it, as " 'the rooster-crow of the spirit of democracy' . . . 'the one democratic club in American life,' the 'great democratic social settlement.' " Roy Rosenzweig, author of a 1983 historical investigation of the working-class saloon, accepts this characterization, despite the fact that most saloons "barred members of the 'wrong' sex, ethnic group, race, neighborhood, or occupation." For the saloon, Rosenzweig writes, "actually was a 'democracy' of sorts — an *internal* democracy where all who could safely enter received equal treatment and respect."[6] There is no evidence that Mary Follett saw the saloon in these symbolic terms; but even if she had, memories of her father's alcoholism and its impact on the Follett family would probably have placed her on the side of those who sought to replace even this "democratic" function of the saloon with effective substitutes.

Although Follett may not have fully grasped the meaning of the saloon in working class life, she quickly saw the potential significance in another neighborhood institution — the public school. Early in the work of her Committee on Substitutes for the Saloon, Follett found her attention drawn to "a movement already begun in London and to some extent in New York — the opening of the Public School buildings, during the hours not occupied by school classes, for what is commonly known as Social work." To residents of poorer neighborhoods, the settlements and other private charitable agencies operating in their midst belonged to outsiders, but the public school buildings were thought to belong to all the people. Follett's appreciation of the symbolic significance of public schoolhouses is apparent in a 1913 lecture to Boston's Ford Hall Forum on community use of the schools, in which she described the public school as a place "where we all meet on common ground with equal rights where there are no races, but all are Americans, where no political party or particular religion has any special privileges, where no commercialism can dominate us."[7]

In 1902, under the auspices of the Boston Equal Suffrage Association for Good Government, Follett applied to the Boston School Board for use of the hall and basement of the Dearborn School in Roxbury. This was the grammar school from which many Highland Union members had graduated and the school whose master, Charles F. King, had helped to acquaint Follett with the "racial, economic, political and other characteristics of the ward" when she first began her work in Roxbury.[8] Follett described the twofold aim of the Dearborn School venture in the 1903 BESAGG report: "first to do something for the boys from fourteen to nineteen years old in a neighborhood where such work was needed, and secondly to prove that the Public School buildings could be used for that purpose, and, with other committees in various parts of the city engaged in the same effort, lead the way to the general use of Public School buildings for social, civic and industrial training."[9] The chairman of the School Committee, Grafton D. Cushing, was sympathetic to these aims and assured Follett and her group that the School Committee would approve their application. On the basis of Cushing's assurances, Follett proceeded with plans for a Roxbury Industrial League, the new organization that would use the space.[10]

Follett seems to have modeled the Roxbury Industrial League on one of Pauline Agassiz Shaw's most successful projects: the North Bennett Street Industrial School. Begun in the North End slums in the early 1880s, the North Bennett Street School soon had an impact far beyond its immediate neighborhood. In 1885 Shaw "offered to finance classes in printing, cooking, housekeeping, and laundering for 150 girls, and printing, carpentry, and shoemaking for an equivalent number of boys, provided that they be released to attend the Industrial School during normal school hours." The arrangement proved so popular that it grew during the 1890s to include more than a thousand Boston school children each school week. What the North Bennett Street educators valued was not so much the hand learning skills themselves, but the opportunity that manual training gave them to inculcate social values.[11]

In his historical investigation of public education in Massachusetts, *Origins of the Urban School*, Marvin Lazerson argues that before 1900 manual training was promoted largely as a means of moral education—a vehicle for combating the evil effects of industrialization and urbanization for children of all social classes. Children of the city did not need more book learning, argued Boston's school superintendent Edwin Seaver; they had to be taught how to work. Only through manual training would children integrate hand and mind, learning the "traditional values of labor: pride, industriousness, and thrift."[12]

In these years, manual training was deemed suitable for every child. Girls as well as boys were trained, although the girls' participation was usually restricted to classes concerned with domestic skills. Sewing, for example, was considered a suitable subject for girls by Superintendent Seaver, "encouraging habits of carefulness and industry; developing a taste for quiet, regular employment; furnishing a resource against idleness; and adding largely to the power of self support." Not only was manual training promoted for children of both sexes, it also was advocated for "both rich and poor." Pauline Agassiz Shaw, for example, offered sloyd and clay modeling classes to students in her upper-class Marlborough Street school as well as to children of the North Bennett Street School's immigrant families. According to Robert A. Woods, Boston's foremost social worker, bringing "the children of the wealthier classes in more intimate relationship with manual labor" would help to "bridge the chasm now broadening so rapidly between the wealthy classes and the breadwinners."[13] The rationale for manual education articulated by Woods echoes a notion popular among the founders of the first social settlements, namely, working in the immigrant neighborhoods would give upper- and middle-class men and women a chance to promote a common value system and thereby bridge the widening gap between social classes.

By 1902, when Mary Follett was planning the Roxbury Industrial League, manual education had become compulsory in the Boston public schools; it was the second of Shaw's private philanthropic initiatives (the first being the kindergartens) to become a formal part of the public school system. However, manual education did not guarantee financial support. According to Lazerson, many training programs in public schools were so poorly equipped and inadequately funded that school systems had little choice but to continue to rely on philanthropic aid.[14] Thus, the need was great, both for Follett's new Roxbury Industrial League and for the private funding provided by the BESAGG.

Follett's initial plans for the league called for vocational classes in printing, woodcarving, and basketry, a recreational class in gymnastics, and study clubs concerned with topics as varied as civics, animal life, electricity, and flags, stamps, and coins. The projected expenses were considerable. Institute of Technology students could be enlisted to serve as volunteer workers, but the head worker, Howard Woolston, and the teachers, janitors, and lecturers would have to be paid. There also would be substantial equipment outlays: industrial classes in printing and sloyd and the gymnastics class required specialized equipment; even the cost of minor items such as games and magazines added up. To fund the new league, Mary Follett and her colleagues raised $3,500 from friends "interested in the movement," one of whom surely was Pauline Agassiz Shaw.[15] But the major factor, Follett told the BESAGG, was "one very large single gift from a young man who most generously came to our aid."[16]

The unnamed donor was almost certainly thirty-eight-year-old James Jackson Storrow, who since 1900 had been a partner in Lee, Higginson & Company, a prestigious Boston investment banking firm. Despite his youth, Storrow had already established a distinguished reputation in Boston. His successful turn-of-the-century campaign to persuade the state legislature to create a freshwater basin at the Beacon Hill–Back Bay end of the Charles River had given Storrow, a suburban resident of Lincoln, an opportunity to focus his attention on city life. Seeing the conditions that Boston's less fortunate citizens had to face, Storrow decided to commit "as much as twenty per cent of his time to public service." A suitable opportunity appeared late in 1901 when the reform-minded Public School Association (PSA) proposed that he run as one of their candidates for Boston School Committee.[17]

Endorsed by both the PSA and the Democratic party, Storrow was easily elected to a three-year School Committee term in 1901. He soon discovered that subcommittee chairmen had almost complete power to rush through just about any scheme "before the average member has a chance to pass an intelligent judgment upon it."[18] Dismayed by the highly politicized and secretive practices of the School Committee, Storrow nevertheless proved quite capable of using them. Assigned by Grafton D. Cushing to the chairmanship of the committee on schoolhouses, Storrow brought forward in February 1902 a plan for the creation of a special committee to consider "the extended use of school buildings" and named himself its chairman.[19]

Storrow was not the first Boston political leader to advocate extended use of the schools. Horace Scudder had raised the matter in an 1896 *Atlantic Monthly* article, and the Boston School Committee gave at least indirect support to the idea in 1899 when it advocated the establishment of societies much like our modern parent-teacher associations. As a part of the same proposal, the committee "authorized use of the schoolhouses for free lectures and concerts and reported the opening of one school in the immigrant North End for evening study," projects that the committee believed could be carried on without creating undue financial burdens on the system. The use of the schools had been further "extended" during the years 1900–1902 when the School Committee agreed to support summer vacation programs and evening lectures. The rationale underlying each of these programs was that "time spent out of school by youth and adults offset the accomplishments of public education, and each group would benefit by exposure to the school environment."[20]

When Storrow first requested the establishment of a Special Committee on Extended Use of School Buildings, his rationale was based largely on more efficient use of the physical plant.[21] But once his committee was in place, Storrow began to reveal a larger purpose. Worried about the "moral and intellectual welfare" of the thousands of children whose education ended after grammar school, Storrow hoped to make "the school-house . . . a natural and wholesome rallying place for those of our boys and girls who are unfortunately obliged to stop their schooling long before they have received what, with the approval of every one, the city freely offers to all."[22]

The need seemed indisputable; in Boston's immigrant North End alone, almost 98 percent of the five thousand day pupils left school at the age of fourteen to earn their own livelihood. Such obvious need helped Storrow make a persuasive case for "extended use of the schools." By the end of 1902 the School Committee had ordered the establishment of "educational centres" in three city neighborhoods: the North End, Jamaica Plain, and South Boston. In addition, the School Committee authorized the Committee on Extended Use to act favorably on the "several applications from responsible parties for permission to use school buildings . . . for work which the committee believe to be of importance and of educational value." It was this subcommittee that gave "official recognition" to Follett's Dearborn School project and committed the School Committee to furnishing light and heat for the project as long as Follett's BESAGG committee paid for the janitor and other expenses.[23]

Although Storrow believed that "the needs of the children are always to be placed first in considering the possible use of the school plant," he also was convinced that "there is no place and no age at which a man's education should stop." He thought it wise, therefore, for the city of Boston to "offer its citizens the use of an appropriate room, with books borrowed from the Public Library, and provided with such other attractions as can well be offered." It was in this supportive context of continuing education for adults that Follett organized a program of Wednesday evening lectures for adults in the Dearborn School, "thus making an attempt in Roxbury," Follett later wrote, "to carry out the idea of having the schoolhouses become neighborhood centres."[24]

The educational centers' first year of operation was so successful that the School Committee publicly endorsed them in its annual report, saying that "the cost of carrying on such centres is surprisingly small, and the amount of good accomplished incalculable." At the same time, however, the committee cautioned that "it will not be possible . . . to extend these new activities much further, and to broaden their scope so that all parts of the city may be equally benefited, without a corresponding increase in the appropriations provided for the support and maintenance of the system." Despite this warning, citizens in neighborhoods that did not yet have an educational center began to lobby for their establishment, and new centers were opened in East Boston and the West End in the fall of 1903. The decision to open new centers even though funds were scarce was undoubtedly a political move on the part of the committee — an effort to increase grassroots support for the centers and thereby enhance the chances of securing an appropriate funding mechanism from the state legislature.[25] Meanwhile, "extended use" advocates such as Mary Follett had to deal with troublesome opposition on two other fronts.

A few masters of the day schools in which the educational centers would function supported the concept of extended use. Two masters even agreed to serve as their neighborhood center's principal, apparently attracted by the chance to work in a new field where "neither academic theory nor official red tape nor municipal politics was allowed to stand in their way." These masters, however, were exceptions. Most school administrators were pleading for greater centralization and control of school operations — not community-based educational centers — and were actively lobbying for public recognition of the special expertise of teachers and school administrators. Thus, when Superintendent Seaver in 1904 "justified using inexperienced college graduates to teach English to immigrant adults by suggesting that the Centres stood outside normal school regulations," the masters' opposition was almost ensured.[26]

Opposition to the educational centers also arose among those who were fearful of the impact they might have on the viability of the evening schools. Evening schools had become fairly common in Massachusetts after the Civil War, but they gained their first formal recognition in 1883, when the state legislature, in an effort to promote literacy among the foreign-born, required that all "cities and towns of more than 10,000 inhabitants offer evening classes for twelve-year-olds and above in 'orthography, reading, writing, geography, arithmetic, drawing, United States history and good behavior.'" Four years later, their legitimacy was assured by legislation that combined "compulsory [evening school] attendance of non-English reading and writing minors … with restrictions upon the employer's right to hire." The switch from voluntary to compulsory attendance greatly increased the numbers of students attending evening classes, and expenditures, as a result, went from being "a nominal expense in most cities to a small but no longer insubstantial part of the regular school budget."[27]

The Committee on Extended Use repeatedly assured evening school adherents that the educational centers would not be allowed to draw students away from evening classes. To avoid conflict with the academic mission of the evening schools, the educational centers emphasized recreational activities and industrial classes in subjects such as carpentry, steam engineering, and mechanical drawing and drafting; as a result, even though women attendees continued to outnumber men by almost two to one, the centers were more successful than the settlements or evening schools had been in attracting men to their activities.[28]

Despite its early successes, the educational centers movement was in a precarious position at the close of 1903. Opposition had arisen among evening school supporters and day school masters, and new centers could not be opened without additional funding authority from the state legislature. Nevertheless, in her 1903 report to the BESAGG, Mary Follett maintained "that at the end of this year we feel as strongly as when we began that the Public School buildings *ought* to be used in the evenings, and we have not found the difficulties so great as to make us think that they *can* not be so used." The "chief" problem, Follett wrote, "is the stationary desk: we must have a desk which can be moved for the evening work and yet which is satisfactory for school use in the daytime." This seems a curious statement given the centers' growing financial plight; perhaps Follett was just putting on a brave face for her supporters. But the statement is interesting in another way, for it shows Mary Follett to be more than just a remarkably facile theoretician; she also was ready to grapple with the mundane problems of implementing grand ideas. If Boston was to realize any of the potential benefits of the school center concept, one of many hurdles that had to be overcome was the stationary desk. Only then could city officials be made to see "that the definition of education should be so enlarged, that it shall mean . . . something which takes account of the adult fully as much as of the child . . . something which tends in short to make men better neighbors, more efficient and intelligent members of the industrial system, and, above all perhaps, better citizens."[29]

In the spring of 1904, just as Follett's part in the educational centers movement was fully under way, her health began to fail. The symptoms appeared gradually: her head felt "tired," her eyes yellowed, and there was a persistent dragging sensation on both sides of her abdomen. At first there was "no pain to complain much of" and only a slight fever, but in May she developed uncontrollable diarrhea and spent several days in bed. G. Carroll Smith, a physician at Copley Square's Hotel Westminster, diagnosed this nonspecific pattern of symptoms as appendicitis. Though by then surgery for appendicitis had become quite common, there was no operation on Follett, perhaps because she was experiencing relatively little pain. Instead, she was confined to the Marlborough Street house under the care of a nurse and stayed there for a month before fleeing with Isobel to Boston's North Shore in search of relief from the city's oppressive midsummer heat and humidity.[30]

Despite the change of scene, Follett's bowel discomfort and the pain in her right side did not abate; she returned to Boston in August to consult Maurice Howe Richardson, a specialist in abdominal surgery at Massachusetts General Hospital (MGH) and professor at the Harvard Medical School. Richardson, like Dr. Smith before him, suspected that Follett had appendicitis and at first advised her to have her appendix removed. The next day, however, he seemed "less positive" and referred her to Dr. Reginald Heber Fitz, Richardson's friend and MGH colleague. It was Fitz who in 1886 had coined the term *appendicitis*, demonstrating to his fellow physicians that inflammation of the appendix was responsible for a pattern of symptoms (sudden severe abdominal pain, nausea, vomiting, and slight fever) that had until then been associated with a variety of organs. Fitz also persuaded his colleagues that early surgery was essential because perforation almost surely meant the patient's death; "the progress of the disease," Fitz wrote, "needs to be watched with knife in hand."[31]

Hardly conservative when it came to surgery, Fitz nevertheless chose not to operate in Follett's case. The only discernible abnormality in her appendix was that it seemed enlarged. Furthermore, a patient suffering from acute, life-threatening appendicitis would have displayed rapidly and dramatically worsening symptoms, whereas Follett's difficulties seemed more chronic. Fitz apparently concluded that she did not have appendicitis, and the source of her troublesome symptoms remained a mystery.

Recounting the Fitz examination for a medical history that she gave six years later, Follett said that Fitz had described the position of her stomach and right kidney as "low" and had called her "very nervous." During this era, Edward Shorter notes in his history of doctor-patient relations, it was common for surgeons to examine "the kidney and stomach to find out whether they had 'dropped' (*ptosis*, as it was called)," for these dropped organs "were thought to cause neurosis and vague, unlocalized abdominal pains." Fitz may well have made this diagnosis, for after his examination Follett briefly wore an abdominal binder before deciding that she "didn't like it."[32]

Follett's illness kept her BESAGG committee from attempting much work during 1904 "except some help towards bills in the Legislature affecting the sale of intoxicating liquors"; but by the end of the year she felt well enough to resume a fairly normal work schedule. Her appetite was good, but repeated bouts of "inflammation of the bowels" after eating made her "fearful of [the] results." In an effort to avoid these painful episodes, Follett radically altered her diet, confining herself to eating the same things each day: milk, potato, pudding — never any "flesh," salad, or soup. To relieve her constipation, she ate fruit and periodically took pills provided by Dr. Fitz. Despite the unpalatable nature of such limited fare, Follett disciplined herself to consume adequate calories and managed for many years to maintain her weight at about 136 pounds.[33]

Seeming to have regained control of her health, Follett may well have concluded that her symptoms were a "nervous" response to recent troublesome events. Her brother, who had continued living with their mother after Mary moved into Boston, married in June 1903; within the year, George had left his mother's home, moving with his wife and infant son to another section of Quincy.[34] George's decision surely reawakened all of Mary's old guilt about her obligations to her mother. Nora Corcoran, an Irish woman who had lived with the Follett family as cook and maid probably as far back as their days on School Street, was convinced that Mary neglected her mother and reportedly had no qualms about saying so.[35]

For a time, Follett probably felt confident that she would fully regain her health despite these familial complications, but she soon discovered that every twelve to eighteen months brought an attack so severe that it was necessary to seek help from Dr. Fitz. Follett may well have attributed these recurrences, like the original attack, to "nerves"; by the fall of 1904 the fledgling educational centers movement in which she had invested so much was in serious jeopardy, a victim of the emerging financial plight of the Boston public schools.

The educational centers initially had been "sold" to the School Committee and the general public as a way of making more efficient use of the massive school plant. Within two years, however, the operating costs incurred by the School Committee for this program had risen "from $3,700 during 1902–03 to almost $24,000." In the absence of legislative action to increase the tax levy, the educational centers had to be funded out of existing accounts — a process that drew the ire of other interests, placed each claim under careful scrutiny, and deflected attention away from the efficient use of the physical plant.[36] Finally, in October 1904, just before the School Committee election, Mayor Patrick Collins came out in opposition to the committee's appropriation for the centers. "I pass no judgment," Collins wrote the committee, "on the object for which this appropriation is deemed to be of civic good . . . But the serious fact faces us all, that, in general, departments center their thoughts and energies in their separate work, and are ambitious to extend it into a wider usefulness; and in their enthusiasm, they sometimes forget that there is an overworked paymaster."[37]

Collins' objection to the committee's appropriation did not faze Storrow, for he had decided to forgo a second term to work for legislative reform of the School Committee's structure. Other PSA incumbents, however, might not have been so sanguine about displeasing Boston's popular Democratic Mayor. The PSA was being challenged by Julia Harrington Duff, a Democratic School Committee member from Charlestown and the first Irish Catholic woman on the board. Duff accused the PSA of favoring Protestant women graduates of private colleges for teaching positions and thereby depriving young Irish Catholic women of opportunities in the Boston public schools. Seeing that she could do little to preserve "Boston schools for Boston girls" without more votes on the committee, Duff decided to take on the PSA at the polls. The Democratic City Committee denied her their support, but even so, Duff's independent Democratic Citizens party was so successful in the elections of 1902 and 1903 that the PSA felt it necessary to sponsor a carefully balanced ticket in the next election: it nominated "four Irish Bostonians with Democratic affiliations" and "four Yankee Bostonians with Republican affiliations." All were nonpoliticians, and one was a woman: Ella Lyman Cabot, who would become one of Mary Follett's dearest friends.[38] When the Democratic City Committee, despite "Mrs. Duff's cries of betrayal," decided to support the Democrats running on the PSA slate, the election of that portion of the PSA ticket was virtually assured.[39]

It is a tribute to Storrow's reputation "for fairness in ethnic matters" that even in the midst of this ethnic and religious turmoil he persuaded the School Committee to disregard the objections of Boston's popular mayor and appropriate funds for the centers. The committee voted twenty in favor, three opposed, to support the centers by drawing on funds that had been set aside for vacation schools and on funds from the regular line-item accounts. Julia H. Duff and two others cast the opposing votes. In some ways Duff's decision seems curious, since she was a champion of community control of the schools and fought against the centralization of authority in the school superintendent. Polly Welts Kaufman, in her informative historical analysis of Boston women in school-city politics, suggests that Duff may have seen the educational centers as "being 'boomed' to build Storrow's reputation at the expense of other school needs [such] as the regular evening schools." This explanation seems plausible, given Duff's conviction that the School Committee should be employing greater numbers of Boston women as teachers; she probably thought that funds given to educational centers should be used instead to lower pupil-teacher ratios and thereby create new jobs.[40]

Just a month before the November election, the committee took up another troublesome issue concerning the educational centers. School administrators were charging that the centers were not being operated "professionally." The School Committee was more responsive to these concerns and promulgated a uniform set of rules and regulations that covered length and time of sessions, pupil-instructor ratios, conditions for employing day school teachers, rates of compensation, and the awarding of certificates of "course" completion. The committee even voted an approved "course of study," a scheme that prohibited the centers from impinging on the offerings of the regular evening schools.[41] Despite these restrictions, the centers managed to establish some innovative activities, such as the West End's free legal aid bureau and classes for salespeople in Jamaica Plain and South Boston. The latter project received special attention from Storrow and another Boston businessman, the department store retailer Edward Filene.[42]

Attendance at the five educational centers sponsored by the School Committee ranged from a low of about 200 per evening in the North End to more than 650 in South Boston, but these substantial figures did not guarantee the centers' future. In March 1904 Mary A. Dierkes, a woman from Dorchester's German Catholic community who had been elected to the School Committee in 1903 as a candidate of Duff's Democratic Citizens party, moved that the centers either be made evening schools or abolished, since the committee had authority only to maintain evening schools.[43] This particular motion did not prevail, but the centers were threatened again later that year when Edwin Seaver, for twenty-four years the superintendent of the Boston Public Schools and a prominent advocate of the centers, was ousted by Duff and her supporters in a battle over the appointment of day school teachers. Seaver's replacement, former deputy superintendent George H. Conley, praised the centers but refused to support them if it meant taking funds away from the evening schools; as a result, the centers' "first term" in the 1904–05 academic year came to an early end on December 9 when the fiscal-year appropriation was exhausted.[44] They opened again for a brief period in 1905 after the School Committee appropriated additional funds, but in his superintendent's report for 1905 Conley issued a stern warning. Unless "a more liberal allowance" to the School Department was forthcoming "from the general tax levy," he was convinced that "these new and highly valuable educational features must be very materially restricted, if not entirely abandoned." Conley's prediction proved to be accurate. The centers closed in the spring of 1905 and were not reopened.[45]

Despite this setback for the "extended use" movement as a whole, the project initiated by Follett's Committee on Substitutes for the Saloon — now called simply the Roxbury League — was thriving. At first there had been problems attracting older boys, "since the presence of an evening school in the same building made any noise impossible, and allowed only the kinds of clubs which could be conducted as classes." The first step toward resolving this problem was taken in January 1903, when Follett's group was allowed the use of two large kindergarten rooms in the nearby Aaron Davis school. Even more satisfactory quarters were secured in the autumn of 1903, when the older boys' clubs were transferred to the Albert Palmer School under the supervision of James T. Mulroy, the young Roxbury resident who had been a charter member of the Highland Union. By this time the work had grown "to such proportions" — 120 boys "from sixteen to twenty years old, organized into self-governed and self-officered groups of twenty each, meeting once a week" — that it "required both more work and more money than [the BESAGG] could furnish." As a result, the Roxbury League was made independent of the suffrage association and by 1905 was fully funded by "persons outside." About this same time, Follett closed the Highland Union, deciding instead to concentrate on the Roxbury League and on other, potentially more productive ventures involving the public schools.[46]

Convinced that the "development of good citizenship should be the direct duty of the city," Follett thought that she could best promote this idea by joining forces with two other BESAGG committees: Prison Reform and Care of the Young, Poor, and Defective. This union, Follett wrote in 1905, promised to strengthen the work of each group "without sacrificing the particular interests of any" because of "the intimate connection of the subjects involved." One of the early activities of the Union Committee involved an analysis of relevant bills pending before the legislature; the committee reported to the BESAGG about those which were "most important, which most needed help, and how that help was to be most effectively given in each case."[47] This project, an extension of work initiated two years earlier by Follett's committee on the saloon, was undoubtedly facilitated by expertise she had gained during her investigation of the Speakership and her work on the elevated railway controversy.

A second, and much more elaborate, undertaking of the Union Committee involved an investigation of civic education in Boston. Confident that the process of inquiry would itself "bring about a closer connection between and co-operation among the various agencies at work for good government and clean politics," Follett proposed to study "the methods used, the results obtained, and the causes of success or failure" in civic education programs in both public and private agencies. To carry out the study, Follett secured the services of Arthur V. Woodworth, a Harvard College graduate who had obtained a Ph.D. at the University of Freiburg before returning to combine a career as a broker on the Boston Stock Exchange with civic work. Woodworth's report, published in pamphlet form by the association in 1907, not only described the status of civic education in Boston; it reportedly also offered prescriptions for reform.[48]

Mary Follett sponsored three civic education projects growing out of Woodworth's investigation. The first concerned the teaching of civics in the Boston public schools. In 1906 the programs of study for the regular and evening high schools were newly revised, but neither required studies in civics or government.[49] The following year, however, the School Committee appointed a joint committee of teachers and lay men and women to prepare a civic primer for use in the evening schools, "the various chapters of which shall deal concretely with those phases of municipal government with which the foreigner first comes in contact." The new joint committee drew part of its membership from Follett's BESAGG Department of Civic Education, where a subcommittee chaired by Meyer Bloomfield was already at work on a "Citizenship Course." The product of the new committee's work, *A Civic Reader for New Americans,* was published in 1908, with the more notable contributors including Bloomfield, director of the North End's Civic Service House, and Wellesley College professors Katherine Coman and Vida Scudder.[50]

Follett was supportive of this project to prepare a civic primer, but she was not satisfied with having people read about government. Follett wanted them to experience the process of government. Two projects sponsored by her Union Committee promised to give young people this experience. The less successful of the projects, conducted in conjunction with the Massachusetts Federation of Women's Clubs and local school departments, was modeled on a system of student government already in use in several other cities. Follett most likely learned about this "school city" plan in April 1905, when, as one of two delegates from the Boston Equal Suffrage Association for Good Government, she attended the annual meeting of the National Municipal League, the nation's premier reform association.[51]

A National Municipal League committee had recently issued a report on the status of instruction in municipal government in secondary and elementary schools. The group described several schemes of student self-government that were being employed in civic education and identified problems commonly encountered in their use.[52] One of these plans, the "school city," organized the school "as a miniature municipality, in which the children, under the guidance of their teachers and with their principal acting as final authority, elected their own officers and exercised legislative, judicial, and executive functions."[53] The school city idea was implemented in Massachusetts through a complex campaign in which information about similar projects throughout the nation was gathered, speeches were given to teachers and school officials by out-of-state experts, and conferences were held to facilitate communication among the various school city teachers. Despite laying this extensive groundwork, many school city projects, Follett observed, were abandoned once "the first flush of enthusiastic interest has passed." And in projects that survived, Follett was disappointed to find a preoccupation with the "police function" rather than "social service and constructive work."[54]

Other critics of the school city program worried about its "thinly disguised" paternalism. Oliver Corman, a Philadelphia principal, contended that a "nominal self-government strictly supervised and directed by the teacher, such as the school city must inevitably become, approximates only too closely (however unintentionally) the form of government — boss-rule under free men's charters — by which our municipalities are actually controlled." Children in a school city "run the danger of having their habits of thought and conduct trained along the very lines a true training of citizenship would lead them to combat." Follett's support of the school city idea lasted only a few years. In March 1909 the BESAGG voted to transfer $400 of the school city funds to other purposes, and a year later the subcommittee on the school city was disbanded.[55]

The second of Follett's experiential civic education projects apparently was modeled on the Political Club that had operated so successfully at Newnham College. Her original plan called for "junior city councils" in four sections of the city of Boston in which "an amateur city council is formed and conducted with regular business procedure, discussing and taking action on questions pertaining to city affairs." Follett's Union Committee proposed the scheme to the Boston City History Club in April 1906 and the next month to the South End Social Union (SESU), a federation of Boston settlements. The SESU decided that the project was not "practical for the Union to take up," but the City History Club saw the plan as having "special value in the case of older boys and young men who can learn best by doing, and to whom the dignity of the idea appeals." The club accepted the plan, with modifications, and gave Mary Follett a seat on its Executive Board.[56] Follett, in turn, assigned responsibility for implementing the plan to a subcommittee of her BESAGG Department of Civic Education headed by Ralph Albertson, a writer and editor who had recently been appointed supervisor of employment for Filene's department store.[57]

The City History Club was the second organization of its kind in the country. It was founded in 1904 to help "the voters of the future to withstand the blandishments of the Ward Boss and the temptation to regard political office from the point of view of the spoils system." The club's president, John Farwell Moors, had actively participated in the early work of the Immigration Restriction League and in 1899 had been named the league's president. A wealthy investment banker of Mugwump/Democrat/free trade persuasion, Moors and other brahmins of his generation were "proud of their ancestral tradition of benevolence," Barbara Miller Solomon writes in *Ancestors and Immigrants,* "but they lacked the older generations' strong certainty that the poor could be transformed."[58] The attractiveness of Follett's junior city council proposal to men such as Moors was that it might prove to be a means of teaching the city's immigrants to conform to Anglo-Saxon ideals of government.

Before the adoption of Follett's junior city council plan, the City History Club had offered its members mostly passive activities — listening to the lectures of prominent public figures, viewing stereopticon shows, and visiting local historical sites. The club was notable, however, for its efforts to bring members of neighborhood branches into contact with each other, thereby giving them a chance to feel a part of the city rather than just their own neighborhood group. "It is not the intention that the boys brought up in different parts of the city under different conditions, should be brought suddenly and frequently together," wrote Frederick J. Allen, the club's executive director. "But at these large meetings all the clubs can come together naturally, each boy at home in his own Club, and meet together, as men do in public life, to discuss subjects of interest to all."[59]

This feature of the City History Club's work was incorporated into the functioning of the junior city councils in 1910, when a Club Congress modeled on the state legislature and national congress was formed. But in 1906, when the council plan was first implemented, there were only two branch clubs, organized locally according to the procedures of the Boston Board of Aldermen. One branch was established at the Palmer School in Roxbury (the school to which Follett had recently moved the activities of her Roxbury League) and the other at Elizabeth Peabody House (a West End settlement). By 1908 the scheme included seven councils, each comprised of about fifteen members; by 1910 the number had expanded to ten.[60]

A major change in the functioning of the councils occurred in 1909, when they were reorganized to conform to the structure and operations of Boston's new nine-person City Council. Officers were elected and committees appointed, with each nonofficer appointed as chair of a committee. The subjects for study and debate in the councils were described by Frederick Allen as "just such matters . . . as come up in the Boston City Council; for instance, improvements of various kinds in all parts of the city; the consolidation of several departments into a single department; the appointment of the Police Commissioner, whether by Governor or Mayor; suggested amendments to the city charter; a saner observance of the Fourth of July; the extension of the right of eminent domain; the repeal of the poll tax law; the granting of public franchises; the establishment of a municipal lodging house; the annexation of Hyde Park to the city of Boston; the veto by the Governor of the bill to limit the application of the Civil Service Examination in the case of misdemeanors." Council members would introduce motions, orders, and resolutions on these subjects and then take "an active part in committee work, in debate upon the floor, and in all that has to do with the passing of orders and city ordinances." In at least two instances, the councils successfully "exerted an influence on city legislation, resulting . . . in improvements in playgrounds and parks in the North End and in Roxbury." On another occasion, a council won "the adoption of an ordinance regulating the exposure for sale of certain food products."[61]

Mary Follett's original plan for the councils called for an evaluation of their work and a prize to be awarded to the group "which has best fulfilled the functions of a city council." The criteria, many of which were spelled out in detail, reflect many of the values Follett had formed during her university education. She would award the prize to the council demonstrating: the "greatest decorum and knowledge of parliamentary law"; the "widest comprehension of public needs"; a commitment to "good citizenship rather than . . . party politics"; a "spirit of alert interest and service rather than of indifference and irresponsibility"; the "independence" of each vote, by which she meant "each measure considered as a measure, and voting not influenced by some individual's lead"; the number of methods suggested by the council for "overcoming tendencies towards corrupt legislation and administration" and for "increasing the efficiency of both legislation and administration"; and, finally, the "greatest number of effective committees."[62] This complex set of criteria, which might have been practicable had there been only two branch councils, clearly could not be used as the number grew larger. But even without formal evaluation, the councils thrived.

In 1910, in recognition of the fact that the junior city councils had become the centerpiece of the City History Club's activities, Mary Follett was chosen the organization's vice-president.[63] Three years later Frederick J. Allen spread the news of his organization's successful nine-year venture in an article in the *National Municipal Review*: "The boys with whom it first began in the various social and educational centers of the city have grown to manhood . . . [and] have exerted a strong influence for good citizenship and good government. They have been conspicuous as leaders in the various sections of the city. Being informed on public matters, and patriotic in spirit, they have caused many of their friends and acquaintances to take a right stand in matters of local and public importance. They have assisted in the naturalization of foreign-born citizens, in the registration of voters, and in bringing them to the polls to vote . . . Their influence has had weight in city legislation, resulting in local improvements in various parts of the city." In light of the mounting evidence that the City History Club was "training the civic leaders and the legislators of the future," Allen felt confident in asserting that his organization had become "preeminently the young men's civic club of Boston."[64]

At mid-decade, Follett's activities on behalf of civic training were progressing satisfactorily, but trouble was brewing in the Boston Equal Suffrage Association for Good Government. During the first five years, there had been agreement about the association's unique dual mission: women's suffrage *and* civic work. Many in the BESAGG, including its primary patron, Pauline Agassiz Shaw, believed that the right to vote could best be won by demonstrating that women desired active public lives and were capable of effective civic work.[65]

By 1907, however, this consensus was beginning to unravel, causing Shaw and Mary Follett to doubt whether the BESAGG was the appropriate home for their civic work.

One factor undermining the BESAGG's commitment to civic work was the illness of key members. Shaw was prevented from giving sustained personal attention to the association, first by the precarious health of her elderly husband and then, after his death in June 1908, by a serious illness of her own. Mary Follett, who had become one of the association's most active civic workers, was similarly incapacitated, suffering a recurrence of her bowel disease late in 1907.[66] About this same time, the BESAGG temporarily lost Maud Wood Park, its extremely competent executive secretary and another supporter of the association's civic work. Park had thrown herself into suffrage activities almost immediately after her 1898 graduation from Radcliffe. She chaired the Massachusetts Woman's Suffrage Association and helped to found both the College Equal Suffrage League and the BESAGG. But when Park's husband died suddenly in 1904, Shaw sensed that Park needed some time to rethink her life. In an effort to avoid losing her altogether, Shaw financed a year-long "vacation" for Park at a San Francisco settlement and then lent her money for a two-year study trip around the world.[67]

During Park's absence, the position of executive secretary was filled by Susan Walker Fitzgerald, a Bryn Mawr graduate who had done social work on the West Side of New York before marrying "a wealthy, Harvard-trained lawyer."[68] She seemed competent enough at first, but within a few months Mary Follett was expressing reservations about Fitzgerald to Shaw. Follett's influence on Shaw was considerable—in part because of their past associations, but also because Shaw's friendship with Isobel Briggs gave Follett access to Shaw even during her husband's illness. The extent to which Shaw was influenced by Follett is apparent in an October 1908 letter from Shaw to Maud Wood Park: "Perhaps . . . you will not mind my asking you to wait [before leaving] till January as we once talked of doing—for tho' Mrs. Fitz-Gerald is executive in one direction it is more that of getting up meetings and putting something through like the Voters' Festival—May Festival—Speakers etc. than it is the planning of the work for our various committees . . . to inspire them with new ideas and to keep up the life of the various enterprises. This I feared a little last winter . . . I have been talking with Miss Follet [*sic*] who will tell you how much we need you to start us *this* winter as you did *last* winter— for without your initiation at those meetings . . . we should have accomplished much less than we did . . . Miss Follett will explain to you how we all feel about it and miss your guiding hand."[69]

Shaw was troubled by Fitzgerald's limitations as a manager, but she also

worried that Fitzgerald "does not seem to care as much for the municipal affairs as she does about suffrage — perhaps she feared not doing enough about
the latter, because she was not an ardent suffragist when she first came." Maud
Wood Park seemed to agree with Shaw's assessment of Fitzgerald's performance. In Boston for a few months before departing on her world trip, Park
remarked to a friend that "I'm frightfully busy just now. Mrs. FitzG. has
got the B.E.S.A. work involved in a bad tangle, & I'm at my wits end for a
way out."[70]

The "way out" that finally made it possible for Park to leave town had three
key elements: first, Shaw agreed to give a lump sum of money to the BESAGG
rather than funding projects on a piecemeal basis; next, the Finance Committee was designated as a "Committee on Plan of Work" to recommend how the
association's money should be spent; and Park was persuaded to remain in
Boston long enough to participate in developing the plan. The key feature of
this blueprint was decided on November 21, 1908, when the Executive Board
voted that "it be the policy of this Association this year to put the emphasis on
Civic work rather than on Suffrage work." According to the minutes, "there
followed a discussion that made it quite clear that it was not the intention of
the Association to do *no* Suffrage work, but that it felt that it was wisest to return to the earlier policy of the Association which held that it could best work
in the interests of Suffrage by doing good Civic work and proving the desire
and ability of women to take an active and useful part in public works."[71]

The Executive Board, which included Mary Follett, also adopted several
other recommendations. In one, the board agreed that the "principal lines of
Civic work" should concern "the Public School and Industrial Conditions."
Others spelled out in detail the secretary's responsibilities for planning and
supervising the work — including a requirement that she keep office hours and
locate her office where she was less likely to be disturbed with "unimportant
demands upon her time." Finally, in what appears to have been an effort by
Fitzgerald's supporters to curb Follett's access to Shaw, it was voted that "the
members of the Executive Board shall not take any matters referring to the
Association or the house [at Six Marlborough Street, where the association's
office was located] to either Mrs. Shaw or [her son] unless authorized by the
Executive Board."[72]

In the days following the November board meeting, the five-person Plan of
Work Committee, of which Follett also was a member, produced a second set
of recommendations — these concerning the association's "departments" of
work. Each of the recommendations was accepted by the board.[73] Follett's
department, Civic Training, was instructed to continue largely as it had been,
working "chiefly for the extended use of school buildings and as opportunity

may occur for the increase of Civic Training in the Public Schools."[74] The remainder of the meeting was devoted to a discussion of a message from Mrs. Shaw in which she expressed regret over the wording of the November resolution that committed the association to an "emphasis on Civic work rather than on Suffrage work." The minutes make no mention of why this wording troubled Shaw, but she surely would not have appreciated either the implication that a choice had to be made between civic and suffrage work or the possibility that some future board might choose a different emphasis.

According to the minutes, a "long discussion" ensued. Wisdom dictated that the board concentrate on allaying the fears of their primary financial supporter; but resentment over the fact that Shaw had chosen Follett to deliver her message made this job extremely difficult. After all, only ten days earlier the board had voted to prohibit unauthorized access to the Shaws. Finally, however, an agreement was reached, and the board voted to have the objectionable provision "expunged from the records." The board's action brought this particular dispute to an end, but it now was fully apparent that two factions existed within the association: one wishing to work directly for suffrage and the other hoping to maintain the original joint commitment to suffrage and civic work.[75]

Thereafter almost every meeting of the Executive Board involved some sort of altercation over the mission of the association.[76] The friction between the two factions was exacerbated by the suffragists' uncertainty about how best to pursue their cause. In 1907 "the movement seemed to have reached a hiatus," Sharon Hartman Strom writes, "in which the convinced reinforced their own convictions. The method of reaching women through the endorsements of prominent citizens, labor leaders, and civic-minded organizations seemed to have reached maximum efficiency." The suffragists were especially dismayed by their inability to reach people who were uncommitted on the suffrage question. "You know how we are hampered," Maud Wood Park protested to Mary Hutcheson Page, "because we are thought to be merely suffragists, how we can seem to go just so far and no farther. For example, when I want to speak to an audience of college girls it's almost impossible to get them together unless someone of great influence works up the meeting. We rarely get a chance to be heard by uninterested persons and when we do get a chance our words carry no weight beyond that of individuals more or less likeable or eloquent."[77] Page, too, was feeling frustrated and complained to Park early in 1909 that "we [in the BESAGG] seem to be always criticising and discussing the past, and *doing* mighty little."[78]

Searching for new tactics, Page devoted much of 1908 to learning about the militant English suffragists. She subscribed to their paper, *Votes for Women*, and corresponded with the editor, Emmeline Pethick-Lawrence. Impressed by the English suffragists' accomplishments, Page wrote a largely favorable article for *Collier's* and began advocating the use of some of their tactics in Massachusetts. Within a year, Page had come to be regarded as the leader of the "direct action" faction of the BESAGG. Page also gained new energy from her growing sense that public opinion was shifting in the direction of the suffragists. In the spring of 1909 Page noted with pleasure that "Mrs. Barrett Wendell who presided at the 'anti' annual meeting the other day announced that it was easier nowadays to be a suffragist than an 'anti.' We *have* moved," Page exclaimed to Park, "when they make such a concession as that, haven't we?"[79]

That summer the BESAGG began to employ some of the more subdued tactics of the English militants. Members traveled throughout the state to conduct open-air meetings, distributed literature in unlikely places such as the floor of the Boston Stock Exchange, and made direct public inquiries of candidates about their views on women's suffrage.[80] In late October, when the English militant suffragist Emmeline Pankhurst visited Boston on behalf of the BESAGG, she scored an impressive triumph. An audience of thousands filled Tremont Temple, generating new interest in the movement and doing much to revive the spirits of the Massachusetts suffragists. At a BESAGG luncheon given in her honor, she urged the Massachusetts suffragists to "lay aside other causes" such as temperance work and social work in the interest of gaining the vote — advice that added fuel to the association's internal controversy.[81]

Capturing the moment, Mary Hutcheson Page proposed that the BESAGG create a ward organization of people interested in suffrage based on a plan already in use in New York. When the board accepted her proposal, Page was ecstatic. "We are no longer," she wrote to Park in December 1909, "so much of an abstract, theoretical society, largely on paper but we are actually *in* the fight — not the thick of it yet, but really fighting. Yesterday afternoon Mrs. FitzGerald & I loaded up a reporter from the *Boston American, who sought us,* with suffrage tales for today's Sunday issue."[82]

As Page saw it, only one person was capable of thwarting her effort to transform the BESAGG into a full-fledged suffrage organization. That person was Mary Follett. Any shift away from civic work was sure to be opposed by her; and since Follett was the only board member having access to Shaw, the association was in serious danger of losing its financial support. The dispute between Page and Follett over the association's mission was acted out in a continuing disagreement over the competence of Susan Walker Fitzgerald, Park's substitute as executive secretary. "Miss Follett's dislike and contempt for Mrs. Fitzgerald," Page wrote to Maud Wood Park in March 1909, "have grown quite unbounded." Concerned that Park might discount her remarks because Page had not always seen eye to eye with Follett, Page added: "I like Miss Follett better than I ever did before, & I get on beautifully with her." Now, however, suspicious of Follett's motives and resentful of her access to Shaw, Page was convinced that Follett "had colored Mrs. Shaw's view of Mrs. Fitzgerald and the B.E.S.A., and made her see it just as she, Miss Follett, sees it."[83] Page was particularly incensed by the emergence of a plan, developed "after much talking and many committee meetings," in which Shaw guaranteed "a salary of $1000 a year to the secretary of the B.E.S.A. until [Park's] return." This plan, Page contended, was a deliberate attempt on Follett's part to get rid of Fitzgerald. "Miss Follett took a violent dislike to Mrs. FitzGerald, and all last year she plotted and planned to get rid of her. She finally, by manipulating Mrs. Shaw and Quincy, the son, got things arranged . . . [Shaw] had been paying $2000 for the secretary and a good sum every month to carry on the work. Miss Follett thought that if only $1000 was to be paid to the secretary, that Miss FitzGerald would have to go."[84] In Page's view, it would be a "great mistake" to get rid of Fitzgerald, but "Miss Follett is as set as the everlasting hills and the more I try to defend or praise Mrs. FitzGerald, the more exasperated she becomes." Well-known for her persuasive powers, Page was accustomed to having her own way. It must therefore have been especially frustrating to discover that she could not "budge [Mary Follett] as regards Mrs. FitzGerald."[85]

In March 1909, confident that Fitzgerald would now be forced to seek work elsewhere, Follett made a conciliatory gesture. Seemingly aware of how much Page resented her exclusive access to Shaw, Follett called a special meeting of the board at which it was voted "that Mrs. Page represent the Board in its relation to Mrs. Shaw concerning the work of the Association and that she communicate with Mrs. Shaw in the name of the Board either personally or by letter." This gesture, unfortunately, accomplished little, for the following month the board voted to retain Fitzgerald. Their vote committed the association to raising an additional $1,000 to supplement Shaw's contribution or, failing that, to pay "the Secretary for one-half time and [allow] the Massachusetts Association . . . to pay her for the other one-half, with the understanding that her entire time is to be devoted to suffrage work."[86]

This vote was less a statement of faith in Fitzgerald's managerial abilities than a symbol of the board's commitment to direct suffrage activity. At the beginning of her tenure, Page had thought well enough of Fitzgerald, saying that "whatever the latter may be and do in civics, in *suffrage* work, she is fine, and it will be a great loss to that branch if she leaves us." But by mid-1910 even Page doubted Fitzgerald's competence, admitting to Maud Wood Park that "I have had to keep an eye on Mrs. Fitzgerald all the time, and it was sometimes wearing."[87] In another letter to Park, Page elaborated on her concerns: "Mrs. FitzGerald has valuable qualities, chiefly her initiative and daring and fearlessness, but she doesn't begin to be as good as you on anything that is steady, like organization work, and the steady putting of two and two together, and working a thing up to a complete result. Every one on that Board will breathe a sign of relief and comfort when they know that you are to return and take charge."[88]

In December 1909 Page reported with obvious relish to Maud Wood Park that the $1,000 needed to retain Fitzgerald had been raised and that "Miss Follett realizes that her plan was frustrated." Page then remarked that Follett had come to her in November, seeming "rather crestfallen at one of the results [of Shaw's new financing plan] which she had not anticipated — namely, that when you come back next year to be at the head of the G.G. that there will be no money for you to work with, unless Mrs. Shaw is so much better that she can be appealed to." Since Shaw was "very ill . . . worse than ever, and sees no one," there seemed little hope for a successful appeal.[89]

Furious about Follett's miscalculation, Page attacked her, claiming that Follett was "no real suffragist" and had "done us real harm by poisoning Mrs. Shaw's mind and cutting off some of our supplies." In December, even after the board decided "that henceforth the activities should be suffrage and not civic," Page still was in no mood to be conciliatory. "We are *in* a movement," she told Park, "we are not merely looking at it as we were before, and *civics* is a side issue."[90]

Even though the board had now made a clear commitment to direct suffrage work, Page's concern about Follett did not abate. In March 1910, in a letter to Park about ways to "strengthen the Board," Follett was identified by Page as one person who could be "spared, as she never worked except when you did her work for her . . . Miss Follett has very much discredited herself with the whole committee."[91] Follett, however, weathered the storm. Apparently having retained considerable support despite Page's active hostility, Follett was nominated for a place on the board and was subsequently reelected by the membership.

No record of Follett's side of the controversy with Mary Hutcheson Page has survived, but it seems almost certain that Follett found her continuing membership on the board more palatable once Maud Wood Park returned. Park, like Follett, believed that the BESAGG was making an important contribution to the future of the city through its civic work. Reflecting on the history of the BESAGG before her departure for San Francisco in 1907, Page noted that "in the first two or three years, we gave a large part of our time to the consideration of private agencies for public good and our work was planned in accordance with their method . . . Little by little, however, we have come to be chiefly interested in the people's work for the people, that is, in the possibilities of government, not mainly in its negative function of relief and control, but as a positive uplifting force in the community. In this field, there are as yet few students compared with the number who have devoted themselves to the workings of private agencies."[92]

During her three-year absence, Park's commitment to the civic portion of the association's dual mission did not waver, even though Page's letters suggested that civic work had become passé. Park worried that she might no longer be the right person for the position of executive secretary: "I wish I saw my way clear to believing that the new method [exclusive devotion to suffrage] is the one for me, too; for I want to be on the same path with you at every turning. But I don't see it yet." Page countered: "Of course you may come back and start us all once again into little committees doing civic work. But I doubt it. The Municipal League is doing all that, and very well too; but no one else is doing our work. We are trying to *win* woman suffrage, and we don't intend to spend our lives at it either . . . Your letter reached me just after I had sent you mine, and it made me quite uneasy to think that you even considered that you and we might not be able to work together."[93]

Page's barbed response may have caused Park to worry even more, because Page felt it necessary to address the controversy again in her next letter: "As to the other part of your letter, your fitness as a leader under what you think are changed conditions . . . [the Board] should be perfectly satisfied to have you act according to your judgment and conscience in the planning and conducting of the work. So, my dear, you cannot escape us. *We want you* . . . We can argue about methods, after you arrive, if you like . . . How glad we shall all be to have your hand on the helm once more! And how gladly we shall work with you!" And then, pointedly omitting any reference to Mary Follett, Page added: "You can do civics with Mrs. Mead, Mrs. Beatley and Mrs. Andrews, and suffrage with Mrs. Ames, Mrs. McCormick and me."[94]

Two weeks after resuming the office of executive secretary in September 1910, Maud Wood Park "outlined a plan for organizing the direct suffrage work and the civic activities of the Association." Among the points included was a provision calling for "the help of the Secretary to be given both to direct suffrage and to civic activities with the understanding that suffrage work should have the greater share of her time during spring and summer and civic activities the greater share during the autumn and winter." Another provision recommended that the new ward and precinct organization be set up "on a joint suffrage and civic basis." Conscious of how much Park's managerial skills meant to the association, the board adopted her plan. But civic work regained only some of its former legitimacy; the momentum now was on the side of suffrage.[95]

It is a mark of Follett's character that she did not feel compelled to leave the association once she recognized that her views had not prevailed. Indeed, even after she found another, more hospitable environment for her civic work, she continued to be active on the BESAGG board. In December 1911, when the English suffragist Emmeline Pankhurst made a second, quite controversial visit to Boston, it was Mary Follett who presided at the BESAGG luncheon given in her honor.[96] And in 1914, after the suffrage amendment finally passed both houses of the Massachusetts legislature, Follett served on the Bay State Campaign Finance Committee that raised funds for the impending referendum battle. Only after this campaign did Follett end her active participation in the association, joining such women as Alice Stone Blackwell, Emily Greene Balch, and Alice Goldmark Brandeis in the ranks of honorary vice-presidents.[97]

Follett's spirited resistance to efforts to limit the activities of the BESAGG to matters directly concerned with suffrage can be attributed not to a lack of commitment to suffrage, as Mary Hutcheson Page had once contended, but to convictions she would express later in her second book, *The New State*. There Follett described the "woman movement" as "merely the end of the movement for the extension of the suffrage" and, as such, a matter that properly "belongs to the past rather than to the present." As Follett put it, "its culmination has overrun the century mark and makes what is really a nineteenth-century movement seem as if it belonged to the twentieth." Furthermore, in her view the mere casting of a ballot could never fulfill the responsibilities of a citizen of a democratic society, for "democracy is not a spreading out: it is not the extension of the suffrage — its merely external aspect — it is a drawing together . . . It is the finding of the one will to which the will of every single man and woman must contribute. We want women to vote not that the suffrage may be extended to women but that women may be included in the suffrage: we want what they may have to add to the whole."[98]

In 1908, just as the civic activities of the BESAGG were effectively coming to an end, Follett was fortunate to find an alternative venue for working out what women might "add to the whole" in the new Women's Municipal League of Boston. For the next several years, this organization would be her vehicle for collaborating with residents from every corner of the city in the establishment of community centers. And these, in turn, were the experiences that would lead her to declare in *The New State* that someday "no question in history will seem more astonishing than the one so often reiterated in these days, 'Should woman be given a place in politics?' Woman *is* in politics; no power under the sun can put her out. We are now beginning to recognize more and more clearly that the work we do, the conditions of that work, the houses in which we live, the water we drink, the food we eat, the opportunities for bringing up our children, that in fact the whole area of our daily life should constitute politics. There is no line where the life of the home ends and the life of the city begins. There is no wall between my private life and my public life."[99]

12

Private Funds for Public Purposes

In January 1909 the front page of the *Boston Globe* announced the establishment of a Women's Municipal League (WML) of Boston. For more than a decade, Mary Follett would exercise creative leadership in the WML. Organized by a group of influential Back Bay women, the league reportedly had no intention of preparing women "for active participation in politics"; nor did it intend "to ascend Beacon Hill to inform the members of the general court what laws are needed for the betterment of the feminine portion of the human family." The avowed purpose of this new women's organization was characteristically restrained: being uncertain about whether "women were taking their fair share in the responsibilities of the municipality," the league wished to "interest and educate women in municipal housekeeping, to influence women to realize and assume their civic responsibilities."[1]

Founders of the WML realized that the public might question the need for yet another civic organization in Boston. For almost twenty years, organizations had been founded for every conceivable purpose—a phenomenon that historians have explained in terms of the pressing needs for municipal services, the seemingly unbounded confidence of reformers in their ability to create societal change, and the determination of a generation of educated women to use their knowledge and skills wherever they were not explicitly excluded. As a consequence, so many new organizations were created, causing such inefficiency and duplication of effort, that a new phenomenon began to appear — the "megaorganization," or federation whose sole purpose for being was the coordination of existing groups. This was precisely the rationale underlying the formation of the Women's Municipal League.

Under the auspices of the league, Mary Follett nourished her lifelong interest in "relations" and achieved a sophisticated understanding of the intricacies of intergroup coordination. By the late 1920s Follett had come to see the concept of coordination as so central to her way of thinking about organizational effectiveness that she made it the cornerstone of her "four fundamental principles of organization."[2]

The founders of the Women's Municipal League spent a full year consulting with men involved in public service before revealing their intentions to the general public. Convinced by these discussions of the need to cultivate a membership that would be representative as well as influential, the founders actively sought members from a cross-section of social, ethnic, occupational, and income groups in Boston.[3] They visited "working women's clubs, church societies and invaded the tenement districts seeking recruits for the movement." Also, in a show of good faith, the founders set the league's dues at twenty-five cents. In the words of the *Globe* reporter, they chose "to be poor in order to attract the women of Boston who needed to be reached to make the organization a success." The impact of these efforts on the league's membership rolls was dramatic: within two years, 1,170 women had joined, and by 1913 that number had almost doubled.[4] To broaden the membership base further, the founders decided to take "no position" on the volatile question of women's suffrage. This decision proved efficacious. The founders attracted to the first two Executive Committees both pro- and antisuffrage women, as well as women who had chosen not to affiliate with either group.[5]

Representativeness, however, was only one of the elements necessary to achieve the founders' aims. To guarantee the organization's future, the league needed immediate, genuine accomplishments.[6] President Katherine Bowlker stressed this theme in her speech at the league's first public meeting and called for action within "the next few months."[7] Believing that "experiments must be tried if the world is to advance," the league's Executive Committee looked favorably on experimentation in municipal government but thought it "manifestly impossible for the city government to try experiments with public funds." This apparent dilemma would be resolved, they argued, if the WML and other, similar organizations used private funds to support experiments "of such enduring benefit to the community, that the city will feel itself justified in incorporating them later into its permanent municipal work." If these "object lessons" were carefully chosen, the league might well come to be seen as "so useful and important, so prominent in the city," that it could not be over-looked.[8] The first of these "object lessons" would be directed by Mary Follett.

The strategy of using privately funded experiments as a means of proving the public value of particular social or educational programs was popular in late nineteenth-century Boston, particularly among upper-class women. This Boston tradition would have been a familiar one to Mary Follett. Her primary link to this movement, of course, was Pauline Agassiz Shaw and her active promotion of kindergartens and manual training programs.[9] But two other Women's Municipal League colleagues—Alice Goldmark Brandeis and Ella Lyman Cabot—had also been socialized to this particular form of private-public collaboration. Each had played an active role in the early Massachu-setts Civic League experiments with privately funded city playgrounds and summer vacation schools.[10] Over the next few years, Brandeis and Cabot would become not only Follett's WML colleagues but also her close friends.

Ella Lyman Cabot was descended from one of New England's oldest fami-lies and related to another by virtue of her marriage to Richard C. Cabot. Like Mary Follett, Cabot had been a Radcliffe "special student" and a teacher (of ethics and applied psychology) in Boston private schools before agreeing to direct the Massachusetts Civic League's summer vacation schools. The imagi-nation and skillful leadership she displayed in directing the schools made Ella Cabot a sought-after figure in brahmin education circles.[11] In 1905 Cabot received appointments to both the State Board of Education and the Radcliffe Board of Governors (where she served until her death in 1934). "Nothing gives such a thrill of joy," Cabot noted in her diary, "as to hear people want your work." Women of her wealth and social standing all too often were courted for their checkbooks rather than for their ideas and talents.[12]

Alice Goldmark Brandeis, the first treasurer of the Massachusetts Civic League and a longtime member of the Governing Committee, became another of Mary Follett's valued colleagues in her school centers work—and later a neighbor and friend. Daughter of Joseph Goldmark, a distinguished revolu-tionary leader of Vienna, Alice Goldmark was imbued with the "ideals of freedom" and the "rich cultural heritage" that characterized the Jews fleeing European political oppression in 1848. She married Louis D. Brandeis, who early in their marriage was involved in a series of controversial, often bitter public cases such as those involving the Public Franchise League. These cases built Brandeis's reputation as the "People's Attorney," but the hostility they generated resulted in anti-Semitic attacks and considerable social ostracism for the Brandeis family. Alice Brandeis remained gracious under pressure and raised their two daughters, but she endured extreme fatigue and headaches, particularly as the demands on her husband's time meant his longer absences from home. By 1908, however, Alice Brandeis felt well enough to become active in two causes close to her heart — education and women's suffrage.[13]

Ella Cabot served on the WML Executive Committee, a position she held by virtue of chairing one of the league's three departments, the Department of Education. By the time of the league's first public meeting in January 1909, the department's Committee on the Extended Use of School Buildings, chaired by Mary Follett, had been functioning for several months.[14] Joining Follett on her WML committee were Alice Brandeis and Anna Clapp Frothingham; the latter's husband was the distinguished pastor of the Arlington Street Church and a tireless worker on behalf of the poor in Boston charitable organizations. Anna Frothingham's presence helped to establish the committee's nonpartisan character: whereas Brandeis's husband was a well-known Mugwump Democrat, Frothingham's brother-in-law was the Republican lieutenant governor of Massachusetts.[15]

At the WML's January meeting, President Bowlker announced that Mary Follett's Committee on Extended Use would undertake the first, and therefore most crucial, "object lesson" for the Women's Municipal League. To this end, an anonymous donor, most likely Pauline Agassiz Shaw, had agreed to finance part of the extended use "of one typical city school for neighborhood work during the next year."[16] Years later in a tribute to Shaw, Bowlker acknowledged that "without her help the work of the committee could not have been undertaken," for she had always "paid more than half the expenses of the Committee on the Extended Use of School Buildings."[17]

Follett outlined the social and civic benefits resulting from the extended use of public school buildings in a report issued immediately after the January meeting. Here Follett made her first bold attempt to contrast the limitations of traditional social settlements with the potential benefits of the extended use of schools. The first advantage that she claimed for the public schools was the "public character" of the buildings. On the basis of her work with the Highland Union and the Roxbury Industrial League, she asserted that "the very boys and girls who most need some influence in their lives often will not go to a Settlement . . . they object to it either because it is a charitable institution, or because they are afraid there will be some one there to 'uplift' them . . . or else they say that it is a place for kids because they know their little brothers and sisters go there." In contrast, many seemed willing to come to school buildings, because "they feel what they call 'independent' there." The second advantage identified by Follett was equally pragmatic: the large classrooms and gymnasiums typically found in public high schools made it possible to offer athletic events and dances — activities that were promising "bait for more serious work" such as industrial classes. Finally, because the 1890s dream of a

settlement in every neighborhood had not materialized, Follett noted that
there were "not enough Settlements and other social agencies to provide for
more than a small number of our young people. Thus on the one hand there is
this urgent need, on the other there are all these empty buildings upon which
we have spent literally millions and millions of our money. Such a waste of
capital seems bad business management on our part."[18]

At the same time, Follett recognized that the financial problems that had
prompted the School Committee to close the first educational centers had, if
anything, grown more serious. Chairman David A. Ellis described the situation in an article in the *Christian Science Monitor*. According to Ellis, the 1901
legislation that had set the school fund tax rate at $2.75 per $1,000 was
"inadequate and has been for a few years back." Forced for several years to
defer the purchase of textbooks, charts, maps, and other supplies, the School
Committee now would need $350,000 in addition to its regular appropriation
in order to make up the deficiencies and provide sufficient resources for the
coming school year. A bill designed to do just that by increasing the tax rate
ten cents per year until the deficiencies were made up was pending in the
legislature.[19]

Cognizant of the financial difficulties facing the schools, Follett acknowledged that the School Committee did not have sufficient funds "to develop
neighborhood use of the schools." But she was confident that this obstacle
could be overcome "if the public is roused to appreciate the good our school
buildings can do when used for evening recreation centres." To this end, Follett and her colleagues on the WML's Extended Use Committee had spent
much time during the winter of 1908–09 not only in "an investigation of
many details, but also [in] the awakening of public opinion, both among
individuals and organizations." Follett did not mind. "Patience," she would
later say of herself, "is the only virtue I have ever claimed."[20] One of the
activities that she undertook during this winter of preparatory work was an
investigation of the extended use of school buildings in New York, Rochester,
and Chicago. Finding that these cities had quite different schemes for the use
of school buildings, she was hopeful that a series of public meetings describing the alternatives might awaken public opinion, inform those already committed to the extended-use idea, and provide a foundation for cooperation
among organizations that wished to promote the concept.

At Follett's urging, several Boston organizations by February 1909 had
agreed to a plan that would have Edward J. Ward of Rochester and Gustav
Straubenmuller of New York, two nationally recognized experts on extended
use, visit Boston to give public speeches and confer informally with leaders of
educational, social, and civic organizations who were interested in furthering

the movement.[21] One of the several groups that agreed to sponsor the visit was the Education Committee of the Twentieth Century Club. James P. Munroe, a member of the club's Governing Council, was yet another descendent of an old New England family and treasurer of the family business, the Munroe Felt and Paper Company.[22] In January 1909, a little more than a month before the Ward-Straubenmuller visit, Munroe was drawn into the extended-use movement when he accepted an invitation to organize and chair the Home and School Association's Committee on the Further Use of School Buildings.[23]

The Home and School Association, a federation of nine parents' associations scattered throughout Boston, was not officially organized until December 1907, but it had its origins three years earlier in a parents' group in the Hyde-Sherwin district of Roxbury. The person responsible for launching this new venture was Fannie Fern Andrews, a 1902 Radcliffe graduate who had received her degree in education and psychology at the age of thirty-four. Having founded the Roxbury parents' group under the auspices of the Committee on Public Schools of the Boston Equal Suffrage Association for Good Government, Andrews quite naturally turned first to the suffrage association's primary patron, Pauline Agassiz Shaw, when funds were being raised to create the Home and School Association.[24] Shaw responded by making major contributions and even agreed to accept the honorary title of president, in part because she hoped that a Home and School Association could play an important role in the larger campaign for a more extended use of the schools. "I think this Association . . . will have it in its power to do more to use the school buildings for the general good of the public (of all ages)," Shaw wrote Andrews in March 1908, "than any other combination of pressure that could now be brought to bear, and you have done it all so wisely, so thoroughly, so quietly, and so practically. I am more happy about it than I can tell you."[25]

Over the next few years the Home and School Association "published a monthly newsletter, recommended children's and parent's books, investigated child attendance at Boston theaters, distributed seeds for home and school gardens, arranged school art exhibitions, and propagandized for improved building sanitation." These endeavors were so warmly welcomed in the city's neighborhoods that by 1909 eighteen branches had been established in Boston school districts. Many of the association's activities implicitly supported the notion of opening school facilities to community groups, but Fannie Fern Andrews wished to go further and explicitly promote the extended use of schools. She was seconded in this aim by the association's treasurer, Robert Treat Paine Jr., who had been a supporter of the extended-use movement since his days as a member of James J. Storrow's educational centers subcommittee.[26] As a result, when Edward J. Ward of Rochester arrived in Boston on

February 15, he was invited to make his first public speech to a meeting of the Home and School Association. He was accompanied on the platform by Boston's Republican mayor, George A. Hibbard, and a Boston schoolmaster.[27]

The Ward-Straubenmuller visit reflects Mary Follett's determination to involve all important constituencies at the earliest possible stage of her work. On the afternoon of February 16, Ward spoke at the Rindge Manual Training School in Cambridge, where he was introduced by a superintendent of schools who wholeheartedly endorsed the extended use movement and hoped "to see Cambridge adopt the policy which has proved so successful in Rochester."[28] The next day, when Straubenmuller arrived from New York, the two visitors spoke to the largest gathering of the week, the masters and public school teachers of Boston. This meeting was cosponsored by the ten major women's organizations in Boston and was presided over by David Ellis, chairman of the Boston School Committee. That evening, at the Twentieth Century Club, Ward and Straubenmuller met with James P. Munroe and others who were particularly interested in the movement, to answer questions and provide estimates of the cost of the work. The next afternoon Ward described "the attitude of the teachers in Rochester toward his work" at a tea for the masters of Boston schools given by the Women's Municipal League.[29] The various events received substantial coverage in the Boston newspapers, presumably because Follett and her colleagues knew the importance of creating a public opinion favorable to extended use and enjoyed access to the local press.[30]

After this highly publicized visit the Home and School Association's Extended Use Committee began work in earnest. The members included Mary Follett, Fannie Fern Andrews, a state legislator who was a former School Committee member, a settlement house director who was a former newspaper reporter, a prominent merchant, a leader in the suffrage movement, the executive officer of the Civic League, and a college dean.[31]

From the beginning, the Home and School Association's committee had a two-part agenda. It would enhance the development of the WML's "object lesson" by assisting Follett's committee in working out answers to certain questions: "Where it would be best to open a Social Centre; What form of Neighborhood Centre would be most useful to the community; Who would be a good director; How shall the money be raised; and the *many* other questions which must be decided before the work can actually begin." The other item on the agenda was development of a citywide plan for the further use of school buildings by existing neighborhood groups. Here the committee's motive was unabashedly political. If the committee could help local parents' associations, United Improvement Associations, and other societies to gain access to the schools for lectures and meetings, it would broaden the base of support for the extended-use concept and thereby improve the chances of obtaining public funds when it was ready to expand the program into other city neighborhoods.[32]

But there could hardly have been a more difficult year than 1909 for Mary Follett and her colleagues to capture the attention of Bostonians. Historians point to this year as a turning point in Boston civic life: the uneasy sharing of power between the Irish and the Yankees collapsed into political warfare. In January, apparently in the hope that a strong mayoral system would foster municipal reform where their public investigations had failed, the Yankee-dominated Finance Commission asked the state legislature to enact a new charter for the city of Boston. The charter proposed "to centralize the government and to take local influence and partisan politics out of the government of the city." There would be a strong mayor, elected for a four-year term and with "near-absolute power over the budget and over appointments." The mayor would be checked only by a small, at-large council and a permanent Finance Commission.[33]

There was enormous divisive potential in the Finance Commission's proposal, but few seemed to recognize it. One who did was brahmin James J. Storrow, who knew that it would be folly for a Yankee-dominated Republican legislature to try to impose charter reform on a largely Democratic and Irish city. In March, Storrow led "several hundred fellow Chamber of Commerce members to the State House," where in dramatic fashion "he addressed the [legislative] committee and an overflow crowd."[34] Although the legislature would not grant Storrow's plea for a binding referendum on the charter, it did agree to a compromise. Provisions relating to fiscal matters were to be enacted without referendum, but voters were given a choice on political issues: "they would choose between the reformers' proposal for non-partisan elections, strong mayor, and small, at-large council or another which allowed for partisan elections and ward councillors (albeit in a single chamber) and a less powerful mayor." After almost a year of hearings and other public discussions, the new charter was narrowly accepted by the voters in the November referendum.[35]

With the new charter in place, public attention turned immediately to the January elections for mayor and City Council. John F. Fitzgerald, the incumbent Irish mayor, was opposed by James J. Storrow, who was favored by the Yankee establishment. During the campaign Storrow inexplicably abandoned "his earlier consensual approach that had minimized attacks on (Irish) politicians and emphasized the public good." His partisan attacks on Irish politicians created such a backlash among Irish voters that they threw their support to Fitzgerald as a matter of ethnic pride. Caught up in the drama of the city's most exciting political contest in decades, more than 90 percent of eligible voters went to the polls. Although "reform" candidates captured seven of the nine seats on the new City Council, Storrow lost to Fitzgerald by a margin of about 1,500 votes.[36]

Fitzgerald's victory over Storrow, following the adoption of the revised city charter, was a watershed event in Boston politics. Unless a new means of integrating interests could be found, Boston politics would be rife with acrimonious ethnic disputes. Political cynicism was already evident in many quarters of the city, and Boston's Yankees, in particular, were finding public life an emotional roller coaster that few wished to ride.[37]

It was in this climate of political cynicism and ethnic mistrust that Mary Follett pressed her campaign for extended use of the schools. She felt little of the resentment and despair that recent events had precipitated in Boston's "best men," in part because she was excluded from electoral politics, but more importantly because she had a quite different vision of democratic political life. Mary Follett was committed not to electing "good men" to govern in place of their fellows but to helping men and women learn to govern *themselves*. In working out this vision, however, Follett repeatedly confronted a troublesome dilemma. If democracy were to be "grown" in Boston's neighborhoods, then members of the intellectual and professional elite, such as herself, would have to use their expertise to organize appropriate opportunities, create a favorable public opinion, acquire funding, and provide suitable training. Yet all this had to be done without usurping the local control that Follett wished to foster.

Over the next few years, this problem reappeared in numerous guises: Should extended-use centers be established by outsiders or opened only in response to neighborhood initiative? Should centers be self-supporting or receive public funds? Should school departments set restrictions on center operations or leave matters of internal governance entirely to local residents? Should managers and club leaders adopt directive roles or act primarily as facilitators? In her 1918 book, *The New State,* Follett would wrestle with this puzzle in a larger context, by struggling to define the appropriate role for the "expert" in a democratic society. Her experience in the social centers movement had demonstrated that "community associations must use expert advice and expert service," but Follett readily admitted that "exactly how this relation will be most satisfactorily worked out we do not yet clearly see." Six years later, in *Creative Experience,* she would return to the problem, and this time she would delineate in considerable detail the dangers of her generation's all-too-ready reliance on experts.[38]

In February 1910, however, Mary Follett was herself the expert. Seeing that the schools' most pressing financial concerns had been alleviated by a recent legislative tax increase, she began a series of meetings with the Boston School Committee in which she reopened the subject of extended use of the schools.[39] All five committee members were professional men (three lawyers, a surgeon, and a banker) committed to bringing efficiency to school operations. But the group was sufficiently diverse in ethnicity, religion, political affiliation, and educational background that Follett thought it wise, first, to confer with each member individually, reportedly "in the endeavor to pass on to them [her] Vision" about the social and civic values of extended use. Only after these individual conferences did she appear formally before the whole body to request their support. School Committee members probably found these one-on-one talks lively and engaging, since a conversation with Mary Follett, one colleague from this era later remarked, provided the kind of stimulation that "none of us who had the privilege of working with her can forget." Follett also could be very convincing. "She was very definite about certain things," this associate continued, "but it was fun to disagree with her and then watch her sharpen her argument against your objections. She would keep discovering more and more points in support of her position."[40] In this particular case, Follett's individual discussions apparently had the desired effect; in the March *WML Bulletin,* she reported that "the School Board has formally approved our plan and promised the use of one of its buildings, including heating and lighting, free."[41]

Curiously, there is no record of this "promise" in the School Committee *Proceedings* — only the vote establishing a twelve-member Advisory Committee on the Further Use of School Buildings.[42] The "off the record" quality of the School Committee's endorsement might have given Follett and her colleagues occasion for alarm had they interpreted it as a sign of lukewarm support, but an alternative explanation was more likely: the Committee — having just requested and received a tax rate increase to ease its financial problems — simply was unwilling to publicize its support for new initiatives. This decision did not disturb Mary Follett; she, too, was inclined to be cautious. "The partial failure of the experiment in two cities," Follett explained in the *WML Bulletin,* "has made us sure that our success depends on going very slowly, on making our plans most carefully, and on waiting until everything is ripe for beginning in just the way we think most wise."[43]

While Follett was busy conferring with the School Committee, action was warming up on another front. On February 9 Mayor Fitzgerald and the new city councilors visited East Boston for the first in a series of district gatherings fashioned after the New England town meeting. More than four hundred men and a few women attended and heard a series of speakers press vigorously for relief of certain neighborhood problems. Twice, speakers called for opening the school buildings for public purposes: one asked that the general public be allowed to use the cleansing baths in the high school; another asked that children be permitted to use classrooms as a place for quiet evening study. The meeting received front-page coverage in the city's newspapers, and at least one of them quoted the mayor as saying that public use of the baths was "reasonable" and he had "made a note of it."[44]

Fitzgerald's apparent openness to the idea of using school facilities for other than traditional school purposes probably was not a total surprise to Mary Follett. During the mayoral campaign, Fitzgerald had publicly pledged to "promote so far as the mayor has any power of influence to secure their adoption, and within the limits of financial practicability . . . the fullest and freest use, under proper restrictions, of our public school buildings and halls for social and neighborhood gatherings."[45] When the new mayor's remarks in East Boston suggested that he would live up to his campaign pledge, the advocates of extended use saw a splendid opportunity. The Executive Committee of the Home and School Association requested an allocation in the mayor's budget for the "furtherance and extension of this movement."[46]

During the winter of 1909–10, Follett felt remarkably well — better than at any time during the previous six years — and as a result was able to do more work. She and Isobel, moreover, were comfortably settled in a new home at Five Otis Place, a four-room, upper-floor apartment at the foot of Beacon Hill to which they had moved when Shaw sold the Marlborough Street residence in 1908. Their new neighborhood, affectionately recreated in Samuel Eliot Morison's *One Boy's Boston*, was home to several of Follett's colleagues and friends — Louis and Alice Brandeis lived across the courtyard at Six Otis Place and Elizabeth Glendower Evans at number Twelve.[47]

The bedrooms were tiny, but the other rooms in Mary and Isobel's apartment were quite spacious. The dining-room featured a "handsome" dining table and chairs and an open fireplace — the high mantel of which was dotted with Japanese and Chinese curios. In the living room, a few fine red mahogany pieces provided a pleasing contrast to the velvet and horsehair upholstery of the overstuffed couch and easy chairs. The curtains were kept partially drawn, but Mary and Isobel could still catch a glimpse of the Charles River from the large living room windows. The walls, covered in dark paper, were "hung close with paintings and photographs" — some of them reproductions of paintings by Jean François Millet owned by the Shaws. Other works of art also figured prominently in the decor, including a Perugini Madonna at one end of the living room and copies of Donatello's relief of St. John and Michelangelo's head of the slave, both of which Mary kept with her throughout her life.

This Victorian décor, dark and even oppressive by modern standards, was enlivened only by the bright living room rug and the green masses of Isobel's ivy plants, but Elizabeth Balch found the Otis Place living room one of the "most delightful" that she knew. "It was a room that you could settle down with and live in and there [Mary] and Miss Briggs worked and played and laughed and discussed and stimulated and criticised one another." They delighted in music, especially the Saturday evening symphony concerts, and took great pleasure in travel and art. Their greatest joy, however, was "the merry, often witty, always stimulating talk . . . sparkling, challenging, analytical, descriptive, it never flagged." The easy intimacy and candor between Follett and Briggs sometimes unnerved Balch: "There was nothing they did not discuss with amazing frankness, nothing they could not say to one another. They deliberately intended to stimulate or restrain one another in order to help self-discipline and to add to one another's stature and powers." She continued: "Often they slashed one another, sometimes they used battle axes rather than rapiers and gave and took hard blows and one was quite used to being called a silly ass or an awful liar. . . Sometimes Mary was almost too frank. Often when I came she would simply tell Isobel to go away and sit in her room as she wanted to talk to me alone and often demurring, but amused, Isobel would go to her tiny room, asking now and then if she might come back."

Isobel Briggs did "endless errands" for Follett, including "spending hours at the Athenaeum selecting books and carrying home armsful of 'light' as well as heavy reading, as Mary must have for every week-end three or four novels or detective stories." These errands, apparently willingly undertaken, no doubt gave meaning to Isobel's life during her postretirement years and provided her a means of expressing her devotion to Mary. Cooking and household duties took little of either woman's time; they shared a set of servants with Inez Gaugengigl, a well-known portrait painter who was also their landlord. Mary engaged and trained the servants, but Isobel set the standards of the household. She was said to be "horrified" whenever Mary, rather than a servant, went to the door; at their small dinner parties, the table was "beautifully appointed" and the service "rather formal." "No one who did not share it," Balch later wrote, "will know what Isobel's contribution was, her charm, her social gift, her sparkling flexible talk, her light hand, her entire subordination of herself to Mary's interests and work."[48]

Despite Briggs's continuous devotion to her welfare, Follett soon suffered another recurrence of her mysterious illness. Only a few weeks after her February 1910 meetings with the School Committee, Mary suddenly "went to pieces." Her symptoms were so trying that even a summertime retreat to Overhills failed to bring relief. The pain and swelling in Follett's right side persisted, as did her "bowel attacks." Once in July and again in September, their severity caused her to fall to the floor "in agony of pain." The "frightful constant" pressure in her head now was accompanied by intense, darting pains — a combination that sometimes drove her to doubt whether she could "get through" the day. Surely most alarming of all were Mary's sudden lapses of memory — episodes that first occurred during April and May; on one such occasion, it took her a full minute to recognize North Station, a major Boston landmark.[49]

These devastating symptoms almost certainly forced Follett to withdraw from an opportunity that had come her way in the autumn of 1909, when she was asked by the National Municipal League to be on a national committee to prepare a "Guide to the Teaching of Civics." Follett surely was disappointed, not so much because of the project itself (civic education was no longer the central focus of her work) but because this invitation symbolized for her how quickly one activity could lead to another. "One of the most hopeful signs we have in all work of this kind," Follett told her WML colleagues, "is the rapidity with which it multiplies itself, that by doing one thing you not only accomplish *that* thing, but prepare the way for many other useful activities."[50]

The weeks of continuing physical anguish made it virtually impossible for Follett to relax, and her suffering was compounded by what she described as a "summer full of complications" at work.[51] Boston's private donors were confused by the multiplicity of organizations campaigning for extended use and were increasingly uncertain about where best to direct their financial support.[52] Moreover, Follett's WML committee was having extraordinary difficulty finding the right director for its experimental project. The position had already been offered twice, both times to "excellent men," but in each case the candidate had been induced to remain in his existing position.[53]

In early October 1909, Follett left Overhills and returned to Boston. Trying to resume her work, she struggled to keep her many engagements, but her symptoms finally forced her to bed.[54] She fought back by consulting colleagues on the telephone, but even a simple phone call could become a frightening experience if a "blank" — one of her unnerving lapses of memory — suddenly descended on her. As the weeks wore on, Mary's problems were exacerbated by difficulties in sleeping. Persistent pains in her head and right side deprived her of badly needed rest, as did twitching leg muscles and a general aching in all her limbs, probably caused by dietary changes resulting in low potassium or calcium. Follett, who by now was quite desperate for relief, made an appointment to see Richard C. Cabot, the physician husband of her friend and colleague Ella Cabot.[55]

Within a few years Richard Cabot would be recognized as the preeminent cardiologist of his generation and would become chief of the medical staff at

Massachusetts General Hospital. But he also was recognized as a maverick and professional gadfly. In 1905, convinced that the Out-Patient Department at MGH was often ineffective because it had no way to see that prescribed treatments were actually carried out, Cabot organized the country's first Medical Social Service and utilized a small group of social workers for this purpose. Another of Cabot's campaigns aimed at improving the accuracy of medical diagnoses. In a paper read at the national meeting of the American Medical Association, Cabot reported patterns of "mistaken diagnoses" in 1,000 autopsies conducted at MGH. Such public revelations of the profession's "mistakes" were not much appreciated by his fellow physicians.[56]

Another form of Cabot's unrelenting criticism of the medical profession appeared in his analysis of "One Hundred Christian Science Cures" for *McClure's Magazine* in 1908. American medicine, Cabot told his readers, had much to learn from the Christian Scientists, who had long had success in treating functional illnesses. "Heretofore," Cabot wrote, the Christian Scientists "have held the field of psychotherapy largely without competition. American physicians have confined themselves mostly to physical and chemical methods (diet, drugs, and surgery), which have a place in the cure of functional disease, but not, I think, the chief place." Cabot was pleased that resistance was breaking down among his colleagues to treatments formerly the province of the mind curists — suggestion, work cure, encouragement. There can be little doubt that Cabot's openness to the validity of mind-cure techniques made it much easier for Mary Follett to reveal, midway through her first examination, that she "had been for years a New Thought person."[57] Follett would also have appreciated Cabot's willingness to give "a straight answer to a straight question." After dealing with this baffling illness for six frustrating years, she surely would have been full of questions about what the future held. Since Cabot's experience had taught him the value of being truthful with patients about their conditions, he almost certainly would have shared with Follett whatever he had learned about her case.[58]

Follett's medical history, recorded by Cabot during her first visit in October 1910, is unusually detailed for the period and supplies much of what is known about her early symptoms.[59] Cabot relied on manual palpation of Follett's organs for his diagnosis; he was enormously skilled in this method, and his book on physical diagnosis, "used the world over as a textbook," appeared in twelve editions from 1901 to 1938.[60] As a result of his examination, Cabot concluded that Follett's pelvis was "o.k.," but he found a "smooth rounded non-tender mass" in the region of her gall bladder that was "not replaceable under [her] ribs." During a second examination five weeks later, Cabot easily located this same mass, which he now called a "tumor," extending below the right rib cage.[61] The tumor's free respiratory mobility seemed to preclude an advanced-stage malignancy, because a mass of this type would have become fixed as it invaded surrounding tissues. Instead, it was likely that one of the three organs in the area — the kidney, gall bladder, or liver — was enlarged.

The "smooth, rounded" nature of the mass was more characteristic of the kidney or gall bladder than the liver, an organ having more of an "edge." Still, one explanation of Follett's symptoms considered by Cabot was "Riedel's lobe," a nonpathological but anatomically anomalous tongue of tissue protruding from the lower edge of the right lobe of the liver. The second organ in this region, the kidney, was not included in Cabot's list of possible causes of Follett's symptoms, but gall bladder dysfunction was.[62] Retention of bile due to the presence of a stone in the duct at the neck of the gall bladder would have enlarged the organ, making it palpable in the general area of Follett's "tumor." The fever, gastric distress, and acute abdominal pain under the right ribs that Follett had been experiencing could have developed as a result of repeated biliary obstructions.[63]

Cabot's third possible explanation of Follett's symptoms was "psycho-neurosis" — a term used in the late nineteenth century to refer "to people who exhibited some psychological disorder but who were not grossly *psychotic,* that is, out of touch with reality."[64] In the first decades of the twentieth century, the colon seemed to be the "body's major battleground for psychic conflict," Edward Shorter writes in *Bedside Manners.* In this era "struggles waged in the unconscious would find expression more surely in abdominal pain, constipation, and diarrhea than in any other physical manner." Generalized symptoms such as these were terribly difficult to treat and were thus a source of enormous frustration to physicians. Cabot probably found the "awful trio" of functional disturbances ascribed to nervous patients — "dyspepsia, constipation, and insomnia" — a reasonable approximation of Mary Follett's symptoms, because in addition to her other complaints, she was feeling "very sleepy all the time" and finding it "hard to quit her working life at night."[65]

Cabot discussed the problems of treating the generic "nervous patient" in a 1906 lecture to the Colorado Medical Society. All too often, Cabot told his colleagues, advice to "nervous" patients ran to "negatives, to prohibitions, and exclusions." The patient was told to "do less; don't work; don't worry; live like a vegetable; empty your mind of its troubles; be calm and quiet." Cabot found these "rest cures," made popular by S. Weir Mitchell and others, exactly the opposite of what most patients needed. Cabot's continuing interest in this subject is reflected in his 1908 book, *Psychotherapy and Its Relation to Religion.* There he wrote that "one half of all the nervous people who come to me are suffering for the want of an outlet, suffering for the lack of some way in which they can put forth their whole power." Rather than urging rest for such a patient, Cabot sought instead to " 'speed her up,' teach the patient to live harder, faster, more intensely, or with some better reason for his activities." Cabot's use of the female as well as the male pronoun to refer to these patients was no accident; his experience had shown that more than half of the ordinary physician's practice consisted of women's nervous disorders.[66]

The "work cure" that Cabot thought might help these women involved neither "drudgery" nor merely keeping busy. In his view, only a genuine vocation had the power to give a woman confidence that she "amounts to something" and a sense that she was "accumulating week by week and month by month something worth while." Cabot, furthermore, was not one who wished to relegate women to unpaid service. Perhaps the experience of having been born to great wealth had taught him about the significance of being paid for one's labors. "After all," Cabot wrote in *Psychotherapy and Its Relation to Religion,* "is there anything in the world that encourages us more than that, — to know that we are really worth while and that some one cares enough to pay something in cold cash because we are on the earth? I do not care how spiritual a person is, I believe he is affected by that consideration, and ought to be affected by it. We have no other equally sure and effective way of finding out that we are needed, and there is no other such stimulant as the thought that somebody else needs us."[67]

Though appreciative of the new European psychotherapies, especially Paul DuBois's *Psychic Treatment of Nervous Disorders* (1905), Cabot based his treatment plan for Follett on his own "work cure."[68] But working would require that Follett rise above the pain, the uncertainty, and the periodic despair engendered by her illness.[69] Pain "must be dealt with largely by physical methods and by the physician," Richard Cabot wrote in 1908, "but *what the man thinks of it,* that goes down deep into his character, involves the whole mental life, his whole point of view, his religion . . . Many a nervous sufferer quavers out in one phrase or another the old lament: 'Why does this trouble come to *me?*' Now, this means: — 'Why do all the forces in the universe conspire to shoot down upon my defenceless head this arrow of misery?' I think it does good to remind such a sufferer that the universe is too busy with other things to bother with any such conspiracy. The world is not a conspiracy against him; it is a conspiracy *for* him, and he will get and give his best only when he works with the spirit of this world, with the spirit of God."[70]

As Cabot saw it, a nervous patient's successful recovery depended largely on that individual's spiritual values and moral character. Mary Follett would have shared this conviction. All her life she had felt driven to do better, to achieve, to prove herself worthy. If a physician whom she trusted told her that her recovery depended on her capacity to suffer nobly and on her determination to be well — in other words, on her moral fiber — she surely would have accepted that challenge. The trials of Mary's childhood, ironically, had prepared her well for this ordeal, and in addition she could count on Isobel's love and care; but still, the mysterious nature of her illness made it a dreadful, lonely burden to bear.

Follett received little or no comfort from her original family — indeed, she most likely kept any news of her illness from them. She visited her mother and brother in Quincy only two or three times a year and avoided all holiday occasions. At this stage of her life, only her young nephew, George Jr., seemed to spark her affection. She presented him at age six or seven with a five-volume set of Kipling bound in red leather and a picture of his namesake, St. George, slaying the dragon. And she delighted him, a few years later, when she asked him to join her in games of cards and cribbage — amusements that other family members thought "terrible." Despite these acts of kindness, Mary remained a rather awesome figure, not the sort a young boy would choose as a confidante, and George Jr. was acutely aware of the lack of real fondness between his aunt and her mother and brother. "It was a duty call when she came out," he later recalled, "it was as if she was someone else's family."[71]

In early November 1910, three weeks after she first consulted Richard Cabot, Follett's health had improved enough that she was able to leave her bed and resume a fairly normal public life. She surfaced first at the School Committee, where she met with the secretary about the practice of charging neighborhood organizations for the use of school property. Concerned that the cost was more than many organizations could afford, Follett hoped that the fees could be rescinded; but after learning that the committee had instituted fees as a way to avoid subsidizing organizations that could afford to pay rent elsewhere, Follett revised her position. Adopting what she would later term an *integrative* conflict resolution strategy, Follett crafted a carefully worded proposal in which "all would be benefitted."[72] A fee would be charged in every case of extended use, but it would not exceed the low rate set for evening school use in those cases "when a school house is used regularly throughout the winter for a certain number of evenings a week, and by people who have the same ends in view as the School Board, that is, the training of young people to fit their social, industrial and civic environment." "We make this request," Follett told the board, "feeling that the School Board can legitimately discriminate between a miscellaneous or sporadic use of school buildings desired chiefly probably to save rent, and a use which might be considered as part of the school system, or rather of an extended school system." She and her colleagues, Follett assured the board, sought uses that would serve educational ends. The details took several months to work out, but the schedule of charges was eventually revised along the lines that Follett had suggested.[73]

Follett's return to work surely buoyed her spirits, but she felt even better when her WML committee finally hired a suitable director for their "object lesson." Ralph E. Hawley, principal of a Michigan grammar school and a graduate of the University of Michigan, had spent the previous summer in Boston, working as a boys' club leader for the Charlestown Episcopal City Mission. "The reputation of these boys for rough conduct and language," Ella Cabot reported, "was such that they were not allowed in any private building. Mr. Hawley organized them into a club on the very curbstone, found a free lot where a house had burned down, started gardening and hammock making, and won the loyalty of every boy." Hawley could not come to Boston immediately because he was obliged to finish the Michigan school year. Nevertheless, he agreed to a three-week visit in February in order to "study the situation in New York, learn to know Boston conditions and possibilities intimately, choose the best available school district and study methods of vocational counselling."[74]

The decision to investigate methods of vocational counseling was undoubtedly Mary Follett's, for she had recently concluded that "the best use of the school buildings during the evening hours is for vocational advice." As a step toward this end, Mary had secured a place both on the Executive Board of the new Vocation Bureau and on its Administrative Committee, a group that met "once a week to work out the practical plans for vocational direction."[75] The Vocation Bureau was yet another of the many worthwhile projects funded by Pauline Agassiz Shaw. Originally proposed in the fall of 1907 by Frank Parsons, an organizer of educational programs for wage-earning men and women at Shaw's Civic Service House, the Vocation Bureau was based on the idea that young men and women needed systematic guidance in the choice of a career as well as vocational instruction. The work had barely begun when Parsons died, creating a several-month hiatus, but the pace picked up dramatically when Stratton D. Brooks, superintendent of the Boston public schools, made an intriguing proposal. Brooks saw benefits to be gained from linking a scheme of vocational guidance with the school system's proliferating vocational education programs and asked the bureau's help in "organizing [vocational] counselling work in the Boston schools." He was particularly hopeful that they might "assist in selecting those pupils who should enter highly specialized courses in industry and commerce in the secondary schools of Boston."[76] The bureau submitted a plan, accepted by the School Committee in June 1909, in which it "proposed the appointment of a committee of six masters and submasters as a 'vocational direction committee,' the appointment of a number of counselors in the schools, and the training of these counselors by meetings to be held under the auspices of the Vocation Bureau."[77]

Realizing that the effective administration of this plan would require an experienced director, the executive board persuaded Meyer Bloomfield, director of Civic Service House and one of Follett's colleagues in the Boston Equal Suffrage Association for Good Government, to accept the appointment.[78] Within a few months Bloomfield was joined by another man with whom Follett was well acquainted, Frederick J. Allen, the secretary of the City History Club. Soon thereafter, probably at Follett's instigation, the board committed the Vocation Bureau to a set of goals that went beyond merely providing vocational advice. Follett, it seems, had had an opportunity to investigate other vocational programs on visits to Edinburgh and London and, as a result, had become convinced that vocational advice was best offered in combination with "placement" and "after-care." Boston could have such a program, Follett argued, if schools, private employers, and city officials would pool and coordinate their efforts in a central bureau.[79]

Funding, as usual, promised to be the most serious problem. The School Committee had implemented the vocational counseling program by appointing 117 vocational counselors, one for each elementary and secondary school in Boston, but the appointments were not accompanied by appropriate financial support. The committee had provided only a pittance for printed materials, training, and conferences and refused either to release the counselors from other duties or to give them additional compensation. Despite this meager show of support, Follett was sufficiently impressed with the bureau's potential that in May 1910 she reportedly told a donor that she was "working with the Vocation Bureau to establish several social centres in as many school houses."[80]

The notion that neighborhood social centers might profitably be married to a program of vocational counseling and placement was inspired by Follett's experiences in Ward 17. It was there that she had seen how ward bosses acquired and maintained political power by satisfying their constituents' needs for jobs.[81] "Urban political machines," writes Alexander Keyssar, author of a fascinating historical study of unemployment in Massachusetts, "emerged and flourished in a world where jobs were scarce and where the threat of layoffs was omnipresent. The strength of those machines was part of the price that respectable Massachusetts had to pay for ignoring the problem of unemployment." Even after the depression of the 1890s made it clear that "honest, industrious workers were sometimes jobless through no fault of their own" and should not be blamed for unemployment, neither public officials nor private agencies did much to help. As late as 1906, job-seekers who wished to avoid being beholden to ward politicians or being exploited by unscrupulous employment agents had only one place to turn: the state-run Free Employment Offices established by the Bureau of Statistics of Labor. Surveying this bleak landscape, Keyssar concludes that the perpetual unemployment of hundreds of thousands of workers remained "one of the best-kept secrets in Massachusetts." Mary Follett, however, not only understood important dimensions of the unemployment problem, but also had a vision of how a citywide vocational guidance and placement system might be integrated with neighborhood social centers to liberate grassroots political life.[82]

The enthusiasm with which Follett approached the idea of affiliating with the Vocation Bureau was not shared by Fannie Fern Andrews, the head of the Home and School Association. Andrews had assumed that her local parents' associations would be the centerpiece of any scheme for neighborhood social centers and was not placated by Meyer Bloomfield's reassurances that "nothing definite was decided on." Convinced that it was time to solidify the Home and School Association's place in the movement, Andrews pressed hard throughout the spring of 1910 for her Extended Use Committee to prepare a citywide plan for the use of school buildings.[83]

The plan, which was drafted by Andrews and De Bruyn and revised in committee, called for seven types of activities: parents' association meetings, vocational activities, junior civic clubs or city councils, classes for mothers in child care and homemaking, popular lectures, evenings with pictures, and music. As there was widespread disagreement about whether the School Committee had the authority to allow noneducational endeavors in the schools, the plan excluded all recreational activities in favor of those that were clearly educational. "Evenings with pictures," for example, would present stereopticon exhibits of pictures from the Museum of Fine Arts rather than popular films. The number of activities included in this citywide plan was deliberately kept small out of a conviction that each neighborhood would have to meet its distinctive needs in its own way. Neighborhoods could best formulate these blueprints for extended use, Andrews argued, if they made use of the twenty-nine local parents' associations, groups of "citizens, already organized, whose main interest is the welfare of its own community, and whose efforts are already pointed in this direction." But despite Andrews' clearly stated preferences, the Advisory Committee left considerable ambiguity about the association's role; parents' associations would provide a valuable "nucleus of organization" in the preparation of local plans, but the ideas generated there still would have to be integrated, in some unspecified way, with those of other individuals and groups.

On purely administrative matters, the plan was exceptionally detailed. It indicated which of the five participating organizations — the Women's Municipal League, the Home and School Association, the Vocation Bureau, Boston-1915, or the City History Club — would be responsible for the initiation, supervision, and expense involved in each type of activity. Public funds were requested only for mothers' classes, which seemed "so apparently a part of the hygiene department of the school system" and therefore were in need of "official sanction." Most of the remaining expenses would be assumed by the Home and School Association and paid through a combination of philanthropy and neighborhood fees. The decision to rely on at least some neighborhood funding was in keeping with the Follett's philosophy that social center work "should be carried on, as far as possible, by the people themselves"; but getting the plan off the ground would require a sizable infusion of private funds.[84] Hoping to generate interest in the plan among donors, Andrews wrote an article in the July issue of *New Boston* claiming that the plan had been "accepted" by the School Committee. This was something of an overstatement of the official record, which reported that the committee "approves in general of the proposition" but declined, "owing to present financial limitations . . . to assume any liability for any expense involved in putting the plan into effect unless it shall have taken definite and favorable action in each specific item."[85]

Mary Follett was nominally one of the people who proposed this funding plan to the School Committee, but her part in the process had surely been limited by poor health.[86] In November 1910, after having been ill for much of the year, Follett finally felt well enough to respond to a request from Edith M. Howes for help in running a club for South Boston working girls founded by the Massachusetts Association of Women Workers. Follett's WML committee, which now included a settlement house director, eagerly accepted the challenge. Not only did it enable them "to help a little in the solution of some of the problems of that most difficult period of youth, the years from fifteen to twenty-one"; it also was "in line with what we hope to do ourselves more extensively next year."[87] After several months with the South Boston project, Follett told colleagues that "nothing could show us more clearly than this actual group of girls, the need of such work as we are planning in our Social Centre. These girls . . . have many needs and few opportunities. They need recreation and companionship, they need friends who will advise them in their lives. The strain of their days and the difficulties they encounter combine with the general lack of interest in their lives to make it really imperative that some definite provision should be made for their leisure time: for recreation, for instruction, and for fitting them to be useful members of the community."[88]

Despite the demonstrable value of clubs such as the one in South Boston, school committees throughout eastern Massachusetts were demonstrating reluctance to open their buildings until the state had resolved all doubts about whether local school committees had the authority to allow recreational uses of school facilities. To correct this problem, extended-use advocates prepared enabling legislation and had the petition filed by a resident of Cambridge, perhaps to discourage the perception that extended use was just "a Boston issue." Large numbers of extended-use supporters appeared at the March 7 legislative hearing and argued vigorously that such work was already being conducted in other parts of the country with great success. The legislators apparently found this argument persuasive. Six weeks later, a bill was enacted that allowed the school committee of any city or town to "grant the temporary use of halls in school buildings upon such terms and conditions and for such public or educational purposes, for which no admission fee is charged as the said school committee may deem wise." In a city such as Boston, the act would take effect upon its acceptance by a two-thirds vote of the City Council and the approval of the mayor. Mary Follett's name does not appear either in the public records concerning this legislation or in the brief news accounts of the hearing, but one of her contemporaries identified her as the person "responsible for the legislation . . . which made it permissible to open school buildings for the leisure time use of adults."[89]

Even while this legislation was still in committee, the Advisory Committee on the Further Use of School Buildings was busy on another front—assessing "the advisability of asking a municipal appropriation for this purpose."[90] As a part of this effort, numerous organizations were contacted, and many responded with support, including the new Boston Chamber of Commerce, the neighborhood-based United Improvement Associations, the Central Labor Union, and the Boston Social Union, a recently organized federation of settlements.[91] But the four organizations "working at this problem in the closest alliance" were the Women's Municipal League, the Home and School Association, the Vocation Bureau, and one other—Boston-1915.[92]

The Boston-1915 movement, a colossal scheme of civic cooperation, was launched by Edward A. Filene squarely in the midst of the public debate over the proposed new Boston charter. What made Boston-1915 different from other "megaorganizations" was its scale and its objectives. The founders proposed in six years to transform their city into an urban paradise of the kind no one had dared to dream since the "White City" of Chicago's 1893 Columbian Exposition—and would do so by coordinating the work of all social, religious, educational, economic, and political entities in the city.[93] In reality, Boston-1915 accomplished no more than a minute fraction of what it had set out to do and went out of business in less than two years, in December 1911.[94]

Fortunately, in 1910 when Mary Follett was looking for extended use allies, Boston-1915 was at the high point of its influence. In addition to being personally acquainted with some of the leaders of Boston-1915 (Brandeis, Storrow, Cabot, Munroe, and Robert A. Woods), Follett found herself connected to this movement in another way.[95] Of the sixteen planks in Boston-1915's original program, several in some way supported the concept of an extended use of the public schools.[96] From the spring of 1910 to the fall of 1911, Follett built a sufficiently close affiliation with the Boston-1915 movement that she was able to make effective use of the directors' access to public officials and other interested civic groups. But she did this without harboring any illusions about Boston's having magically entered a new era of cooperation. A pragmatist with ideals, Follett would later write in *The New State* that "it is a mistake to think that such abstractions as unity, brotherhood etc. are as self-evident to our wills as to our intellect."

> I learn my duty to my friends not by reading essays on friendship, but by living my life with my friends and learning by experience the obligations friendship demands. Just so must I learn my relation to society by coming into contact with a wide range of experiences, of people, by cultivating and deepening my sympathy and whole understanding of life . . . We talk of fellowship; we puny separatists bristling with a thousand unharmonized traits, with our assertive particularist consciousness, think that all we have to do is to *decide* on fellowship as a delightful idea. But fellowship will be the slowest thing on earth to create. An eager longing for it may help, but it can come into being as a genuine part of our life only through a deep understanding of what it really means.[97]

The momentum that was building around the cause of extended use received yet another boost on March 6, 1911, when the directors of Boston-1915 announced their program for the coming year. The eleven program objectives, heralded on the front page of almost every Boston newspaper, included one of special concern to extended-use advocates, namely, Boston-1915's commitment to "organizing a larger use of school houses."[98] Taking advantage of the favorable publicity, James P. Munroe, who had recently been named Boston-1915's executive director, wrote to Mayor Fitzgerald and solicited his support for a municipal appropriation for extended use. As of this moment, the campaign to establish social centers in Boston's neighborhood schools was fully under way.[99]

13

"My Beloved Centres"

Mary Follett's contemporaries saw her as both "the leading spirit" and the primary architect of the Boston school centers movement. At a 1937 occasion celebrating the centers' twenty-fifth anniversary, the first citywide director acknowledged that it was to Mary Follett "more than to any other individual or group of individuals [that] we owe the School Centers of Boston."[1]

The exceedingly convoluted path that Mary Follett had to travel in her quest for public financial support for school centers, described in detail in this chapter, should dispel any notion that Follett was naive about the difficulties involved in creating "integrative" forms of conflict resolution or that she was inexperienced with respect to matters of power and control. Later in her career, Follett took considerable pride in the "reciprocal relatings" of her experience and theory development and was impatient with suggestions that she was an "armchair philosopher." "I think what I rather object to is this," Follett told a young questioner during a 1927 Harvard graduate seminar on the fundamental principles of the social sciences, "that I have not sat and read books on philosophy and decided that the deepest fundamental principles of the universe were three." On the contrary, "I have simply for about 25 years been watching boards and groups and have decided from that watching on these principles of interacting, unifying and emerging. And it seems to me that you are supposing that I began the other way around. In my experience that is what happens when you have fruitful results. I am giving my experience. I am not giving philosophy out of a book."[2]

From the beginning, the campaign to acquire public funding for Boston school centers was enmeshed in a complex of relations involving the mayor, City Council, Finance Commission, and School Committee. Since women had little credibility with public officials and were expected to keep a low public profile, Follett would have to rely often on sympathetic male colleagues to represent her concerns.[3] Although her activities were usually confined to the less visible or less newsworthy aspects of the campaign for public funding, any resentment that Follett might have felt was largely assuaged by her rich appreciation of behind-the-scenes work. Her consideration of the "brilliant and creative leadership" of Henry Clay as Speaker of the House of Representatives had convinced her that bold policy initiatives are best undertaken in an atmosphere of fairness, nonpartisanship, and personal consideration for others — a spirit that her less public contributions might help to create; and her intimate association with the collaborative ventures of Pauline Agassiz Shaw had shown her how much could be accomplished by choosing good people and then providing them a sense of direction, sympathetic understanding, and emotional support. Follett also relished the planning and coordination of a collaborative endeavor — something she may have witnessed in Albert Bushnell Hart's editorship of several complex publishing ventures. "It really is great fun," Hart wrote of his editorial experiences, "to drive a hundred horse team."[4]

Much of the difficulty that Follett and her colleagues would encounter in acquiring public funding for social centers derived from the troubled relations among Boston's elected officials. Fitzgerald's victory put the newly strengthened mayor's office in the hands of the city's Irish Democratic majority, but "efficiency-style reformers" controlled both the City Council and the School Committee and dominated the independent Finance Commission.[5] Despite their internecine struggles, by April 1911 the mayor, Finance Commission, and School Committee each had gone on record as favoring the idea of expending public funds for extended use. Unfortunately, no funds had actually been committed. The mayor was still hoping that the School Committee could be pressured into accepting financial responsibility for extended use, since that would validate his charge of "fat" in the school department's budget. The School Committee had so far doggedly resisted the mayor's pressure; however, if this stalemate continued, it risked either losing a part of the school department's operations or damaging its relations with center advocates, many of whom had been longtime supporters of the "reform" school board.

A new round of activity on behalf of extended use was initiated in May when the Education Conference of Boston-1915 reminded first the mayor and then the School Committee that a number of organizations, including the Chamber of Commerce, the Central Labor Union, and the United Improvement Association, were giving active support to the extended-use plan.[6] The committee, however, refused to provide funds, "especially at this time, when there are so many imperative demands for larger expenditures for strictly school purposes."[7]

The School Committee, Follett remarked with growing dismay, seemed to consider extended use as somehow outside *regular* school purposes and not really part of its educational responsibilities. Follett acknowledged that some of the difficulty that her WML committee was having in obtaining funds from the School Committee was her group's own fault, because the WML had placed too great an emphasis on *efficiency* in the use of buildings. "I have no interest in the extended use of school buildings *in itself*," Follett said in a 1912 speech. "I stand for a great unmet need in our community, and I believe we can meet that need with our schoolhouses . . . I am pleading for an extension of our educational system, rather than for the extended use of school buildings."[8]

Follett's view of the matter, however, did not prevail with the School Committee, and extended-use advocates were again forced to turn to the mayor for help in securing an appropriation from other municipal accounts.[9] They were gratified when Fitzgerald finally recommended that the City Council pass an order providing $13,000 from the reserve fund to be expended (half for supervision, half for heat, light, and janitorial costs) under the direction of the superintendent of public buildings.[10] By involving the public buildings department in school business, Fitzgerald made no secret of his displeasure with the School Committee.[11]

Mary Follett would have had every reason to feel hopeful about the outcome, given that the mayor's recommendation reportedly was favored by a majority of the City Council. Yet immediately after Fitzgerald temporarily left the country with a Chamber of Commerce group, a series of problems began to appear. First, the appropriation order was laid over as a result of the intervention of Thomas Buckley, one of three "Fitzgerald men" on the council, who in a surprise move argued that "such use of school buildings should not be limited to the women's home and school association, the Boston-1915 movement and the improvement associations . . . [but] should be open to all gatherings of a public nature."[12] Buckley's objection naturally worried Follett, and she took the matter up at some length in a speech to the Playground and Recreation Association.[13] Such "miscellaneous use," Follett told her audience, would be inefficient: there would be only an occasional use of the schoolhouses; the committee would be subsidizing organizations that could afford to pay for halls elsewhere; and it would be impossible "to get a satisfactory guarantee for the proper use of the buildings." Furthermore, such a system would exclude "the very people who need such places and opportunities most, those, namely, who have not sufficient initiative and knowledge of the world to organize clubs and get guarantees for the proper use of property." Follett did not consider "an isolated and occasional use entirely out of the question" but felt "strongly that such miscellaneous and occasional use should not be allowed *to stand in the way* of a much needed regular use."

The form of "regular use" that Follett had in mind was the establishment of new clubs *"in* the schoolhouses." She observed: "We know the evils existing in certain self-formed clubs in many neighborhoods; they are often tools of the political machine; their existence is frequently a menace to the morals of the girls in that neighborhood; or at best they are often mere lounging places, forces for disintegration rather than for helpful up-building . . . There is a greater chance of having clubs which shall upbuild if they are organized *in* the school buildings than if they come in from the outside, for the very atmosphere of the schoolhouse suggests decent behavior, some sort of *motive,* and some connection with the rest of municipal life. Moreover, under our plan, the city, while encouraging all clubs to be as independent and self-governing as practicable, would offer some form of leadership." Follett also worried that clubs coming into the schools under the "miscellaneous and occasional use" being promoted by Councilman Buckley would be exclusive to particular ethnic groups. What she wanted, instead, were "clubs of Americans, no matter where they were born, learning the American language and customs and ideals, and helping to form an American nation."[14]

Even before the issue of "miscellaneous use" was resolved, other complications arose. Corporation Counsel Thomas M. Babson rendered an opinion that the City Council could not appropriate money "for the purposes intended," and the appropriation order was tabled on June 28.[15] In September the municipal funding campaign began again when reform councilman Daniel J. McDonald introduced an order designed to authorize the School Committee, in accordance with chapter 367 of the Acts of 1911, to open school buildings "for other than school purposes."[16]

In early October, while the City Council's order was still pending, the Finance Commission recommended that "the existing policy of permitting the use of school buildings for other than school purposes be extended as funds become available" and that, "if necessary, the Legislature be asked to grant a larger appropriation for school purposes." This larger school appropriation could be made "without materially raising the tax rate," the commission argued, if the mayor would follow its recommendations and reduce political patronage and waste in other municipal departments.[17]

Mayor Fitzgerald angrily responded to the Finance Commission's report with a proposition that further threatened the School Committee's turf. Asserting that the commission's report "contains only a passing allusion to the subject" of who should pay for the extended use of schools, Fitzgerald proposed that the City Council create a "Department for Extending the Use of School Buildings Within the City of Boston." "This action," Fitzgerald asserted, obliquely referring to the School Committee, "will at least focus attention upon a problem which seems to be ignored by those whose proper function, in my opinion, it is to arrange such matters." The new Extended Use Department would be comprised of three nonsalaried mayoral appointees, at least one of whom would be a woman. It would have the "power to negotiate with the School Committee a lease or leases of school buildings during school vacations and for such days and parts of days as the public schools are not in session, and . . . to issue permits for the use of such leased school buildings for meetings of the people for general education, recreational and public purposes." Events scheduled in this manner would be directed and supervised by the new department and would be "subject to such regulations as it may make to govern the same." Finally, the department would have the authority to expend "whatever sums of money may be appropriated in any one year" and would be accountable for these expenditures to the City Council. The appropriation for this first year of activity would be $13,000, a sum that would be transferred from the reserve fund.[18]

At first it seemed highly likely that the mayor's proposal would be approved by the City Council. The proposition had the endorsement of the state commissioner of education, the Chamber of Commerce, the Women's Municipal League, and numerous other individuals and organizations. Furthermore, the movement was receiving favorable coverage in the press, a development facilitated by the addition to Follett's WML committee of Livy S. Richard, the respected former editor of the Rochester (N.Y.) *Times* and a veteran of the social centers movement.[19]

The most extensive and favorable coverage of the extended-use movement appeared in the *Christian Science Monitor,* the newest of Boston's newspapers. Founded in 1908 to "counteract the sensationalism rampant in the press at that time," the *Monitor* heartily endorsed Mayor Fitzgerald's proposal for a new city Department of Extended Use and argued that it "deserves the aid of all citizens of intelligence and ordinary prudence." The great virtue in the proposal, according to the *Monitor,* was that the new department's leasing authority would provide the mechanism by which private funds could be expended to support extended use until such time as "public opinion supports taxation for such use." The *Monitor* reminded its readers that "both the kindergarten and manual training first found their way into Boston's scheme of education by a woman's generous aid in proving that each new feature was needed," and contended that "it is by this combined action of individuals and communities that America, without the centralized imposition of methods as in Germany, keeps well to the front in educational reform."[20]

Fitzgerald's proposal was vigorously opposed by the Finance Commission, especially since it would result in a divided jurisdiction for the schools. Instead, the commission wanted the mayor to petition the incoming legislature for an act authorizing "the School Committee to appropriate [a sum] not exceeding two cents upon each $1,000 of the valuation on which school appropriations are based . . . to be used for the extended use of school buildings under rules and regulations established by the School Committee."[21] Boston-1915's Education Conference finally endorsed the recommendation of the Finance Commission, confident that legislation could "doubtless be secured within a few months" that would put "the whole matter on a firm legal basis."[22]

As this second episode in the quest for public funding for social centers drew to a close, public opinion was divided over which city officials deserved commendation. The *Christian Science Monitor* applauded the Finance Commission's "practical recommendations to the mayor by which legal obstacles now in the way can be overcome" and implicitly agreed that authority for extended-use activities should be lodged in the School Committee rather than being divided. But Mary Caroline Crawford, then the executive secretary of the Ford Hall Forum, a respected public lecture society, was not nearly so sanguine about giving entire responsibility for extended use to the School Committee. She had seen enough, she complained, of committee members who said "that nothing can be done because no money is at hand for the work" and had began wondering "if all the *backing and filling about the money* were only a device to conceal from us the Board's lazy evasion of its clear duty in the matter of working out a *plan*."[23]

The School Committee had been so reluctant to expend existing funds on extended use that Crawford thought it "almost by inadvertence" that these particular men were "acting as godfathers" to the city's first social center. This center, which had opened without fanfare six weeks earlier, in October 1911, was the product of a process initiated almost two years earlier by Mary Follett. Realizing this, Crawford publicly assigned the credit for opening the new center not to the recalcitrant School Committee, but "chiefly to Miss Mary P. Follett."[24]

The decision to put the first social center in East Boston, a large harbor island immediately northeast of downtown Boston, was made in the spring of 1911, after Ralph Hawley, the man whom the WML had hired to direct its first "object lesson," had carefully studied possible sites in South Boston, Charlestown, and East Boston. Although the site was somewhat isolated from the mainland and reachable from Boston proper only by ferry or the East Boston subway tunnel, it had certain advantages that were neatly summarized by Ella Cabot: "East Boston has a mixed population, including Jews and Italians as well as Irish. The school is very central, instead of on the extreme edge of the population, as in South Boston. The day and evening school-masters are heartily in sympathy with the plan, and [Superintendent] Stratton Brooks strongly recommends East Boston as a field needing just what the Recreation Centre can give."[25] The opening of the center was not announced through existing community organizations; instead, invitations were delivered directly to East Boston residents as they came through the ferry exits on their way home from work. The invitations were in the form of 6,000 flyers announcing that "free opportunity clubs for young men and young women" were being formed at East Boston High School. All young people "over 14, and not in day school" were invited to appear on October 26 to register for a variety of clubs.[26] Nearly 140 boys and girls decided to take advantage of this new opportunity.

Convinced that center advocates must be "neither hasty nor careless in our advocacy of the extended use of school buildings," Mary Follett was determined first "to find the true principles upon which such an extended use should rest, and then . . . use every effort of which we are capable to secure a public acceptance of these principles."[27] Following her own advice, Follett had designed the East Boston center around the answer to one central question: "What do these boys and girls need most in their preparation for life?" Her answer — rooted in Idealism, but far more heavily influenced by her experience — was that these youngsters needed "a social training for a life which is one of relationships. In the factory, in the office, everywhere, this relational, this social activity is to a greater or less extent the basis of all work. Each worker does only a part of some greater whole whose success depends largely on subordination of the parts to the entire scheme. For example, in a shoe factory each worker carries the shoe one stage nearer completion, but his work is of value only when it is done in such a way that it is ready to be carried forward by the next worker beyond, and on a plan already formulated by the head-worker."[28]

It seemed to Follett that more such "social training" was needed, especially for those who left school at age fourteen. Toward this end, Mary chose as the central object of her evening center work "the teaching of this lesson of co-operative helpfulness: that all our work in life is interdependent, and that in the factory, in business, in political and in social life, all our success is measured by our ability to subordinate ourselves, and yet to play a strong part in some larger whole whose success is dependent on the fact that all work together for a common end."

Some social center advocates were content merely with giving people a chance to become better acquainted with their neighbors, but Follett had more complex goals. In her experiments in Roxbury and South Boston, she had seen how she could increase the interest of participants and give each person "a sense of his individual responsibility and of the solidarity that must underlie all effective activity" by engaging them in activities "which required pulling together." She had also seen how the club as an organization, with its constitution, officers, and weekly business meetings, provided a fertile training ground for "group life." By joining these two elements — group activities and self-governance — in the design for the East Boston Opportunity Clubs, she would be giving the young men and women of East Boston a chance to learn more than "the mere part in some play, or the added skill on some musical instrument." They would learn what Follett then thought of as the central lesson of life — that "social power is increased in proportion as the individual sinks himself in the body he serves."[29]

Follett knew from her previous experience that clubs of the sort she envisioned would require unusually skillful leadership; each club leader would have to act not as a teacher but "as far as possible to assert his leadership by the force of his own personality, as a member of the group." Follett and her coworkers therefore exercised great care in their choice of club leaders, attending to what one observer called "inspiring personal qualities no less than to teaching ability." In return, all club leaders were paid, "thus differentiating their service sharply," Mary Caroline Crawford thought, "from the more or less casual leadership offered in many settlement houses by volunteer workers." Follett's committee retained one valuable element of the traditional social settlement leadership model when they stipulated that the director and his wife should live in East Boston. This residential arrangement worked so well that at the end of the center's inaugural year, Follett gratefully attributed "much of the success of our Centre . . . to the enthusiasm of our Director and his wife, to their untiring devotion, and to their zealous identification with the interests and needs of the young people of East Boston."[30]

Having found that clubs could "hold our young people, give them an *esprit de corps*, a greater interest, and a greater individual responsibility," Follett tried to carry her commitment to self-governing groups one step farther by having each club send its president and one elected delegate to a central governing body.[31] "It is our aim," Follett wrote, "that this Committee shall make all our members feel that they belong to something larger than a Glee Club or a

Gymnastic or Dramatic Club, or whatever their particular interest may be, shall make them feel that they are a part of a living and radiating centre of municipal activity, and that *they* are responsible for its success and for its accomplishment of the aims it has set before itself, aims which they *approve* merely at present, but which in the future we expect they will help to formulate, initiate and execute." Follett hoped that "some day this body will be sufficiently trained to take practical control of the Centre." Having learned "how to work for larger things than their own self-development," they would eventually be "helped to any social or civic work for their community for which they show willingness and aptitude."[32]

Follett's design for the East Boston center relied heavily on the results of her earlier experiments in Roxbury and South Boston, but she also investigated other cities' experiences with extended use. By the end of the century's first decade, many cities had opened their public school buildings for public lectures and certain forms of recreation, but "the first impetus to the school centre movement in the United States" came from the work of Edward J. Ward in Rochester. Ward, a Social Gospel minister who as a young man had left the clergy and joined the Socialist party, was deeply committed to public service. He was blessed with a sympathetic school board, one that "understood its position as a servant of the people," but it was Ward's vision — what one person called his "sublime audacity" — that was the telling factor in the 1907 decision of Rochester's city officials to open the schoolhouse doors to the public. In preparation for his experiment, Ward studied other publicly funded social centers, particularly those in Chicago and New York. Although the Chicago system did not involve the extended use of school buildings, since its programs were run by the Parks Department in newly constructed field houses, in virtually every other way the New York and Chicago programs were similar. Each offered "clubs of every kind and classes on every subject" to people of all ages and were "tightly controlled, financially and administratively, by public agencies" rather than being run by neighborhood residents.[33]

Ward decided that his Rochester experiment would differ from these existing models on four key dimensions. First, Ward's centers would exclude children, a practice that was based on a conviction that "if it becomes an adult movement, the young will imitate their elders." Next, he was careful to locate the first Rochester center in a middle-class neighborhood. He hoped thereby to differentiate his intentions from the New Yorkers' penchant for doing something "for the unfortunates" and to "prevent the movement at its start from being stamped as one especially for either poor or rich." In Rochester, Ward said, "we are simply bringing folks together . . . When we come together in our 'social centre,' there isn't race, nor creed, nor class, but just human beings. It's a social centre for social exchange, not for social service." The activities that constituted these social exchanges, to the extent possible, would be recreational or civic rather than educational. Ward hoped to "keep off the educational idea, because most people don't want to be uplifted . . . Everywhere else the idea has started as an attempt to uplift — and it stopped there."[34]

The real heart of the Rochester experiment, however, was the neighborhood civic club — a place where adults could meet in nonpartisan groups "for the purpose of developing intelligent public spirit by the open presentation and free discussion of matters of common interest."[35] In the end, the civic clubs operated only briefly before Rochester's political bosses cut off their funding, but even this brief success prompted numerous discussions about civic uses of the public schools in the National Municipal League, the Playground and Recreation Association of America, and the National Education Association. As a result of the Rochester experiment, even the New York Board of Education, the bastion of the "paternalistic recreation center," finally agreed in the fall of 1911 to participate in creating a "largely self-governing, self-supporting neighborhood social centre." This new social center would differ from the board's previous extended-use enterprises by being "a neighborhood institution produced through the application of resident energy, commitment, and ideas, and run 'from the bottom up instead of the top down.' "[36]

Despite this burgeoning interest in neighborhood civic clubs and local control of extended use, there still was relatively little agreement "as to just what a social center really is." This fact became abundantly clear when the first national conference on social center development was held in Madison, Wisconsin, in October 1911. A reporter for the *Boston Common* wrote: "Some there were particularly interested in the civic side, that is in what was termed the gathering in public places for open discussion of public questions . . . And some . . . were particularly interested in the social possibilities of the school center, in the idea of bringing the families of a given community into closer friendliness with one another so as to create that spirit of co-operation which can be gained only by mutual understanding. Still others were chiefly interested in the educational side, 'seeing in the social center a medium for the education of parents, who are usually so neglected in our modern educational system.' "[37]

Follett knew about the Madison debates — probably firsthand, since only poor health could have kept her from attending an event so central to her interests. She agreed with those who saw value in the "frequent public discussion by adults of civic and national issues" and hoped eventually to incorporate an adult civic club into the East Boston experiment. However, "as one cannot . . . do everything one wishes at the same time," her committee had decided "that we ought to begin with the boys and girls." Their needs were "more pressing," and satisfying them would create a generation of adults who would make "future Centres a powerful force for good in the city."[38] Follett's decision to begin the East Boston work with young people rather than adults was also influenced by her appreciation of the political problems that had led to the demise of the Rochester civic clubs. Given the animosities that existed among Boston's city officials, it probably seemed wise to forgo the establishment of adult civic clubs until the centers' funding base was firmly established.[39]

Because Follett sought to use the social centers to offer opportunities for training in social relations and nondirective styles of leadership, her design for the East Boston center originally excluded already-established organizations — even though she realized that they must eventually be integrated if for no other reason than that politicians like Councilman Buckley would demand it. Follett remained firmly opposed, however, to the practice of "letting in existing outside organizations not in sympathy with the purposes for which the school buildings have been opened to the public, but who come simply to save rent" and was therefore gratified to find that groups formed outside the center in East Boston seemed "willing to conform to certain general requirements" set by the School Committee so long as they were "allowed eventually to make those requirements." To those who felt that this approach was undemocratic, Follett replied (just as she had fifteen years earlier when supporting the idea of a strong Speakership) that "*leadership* is not incompatible with democratic organization."[40]

In February 1912, legislative hearings began on bills that would provide an appropriation for the extended use of the Boston public schools. The extended-use bill had been introduced by the Republican chairman of the House Ways and Means Committee, but it quickly garnered broad bipartisan support. Every major Boston official endorsed the legislation even though the city was embroiled in another controversy over proposed increases in the size of the School Committee.[41] Numerous civic groups also gave their support to the appropriations bill, including the Massachusetts Civic League, the Chamber of Commerce, the United Improvement Associations, and the Public Recreation League.[42] Even the Boston Social Union, whose leadership might well have resented the attention being given to the social centers, endorsed the legislation. Mary Follett had worked hard to maintain good relations with the leaders of Boston's social settlements and had succeeded; in November 1911, at the height of the social center funding campaign, Follett was elected the union's vice-president.[43]

Ten days after the passage of Chapter 195, Mary Follett took the next, crucial step in the development of Boston's social centers. She wrote to the

Boston School Committee requesting an appropriation that would allow the already-established East Boston center to continue its operations during the coming school year. Follett reminded the committee that the Women's Municipal League had undertaken the East Boston project, "not in any way as a supplement to the present school system, but purely as an experiment, since the city had not the money with which to try such an experiment itself." The project work had demonstrated "that there are certain vital, pressing needs in any neighborhood where there are large numbers of working boys and girls, and secondly, that such a neighborhood is likely to respond to the attempt to meet these needs by schoolhouses open evenings with well-organized activities." Having shown the need for the enterprise and having proved its viability, Follett's committee felt that its work was concluded.

Follett proposed three methods of organization, each of which would allow the project to continue under the auspices of the school department. The first method called for making the East Boston Social Centre into a full-fledged "Neighborhood Centre," a laboratory in which practical suggestions could be developed for use in other parts of the city. If the School Committee felt unable to go beyond the social center concept, Follett suggested hiring a full-time director of social centers who could then establish four or five centers, each having a local part-time director.[44] If the committee felt that it could do no more than the minimum, maintaining the single East Boston center, Follett suggested making the operation an extension of the evening school system.[45]

Suddenly, on the very day that the School Committee referred Follett's proposal to the superintendent "with instructions to report some general plan for extending the use of the school plant," Superintendent Brooks submitted his resignation. According to the *Boston Herald,* the School Committee had tried valiantly to keep him, extending his term of office through 1918 and offering to meet any financial offer he received from the University of Oklahoma. However, after the bitter School Committee campaigns during which his performance had been the focus of many attacks, Brooks apparently had had his fill of Boston school politics. Fitzgerald was delighted with Brooks's impending departure. The mayor told the *Globe* that he had long been frustrated by Brooks's unwillingness to appoint an assistant superintendent who was "a specialist in industrial education." Fitzgerald was disturbed by the fact that only "12 percent of the boys who enter the elementary schools graduate from the High Schools," and thought that something must be done for "the boys who cannot go to college, but who must work out their existence with hand and brain."[46]

Before he left for his new post in Oklahoma, Brooks submitted an extended-use plan. His doing so was a tribute to Mary Follett's good relations with the superintendent and to the nearly one thousand persons who had petitioned the School Committee on behalf of the East Boston center. The superintendent recommended "three general lines of work": first, he would expend $10,000 to establish four social centers "similar to the one successfully conducted by the Women's Municipal League in East Boston during the past year"; next, he would devote $5,000 to "educational and recreational lectures and concerns to be conducted throughout the city"; and finally, he would furnish heat, light, and janitorial service for organizations and events such as "parents' associations, alumni meetings, and courses of lectures conducted by philanthropic organizations." Brooks proposed that responsibility for the "general management of school extension" be placed in the hands of "an assistant director of evening and continuation schools, at a salary of $2,580."[47] Two weeks after Brooks submitted this proposal, the School Committee voted to adopt it; and on April 22, 1912, in a unanimous vote, the committee appropriated for this purpose the sum of $28,000. An Advisory Committee on Social Centres was established soon thereafter, and all the individuals appointed to serve were members of Mary Follett's WML committee. This action by the School Committee marked the end of its relationship with the Home and School Association's Committee on Extended Use.[48]

With the School Committee finally assuming formal responsibility for the development and operation of school-based social centers, Mary Follett now was able to turn her attention to developing the vocational guidance and placement component of the social center system. Eighteen months earlier, the School Committee had asked one of its administrators to create "practical plans for the establishment of vocational guidance of pupils in the public schools," but disputes with teachers and a bitter election campaign had distracted committee members from the vocational guidance issue. As a result, the only activities under way during the 1911–12 school year were the Vocation Bureau's lectures for guidance counselors and the continued production of information pamphlets about occupations.[49]

As before, neither of these Vocation Bureau activities received much financial support from the school department, a problem that one observer of vocational guidance during this period attributed to the director's limited knowledge of the public schools and his inability to formulate concrete plans. Meyer Bloomfield was better at "stirring up the school people themselves to improved work in vocational guidance," according to John Brewer in his history of vocational guidance, than in developing workable plans.[50] Mary Follett, by contrast, was not only a remarkable theoretician and articulate spokesperson for the causes she favored, but also an adept program planner and implementer. Convinced that any viable scheme of vocational guidance had to include provisions for placement, Follett grew increasingly frustrated by Bloomfield's neglect of placement activities. According to Brewer, it was criticism of Bloomfield's performance that was the "central, culminating factor" in the establishment of the Placement Bureau.[51]

Even before there was any idea of establishing the Placement Bureau, Follett had tried to make some progress on the issue by including a vocational guidance scheme in the East Boston experiment. Whatever detailed plan was finally developed, Follett was convinced that it must contain "three parts, not only *advice*, but also *placement* and *follow-up*. It is not enough to advise the boy to be a baker rather than a clerk, he must be helped to find just that firm where he will be happiest, where he will get the greatest amount of training, and where the conditions will be most favorable to *his* development. If he is left to himself to find his first place, he will more likely than not get into the wrong one, and then begin that fatal drifting . . . When there is once established a close three-fold relation between the employer, the child, and the adviser, for the first two to four years of the child's working life, the drifting from job to job will become so diminished that the gain to society will be incalculable."

When Follett proposed her threefold concept to Superintendent Brooks, it "met with his warm approval and assurances of support and help." Brooks reportedly told Follett that he "hoped that the experiment we were planning could be carried on in such a way that it would be semi-official from the first in order that it might easily be taken over by the School Committee at any moment that body wished to incorporate it in the school system." Toward this end, Follett's group agreed to act "in closest co-operation with the masters of the grammar schools, with whose graduating pupils we were to begin our work," and would locate their operation in one of the school buildings.[52]

Follett had hoped to begin her East Boston placement experiment immediately after the center's first season was concluded; this would allow the work to be "sufficiently well-organized by graduation day in June to handle the numbers who would be seeking employment in the summer." Her timetable, however, was disrupted when the School Committee decided to assume responsibility for the social centers and enlisted Ralph Hawley's services. With Hawley no longer available to participate in the vocational guidance experiment, Follett decided to postpone the project. She recognized that anyone new to the district "would have to spend much time over the preliminary work of getting acquainted with local conditions."[53]

Then, just as suddenly, the prospects for a placement experiment brightened when Follett learned that the Children's Welfare League of Roxbury, an affiliate of the Society for the Prevention of Cruelty to Children, was hoping to organize a placement system. The Welfare League simultaneously discovered that Follett's committee "had a plan very like theirs" and proposed that the two groups join forces.[54] Follett's WML committee happily assented to an eleven-week placement experiment in Roxbury and asked only that the Welfare League "add to their plan our scheme for a close connection with the Social Centre of the district." Expenses were shared, with Follett's committee supplying the two placement secretaries (James T. Mulroy, director of the Roxbury League, and Laura F. Wentworth, vocational assistant at the High School of Practical Arts) and the Welfare League contributing their executive secretary, Helen W. Rogers.[55] In a December 1912 report to the Women's Municipal League, Follett expressed her delight with Rogers' work: "while Mrs. Rogers presented her plans to us at every stage, and while we met frequently for discussion," all elements of the plan (except for the Placement Bureau's connection with the Evening Centre) were hers and the "success of the experiment entirely due to her ability in carrying it out."

Follett now felt confident that the two forms of extended use with which she had been experimenting would strengthen each other. Her description of how this would occur anticipated the notion of "reciprocal relating" that would become the central process in her social philosophy. The centers would help the Placement Bureau because "follow-up work can be done more naturally, easily and effectively in connection with the School Centres than in any other way"; moreover, "guidance can be given at all times as far as tact and good sense dictate, and the young people will allow." At the same time, the placement bureaus would act as "feeders" to the centers, since Follett intended to make the placement services available "not only to those leaving school, but to all members of the Evening Centre who claim it." Follett thus envisioned an evening social center and a placement bureau in every district of the city, "acting and reacting on each other, playing directly and indirectly into each other's hands, and the two together forming a giant combination for the good of the city."[56]

At the end of eleven weeks, the group supervising the Roxbury Placement Bureau sought the School Committee's permission to establish a headquarters in the Roxbury High School and continue the experiment for another year. This would allow time to establish a central office or bureau that could "bind together all the local units" and "affiliate all those agencies interested in vocational guidance, industrial education, investigation of industrial condition, and the employers, in order that duplication might be eliminated, uniform methods adopted, and the momentum of united and concentrated effort be given to the whole movement of vocational guidance." To secure the necessary funds, an arrangement was developed with Edith M. Howes and the Girls' Trade Education League. The Education League would pay half the expenses and provide the services of a trained investigator to "discover the industrial opportunities in Roxbury and to visit all the employers who apply to the Bureau for the services of young women." Help also was forthcoming from the WML's Committee on Opportunities for Vocational Training, whose student volunteers made studies of opportunities for employment in various stores and factories.[57] The students performed so well in this capacity and showed such great interest in the project that several began working directly for Follett's committee. Together, the bureau's staff and student volunteers added to the files of the Placement Bureau 400 profiles of working conditions in specific industries; they accumulated a "total of over a thousand" by May 1913.[58] The involvement of these college students (fourteen of whom came from states other than Massachusetts) was especially pleasing to the bureau's organizers, since the students would "carry back to these States the practical training in municipal work which they have had in Boston through their connection with the Women's Municipal League."[59]

The Roxbury Placement Bureau officially served only the "the ten grammar schools of Roxbury and the High School," but by May 1913 "so many calls" had been received "from other districts for the services of the Bureau, that a perfectly natural way has been opened for the extension of the Bureau's activities." If the School Committee gave its approval, Follett felt certain that work could begin "at once in Dorchester, South Boston and East Boston." To prepare for a likely extension of the work to other areas of the city, the original supervisory committee was enlarged to include representatives from the School Committee, the Board of Health, the Free Employment Bureau, the Vocation Bureau, the Employment Managers' Association, and the headmasters of schools served by the Placement Bureau. It was Follett's hope that an executive committee of this group, affiliated with a committee of the Chamber of Commerce, would "direct the development of the present Bureau" into an organization that would serve all children from Boston's public schools.[60]

To prepare for this enlarged function, the Placement Bureau established a close connection with the school department's newly established Department of Vocational Information. The creation of this department, which replaced the work done by Bloomfield's Vocation Bureau, marked the first real step in incorporating vocational guidance into the official responsibilities of the school department. The Vocational Information Department and the Placement Bureau functioned for almost two years as separate but cooperating agencies, with the former supported by tax dollars while the expenses of the Placement Bureau were borne entirely by the Girls' Trade Education League and the Women's Municipal League.[61]

By the spring of 1913, the various agencies cooperating in the work of the Placement Bureau agreed that placement services should be extended to all the public schools of Boston. The School Committee gave the necessary permission, subject only to the approval of the masters of the respective schools. Since numerous masters had already endorsed the idea, this condition was easily met. The bureau began its citywide operations "not only with the *approval* of the masters of the schools, but in most cases at their request and with their more than sympathy: a number of them said that it was the thing which the schools of Boston needed more than anything else, and they would work with the Placement Bureau for the success of this experiment."

Operating on a citywide scale required a reorganization of the supervisory board to include "the organizations most directly interested" in the work. As a result, in November 1913 a five-member Board of Directors was named that included (in addition to Follett and Howes) Michael H. Corcoran, chairman of the Boston School Committee; Caspar Isham, master of the Hyde School; and Henry S. Dennison, representative of the Boston Chamber of Commerce and an officer in the Dennison Manufacturing Company in nearby Framingham.[62] Eighteen months after accepting this appointment, Dennison was named chairman of the Massachusetts Committee to Promote Work, a group formed by Governor Walsh in response to the severe unemployment of 1914–15. The collaboration between Dennison and Follett on behalf of the Boston Placement Bureau was the beginning of a friendship that both would find instructive — for Follett in her later work on business management and for Dennison in his practical experiments on worker participation and control.[63]

Once the Placement Bureau was "firmly established," Helen W. Rogers felt able to leave her post and was replaced in November 1913 by Susan J. Ginn, a Roxbury master's assistant who had worked two summers as a placement secretary and for a few months as the bureau's acting director. Follett, who was extremely pleased by this choice, said that Ginn's "very marked executive ability, her understanding of the whole problem of vocational guidance and its relation to the schools, and her general efficiency, made her eminently fitted for the position." Almost immediately after her acceptance, Ginn was also named the half-time director of vocational counselors and head of the Division of Assignment and Records in the Continuation School. Ginn's multiple appointments created the first formal connection between the school department's vocational counselors and the Placement Bureau, and, in Follett's words, "strengthened the work of both."[64]

Follett had always understood how influential a new organization's name could be in determining the way it came to be perceived. In the case of the Boston Placement Bureau, she thought the name "unfortunate, for the last thing we wish to do is to *place;* all our efforts aim to get the child to continue his education." Indeed, the bureau's efforts "to get every boy and girl back into school" had led the Board of Control to conclude that "it is seldom economic necessity that takes the child of fourteen to work." Instead, this decision often was made hastily, driven by feelings on the part of the child that "he is 'tired of school' and wants a change, or longs to get free from authority, fondly believing that industry will give him more independence than 'school-teacher'!" In cases such as these, the placement secretaries had tried to convince parents and children of the advantages of further education, and they sometimes succeeded. Of the 2,200 children registered with the bureau during its first year and a half of existence, 551 returned to school.[65]

Whenever the young person's education was not resumed, the placement secretaries did their best to find an appropriate job, but they were constantly reminded that they were engaged in "a *placement,* not an *employment,* bureau." Their duty was "to find permanent positions, not stray jobs, to sacrifice no child to industry, and to fit each child as wisely and as well as we knew how." The placement secretaries apparently "held steadfastly" to this purpose even in the first months of the Roxbury Bureau's existence, when few employers were offering jobs and, as a result, the young people were losing faith in the bureau's ability to help them. Mary B. Gilson, who would go on to do pioneering work as an industrial personnel manager, was employed as a vocational counselor for the Trade School for Girls during this era. Gilson tracked down jobs requiring power-machine skills in garment, curtain, and straw-hat manufacturing firms and then placed girls in these jobs after they had been trained. She was appalled by what she found in many workplaces: "Newspaper columns gave leads for hunting openings, but the most effective method was to tramp up and down loft stairs and visit factories and shops where power machines were used. Sometimes physical working conditions were impossibly bad, and in that case I put those shops on my black list. But I had to do a good deal of compromising with decent standards, for relatively few workplaces had good ventilation and good light and anything that approached good housekeeping. Toilets in many of these shops were nothing short of vile . . . windows and floors were often dirty and workers crowded in small working space. Frequently fire exits were blocked." Even the best placements required the girls to work long hours for extremely low wages. It seemed to Gilson that the majority of employers were "either unconcerned about the health and comfort of their workers or else were caught in a vise of competition which forced them to divert all their energy to keeping up with or ahead of their competitors."[66] The vocational counselors and placement secretaries were determined, nevertheless, to serve the *child's* interests as best they could — a commitment that is all the more remarkable in light of the fact that many vocational guidance enthusiasts during this era settled merely for "fitting the child to the job."

The work of Follett's Placement Bureau was extraordinary in another way as well. Like most other educational and vocational guidance organizations, the bureau's Board of Control espoused no broad vision of how it would promote industrial reform; its work might "ultimately tend to better the working conditions for adolescent children in Boston," but the process was likely to be so slow as to be "almost imperceptible." Over the years, however, it was possible to see that the bureau was doing more than finding individual children suitable jobs. Detailed investigations of job openings and extensive follow-up work helped to protect children from exploitation and convinced some employers to raise their wage scales "in order to secure the child recommended by the Bureau."[67]

The bureau's commitment to investigating each placement opportunity became a massive undertaking, particularly when its jurisdiction was extended to all parts of the city. During 1914–15, for example, the college students working for the bureau made more than 5,200 visits to firms, recording information about "the nature of the work offered, the working conditions as to hours, light, ventilation, cleanliness, class of fellow employees, sexes, race, scale of wages, and opportunities for advancement. The data about jobs and firms were examined in conjunction with information about the children registered with the bureau in an effort to "adjust one to the other, keeping constantly in mind the cardinal principle, — that the good of the child is of primary importance, the good of the employer secondary, although mutually interdependent."[68]

Any program concerned with the "good of the child," Follett argued, must offer opportunities for "the largest amount of development and training of which he is capable, and which will at the same time enable him to give to society what *he* is particularly fitted to give." In keeping with this commitment to development, the Boston Placement Bureau implemented a three-part follow-up process. First, each child and parent signed a card agreeing that the child, in return for the bureau's services, would "not leave any position until he has reported to the Bureau and received the Bureau's reply" and would report to the bureau if dismissed by the employer. The employer, similarly, agreed not to discharge the child "without notifying the Bureau in advance." This notification system allowed the bureau to intervene in a timely way in numerous difficulties, helping to resolve problems that otherwise would have terminated the placement.[69] Another component of the follow-up system was a questionnaire that was sent to employers at regular intervals. The questionnaire asked (1) whether the employee's grade of work was "excellent — good — fair"; (2) how it could be improved; (3) whether the child had any "habits which are interfering with his efficiency"; and (4) whether the child was demonstrating "the capacity for advancement and increase in wages." The employer's replies formed the basis of the third "after-care" component, a monthly meeting between the placement secretary and the child, preferably at an evening center.

This follow-up system produced amazingly good results. Follett reported that "at the end of the first year 95 per cent. of our children were doing excellent or good work; only 5 per cent. had been poor or unsatisfactory." The bureau's turnover rates, furthermore, compared favorably with rates reported in "investigations which have recently been made of *unguided* children in their first year after leaving school." In studies of these unguided children, it was frequently found that "young people change [jobs] so constantly that they can hardly be kept in sight"; but at the Placement Bureau, "60 per cent. were still in their first positions, 25 were in their second, 11 in their third, and only 4 per cent. had made frequent changes."[70]

By the middle of 1915, Follett felt confident that the experimental phase of the Placement Bureau's work was over. Relations with employers continued to improve, and, perhaps as a result, placements increased even during periods of severe unemployment.[71] Follett attributed these improved relations to the employers' having "found out that we are working from their point of view as well as the child's. While the child himself stands at the centre of all our work and must be the primary consideration of the Bureau, yet we have always felt that we must hold before us both points of view, the employer's *and* the child's. That the employers have begun distinctly to appreciate this fact in regard to the Bureau is a decided gain for this year." During 1915–16, employers "offered the Bureau so many positions without solicitation" that the person who had been assigned to "digging up jobs" was no longer needed.[72] The only truly disappointing aspect of the bureau's development was its relation to the evening centers. There were considerably fewer applicants from the centers than had been expected; but all interested parties were in "frequent consultation . . .

as to how the Bureau can be helpful to larger numbers in the centres," and Follett felt confident that in "another year the way would be found to accomplish this."[73]

Follett had originally set the "magic year" of 1915 as the date by which she hoped the School Committee would assume responsibility for the Placement Bureau. But in spite of favorable local publicity and even some national recognition of the bureau's accomplishments, the transition was not officially completed for two more years.[74] The process was helped along by the establishment of Boston's first "continuation school," a concept introduced by the new superintendent of schools, Franklin B. Dyer. In the continuation school scheme, all working children between the ages of fourteen and sixteen were required to spend four hours a week at a special school that utilized the wage earner's daily experience in practical instruction. The Continuation School, which did its own follow-up work, established a "close and cordial working relation" with the Placement Bureau, an arrangement "recognized by the school authorities" and welcomed by vocational guidance advocates.[75] The other milestone — on the way to formal school department responsibility for placement — was passed when the School Committee established a Department of Vocational Guidance and appointed Susan J. Ginn, the Placement Bureau's director, as its head. Since the new department was charged with the placement of high school students, the privately funded Placement Bureau now had few remaining duties.[76]

Ginn organized a committee of "influential citizens" to advise her on matters of vocational guidance and was delighted when Mary Follett agreed to join the group.[77] Ginn considered Follett "a woman of rare vision and foresight" and was convinced that she had exercised a "powerful influence in developing the policies that had been followed" in vocational guidance. She was "an inspiration," Ginn wrote in a 1933 memoir. Her "quickness in grasping the situation, her wisdom in advising and her cleverness in interesting those in authority in the schools went a long way in assuring the Placement Bureau of success . . . Whenever she spoke she commanded attention and respect."[78]

Follett's six-year effort to establish a publicly funded system of vocational guidance and placement for the young men and women of Boston was finally crowned with success in the summer of 1917. On June 29 Follett wrote with relief and pleasure to Ella Cabot that "the School Committee last night took over the Placement Bureau." Thanking Cabot for her "generosity & farsightedness about it, & all your work and interest," Mary readily acknowledged that "I could never have gone on with it without your constant help & support." The two of them should rejoice "over this splendid ending (or begin-

Ella Lyman Cabot, ca. 1915. The Schlesinger Library, Radcliffe Institute, Harvard University.

ning!)," Follett continued, because many of the employers had become "not only clients, but friends in working out the great problems of the relation of industry to education, and of the relation of the child to the community." The bureau's "steady growth in usefulness to the schools, the children, the parents, and the employers of Boston" had made it into "a true civic institution."[79]

Despite her pride in this "valuable piece of work," the Placement Bureau was "so much less personal a work" for Follett than her "beloved centres." It was to these, Mary told Ella Cabot, that "I am now giving all my time."[80] By 1916 Follett was concentrating more on the national movement for social centers than on local issues, but she was still available to the Boston centers in her role as chair of the school department's Advisory Committee.[81] Follett was mobilized into action on their behalf on three occasions during the period 1913–1916. She no longer found it necessary to restrict herself to acting behind the scenes: the credibility she had gained through the successful East Boston experiment had freed her to emerge publicly as the centers' most eloquent champion.

At first the Boston centers had experienced no real financial problems. The $44,000 of public funds appropriated under Chapter 195 and a small amount of continuing private contributions were more than adequate to meet the needs of the original four centers. But the economic downturn of 1913–1915 reduced the centers' appropriation by almost 25 percent just as the number of centers was doubling. Each neighborhood wanted its own evening center; and the School Committee, under pressure from neighborhood groups and the mayor, had tried to meet the demand. Expanding from one center to nine in five years was difficult enough, but these organizational problems were exacerbated by politicians' demands that the centers make patronage appointments and start up specific activities that the politicians deemed desirable.[82]

Follett first came to the aid of the centers early in 1914, shortly after James Michael Curley succeeded John F. Fitzgerald as mayor of Boston. In the weeks following his election, Curley filled Boston's newspapers with stories of how he was struggling to correct the abuses of Fitzgerald's administration by dismissing unnecessary city employees and reducing inflated salaries.[83] Each week brought new terminations: one day it was thirteen engineers from the Bridge and Ferry Department; a few days later it was nineteen employees of the Parks Department.[84] The school department was bound to come under attack as well, but since the mayor's only formal means of controlling school department operations was his veto of appropriations, Curley could not unilaterally dismiss current employees. The School Committee's budget for the new fiscal year, however, was subject to the mayor's veto, and Curley's budget-cutting knife was poised.

Instead of waiting for Curley to act, Follett rushed to preempt. On April 1, 1914, citing "the disturbing prospect that Mayor Curley, in his continuing search for municipal economy, will either reduce or eliminate entirely the appropriation proposed for the work of the Evening Centres," Follett authored a four-column account in the *Evening Transcript* of the purposes and accomplishments of Boston's six evening centers. Follett's piece included a detailed listing of the activities available to neighborhood residents and reported the obligatory attendance statistics, but the real power of this article lay in Follett's evocation of the center spirit. She took her readers inside the centers, painting intimate sketches of how social theory was being put into practice and enlivening her accounts of center activities with enthusiastic endorsements from the men, women, and children who came there as participants. "To make a round of the Boston Evening Centres," Follett assured the brahmin *Transcript* readership, "is indeed a thrilling experience."

Follett gave special attention in this article to the "large numbers of older people one sees" at the centers—something she saw as the Boston centers' "most promising feature": "In the larger civic clubs of men and women . . . the members hear such questions discussed as 'New Laws,' the local senator or representative giving an account of the mothers' pension law, the child labor law and the pure food law; or the garbage question is discussed by a city official, a housewife, and a representative of the Women's Municipal League. The port of Boston, the curfew law, housing, municipal opportunities at our doors, savings bank insurance and cooperative banks are a few of the many interesting subjects considered at the meetings of the civic clubs." Even accomplishments such as these would not be worth the money expended, Follett readily admitted, if the object of all "these lectures and entertainments, these clubs and classes" was merely "to keep young people off the streets, to inform or entertain older people." Follett's social centers had larger aims. They would "give social worth to the individual—free his initiative and his power of expression, create habits of social value, above all strengthen and develop his sense of responsibility." And they would give people training "for that larger degree of democracy which we see coming, to help them to learn how to work and play together, how to live together not only harmoniously but also effectively."[85]

There is no way of knowing whether Mayor Curley saw Follett's article or was moved by it. But on April 3, when Curley announced his proposed reduction of $147,000 in the school department budget, the centers escaped unscathed.[86]

Almost as quickly as this budget-cutting episode passed, another crisis arose. On May 25 Ralph Hawley wrote a letter to the superintendent resigning his position as acting director of extended use. This decision did not take Follett by surprise. Two months earlier she had closed her *Evening Transcript* article with the remark that as "the Centres are new, there are many perplexing questions connected with their management, many and very difficult problems to be solved."[87] Indeed, trouble had been brewing over Hawley's status for almost two years.[88]

It had been rumored "that in the event of Mr. Hawley's leaving, Mrs. Eva Whiting White might be asked to conduct the centers." White would have been an extremely attractive candidate. Experienced in social service and educational matters, White was highly thought of in all quarters of the city. She had directed Elizabeth Peabody House, a settlement in Lomasney's West End district, and since 1910 had overseen the vocational work of Boston's day and evening schools in her capacity as director of the Vocational Department of the Massachusetts Board of Education. White later recalled that the person behind the movement to draft her was Mary Follett. Follett, she said, had engaged in a full-scale campaign to get her to accept the job, even using White's friendship with Katherine Lowell Bowlker, the head of the Women's Municipal League, as a means of influencing her decision.[89] Follett succeeded in time for the May 25 meeting, and Superintendent Dyer was able to propose White's appointment. The matter might have been pushed through that same night under a suspension of the rules, but one of the centers' opponents, Michael H. Corcoran, objected, and the appointment was held over. In the end, however, Corcoran decided not to oppose White, and she won the board's unanimous approval.[90]

With White's appointment, Follett relinquished control of the development of the Boston evening centers. Unlike many other women who founded organizations during this era, Follett seemed not to need an organizational "home." Each project, no matter how dear to her heart, was eventually turned over to a capable colleague. If a crisis arose, Follett could be counted on to help; but perhaps following the example of Pauline Agassiz Shaw, Follett most often restricted her involvement to offering praise and encouragement. "I have not seen you for some time because I thought it was best," she wrote to Eva Whiting White several months after her appointment as director, "but I cannot let the Xmas time go by without sending you warm greetings & the deepest appreciation of the work you are doing. There is no one else I am sure who can understand & sympathize as completely as I can, no one else who can so keenly appreciate both what you are trying to do for the city & also the *herculean* effort it takes to do it. The discouragements must be many, but I *know* the end is worth them all. At any rate I want you to know that there is some one entirely in sympathy with you. I hope you are going to take a little holiday now & let the Xmas peace get at you."[91]

The centers emerged from the crises of 1914 relatively unscathed. Funds were budgeted for seven school centers, and authority for their management was lodged in a director who commanded widespread respect. Of the two School Committee members who had tried to thwart the centers' development, one chose not to run for reelection, and the other, Michael H. Corcoran, became chairman of the School Committee. Somehow, Corcoran was eventually won over to the cause. In October 1915 both he and Mayor Curley played central roles in the festivities celebrating the opening of the newest school center in Boston's North End, and Corcoran became an ally in the centers' next financial crisis.[92]

This third crisis bringing Mary Follett to the aid of the school centers occurred in May 1916.[93] In an effort to serve more city neighborhoods, the number of centers had increased beyond the ability of the Chapter 195 appropriation to pay for the costs; and now, with the downturn in the state's economy, even that appropriation was shrinking. To help compensate for this loss of funds, center advocates were working to secure passage of a legislative petition filed by Michael H. Corcoran that would permit the school centers to collect admission fees for events in school buildings. Passage of this bill, Eva Whiting White told her colleagues in the Boston Social Union, was crucial, for "it would mean the practical closing of the school centres if the bill failed." The primary opposition came from proprietors of "picture shows" and other commercial interests who hoped to block the centers from competing for their clientele. The bill was also opposed by a Dorchester state senator who thought that "public schools should be entirely free," but language apparently was found that met his concerns.[94]

With the February passage of Chapter 86 of the Acts of 1916, the centers for the first time could supplement their public appropriation and voluntary contributions with admission fees; but their financial problems apparently were still not resolved, because word was circulating that the School Committee planned to cut both the director's salary and the rates paid to center managers.[95] White's salary, which had remained constant at $3,420 since her appointment in 1914, was comparable to those of persons with similar responsibilities; first-year head masters, for example, were paid $3,204 and through years of service could earn a maximum of $4,068.

Center managers and assistant managers were not so fortunate. In 1914 their salaries were comparable to those of persons at the bottom of the school department administrative hierarchy: managers were paid $1,500; assistant managers were paid $1,200.[96] Although these rates created a salary differential between men and women (the department always named men as managers and women as assistant managers), the disparity was much less egregious than was often the case in the school department.[97] This situation grew sharply worse, however, when this salary scale was replaced after only a few months by a system of daily rates and limitations on the number of days center officials could work. Most managers now could earn no more than $760, half of what they had previously earned. The assistant managers, who apparently were allowed almost twice as many days of service, still earned only between $630 and $800. The rates for assistant manager apparently became the target of considerable criticism, for they were soon retroactively increased to a level that allowed earnings of between $740 and $950 for 180 days of service.[98]

In the spring of 1916, these already low salaries became the focus of a genuine crisis when Chapter 195 generated an appropriation of only $34,250 for 1916–17 — a reduction of almost $10,000 from previous years. The School Committee, in an effort to cope, was considering cuts in the salaries of all extended-use administrators. Fearing that these cuts "would impair the efficiency of the centers by causing the present workers to retire and making it possible to secure only inferior workers," Mary Follett mobilized the advisory committees of the various centers. The committee in East Boston drew considerable attention to the accomplishments of the centers by inviting Governor Samuel McCall to a huge celebration marking the end of the school center year. McCall was called away at the last minute, but the event still was extremely well attended. Lieutenant Governor Calvin Coolidge and members of the governor's staff filled in and were greeted by "a committee of seventy-five members made up of the Advisory Board of the Center, and delegates from the various East Boston organizations, together with the Senator and Representatives from the district." The event reportedly drew such a crowd that "every available spot in the hall was used for standing room," with several hundred people unable to get in.[99]

Local advisory committees also were urged to demand that the School Committee hold a public hearing on the salary question. Responding to these pleas, the School Committee cut short its regular business on May 15 in order to give "more than 100 prominent men and women interested in the school centres of Boston" an opportunity to express themselves. The petitioners' portion of the meeting was conducted by Mary Follett.[100]

Follett reportedly used her opening remarks to make four arguments on behalf of maintaining the director's salary. Speaking first to concerns about efficiency and economy, Follett argued that "experts in the study of financial organization have decided that an increased cost at the head of a system, up to a certain point, means a decreased total cost." She also reminded the board that the director of a new program such as this had to have skills of the highest caliber so that she might solve "unconsidered problems," organize "chaotic material," and arouse general interest in the enterprise. The director's role was further complicated by the fact that she had "to create a large part of her funds and all her attendance" and had to train her managers and club leaders. It seemed to Follett that Eva Whiting White, instead of costing too much, "had saved a large part of her salary to the city by being a person of such a caliber and such standing in the community that she had secured much outside help."[101] Follett then turned to the matter of the managers. A member of the School Committee had been quoted as saying that the managers were paid $8 per night, but Follett thought it more accurate to describe their salaries as $24 a week, since they were restricted in the number of days they could work. The present $800 salary of managers was "none too much," Follett argued, "when the breadth and scope of their work was taken into consideration"; in addition to "leading the members, forming classes and caring for its various needs," center managers were responsible for raising funds. In cities that she had visited, "all of them smaller than Boston," people in positions comparable to those of Boston's managers were being paid from $2,500 to $4,000 a year.

Follett then introduced a series of speakers representing the centers' ethnic and religious diversity. Since each speaker took a somewhat different tack in his presentation, by the time they had finished almost every possible argument that might have been made on behalf of the centers had been made. Augustus Bacon, a Roxbury Yankee, told the committee that the Roxbury center had become the "gathering place of the community" and reminded them that the centers needed time to develop their full potential. Major P. F. O'Keefe of Dorchester spoke "from the standpoint of a boy who had been brought up in the city proper and knew what temptations the streets afforded." Without the centers as a place for recreation, boys from neighborhoods such as his own were constantly tempted by vices such as drugs and were almost certain to "land in some reformatory, where bad practices would be acquired from experienced criminals." O'Keefe closed his remarks with a plea for increases in the managers' salaries by noting that less than half of one percent of the seven-million-dollar school budget went to extended use. Frank Leveroni, a juvenile court justice, was particularly impressed with how the school centers were teaching American ideals. "It would be no less than a crime against America," Leveroni asserted, "to stop this great work, or to lower the present high standard by cutting the salaries of the leaders." Joseph B. McCabe, editor of the *East Boston Argus Advocate*, had even more florid praise for the centers: their abolition "would militate against East Boston success and the development of the brotherhood of man."

A few other neighborhood leaders made brief presentations, but the other major speech of the evening was given by James P. Munroe. Introduced by

Follett as "a representative of the municipal manufacturer and the business man," Munroe told the committee that "one of the chief criticisms of business men against the school management is the enormous overhead expenditures on the plant without corresponding efficiency." This problem, Munroe asserted, could be solved "by simply employing the school buildings more," as was being done with the centers. Munroe assured his listeners that business leaders were pleased rather than distressed by the $40,000 expenditure for the centers and would happily see that amount "even doubled or trebled," for they realized that the managers "must be the best procurable, and money must be paid for good people."

At the conclusion of the presentations, Chairman Scannell "commented on the strong hold the evening school centre plan had on the people of Boston . . . [and] said that it was farthest from his mind to vote in favor of stopping the work."[102] The School Committee took no action on the salary issue at this meeting, but three weeks later, when salary rates were set for the coming year, the impact of the hearings was apparent. The rates showed no further reductions in either the director's salary or the amount that managers could earn.[103] Six months later the Boston school centers received another vote of confidence when the Finance Commission issued the results of an investigation of school department expenditures conducted at the request of Mayor Curley. The outside experts, hired as consultants for this investigation, had high praise for the centers and told the Finance Commission that "no city has yet devised a better solution of the problem presented by its adult foreigners than the establishment of school centers under control of the School Department. In Boston this work is being carried on effectively at a small cost entirely out of proportion to the value of the service rendered."[104]

Modern writers frequently describe Mary Follett as someone who "never met a payroll," and they marvel that a woman with such limited managerial experience could develop such sophisticated ideas about organization and management. But as we have seen in the preceding chapters, Follett was not a managerial dilettante. In her work on behalf of women's suffrage, civic education, vocational guidance and placement, and the development of neighborhood community centers, she successfully enacted all the major roles we commonly ascribe to managers.

Follett, above all, showed great savvy as an entrepreneur. Sensitive to the social, political, and economic conditions of her times, she was remarkably proficient in developing programs responsive to the problems and opportunities she saw around her. She investigated activities already under way in other locales and, with an eye toward possible future collaborations, also acquainted herself and her colleagues with the undertakings of the many private organizations and public agencies in Boston. In the early stages of program development, Follett articulated for participants a social philosophy that would guide program planning, form the basis of criteria against which accomplishments might eventually be judged, and help to ensure the program's long-term integrity. In developing strategy, she relied heavily on experimentation — usually beginning with a small pilot project and then, after the results of that experiment were in, proposing alternatives for program expansion that would ensure capable leadership, a stable funding base, and continuing responsiveness to relevant constituencies.

Although Follett was an astute and inventive planner, her skills were not limited to conceptualization. She personally cultivated the support of politicians, neighborhood residents, school officials, and others; creatively negotiated conflicts of interest; orchestrated publicity favorable to her various causes; championed the passage of enabling legislation; raised funds from private as well as public sources; allocated and controlled the expenditure of scarce resources; and vigorously defended her fledgling programs in public speeches, private discussions, and in print whenever political squabbles or resource cutbacks threatened their viability. Aware that the social philosophy underlying her programs would demand unusually sensitive and skillful leadership, Follett personally recruited committee members and key program officials; fought to provide the professionals among them with appropriate compensation, training, and opportunities for advancement; and continually sought better means of empowering those whom she was trying to serve. Follett also provided a more intimate kind of support — inspiring her colleagues with a vision of the pioneering nature of their work, encouraging their creativity, proffering wise counsel, and liberally praising their accomplishments.

The sweeping nature of Mary Follett's contributions to the projects she undertook was cogently captured by a student of the Harvard Graduate School of Education in his 1912 report on Boston's school centers: "The agitation for School Centres in Boston was begun by the Women's Municipal League, but as in all such movements there was one individual who was the mainspring of the whole agitation. As Mr. [Ralph] Hawley the present head of the system said to me: — "Miss Mary Follet [*sic*] is the heart and brain of the whole movement."[105]

Mary Follett's involvement in the social and civic life of Boston already had begun to shape her ideas about power, authority, leadership, conflict, coordination, and group process; but in 1916 her attention was still focused on furthering the community centers movement. After almost five years of reacting to threats to the existence of the Boston centers, Follett finally was able to concentrate on extending rather than defending the movement. Convinced that the long-term accomplishment of her aims would depend "upon the manager more than upon anyone else," Follett turned her efforts to defining the roles of these new community workers and creating training experiences that would develop their informed commitment to the concept of community self-direction. She also emerged during this period as a major figure in the national centers movement, where she would contribute her talents to the development of the National Community Centers Association.

14

The Functions, Financing, and Control of Community Centers: Issues for the National Movement

Even as Mary Follett worked in 1915 and 1916 to stabilize the political and financial position of evening centers in the Boston public schools, she was becoming more widely recognized outside Boston. By 1917 she would be acknowledged as one of the national leaders of the community centers movement. In her work on this national stage, she would directly experience intractable ideological and personal conflicts, regional struggles for power, challenges to freedom of speech, and red-baiting. All these experiences were grist for her forthcoming book *The New State* (1918), Follett's first systematic explication of her emerging ideas about conflict, leadership, power, and authority.

The national community centers movement was experiencing remarkable growth. In 1910 only 31 cities had reported using their schools as social centers, but by 1916 this number had risen to 463. During these early years, important roles were played by eastern cities such as Rochester, Boston, and New York, but "western" states such as Illinois, Wisconsin, Kansas, and Texas also were prominent.[1] The movement's national character and the involvement of rural as well as urban constituencies soon attracted the attention of aspiring politicians — among them Woodrow Wilson, then governor of New Jersey. In October 1911, when 150 delegates from sixteen states convened in Madison, Wisconsin, for the First National Conference on Social Center Development, it was Wilson who delivered the keynote speech.[2]

A newcomer to the social centers movement, Wilson was intrigued by the possibilities that the centers offered "for the restoration of the unity of communities." The fundamental problem of American economic and political life, Wilson told his audience, was the difficulty of "accommodating the various interests in modern society to one another." Just as he had sought in his book *Congressional Government* to expose the secrecy and collusion of the congressional committee system, Wilson now was decrying the presence of "secrecy" and "concentration" in the operation of special economic interests and the "reign of management" in politics. And just as he had prescribed competitive, parliamentary-style debates as the antidote for the evils of the congressional committee system, Wilson now advocated the free and open debate of political questions in the nation's schoolhouses. "The treatment for bad politics," Wilson told the delegates, "is exactly the modern treatment for tuberculosis — it is exposure to the open air."

Wilson praised the social centers for fostering a "town meeting" spirit. "Is it not significant," he asked his audience, that this movement "is being erected upon the foundation originally laid in America, where we saw from the first that the schoolhouse and the church were to be the pillars of the Republic? Is it not significant that as if by instinct we return to those sources of liberty undefiled which we find in the common meeting place, in the place owned by everybody, in the place where nobody can be excluded, in the place to which everybody comes as by right?" For Wilson, "the very definition of community is a body of men who have things in common, who are conscious that they have things in common, who judge those common things from a single point of view, namely, the point of view of general interest." Such commonality was impossible without "close communication," and this, he hoped, might be fostered by the establishment of social centers in the nation's schoolhouses.

No doubt aware that some might consider the commonality he espoused as a threat to traditional American individualism, Wilson further argued that "liberty as now expressed is unsatisfactory in this country." The individual was free only "in proportion to his perfect accommodation to the whole or in proportion to the perfect adjustment of the whole to his life and interests."[3] The first part of this assertion was merely a restatement of the Idealist formulation of individual liberty. The latter half, however — the notion that one might achieve freedom by adjusting the whole to one's own life and interests — was pure Woodrow Wilson. Years earlier there were signs of this rather audacious philosophy in Wilson's advocacy of cabinet government — a form particularly suited to his personal talents — and it would appear again at Versailles in Wilson's struggles to bend the world to his personal vision of peace.

Wilson's advocacy of political discussion and debate in the nation's social centers probably caused a certain amount of consternation among the Madison conference delegates, because he had allied himself, perhaps unwittingly, with one of the "sides" in an emerging controversy in the movement. The cosponsors of the conference — the Extension Department of the University of Wisconsin and the Social Center Association of America — represented different lines of social center development. The Social Center Association of America, whose offices were located in New York, was financed by a wealthy Pittsburgh woman, Frances G. Vandergrift, and drew its board largely from the eastern states. This branch of the movement was concerned largely with the "nonpolitical" aspects of social centers, namely recreation and education.[4] The University of Wisconsin, by contrast, was identified with the neighborhood civic club concept; when Rochester's boss-dominated city administration virtually eliminated public financial support for Edward J. Ward's three-year-old civic club experiment, the university regents invited Ward to Wisconsin to promote the statewide development of social centers. Even in this new setting, however, public officials were divided in their support for open political discussion and debate.[5]

With the conference sponsors themselves uncertain about whether social centers should be recreational or political in character, the issue was hotly debated by the delegates. In the end, a majority decided that the new National Association of Social Centers and Civic Development should embrace both forms of extended use. Two commentators for the *National Municipal Review*, Charles Beard and Roger N. Baldwin, found that "a large and overwhelming majority took or endorsed the stand that if any subject of discussion was permissible at such centers of exchange in view and ideas, it was the subject of government, which touches so nearly the daily and personal welfare of every human unit in the country."[6] The faction with which Woodrow Wilson had allied himself early in the conference apparently had prevailed.

Eight months after delivering the conference keynote address in Madison, Wilson was named the presidential nominee of the Democratic party. As a presidential candidate, he continued his campaign for the restoration of the unity of communities: he told Americans that they could revitalize their politics and transcend the increasingly problematic special interests of big business only by discovering "what is in the common interest." But as the campaign unfolded, the differences between the two major candidates — Wilson and Theodore Roosevelt — centered upon one key question: "In an age of big business, what was the role of the government in preserving democratic values?"

The turn-of-the-century merger movement had changed the face of the American economy: the two thousand largest firms in the United States made up less than one percent of the nation's businesses, but they produced 40 percent of the total value of the nation's industrial goods. Wilson's economic adviser, Louis D. Brandeis, believed that American democratic values could not endure in a society dominated by large economic units, but he also was convinced that bigness had to be controlled without interfering with personal liberty. Wilson's "new freedom," therefore, proposed a government antitrust program that would intervene only to "keep the market place expanding, deprive would-be monopolists of their anticompetitive weapons, and break up conspiracies for restraint of trade." Theodore Roosevelt and his adviser, Herbert Croly, harbored none of Brandeis's predispositions against bigness — either in business or in government. Their "new nationalism" proposed the creation of a federal regulatory and welfare bureaucracy of professional experts who would utilize the productivity and efficiency of big business on behalf of "social and economic amelioration."[7]

There is no evidence that Mary Follett was involved in the 1912 campaign on either candidate's behalf; she had come to abhor political parties, and, as a woman, she was unable to vote. But when Wilson prevailed in the November election, Follett surely was intrigued by the prospect of having in the White House someone who believed, as she did, that American society was being undermined by a faulty notion of individual liberty. At this stage in the evolution of her social philosophy, Follett was convinced that the problem of individual liberty in a democracy could be resolved only as the Idealists had long argued — by increasing the individual's willingness to subordinate his or her interests "to the well-being of all."[8]

Speaking in December 1913 on "The Social Centre and the Democratic Ideal" at Boston's respected Ford Hall Forum, Follett argued that "we have talked a good deal *about* democracy but we haven't yet seen much of the actual stuff of it." The problem, she told her audience, lay in our persistent linking of democracy with "the philosophy of the individual." All too often, Follett said, people "define democracy as equal opportunity, and then think of opportunity as every man having a chance to get to the top and rule others! There could be no more mistaken idea. Democracy is not the glorification of the individual in any form, but the subordination of the individual to the well-being of all. It is not the liberty of the individual, but the restraint of the individual, by himself, for the good of all . . . We must emphasize unity rather than equality, brotherhood rather than liberty if we would understand the meaning of a larger democracy."[9]

Making real what now was only an ideal would require personal acquaintanceships of the kind that social centers could foster. In this Follett and Wilson were agreed. And Follett saw merit in Wilson's advocacy of "frequent discussion and . . . a certain amount of direct civic teaching" in the social centers. In her Ford Hall address, she applauded his prescription for bad politics — "exposure to the open air." But Follett did not exaggerate the advantages of people's simply getting together to talk. Although she was impressed by the plethora of municipal movements, national associations, labor organizations, cooperative societies, and employer-employee associations spawned in the early part of the twentieth century and by the "passion for solidarity" that they seemed to represent, the real problem was making this togetherness count. "It is one thing," she said, "to live together *harmoniously* and quite another to live together *effectively.* What we want is to make our democracy effective, telling, an actual fact. Association ought to mean action for common ends."[10]

Fifteen years of experience in social and civic enterprises had convinced Follett that civic effectiveness was grounded in a particular kind of group activity, "where the wishes of the individual must be constantly sacrificed to the needs and interests of the group, where the loyalty developed will be group loyalty, where every one will feel that he as part of the group is something bigger and finer than just one man all alone by himself, that he partakes of the strength and power and potentiality of the whole." These characteristics might emerge in groups organized to discuss political questions, but social or recreational endeavors might be even better. "I can read by myself, or work by myself," Follett told her listeners; "I can talk to you and you can't talk back, (yet!) but if I want to play, I must find some one to play *with*. Now the essence of democracy also is doing things together, therefore it is particularly appropriate that we should have as much play as possible in a place which we hope above everything else is to prepare people for a larger degree of democracy."[11]

The real value of group activities in social centers, then, was that they were providing "a larger opportunity than we have ever known before, for an associated life, for a training in citizenship, and for the *practice* of democracy." Follett thought it "particularly tragic that our modern industrial system does not give large opportunities to develop these qualities." She explained: "Many men and women work all day in occupations which tend to repress and stifle all initiative, all power of decision or of self-dependence. Every movement, the very pace of the work, may be regulated by the machine. Or . . . there is at any rate the ever-present foreman, and one must obey every moment orders from above, and never have the education of making one's own decisions and failing or succeeding from one's own initiative . . . With this lack in the day-time occupations of men and women, it is of the utmost importance that the Social Centres should give every opportunity for self-expression, that most fundamental need of man, and for the development of initiative and will-power."[12]

In making this plea, Follett was not addressing a select group of Boston's social and economic elite. The audience of the Ford Hall Forum, which usually numbered about five hundred and frequently reached almost three times that size, was perhaps the most heterogeneous in Boston. According to one writer, most of the attendees had occupations as clerks, salespeople, and tradespeople; men usually outnumbered women two to one, but women were "well represented"; and although the largest percentage had no affiliation with any church, a quarter of them were Jews, and a smaller percentage Catholics.[13] Thus, when Follett asked her Ford Hall audience "to help in the development of the Boston Social Centres, in making them mean what they ought to mean in the life of the city," she was asking her audience not to "uplift" someone below them in social status but to help themselves. Early in the development of evening centers, the Boston School Committee had played a crucial role, but now, Follett told her audience, "the thing I feel more strongly about our Centres than any other is that they will never be successful if they are directed by the School Committee or the agents of the School Committee. They must be community affairs, organized by community initiative, for community ends."[14]

Even community-sponsored groups, however, would need leadership, and Follett wisely anticipated that the leaders must be carefully trained. Convinced that the long-term success of the movement would not be secure unless center managers and leaders developed a commitment to centers as true community enterprises, Follett "looked forward to the time when men and women shall prepare themselves for evening center management as they do now for other departments of social service." Unfortunately, there did not yet exist a detailed description of the attitudes and behaviors expected of center managers and leaders — the kind of definition on which an effective training program might be based. Follett herself, had only recently turned her attention in that direction. In January 1913 she had spoken to the ninety-eight managers and leaders of the new Boston evening centers about the role of these new community workers. At the core of Follett's remarks was a warning: "In a short time we shall have no centers at all unless we make them self-governing. If I cannot impress this upon you I see no hope for the evening center movement in Boston . . . These are not children we are dealing with, chiefly, they are young men and women; we cannot force them to the centers, they will come if they feel that they have a place and a part there, that the centers are theirs."[15]

Always pragmatic, Follett recognized that self-government was not something to be "permitted" or "given." It was, she said, "like almost everything else in life, a thing which you must win, must conquer for yourself." But she saw it as the responsibility of center managers and leaders to show young people "how to win self-government, to train them in the ways of self-direction." Similarly, center managers were to help the adults of the neighborhood "develop the machinery by which they themselves can furnish the satisfaction of their desires. The evening center movement can never be successful in the long run if things are imposed upon a district from without . . . He is not the best manager who imposes the most progressive ideas on his district — he is the best manager who guides the people of his district to express and develop the best in themselves."[16]

Having learned through experience that self-government was best taught and nurtured in an atmosphere of togetherness, Follett impressed on her audience the importance of developing a "club spirit." This could be done, she argued, both through the appropriate conduct of business meetings and through clubs in which center members could "feel their fellowship and the fun of planning and doing things together." The good feelings that these activities might produce seemed to Follett their most important product. "It is all very well," Follett reminded her listeners, "to say that we do know already that we are parts of a larger whole than just our family or our group of friends, but is it quite another thing to feel it, — we shall never really know it until we feel it, and this is what the Centres are going to do for us — make us *feel* our oneness."[17]

Follett's "hands-on" experience in Boston's first school centers enabled her to provide unusually detailed guidance about center operations. She knew, for example, that it was not enough "that the members of a center should be allowed to vote on questions pertaining to the center; all these questions should be put before them in such a way that their consideration of them should be a real training in self-government." At a minimum, this required putting before members questions "in which they will be genuinely interested, and yet in which we, as managers, are willing to give them the final decision, without claiming a right of veto." Even more important, however, was her conviction that managers and club leaders must avoid seeking to influence "by preaching or by any direct method." Sensitive to the resentment felt by young people when outsiders attempt to "improve" them, she urged that they "be careful from the first, and particularly at first, that the attitude of manager and leaders is that all are there to help the young people get what they want, not to 'uplift' them."[18]

Follett was equally specific in her suggestions about the nature and conduct of club activities. She urged each club leader to remember that the subject being "taught" was merely a means to the real end of developing a "true social spirit." Each leader periodically should ask, "Have I analyzed my particular subject to see how the things which we want to teach can be taught through it, — self-control, fair play, patience, steadiness, generosity of feeling toward the efforts of others, perseverance, courageous facing of difficulties, etc.?"

Many of her listeners, Follett realized, would find this an onerous responsibility and would demur, saying, " 'Yes, I know the evening centers exist for these ends, but that is not my part; I must teach this boy to be a good Tom Pinch, or a good cornetist, or a good basket ball player; some one else will teach him these other things.' Don't make this mistake," Follett pleaded. "There is no one else."[19]

Leadership of the kind she hoped to evoke would require of center managers an impressive list of personal qualities: "originality, perception, adaptability, insight, vision and imagination of the highest order, and at the same time a practical grasp of detail, a shrewd knowledge of human nature, and an ability to handle groups." Some would find these demands daunting, but to Follett they represented an enviable opportunity — a chance to "blaze the way and show all the possibilities of these centers." "Pioneer work," she told the novice managers, "is the work that thrills us all — it is more interesting to make the path than to walk in it."[20]

Follett's Ford Hall speech surely informed Boston's center managers and leaders and no doubt also inspired them, but the training of these new professionals had to be made more comprehensive and systematic if Follett's ideas were to take root and endure. Hoping to spark interest in the development of professional training for center workers, Follett read her Ford Hall paper to colleagues at the Boston Social Union and persuaded the Boston School Committee to distribute a printed version to interested parties across the nation. She then approached Dr. Jeffrey R. Brackett, head of Boston's ten-year-old School for Social Workers, a coeducational enterprise jointly begun in 1904 by Harvard University and Simmons College. Follett urged that the school establish a course "which shall meet the needs of leaders and managers of the Evening Centres as of club-workers generally."[21] Perhaps because she was already involved with the school as a member of the advisory committee for Eva Whiting White's recreation course, Dr. Brackett gave Follett's request his quick assent.

Boston's first course in "Neighborhood and Community Work" was offered during the 1913–14 academic year. Designed for second-year social work students, the course included weekly lectures, supervised fieldwork, and a "special study." Some of the area's most esteemed social and neighborhood workers — Joseph Lee, Richard C. Cabot, Robert A. Woods, and Mary Follett — appeared as lecturers, speaking on topics such as forms of neighborhood activity, boys' and girls' clubs, school and social centers, individual and group psychology, group techniques, and social aspects of the modern industrial era. Follett also participated in the special study portion of the course by helping Eva Whiting White supervise student investigations of problems in the field.

This aspect of the course, reminiscent of Follett's own undergraduate research training, was intended "to give the students an opportunity to learn something of the methods of social inquiry for practical purposes."[22]

As news of Boston's accomplishments in center development and management spread throughout the nation, Follett began to receive invitations to speak.[23] Even as a young woman, Follett had been able to captivate an audience. Not only was she bright and articulate, but she also found ways to make both her message and her presentation compelling. She challenged her listeners to see the larger significance of day-to-day issues — placing them in philosophical, political, economic, and social context — and, at the same time, she was remarkably adept at illustrating difficult concepts or principles in anecdotes that her audience could easily grasp and appreciate. Follett never patronized her listeners; on the contrary, she frequently reached out to enlist their aid. "Here is where I want to ask you," she would say at the close of a typical lecture. "Will you help to get people together in our school buildings to know one another, to discuss together, to learn to act together?" Follett's rhetorical success must also be ascribed in part to her mastery of the rhythms of public speaking. In the following passage, for example, she uses parallel phrasing and repetition to sweep her listeners along to an inspiring climax: "There has gradually come into the world a new idea of democracy . . . if we here to-night pledge ourselves to the new democracy, a new force will be created in the world. For we no longer think of democracy as a form of government. We know now that it is far more than that. It is the substance of our life. It is the flame at the heart of man, the flame which binds us together, makes us one, not many. Democracy is not a goal, it is the path; it is not an attainment, but a process. It is the 'more abundant life.' It is the attitude of man towards his fellow-man. It is the only true method of living. When we once grasp this and begin to *live* democracy, then only shall we *have* democracy."[24]

In May 1913, Follett gave her first paper outside New England at the Seventh Annual Congress of the Playground and Recreation Association of America — the parent association of the New England Institute to which she had spoken the previous year. Almost five hundred people from twenty-eight states registered for the Richmond, Virginia, meeting; thus, Follett had access to her most extensive audience to date.[25] Other presentations allowed her to become personally acquainted with social workers from her own local region. In March 1913 more than fifty representatives of settlement houses in New York, Rhode Island, and Connecticut traveled to Boston to meet with members of the Boston Social Union in a three-day "Inter-City Settlement Conference." Follett was part of a four-member panel entrusted with providing a "Perspective and Forecast" in the closing conference session. Joining her were the presidents of the sponsoring settlement federations (Robert A. Woods of Boston and Rev. Gaylord S. White of New York) and Mary K. Simkhovitch, a former Bostonian who was the founding director of the Greenwich House settlement in New York. Follett appeared on the platform with another New York settlement leader later that year when she and John Lovejoy Elliott of the Hudson Guild, who shared Follett's enthusiasm for fostering neighborhood self-government, spoke at Boston's Ford Hall Forum.[26]

The chance to get to know her East Coast counterparts would prove beneficial to Follett, for the national social centers movement increasingly coalesced around New York.[27] The next conference of note — the April 1916 National Conference on Community Center Problems — was called by the People's Institute, the body that had overseen the effort to transform New York's social centers from a centralized, authoritarian School Board operation to a self-governing set of neighborhood associations.[28] The conference was to be organized by John Collier, the head of the institute's Training School for Community Center Workers. Mary Follett's name appears on a brochure calling for the conference, but she was not named to any of the six committees whose preconference reports formed the basis for deliberations at the meetings.[29] Family matters apparently intervened.

About this time, Follett's seventy-five-year-old mother fell down a flight of stairs while visiting a friend and suffered a serious head injury. At first it seemed that Mrs. Follett might recover completely; she was receiving good care from her longtime servant, Nora Corcoran, and her son George and his family, who lived right next door. But it soon became apparent that Mrs. Follett, who once had been quite active in managing her business affairs, was suffering a gradual diminution of mental powers. The responsibility for disposing of Mrs. Follett's real estate and managing her investments most likely fell to Mary, and in January 1922 Mrs. Follett would write a will naming Mary as the executor of her estate.[30]

Follett had to spend more and more time on her mother's affairs, but she was able to be in New York when the community centers conference convened in April 1916. This conference, like the one in Madison, was the scene of considerable controversy. The delegates to the 1911 Madison meetings had struggled with the question of whether social centers should foster political debate. In 1916 the issue reappeared in the form of a dispute over the wisdom of fostering freedom of speech in community centers. On the last day of the conference Charles Beard, the Columbia University historian, told the delegates that he rejected the position favored by some that would have public and community center forums subject to the "official censorship" of an appointed or elected school authority such as the board or superintendent. Instead, Beard argued, the schools should be open "to responsible organizations of citizens for the discussion of all matters of public concern, even those partisan in character," and this privilege withdrawn by school authorities only if the group in question abused them.[31] Beard later recalled how these seemingly innocent remarks became a *cause célèbre:* "A few weeks before, a speaker at one of the school forums was alleged to have said, 'To Hell with the Flag,' and for that reason a number of persons had urged the closing of school centers altogether. Indeed, some of the speakers at the above-mentioned conference advocated a sort of censorship for all school forums. In my address I merely took the reasonable and moderate view that the intemperance of one man should not drive us into closing the schools to others. The reports in the newspapers, with one exception, were fairly accurate. But one sensational sheet accused me of approving the sentiment, 'To Hell with the Flag.'"

Since these remarks were made just as prewar suspicions about subversive activities were on the rise, Beard's "impassioned plea for radical freedom of speech in school forums," John Collier later recalled, "quite swept the conference away, crowded out the war news on the front pages of newspapers, and is said to have occasioned a trustee meeting at Columbia University." Beard wrote to the newspapers in an effort to "remove the misunderstanding that had arisen," but he was "summoned" before the trustees' committee on education. They reportedly subjected Beard to an "inquisition" into his views and teachings and instructed him to "warn" his department "against teachings 'likely to inculcate disrespect for American institutions.'" This proved to be the first in a series of altercations between Beard and the Columbia trustees, and in October 1917, in one of the landmark academic freedom cases in American higher education, Beard resigned from the Columbia faculty.[32]

The question of whether the nation's community centers should be places of free and open debate on political matters was not the only source of discord at the New York conference. An equally impassioned debate — reflecting ideological differences, regional jealousies, and struggles for personal power — raged over the appropriate financing and control of the centers.[33] According to the sixteen-member Committee on Financial Support of Community Center Work, chaired by John Collier, neither private philanthropy nor public taxation would allow the full development of the community center movement. "Nothing short of progressive self-support through the performance of economic services," the committee declared, "can provide the self-maintenance, or create the needed capital, for the complete development of community center work." Private giving and public taxation, which had long been the basic sources of regular operating funds, should instead be used as working capital for service ventures such as cooperative medical care, cooperative purchases of consumer commodities, substitutes for commercial entertainment, and certain types of formal education. Self-support, the committee concluded, "is not only possible but is morally desirable in the case of community centers, and is in fact necessary [if] genuine group-government or neighborhood self-government is to be developed through the community center."[34]

Mary Follett was well acquainted with the problems of center funding and no doubt saw merit in the Collier committee's advocacy of self-support. Boston's tradition of experimenting with private funds for public purposes had taught Follett the importance both of philanthropic initiatives and of adequate public support; however, she believed that some aims could better be achieved through self-support. Each Boston school center, beginning with the one in East Boston, encouraged its clubs in the most elementary form of self-support — setting dues. Another form of self-support that Follett sought to promote was the collection of admission fees for concerts, plays, and similar performances given by center members for the community. In 1912 Follett met with the Boston Social Union to seek its assistance in securing the passage of state legislation that would allow the collecting of fees in school centers. They could not succeed, Follett told the Union, unless people like them influenced "the school board to see that, in the large use of schools, some sharing of the financial responsibilities would make the undertaking more valuable in the eyes of the public, especially adults." It would prove to be an uphill battle. Some opponents of the fee legislation argued that it would allow "commercialism" to creep into the schools; others worried that the School Committee might profit financially. These objections were finally overcome, and the enabling legislation was passed in 1916.[35]

Follett's experiences with the financing of the Boston school centers did not include any of the more elaborate schemes of cooperative self-support put forward by Collier's committee, but she probably would have given her hearty support to experimentation along these lines. Others in attendance at the New York conference looked less favorably on the committee's recommendations, and the 175 people there again split into factions. One group, comprised largely of delegates from New York and other eastern cities, was led by the conference organizer, John Collier. During his tenure as editor of the People's Institute newspaper, Collier had supported anti-Tammany reform programs — a position with which many center advocates could easily agree, but Collier's participation in the weekly salons of the avant-garde writer Mabel Dodge aroused suspicion. Social and cultural radicals, including Margaret Sanger, Emma Goldman, Max Eastman, Bill Haywood, and John Reed, frequented these gatherings — a situation that led some to label Collier, despite his North Carolina roots, an effete eastern radical.[36]

The "western" faction in this dispute was led by the most celebrated figure in the center movement, Edward J. Ward.[37] Ward, who had left Wisconsin to become head of community organization work at the U.S. Bureau of Education in Washington, leveled a vicious attack on Collier. He charged that Collier and his colleagues on the Committee on Financial Support "represented the ideas and philosophy of 'Bill' Haywood, the I.W.W. leader, and was 'syndicalism' of a pronounced type." Ward's red-baiting remarks received extensive coverage in the *New York Times*.[38] For delegates who were familiar with the history of the community centers movement, there was considerable irony in Ward's allegations. Only a few years earlier, Ward had been the one defending himself, first in Rochester and then in Wisconsin, against accusations that his neighborhood civic clubs were a seedbed for socialist and other radical causes.

Nevertheless, Ward's hostile rhetoric served its purpose, and a "compromise" ensued. A three-part agreement provided "first, that public buildings in general should be available to the people as a right, instead of by permission; second, that community centres should be administered through responsible public officials; and, third, that tax money should be used in the promotion and maintenance of community centres."[39] Ward was quick to hail the adoption of these principles as "a victory," but Collier and the "eastern" faction were the clear winners in the next contest — the selection of officers.

The presidency went to a Chicago man, but both of the "working" positions — secretary and editor of the new periodical, the *Community Center* — were awarded to John Collier. Joining Collier and Ward on a twelve-person Executive Committee were Mary Follett and several other national figures: Clarence A. Perry, the Russell Sage Foundation staff member whose books documented the growth of the movement; Wilbur C. Phillips, whose National Social Unit experiment in Cincinnati soon would be praised nationwide; and Edward L. Burchard, a pioneer in Chicago's community center movement and organizer of a federation of local centers.[40] Follett's inclusion in this group marked her ascendance into the leadership ranks of the national movement, and she soon would emerge as one of the key members of the Executive Committee.

Even before the Executive Committee began its work, Follett probably suspected that Collier and Ward would be better at inspiration and oratory than at organizing. Collier's prowess as a speaker was legendary, but his success as a community organizer perplexed even fervent supporters such as Mabel Dodge, who thought her small, rather disheveled southern friend to be "intense, preoccupied . . . all in the air, wind-blown . . . not down on the solid ground."[41] Edward J. Ward evoked even greater ambivalence from those with whom he had worked. One Wisconsin newspaper called him "absolutely too impractical and theoretical to get down to earth where he can work out any of his ideas." To make matters worse, Ward often behaved in ways that local leaders found "egotistical, overbearing and snobbish." "Again and again have I heard people ask him for advice and direction," one university extension officer complained, "and again and again have I heard him go off on a tangent about the theory of government or the idea of the state or something of that kind."[42] Follett also worried about Edward Burchard, wondering if he could provide the managerial skills that Collier and Ward lacked. But after a year, a relieved Follett reported to Ella Cabot that "my doubts about the National are disappearing, for Mr. Burchard seems to me more and more able as I go on with him. And his energy, devotion and willingness to sacrifice every personal interest are most striking even in this year of 1917."[43]

The most intractable problem for Follett during this period proved to be not her professional colleagues but her own health. Shortly after the New York conference, yet another attack of her mysterious, recurring illness forced Follett to enter Brookline's private Corey Hill Hospital under the care of William P. Graves, a renowned gynecological surgeon at the Harvard Medical School. This time Mary was met with the frightening news "that the chances were against my living."[44] Nothing else is known about this episode. Perhaps it was the appearance of certain menopausal symptoms that led forty-seven-year-old Follett to consult Graves; she may have thought the menopause was exacerbating her long-standing pain and gastric distress. It is even more likely, however, that she sought out Graves for other reasons. During this era, kidney disorders fell within the gynecologist's purview, and Follett's right kidney had been diagnosed as enlarged six years earlier. This enlarged kidney along with Mary's other symptoms may have led Graves to diagnose her condition as cystic kidney disease. In this condition the patient may experience the first symptoms as early as age twenty, but signs of uremia (serious kidney dysfunction) usually appear later. Both kidneys are usually affected, with normal kidney substance replaced by cysts and fibrous tissue, but "one may be worse than the other and much bigger," so that only one appears to be affected. Not only does this condition fit what then was known about Follett's symptoms, but it also is a disease for which no treatment then existed.[45]

Remarkably, however, Follett began slowly to recover, and in doing so defied yet again her doctors' understanding of her illness. The good news was reported by Elizabeth Balch to George Coleman (of the Ford Hall Forum) in a late October letter discussing their work on behalf of Italian-American immigrants. "Please do not speak to anyone of Miss Folletts [*sic*] being ill," Balch implored Coleman, "she is getting better."[46] Indeed, Follett's health improved just in time for her to participate in a new phase in the controversy over the financing and control of community centers.

This phase began in April 1917, when five hundred delegates from twenty-six states came to Chicago for the next annual community centers meeting.[47] Representatives from both the "eastern" and "western" factions appeared on the program, and this inclusiveness initially had salutary effects; but by the fourth day, tensions were rising. Only two weeks before the conference convened, the U.S. Congress had declared war on Germany. The entry of the United States into this bloody conflict was enormously dispiriting for many in the center movement, but the sense of national crisis was also energizing, for it had the effect of raising the stakes for control of the new association; the leaders of the winning faction stood to gain considerable national stature in the likely event that the center movement was asked to help the nation organize for war.

The simmering factional struggle for control of the association erupted when the delegates assembled to adopt a set of bylaws and elect the association's three major officers: the president, the first vice-president, and the secretary, the last being the permanent executive. Normally the president would have been the first officer elected, but on this occasion the nominations for secretary were taken first. This politically astute maneuver, orchestrated by John Collier, allowed him to make a seemingly conciliatory gesture: he nominated a "westerner," Edward Burchard of Chicago, for the influential position and suggested that the headquarters of the national organization be located there rather than in New York. Collier's gesture apparently had its desired positive impact; the delegates cast a unanimous ballot for Burchard.[48]

Attention then shifted to the election of the president. Collier's new "western" allies nominated him and proposed a unanimous ballot. But Edward J. Ward vociferously objected and launched into a lengthy diatribe directly largely at Collier.[49] When Ward finally ended his remarks, he did so with the weak assertion that his dispute with Collier was not at all personal. The laughter that this claim elicited suggests that the delegates saw in Ward's strident attacks on Collier what he could not — evidence of professional jealousy and a desire for power.[50] The delegates, with only two objections, cast a unanimous ballot for Collier.[51]

The secretary and president having been elected, the next order of business was the election of the first vice-president. It was for this purpose that the chair recognized Clarence A. Perry of the Russell Sage Foundation. "It is a truism," Perry told the delegates, "that the heavy end of modern, social and civic effort is being borne by women. If we are going to have a set of officers which will truly represent the forces which are working in this field we want a woman as first Vice-President. We are in the fortunate position of being able to place in this position a woman who is not only a representative of social and civic work but who has also been a leader in this very movement." That person was Mary Follett. She apparently had worked well with other members of the Executive Committee and undoubtedly had won Collier's support. Follett, after all, shared his preference for organizing centers as self-governing groups rather than, as Ward would have it, as individuals "forming de novo constituencies, self-governed by the mass-meeting method." Nominations were quickly closed, and a unanimous ballot was cast naming Mary Follett the first vice-president of the National Community Centers Association.[52]

The spirited debate engendered by the election of officers moved some delegates to raise other matters of concern about the conference program and organization. Surely the most significant of the complaints registered during the final hours of the conference was raised by the New York settlement leader Mary K. Simkhovitch. Simkhovitch found it ironic that despite all the talk about the democracy of the centers movement, no plan had been developed "by which representatives of the people themselves who make up these community centers can get on some of these committees."[53]

In response to this criticism, five geographical regions were established and charged with developing "a system of representation from the bottom up."[54] The New England region was headed by Mary Follett and George W. Coleman, director of Boston's Ford Hall Forum and president of the national Open Forum Council.[55] Governance by community center members was an idea to which Follett had long been committed, but experience had taught her that progress would be made very slowly. A citywide representative body had been a part of Follett's dreams for the Boston centers from the beginning, but the only citywide body created to date was the Club Congress of the Junior City Councils. Representative schemes at the state and regional levels were sure to be doubly difficult to achieve. In January 1918, seven months after the Chicago conference, Edward Burchard surveyed the progress of the state and regional units for the association's "Half-Yearly Report." Although Follett was accomplishing more than the heads of most other units, even she had succeeded only in initiating plans for a New England conference.

In his remarks closing the Chicago conference, John Collier expressed gratitude for the criticisms that had been offered during the final conference sessions, saying that "it is this tension, this passion, this pugnacity which is the hope of our Movement . . . Let this be one national body which shall be

hospitable to the independent, not only to strange ideas but equally to un-
curbed temperaments. Let that be our distinguishing character. It will be."[56]

Years later, as she worked out her ideas about constructive conflict and
integrative conflict resolution in *Creative Experience* (1924) and her lectures
on business administration, Mary Follett no doubt had occasion to recall these
community center disputes. It was from experiences such as these that Follett
became convinced, first, that conflict could be beneficial, and second, that even
the most controversial matters often include threads from which an integrative resolution can be woven. For example, partisans of each of the various
functions of community centers — recreation, education, or civic discussion
and action — might have integrated their concerns around an idea that had
been central to Follett's work in Boston, namely, that any activity is appropriate to a community center as long as it helps participants learn to work together and develops a social spirit. And those who battled over the financing of
community centers might have been united around the notion that each form
of financial support has a place in the long-term development of a center:
private funds being especially useful as seed money, public funds providing a
solid operating base, and self-support fostering a sense of local responsibility
and encouraging the development of local leadership.

The issue of the control and governance of the centers was perhaps the most
intractable problem. Many people in the movement, like Follett, were committed to the ideal of self-governing centers but believed that self-government
had to be learned rather than "granted." This meant that center members
needed, at least for a time, the expertise that professional workers could provide; yet the experts must create ample opportunities for the members to
become skillful practitioners of self-government rather than simply running
the centers themselves. Follett's experience with this difficult issue in the Boston centers undoubtedly influenced her emerging notions about effective leadership and helped to shape aspects of her ideas about "integrative" conflict
resolution — particularly the importance of seeking integrations in action and
experimentation rather than in ideological debate.[57]

The national disputes over the functions, financing, and control of community centers (following as they did on a series of local struggles over school
center development and women's suffrage in Boston) left Mary Follett with a
sober appreciation of the difficulties inherent in finding integrative resolutions
to conflict — difficulties that could be exacerbated by personal antagonisms
and stubborn adherence to ideology. The process of unifying differences of
interests and standards, Follett would later write, places significant intellectual demands on the participants, for it requires of them "a high order of

intelligence, keen perception and discrimination, and more than all, a brilliant inventiveness" — and even this often was not enough.[58] Bringing out differences and integrating them into a unity requires that we learn better skills of working together and that we use those skills in processes that encourage the reciprocal interplay of thought, will, and action. This was an agenda to which Follett would return again and again during the last decade of her career. She would make her first serious attempt to explicate this aspect of her social philosophy in *The New State,* the book she was just beginning to write.

15

The War Years

The year 1917 brought sorrow and anxiety to the Follett-Briggs household as well as pride in professional accomplishments. On February 10, Pauline Agassiz Shaw, Isobel's great good friend of almost forty years and Mary's primary patron, died at the age of seventy-six. A "painfully sore-hearted" Isobel, writing to thank Mary Hutcheson Page and her husband for a commemorative sonnet, disclosed that their tribute "unseals the fountain of hot tears, but it relieves, too." "It is that 'gratitude unsaid' that kills me," Briggs confided, "and yet it seems to me that I was telling her all the time — as much, that is, as her noble reticence would allow."[1] Shaw's death had a special poignancy for sixty-eight-year-old Isobel. Not only had a dear friend passed from her life, but only six months earlier Mary Follett, her partner of more than twenty years, had been told she might not live.

The death of Pauline Agassiz Shaw also generated anxieties for Briggs and Follett of a more mundane variety. From the beginning, Shaw had provided seed money for many of Follett's social and civic projects, and she apparently also had paid Follett and Briggs stipends for their work. Now both forms of support were threatened. The terms of Quincy Adams Shaw's will prevented his wife from leaving bequests; upon her death, the money he had left to her almost a decade earlier was to revert to their children. In a November 1916 letter, Pauline Agassiz Shaw expressed her anxiety about this state of affairs and exhorted her children to continue the kinds of endeavors that had given meaning to her life: "I had too much — you will all have too much — and it will require great effort with God's help to determine 'to give' rather than 'to hold,' and to think deeply as you spend: to spend for progress and welfare rather than for 'pleasure' — or mere temporary amusement . . . What I had, I chose to spend in asking others to work with me. Now, this continues till I go and then, you must decide how to adjust this problem so that all these faithful workers and friends will not suffer in the re-adjustment but may gradually adjust their own lives to any change you may decide to make." Shaw urged her children to "take several years" in making these adjustments, but her advice was not heeded. According to the records of the administration of Shaw's $630,000 estate, support of all forms was quickly terminated. The stipends to Briggs and Follett were discontinued after a $600 payment to Briggs in June and a $2,000 payment to Follett in October.[2]

The loss of Shaw's support caused Follett and Briggs anxiety about their own personal finances, but the loss was doubly troublesome because it came just as Follett was trying to raise funds for the new National Community Centers Association. In seeking the financial support of Boston contributors, Follett was forced to compete with war bond drives and other war-related fundraising campaigns; even so she managed to raise almost 40 percent of the revenues for the NCCA's 1917 operating budget. The next year, in a remarkable display of commitment to this new venture, Follett and Briggs together contributed $1,100 to the NCCA, a sum representing almost 55 percent of the association's operating revenues.[3]

It was early in this period, in the spring of 1917, that Follett decided to write a chronicle of the community centers movement. Needing an alternative to the stipend she had received from Shaw, Follett may have hoped that a book on a topic of contemporary interest would generate sizable royalties. Then, too, Shaw's death together with Mary's own unfavorable prognosis surely must have heightened forty-eight-year-old Follett's sense of her own mortality. If she had anything to say to the world, she had best not delay.[4]

Having made the decision to write the book, Follett devoted herself quite single-mindedly to the task. She surrounded herself with stacks of books and papers and worked from "very early morning all day long in fierce absorption." Before long the living-room floor was littered with "piles and piles of yellow paper, some with but a word or two scribbled on them." Her method of working was to "jot down a thought, a quotation, a reference, on a separate sheet, then shuffle and analyse them ready for future use." Once Follett began to write, she was "so absorbed, so utterly concentrated on the creative chapter that was shaping and formulating itself out of what looked like a mere scattering of papers, that ordinary living and intercourse was for the time suspended." It seemed, Elizabeth Balch would later recall, that "everything was burned up in a fierce white creative glow which left her exhausted, physically, nervously and mentally. She was so depleted that to come to a lunch table where there was a quick clever chatter and talk would have been impossible. To do creative work in the sense of finding forms for her intensive thinking left nothing over."[5] Still, Mary was anxious to get others' opinions about her work and actively solicited feedback. She discussed every word thoroughly with Isobel and made telephone calls to colleagues asking them to come over so that she "could read something she had just written and discuss it."[6]

Briggs did what she could to protect Follett from unwanted intrusions, but some distractions were unavoidable.[7] One concerned Mary's younger brother, George. One Saturday around this time, George Follett stayed home with a cold instead of going to his job as a salesman of cotton and woolen yarns at Arlington Mills. When a coworker mentioned that he had seen George outside in his yard earlier that same morning, the mill owner reportedly "picked up the phone and fired him." George had worked at Arlington Mills for seventeen years, but his long tenure was of little help in securing a comparable position with another firm.[8] George already was in his early forties, and this was the worst possible time to be looking for work: the end of World War I brought "serious and irreversible losses" to the textile and shoe industries in Massachusetts; firms "cut production, slashed wages, and sometimes closed their plants altogether."[9] George was unemployed for almost five years before he landed a sales position with a Philadelphia firm; in the meantime his resourceful wife, Edna, sewed and gardened, and the older of the five children took odd jobs. Mary, too, did what she could to help. She supervised the sale of her mother's Quincy Point real estate holdings, keeping only the house at 105 Putnam Street, and used a portion of the proceeds to purchase the mortgage on George and Edna's house at 109 Putnam Street.[10]

In addition to these familial obligations, Follett had pressing professional responsibilities with the school centers. When Eva Whiting White, the director of Boston's Department of Extended Use, left for Washington to help with the war effort, Follett "very energetically [undertook] to hold the Boston situation together" until an appropriate replacement could be found and commitments to that person's appointment could be secured. White helped by taking a leave of absence rather than simply resigning — allowing time, as White later put it, to "get her own Irishman in." The eventual appointment of James Mulroy as director reportedly delighted Follett, for Mulroy had been one of the charter members of her turn-of-the-century Roxbury debating club.[11]

Mulroy's appointment was only one of the several professional matters demanding Mary Follett's attention. As an officer of the National Community Centers Association, she had to devote considerable time to fundraising. Follett, Collier, and Burchard were each charged with raising one-third of the $6,000 operating budget for 1917–18, a good portion of which would be used to fund the association's monthly newsletter, the *Community Center*. During these early years the *Community Center* would be the primary vehicle by which the NCCA carried out the spirit of the mandate of the Chicago conference that "each local Community Center, as far as possible, [should be] represented in the membership and voting power of the Association." The *Community Center* would report "significant events and progress in the Centers themselves" and would do so in "popular rather than technical style." Subscription rates were set at only fifty cents a year so that members of local centers as well as professional workers could afford to subscribe. Contemplating the fundraising tasks that lay ahead, Follett told Ella Cabot that she expected to "have to work pretty hard to get $2000," but the job would perhaps be "easier now that we are definitely contributing to the war work, now that people see that we are taking a real part in solving the present problem of the world."[12]

Follett had not initially supported the entry of the United States into the European conflict; before the declaration of war on Germany, she had promoted planning for a "constructive peace." In January 1915 Follett was one of seven women who sponsored a controversial Tremont Temple lecture by the militant English suffragist and peace advocate Emmeline Pethick-Lawrence.[13] Pethick-Lawrence's appearance in Boston followed successful speeches in New York and Chicago and a rally in Washington, where she helped to inaugurate Jane Addams' Woman's Peace party.[14] More than a thousand women turned out for the Boston lecture, and they heard a passionate appeal from Pethick-Lawrence for "the inclusion of the mother-half of the human race into the ranks of articulate citizenship," for a more democratic control of foreign policy, and for the creation of a United States of Europe.[15]

Although Follett's sponsorship of the Pethick-Lawrence speech has been documented, there is as yet no other information about her involvement in peace-related activities. Isobel Briggs became a member of the Boston chapter of the Women's Peace party, but Follett apparently did not join.[16] Perhaps she doubted the viability of a group that limited its membership to women; or perhaps the public vilification suffered by Jane Addams in the summer of 1915 convinced her that further work in the peace movement could result in the crippling of the community centers movement — the cause she held most dear. Or perhaps Mary was once again troubled with poor health and was trying not to overextend herself.[17] One thing at least is clear: Follett was convinced that "you can never aim directly at peace, peace is what you get through other things." Writing about the movement in *The New State* (1918), Follett would say that "much of the peace propaganda urges us to choose peace rather than war. But the decision between 'war' or 'peace' never lies within our power. These are mere words to gather up in convenient form of expression an enormous amount that is underneath. All sorts of interests compete, all sorts of ideas compete or join: if they can join, we have peace; if they must compete, we have war. But war or peace is merely an outcome of the process; peace or war has come, by other decisions, long before the question of peace or war ever arises." In other words, she had become convinced that any hope for "future international relations lies, not in the ethical exhortations of the pacifists, nor in plans for an economic war, but in the recognition of the possibility of a community of nations."[18] It was toward that end that she would bend her efforts — toward discovering the principles of community wherever they might be found, in the neighborhood, the nation, or in international relations.[19]

Follett was far more successful than her colleagues in raising funds to support the NCCA's contributions to the war effort. By December 31 she had raised $1,400, compared with only $500 for Collier and none for Burchard. Impressed by her performance, the Executive Committee asked Follett to form a finance committee and suggest a treasurer for the association.[20] The "contributions to the war work" that Follett so successfully employed in her fundraising efforts were concerned mainly with the NCCA's involvement in food conservation.[21]

In May 1917 Herbert Hoover had returned to the United States from his Belgian relief efforts to take up additional duties as the nation's food administrator in President Wilson's unofficial war cabinet. Hoover's method of organizing the Food Administration relied heavily on voluntary action and compliance and on institutional cooperation. Follett's colleague Edward Burchard and leaders of other prominent social and civic organizations were enlisted to publicize the need for food conservation and to educate people at the local level in its techniques, all under the direction of Ray Lyman Wilbur, the Stanford University president who had been appointed director of Hoover's Conservation Division.[22]

Among the measures being advocated were "the substitution of less critical commodities in American diets, the gospel of the 'clean plate' and the 'meatless days,' and a whole battery of new foods, new menus, and canning techniques." The food conservation campaign gave the women of America their first opportunity to make a direct personal contribution to the war effort, and many were inspired by the notion that "food could win the war." Achieving an Allied victory, however, was not the sole aim of the Food Administration.

Hoover repeatedly stressed that conservation was an essential part of helping the people of Europe survive the devastation of war. It was this dual purpose — European relief as well as an Allied victory — that made it possible for pacifists such as Jane Addams to speak on behalf of food conservation.[23]

The National Community Centers Association saw food conservation as a new field of educational activity. Although the NCCA participated in the campaign to secure written conservation pledges from neighborhood women, the association was not involved with any of the compulsory activities of the Food Administration.[24] "Our cooperation," Edward Burchard wrote in September 1917, "is devoted completely to the effort to bring to bear the educational forces of the school system during the leisure time hours, and on the other hand to help promote such complete organization of the neighborhood as will bring the family and the individual to the school centers where they may learn the need for cooperation in this great national endeavor." Many people associated with the movement heartily supported this strategy. "You have a great idea," wrote University of Michigan sociologist Charles Horton Cooley in a letter to the *Community Center,* "and I feel sure this is the time to put it through."[25] At first Mary Follett wasn't so sure, but by the summer of 1917 she, too, was supportive of the NCCA's involvement. "That we can help Hoover is obvious," Follett wrote Ella Cabot. "That Hoover and food conservation can help us is now becoming clear to me, although I held off at first, but all this will help us teach the members of the Centres what civic life and civic responsibility and national life and national responsibility really mean in their own lives." But Follett's major concerns continued to center upon "building up the association," and she "extracted an oath from Mr. Burchard that he will also do the things I think necessary to be done" before she gave the food conservation campaign her full support.[26]

Burchard's first step to build up the association involved persuading the newly formed Council of National Defense (CND) to "perfect its Community Councils of National Defense in every School District on a cooperative and educational basis."[27] The Council of National Defense, a prewar creation of the federal government, was organized in October 1916 to "coordinate industries and resources for the national security and welfare" and to investigate and make recommendations to the president concerning the production, distribution, and consumption of materials needed by military and civilian populations.

The federal legislation establishing the Council of National Defense called for decisions to be made and actions taken at the state and local as well as at the national level. To carry out this mandate, the CND called for the creation of a council of defense in every state in the Union (either by appointment of the governor or by act of the legislature) and established a State Councils Section to coordinate the work of men in these state-level groups.[28] To organize the wartime work of women, the CND appointed a separate Woman's Committee led by the distinguished suffragist Anna H. Shaw.[29]

Months before the community-organizing activities of the State Councils Section and the Woman's Committee were fully under way, the NCCA's Executive Committee recognized that the wartime creation of a network of community councils of defense could be a real boon to the community centers movement. If local community councils were successfully organized during wartime, "the full strength of each neighborhood" during the *postwar* period could be devoted to preparing "citizens to do their part for the new health and housing of a garden city; for vocational and cultural opportunity for every youth and adult; for an increasing share for the worker in industrial management; for the restoration of the neighborhood; and for the more intimate understanding and control by everyday men and women of the mechanism of administration for the public weal."[30]

The NCCA was only one of many social and civic groups enthusiastically supporting the wartime mobilization. "Settlement workers, like many other reformers," writes historian Allen F. Davis, "deluded themselves into thinking that the social experiments and social action of the war years would lead to even greater accomplishments in the reconstruction years ahead."[31] Compared with some of its counterparts, the Executive Committee of the NCCA seems to have maintained a healthy skepticism about what the government could accomplish if left to its own devices; as a result, the NCCA kept its independence and was quite assertive in its dealings with government agencies. Believing that the community councils of defense would fulfill their postwar promise only if they were developed along the lines of the "Community School Center," the NCCA worked intensively to influence the plans of the Council of National Defense. In December 1917, after "several months of work" and "appeals, verbal and written," Burchard reported to his colleagues that the CND had officially adopted the NCCA's school-centered approach to community council organizing.[32] President Wilson applauded the council's decision as an "advance of vital significance." When thoroughly implemented, the president believed, it would succeed "in welding the nation together as no nation of great size has ever been welded before."[33]

The impending infusion of governmental resources into school-based community organizing was warmly welcomed by the NCCA, but the Executive Committee realized that the proselytizing done by these federal and state agencies would generate a plethora of new demands for "professional assistance in the establishment and maintenance of war centers" and in techniques of neighborhood cooperation. These demands, cautioned Burchard, would almost certainly impose "a heavy obligation on any Association, like ours, standing for high professional ideals."[34]

Believing that the strain would be lessened if the technical assistance and clearinghouse functions of the NCCA were assured adequate financial support, Burchard wrote a fundraising prospectus based on the arguments that he had successfully used in his discussions with the CND. In this prospectus, which was "carefully reviewed" by both Mary Follett and Alice Brandeis, Burchard warned that community organization, whether for wartime or postwar reconstruction, should not be left solely to government agencies. Community organizing was "basically an educational process for the entire population of a neighborhood" and, as such, "requires more than press publicity, advertising posters, occasional meetings or canvassing of a neighborhood when a drive is on." The creation of an effective network of community councils would require "the whole-hearted and intelligent support and help of the educational forces of the country." Unfortunately, the nation's teachers, administrators, and school patrons, Burchard continued, "do not begin to understand their strategic importance and obligation in developing these Community Councils of Defense and need a campaign of educational propaganda." As he saw it, "The community center is succeeding but primarily because of the demand of the public for more recreational and educational opportunity. Its greatest obstacle today is the resistant attitude of these educational forces who do not understand it, or fear its democracy."[35]

Assisting the Council of National Defense in gaining direct access to the nation's educators represented yet another way in which the NCCA offered the federal government uniquely valuable assistance. In city after city, organizers of school-based community centers had developed expertise in creating productive relations with educators. In Boston, for example, Follett had worked closely with each successive superintendent and had taken special pains to involve the masters in each school-related activity.[36] But it was through a national-level partnership with the National Education Association (NEA) that the NCCA had the best hope of facilitating meaningful contacts between the Council of National Defense and the educational establishment.[37]

When Edward Burchard made his initial contacts, he sought both permission for the NCCA to participate formally in the NEA's 1918 national meeting and closer ties with the Department of School Patrons. The School Patrons, a federation of women's organizations (five national and one regional) committed to strengthening public education, was a particularly influential group because its members were in a position to "react both on the school and the community, on the school board, the teacher, the local editor, and other 'opinion makers.' "[38] Burchard also explored ways in which the NCCA might make use of the NEA's newly established Washington office. This office proved to be a powerful tool for communicating with educators and legislators; it expanded in only five years from a staff of four in two rented rooms to a group of fifty working out of its own building.[39]

By the summer of 1918, as Follett was completing a draft of her book manuscript, the NCCA's two-pronged strategic plan — building up the association while contributing to the war work — seemed to be bearing fruit. In July 1918 the NCCA joined the NEA for a successful national meeting in Pittsburgh and agreed to prepare, in conjunction with the Department of School Patrons, a program on community work for the NEA's Chicago conference the following February.[40] The NCCA's working relationship with the Council of National Defense also seemed to be unfolding well. Frederick Lewis Allen wrote a highly favorable article about the state councils and their local affiliates in the December 1917 issue of *The Century*. "One wonders," Allen exclaimed, "whether ever before in American history there has been anything like this system of bodies appointed by the States, working together at the suggestion of Washington, and undertaking everything from the construction of warehouses to the supplying of free dental service and the distributing of patriotic pamphlets . . . By the very looseness of its organization, [the state council system] enlists local pride and local energy in the cause not of the locality, but of the nation . . . They and millions like them in other counties and other States are taking part in government by the people, for the nation." By means of impressive teamwork, the councils reportedly were stimulating the production and conservation of food, recruiting home guards to take the place of federalized state militia, registering and educating aliens, surveying railroad equipment, organizing volunteer motor brigades, equipping mobile hospitals, entertaining men in training camps, and arbitrating labor crises.

Allen struck only one cautionary note in his article — this concerning the penchant of some state councils to use heavy-handed intimidation to shape public opinion. "Missouri and Iowa do not compromise with sedition," Allen noted. "When disloyal utterances are reported to Mr. Young, chairman of the Iowa Council, he writes to the supposed traitor and asks him point-blank to declare whether he is for the United States or for Germany. The chairman in Henry County, Missouri . . . sends a white card of caution to any man reported disloyal. If the complaints continue, he sends a blue card of warning. If this does not serve, out goes a red card, asking the man to report to the local postmaster; the final step is to write the Department of Justice about the offender. At least that is the plan . . . Mr. Lindsay has not found it necessary to send any red cards yet; the white and blue ones have done the trick." Whatever

concern Allen had about this sort of intimidation was mitigated by his conviction that the councils relied less on threats and coercion than on rational
means of influencing public opinion. "One may approve of such methods or
not," Allen concluded, "but the state councils happily have not been content
with intimidation of the disloyal; they have generally realized that persuasion
and education are the surest avenues to public unity."[41]

The performance of the Council of National Defense and its state and local
affiliates occasioned one other sort of concern, this time among the members
of the NCCA's Executive Committee. The Executive Committee heartily endorsed the principle of "decentralizing" that had been adopted for the activities of the Council of National Defense and Bureau of Education, but the
NCCA soon found that when making policy these federal agencies usually
ignored both experts and members of local communities.[42] Each of the agencies of government, Edward Burchard wrote, should do its "proper work of
statistics, guidance and supervision, but [it must] not arrogate to itself the
rights of self-activity that belong to the locality and individual." Government
officials at every level "are but means to an educational end, and that is to
secure the utmost cooperation of each individual in the National struggle we
are all in."[43]

Mary Follett, having seen that the network of community councils was
being used almost exclusively to communicate policies already established in
Washington to the nation's neighborhoods, took up this problem in *The New
State.* "In a country which is even nominally a democracy," she wrote, "you
cannot win a war without explaining your aims and your policy and carrying
your people with you step by step. If beyond this the country wishes to be
really a democracy, the neighborhood groups must have a share in forming the
aims and the policy."[44]

The intensity of Follett's efforts on behalf of the NCCA, coupled with her
concern about her brother's financial difficulties, forced Follett and Isobel
Briggs to give up their usual summer retreat to Overhills. But by working
continuously through both the summer and a frigid winter plagued by coal
shortages, Mary produced a draft of her book manuscript by April 1918.[45]
Although she had begun this book simply as a chronicle of her experiences in
the community center movement, what finally emerged was an impassioned
and complex critique of modern representative government.

Recognizing that her manuscript was quite different from the book she and
others had originally envisioned, Follett thought it wise to seek comments
from colleagues before sending the manuscript off to the publisher. She first
took it to Anna Boynton Thompson and Albert Bushnell Hart, whose opinions she respected and who would give her personal support. Follett then

sought advice from people outside her immediate circle. One of her readers was Harry A. Overstreet, a philosophy professor at the City College of New York who was a pioneer in adult education and a promoter of vocational schemes of political representation. In later years Overstreet remembered his surprise at finding "that a mere woman was diving into the complexities of psycho-social problems," but he "soon learned that this 'mere woman' could hold her own with the best thinkers of them all."[46] Another from whom Follett sought advice was Dean Roscoe Pound of the Harvard Law School, the internationally renowned advocate of "sociological jurisprudence."[47] Follett later confided to Pound that she had wished for his critique "much as I might wish for the moon, thinking you would not want to be bothered with a nonentity like myself," but Albert Bushnell Hart encouraged the idea and offered to approach Pound on her behalf. "What is it that you do," Hart inquired of Pound with his characteristic wit, "that so arouses hard-thinking young minds? . . . I don't know where [Follett] got these revolutionary ideas — certainly not from me when I was her teacher. You take the responsibility of upsetting people's cherished formulas."[48]

Pound agreed to read the manuscript and seemed a likely candidate to write the introduction. But the Follett-Pound relationship got off to a rocky start when Pound suggested that Follett seek a critique of her ideas from Harold J. Laski, the brilliant young political theorist who in the autumn of 1916 had come to Harvard from McGill University in Montreal. Follett thought highly of Laski's work and originally had been anxious to meet him; but when she began to hear that Laski was "arrogant" and "insufferable" — the kind of person who would "talk over [her] ideas with every one freely" before she had a chance to present them herself — she had second thoughts. Follett expressed reservations to Pound and no doubt quickly wished that she had kept her concerns to herself. Pound was incensed, and their relationship seemed permanently damaged.

Roscoe Pound had become acquainted with Harold Laski during the summer of 1915 through Felix Frankfurter, one of Pound's Harvard Law School colleagues. Laski, who was still at McGill and deeply desirous of a Harvard appointment, made the most of Frankfurter's entrée by quickly beginning a correspondence with Pound. Indeed, when Pound was named dean of the Harvard Law School later that year, Laski wrote an ingratiating letter of congratulations that, according to his biographers, "knew no bounds in its flattery." Laski's association with Pound was considerably strengthened the following year when Laski received a Harvard teaching appointment and, at the same time, enrolled as a student in the Law School. Although Laski found that he was capable of sustaining this demanding workload for only a single semester, he served for almost two years as the *Harvard Law Review*'s book review editor. In this capacity, he brought to the *Review* a "heightened sensitivity . . . to the relationship between law and the social sciences" for which Pound, a pioneer of sociological jurisprudence, was openly grateful.

Follett, who obviously had not been aware of the intimacy of the Pound-Laski association, immediately sought to salvage her own fledgling relationship with Pound. First, she offered him a written apology. "I now accept what you say about Mr. Laski," Follett told Pound, "as you are in a much better position to know than these other people, and I hope that next winter Mr. Laski and I may meet and join forces to work for the same end. Our differences are very few compared to our agreements. Mr. Laski has erudition, natural brilliance of mind etc. I have no such qualities in any degree. The only justification I have writing this book is in the fact that most students have not had so much practical experience as I have had, and on the other hand, the majority of social workers have not been even as much of a student as I have been. The combination I thought gave me perhaps a right to speak."[49]

Follett found that Pound's anger was not easily assuaged. "Good ideas are *res communes,*" Pound icily replied, "and if you have any which you wish to put forth unspotted by the world my advice would be to keep them strictly to yourself and not ask anyone to read your manuscript." This chilling retort would have intimidated most people, but Follett tenaciously worked at resolving the dispute. She wrote again, first reiterating her apology and explaining her reasoning; then she cleverly appealed to Pound's sense of justice. "You have got a wrong impression of me," Follett told Pound, "exactly as certain people have of Mr. Laski. You would like those people to erase that wrong impression and substitute the true idea. Won't you please do the same for me?" This letter apparently did the trick. The relationship was salvaged, and Pound soon supplied Follett with useful clarifications of several matters discussed in her chapters on jurisprudence. Although Pound did not write the hoped-for introduction, the Follett-Pound correspondence suggests that this outcome was due less to any fundamental reluctance on his part than to his demanding schedule and to Longmans, Green's desire to have the book published by September.[50]

Follett, too, was anxious to get the book out and was quite explicit about her reasons. "Our political life is stagnating," she warned in the book's opening sentences; "capital and labor are virtually at war, the nations of Europe are at one another's throats — because we have not yet learned how to live together." Convinced that the "twentieth century must find a new principle of association," Follett tried to provide just that in *The New State.*[51] Her theorizing about the effective functioning of groups would provide the foundation for much of her later writing on business management and would give meaning and direction to the rest of her life.

16

The New State

In September 1918, after months of intensive manuscript revisions, Follett allowed herself one of her few "larks" of the summer. She celebrated her fiftieth birthday at the summer home of Louis and Alice Brandeis southwest of Boston. Writing to thank Alice for her family's delightful company and for a meal that included Mary's favorite food — chocolate blancmange — Follett added a lengthy postscript about the experience of writing *The New State*. "In order to write that book," Follett told Brandeis, "I have had to think everything out pretty carefully & I know now what I would go to the stake for. That isn't either a joke or highfalutin. I mean it pretty literally. I have come to certain conclusions which I am willing to give up everything for."[1]

When Follett published her 1896 book on the Speakership, more than one reviewer had chastised her — an inexperienced woman — for daring to speak on contemporary political matters. Now, more than twenty years later, Follett was not dissuaded by the memory of these stinging criticisms. With a courage born of years of social and civic experience in the complex milieu of Boston politics and the national community centers movement, Follett moved boldly and confidently. She opened *The New State* with the startling assertion that "representative government has failed. It has failed because it was not a method by which men could govern themselves." Democracy should be "a genuine union of true individuals" — and this sort of union, unfortunately, had never existed in America.

To learn how to attain such a union, Follett wrote, we must "leap at once from the region of theory, of which Americans are so fond, to a practical scheme of living . . . it is not merely that we must be allowed to govern ourselves, we must learn how to govern ourselves; it is not only that we must be given 'free speech,' we must learn a speech that is free; we are not given rights, we create rights; it is not only that we must invent machinery to get a social will expressed, we must invent machinery that will get a social will created."[2] To replace a mythological democracy with the actual workings of democracy, the American people would first have to "find a new principle of association." Her goal in The New State was to elucidate that principle.

Follett's search for this new principle of association resulted in a book that Benjamin R. Barber, Kekst Professor of Civil Society at the University of Maryland, called "an American classic of participatory democracy." Lamenting in 1998 that The New State "has remained in the shadows of American political theory for too long," Barber asserts that it is especially relevant to our times — an era in which there is much skepticism from all quarters about whether our institutions of government have any real significance for the lives of average Americans or for the major issues facing our nation. In 1998 Jane Mansbridge, Adams Professor of Political Leadership and Democratic Values at Harvard University, described Follett's book as having made lasting contributions — most notably her "recognition of the root dependence of all democracy on local democracy and institutions, and her insistence that the associations on which democracy should be based can maintain difference within unity, conflict within integration."[3]

Follett's book was widely reviewed after publication and sold well enough to be reprinted five times in the early 1920s. Since then The New State has been mostly ignored. Yet according to Rutgers University political scientist Kevin Mattson, Follett's critique of the American political system is far more grounded in the practical realities of democratic participation than the work of most of her male contemporaries such as John Dewey, Herbert Croly, Walter Lippmann, and Harold Laski.[4] Follett's experience in Boston community centers had taught her well about the psychological processes involved in self-government.

The New State also is notable for what it reveals about Follett's intellectual mastery of new scholarship being generated in the emerging social sciences. Sociologists for the first time were exploring the psychological aspects of collective behavior, psychologists were writing about societal influences on

individual mental phenomena, and political scientists were once again studying human nature as well as political institutions. Follett was intrigued by
this intellectual activity. An impressive array of groundbreaking works appeared around the turn of the century, many of which would become classics.
These included works in sociology by Charles Horton Cooley, George Herbert
Mead, and Edward A. Ross; in psychology by James Mark Baldwin, G. Stanley Hall, Sigmund Freud, and William McDougall; and in political science
by Graham Wallas, Herbert Croly, Walter Lippmann, Robert Michels, John
Dewey, and Harold J. Laski.[5]

In *The New State*, Follett displays no interest in depicting herself as an
original thinker and readily acknowledges her intellectual debts. Indeed, she
asks her readers to think of the word "new" in the title as connoting ideas that
she had found alive, real, and vital in modern political life even if they had
been "familiar to Aristotle or Kant." But she deliberately avoids any systematic tracing of the "strands of thought which have led us to our present ideas"
and refuses for the most part to identify herself with particular schools of
thought in ongoing academic disputes. Convinced that "much interweaving of
thought will be necessary before the form of the new state appears to us," in
The New State Follett uses a style of discourse quite different from the tightly
knit argument of her book on the Speakership. Eschewing for the most part
citations, explanatory footnotes, references, and even an index, Follett adopts
an informal style, one better suited to "the tentative, the partial, the fragmentary thought, the isolated flash of insight from some genius, all of which, is
being turned to the solution of those problems which, from our waking and
our sleeping, face us with their urgent demand."[6]

To modern readers who are not conversant with Follett's numerous informal, cryptic references to ideas and issues of the day, her book often
seems obscure, peculiarly organized, and badly in need of condensation.[7]
Readers are also challenged by Follett's erudition: a plethora of academic
disciplines (philosophy, political theory, sociology, psychology, and even biology) informs her thought. To make her book more accessible, this chapter
explicates in some detail the major issues she raised—wherever possible in
her own passionate voice. The power of her rhetoric helps us appreciate
why Follett's postwar audience found both new direction and hope in *The
New State*.

Follett divides *The New State* into three major sections: a description of the
"fundamental principles that must underlie the new state," an analysis of
"how far they are expressed in present political forms," and suggestions about

"how they can be expressed." Each of the principles underlying Follett's *New State* has as its starting point an integrative group process.

Democracy Must Be Created through an Integrative Group Process

It had long been thought that the primary vehicle for creating the social will was the state, but the state, Follett asserts, is "now discredited in many quarters." Many currents had fed the "stream of reaction against the state." Some thought the state was dependent on an electorate disparagingly characterized "as a crowd hypnotized by the party leaders, big words, vague ideas and loose generalizations." The state also felt "remote and foreign" to many citizens, especially when contrasted with the "real and intimate" experiences they were having in voluntary associations. Still others believed that the state had failed to respond adequately to changing economic realities such as labor's demand for a share of political power and the increasing tendency of both economic and social interests to cut across national boundaries. And finally, the state was being discredited by intellectuals such as the pluralists who saw the state merely as an umpire, its sole role being to settle conflicts among other societal groups.[8]

Having enumerated these various forms of reaction against the state, Follett concluded that "every one of these reasons has force. Almost any one of these reasons is sufficient to turn political theory into new channels, seeking new currents of political life." As Follett saw it, the fundamental issue was the need to find "some method by which the government shall continuously represent the people." How was this to be attained?[9]

Follett had struggled with issues of democratic control throughout her years in the community centers movement and, as a result, was convinced of the importance of creating effectively functioning groups. At the same time, however, she had seen that people often do not know how to work together. Thus, when she asserted that "the fundamental reason for the study of group psychology is that no one can give us democracy, we must learn democracy," Follett was arguing from experience rather than from *a priori* social philosophy. "To be a democrat is not to decide on a certain form of human association, it is to learn how to live with other men."[10]

Follett begins her discussion of the principles on which the new state should be founded with a description of an effective group process. The example she uses is a committee meeting — a setting certain to be familiar to most of her readers. "The object of a committee meeting," Follett writes, "is first of all to create a common idea. I do not go to a committee meeting merely to give my own ideas. If that were all, I might write my fellow-members a letter. But neither do I go to learn other people's ideas. If that were all, I might ask each to write me a letter. I go to a committee meeting in order that all together we may create a group idea, an idea which will be better than any one of our ideas alone, moreover which will be better than all of our ideas added together. For this group idea will not be produced by the process of addition, but by the interpenetration of us all. This subtle psychic process by which the resulting idea shapes itself is the process we want to study."[11]

If we succeed in creating a "group idea," we become "tremendously civilized people, for we have learned one of the most important lessons of life: we have learned to do that most wonderful thing, to say 'I' representing a whole instead of 'I' representing one of our separate selves. The course of action decided upon is what we all together want, and I see that it is better than what I had wanted alone. It is what *I* now want." The creation of such unities gave Follett extraordinary pleasure, for she saw in them the realization of the promise of her youthful Idealism freed from its deadening metaphysics. "We see now," Follett continues, "that the process of the many becoming one is not a metaphysical or mystical idea; psychological analysis shows us how we can at the same moment be the self and the other, it shows how we can be forever apart and forever united."[12]

What is required of the individual in order that this sort of group idea be produced? "First and foremost," Follett writes, "each is to do his part." This would require getting rid of "some rather antiquated notions." For much of her life, Follett had subscribed to the idea that the individual should subordinate himself or herself to the Whole. But now, after careful reflection, she concluded that the subordination called for in Idealist philosophy was a mistake. To create a genuine group idea, "every man must contribute what is in him to contribute. The individual is not to facilitate agreement by courteously (!) waiving his own point of view. That is just a way of shirking. Nor may I say, 'Others are able to plan this better than I.' Such an attitude is the result either of laziness or of a misconception . . . I must not subordinate myself, I must affirm myself and give my full positive value to that meeting." A majority vote, or "even the passing of a unanimous vote by a group of five," Follett warned, "does not prove the existence of a group idea if two or three (or even one) out of indifference or laziness or prejudice, or shut-upness, or a misconception of their function, have not added their individual thought to the creation of the group thought."[13]

An important practical implication of this sort of self-affirmation is that "a readiness to compromise must be no part of the individual's attitude." This relinquishing of compromise and concession "is the heart of the latest ethical teaching based on the most progressive psychology: between two apparently conflicting courses of action, *a* and *b*, *a* is not to be followed and *b* suppressed, nor *b* followed and *a* suppressed, nor must a compromise between the two be sought, but the process must always be one of integration."[14] This "latest ethical teaching" would eventually become the focal point of Follett's ideas about integrative conflict resolution.

The scholars involved in this marriage of psychology and ethics are not mentioned by name, but Follett most likely was referring to work being done at Harvard. Josiah Royce had long argued that prudence demands giving consideration to all future consequences of action—including consequences for one's neighbors as well as for oneself. William James made a similar point in his 1891 lecture "The Moral Philosopher and the Moral Life," when he said that "those ideals must be written highest which *prevail at the least cost,* or by whose realization the least possible number of other ideals are destroyed. The course of history is nothing but the story of men's struggles from generation to generation to find the more and more inclusive order. *Invent some manner* of realizing your own ideals which will also satisfy the alien demands—that and that only is the path of peace." The generation of Harvard philosophers that followed Royce and James—most notably Ralph Barton Perry and Edwin B. Holt—continued their predecessors' efforts to create an integrative ethics.[15] This Harvard tradition clearly had an impact on Follett's thinking.

In order to satisfy not only our own demands but also the demands of others, we must offer fully what we have to give and "be eager for what all others have to give." Both giving and receiving are required if a truly collaborative idea is to be produced. Too many people "conscientiously go to their group thinking it their duty to impose their ideas upon others." But "we have no more right to get our own way by persuading people than by bullying or bribing them. To take our full share in the synthesis is all that is legitimate." Follett had little patience for people who came to groups determined "to score, to be brilliant, rather than to find agreement. I asked a man once to join a committee I was organizing and he replied that he would be very glad to come and give his advice. I didn't want him—and didn't have him . . . what I wanted was to get a group of people who would deliberately work out a thing together." Follett also warned that "throughout our participation in the group process we must be ever on our guard that we do not confuse differences and antagonisms, that diversity does not arouse hostility."[16] This, of course, was precisely what she had seen in the heated interpersonal dispute between the NCCA's Edward J. Ward and John Collier.

In sum, the essence of a "group" must involve "an acting and reacting, a single and identical process which brings out differences and integrates them into a unity." Through this process, we evolve the collective thought and the collective will. As a pragmatic test of the quality of a group, Follett suggests the following question: "do we come together to register the results of individual thought, to compare the results of individual thought in order to make selections therefrom, or do we come together to create a common idea? Whenever we have a real group something new *is* actually created."[17]

Advancing Democratic Ideals Requires an Interplay of Thought, Will, and Action

Although the collective thought and the collective will are created in the group process, they are not yet complete: "they complete themselves only through activity in the world of affairs, of work, of government." Here, Follett's thinking was guided by the pragmatists, who had argued that thought and action are parts of the same process, but also by her reflection on her own experience: "We see this in our daily life where we do not finish our thought, construct our will, and then begin our actualizing. Not only the actualizing goes on at the same time, but its reactions help us to shape our thought, to energize our will. We have to digest our social experience, but we have to have social experience before we can digest it. We must learn and build and learn again through the building, or we must build and learn and build again through the learning." This continual interaction among thought, will, and action is an all-important principle when applied to politics: "Democratic ideals will never advance unless we are given the opportunity of constantly embodying them in action, which action will react on our ideas. Thought and will go out into the concrete world in order to generate their own complete form. This gives us both the principle and the method of democracy. A democratic community is one in which the common will is being gradually created by the civic activity of its citizens. The test of democracy is the fulness with which this is being done."

Right, Conscience, and Duty Are Created in the True Group Process

Conceptualizing the social process as a unity of thought, will, and action has important implications for certain ethical concepts, among them our notions of right, conscience, and duty. "It is often thought vaguely," Follett says, "that our ideals are all there, shining and splendid, and we have only to apply them. But the truth is that we have to create our ideals." In particular, we have been told that we must conform to standards that others have created for us to have a sound foundation for society. This, Follett boldly argues, is a fallacious idea. *"The true test of our morality is not the rigidity with which we adhere to standard, but the loyalty we show to the life which constructs standards."*[18]

Conceiving of "right" as a group product changes our notion of duty. For twenty or thirty years, the social ethicists had promoted the idea of altruism, claiming that our duty is to others. But Follett could now see emerging "an idea of ethics entirely different from the altruistic school, based not on the duty of isolated beings to one another, but on integrated individuals acting as a whole, evolving whole-ideas, working for whole-ideals." Conceiving of "right" as a group product also "shows us that there is no such thing as an individual conscience in the sense in which the term is often used." No man can be subject only to his own conscience. "Has not my conscience been produced by my time, my country, my associates? To make a conscience by myself would be as difficult as to try to make a language by myself." At the same time, however, "the individual is not for a moment to yield his right to judge for himself; he can judge better for himself if he joins with others in evolving a synthesized judgment . . . Those of us who are not wholly in sympathy with the conscientious objectors do not think that they should yield to the majority." However, Follett continues, "Before they range themselves against society they must ask themselves if they have taken the opportunities offered them to help form the ideas which they are opposing. I do not say that there is no social value in heresy, I only ask the conscientious objectors to ask themselves whether they are claiming the 'individual rights' we have long outgrown."[19]

Follett's view of the social process — as continual unifyings of thought, will, and action — has important implications, not only for the concept of "right," but also for the notions of "purpose" and "loyalty." Many believe that the purpose (goal or objective) of a group is developed prior to action, but Follett sees this idea as too limited, arguing that "purpose is involved in the process, not prior to process. The question is often asked, 'What is the proposed unity of European nations after the war to be for?' This question implies that the alliance will be a mere method of accomplishing certain purposes, whereas it is the union which is the important thing. With the union the purpose comes into being, and with its every step forward, the purpose changes."[20]

Loyalty likewise is "awakened through and by the very process which creates the group." Our task is not, as Josiah Royce had urged in *The Philosophy of Loyalty* (1908), "to 'find' causes to awaken our loyalty, but to live our life fully and loyalty issues." Nor are we obliged, as Herbert Croly had asserted in *The Promise of American Life* (1909), to be loyal to the nation. "Loyalty to a collective will which we have not created and of which we are, therefore, not an integral part," Follett argues, "is slavery. We belong to our community just in so far as we are helping to make that community; then loyalty follows, then love follows."[21]

Democracy as a Process Requires That We Learn about Groups, Not Crowds

Having concluded that democracy depends on the functioning of groups which are committed to integrating "difference, related difference," Follett was struck by how many of the intellectuals of her era had made conformity the *sine qua non* of society.[22] Convinced that society was disintegrating under the combined impact of industrialization and urbanization, many of Follett's contemporaries in Europe and America were deeply concerned about the future of democratic institutions of government. Charles Horton Cooley, the University of Michigan sociologist, put the question this way: "Is democracy, then, the rule of the crowd, and is there a tendency in modern times toward the subjection of society to an irrational and degenerate phase of the mind?" Cooley answered this question in the negative, but he knew that many others would disagree.[23]

Crowd psychology, a term coined by the French social theorist Gustave Le Bon (1841–1931), formed the basis of many of the early twentieth-century attacks on democracy. As a result, Follett devotes a substantial portion of the first section of *The New State* to exposing the deficiencies of crowd psychology as an explanation of social conduct. Follett argues, first, that Le Bon had lumped together under the concept of "crowd" too wide a diversity of social groups. Like others before her, she believed that careful conceptual distinctions must be drawn among types of groups so that the more productive forms of human association were not made to suffer from the stigma attached to others.[24]

Even more central to Follett's critique of crowd psychology, however, was her conviction that "the difference between a group and a crowd is not one of degree but of kind." Specifically, "suggestion is the law of the crowd, interpenetration the law of the group. Suggestibility, feeling, impulse — this is usually the order in the crowd mind . . . There are no 'differences' in the crowd mind. Each person is swept away and does not stop to find out his own difference. In crowds we have unison, in groups harmony. We want the single voice but not the single note; that is the secret of the group."[25]

Follett realized that there had not yet been the kind of "scientific analysis" of groups that would enable us to know how best to create the integrative processes she prized. For example, more would have to be learned about the significance of group size, or more particularly "the number . . . which will bring out as many differences as possible and yet form a whole or group." Follett also recognized that such apparently inconsequential matters such as seating arrangements and temporary changes in the composition of the group's membership could have a profound influence on group dynamics. Group members are "reciprocally conditioning forces none of which acts as it would act if any one member were different or absent. You can often see this in a board of directors: if one director leaves the room, every man becomes slightly different." Yet another area of study that Follett thought might prove fruitful concerned the impact of group participation on individual performance. At the time, it was widely believed that individuals are more rational, more innovative, and more productive working alone than when joined with others in a group. Follett disagreed, and in so doing anticipated some of what would later be called the psychological process of social facilitation. "Men descend to meet? That is not my experience. The *laissez-aller* which people allow themselves when alone disappears when they meet. Then they pull themselves together and give one another of their best. We see this again and again. Sometimes the ideal of the group stands quite visibly before us as one which none of us is quite living up to by himself."[26]

There was much yet to learn about the functioning of groups, but crowd association had so far received more attention because, Follett trenchantly remarks, "as a matter of fact there is at present so much more of the former than of the latter." But, she continues, "we need not only a psychology which looks at us as we are, but a psychology which points the way to that which we may become."[27]

Interpenetration, Not Imitation, Is the Heart of the Social Process

Despite the widespread interest in the crowd phenomenon, no one writing in the early twentieth century had as yet really accounted for this apparently "radical transformation of the individual's psychic state and disposition" when placed in a crowd. Most social theorists tackled this problem by focusing on the processes by which individuals are molded into likeness and conformity. The major approaches under consideration — the "imitation theory" of the French magistrate and sociologist Gabriel Tarde (1843–1904) and the "consciousness of kind" theory of the Columbia University sociologist Franklin Giddings (1855–1931) — came to represent the theoretical underpinnings of "crowd psychology." Tarde's imitation theory, in particular, held great appeal for American academics, largely because traditional psychological theory had come to be seen as too exclusively focused on rational phenomena, and in particular on the investigation of individual sensory perceptions.[28]

For those dissatisfied with traditional theory, the work of the new imitation and likeness theorists provided a breath of fresh air, bringing to the fore new concerns about instinctual, unconscious mental processes and the social dimensions of psychological experience — both of which were thought to involve irrational aspects of human behavior.[29] Follett acknowledged the importance of the imitation and likeness theorists but also saw crucial errors in their work. For Follett, "interpenetration," not imitation, was the significant social process.[30]

Follett devotes much of the first section of *The New State* to exposing the deficiencies of Giddings' efforts to use a "consciousness of kind" to explain social conduct and the efforts of Tarde, Ross, and others to make "suggestion" and "imitation" the heart of the social process. To say that the social process is merely the spread of similarities, whether biologically given or produced through imitation, seemed to Follett to "ignore the real nature of the collective thought, the collective will." In Tarde's theory, a social idea is an individual idea that has been communicated or disseminated to others; in Giddings' theory a group idea exists whenever "every member of a group has the same thought . . . when all respond simultaneously to the same stimulus." Follett saw the difference between these notions and her notion of the production of a collective idea as being "one of kind." According to Follett, "a collective thought is one evolved by a collective process. The essential feature of a common thought is that it has been produced in common."[31]

Unifying in the True Group Process Creates Empathy as Well as a New Notion of Service

Follett's notion of unifying draws in part on the Hegelian method of exposition: thesis, antithesis, and synthesis. But she specifically cautions her readers not to "confuse the type of unifying spoken of here (an integration), which is a psychological process, with the 'reconciliation of opposites,' which is a logical process."[32] Here Follett emphasizes that she is concerned not only with cognition — the unification of thought — but also with "the unification of feeling, affection, emotion, desire, aspiration — all that we are." In this regard, she objects to the efforts of the likeness theorists to define "sympathy" as an automatic byproduct of an "inherited gregarious instinct."[33] Instead, just as the collective idea is born in the group process, "sympathy too is born within the group — it springs forever from interrelation . . . only from the group comes the genuine feeling with." From Follett's new conception of sympathy (which today we would more likely call "empathy"), we learn two lessons, namely, "that sympathy cannot antedate the group process, and that it must not be confused with altruism."[34]

One can see these errors, Follett says, in the discussion of group cooperation in the business world. "The question often asked, 'Does modern cooperation depend upon self-interest or upon sympathy?' is entirely misleading as regards the real nature of sympathy." If "six manufacturers meet to discuss some form of union," the new psychology teaches us "that what these men need most is not altruistic feelings, but a consciousness of themselves as a new unit and a realization of the needs of that unit. This true sympathy, therefore, is not a vague sentiment they bring with them; it springs from their meeting to be in its turn a vital factor in their meeting." For Follett, then, sympathy was always "a group product; benevolence, philanthropy, tenderness, fervor, ardor, pity, may be possible to me alone, but sympathy is not possible alone."[35]

Continuing her brief exploration of the workings of empathy (or what she called sympathy) in business, Follett argues that employers and employees "cannot be exhorted to feel sympathy one for the other; true sympathy will come only by creating a community or group of employers and employed." Commenting on the paternalistic efforts of businessmen in this era to hire social welfare secretaries to improve the lives of their workers, Follett saw little that was truly unifying employer-employee concerns: "The men who provide rest rooms, baths, lectures, and recreation facilities for their employees, do not by so doing prove themselves to be socially-minded; they are altruistically-minded, and this is involved in the old individualism. Moreover, in our attempts at social legislation we have been appealing chiefly to the altruism of people: women and children ought not to be overworked, it is cruel not to have machinery safe-guarded, etc. But our growing sense of unity is fast bringing us to a realization that all these things are for the good of ourselves too, for the entire community."[36]

"Our interests," Follett says, "are inextricably interwoven. The question is not what is best for me or for you, but for all of us." We must, as a result, change our notion of service. "The other day," Follett continues, "it was stated that the old idea of democracy was a society in which every man had the right to pursue his own ends, while the new idea was based on the assumption that every man should serve his fellow-men. But I do not believe that man should 'serve his fellow-men'; if we started on that task what awful prigs we should become. Moreover, as we see that the only efficient people are the servers, much of the connotation of humility has gone out of the word service! Moreover, if service is such a very desirable thing, then every one must have an equal opportunity for service." Through her own struggles to reconcile a passionate desire for self-realization with the Oxford Idealists' ethic of service, Follett had become convinced that "public spirit will sometime mean, as it does to-day in many instances, [not only] that my city, my nation needs me, but that I need it as the larger sphere of a larger self-expression."[37]

The "Gap" between Individual and Society Is a Fiction

Follett's consideration of the meaning of concepts such as "the social consciousness" and "the social mind" led her next to a consideration of the widely held dualism of individual and society. In her reading, she had found that people were increasingly talking of the social mind "as if it were an abstract conception, as if only the individual were real, concrete." "The two," Follett says, "are equally real. Or rather the only reality is the relating of one to the other which creates both. Our sundering is as artificial and late an act as the sundering of consciousness into subject and object." But, Follett contends, "there is no way of separating individuals, they coalesce and coalesce, they are 'confluent,' to use the expression of [William] James, who tells us that the chasm between men is an individualistic fiction, that we are surrounded by fringes, that these overlap and that by means of these I join with others."[38]

"The old psychology," Follett reminds us, "was based on the isolated individual as the unit, on the assumption that a man thinks, feels and judges independently. Now that we know that there is no such thing as a separate ego, that individuals are created by reciprocal interplay, our whole study of psychology is being transformed." Imitation had been made "the bridge to span the gap between the individual and society, but we see now that there is no gap, therefore no bridge is necessary." Using compelling imagery, Follett argues that "the individual is not a unit but a centre of forces (both centripetal and centrifugal), and consequently society is not a collection of units but a complex of radiating and converging, crossing and recrossing energies." For Follett, society is a dynamic, "psychic process" rather than either "a crowd" or a collection of already-developed individuals.[39]

Follett was not the first to object to the long-standing dualisms of self and other, individual and society. Charles Horton Cooley in 1909 had called self and society "twin-born, we know one as immediately as we know the other, and the notion of a separate and independent ego is an illusion." George Herbert Mead likewise rejected the idea of the autonomous individual, seeing human psychology in its most distinctive aspects as basically social in both origin and function. Mead actually seemed to invert the traditional argument, saying that "for social psychology, the whole (society) is prior to the part (the individual), not the part to the whole; and the part is explained in terms of the whole, not the whole in terms of the part or parts."[40] And in a 1916 speech to the American Psychological Association, John Dewey deplored the tendency of the imitation-suggestion theorists to oppose the individual and society — to see the individual as rational until placed in association with others; this view of the social process, Dewey argued, involves the relating of mythical isolated individuals to an even more mythical social or crowd mind.[41]

Despite the vigor with which James, Cooley, Mead, and Dewey argued against the dualism of individual and society, the myth continued to flourish. Much of its staying power, Follett thought, could be attributed to the way Americans think about the "subordination of the individual to society." We usually think this means "the subordination of the individual to 'others,'" whereas it does not at all, it means the subordination of the individual to the whole of which he himself is a part. Such subordination is an act of assertion; it is fraught with active power and force; it affirms and accomplishes. We are often told to 'surrender our individuality.' To claim our individuality is the one essential claim we have on the universe."[42]

Certain "continental sociologists," Follett noted, had attempted to construct a social hierarchy in which "one man or group of men is the sensorium, others the hewers and carriers," but Follett denounced this approach: "It is exactly this despotic and hopeless system of caste from which the true democracy frees man." Unfortunately, remnants of this sort of hierarchical thinking persisted even in the work of such "democratic" thinkers as Cooley and Dewey. The difficulty lay in their conception of society as "an organism."[43]

"The organic theory of society has so much to recommend it to superficial thinking," Follett says, "that we must examine it carefully to find its fatal defects." The term *organism* is "valuable as a metaphor," but it lacks "strict psychological accuracy." The social bond, being "a psychic relation," cannot be expressed either "in biological terms or in any terms of physical force." Our "psychical self-unitings knit infinitely more closely and in a wholly different way." Freed from the limitations of time and space, "minds can blend, yet in the blending preserve each its own identity." Furthermore, in society "every individual may be a complete expression of the whole in a way impossible for the parts of a physical organism." While the cell of an organism "has only one function, the individual may have manifold and multiform functions: he enters with one function into a certain group of people this morning and with another this afternoon. This saves us from the danger to democracy which lurks in the organic theory. No man is forced to serve as the running foot or the lifting hand. Each at any moment can place himself where his nature calls."[44]

In the same vein, Follett objects to the penchant of Tarde, Ross, and Giddings to reserve to a few particularly creative individuals the initiation of social change. Because interpenetrating is the "fundamental law of existence," it cannot be left to experts or to the elite of any particular class, sex, or race but demands, instead, "the continuous activity of every man." Convinced by her experience that creative potential is universal, Follett is frustrated by those who forgo creative unifying in favor of associating with their own kind: "Imitation is for the shirkers, like-mindedness for the comfort lovers, unifying for the creators . . . Some one ought to write an essay on the dangers to the soul of congeniality. Pleasant little glows of feeling can never be fanned into the fire which becomes the driving force of progress." Nor does she have much patience with those who "think that certain kindred souls should come together, and then by a certain intensified thinking and living together some noble product will emerge for the benefit of the world." Most utopian communities, she says, "have died simply of non-nutrition. The bond created had not within it the variety which the human soul needs for its nourishment. Unity, not uniformity, must be our aim. We attain unity only through variety. Differences must be integrated, not annihilated, nor absorbed."[45]

Social Progress Depends on the Continual Integrating of Difference

Follett's conception of social progress represents yet another way in which she disagreed with the imitation and likeness theorists. In the first place, these theorists seemed to Follett to emphasize in society the "given similarity" rather than the similarity that is "achieved." "The common at any moment is always the given; it has come from heredity, biological influences, suggestion and imitation, and the previous workings of the law of interpenetration. All the accumulated effect of these is seen in our habits of thinking, our modes of living." But Follett cautions, "we cannot rest in the common. The surge of life sweeps through the given similarity, the common group, and breaks it up into a thousand differences."[46]

The importance of reaching for the "achieved" similarity is illustrated in Follett's prescient comment about the negotiations that would follow World War I. "The Allies are fighting to-day with one impulse, one desire, one aim, but at the peace table many differences will arise between them. The progress of the whole world at that moment will depend upon the 'similarity' we can create. This 'similarity' will consist of all we now hold in common and also, of the utmost importance for the continuance of civilization, upon our ability to unify our differences. If we go to that peace table with the idea that the new world is to be based on that community of interest and aim which now animates us, the disillusion will be great, the result an overwhelming failure." To prevent this sort of disillusionment, you must "never settle down within the theory you have chosen, the cause you have embraced; know that another theory, another cause exists, and seek that." We must remember always that "progress does not depend upon the similarity which we *find* but upon the similarity which we *achieve*."[47]

In working out her conception of social progress, Follett expressed reservations about the way the Darwinian notion of "the survival of the fittest" was being applied to society. Struggle need not mean "strife, opposition, war," but rather "effort, striving, the ceaseless labor of adjustment" and the progressive unifyings that can result. Science, she was convinced, was on her side in this argument. Charles Darwin had maintained "that the cause of the advance of civilization was in the social habits of man"; and the recent investigations of the Russian zoologist and social theorist Petr Kropotkin had demonstrated that "the animal species in which the practice of 'mutual aid' has attained the greatest development are invariably the most numerous and the most prosperous." Thus, "the 'strongest' man has been to science the being with the greatest number of points of union, the 'fittest' has been the one with the greatest power of cooperation. The test of our progress is neither our likenesses nor our unlikenesses, but what we are going to do with our unlikenesses. Shall I fight whatever is different from me or find the higher synthesis? The progress of society is measured by its power to unite into a living, generating whole its self-yielding differences."[48]

"Lately," Follett says, perhaps alluding to Walter Bagehot's claim that "discussion" should be considered the highest form of social conflict, "the struggle theory has been transferred from the physical to the intellectual world." But this seems to her to spell little progress, for "as long as we think of discussion as a struggle, as an opportunity for 'argument,' there will be all the usual evil consequences of the struggle theory." Instead of validating struggle in this intellectual form, she urges the learning of "cooperative thinking, intellectual team-work."[49]

Follett has been criticized for assuming that "the intense solidarity she prized was easily achieved," but this seems a curious charge in light of the fact that she repeatedly acknowledged the difficulties involved in unifying — difficulties she had personally experienced both in the Boston Equal Suffrage Association and in her local and national work on behalf of community centers. In one place, for example, she writes: "Suppose I disagree with you in a discussion and we make no effort to join our ideas, but 'fight it out.' I hammer away with my idea, I try to find all the weakest parts of yours, I refuse to see anything good in what you think. That is not nearly so difficult as trying to recognize all the possible subtle interweavings of thought, how one part of our thought, or even one aspect of one part, may unite with one part of one aspect of one part of mine etc. Likewise with cooperation and competition in business: cooperation is going to prove so much more difficult than competition that there is not the slightest danger of any one getting soft under it." Follett did not doubt that "it takes more spiritual energy to express the group spirit than the particularist spirit. This is its glory as well as its difficulty. We have to be higher order of beings to do it — we become higher order of beings by doing it."[50]

Follett concludes her brief against the struggle theory of social progress by taking on the problem she considers "the most profound," namely, that the struggle theory "always erects a thing-in-itself. If I 'fight' Mr. X, that means that I think of Mr. X as incapable of change — that either he or I must prevail, must conquer. When I realize fully that there are no things-in-themselves, struggle simply fades away; then I know that Mr. X and I are two flowing streams of activity which must meet for larger ends than either could pursue alone." Much of our fear of difference, Follett argues, is attributable to our tendency to see it as static, as given; but difference "also is involved in the world of becoming." The social environment, likewise, "is not a hard and rigid something external to us, always working upon us, whose influence we cannot escape . . . both self and environment are always in the making." This was no fantasy of an armchair psychologist; it was a conviction born of Follett's social and civic work. Whenever her Women's Municipal League committee or representatives of Boston- 1915 approached the mayor or the Boston School Committee or the Finance Commission on behalf of Boston's community centers, they did not for a moment dare to forget the complex and continually changing patterns of relations among these myriad political actors. "It is not," Follett observes, "that formative influences work on a dead mass of inertia, but formative influences work on an environment which has already responded to initiatives, and these initiatives have been affected by the responses. We cannot be practical politicians without fully understanding this."[51]

Finally, Follett's conception of social progress is also dynamic. She respects "the creative process not the created thing; the created thing is forever and forever being left behind us." Just as Follett in her own life had disavowed the metaphysics of Idealism and ended certain organizational affiliations in order to move on with her work, she urges her readers to "get away from 'the hell of rigid things.'" "To live gloriously is to change undauntedly — our ideals must evolve from day to day, and it is upon those who can fearlessly embrace the doctrine of 'becoming' that the life of the future waits." This does not mean, however, that we must give up the abiding. "The unchangeable and the unchanging are both included in the idea of growth. Stability is neither rigidity nor sterility: it is the perpetual power of bringing forth."[52]

Socialism Is Not a Substitute for the Gradual Process of Evolving the Collective Will

In her musings about democracy, Follett had been much taken with the recent work of Graham Wallas, a longtime socialist member of the London Common Council and London School Board. Like Follett, Wallas was deeply troubled by certain flaws in democratic theory — "the excessive faith in elections, the lack of provision for the necessity of organizing the electorate, the lack of foresight about the increasing difficulty of generating public interest in an ever larger and more complex society."[53]

Wallas favored no political doctrine or ideology in its entirety, but he made collectivism, or the socialist control of economic life by the state, the centerpiece of his *Great Society*. Follett did not share Wallas's faith in a socialist future. "We cannot have any genuine collectivism until we have learned how to evolve the collective thought and the collective will . . . The wish for socialism is a longing for the ideal state, but it is embraced often by impatient people who want to take a short cut to the ideal state. That state must be grown — its branches will widen as its roots spread. The socialization of property must not precede the socialization of the will. If it does, then the only difference between socialism and our present order will be substituting one machine for another."[54]

New Forms of Association in American Society

Follett was no believer in utopias, but she did see many promising signs of the group principle at work in American society and devotes the final two chapters of the principles section to these new forms of association. Follett discusses positive developments in areas as diverse as education, medical social service, city planning, criminal justice practices, labor-management relations, and immigration. With regard to immigration, she had been pleased to find that the idea of community was gradually replacing mandates for assimilation on the one hand, or separation of immigrant groups on the other. "We want all these different peoples to be part of a true community. Only by a mutual permeation of ideals shall we enrich their lives and they ours."[55]

But nowhere in American national life did Follett see more compelling evidence of the growing recognition of the group or community principle than she had found in the modern theory of law. Drawing heavily on Roscoe Pound's *Harvard Law Review* articles (1910–1912) on sociological jurisprudence, Follett contends "that law is the outcome of our community life" and "that it must serve, not individuals, but the community." Sir Henry Maine had once stated that "the movement of progressive societies has hitherto been a movement *from Status to Contract*"; but this change, Follett says, "we do not now consider the history of liberty but of particularism — the development of law through giving a larger and larger share to the particular will. The present progress of law is from contract to community. Our particularistic law is giving way to a legal theory based on a sound theory of interrelationship."[56]

Follett applauds the trend in jurisprudence toward considering "individuals not as isolated beings, but in their relation to the life of the whole community," and she extracts from Pound's articles a number of illustrations of the "growing recognition of community as the basis of law." These include limitations on the use of property, as in laws governing the construction and maintenance of buildings; limitations on freedom of contract, as in statutes regulating the hours and conditions of labor; limitations on the part of creditors or injured parties to extract satisfaction, as in homestead exemptions; imposition of liability without fault, as in workmen's compensation; limitations on private use of water rights; and societal protection of dependent members of households. But no matter how valuable we find any particular form of the community principle, Follett warns, we must never consider the law as "finished." Sharing Pound's faith in "the efficacy of effort" — in the idea that the law "has been and may be made consciously" — she is confident that the law is "always in evolution."[57]

Having established in the first section of *The New State* that "the very essence and substance of democracy" is the creating of the collective will through psychic interpenetration in the true group process, Follett examines some past notions about democracy and traces the "growth of true democracy in America." Democracy, Follett says, "has meant to many 'natural' rights, 'liberty,' and 'equality,' " but these terms acquire new meaning if we accept the group principle as the basis of democratic association.[58]

Individual Rights Derive from the Workings of the True Group Process

"Natural" rights are the rights that all people are thought to possess and that obligate them to act, or to refrain from acting, in certain ways. People have a natural right to life, Thomas Hobbes had argued, "which no society can abridge arbitrarily"; all obligations are derived from this right, and no man is bound to regard as a duty whatever he regards as destructive to the security of his life. To this "natural" right to life, John Locke had added two others: the rights to liberty and to property. The "natural law" derived from deductions concerning this triad of rights, in traditional thinking about democracy, forms the basis of civil society.[59]

The English philosopher Thomas Hill Green opposed this traditional idea of natural rights, contending that "[n]o one possesses abstract rights independent of his membership in a society in which the members recognize some common good as their own ideal good." Rights, being founded on a concept of social good, cannot predate society. They may, however, exist independently of the state: "A man may thus have rights as a member of a family or of human society in any other form, without being a member of a state at all, — rights which remain rights though any particular state or all states refuse to recognize them." What, then, is the role of the state in regard to rights? The state, Green said, "does not create rights, but gives fuller reality to rights already existing." Furthermore, "since all rights derive from society, in the sense that they require social recognition to become 'real,' '[a] right against society as such, a right to act without reference to the needs or good of society, is an impossibility'; for no community could possibly see the granting of such a right as forming an element in its conception of social good."[60]

Follett's argument about rights runs parallel to Green's — the significant exception being that she makes concrete in the group process the evolution of the social good and associated rights.[61] "If my true self is the group-self," Follett writes, "then my only rights are those which membership in a group gives me. The old idea of natural rights postulated the particularist individual; we now know that no such person exists. The group and the individual come into existence simultaneously: with this group-man appear group-rights."[62]

Freedom Inheres in Obeying the Collective Will We Have Helped to Make

Follett's conviction that the group principle is the basis of democratic association requires not only a new conception of "rights" but also a new notion of "liberty." "The idea of liberty long current," Follett says, "was that the solitary man was the free man, that the man outside society possessed freedom but that in society he had to sacrifice as much of his liberty as interfered with the liberty of others. Rousseau's effort was to find a form of society in which all should be as free as 'before.' According to some of our contemporary thinkers liberty is what belongs to the individual or variation-giving-one. But this tells only half the tale. Freedom is the harmonious, unimpeded working of the law of one's own nature. The true nature of every man is found only in the whole. A man is ideally free only so far as he is interpermeated by every other human being; he gains his freedom through a perfect and complete relationship because thereby he achieves his whole nature."[63]

Contrasting this idea with other notions of freedom then current, Follett judges "most superficial" the notion that free-will "consists in choice when an alternative is presented." Freedom, Follett says, "is obedience to the law of one's nature. My nature is of the whole: I am free, therefore, only when I choose that term in the alternative which the whole commands. I am not free when I am making choices, I am not free when my acts are not 'determined,' for in a sense they always are determined (freedom and determinism have not this kind of opposition). I am free when I am creating. I am determined *through* my will, not in spite of it."[64]

"The particularist idea of liberty," Follett continues, "was either negative, depending on the removal of barriers, or it was quantitative, something which I had left over after the state had restrained me in every way it thought necessary." As a corollary of this idea, it is often thought "that when some restraint is taken away from us we are freer than before, but this is childish. Some women-suffragists talk of women as 'enslaved' and advocate their emancipation by the method of giving them the vote. But the vote will not make women free. Freedom is always a thing to be attained."[65]

Follett sees certain practical implications emanating from the idea "that we are free only through the social order, only as fast as we identify ourselves with the whole." First, "we must take part in all the life around us: join groups, enter into many social relations." In her view, "We do not curtail our liberty by joining with others; we find it and increase all our capacity for life through the interweaving of willings. It is only in a complex state of society that any large degree of freedom is possible because nothing else can supply the many opportunities necessary to work out freedom."[66]

The formation of this conviction surely was influenced by Follett's own experience. She had found the opportunities to work out her freedom in the complex social and civic life of Boston — but she had first found it necessary to escape a stultifying family life in small-town Quincy and then, a few years later, to relinquish a self-imposed exile in the mountains of Vermont. "We have considered ourselves bound in thousands of ways," Follett writes, " — by tradition, by religion, by natural law, by inertia and ignorance, etc., etc." But the idea that "we are not free has been the most deadening fallacy to which man has ever submitted. No outside power indeed can make us free. No document of our forefathers can 'declare' us 'independent.' No one can ever give us freedom but we can win it for ourselves." Freedom, furthermore, is not a static condition. "As it is not something possessed 'originally,'" Follett contends, "and as it is not something which can be given to us, so it is not something won once for all. It is in our power to win our freedom, but it must be won anew at every moment, literally every moment."[67]

Follett's idea of freedom shares some of the language of Idealism, but she clearly has dispensed with the notion of the Absolute. The "whole" in which the individual finds freedom is not something given, something eternal; it is being continually created by the members of the group in the group process.

Follett's notion of freedom, like her idea of rights, almost certainly was influenced by the writings of T. H. Green—particularly by his idea of "positive" freedom. Freedom, according to Green, is "a *positive* power or capacity of doing or enjoying," not "merely freedom from restraint or compulsion." And freedom is " 'something that we do or enjoy *in common with others*,' not 'a freedom that can be enjoyed by one man or one set of men at the cost of a loss of freedom to others.' " Thus, I. M. Greengarten concludes in his study of Green's political thought, "it is the pursuit of a personal good that is at the same time a shared good, a good that is personally satisfying only in so far as it satisfies others as well, as opposed to a good that is exclusive and can only be achieved at the expense of others."[68]

Green is careful to distinguish his idea of liberty from the Hegelian concept of the state, and Follett shares his concern.[69] We are obeying ourselves and therefore are free, she says, only when we are obeying the group that we have helped to make and of whose collective ideas, spirit, and will we are an integral part. "Ideally," Follett continues, "the state is such a group, actually it is not, but it depends upon us to make it more and more so. The state must be no external authority which restrains and regulates me, but it must be myself acting as the state in every smallest detail of life. Expression, not restraint, is always the motive of the ideal state . . . We are beginning to know now that our freedom depends not on the weakness but on the strength of our government, our government being the expression of a united people. We are freer under our present sanitary laws than without them; we are freer under compulsory education than without it. A highly organized state does not mean restriction of the individual but his greater liberty."[70]

More than one writer has accused Follett of being insensitive to the importance of negative freedom, of "freedom from."[71] But this insensitivity is apparent rather than real—an artifact of her focus on the potential inherent in the group process for resolving the duality of individual freedom and collective control. Follett's position on negative freedom is clear. She adamantly rejects any notion of freedom that involves subservience to an external purpose. When I am participating in an integrative group process, Follett says, I may consider myself free for two reasons: "(1) I am not dominated by the whole because I *am* the whole; (2) I am not dominated by 'others' because we have the genuine social process only when I do not control others or they me, but all intermingle to produce the collective thought and the collective will. I am free when I am functioning here in time and space as the creative will."[72]

Equality: The True Group Process Requires the Differences of All

The third of the concepts traditionally identified with democracy is "equality," and it, too, would acquire new meaning if the integrative group principle were to become the basis of democratic association. "Much of our present class hatred," Follett says, "comes from a distorted view of equality. This doctrine [of equal rights] means to many that I have as much 'right' to things as any one else, and therefore if I see any one having more things than I have, it is proper to feel resentment against that person or class. Much legislation, therefore, is directed to lopping off here and there. But such legislation is a negative and therefore non-constructive interpretation of equality."[73]

Follett was convinced that a much more promising conception of equal rights could be found in the group process. Here, she says, there are "no mechanical, no quantitative equalities," but if the group members are committed to unifying, we are nevertheless equal from two points of view. The first is procedural: "I am equal to every one else as one of the necessary members of the group." Indeed, social progress depends on confronting and unifying our difference. "Democracy in fact insists on what are usually thought of as inequalities. Of course I am not 'as good as you' — it would be a pretty poor world if I were, that is if you were not better than I am. Democracy without humility is inconceivable. The hope of democracy is in its inequalities. The only real equality I can ever have is to fill my place in the whole at the same time that every other man is filling his place in the whole."[74] The second form of equality is substantive, but it involves our human potential rather than our ascribed or achieved social status. We are equal in that each of us has capacity for growth, for change — or, as she puts it, "in every man lives an infinite possibility."[75]

Rethinking Other Traditional Notions of Democracy

Having concluded her discussion of the concepts of rights, liberty, and equality, Follett turns her attention to other prominent errors in our traditional ways of thinking about democracy. Many people identify democracy with "majority rule," but we "are beginning to see now that majority rule is only a clumsy makeshift until we shall devise ways of getting at the genuine collective thought." Those who fear the "tyranny of the majority" have identified democracy with respect for the "rights of minorities," but Follett had learned through her research on the Speakership that a minority has no more inherent virtue than a majority. As a result, she saw little to be gained in giving minorities more power on election day. No doubt thinking of the sort of civic "intermingling" she had witnessed in Boston's community centers, Follett insists that the integration of majorities and minorities "must begin further back in our life than this." "Representation," she argues, "is not the main fact of political life; the main concern of politics is *modes of association*. We do not want the rule of the many or the few; we must find that method of political procedure by which majority and minority ideas may be so closely interwoven that we are truly ruled by the will of the whole. We shall have democracy only when we learn to produce this will through group organization."[76]

Another of the traditional ideas that Follett rejects as "insufficient" is the notion that "democracy is an attitude and must grow up in the hearts of men." Unity involves "more than a sentiment; it must be an actual system of organization." This conviction, which sprang originally from Follett's analysis of the failures of the congressional committee system, was later nurtured in Boston's community centers and reinforced by her observations of a nation mobilizing for war. As a result of these experiences, Follett concluded that the value of history and tradition in creating unity and community had been "overemphasized." If this were "the only way of getting unity, there would be little hope for the future in America, where we have to make a unity of people with widely differing traditions, and little hope for the future in Europe where peace is unthinkable unless . . . new ties can be made on the basis of mutual understanding and mutual obligation."[77]

In the final section of her book, Follett reports mounting evidence of "the steadily increasing appreciation of the individual and a true understanding of his place in society, his relation to the state." She mentions the movement toward industrial democracy, "the woman movement," the increase of direct government, the introduction of social programs into party platforms, and the increasing recognition of the necessity of joining expert service with an active electorate. But her hopes for the growth of democracy in America are tempered by the fact that the theory of government based on individual rights "still occupies a large place in current thought, in the speeches of our practical politicians, in our institutions of government, and in America in our law court decisions." Follett attributes the continued dominance of this idea, first, to an almost automatic resistance to any idea that even "*seems* to enthrone the state and override the individual"; next, to the role played by the suggestion and imitation school of sociology in retarding development of new forms of social and political organization; and, finally, to the widespread conviction in America that economic development depends on continued adherence to the traditional idea of individual rights.[78]

Valuing Integrative Neighborhood Groups

Convinced that group organization is the method of democracy and the basis on which the new state should be founded, Follett begins the last major section of her book — her explication of how the new state might be expressed — with a discussion of the neighborhood group. Drawing on her experience in the community centers movement, Follett identifies the several advantages of neighborhood group organization. She notes, for example, that "as a member of a neighborhood group we get a fuller and more varied life than as a member of any other kind of a group we can find, no matter how big our city or how complex or comprehensive its interests"; and she places particular emphasis on the opportunities that neighborhood groups provide for practicing new methods of human association. Follett also applauds the diversity of neighborhood groups, seeing in their "different education, different interests, different standards" opportunities to bring out differences and integrate them into a unity. She recognizes, however, that some neighborhoods have been formed selectively on the basis of race, ethnicity, or social class, and these, Follett says, are not "so good for our purpose."[79]

Although she is clearly enthusiastic about the potential for neighborhood association, Follett never suggests that it be "substituted for other forms of association — trade union, church societies, fraternal societies, local improvement leagues, cooperative societies, men's clubs, women's clubs etc." Instead, the neighborhood group should be conceived as "the means of coördinating and translating into community values other local groups," as a "medium for interpretation and unofficial integration." Follett had seen firsthand the pressing needs for social and civic coordination and hoped that neighborhood groups might be the vehicle for learning "how to gather up into significant community expression these more partial expressions of individual wants."[80]

In considering how an integrated neighborhood consciousness might be evolved, Follett once again draws heavily on her community centers experience, describing what she had learned from observing integrative neighborhood groups. Among the key elements of this new method of human association are a commitment to fostering genuine discussion, developing integrative local leadership, and creating methods whereby neighborhoods might join with other neighborhoods.

FOSTERING GENUINE DISCUSSION RATHER THAN DEBATE

It was in the community centers of Boston that Follett first became convinced of the need to learn and practice a genuine discussion, "that is, a discussion which shall evolve a true collective purpose and bring the group will of the neighborhood to bear directly on city problems." Follett herself had been a debater and had made her first civic club a debating society, but she now insists that these "pernicious" societies must be abolished "in colleges, schools, settlements, Young Men's Christian Associations, or wherever found." "The object is always to win, it is never to discover the truth," Follett complains. "This is excellent training for our present party politics. It is wretched preparation for the kind of politics we wish to see in America, because there is no attempt to think together . . . You do not try to see what ideas of your opponent will enrich your own point of view; you are bound to reject without examination his view, his ideas, almost I might say his facts." Follett suspects that we are often reluctant "to get acquainted with the arguments of our opponents for fear we might sympathize with them." But genuine discussion helps us to overcome this reluctance, for it not only brings out difference "but at the same time it teaches us what to do with difference." Genuine discussion, therefore, provides the opportunity for experimentation, change, growth — for the chance to "overcome misunderstanding and conquer prejudice."[81]

DEVELOPING INTEGRATIVE LOCAL LEADERSHIP

Neighborhood groups not only are capable of evolving a collective will to replace the "crowd opinion" on which political parties depend; they also are a seedbed for the development of leaders to replace party bosses. Definitive statements about leadership could not be made, Follett believed, "until it is studied in relation to group psychology," but certain of the ideas she offers in *The New State* about neighborhood leadership would reappear in her later writings on business management.[82]

The first important quality of leadership, according to Follett, is that "the leader guides the group and is at the same time himself guided by the group, is always a part of the group." Then and only then does personal loyalty to the leader merge with loyalty to the group, which is a product of the group process. A second, and equally important, quality of leadership is the leader's "power of integrating." "The leader of our neighborhood group," Follett says, "must interpret our experience to us, must see all the different points of view which underlie our daily activities and also their connections, must adjust the varying and often conflicting needs, must lead the group to an understanding of its needs and to a unification of its purpose. He must give form to things vague, things latent, to mere tendencies." The leader undertakes this integrating not so that he or she can impose "wise" decisions upon us, but to enable us to reach our own decisions. "We need leaders," Follett warns, "not masters or drivers." The skillful leader "does not rely on personal force; he controls his group not by dominating but by expressing it. He stimulates what is best in us; he unifies and concentrates what we feel only gropingly and scatteringly, but he never gets away from the current of which we and he are both an integral part. He is a leader who gives form to the inchoate energy in every man. The person who influences me most is not he who does great deeds but he who makes me feel I can do great deeds. Many people tell me what I ought to do and just how I ought to do it, but few have made me want to do something. Who ever has struck fire out of me, aroused me to action which I should not otherwise have taken, he has been my leader."[83]

The leader also must be a "practical politician," knowing first "how the smallest needs and the humblest powers of his neighborhood can be fitted into the progressive movements of our time" and then interpreting a neighborhood "not only to itself but to others." The neighborhood leader's "guiding, embracing and dominant thought" should always be to make the group's evolving community consciousness "articulate in government."[84] With enabling leadership of this kind, the neighborhood group is capable of evolving "a responsible government to take the place of our irresponsible party government." Reform associations, "while they have fought party, have often endeavored to substitute their own organization for the party organization. This has often been the alternative offered to us — do we want good government or poor government? We have not been asked if we would like to govern ourselves."[85]

We should concern ourselves, Follett urges, with "how the increasing activity of the individual can be state activity, how the widening of the sphere of state activity can be a widening of our own activity." Our modern political problem is always how to *be* the state. In the ideal state the individual and the state are one, yet "this is pure theory until we make them one."[86]

CREATING METHODS WHEREBY NEIGHBORHOOD
GROUPS MIGHT JOIN WITH OTHERS

Although she advocates the development of neighborhood association, Follett's aim is not "to keep people within their neighborhoods but to get them out." The neighborhood provides a useful, perhaps even necessary, starting place for building the new state because psychologically "we are ready for membership in a larger group only by experience first in the smaller group"; but our aim should be to "get people to identify themselves actually, not sentimentally, with a larger and larger collective unit than the neighborhood." For the neighborhood group to be the foundation of the new state, methods should be devised for joining neighborhood with neighborhood. All too often, Follett notes, representatives of a group go to citywide or statewide bodies to "try to push through the plan of action decided on by our own local group," but the process she has in mind is quite different: the continual integrating through "reciprocal interaction and correlation" of standards as well as interests.[87]

Follett's conviction that neighborhood groups might eventually be joined "through larger intermediary groups, into a true state" seems quite unrealistic today; but the rapid growth of the community centers movement and the county and state organization of community councils under the wartime auspices of the Council of National Defense gave considerable contemporary credibility to Follett's claim.[88]

Follett recognized that the neighborhood group could become the basis of the new state only if there was widespread acceptance of two critical assumptions: first, that "the state" was worth creating, and second, that the neighborhood provided a better basis for creating the state than either occupational groups or some other sort of group association. Each of these assumptions, Follett admitted, have been "denied by some of our most able thinkers."[89]

The Pluralist Critique of the State

The doctrine most closely identified with this denial was political pluralism. In the period before World War I, Europe "witnessed a burgeoning of intellectual interest in reconstructing institutions for the protection of individuals — individuals who seemed increasingly lost in the mass, debased by the industrial division of labor and exposed to manipulation by an unrepresentative state." In place of a state founded on liberal or Idealist conceptions — the atomistic individual or the sovereign all-powerful state — the pluralists argued for recognizing the rights of a plethora of intermediary groups that would provide individuals a sense of community while shielding their members against undue state power. Under a pluralist regime, the state "would become a passive coordinating authority, acting merely in response to group desires." These views found particularly cogent expression in the work of the English pluralist thinkers, among them Frederic Maitland, John Neville Figgis, A. R. Orage, Ernest Barker, Harold J. Laski, and G. D. H. Cole.[90]

Follett devotes several chapters of *The New State* to a consideration of the pluralists' arguments, calling pluralism "the most interesting, the most suggestive and the most important theory of politics now before us." The pluralists, she says, rightly "prick the bubble of the present state's right to supremacy"; they recognize that the interests of the state, at least as presently constituted, are not always identical with the interests of its parts, and they willingly struggle with the practical problems of federalism. The pluralists, furthermore, believe that the state, like any other association, must prove itself pragmatically by what it achieves, and this, they argue, is an infinite task. "The great lesson of Laski's book," according to Follett, "is in its implication that we do not have a sovereign state until we make one."[91] But the primary contribution of the pluralists to political thought lies in the recognition they give to "the value of the group," to the notion that "the variety of our group life to-day has a significance which must be immediately reckoned with in political method." This, Follett feels certain, marks "the beginning of the disappearance of the crowd" in political life. Follett, finally, gives hearty approval to the pluralists' pleas "for a revivification of local life" — for substituting our current "pretence" of democracy with "the awakening and invigorating, the educating and organizing of the local unit."[92]

Follett's Critique of Pluralism

Despite the pluralists' generally positive contributions to political discourse, Follett is firmly committed to the idea of a "unifying" rather than a "pluralistic" state. The viability of the latter, she argues, is undermined by certain fundamental weaknesses in pluralist thought. The first of these shortcomings involves the pluralists' interpretation of William James's pragmatism. As Follett saw it, James had emerged from his struggles with the problem of how to make "the parts live fully in the whole, the whole live fully in the parts" with a firm conviction that, as he explains, "states of consciousness can separate and combine themselves freely and keep their own identity unchanged while forming parts of simultaneous fields of experience of wider scope." But the pluralists deny the possibility of the collective and insist that multiple sovereignty must mean parallel rather than ascending groups.[93] This, Follett is convinced, is a serious error.

The second of the weaknesses that Follett sees as underlying pluralist doctrine is their misunderstanding of Hegelianism. "Do they adopt the crudely popular conception of the Hegelian state as something 'above and beyond' men, as a separate entity virtually independent of men? Such a conception is fundamentally wrong and wholly against the spirit of Hegel." Unfortunately,

Follett continues, "there is the real Hegel and the Hegel who misapplied his own doctrine, who preached the absolutism of a Prussian State." The pluralists had responded to this distorted Hegelianism not only by rejecting the state as currently constituted but also by denying the possibility of collective sovereignty. Follett demurs, being firmly convinced that collective and distributive sovereignty can exist together. Perhaps when the pluralists "accept the compounding of consciousness taught by their own master, James, then they will see that true Hegelianism finds its actualized form in federalism."[94]

One of the major obstacles to a reconciliation of the distributive and collective in pluralist thought seemed to Follett to lie in the pluralists' fascination with the Middle Ages — or more specifically, with the prospect of recreating a lost feudal utopia of guilds, municipalities, churches, universities, and the like. But Follett, who had studied at Radcliffe College with one of the preeminent medieval scholars, William James Ashley, harbored no such illusions about the Middle Ages. The great triumph of that era, according to Ashley, was the emergence of the individual — "not as a member of a group but as a member of a nation."[95] And despite the fact that "the individual as the basis of government has remained an empty theory," Follett believes that "we have always considered this on the whole an advance step." Furthermore, groups were separated from one another during that era by status and class, and no method existed "by which the parts could be related to the whole without the result either of despotism of the more powerful parts or anarchy of all the parts."[96]

To this growing catalog of errors and misconceptions in pluralist thought, Follett adds yet another, this one the "most serious." The pluralists, like other social and political theorists, "have not begun a scientific study of group psychology"; they profess admiration for empiricism, but they do not submit to rigorous scientific examination the claim that voluntary associations will be more representative than the existing state. Furthermore, in considering "how acrimonious disputes between guilds are to be avoided," the guild socialists "say that 'the labor and brains of each Guild naturally [will evolve] a hierarchy to which large issues of industrial policy might with confidence be referred,' and 'at the back of this hierarchy and finally dominating it, is the Guild democracy.'" But if this is true, Follett soberly observes, "then guild socialism is to have no different psychological basis from our present system. This is exactly what we rely on now so patiently, so unsuccessfully — the lead of the few, the following of the crowd . . . We need a new method: the group process must be applied to industrial groups as well as to neighborhood groups, to business groups, to professional societies — to every form of human association."[97]

These shortcomings of pluralist thought — the inability to reconcile the distributive and collective, the overreaction to a misunderstood Hegelianism, the obsessive fascination with the Middle Ages, and the failure to study group psychology — create additional difficulties, Follett submits, when the pluralists develop their concepts of sovereignty, group rights, balance of power, and federalism.

Sovereignty Evolves within an Integrative Group Process

Turning her attention first to sovereignty, Follett agrees with the pluralist school "that the present state has no 'right' to sovereignty," but a new conception of sovereignty — one based on group psychology — is "perhaps the most vital thought of the new politics." "The pluralists always tell us that the unified state proceeds from the One to the Many; that is why they discard the unified state. This is not true of the unify*ing* state which I am trying to indicate . . . When we say that there is the One which comes *from* the Many, this does not mean that the One is *above* the Many. The deepest truth of life is that the interrelating by which both are at the same time a-making is constant." The challenge of political life, therefore, is to "seek those methods by which a genuine authority *can* be evolved, by which the true social process shall be everywhere possible."[98]

"Individualism and concentrated authority," Follett acknowledges, "have been struggling for supremacy . . . since the beginning of our government." Herbert Croly was one of many who had sought a synthesis, arguing in *The Promise of American Life* (1909) that the operation of large corporations and a strong federal government, rather than being inimical to democracy, were essential to its aims and ideals. Follett agrees. The average American, she says, has long feared the growth of strong corporate bodies. "But this prejudice must go: we need strong corporate bodies not to compete with the state but to minister to the state." She is critical of the pluralists' desire to shear "the Samson locks of the state" by taking away power from the state and giving it to the group. "This," Follett says, "I do not believe we want to do. We should instead give more and more power to the groups, or rather, because we can never 'give' power, we should recognize all the power which springs up spontaneously within the state, and seek merely those methods by which that self-generating power shall tend immediately to become part of the strength of the state."[99]

Unifying, Rather than Balancing Power among Groups, Should Be Our Aim

Follett is also troubled by the pluralists' attraction to the balance-of-power theory, calling it the "most pernicious part of the pluralists' doctrine." Unifying interests, not balancing power among groups, is her aim.

Recognizing that the process of unifying is fraught with difficulties, Follett readily acknowledges that "we have no more difficult, as we have no more important, problem before us than the relation within the state of one powerful organized body to another and of these bodies to the state." But she will not concede the pluralists' claim that unity and a plurality of groups are incompatible: "The true monistic state is merely the multiple state working out its own unity from infinite diversity. But the unifying state shows us what to do with that diversity. What advantage is that diversity if it is to be always 'competing,' 'fighting,' 'balancing'? Only in the unifying state do we get the full advantage of diversity where it is gathered up into significance and pointed action."[100]

Follett illustrates her point by looking specifically at guild socialism, the most prominent embodiment of pluralist thought. This form of pluralism was organized around producer control of the conditions of production and consumer ownership, through the state, of the means of production. These principles, Follett writes, are "the next step in industrial development, in governmental form," and their increasingly widespread acceptance "gives us large hope for the future."[101] But such a system will work, only if the meetings of group representatives — guild with guild, consumer group with consumer group, producers with consumers — are preceded by some unifying of interests and standards. Otherwise, Follett cautions, it often "is too late to expect agreement" because the "desire to prevail is . . . keenly upon us [and] we behave very differently than when our object is the seeking of truth."[102]

Federalism Is Not Distributed Sovereignty, Consent, and the Balance of Power

Follett focuses the final aspect of her critique of pluralism on what she perceives to be a misinterpretation of federalism.[103] She begins with the pluralist conception of society as a universe of sovereign occupational groups. Follett vigorously opposes this idea. "Man has many functions or rather he is the interplay of many functions . . . All the different sides of our nature develop by the process of compounding. If you shut a man up in his occupation, you refuse him the opportunity of full growth . . . Man must identify himself with humanity. The great lesson which the pluralist school has to teach is that man cannot do this imaginatively but only actually, through his group relations. What it leaves out is that the task is manifold and infinite because man must identify himself with a manifold and infinite number of groups before he has embraced humanity." "Some of the guild socialists tell us," Follett continues, "that a man has as many 'rights' as he has functions: a shoemaker is also a father and a rate-payer. But they do not give us any plan for the political recognition of these various functions . . . The state will never get the whole of a man by his trying to divide himself into parts. A man is not a father at home, a citizen at the polls, an artisan at work, a business man in his office, a follower of Christ at church. He is at every moment a Christian, a father, a citizen, a worker, if he is at any time these in a true sense. We want the whole man in politics."[104]

Follett also sees pluralist schemes of occupational representation as deficient because they fail to recognize that a single person may be a member of several different (and perhaps opposing) interest groups. These "cross lines," Follett writes, are "of inestimable value in the development of society," for the new psychology warns that the "law or right . . . evolved by men of one occupation only will represent too little intermingling to express the 'community' truth." We must therefore work for "a plastic social organization: not only in the sense of a flexible interaction between the groups, but in the sense of an elasticity which makes it possible for individuals to change constantly their relations, their groups, without destroying social cohesion."[105]

Having made the case that sovereignty, based on the principle of interpenetration, is generated within the group and that the individual joins many groups in order to express his multiple nature, Follett is now ready to compare her notion of federalism with that of the pluralists. The pluralists, she contends, advocate "a conception which includes the false doctrines of division of power, the idea that the group not the individual should be the unit of the state, the old consent of governed theory, an almost discarded particularism (group rights), and the worn-out balance theory." Follett disputes each of these doctrines. The United States "is neither to ignore the states, transcend the states, nor to balance the states, it is to *be* the states in their united capacity." She readily admits that many Americans "think of our government as a division of powers between central and local authority, therefore there is as a matter of fact much balancing of interests. But as far as we are doing this at Washington it is exactly what we must get rid of. The first lesson for every member of a federal government to learn is that the interest of the different parts, or the interest of the whole and the interest of the parts, are never to be pitted against each other. As far as the United States represents an interpenetration of thought and feeling and interest and will, it is carrying out the aims of federalism."[106]

The pluralist notion of federalism errs not only in its acceptance of the traditional idea of division of powers — a doctrine that Follett had found lacking as far back as her analysis of the Speakership — but also in its assertion that the group rather than the individual should be the political unit. Follett, by contrast, is "advocating throughout the group principle, but not the group as the political unit . . . Our present method is right so far as it is based on individuals, but we have not yet found the true individual. The groups are the indispensable means for the discovery of self by each man . . . The different groups bring into appearance the multiple sides of me. I go to the polls to express the multiple man which the groups have created. I am to express the whole from my individual point of view, and that is a multiple point of view because of my various groups." The "essence of democracy," therefore, "is the expression of every man in his multiple nature." Because the individual comes into "being and functioning through groups of a more and more federated nature," the unit of society "is neither the group nor the particularist-individual, but the group-individual." Or, put another way, "The individual must always be the unit of politics, as group organization must be its method."[107]

Follett's notion of federalism is thus grounded not on a distributed sovereignty, consent, and the balancing of a plurality of groups, but rather on unifying — both within and among groups. The federal state must therefore express "the two fundamental principles of life — the compounding of consciousness and the endless appearings of new forces." Federalism is "the only possible form for the state," not only because it means an infinite seeking for relation, but also "because it leaves room for . . . the myriad centres of life which must be forever springing up, group after group, within a vital state. Our impulse is at one and the same time to develop self and to transcend self. It is this ever transcending self which needs the federal state."[108]

Although Follett is committed to the "genuine group" as the foundation of the new state, she recognizes that the creation of such groups would "be a matter of experiment and experience, of patient trial and open-minded observation." In this she resembles the progressive thinkers examined in James T. Kloppenberg's comparative intellectual history, *Uncertain Victory*. Follett frankly admits uncertainty and denies in principle that she or anyone else is capable of devising completely adequate solutions to social and political problems. Kloppenberg notes that the refusal of theorists such as Croly, Lippmann, and Dewey to put forward detailed schemes of social reconstruction left them open to charges of intellectual "cowardice"; but after examining the ideas about knowledge and action underlying their political thought, Kloppenberg is convinced that theirs was a principled refusal, traceable to the ideas of the late nineteenth-century philosophers of the *via media*. For thinkers such as T. H. Green, Henry Sidgwick, and William James — men whose work had a profound influence on Follett — politics "originated not in a priori notions of reason, virtue, or justice, but instead in a new conception of experience and a new awareness of uncertainty. Using the tools of radical empiricism and the experimental method of pragmatism, these thinkers fashioned a theory of social action stressing the reciprocal relation between individual choices and historically developing cultural values. According to that theory, moral and political principles are not brought to experience but grow from it; like all ideas, they are subject to endless testing in practice . . . Steady, incremental change through the democratic process, with all its confusions and imperfections, is the political expression of this philosophical creed." Follett reflects this philosophical heritage when she insists that "democracy must be conceived as a process, not a goal. We do not want rigid institutions however good. We need no 'body of truth' of any kind, but the will to will, which means the power to make our own government, our own institutions, our own expanding truth. *We progress, not from one institution to another, but from a lesser to a greater will to will.*"[109]

Follett's work reflects the legacy of the philosophers of the *via media* in yet another way. Their "ethics of rational benevolence" echoes in her conviction that morality is never static — that what is "right" is continually being created — and her belief that this continual revaluing is a group rather than an individual product. As philosophers such as Sidgwick, Green, and James understood it, Kloppenberg writes, our ethical ideas "like the rest of our knowledge . . . cannot conform to prescribed standards but derive instead from reason reflecting imperfectly on experience"; the right and the good, therefore, "like truth, must be unhitched from certainty and made historical."[110]

For political thinkers such as Croly, Dewey, and Follett, the state plays a vital role in this process of working out the right and the good. The state, as "the natural outcome of the uniting groups," must be, according to Follett, "the collective mind embodying the moral will and purpose of All." "It must appear," Follett continues, "as the great moral leader. Its supreme function is moral ordering." But the contemporary state, Follett admits, had proven itself morally bankrupt. How, then, could the state gain moral and spiritual authority? The neighborhood group, which Follett had often found an arena bubbling with diversity, seems to her a particularly suitable forum for the process of creating the moral state, "because we have daily to consider the wants of all in order to make a synthesis of those wants; we have to recognize the rights of others and adapt ourselves to them. Men must recognize and unify difference and then the moral law appears in all its majesty in concrete form. This is the universal striving." After all, the "chief object of neighborhood organization is not to right wrongs, as is often supposed, but to found more firmly and build more widely the right."[111]

Just as the bringing out and unifying of difference through interpenetration gives rise to the new state, "Through the further working of this principle,"

Follett tells us, "the world-state appears." But in the international arena, as elsewhere, the pernicious influence of the imitation and likeness theorists must first be overcome: "Superficial moralists try to get us to like some other nationality by emphasizing all the things we have in common, but war can never cease until we see the value of differences, that they are to be maintained, not blotted out. The white-man's burden is not to make others like himself. As we see the value of the individual, of every individual, so we must see the value of each nation, that all are needed." And just as Follett will not be satisfied with compromise and concession as strategies for dealing with difference within the group, she finds these strategies equally destructive in the international arena. "The pacifists," she writes, "have wanted us to tolerate our enemies and the more extreme ones to turn the other cheek when smitten. But tolerance is intolerable. And we cannot dwell among enemies . . . The old-fashioned hero went out to conquer his enemy; the modern hero goes out to disarm his enemy through creating a mutual understanding." Just as one must be anxious in the group for what others have to give, the nationalism Follett seeks is one that "looks out as well as in." Nationalism "means, in addition to other meanings, every nation being responsible to a larger whole . . . Nationalism is not my nation for itself or my nation against others or my nation dominating others, but simply my nation taking its part as 'an equal among equals.' "[112]

Follett saw considerable reason for hope in the possible creation of an international League of Nations, but she felt certain that such a league would fail unless all nations — including Germany — were included. She reminded her readers that "we do not join a league of nations solely to work out our relations to one another, but to learn to work for the larger whole, for international values. Until this lesson is learned no league of nations can be successful."[113]

Whether a lasting international peace was possible seemed to Follett to depend upon "whether we have advanced far enough to be capable of loyalty to a higher unit, not as a substitute for our old patriotism to our country, but in addition to it." This could not be done through "the imagination alone . . . Men go round lecturing to kind-hearted audiences and say, 'Can you not be loyal to something bigger than a nation?' And the kind-hearted audiences reply, 'Certainly, we will now, at your very interesting suggestion, be loyal to a league of nations.' But this is only a wish on their part, its realization can never come by *wishing* but only by *willing*, and willing is a process, you have to put yourself in a certain place from which to will. We must, in other words, try experiments with a league of nations, and out of the actual life of that league will come loyalty to it."[114]

Follett suspected that many would see her vision of the new state as denying some of the most important principles of the American tradition, but this prospect did not dissuade her. "We need to-day new principles," she wrote. "We can reform and reform but all this is on the surface. What we have got to do is to change some of the fundamental ideas of our American life. This is not being disloyal to our past, it is exactly the opposite. Let us be loyal to our inheritance and tradition, but let us understand what that inheritance and tradition truly is. It is not *our* tradition to stick to an outworn past, a conventional ideal, a rigid religion. We are children of men who have not been afraid of new continents or new ideas. In our blood is the impulse to leap to the highest we can see, as the wills of our fathers fixed themselves on the convictions of their hearts. To spring forward and then to follow the path steadfastly is forever the duty of Americans. We must *live* democracy."[115]

A vivid rhetoric permeates *The New State,* and more than one reviewer would find fault with it; but the presence of such intensely dramatic language throughout the text tells us that the writing of *The New State* was more than an academic exercise for Mary Follett. Indeed, as she finished the manuscript, Follett was exultant. She now knew what she was living for — she knew what she would "go to the stake for." Americans must overcome "the conviction of separateness"; they must find "a new principle of association." "We find the true man," Follett was convinced, "only through group organization." "The group process contains the secret of collective life, it is the key to democracy, it is the master lesson for every individual to learn, it is our chief hope for the political, the social, the international life of the future."[116]

In *The New State* Follett asserts again and again that every difference must be cherished, must be related — all must participate in creating the state: "Every man sharing in the creative process is democracy; that is our politics and our religion." She elaborates: "The true state has my devotion because it gathers up into itself the various sides of me, is the symbol of my multiple self, is my multiple self brought to significance, to self-realization. If you leave me with my plural selves, you leave me in desolate places, my soul craving its meaning, its home. The home of my soul is in the state."[117] But being a woman in turn-of-the-century society, Follett had been denied participation in much of public life. She had an obvious affinity for political and economic analysis, but these talents had so far found expression only in her book on the Speakership. She was denied an academic career of the stature available to her male intellectual peers and, in the political arena, could not even vote. After abortive attempts at other sorts of careers proved unsatisfactory, Follett turned, in considerable desperation, to Pauline Agassiz Shaw and settlement work.

It was here, in the neighborhoods of Boston, that Follett began to realize that politics as it was often practiced — the politics of "interests" and social classes — often did not touch the real needs of the people. In *The New State* Follett paints a vivid portrait of the dissociation she found:

> We work, we spend most of our waking hours working for some one of whose life we know nothing, who knows nothing of us; we pay rent to a landlord whom we never see or see only once a month, and yet our home is our most precious possession; we have a doctor who is with us in the crucial moments of birth and death, but whom we ordinarily do not meet; we buy our food, our clothes, our fuel, of automatons for the selling of food, clothes and fuel. We know all these people in their occupational capacity, not as men like ourselves with hearts like ours, desires like ours, hopes like ours. And this isolation from those who minister to our lives, to whose lives we minister, does not bring us any nearer to our neighbors in their isolation. For every two or three of us think ourselves a little better than every other two or three, and this becomes a dead wall of separation, of misunderstanding, of antagonism.[118]

"How," she asks, "can we do away with this artificial separation which is the dry-rot of our life?" The answer, she thought, could be found in the work of the community centers of Boston: "Community must be the foundation stone of the New State," and its method must be the group. "Group organization is to be the new method in politics, the basis of our future industrial system, the foundation of international order. Group organization will create the new world we are now blindly feeling after, for creative force comes from the group, creative power is evolved through the activity of the group life." This was an exhilarating discovery, for Follett now felt certain that she and others like her "are coworkers with every process of creation, that our function is as important as the power which keeps the stars in their orbits."[119]

That women were numbered among the creators of the new state was a stirring revelation. Many of the century's "New Women," feeling a special urgency about finding ways to marry their commitments to self-realization and service, had devoted their lives to social and civic enterprises. "Each of us," Follett writes in *The New State*, "wants to pour forth in community use the life that we feel welling up within us . . . The woman suffrage movement, the labor movement, are parts of this vital and irresistible current. They have not come from surface springs, their sources are deep in the life forces of our age. There is a more fundamental cause of our present unrest than the superficial ones given for the woman movement, or the selfish ones given for our labor troubles: it is not the 'demand for justice' from women nor the 'economic greed' of labor, but the desire for one's place, for each to give his share, for each to control his own life — this is the underlying thought which is so profoundly moving both men and women to-day." If, as Follett now believed, the most pressing problem of society was the working out of new principles of association, the lives of thousands of talented women were given new meaning. "This is the deeper thought of neighborhood organization," Follett tells her readers, "that through performing my humblest duties I am creating the soul of this great democracy."[120]

Follett concludes *The New State* by reaching out to her readers, and in so doing sets for herself a new agenda. "This book," she tells us, "is a plea for the more abundant life: for the fulness of life and the growing of life . . . It is a plea for a splendid progress dependent upon every splendid one of us. We need a new faith in humanity, not a sentimental faith or a theological tenet or a philosophical conception, but an active faith in that creative power of men which shall shape government and industry, which shall give form equally to our daily life with our neighbor and to a world league."[121]

Admittedly, the scope of her vision was enormous and the tasks of building the new state formidable, but challenges had always energized rather than discouraged Mary Follett. The important thing was to begin. "I am sometimes told," she says, "that mine is a counsel of perfection only to be realized in the millennium, but we cannot take even the first step until we have chosen our path."[122] This the writing of *The New State* had enabled her to do. Follett had begun the book as a chronicle of the community centers movement, but through the sort of "interpenetrations" she had come to advocate, she had uncovered the meaning of her experience for practical politics, for contemporary social theory, and for her own life. "It is a glorious moment to come to one," she told Alice Brandeis, " — really to know for the first time what you are living for & to know it so completely that you are willing to make any sacrifice for it, that the whole of life takes on a new significance & new proportions. To many, happily, it comes when they are much younger, but I am thankful to have it at all."[123]

17

Not Neighborhood Groups but an Integrative Group Process

As reviews of *The New State* began to appear, Follett found her most appreciative academic audience among philosophers. The 1919 president of the American Philosophical Association, Hartly Burr Alexander, pronounced himself "in hearty concord" with the "practical programme suggested in *The New State*" even though he was a bit suspicious of Follett's conception of a "liaison-inviting self driven on by the vital impulse to the formation of a social Whole." Alexander was also impressed by Follett's ability to weave together threads of ideas from a remarkably diverse collection of thinkers.[1] Indeed, her penchant for drawing ideas from opposing schools of philosophic thought drew accolades from monists as well as pluralists. "The most interesting thing that has happened about my book," Follett wryly confided to a colleague, "is that (the 'third position' not being usually recognized) each side thinks I am with them."[2]

Although Follett was clearly not a monist in any traditional sense, England's leading proponent of Absolute Idealism, Bernard Bosanquet, judged *The New State* to be "a very excellent book." He wrote "two very nice letters," Follett remarked to a colleague, "in one of which he says that I have made an advance in thought, but adding that on the whole I am on his side and must be prepared for much opposition from the political pluralists."[3] James H. Tufts, the University of Chicago professor with whom John Dewey had produced the classic text *Ethics,* called the "distinguishing merit" of *The New State* "its employment of social psychology." Follett's book, Tufts continued, was "singularly fresh in its treatment, and frequently brilliant in its style"; it "essays a critical analysis of our political situation and a constructive principle for its improvement." Tufts, however, had one major problem with Follett's approach—at least as he interpreted it. He doubted "the adequacy or workability of the neighborhood group, for the task put upon it," arguing that the increasing preponderance of renters made "neighborhood consciousness almost impossible." The philosopher from whom Follett received her highest accolades was Harry A. Overstreet, the pluralist proponent of vocational schemes of political representation. Mary was enormously grateful for Overstreet's reviews, not merely because he lavished praise on her work but because, as she later told him, "you so generously (as I can never forget) endorsed The New State before you knew how it would be received."

Writing in *The Survey,* Overstreet applauded Follett's distinction between the group and the crowd and called her analysis of the group "a contribution to a new sociology and a new politics, as truly so as the contributions, in their day, of Bentham and of Tarde." And in the *Journal of Philosophy, Psychology and Scientific Methods,* Overstreet characterized *The New State* as "a philosophy come back to earth. The One and the Many are there; the Universal and the Particular; Monism and Pluralism; objectivism and subjectivism; real personality; unity of opposites; compenetration, and all the rest; but they do not float in the metaphysical ethers. They are tied to the homely behaviors of men and women in society." Overstreet assured his fellow philosophers: "There are few books published in recent years that go so deeply to the foundations of our social and political problems." It seemed to him that political philosophy had so far paid very little attention to the group, focusing instead on "the puzzle of the individual *versus* society." Mary Follett, by contrast, recognized both "that man lives his social life most effectively in groups—neighborhood, occupational, artistic, scientific, *etc.* —and that in his group life 'the fallacy of the self and others fades away.' "[4]

Overstreet's remarks gave Follett one important supporter among the pluralists, but the pluralist thinker from whom she was most desirous of a favorable review was Harold J. Laski. Laski, Follett confided to Alice Brandeis, could be "a fellow-worker for the same ends if he does not misunderstand me." Even before the publication of her book, Follett worried about how Laski would react to her critique of pluralism, telling Brandeis that she hoped to "meet him personally when our similarity of view can be emphasized before he reads my book where the difference there is inevitably between 2 minds has perhaps more prominence than a cleverer writer than myself need have given it." Follett had at one time considered going to Canada to meet Laski, thinking of him "from his writings as hoary with the wisdom of a long life!" But when she discovered that he was only twenty-five, she discarded the idea. Now, however, with Laski in Cambridge as a Harvard lecturer, Follett appealed to Brandeis as "a valedictory blessing on the book" to create an occasion on which she and Laski might meet *"in a natural way."* "He wouldn't stir a step of course to see *me,*" she said in one letter, "but he would come up from Rockport gladly to see *you,* & then I could be tucked in."[5]

There is no record of whether this prepublication meeting actually took place, but when Laski's review appeared in the *New Republic* in February 1919, it was clear that Follett had had reason to be concerned. Laski's opening remarks were derisive and patronizing. *The New State,* Laski wrote, "suffers from being written in a hideous journalese that deprives it of no small part of its effectiveness. It is at times confused upon the theory involved in the practical facts at issue. It has a somewhat jejune habit of making large assumptions as to the results of ethical and psychological inquiry. It will not assist a specialist anxious for discussion upon the comparative merits of the new ideas. But for the general reader who is aware of a debate, and anxious for information as to its subject, Miss Follett's is, on the whole, the best book as yet to be had. It is at least decisively clear as to the large outline of its subject, even if it lacks a meticulous accuracy of thought."

Laski's critique often seemed less a review of *The New State* than a restatement of his attack on sovereignty. Ignoring Follett's conviction that sovereignty cannot be assumed but instead must be "grown" through the law of interpenetration in ever-widening federations of groups, Laski charged incorrectly that Follett "is still in the stage where the state, for her, is the supreme representative of the community." He also judged *The New State* deficient with regard to another of his critiques of sovereignty — the objection on moral grounds. "Miss Follett's implied warning that our denial of the sovereignty of the state must not result in the erection of the sovereignty of the individual has real merit," Laski writes; "but it is ethically unsatisfactory insofar as it does not admit that my duty to the state is to do right as I see it and, if need be, pay the penalty." The state, Laski argued, has no absolute right to the obedience of its citizens — the individual must at all times obey only his own conscience. But here, too, Laski misinterpreted Follett's argument. Follett did not throw out individual conscience; on the contrary, she insisted that "the individual is not for a moment to yield his right to judge for himself." The point Follett was trying to make was twofold: first, there is no such thing as a truly "individual" conscience, and second, the individual "can judge better for himself if he joins with others in evolving a synthesized judgment." Laski also criticized Follett for advocating a political process based not on majority rule, but on creation of the collective will. His critique was not based on a serious evaluation of the strengths and weaknesses of the process by which Follett believed the collective will might be created; instead Laski merely charged, again incorrectly, that Follett's position was identical with the discredited ideas of Rousseau.

Laski's final objection to *The New State* rested on his conviction, at least at this stage of his career, that genuine political reform is impossible. Impressed with how thoroughly the capitalist oligarchy had come to dominate traditional political organization, Laski was convinced that "the state is hostile to the aspirations and claims of the workers and their unions," and, as a result, "the simple weapons of politics are alone powerless to effect any basic redistribution of economic strength." Laski believed that writers such as Follett, rather than focusing on political reforms, should seek to create new forms of worker control of industry. He was particularly put off, as Follett suspected he would be, by her critique of guild socialism, charging that she had failed to appreciate the intimate interplay of economic and political power. But here, as elsewhere, Laski misrepresented Follett's views. She was firm in her conviction that "political and economic power cannot be separated" and, indeed, criticized the guild socialists for failing to give adequate recognition to the relationships between economic and political life.[6]

Laski was not the only political scientist to react unfavorably to *The New State*. Others charged that Follett's ideas not only were impractical but also were expressed with a fervor akin to "religious ecstasy."[7] Committed as these new social scientists were to what they considered "objective" investigation, Follett's sometimes passionate prose made them uneasy. The *Political Science Quarterly* "says it is worthless," Follett noted in a letter to Overstreet; "I forget whether it uses that word, but it says its only value is to show the restlessness of the times." Fortunately for Follett, the political scientists' negative notices mattered less, given her aims, than reviews in the popular press — and there she received unstinting praise. The anonymous writer for *The Nation* called her book "almost unique among reconstruction books because it really drives down to fundamentals" and is "intensely and immediately practical." Follett offered "a suggestion of political organization through the neighborhood group which is not only fascinatingly simple and sane but deep-reaching in its social and political implications."[8]

The writer for the *Times Literary Supplement* was even more effusive. He was particularly impressed with how "Mr. M. P. Follett" elucidated the connections between economic and political democracy: "The only promise of a solution [to increasing conflict between employers and wage earners] is in the group system applied to industry as to government and all other activities that men must carry on in common . . . Our need now is to find the right and natural means to democracy in industry, and then to apply that to politics." This glowing *TLS* review gave Follett enormous satisfaction. "They gave me the whole front page," she told Harry Overstreet with pride, "and it was written by some one who really understands the book — it is indeed a pleasure." Follett also confessed to some delight at seeing Harold Laski's opinion swayed by the appearance of these complimentary reviews. Follett reported to Overstreet that Laski was now writing "of course 'you and I' think so and so, 'you and I' want so and so, and proposing that I do certain things with him, and then just a week or so ago he writes and congratulates me on the review in the Times and also Bosanquet's review, saying, 'But how can Bosanquet have any doubts about your belief in a pluralistic state?' " Laski's newly "professed 'gladness' over the favorable reception of my book" quite amused Follett; it "seems to indicate," she remarked to Overstreet, "that [Laski] thinks he wrote a favorable review of it!"[9]

Follett's book not only drew notices from philosophers, political scientists, and the general press; it also was of interest to the sociologists. Charles A. Ellwood, a University of Missouri professor and one of the most prominent American exponents of the new psychology, reviewed the book for the *American Journal of Sociology. The New State,* Ellwood wrote, was "a notable contribution to social and political theory. Not only is it indispensable to those who wish to think intelligently about the political reconstruction which is evidently before us, but also to all who wish a clear summary of the results of modern psychological sociology. In no other work is the modern sociological point of view brought out more clearly." Ellwood would have been particularly well qualified to judge. Harry Elmer Barnes says in his history of sociology that Ellwood "showed a wider mastery of the technical literature of psychology and social psychology than any other American sociological writer of his generation."[10]

Ellwood was particularly impressed with what he saw as a "remarkable elaboration" of Charles Horton Cooley's idea of the importance of primary groups in social life.[11] Follett's book, Ellwood wrote, did "for the neighborhood group in particular what other books have attempted to do for the family, and it points to the revitalization of neighborhood group organization as the most necessary step toward the revitalization of our political life." But this equation of Follett's ideas about the neighborhood group with Cooley's notion of "primary groups," however complimentary in its intent, reflected a fundamental misunderstanding of Follett's argument — a misunderstanding that persists to this day.[12]

Cooley believed that the "more elaborate relations" of society were based on the social consciousness developed in the early primary relations of family and neighborhood. "The result of intimate association, psychologically, is a certain fusion of individualities in a common whole, so that one's very self, for many purposes at least, is the common life and purpose of the group." Cooley left largely unexplained the process by which this "fusion" was accomplished; but, appreciative of the theoretical contributions of Tarde and Baldwin, he emphasized the workings of an instinctual sympathy, suggestion, and imitation.

The "genuine" neighborhood groups that Follett was seeking to create, by contrast, were characterized by a more dynamic process — by interpenetrations, by the bringing out and integrating of differences into continually evolving unifyings. Furthermore, it was this *process* to which Follett was committed, not to neighborhood groups per se; neighborhoods interested her only because her social and civic experience had demonstrated that neighborhood groups had the potential for developing this sort of process. "Neighborhood groups, economic groups, unifying groups, these have been my themes," Follett writes in *The New State*, "and yet the point which I wish to emphasize is not the kind of group, but that the group whatever its nature shall be a genuine group, that we can have no genuine state at all which does not rest on genuine groups."[13]

Ellwood, despite his apparent failure to appreciate Follett's concern with a dynamic group process, was clearly impressed with the ideas expressed in *The New State*. Indeed, the only aspect of the book that caused him any real concern was Follett's "tendency toward paradoxical and extravagant statements," noting that "those who feel strongly the necessity of a very exact use of words in a scientific work will undoubtedly be repelled by this fault in the author's style." Personally, however, Ellwood was not put off.[14] He "fought valiantly" throughout his career, against "a sterile 'objectivism' in social science" and fervently believed that "sociology should be a normative and ameliorative social philosophy."[15]

It was Follett's stirring rhetoric, particularly as it proclaimed the virtues of creating the collective will, that opened her work to another sort of attack that was common during the immediate postwar period: she was labeled a communist sympathizer. Follett's accuser was Thomas P. Bailey, a professor of ethology at the University of the South. Follett's "many instances of over-emphasis and exaggeration," Bailey charged, suggested " 'yellow' sensationalism and muckraking, and her obsession by the one idea of the Saving Group gives a 'red' halo to much of her thought." Continuing in this vein, Bailey warned that the "spirits that [Follett's] 'groups' may call forth from the vasty deep *may* turn out at best only 'sincere' fanatics like Lenine [*sic*]. He seems to be a past-master in the ability to 'integrate' and 'interpenetrate' his soviet of soviets."[16]

Bailey's easy linking of Marxist-Leninist ideology with Follett's commitment to creating the collective will indicates how frenzied the postwar political debate had become. The successful Bolshevik revolution in Russia, uprisings in Hungary, and unrest in Germany provided a somber backdrop to America's domestic conflicts and dislocations. Postwar inflation was rampant; cancellations of war orders resulted in an abrupt economic depression in late 1918 and early 1919; women and blacks, who had temporarily gained new status through their employment in wartime industries, now found themselves without jobs; and returning soldiers could not find work. The resulting economic tensions produced more than three thousand strikes, which were quickly translated by some "into a full-blown Red Scare." Businessmen and their allies created "open shop" committees to smash the unions, and consequently union membership "fell from a peak of more than 5 million in 1920 to about 3.6 million in 1923."

Those who experienced the greatest oppression during the early 1920s were the immigrants from southern and eastern Europe and from Asia — people "who faced not only social and economic problems but also widespread charges that their alien influences were permanently corrupting American society." The Ku Klux Klan, which by 1924 had 4 million members nationwide, was on the march. The Klan's enemies were blacks, aliens, and "moral degenerates," and these groups were regularly terrorized by personal intimidation and violence. During this same period, "a host of private vigilantes and public officials moved with devastating effect against organized radicalism." A. Mitchell Palmer, the U.S. attorney general, "marshaled the resources of the Justice Department and launched a series of raids that were decried by one civil libertarian as 'the greatest executive restriction of personal liberty in the history of this country.'" Although the most flagrant phase of the Red Scare ended "when Palmer predicted that there would be massive bombings on May Day of 1920 and nothing happened," a general antiradicalism persisted throughout the early 1920s. The Red Scare eventually subsided, but suspicion of immigrant groups remained high. The restrictive 1924 immigration law not only "placed a ceiling on immigration that was less than one-fifth of the normal prewar flow," but also skewed quotas in favor of northern Europeans and totally excluded Asians.[17]

Mary Follett was not the only leader of the community center movement who was singled out for criticism during the height of the Red Scare. John Collier, who had gone to California from New York in September 1919 "to undertake the leadership of adult education in the state," soon found himself under attack.[18] The leaders of the National Social Unit experiment, Wilbur and Elsie Phillips, were also accused of being "Red." As a result, the "social unit" idea lost its funding and by mid-1921 was dead, not just in Cincinnati but nationwide.[19]

This hostile postwar social and political environment made it nearly impossible for the community centers movement to retain the momentum it had gained during the war. Only a few months before the armistice, the Executive Committee of the NCCA had felt extremely confident about the future: all but one of its functions — enlisting teachers in the movement and persuading them to assume civic secretaryships — had been absorbed to some degree by the federal government working through its various departments and the Council of National Defense.[20] Even when the war ended, it seemed that federal support for the community centers movement not only would be maintained but would actually be enhanced by the participation of the Red Cross and the War Camp Community Service, "quasi-official agencies" which had grown to enormous size and enjoyed wide popular support.[21]

In the spring of 1919 the secretary of the interior, Franklin K. Lane, demonstrated his continuing support for the community centers movement. He asked Congress for an appropriation of $100,000 for a Division of Educational Extension in the Bureau of Education, a group that had so far been maintained by President Wilson's War Emergency Fund. Established only a few months earlier, one of the division's primary functions was to cooperate with state extension officials in promoting community centers.

But in the midst of these promising indications that federal support for the community centers movement would continue, warning signs began to appear. By the end of 1918 President Wilson, rather than promoting a great program of reconstruction, seemed to be seeking a rapid return to prewar social and economic conditions. Wilson's position reflected a tension that had existed throughout the war — two currents of thought that, according to a historian of the period, Emily N. Blair, ran "almost side by side and often intermingling. One was a desire that the war machinery should be available after the war for reconstructing the social fabric and making America all that true Americanism might desire it, that the cooperative spirit developed under war needs might be salvaged; the other was a distinct fear that organizations built up for war needs might be perpetuated during peace times until they became a heavy incubus on the social structure, that the personal liberty yielded for the sake of national strength should not be returned, that Federal authority would usurp State Control."[22]

Despite these postwar debates about the proper relationship among individual freedom, states' rights, and federal control, the immediate cause of the termination of federal funding for the community centers movement was much more mundane. Angered over Wilson's failure to include an active Republican

leader in the delegation to the Versailles Conference, senior Republican senators resolved to punish him. When the appropriation bill came up for debate,
the Republicans led a successful filibuster that had the effect, among other
consequences, of cutting off funding for programs of importance to the community centers movement, including the Division of Educational Extension.[23]

According to Emily N. Blair, the withdrawal of federal support had had a
devastating effect on the whole state council system. By May 1919 "the line of
communication between the Field Division and the State Councils was entirely
down, due to the fact that the receiving stations had gone out of business.
Twenty State Councils had either adjourned or disbanded; 3 had paper organizations or were inactive; 8 had greatly reduced their force, although still in
existence; 3 had turned their business over to new agencies. Only 12 were
really alive."[24]

The withdrawal of the federal government from the promotion of the community centers movement forced the National Community Centers Association to reevaluate its agenda. In the fall of 1920 the NCCA reluctantly
renounced its earlier commitment to making itself into a grassroots representative organization; a committee was appointed to draft a new constitution
that would make the association "the official body of those professionally
engaged in Community Center work" — a path already taken by numerous
groups of emerging professionals during the Progressive Era.[25] The following February, in a continuing effort to sort out this new mission, the Executive Committee considered two radically different proposals: disbanding the
NCCA in favor of affiliation with the National Education Association or the
National Conference of Social Workers, or reconstituting the association as
the national coordinating body for community organizing.[26] One of the conference speakers, Eduard C. Lindeman, a young professor at the Women's
College of North Carolina who would soon become involved in a research
project with Mary Follett, put the need for a new national coordinating group
this way: "People are now bewildered by the fact that a host of organizations
are attempting to organize them . . . Unless some such coordination takes place
very soon the people will lose confidence in the entire community movement.
The country is vitally interested in a democratic community movement but
they are insisting that it shall be free from institutional selfishness."[27]

By 1922 the transformation of the National Community Centers Association into a professional association of community workers and researchers
was virtually complete. The NCCA held its annual meeting in conjunction
with the American Sociological Association, and two prominent sociologists
were elected to senior positions: Robert E. Park of the University of Chi-

cago became president, and Arthur Evans Wood of the University of Michigan vice-president.[28]

There is no evidence that Mary Follett played a significant role in this transformation. Follett had been named to a sixteen-person NEA-NCCA committee charged with planning the February 1920 annual meeting, but she apparently did not attend; and when the NCCA elected officers for 1920–21, Follett was continued as a vice-president but in an "honorary" capacity.[29] Follett's withdrawal from active participation in the NCCA almost certainly was a sign that she no longer saw this organization as the proper vehicle for the important work ahead of her. Instead, the challenge facing Mary Follett was to work out new methods of human association through integrative group processes — and she would do so in whatever arena integrative groups might be found.[30]

During the years following the war, many of Follett's contemporaries were thoroughly disillusioned — some by the war itself, but many more by the subsequent political and racist hysteria and by their failure to persuade business and government leaders to support a period of reconstruction that would consolidate and expand the social programs developed during the war. Even Follett, who had a determinedly optimistic temperament, was not immune to these frustrations. "Think how we felt," Follett reminded an audience some years later, "during the great war. It was horrible, it tortured anyone with any imagination, and yet all the time underneath was the exultant feeling that the Time had come — our Der Tag — the time had come when man was to awake to a great and new understanding of the possibilities of human fellowship. We could go through all the horrors of that war because we were looking beyond." Follett continued: "We have been grievously disappointed, yet the faith is still there, will I believe always exist in the hearts of men as the strongest urge of human life . . . that the next generation shall realize what he sees only as in a vision."[31]

Writing *The New State* had been an expression both of Follett's faith in the future and of her willingness to press on in the face of anguish and disappointment. Her courage gave others strength. Eduard Lindeman, who would soon begin a two-year collaboration with Follett, later recalled that the "*New State* came into my hands during that perplexing post-war period when I, like so many others who had hoped to bring a gift to life and were baffled with purposes out of harmony with prevailing force and coercion, sought expression in some creative channel. Miss Follett's challenge to the atmosphere of fatigued futility of that period set off the 'trigger' which gave new direction and new hope to researches already partially conceived."[32] But it would be two years before the Follett-Lindeman collaboration would take center stage; in the interim, Follett was involved in a number of other projects.

Convinced that the future of the community centers movement was dependent in part on the nature of the training available to community center workers, Follett became involved in an effort to improve the quality of that training. In June 1919 she was one of two Radcliffe alumnae appointed to a four-person committee of the Radcliffe Union, a club of former nonmatriculating students. This committee was charged with conferring with Harvard officials about the establishment of a Harvard University "graduate school of applied sociology, to be open to graduate students of Radcliffe College."[33]

The Radcliffe Union committee was chaired by Ada Eliot Sheffield, a well-known Boston social worker and the sister of T. S. Eliot. At this point in her career, Sheffield's interests lay in the education of social workers — particularly in fostering improvements in the writing of cases and their use in the classroom. Sheffield, like many other local social workers, had regularly supplemented her meager social work salary by giving paid lectures at the Simmons College School for Social Workers, but in the spring of 1917, two years before the formation of the Radcliffe Union committee, she ended this arrangement. Deeply discouraged about the state of social work training in Boston, Sheffield turned to research and to writing about the importance of studying the multiple, changing factors that make up a case situation. Sheffield's ideas so impressed Mary Follett that in *Creative Experience* (1924) she used excerpts from Sheffield's articles to illustrate the concept of "the total situation."[34]

Blessed with the informed and committed leadership of Sheffield and Follett, the Radcliffe Union committee reportedly drew up plans for an applied sociology program, probably based on the case method of instruction. In January 1920, before the plans for this new "applied sociology" program could be put into effect, Richard C. Cabot was appointed to a chair in the Harvard Social Ethics Department.[35] Cabot's public service had included a stint as a member of the board of the Boston Children's Aid Society, where he had been so taken with the casework method that he made it the cornerstone of the medical social service unit during his tenure as chief of staff of Massachusetts General Hospital. Cabot's track record on casework methods of instruction led the Radcliffe Union to feel so comfortable with his appointment that it terminated its campaign for the applied sociology program. Under his leadership, the Department of Social Ethics seemed likely to fill the need that had been under discussion.[36]

Although the Radcliffe women disbanded their committee, they kept a watchful eye on developments in the Department of Social Ethics and did not hesitate to try to influence the curriculum. Neither Sheffield nor Follett, however, became a paid lecturer in the program, and Follett seems to have dispensed with the idea of teaching even before Cabot's appointment. "I have decided definitely that I am not going to teach anywhere," she told Harry Overstreet in September 1919. "I want to study the group, or better, to get a group to study the group."[37]

Follett's decision to pursue group studies was probably influenced by the favorable reactions she was receiving from readers of *The New State*. Walter Lippmann, the author and political commentator who in two years would publish *Public Opinion* (1922), had written to say that "Laski has allowed me to see your letter of August 16, and I am writing you just a line to say that I think you have put your finger on a very critical point. I agree as to the necessity for what you call group psychology, and in the book for which I am now studying I am struggling with aspects of that question . . . I do hope that you will come to New York soon. Graham Wallace [*sic*] will be here and I shall be glad to take you to see him, so that we three could talk over the thing together."[38] Wallas was coming to New York at the invitation of Herbert Croly to give "the star course of the year" during the inaugural semester of the New School for Social Research.[39]

Follett was intrigued by the idea of meeting Wallas, but first she had to fulfill some pressing obligations. Apparently at Harry Overstreet's instigation, Follett had been invited to write a 5,000-word article on community for the November issue of the *Philosophical Review* and then to present a companion paper at the December meeting of the American Philosophical Association.[40] Wilbur Urban, the Trinity College philosopher charged with organizing the paper session, described the underlying premise for the meeting in the *Philosophical Review*. Urban believed that there was heightened interest in the concept of community because "life within the community and relations between communities have become strangely difficult and unsatisfactory. The community as we have known it is rapidly becoming unrecognizable . . . What is this thing, society or community? What is its matter and its form? Is it something made or does it grow? or is it partly a growth and partly a construction? What are the limits of its modifiability? Is it a collection, an organism, or a person? Which is more ultimate, individual, society, or group? What of the *communitas communitatis* or state? What is its relation to other communities or groups? Is it omni-competent and omnipotent, or is it but one among equally sovereign groups?" Recognizing that "expertness in many fields of knowledge and practice" was required to deal adequately with these questions, Urban invited "specialists in sociology, jurisprudence, and political science" to meet with the philosophers.[41] Those invited included Follett, Harold J. Laski, James H. Tufts (University of Chicago), Wilbur M. Urban

(Trinity College), Morris R. Cohen (City College of New York), and apparently also Roscoe Pound (Harvard Law School).

In letters written before this rather formidable occasion, Follett's characteristic insecurities are fully apparent, but she also demonstrates a stylish wit. "I think that it was probably you," she told Harry Overstreet, "who suggested that I take part in the Conference, therefore I don't want you to be ashamed of [my paper], so please, please tear it to pieces. Or if you think it is not equal to the occasion and can't be made so, I beg you to say so frankly, and I can be ill or lose the paper or commit suicide — anything to save your reputation! . . . Another thing — will they think it awfully cheeky of me, not a philosopher, to say that both the monists and pluralists are wrong? I suppose I shall not have a friend left after December, for I only stop belaboring the pluralists long enough to have a go at the monists."

In early November, having learned that the upcoming meeting would be held in Ithaca, New York, rather than in nearby Providence, Mary joked with Overstreet about the change, confessing that "I am the most provincial person I know, not to say parochial, or whatever word expresses that I *always* view with 'dismay' the idea of moving from my own door-step. And Ithaca!"

> Still I think I won't now give up this chance of regeneration for my soul, as you consider it! And are Pound and Laski, Tufts, Urban and Cohen all to be regenerated at one fell swoop? If you take a different six every year, it is only a question of arithmetic when the world will be saved.
>
> Are all philosophers like you and Dr. Urban? And have I lived to this hoary age missing the best thing in life? If the meeting at Ithaca is at all as you and Dr. Urban describe it, I shall give up all other associates and humbly beg to spend the rest of my life with philosophers. I could sweep out the office or black boots, or something like that.
>
> . . . Pay no attention to this letter. But do forgive my frivolity. I will try to murder it or hide it away before I enter the Presence in December.

Follett was quite taken with the philosophers' strategy of pairing preconference publications with presentations, since this format suggested a deliberate attempt to foster "interpenetrations." But upon reflection, thinking it more likely that the meeting would involve little more than the usual "give and take" of an academic conference, Follett thought it best to check with Harry Overstreet about what her presentation should include: "Dr. Urban says it is to be this same paper which is coming out in the Philosophical Review with the 'modifications' which my reading of the other papers will entail!! (I had not imagined there was a whole association which so completely followed the true doctrine!) But unless you are all too good to be true I cannot quite believe this. Aren't the December papers more likely to be in the nature of a rebuttal? Or is it understood that they are to be practically the same papers, and then that the discussion comes *after* the reading of the papers? In that case won't the people who have already read them be bored to tears. Please let me know. I am not criticizing your methods. They have seemed to me particularly enlightened — this getting the material of the discussion before the members beforehand."[42]

Follett's suspicion that the meeting would center upon statements and rebuttals rather than "interpenetratings" and "unifyings" proved to be well founded. Even the published papers seem to consist largely of expressions of already-defined positions in the continuing monist-pluralist debate. Wilbur Urban, the primary proponent of monism, argued in his paper that the state was not *omnipotent*, that is, having ultimate authority in all things, but that it was *omnicompetent*, having the "final authority in certain things which concern all the elements of community." Harold Laski, predictably, took a quite different view, arguing that the monistic state was not only an intellectual fiction but was also "administratively incomplete and ethically inadequate." The defects of the monistic state could be remedied, Laski contended, only in a pluralistic state where coordination would replace hierarchical structure. Laski's denial of the existence of "over-individual" or "communal minds" was seconded by Morris Cohen, but Cohen then warned that political pluralism was itself open "to serious practical and theoretical objections." Small groups or communities "may be far more oppressive to the individual than larger ones," and "if the state gives up its sovereignty over any group there will be nothing to prevent that group from oppressing the rest of the community." James H. Tufts adopted a quite different angle of vision; he contended in his preconference paper that debating the future of community solely in political terms was outdated, for "economic power appears to be steadily gaining in effectual control over all living conditions, and in the view of some is rendering political power obsolescent."[43]

Follett's *Philosophical Review* paper, like those of the other participants, consisted largely of arguments already made elsewhere. Follett's agenda seems to have been twofold: to reiterate the "third" (neither monist nor pluralist) position she had taken in *The New State* and to clear up misunderstandings that had become apparent in recently published reviews of her book. With regard to the latter, Follett seemed particularly intent on reiterating her conviction that it was new modes of association that were needed — a new group *process* — rather than neighborhood groups or occupational groups per se. In making this point, she recapitulated portions of earlier arguments, but she prefaced them with something new — a lengthy reference to what she saw as a remarkable "correspondence" between recent biological and psychological research about individuals and integration in groups. Follett's interpretation of this new individual-level research drew heavily on *The Freudian Wish and Its Place in Ethics* (1915). Follett had persuaded the author, the recently retired Harvard psychologist Edwin B. Holt, to read and critique her *Psychological Review* paper.[44] Focusing on Holt's interpretation and "expansion" of Freud, Follett argued that Freudian psychology "shows us that personality is produced through the integrating of 'wishes,' that is, courses of action which the organism sets itself to carry out. The essence of the Freudian psychology is that two courses of action are not mutually exclusive, that one does not 'suppress' the other. It shows plainly that to integrate is not to absorb, melt, fuse, or to reconcile in the so-called Hegelian sense. The creative power of the individual appears not when one 'wish' dominates others, but when all 'wishes' unite in a working whole." The value to Follett of Holt's interpretation of Freud was that she had now amassed two lines of study — one focused on individual personality and the other focused on the group — which suggested that "community, the essential life process, is the activity of integrating."[45]

Having established the significance of "integrating," Follett focused squarely on the conference topic. "What then," she asked, "is the law of community? From biology, from psychology, from our observation of social groups, we see that community is that intermingling which evokes creative power. What is created? Personality, purpose, will, loyalty." Follett, of course, felt strongly that the creative power of groups could be understood and appreciated only by the study of actual groups. The endless debates of the monists and pluralists over whether "the community may be a person" no longer interested her. "There is only one way to find out," Follett told her readers. "My idea of ethics is to lock three people into a room and listen at the keyhole. If that group can evolve a common will, then that group is a 'real' person. Let us stop talking about personality in ethics and sovereignty in political science and begin to study the group."[46]

Conceiving of community as a process, Follett continued, "does away with hierarchy, for it makes us dwell in the qualitative rather than in the quantitative." Taking up the issue of hierarchy explicitly for the first time, Follett anticipated her later ideas about "power-over" and "power-with": "Much of the pluralist objection to the state is because of the words often applied to it by the monists: it is 'superior,' it is 'supreme,' it is 'over and above.' What we need is to discard this quantitative way of thinking and speaking . . . The state, as state, is not 'the supreme object of my allegiance.' The supreme object of my allegiance is never a thing, a 'made.' It is the very Process itself to which I give my loyalty and every activity of my life."[47]

In late December, when the philosophers convened to discuss the published papers, half of the expected presenters (Pound, Laski, and Tufts) were prevented from attending by the flu epidemic. The affair nevertheless seems to have been a success. James Creighton, a proponent of self-realization philosophy at Cornell, reported to Harvard's W. Ernest Hocking that "Miss Follett, Urban, and Cohen did well in the Discussion . . . and the interest was maintained surprisingly well . . . I was much interested in meeting Miss Follett, who is, as I have told her, a perfectly good Hegelian, and also a very charming lady." Helen Huss Parkhurst of Barnard College, who published an account of the meeting in one of the philosophy journals, noted that "this year as in many previous years not the least of the inspiration and pleasure came from impromptu speeches, witty repartee, chance remarks uttered at luncheon or in intermissions, or in the glow of the blazing log fires lighted in Prudence Risley Hall after dinner." At this affair, unlike Follett's experience almost thirty years earlier at the American Historical Association meeting, women were welcomed at the informal gatherings as well as at the formal presentations. Indeed, Parkhurst explicitly praised "the lack of discrimination against women on the ground of sex which characterizes men who are philosophers from men of some other persuasions. Not every learned society treats the presence of women with a cordiality that is untainted by a perfunctory tolerance."[48]

Follett devoted a substantial portion of her conference presentation to rebutting arguments made in the published remarks of the other participants. Replying to Wilbur Urban, who had failed to see how Follett's "inter-individual" community was any less mystical than his monist "over-individual" community, Follett said that her "inter-individual" community was an actual process — the continual creation of interpenetratings and unifyings. "If we can find an activity of the actual and literal interpenetrating of individual wills," Follett told her audience, "then we have a collective will which is wholly concrete . . . the only kind of collective will I can be interested in is one which we can actually evolve."[49]

Follett's reply to Morris Cohen was more extensive, for Cohen had leveled harsher, more fundamental criticisms against *The New State*. "I should be lacking in candor," Cohen had written in his published paper, "if I refrained from saying that [*The New State*] appears to me strikingly deficient in cogent factual evidence or clear, convincing analyses of fundamental ideas." In Cohen's view, Follett was guilty of a "failure to maintain a critical attitude." Her book was "a work of exhortation," written in the "inspired style and absolute confidence of the prophet such as Buddha or Mohammed." Responding to this disparaging characterization, Follett demonstrated remarkable equanimity, but she either refused or was simply unable to acknowledge the excessive passion that others perceived in her rhetoric. Ignoring the charge of excessive emotionalism, Follett interpreted Cohen as claiming that her judgment had been impaired by a failure to critically examine abstract intellectual jargon. "I agree with Mr. Cohen's general principles," Follett told her audience, "but object to their application to me. For I too deplore, as our greatest foe to progress, the lack of the critical attitude. I too deplore the jargon of much of our political science which accepts without analysis time-consecrated phrases and notions, which treats as fundamental ideas the crude, primitive attempts to get at democracy by rule of thumb. The world has long been fumbling for democracy but has not yet grasped its essential and basic idea." What Follett wanted to urge was "the study of community. Almost every problem at present discussed needs for its solution a better understanding of the laws of human association. This we can get only through a study of men interacting, through as careful and penetrating an analysis as the Behaviorists are giving to the individual. Not governmental machinery but modes of association is the fundamental thing today."[50]

Cohen, like most reviewers of *The New State,* had interpreted Follett as calling for neighborhood groups as the basis of political life. Some reviewers looked on this prospect with favor; Cohen did not. "How the principle of neighborhood organization really differs from the present much-berated principle of geographical representation," Cohen wrote, "is not made very clear — except that Miss Follett like other reformers seems to suppose that the limitations of human nature, ignorance, jealousy, *etc.,* will not operate under her dispensation. Perhaps they will not. But how with our present imperfections can we attain her state of perfect cooperation?"[51] This element of Cohen's critique, with its focus on the neighborhood group per se, suggests that he had failed to grasp the essence of Follett's argument. It was not the ascendance of neighborhood groups in political life that Follett was seeking but new modes of association — a new kind of group process.

Cohen had also criticized Follett for her "too facile reconciliation of incompatible alternatives." But Follett, convinced that conceiving of community as a process tended to do away with some of the antagonisms that separated monism and pluralism, concluded her presentation with a powerful restatement of her "third position." "The most fundamental idea we get from studying group action," Follett told her audience, "is that integrating is the true law of association."

> I believe any talk of sacrifice of interests on the employers' part because of altruistic feelings, any talk of sacrifice of sovereignty in a League of Nations, is ruinously sentimental. We must learn the process of evolving a unifying purpose where all interests and purposes appear in that new moment which is the increment of the unifying. As we study group action, the community process, we become monists as we see the One a-making, as we see purpose as the

appearing of the power of unifying, as the One holding Many, as the gathering together into One of every moment, every act, every changing circumstance, the ranging of multiplicity into that which is *at the same time means and end.* But we become pragmatists as we see that the responsibility for this process is ours, that there is no a priori One (Hegel and Royce), and we become pluralists as we find it imperative that we should always begin with the individual and the self-creating units. Not neighborhood organizations or trade unions, necessarily, but wherever we can find the conditions most favorable for freeing the way for a fructifying relating.[52]

A month after the Ithaca conference, in January 1920, Follett received a letter from Viscount Haldane, the English statesman, lawyer, and philosopher, asking if she would allow him to compose an introduction to a new printing of *The New State.* Though pleased, Mary was cautious in her response. "I fear I don't know much about him except what I have read in the papers during the war," Mary remarked in a letter to Harry Overstreet, and then added, "He must, at any rate, think a lot of himself to offer it!"[53]

Haldane, indeed, had a career about which one might boast. It was under his leadership as secretary of state for war (1905–1912) that England had prepared for the European conflict, and he subsequently served for three years as lord chancellor before a internecine party quarrel forced him to resign. Haldane remained popular with the Liberal rank and file despite this dispute, but thereafter he was increasingly estranged from the official Liberal party. After his 1915 resignation, Haldane's long-standing interests in higher education and administration occupied more and more of his time. Early in the century, he had led the effort to establish provincial or "civic" universities and in 1904 had chaired the committee whose work resulted in the creation of the University Grants Committee.[54] After the war, it was adult education that interested Haldane, and it was largely through his leadership that the British Institute of Adult Education was founded in 1921.[55] One writer who has analyzed Haldane's efforts to promote workers' education charged that as late as 1924 "Haldane still nursed the illusion that education of the masses would 'tranquillise' them; once they understood both sides of the tensions between capital and labour they would go back to their mines and railways and factories content." But whatever Haldane's motives, there is no question that he saw "training for citizenship" as the "first need of democracy" — and it was this conviction that sparked Haldane's interest in *The New State.*[56]

Follett did not immediately respond to Haldane's proposal. She was worried about whether including Haldane might be taken as a sign that she had allied herself with a particular school of philosophical and political thought. "I don't know whether it would help the book or not," Follett told Harry Overstreet. "Longmans thinks it problematical . . . I think I am rather against it for the reason that as I am trying to bring different schools together, I would rather it wasn't stamped with any one. For instance much as I care for Prof. Bosanquet's writings, I shouldn't want him to write an introduction. But perhaps Lord Haldane isn't of any particular [philosophical] school." In an effort to sort out Haldane's philosophical pedigree, Follett discussed the matter with two Harvard philosophers, R. F. Alfred Hoernlé and W. Ernest Hocking. This only confused matters. "Mr. Hoernlé strongly advises the Haldane introduction," Follett told Overstreet. "Mr. Hocking . . . advises as strongly against it — says an introduction always makes a book look as if it needed propping." Hoernlé, furthermore, had mentioned "that Haldane was known by every one as a pronounced Hegelian." This piece of information led Mary to decide "at first instantly against it"; but then Hoernlé "ingeniously suggested as a way out of that, that I should write to Lord Haldane telling him how and in what way I wish to unite the two schools (of course I am not capable of attempting any thing of the kind for philosophy, I mean always from the political science point of view), that Lord Haldane would undoubtedly incorporate what I said in the introduction. Yes, the more I think of it, the better I like the idea, for it is of course true, as Prof. Hetherington (philosophy at Cardiff, who was in Boston for a day and came to see me) said naively, 'Why, no one had ever heard of you.'!"[57]

This strategy seems to have worked, resulting in what Follett liked to call a genuine integration of desires. Haldane's ten-page "Introduction," published in the September 1920 edition of *The New State*, focused largely on the theory underlying the book and, just as Mary had wished, emphasized her "third position." Haldane also wrote that although Follett might not agree with all the inferences he had drawn from her book, he was confident, that "the principles relative to the future of the state, set by her before the public in the scientific and systematic fashion which is characteristic of her volume, ought to influence opinion deeply, not only in her country but in my own."[58]

By the time the Haldane introduction appeared, Follett was already deeply involved in another project — one that she had hinted at in her letter to Overstreet about Haldane. "I have been asked recently to do some articles for this and that, and one attracted me," Follett wrote, "but I have decided to give everything up for the group studies, all but one thing which I shall speak to you about when I see you."[59] The "one thing" to which Follett was almost certainly referring was her impending participation on the wage boards of the Massachusetts Minimum Wage Commission.

The Massachusetts minimum wage bill, the first in the country, had become law in 1912 through the initiative and hard work of Florence Kelley (then general secretary of the National Consumers League), the Boston Women's Trade Union League, and two Boston women, Elizabeth Glendower Evans and Mary Dewson. The decision to press for a minimum wage aroused strong opposition, including charges of inappropriate government interference in the workplace; but the labor unrest of 1912, most notably the three-month Lawrence textile workers' strike, finally moved the Massachusetts legislature to act. The law established a permanent three-member commission (one of whom, according to the legislation, "may be a woman") with authority to investigate wages on an industry-by-industry basis and to recommend appropriate pay levels. Only women and children under eighteen were covered under the new law's provisions; hostility to the idea of including men was just too great. The law had one other significant limitation: the new commission's recommendations would not be legally binding; enforcement would depend on "an educated public's willingness to force employers to follow the suggested wage guidelines."[60]

Six years after its enactment, the law was amended, abolishing the independent Minimum Wage Commission and transferring its functions to the Department of Labor and Industries, where the work was assigned to the three male associate commissioners. The commissioners did their work through a series of appointed "wage boards," each of which included representatives of employers, employees, and the public. The Massachusetts law, James T. Patterson writes, largely "followed procedures then practiced in Europe," but there was one important deviation: the method of determining the recommended wage. In Massachusetts, "wages were to be set according to the 'necessary cost of living,' not according to some acceptable compromise promulgated by a 'socialistic' government arbitration board after intervening in a labor dispute. 'Necessary costs' — to be determined by careful statistical studies of living costs — were to be adequate for the 'health and morals' of the workers."[61]

This procedure for determining the minimum wage — based more on careful investigation of the facts than on political compromise — intrigued Follett. It reminded her of something she had seen with increasing frequency in the opinions of progressive jurists: cases were being decided, not in favor of one party at the expense of the other, but with appropriate regard for the complex, reciprocal relations of all parties concerned. "Our progressive judges," Follett had written in her 1919 *Philosophical Review* article, "seek always the law of the situation, which means in the language of this paper the discovery and formulation of modes of unifying." Apparently sensing that the new minimum wage boards were likewise seeking the "law of the situation," Follett sought to join these boards in order to observe and study their methods. She acknowledged as much in remarks made at a public hearing on the recommendations of her first wage board. The board, she said, had come to a "unanimous conclusion and I am interested in the process which brought it to that conclusion . . . The employers stated over and over again that they thought the girls had to be well nourished, had to have vacations, had to have something in the way of recreation in order to do the very best work. Both sides recognized that that figure could be found . . . On Boards that I used to be on there seemed to be a good deal of moral talk. We must be fair, we must be considerate, we must be courteous, we must make the big sacrifices in this life, we must be Christian. On this Board it seemed to be a recognized fact, for us to consider that it was more a matter of intelligence than morals, if we could be intelligent about it, to find that figure between $10, $11 [what was usually paid] and $13.50, which would be of equal interest to both sides."[62]

Follett was appointed to her first wage board in the fall of 1920. Wage board members were compensated for their service at the same rate as jurors, four dollars per day in 1920, and were reimbursed for traveling and clerical expenses. Although it is not known with certainty how Follett came to be nominated and selected, she was well acquainted with leaders of the minimum wage movement: Elizabeth Glendower Evans, a close friend of the Brandeis family, had been a neighbor on Otis Place, and Louis Brandeis was writing briefs for minimum wage cases nationwide.[63]

The fifteen-member board to which Follett was appointed as one of three public representatives was convened to consider the wages of women employed in the "manufacture of minor lines of confectionery and food preparation."[64] After meeting weekly for more than a month, the members of the Confectionery Board found themselves in significant disagreement about the employees' cost of living. These early disagreements at first seemed insurmountable, and the board considered an "indefinite adjournment," but Follett advised against it "as failing to meet the responsibilities of the Board."[65] After much deliberation, the board agreed to a two-month adjournment in the hope that the business situation and the fluctuating prices "might be more stable when the work was resumed."[66]

When the board reconvened in February 1921, Follett and two others were named to a subcommittee to study a change in the three principal items of the cost-of-living budget by which the minimum wage was determined.[67] This proved to be a most instructive experience. Follett saw firsthand the folly of thinking that important public policy questions would automatically be resolved merely by uncovering "the facts." Writing in *Creative Experience*, she said that "those who wish conclusions to be drawn always from precise measurements forget that many of our problems defy the possibility of precise measurement. For instance, what is the minimum a girl can live on 'in health and decency?' — the phrase used in the Massachusetts Minimum Wage Law."[68]

Follett also learned a good deal about how to facilitate the confronting and integrating of difference. The Confectionery Board, Follett observed, made more progress in its deliberations when it investigated the cost-of-living elements one by one rather than trying to make a summary determination about the matter. This process — what she called "breaking up wholes" — would later be incorporated into her formal suggestions about how to foster the integrative resolution of conflicts: "One way of breaking up wholes in conference is to split the question up as minutely as possible and take the vote as you go along. I have seen this done with marked success . . . Instead of voting on the amount of wages, in which case the line-up would of course have been according to sides, we voted on the amount needed for board, lodging, clothes, recreation, self-improvement, savings, etc. On many of these questions the vote showed employers and employees on both sides."[69]

Yet another instructive aspect of Follett's Confectionery Board experiences concerned the advantages of "cooperative" fact-finding; elements of this idea would find a place in her writings about leadership and coordination as well as in her proposals for integrative conflict resolution. "From my experience on Minimum Wage Boards," Follett wrote in *Creative Experience,* "I see that there is possible a cooperative gathering of facts which is more useful to the resolution of conflict than for each side to get them separately and then try to integrate them, for when each side gets them separately there is a tendency for each to stick rigidly to its own particular facts."[70] This cooperative fact-finding technique had been used successfully by the Confectionery Board in determining employees' cost of living.

Once the Confectionery Board had agreed on the cost-of-living budget, it turned its attention to the financial condition of the industry. Some board members argued that "the minimum wage would have to be below the established cost of living budget if the industry was to continue to make a profit." Follett initially argued against this idea, saying that "she felt that little definite evidence had been presented on this subject."[71] In the months that followed, however, additional investigation apparently yielded evidence that Follett found convincing. She described this sequence of events in *Creative Experience:* "On a Wage Board, one year, we were up against an interesting objective situation: a drop in prices, indications of unemployment, and at the same time a demand for higher wages in that particular industry. In anticipation of the proposed heightened wage scale which our Board was to effect, some employers were turning off their less efficient workers. We had to ask each week the changes in that respect in the objective situation; those changes had been brought about by the trend of our deliberations, but also our deliberations were very much affected by these changes. We saw that it would be a disadvantage to the employees as well as to employers to have the minimum wage too high, since we had evidence in the actual situation, not mere threats, that that would mean a certain amount of unemployment." Follett would later use this experience as an illustration of "circular response" — a process in which the various factors in a situation not only are constantly evolving but also are continually influencing each other.[72]

In June 1921, after sixteen meetings, the Confectionery Board submitted a unanimous recommendation. The board found the "cost of living" for a self-supporting woman in the occupation to be $13.50 a week, but because of the financial condition of the industry it recommended a minimum rate below the cost of living. It was Follett, finally convinced of the perilous condition of the industry, who moved that the minimum be reduced from $12.50 to $12.00; at the same time, however, she moved that the age limit at which this minimum was to be received be reduced from eighteen to sixteen.[73] The Confectionery Board unanimously adopted Follett's motion, the minimum wage commissioners accepted the recommendation, and a decree was entered effective November 1. The terms apparently were widely accepted — at least by employers; by the end of the year, only two of the twenty-one firms inspected were out of compliance with the decree.[74]

Follett considered the Massachusetts Minimum Wage Law "far from perfect," but she thought it a matter of the utmost importance that the law "has recognized the principle that a conference should not merely record existing differences of opinion, nor should it be a fight, with the vote registering the outcome of the struggle, but a sincere attempt to find agreement." As it turned out, careful adherence to this principle was a major factor in enabling the members of Follett's second wage board to reach a recommendation.

Established in December 1921, the Brush Wage Board was one of five reconvened by the Minimum Wage Commission to revise existing rates.[75] Almost immediately, Follett later wrote, it became apparent that "to a number of the Board cost of living and the condition of the industry were by no means the main facts of the situation, but the relative strength at that moment of labor and capital. When those members brought in a demand for a Minimum wage of $21.40, these figures did not represent the cost of living in Boston in 1922, they represented an estimate of labor strength in Boston in 1922."[76] Further evidence quickly appeared that an adversarial confrontation was in the works.

The single male member among the six employee representatives—a labor leader from a strong union—"long before the questions involved had been threshed out, suddenly proposed that the vote be taken on the Minimum wage for that industry." It was at this point that the principles underlying the wage law assumed their full significance and at least temporarily saved the day. Follett described the moment in *Creative Experience*: "Before the chairman could say anything . . . the Secretary of the Board of Labor and Industry, who sits with all Minimum Wage Boards, announced that the Board of Labor and Industry did not convene Minimum Wage Boards in order that they should take a vote, in order, that is, that they should register the preexisting opinions of employers and employees; they were called together to see if by discussion based on a review of all the facts involved they could come to some agreement . . . It was thus expressly pointed out by an official of the state that this group of employees, employers, and public had been called together and given the job of trying to create unity."[77]

This statement of principle, however helpful, did not resolve all the Brush Board's problems. The dynamics of group representation—a subject about which Follett had thought deeply in the context of political representation— proved to be the source of the board's most intractable problems. The employee representatives tended to be among the most highly paid in the industry and, as such, "are often willing to concede too much, are less urgent than the girls actually suffering from the lowest wages. On the other hand the labor leader is far more urgent than any minimum wage girl would be. Neither represents those she is supposed to represent." Follett came away from her wage board experiences convinced that each form of representation—shop or union—had its own incentives and tendencies; but she did not declare a preference, believing that "much more study is needed before anyone is competent to do that."[78]

As it turned out, the Brush Board was not a success; it neither fully confronted nor integrated its differences. In January 1922, after only six meetings, the board submitted a report signed by twelve of the fifteen members (among them Follett and the other two public representatives), recommending a minimum of $14.40 for experienced employees for a week of forty-eight hours, less for learners and apprentices. The commissioners apparently found the wage rate too high and returned the recommendation for reconsideration, but the wage board voted to resubmit its original findings. The impasse was broken only after the commissioners voted to establish a new board; this group, within a few months, submitted a lower rate of $13.92 a week.[79]

The richness of Follett's experiences as a member of the Massachusetts minimum wage boards whetted her appetite for further group studies. Now more than ever, Follett was convinced that the future of American social, political, and economic life depended on the working out of a new kind of group process. Determined to make a contribution to finding these new modes of association, she once again took the initiative and embarked on a two-year collaboration with a young social scientist, Eduard C. Lindeman.

18

"Too Good a Joke for the World"

The Follett-Lindeman collaboration, which resulted in the 1924 publication of Follett's *Creative Experience* and Lindeman's *Social Discovery,* was as stormy as it was productive. About a year into the project, Follett appealed to her frustrated colleague not to "speak again of 'throwing up your job,' for it would be too good a joke for the world, while we are teaching everyone how to resolve conflict that we cannot resolve the differences between ourselves. Let us face them and integrate them."[1]

Mary Follett was familiar with Eduard Lindeman by reputation if not personal contact as early as 1920 because both had worked in the National Community Centers Association; in the early months of 1920, Lindeman participated prominently in the debate over the future of the NCCA and was elected the following year to a place on the Executive Committee.[2] Although this thirty-five-year-old husband and father of four small daughters was by 1920 a professor of sociology, he had never received a doctorate. The tenth child of a poor immigrant family in eastern Michigan, Lindeman had endured years of hard manual labor and had had little opportunity for education. He nevertheless entered the Michigan Agricultural College under a special program and in 1911 received his baccalaureate degree at age twenty-six.[3] During the period following his graduation, Lindeman spent two years organizing young people's clubs for the local Congregational church, four years with the

Agricultural College's Division of Extension founding a statewide program for young people (now the "4H Clubs"), and one year teaching courses at the Young Men's Christian Association College of Chicago.[4]

Lindeman's departure from the Extension Division and YMCA jobs was on less than friendly terms. The impact of the Extension Service upon rural people, Lindeman later wrote, " 'is overwhelmingly materialistic, prosaic, dull and uninspiring.' The Extension instructors 'are uniformly persons who have been trained to view life through the lens of some technical specialty . . . They look at the farmer in relation to hogs or alfalfa, but they almost never see hogs and alfalfa in relation to the total personality of the farmer.' "[5] His experience at the YMCA College was hardly better, frustrated as he was by the conservatism of his administrative superiors.[6] Lindeman's willingness to fight for change was even more evident in his next position, as a member of the Sociology Department of the North Carolina College for Women in Greensboro. By 1921 Lindeman had become the object of newspaper attacks orchestrated by the Ku Klux Klan because his family treated "their black cook as a member of the family."[7] It was during this period that Mary Follett, apparently intrigued by Lindeman's recently published account of the nature of community organizing, *The Community* (1921), paid him a visit in North Carolina.[8]

There was much in this young professor's book that Follett would have found appealing. Lindeman, like Follett, believed that the "essential problem of Democracy is not yet solved," and he was persuaded by his experience that "its only hope of solution lies in practical demonstrations carried out in small communities."[9] In his discussion of conflict in *The Community,* and specifically in his notion of the "integration of solutions" in resolving conflicts, Lindeman drew explicitly on Follett's *New State.*[10] Lindeman also shared Follett's sense of urgency about the study of groups and group process; as he saw it, the individual could be brought into the community process only through groups — "through the expression of his most vital interests." Given the ever-growing numbers of societal groups, Lindeman thought it imperative to learn how best to coordinate their interests.[11]

It was during Follett's visit to North Carolina in the spring of 1922 that the idea for a research partnership was born. Follett's intellect and quick wit no doubt captivated this young, untested scholar, and Lindeman's appreciation of the potential inherent in groups as well as his "magnetic" personality apparently had its effect on Follett. "There was an air of enticement surrounding Lindeman which invited personal approach," writes David Stewart, one of Lindeman's biographers. A lean six-footer with deep blue eyes and a fair Nordic complexion, Lindeman had a "strong and vibrant bass voice" and a lively, unceremonious demeanor; he "liked food and drink, socializing informally, jokes and laughter, baseball and tennis." At the same time, however, when the conversation turned to the pressing issues of the day, he was deadly earnest.[12]

Returning from North Carolina, Mary Follett took it upon herself to find Lindeman sufficient financial support to enable him to leave his teaching post and come north.[13] "Realizing how impossible Lindeman's position in Greensboro had become," writes Gisela Konopka, another of Lindeman's biographers, "Mary Follett introduced him to Herbert Croly and Dorothy Whitney Straight."[14] Straight was a young New York heiress whose financial support had made it possible for Croly to found the *New Republic* magazine; and in 1918, a few months before her husband died in the worldwide influenza epidemic, she agreed to provide much of the funding for another of Croly's ventures, the New School for Social Research.[15] Follett, too, was a great admirer of Herbert Croly and was much taken with the "possibilities of the development of democracy and of the meaning of citizenship" expressed in his *Progressive Democracy* (1914) and *The Promise of American Life* (1909).[16]

The years immediately following the war had been "catastrophic" for Croly. Having committed the *New Republic* to the support of President Wilson and believing that the war might offer "a chance to focus the thought & will of the country on high and fruitful purposes," Croly and his colleagues felt personally betrayed by the postwar, government-sanctioned attacks on civil liberties and Wilson's abandonment of principle at Versailles. "After much searching of heart and prolonged discussion," Croly decided to oppose the treaty, a position that both threatened the magazine's financial future and created bitter animosities with longtime friends. Exhausted and demoralized, Croly's spirits were raised only by the proposed establishment of a school dedicated to the systematic investigation of societal problems, and he "plunged enthusiastically into [planning] discussions" with John Dewey and a group of exiles from the Columbia faculty.[17]

Croly actively enlisted the financial support of Dorothy Straight and other philanthropists, and in February 1919 the New School for Social Research opened for classes in six renovated Victorian mansions a few blocks from the offices of the *New Republic*. At first the experiment, with its small cadre of founding faculty and a steady stream of distinguished visiting lecturers, seemed a success. But by April 1922 "the original excitement had begun to dissipate. The school's chronic indebtedness, the difficulty of operating an egalitarian educational institution, and the growing recognition that teaching the popular lecture courses must be given higher priority [than research] all contributed to growing dissatisfaction." When the Board of Trustees decided to deemphasize research in favor of the adult lecture program, Croly left the New School.[18]

Shortly thereafter, in May 1922, Mary Follett broached with Croly the idea of a collaborative study of the constructive nature of conflict.[19] Precisely how Follett arranged the meeting is not known, but Follett's friends, the Cabots and Brandeises, were personally acquainted with both Croly and Straight. Follett, furthermore, had met Straight in August 1921 when Straight had the Brandeises, Follett, and Elizabeth Glendower Evans to lunch at Woods Hole on Cape Cod. Straight was sufficiently impressed with Follett to mention the meeting in a letter to Leonard Elmhirst, the Englishman she would eventually marry: "Our friends, the Brandeis's, have been several times — and yesterday they came to lunch bringing with them a lady called Miss Folette [sic], whose book "The New State" you may know. . . Some time, if you ever come across her book, do read it — for it is, I believe, the first serious political study made by a woman."[20]

Dorothy Whitney Straight was a most unusual woman. Despite her privileged social class, she supported a number of radical causes, including the Women's Trade Union League and the National Social Unit Organization, and worked actively on behalf of women's suffrage. During the war she helped to unite the New York City women's organizations for war work; after the war, she advocated on behalf of disarmament.[21] As the founding president of the Association of Junior Leagues of America, she pressed other women of her social class into investigating the industrial and living conditions of the poor and taking corrective action.[22]

This thirty-four-year-old widow and mother of three young children not only was a serious-minded social reformer; she also was drawn to difficult intellectual questions. Straight regularly took college-level courses in subjects such as philosophy, economics, and Greek literature, and in 1921, a month after meeting Mary Follett, she enrolled in two Columbia University psychology courses, one of them with John Dewey.[23] Straight's studies in psychology surely enhanced her appreciation of Follett's approach to studying conflict, and her personal experience impressed on her the urgency of ascertaining the *constructive* nature of conflict. "The cruel intolerance of this post-war period," Straight would later write, "challenged me to withstand the terrifying wave of fear and prejudice that seemed about to crush all the liberal movements in which I believed. And thus, I became a target for attack by the entrenched interests of the right wing. Not being by nature a fighter I found this struggle to maintain my integrity extremely hard and exhausting."[24]

Given their respective passionate commitments to finding solutions to the problems of American society, neither Straight nor Croly needed much convincing when approached by Follett with the idea of investigating social conflict. Croly, in particular, having seen how the New School faculty had been distracted from their scholarly endeavors by teaching responsibilities, surely found much in Follett's suggestion that was intriguing. Perhaps the kind of social research he envisioned could be done by "independent" scholars — and for a fraction of what it would cost at the New School. Within weeks, Dorothy Straight agreed "to finance Lindeman so that he could do free-lance writing and private research from 1922 to 1924."[25] Follett did not originally seek funding for herself, but by the first week in October it was agreed that she, too, would be funded, receiving $4,000 for the year to cover salary and expenses.[26]

In September 1922 Follett invited Lindeman and Albert Dwight Sheffield to spend a week in Putney planning a program of research.[27] Sheffield, the husband of Ada Eliot Sheffield, Follett's colleague in the Radcliffe Union's applied sociology venture, was a Wellesley College professor of rhetoric and composition with particular interests in language, methods of analysis, and group discussion. For more than ten years Sheffield had taught classes for trade unionists in the practice of "directed discussion" and in 1919 helped to found Boston's Trade Union College; two years later, the Workers' Educational Bureau of the American Federation of Labor published Sheffield's first book on the subject, *Joining in Group Discussion*. Sheffield acknowledged that Follett's *New State* had had a profound effect on his thinking. Groups, Sheffield argued, should seek neither a "majority" idea nor a "compromise" but a " 'consensus' on the matter discussed — that is, a conception to which each has contributed and on which all are disposed to act." For Sheffield, discussion was the "technique of democracy."[28]

Believing that Sheffield's expertise and experience would enhance the quality of their proposed study of the constructive nature of conflict, Follett included him in the planning discussions and hoped that Dorothy Straight could eventually be persuaded to provide him some financial support. "He *is* a good one," Follett remarked in a December letter to Lindeman, "& the way our 3 minds are working together is extraordinary."[29] Neither Follett's nor Sheffield's impressions of the September meeting have survived, but Lindeman wrote excitedly to a friend: "My visits in Vermont with Miss Follett have been most successful . . . There are advantages such as mountains, good food, woods, streams, and much good talk. We worked every morning from 8 a.m. until 1 p.m. What a marvelous mind she has!" As the years passed, Lindeman came to consider the Putney discussions "the most exciting intellectual event of my total experience." Reviewing his notes of this "three-cornered dialogue," Lindeman found "that we three had set for ourselves a most ambitious program including such questions as: What is the nature of social conflict? What is the relation between the situation and the evolving situation? How do purposes evolve? What is the relation between compromise and integration? To what extent does the emotional content of words impede human relationships? How do short-term and long-term interests come into conflict? What is the nature of representativeness? What distinctions need to be made between the leader and the expert? What relation does responsibility bear to the consenting procedure?"[30]

Throughout the autumn months, largely through correspondence, Follett and Lindeman exchanged ideas about a proposed "Manifesto" in which they would make public their reasons for studying social conflict and the nature of their approach.[31] The first outlines of the Follett-Lindeman collaboration called for an early January announcement to the public of the creation of a "Committee for the Study of The Constructive Nature of Conflict," to be located at 421 West 21st Street in New York, the editorial offices of the *New Republic* magazine.[32] There apparently was some question about who was best able to write the "Manifesto." Follett thought it should be a group product rather than hers alone and can be seen trying to bolster Lindeman's self-confidence: "Did I take the time," she said in a typical letter, "to tell you how *perfectly splendid* I think your stuff. Don't talk about my writing [the 'Manifesto'] after that capital piece of work."[33]

The first significant difficulties in the collaboration arose in late December 1922 as Follett struggled to get Lindeman to respond to her inquiries about how best to persuade Dorothy Straight to fund Sheffield's participation.[34] Perplexed, Follett opened her third letter with an unmistakably acerbic edge: "I think if we are working together, you ought to be willing to answer a letter. Several weeks ago I wrote you asking you a perfectly definite question: whether you were going to take up the matter of Mr. Sheffield with Mrs. S. or whether I should. I received no reply! I therefore wrote again, a very urgent letter not pressing anything myself, saying I was perfectly ready to follow your wishes in the matter, but that I wanted to know what those were. Again no reply! (for the telegram said nothing) . . . Now remember, if you are finding it difficult to arrange anything with Mrs. Straight, do not press her because of this letter, because people do not like to be pressed, & that is *not* the object of this letter . . . I want you to use your judgment, but I do what to know what your judgment is, & I think I have the right to ask that, have I not?" The next day Follett sent another letter in the same vein, but this time she expressed a new frustration: "I am putting it all before you so that you will know what is in my mind. As I say, you may be arranging it all today. Or you may be in the

South! You see I do not even know your whereabouts, & I think people working together shd. have each other's addresses."[35]

Problems were bound to arise in a partnership that placed one principal in New York with the project's intellectual and financial patrons while the other remained in Boston. In the four months since the inception of their work, Follett's only contact with either Croly or Straight was a single meeting with the latter in New York.[36] Lindeman, by contrast, saw Croly on a regular basis and had periodic access to Straight. Follett quite reasonably might have worried that there were discussions taking place in New York to which she was not privy and that they would come to shape the direction of the project. Other fears, too, almost certainly were at work, for Lindeman's "disappearance" played directly into Follett's own — and most fundamental — insecurities. The child of an alcoholic father, she had painful memories of unexplained disappearances and other sorts of unpredictable, unreliable behavior; and she tended, as a result, to become more than a little anxious when the erratic behavior of a colleague or friend suggested that events were careening out of her control.[37]

Lindeman's wife and children might well have grown accustomed to his absences. Eduard had spent considerable time "in the field" in order to meet the demands of his first jobs in Michigan and Chicago, and by the time he and Follett were working together in the early 1920s, his obligations required frequent separations from his family for weeks or months at a time. Indeed, for seven years beginning in 1928, Lindeman would live almost a "dual life," sharing an apartment with Roger Baldwin, the founder of the American Civil Liberties Union, and enjoying a "frequently changing throng of friends" in Greenwich Village. Baldwin would later describe Lindeman as having had relationships with many women (and "no intimacy" with his wife), and Lindeman's daughter reports that her father had "had a serious affair with a 'Mrs. C.'"[38]

Little is known about the impact of Lindeman's peripatetic behavior on his family, but Mary Follett was not the only professional colleague who was dismayed by Lindeman's unpredictability and frequent inaccessibility. His biographer recounts a 1926 altercation between Lindeman and John Hader, the young colleague with whom Lindeman would write *Dynamic Social Research* (1931). Hader told Lindeman's biographer that he all too often had time on his hands because Lindeman, then his boss, was rarely in the office: " 'I wouldn't see him for days, sometimes for weeks. I had trouble keeping the ship going — for direction.' All Hader knew was that Lindeman was often traveling outside New York. When he returned, not much was said about where he had been.

Eduard C. Lindeman, ca. 1929. Photo by John Hader, from the David Stewart Papers, Syracuse University Library, Department of Special Collections; permission of Elizabeth Lindeman Leonard.

'We didn't ask too many questions,' remembers Hader. It didn't seem as if such questions would be encouraged." Hader, frustrated and desperate for advice, went to see Herbert Croly. What Hader had to say about his boss reportedly "came as no surprise to Croly," who by then was well aware of his friend's "frailties." Croly apparently decided that the best course of action was to pass the complaint on to Lindeman — precipitating a discussion between Lindeman and Hader "that was very uncomfortable for them both," and thereafter "the matter was dropped."[39]

When Mary Follett, three years before the Hader incident, was confronted with one of Lindeman's "disappearances," she tried to work out the situation directly with Eduard, sending letter after letter to her recalcitrant colleague describing the difficulties engendered by his erratic behavior. When her increasingly insistent letters finally elicited a reply, Lindeman not surprisingly was quite defensive. His reply has not survived, but subsequent correspondence suggests that the retort had been punctuated with a series of accusations: Mary was impatient; she was suspicious; and she obviously lacked confidence in him. Lindeman, Follett soon discovered, was extraordinarily sensitive to criticism — at least when it involved his personal behavior. Many of Lindeman's friends and colleagues were troubled by this aspect of his character. It took Dorothy Straight five years before she felt able to broach the subject with him: "You see, I still don't understand, Edward, why you are so frightfully sensitive to criticism, — why it seems to knock you all to pieces. I have been conscious of that fact for years but I see it now more vividly — I don't know what the answer is, but I'm sure you could enormously increase your power and stability if you could discover the source of those particular fears."[40]

Confronted with Lindeman's defensive hostility, Follett responded much as she had earlier in her career in altercations with Mary Hutcheson Page and Roscoe Pound: she plunged in and tried to repair the damage. "What could that wretched letter of mine have contained!" Follett wrote remorsefully. "I cannot tell you how sorry I am that my letter disturbed you. I never imagined such a thing. I thought the basis of understanding between you and me was already established in the inner harmonies of the universe which you and I both have some faith in. But I did not know how to get you to send me that mere — yes or no — postcard which was all I was asking, and yet I did not know how to proceed without it for I thought I might make an awful muddle by going on without your approval . . . You will understand, won't you, or at any rate reserve judgment until I see you."[41]

This combined explanation and apology might have placated Lindeman and provided the opportunity for a reconciliation; but the underlying difficulties deepened a few days later when Follett received in the mail a copy of a paper that Lindeman had chosen to share in advance with Croly and Straight. Struggling to maintain her composure, Follett fired off this response: "Do you not think the time has come for us to plan more definitely for team work, since that was the basis on which we began this undertaking? About your Paper: it was definitely and explicitly arranged between us that nothing should be circulated concerning this enterprise which you and I did not both endorse. I do not endorse this Paper. I feel so strongly about it that I do not think it enough for you to ask Mr. Croly and Mrs. Straight not to read it. I think it ought to be taken away from them to prevent the possibility of anyone reading it. You can easily make the excuse of wishing to revise it." Though indignant, Mary was able to see the irony of their situation, for this was the moment when she remarked to Lindeman that "it would be too good a joke for the world, while we are teaching everyone how to resolve conflict that we cannot resolve the differences between ourselves."[42]

Since Lindeman was in the midst of another of his cross-country trips and probably would not receive her letter for some time, Follett decided to arrange a personal meeting in New York with Croly and Straight. There, "to my astonishment," she told Lindeman in her next letter, "[I] found there had been some misunderstanding, which shd. be put right immediately." This misunderstanding most likely centered on who was to write the "Manifesto."[43] In a letter to a friend written about this time, Lindeman said that "there has been some question about whether Miss Follett or Mr. Croly were to do the writing," acerbically adding: "It now seems we will have to get on without Miss Follett for she seems thoroughly incapable of working with a group and she gets nothing done. I'm going up to Boston on Monday to make a last effort to get something out of her."[44]

Lindeman's unjust characterization of Follett, whose distinguished social and civic career provides ample evidence of her skillfulness in working with others, was almost certainly born of his own guilt. His outburst occurred just about the time he learned that Croly and Straight had decided not to fund Sheffield's participation in the project. Lindeman no doubt experienced the Croly-Straight veto as a personal failure, for it was he in the preceding weeks who had demanded that Follett be patient in the Sheffield matter and show greater confidence in his judgment. Given the discretion he had demanded, the failure in the matter now was undeniably his. Feeling guilty, but still incensed over what he perceived to be excessive earlier criticisms, Lindeman privately lashed out at Follett, writing disparaging remarks to a friend about her productivity as well as her ability to work in groups. With Follett directly, however, Lindeman was considerably less contentious, even admitting to feeling "chagrinned" about the Sheffield matter. "Don't you do anything of the kind," Follett generously responded. "[Sheffield] must have known that it all depended on H. C. & Mrs. S. You have nothing to reproach yourself with."[45]

In late January Follett and Lindeman finally met to resolve their differences and decided to proceed with the project. Follett was to write a book explaining the psychological and interdisciplinary underpinnings of their approach to the study of conflict, and Lindeman would follow with an explication of what they had learned about new methods for investigating conflict.[46] Follett's willingness to let go of the animosities engendered by past disputes, a quality of character already evident in her relationships with Roscoe Pound and Mary Hutcheson Page, is again noticeable in the thoroughly professional and congenial tone of her letters to Lindeman following the January reconciliation.[47] "I am immensely pleased with your material," Follett wrote after seeing Lindeman's notes on the functioning of southern agricultural cooperatives.

> I think what you have avoided almost as striking as what you have done: it would have been so easy to emphasize the picturesque or dramatic moments, or to take up the more obvious problems, but, in your effort to follow the plan we laid down, you have not balked at any of the difficulties. I think your persistence in this unusual — people so often take the line of least resistance.
>
> Your material is very rich. What I am doing is to go over it carefully, interpreting it from our point of view, making notes all the time for you . . . When I send your material I shall send you my seventy pages or so on conflict, for I feel sure that you will find in that food for thought, and suggestions for your observation. For the whole seventy pages consist of questions and problems — they are the things I *don't* know about conflict![48]

Although Follett's letters in the spring of 1923 were full of praise for Lindeman's accomplishments, they also contained suggestions about how the work might be improved. "Now I want to speak to you about your paper on 'Technique,'" Mary wrote Eduard in April. "I do not care much for it. But your actual technique is so much better than your on-paper technique. What you are *doing* is very unusual, *is* an addition to technique, but you have not done yourself justice in the paper . . . I think I can show you how you can make the paper on 'Technique' valuable — by putting in what you are *doing* instead of what you are *thinking:* the former has gone ahead of the latter."[49] Lindeman's thoroughly professional response to these remarks suggests that he found it much easier to accept criticism of his ideas than of his working style. "These are only partial attempts at answers to some of your queries," he wrote after thoughtfully considering each of Follett's questions and comments. "Your questions have thrown light on the very problems with which I have been wrestling. It is really quite startling the way the nodes of our parallel lines come together — but also most promising."[50] Follett, too, was encouraged: "I feel now that we are going to have something that may repay Mr. Croly and Mrs. Straight . . . Their initial faith in the project . . . was so splendid that I should feel very sorry if any difficulties or slowness in getting under way should have given them misgivings, for I think now that we are going to be able to justify their faith in us."[51]

Just when everything seemed to be going so well, a new problem arose. On April 22, 1923, Follett wrote to say that the conference she had been planning with Lindeman for Vermont would have to be postponed because her mother was gravely ill.[52] Although Follett's mind was "in a whirl with a hundred details & the great anxiety," she characteristically sought both to fulfill her filial obligations and to continue her work on the manuscript. The combination, not surprisingly, proved injurious to her own health. "I am pretty exhausted at present," Follett confided to Lindeman, "because I have been trying to get up at 5 & have all my work done by 2 & spend the afternoons & evenings with her."[53] Two weeks later, little had changed, and now it seemed that Follett and Briggs would have to forgo their trip to Vermont. "I don't mind for myself," Follett told Lindeman, "as I am working too hard to notice where I am, but Miss Briggs is terribly disappointed, & I know she *needed* to get out of the city this year more than she ever has before, but it looks as if I should have to sacrifice her . . . I want to keep on, on the book, now without interruption, so that I can have it ready for Mr. Croly when he gets back [from Europe]."[54]

Within another month, however, it was Follett herself who was sick. This time there was blood in her urine.[55] Hospitalized, Follett was examined by two of Boston's most prominent physicians: Dr. Elliott Joslin, chief physician at New England Deaconess Hospital and a Harvard Medical School professor renowned for his work on diabetes; and Daniel Fiske Jones, staff surgeon at the Massachusetts General Hospital.[56] These two doctors were aware, just as Richard Cabot had been in 1910, of the presence of some sort of "tumor" in the lower portion of Follett's right kidney, but they had difficulty ascertaining its nature. If Drs. Joslin and Jones "had made any definite statement to me of an organ diseased & wished to remove it," Mary later wrote to Cabot, "I should have consented, but until Dr. Joslin's letter came to Miss Briggs, I did not know that they had any idea what was the matter with me. They spoke as if it might be any one of a number of things, that they could not tell until they looked inside me. They gave me the impression that I was in for, not one operation, but perhaps several, & very likely then with no good results. If they had been frank with me I should undoubtedly have gone on with their treatments, but they surrounded me with an air of mystery, very different from the openness 7 years ago of Dr. Graves who trusted me with what he knew as fast as he found out, even although he had to tell me one day that the chances were against my living."[57]

The alternative diagnoses being considered most likely were three: a urinary tract infection in conjunction with an unusually shaped but otherwise healthy kidney; congenitally cystic kidneys in which one (or both) of the kidneys is enlarged and its normal substance is replaced by cysts and fibrous tissue; or a malignancy — either in the right kidney or an adjacent organ. In the 1920s it was extremely difficult to make a correct differential diagnosis without surgery; and even with surgery, the outcome was uncertain. If surgery revealed polycystic kidneys, no treatment was possible; if it uncovered a malignant kidney tumor, surrounding tissues often were so involved that removal of the kidney either would be deemed impossible or would produce little improvement in Follett's prognosis.[58]

Uncertain about their diagnosis, the doctors apparently were not completely frank with their patient, and it was their paternalistic attitude that finally drove Follett to seek an alternative form of treatment. "I am not criticising Dr. Joslin," Follett continued in her letter to Cabot; "his large experience probably tells him that his way is the best in the majority of cases, but the result for me was that, thrown back on myself by all the mystery (Dr. Dan Jones said, 'I can't tell you what I think because you are Dr. Joslin's patient & he must be the one to tell you' — you see how mysterious, I might almost say sinister, it all sounded) — that I thought I would try to clear up the whole condition by a different process. So by the time Dr. Joslin made up his mind to speak, I had made my decision."[59] That decision was revealed in a late July letter from Isobel Briggs to the Sheffields: "After much agonizing discussion at the hospital, for the doctors and surgeons found the case grave and puzzling, we decided to try a different treatment." Follett was "put . . . to bed in a stateroom on the train," and the two of them headed for Kansas City and the headquarters of the Unity School of Christianity.[60]

Mind cure as a method of healing had fascinated Mary Follett ever since her youth, and in 1910 she reportedly told Richard Cabot that she "had been for years a New Thought person."[61] Given her long-standing interest in mental and spiritual healing, it is not surprising that Follett turned at this moment of crisis to the principles and practices of New Thought. "She is in the care of a healer who has made many remarkable cures of cases fully as grave and of the same nature as hers," Briggs told the Sheffields, "and who in personality, mentality and spirituality is able to cope with a person of Miss Follett's trend of mind and power of thought. We are in good quarters [at a nearby hotel], she has a pleasant garden to sit in, and is able to be up most of the time. She and I both feel sure that she will get well."[62]

The Unity School of Practical Christianity, founded in Kansas City in 1889 by Charles and Myrtle Fillmore, had become after more than thirty years the "largest of the movements collectively known as New Thought."[63] By 1923 Unity School had grown so large that three downtown buildings were required to house its spiritual healing activities and its administrative and publications offices.[64] The fundamental principle underlying the Unity movement, writes James D. Freeman in *The Story of Unity*, was the notion that the body could be healed through prayer. The Fillmores "instructed the student to relax in mind and body, to turn to God in thought, to think not about the problem but about God, whose wisdom, love and power are mighty to solve every problem."[65]

The Fillmores had no desire to have Unity function as a church. Their concern was to help people of all faiths to "apply spiritual principles to their daily problems."[66] Indeed, it was not until thirty years after the founding of Unity that Charles Fillmore, "at the urgent request of some of his followers, wrote out a *Unity Statement of Faith*," but he appended to this declaration an important caveat: "We may change our mind tomorrow, and if we do we shall feel free to make a new statement of faith in harmony with the new view-point."[67] The Fillmores' rejection of a fixed creed and their emphasis on the legitimacy of each individual's search for truth surely resonated strongly with Mary Follett's own personal beliefs. Follett was probably also impressed by the "great informality" of the public meetings and the "give and take between leader and people." According to Charles S. Braden's *Spirits in Rebellion*, Charles Fillmore "was more a teacher than a preacher, and he welcomed questions and discussion of the subject with which he was dealing."[68] The classes led by the Fillmores also were notably "joyous." The symbol of Unity was not the cross but the winged globe of Spirit.[69]

About seven weeks after her arrival at Unity School, Follett felt well enough to write Richard Cabot a letter. "I have been through deep waters since coming to K.C.," she soberly confided, "but I have stuck to the belief that what I needed was a deeper spiritual understanding & that when I got that I should be able to heal my body. I spend many hours a day in meditation & prayer & in trying to attain that consciousness of oneness with God which I think can then be made operative in the body to cleanse & purify it, nourish & upbuild, harmonize & free. I think that creation is a dual process of God & man, & that man has to learn how to do his part consciously. . . I think that I shall conquer for I have never before honestly (I can see now) wholly consecrated myself to God. I do now. Not to save my body, but because at last I truly want to."[70] The integration of self with a larger Whole that Follett had long pursued in her studies of philosophy and sociology, her social and civic work, and her writing about democracy had now become the object of a spiritual exploration.

Follett surely suspected that Richard Cabot was not pleased with her decision to leave the hospital and go to Kansas City. Although Cabot had long deplored the tendency of his fellow physicians to ignore the interactions between their patients' mental and physical health and had actively participated in an effort by one of Boston's oldest Episcopal churches to join the known principles of psychotherapy and religious faith with competent medical practice, he was convinced that physicians should be in control. The leaders of the Emmanuel Movement took great pains to distinguish their practices from those of Christian Science, which had no place in its creed for academic medicine; but they made little effort to understand the various spiritual healing movements known as New Thought or to appreciate the ways in which New Thought differed from Christian Science.[71]

The differences, however, were profound. Stephen Gottschalk argues that Christian Science was "a negative reference in contrast to which [many in New Thought] defined their own character." The primary distinction between New Thought and Christian Science was the controversy over the individual's relationship to God: whereas New Thought adherents believed that "any inspired individual could have his . . . private revelation of basic divine truth," Christian Science doctrine stated that "revelation had to come from outside, from above, from the top down."[72] Other differences existed as well. Christian Science, for example, denied the existence of sickness and death; New Thought admitted their existence but sought through "beneficent human thought" empowered by "the God within" to project "a more healthy image upon the mind of the sick person, whose body then externalizes this more healthy picture." Christian Science, furthermore, traditionally resisted cooperation with medical practitioners, while the Unity movement considered science and religion as "but two different approaches to the same Truth."[73]

Richard Cabot's failure to appreciate the ways in which Mary Follett's experience at Unity School might differ from the practices of Christian Science is apparent in his cryptic note in her medical record describing her decision to pursue another form of treatment: "Kansas . . . to Christian Scientists."[74] Aware of Cabot's bias, Follett closed her letter from Kansas City with a plea: "Oh trust me Richard & Ella Cabot & love me right through all this even if you think I am wrong . . . I believe I have been guided by God throughout, & I am thankful for all the steps which brought me here — to this place & to this period of communion."[75] Richard, to his credit, responded graciously to her plea, setting aside his reservations and immediately sending a letter of love and support; this letter, unfortunately, seems to have been lost in transit, but another sent by Ella two weeks later found its way to Mary in Kansas City: "I am most sorry that Richard's letter did not reach you, for it said as only he can say and with my full Amen, our love & honor for you. Of course we might differ (with *you* of all people) in a decision or judgment & love even more, for who but you taught us that to differ & learn is itself a new creation? You would not want us to argue now for you are drinking in an experience that must mean listening to other voices but of our love you must feel surer than ever & of our wish to share . . . Blessings to you always dear Mary."[76]

Eduard Lindeman received his first news of Follett's illness when A. D. Sheffield wrote on June 22, 1923, to say that "Miss Follett is seriously sick. What the trouble is I do not know, but the enclosed note from Miss Briggs makes me fear that she is trying to 'integrate' a conflict that calls for surgery."[77] A week later Lindeman received a note from Isobel Briggs, telling him of their hurried flight to the Midwest.[78] Briggs tried throughout the ordeal to keep him informed, but it was not until late August that she had good news to report. "Miss Follett has had some dreadful days, going through terrible suffering," Briggs confided in a discreet reference to a three-day period of hematuria and hours of agonizing pain; "but we think that that was the crisis and that she will now improve. She sent for her MS. a few days ago, and hopes to be able to work a little on it every day — on the book which is so near completion. She is still in no condition to leave here and the treatment she is having here, which we both believe is going to cure her." Briggs also made an attempt in her letters to Lindeman to revive the joint project, seeing how agitated Mary was at the thought that her illness might be undermining it. "To discuss how your work and her work is to fit together, and how much you will be able probably to do, will be, I think, fruitful and helpful to you both." Hoping further to entice him, Isobel added: "You will of course be our guest while you are here."[79]

It was not until late August that Lindeman's own poor health began to be discussed. In 1917, after taking a physical to assess his fitness for military service, Lindeman had been told that he had Bright's disease, now called glomerulonephritis. Lindeman's nephritis would prove to be relatively slow in developing — his death from renal failure did not come until thirty-five years after the diagnosis — but he would suffer throughout his life from infections, persistent low-grade fevers, repeated episodes of blood or protein in the urine, hypertension, and fatigue. "Most friends and associates knew that Eduard's health was precarious," writes David Stewart, "but few, if any, knew how serious the difficulties were."[80] Follett and Briggs, however, may well have been among the few who knew. Eduard was very fond of Isobel, as she was of both him and his family, and he seems first to have confided in her. "Miss

Briggs has . . . let me read your letter to her as it was all right that I should know," Mary wrote Eduard, remarking on his late September illness; and then, in an apparent reference to the nephritis, added: "I am so relieved that it is not the other thing [probably meaning cancer or polycystic kidneys] . . . How happy Mrs. Lindeman must be over your good news."[81]

Encouraged by the news of Lindeman's recovery and feeling somewhat better herself, Follett soon began to show her old enthusiasm. "I think that we are on the track of a big idea," she wrote in late September. "[Professor] Lawrence Henderson (you have read his books of course) said to me just before I was taken ill 'You've got hold of the idea which a few of the greatest minds in the course of the last few thousand years have tried to say, but no one has said and I don't believe you will.' But he was immensely interested in the idea, and some people think he has the best mind at Harvard. I want our two books together to say that thing and I believe we can, but it means, as you say, in this letter, some conferences." This late September letter is also notable for the reappearance of Follett's quick wit. After hinting mysteriously at a "big idea" she thought would benefit Lindeman's work, she told him that when she finally revealed it, "You will either think it splendid or that I am a lunatic and should be shut up (I see that has two meanings!)."[82]

The reprieve was brief. By early November, Follett's hopes for a steady recovery had been dashed. "We have decided to spend the winter here," she announced to Lindeman with evident disappointment. "I have been in bed & behaving badly again. However, I only lost 2 days of work, for I kept on even those days when I had to be flat on my back. I am up again now & working hard & know I shall be wholly well sometime. But I think I must stay here at present." Before his own illness had prevented it, Lindeman had proposed coming to Kansas City to consult with Follett. She now resurrected this idea, offering to help pay his expenses; she suggested, however, that the trip be delayed until they had had an opportunity to exchange manuscripts. Follett was having a copy made for Roscoe Pound, who had just agreed to critique the five law chapters, and she was also planning to send copies to Lindeman and Croly. "Then when you have read mine & I have read yours, we shall *have* to consult," Follett pleaded. "For I think there are a good many ideas in both our minds which are the joint property of both of us, & the question is already in my mind as to what use it to be made of them for the joint undertaking. Or rather, perhaps I ought to put the question in this form: just what *is* the *joint undertaking?*"[83]

Before the details of this meeting could be worked out, everything changed again. Follett and Briggs "came flying home because of some alarming developments and [Follett] went at once to the hospital."[84] Among the first to examine her when she arrived at Massachusetts General Hospital on November 22 was Richard Cabot. Just as during their first consultation in 1910, Cabot found a "smooth, solid non-tender mass" in the area of Mary's right kidney that could be moved a few inches in each direction. Now, however, it was almost twice its previous size. A series of tests would first have to be done, but Cabot thought an operation unavoidable.[85] Nothing could relieve the anxiety Follett was feeling, but at least she was in comfortable surroundings. MGH's Phillips House had been opened in 1917 in an effort to attract private-paying, "well-to-do" patients, many of whom had considered hospitals suitable only for charity cases. Phillips House not only was "luxuriously furnished" and offered amenities rivaling those of a fine hotel; it also was "lavishly equipped." It was most definitely a modern hospital.[86]

Two of the tests that Follett would have to endure — a cystoscopy and a pyelogram — required both the latest equipment and highly trained physicians. The cystoscopy procedure could be "trying and embarrassing," but it was only in this way, Follett's physicians no doubt assured her, that they could obtain the sort of data that would enable them "to determine the source of the hematuria, to ascertain the origin of pain and to identify an otherwise symptomless tumor." In Follett's case, however, the results were not definitive. Follett was next taken for a pyelogram. This procedure, involving an X ray of the kidney, necessitates the injection of a contrast medium, which then shows up on the X-ray plates. Like the cystoscopy, this procedure also could be unpleasant, with patients suffering flushing sensations and pain. The situation was further complicated by the fact that the X-ray equipment of this period was clumsy and difficult to use. Just a year earlier, a new substance, lipidol, had been introduced to provide a bland and harmless contrast that permitted effective photography; but the reading of X rays involving soft tissue such as tumors remained extraordinarily difficult. In Follett's case, the radiologist could discern no definite pathology in either the urinary tract or the kidneys.[87]

With this first series of tests providing no conclusive answers as to the cause of Follett's recurrent pain and hematuria, the doctors decided to schedule a second round; but since her skin was now too sensitive to withstand additional X rays, she was discharged, and the tests were delayed until early January.[88] Follett was well aware that her condition "could hardly be more precarious." In late December she told Lindeman that the doctors were reluctant to operate because of an unnamed "complication" — most likely the possibility that she had congenitally cystic kidneys. In such a case, surgery would not help. If the doctors' "final verdict" was that they could not operate, Follett admitted with characteristic candor, "then I cannot live long." But she did not linger long over this prospect. Instead, she assured Lindeman that she felt "fairly well in general health," with the pain only "local & intermittent," and thought she looked well, too; still, "with this trouble that is no encouragement. The local condition is what it is."[89]

Despite the uncertainties surrounding her medical condition, the joint project with Lindeman was never far from Follett's mind. "I am going to beg the doctors to let me stay out [of the hospital] until the book is finished," she assured her colleague, "by which I mean until you have been here. As I am feeling fairly well, I hope they will concede this. Meanwhile, please let me know your plans for January."[90] Less than two weeks later, a note from Lindeman arrived, mixed in among the Christmas greetings: not only would he not be visiting Boston, but he saw no need for an exchange of manuscripts. Stunned, Follett spent Christmas Eve composing a frantic, disjointed reply. "I am somewhat startled at your note, not because you are not coming on; for I *quite* understand that," she told Lindeman, "but at your apparent repudiation of our joint undertaking when you seem to think that it is possible for me to publish my book without your seeing it. And I do not understand such repudiation, for I do not see how I have been remiss . . . You may say that I have been ill for 6 months. Yes, but I have worked since Sept. first. I have worked lying flat on my back, under the greatest difficulties, & in great pain, but I *have* worked, & many hours a day. I have been home from K.C. now 5 weeks & I have not even seen my aged Mother (!), my sense of obligation to you has been so great . . . It is impossible for you to realize the extent of my sacrifices, for the doctors say I may not recover, & there are some very close & dear friends I should have liked to see, some business I shd. have like to arrange, before going back to the hospital, but I have refused myself everything in order to get on with this work . . . *solely that I should not keep you back*."

Stung by Lindeman's rejection, it is only after this lengthy expression of resentment and indignation that Follett adopts a more reasoned tone: "But perhaps I entirely misunderstand your letter. Perhaps I should have put no such construction on it. But I should consider it an absolute breaking of our agreement for me to publish anything without consulting you, or for you to publish anything without consulting me." Before closing, Follett changes her tone yet again: "You know, dear Mr. Lindeman, there is something else I care for besides the joint undertaking, we have been associated long enough now for me to care very much for your interests. I want this book to do a great deal towards establishing your reputation. Parts of it are *very* good, but I am sure that as a whole it can be better, & I shd. like to talk it over with you on that account too if you would care to have me . . . The standing this book takes will probably make a difference to all the rest of your life."[91]

After a night's reflection, Follett spent part of Christmas Day composing a second letter. This time she opened with admiration for Lindeman's work. "I have only dipped in [your manuscript] here & there," Follett told him, "but it so much more than fulfills my greatest expectations of it — wh. were not small. I admire the way you were able to do yourself without any pioneer in front of you the kind of social research wh. you are advocating . . . You remember that I thought we must be so careful we didn't *talk* about a new method of research & then after all *do* about the same kind that had been always done. I was afraid also of descriptions that might be merely journalistic. I need not have been afraid of either danger. You have got from your trips & studies something very different, just what I had hoped for, but I hardly believed the first pioneer could clear the forest so well." Her admiration notwithstanding, Follett still felt indignant about Lindeman's abandonment of the joint project, and her resentment soon surfaced. "It is Xmas day. I rose at 6.30 & have worked until 4 with a half hour for luncheon. I shall go on after a little rest. I worked all Xmas Eve day & evening. I did not even look out the window at the carol singers but sat right here until 10 p.m. I do want you to know that I am doing my best, & not without results that I think will interest you."[92] This pointed account of her holiday labors surely was intended to arouse Lindeman's guilt, but something more complex was also at work here.

From the time she was a child, Mary Follett had tried desperately through her accomplishments to prove herself worthy of the love and affection of others. Even at age fifty-five, this inner pressure to perform was intense. Almost from the beginning of the joint project, Follett was haunted by the fear that she might disappoint her benefactor Dorothy Straight or, much worse, might produce work that Herbert Croly would find unworthy of the confidence he had shown in her intellectual prowess. These concerns, exacerbated when she was taken ill, are evident in many of Follett's letters. In late September, for example, Follett expressed her disappointment about not having the book manuscript ready for Croly and Straight in July. "About the time I have lost this summer," Follett told Dorothy Straight, "I would like to explain that although I did nothing for two and a half months, I almost, perhaps quite, made up for that by my long hours last winter when I very foolishly, worked days and evenings, Sundays and holidays. But it is rather absurd to mention this, as of course what you will be interested in is not the time spent but the quality of what is produced. I do hope you will like that. I hope you will think the whole joint undertaking worth while. The work that I did . . . convinced me that we, as a group, are on the track of a bigger idea than we have perhaps realized, one that ought to make some difference to all the social sciences if we can get it expressed convincingly."[93] Three months later, in a letter to Lindeman, Follett focused her anxieties on Croly's opinion of her work: "I have not written to Mr. Croly for a long time, but I think always, in whatever I am doing, whether he would approve . . . I somehow feel that he is trusting me, but at any rate time will show him that I have not wasted any time."[94]

When Lindeman decided to abandon the project and go his own way, Follett was distraught—not simply because his leaving meant they would not finish what they had started or because they now would have to engage in the unseemly process of sorting out which of the ideas expressed in the manuscripts were his and which were hers, but also because she felt an enormous burden of guilt. It was her illness, or so Follett thought, that was responsible for their failure; she was the reason they were losing the opportunity to work out the grand ideas they had envisioned when they embarked on the joint project.[95]

Isobel Briggs, who was acutely aware of her partner's distress, also became involved in the dispute, interceding with Lindeman on Mary's behalf. She wrote a note of gratitude to Lindeman's family for their Christmas greetings and for their repeated invitations to visit whenever she happened to be in New York. Recalling happy scenes from the family's visit to Putney the previous year, Isobel added wistfully, "I should like to see you again in country togs, mowing with that practised, graceful swing, and incidentally saving my short and ungraceful dabs! But even better than that would be to see your young barbarians playing on some hillside round there like the young savages they may be in such remotenesses." But such pleasantries, Isobel realized, would have to wait until she was less preoccupied with Mary's illness. "I have been very appreciative [of your invitations]," she told Eduard, "and have always paved a large area with intentions to acknowledge them. But I have never, since last summer, been without the disquietude that anxiety about the health of one's family occasions, and you will understand now how paralyzing that has been since you know its culmination and our long exile in the Middle West—and our disconcerting return here." Perhaps hoping that Lindeman might be moved to resume the joint project if only she could make him see how arduously Mary had labored, Isobel continued in this vein, divulging even more about her distress over Mary's suffering: "This [situation] has only been made bearable by Miss Follett's marvellous courage, patience, endurance of pain, and even rather grim determination to finish what she had undertaken to do. Even so, it has about broken my heart to watch her (and hear her day and night) doing it."[96]

Neither Briggs nor Follett seemed to realize that Lindeman's decision to abandon the joint undertaking was driven not by Follett's illness, but by something that Follett did not cause and could not control—Lindeman's increasingly intense yearning for the approval and affection of Dorothy Straight.[97] After the death of her husband in 1918, the thirty-five-year-old Straight (who

was one year younger than Lindeman) had had no dearth of male companionship. "She was attractive enough," writes her biographer, "with sparkling light
blue eyes in an oval face, wavy brown hair piled high on her head, and her soft
voice and her manner to have drawn men to her even if she had not been an
heiress." But Straight was understandably wary about her suitors' motives,
and her shyness and ambivalence about physical intimacy combined to keep
these relationships quite platonic.[98] Even Leonard Elmhirst, the most determined of her suitors and a man to whom she was deeply attracted, was kept
quite off balance by Straight's demeanor. An Englishman, Elmhirst was a
twenty-seven-year-old student of agricultural economics at Cornell when he
and Dorothy met in 1920.[99] Less than two years later, in January 1922, Elmhirst wrote from India, where he was doing rural development, and asked
Dorothy to marry him. Not only did she say no; she called marriage "out of the
question. She wanted them to give each other love, comfort, co-operation and
understanding, but marriage, no." Their lives, Straight told him, were to be
committed to doing good works — his in India and hers in America. Elmhirst
persisted, repeating his proposal at regular intervals, but few who knew them
thought that Elmhirst's courtship of Dorothy would succeed.[100] Still, whatever
her wariness about marrying him, there is no doubt that Elmhirst was at the
center of Dorothy's emotional life almost from the first moment they met.

Eduard Lindeman seems to have been quite oblivious to the Straight-
Elmhirst relationship. Lindeman did not meet Leonard Elmhirst until August
1924, just about the time Straight finally decided to marry; and even then,
Lindeman seems not to have recognized the true nature of the relationship.[101]
The wedding plans were kept secret from all but a few, and Lindeman, while
on a family vacation in Italy arranged by Straight, was both stunned and
deeply distraught when he saw in an April 1925 newspaper that Straight had
married Leonard Elmhirst. Straight's decision not to confide in Lindeman
about her impending marriage tells us something about the limits of their
relationship: perhaps she doubted that Lindeman could give her the kind of
emotional support she had often provided for him; or perhaps she thought
silence was the only way of avoiding the embarrassment they both would
endure if Lindeman was overwhelmed by jealousy.[102]

Lindeman's feelings of gratitude toward Dorothy Straight as his benefactor
had first been transformed into something more complex in the autumn of
1923, the period when Follett was confronting her illness in Kansas City.
Lindeman himself was taken ill, and when Straight learned of his plight she
sent a message of admiration and concern. "It was a shock to hear of your
illness and I have been very distressed about you," Straight wrote in late
September. "It made me realize how much I cared for you and how important

you had become in my life as well as in the larger life of mankind. For you know, I feel sure that your book is going to prove the most important contribution to social thinking, that has been made in many generations. I'm grateful to you for having sent me the advanced pages and for giving me a chance to share in the work from the start."[103] Emboldened by Straight's letter and her visit a few days later, Lindeman reciprocated with his own letter of concern when Dorothy was debilitated by a thyroid condition later in the year. Still addressing her as "Mrs. Straight," Eduard's tone was cautious. Not until the end of his letter does he reveal his true purpose: "Would you mind greatly if I dedicated my book to you? I haven't mentioned this to anyone but it has been in my mind. I should like it to be very simple — without embellishments or qualifications — just TO D. W. S. and, it would give me so much pleasure. Please! At any rate, don't decide until I can see you."[104]

When Straight did not immediately reply, Lindeman sent off a second letter, revealing considerably more about the place Dorothy was assuming in his life. "I recall a Christmas long ago in our Michigan home," Lindeman confided, "when my Mother presented me with woolen mittens and woolen stocking which she had made by lamplight. My joy was so great that I still remember with vividness her expression: '*Deine augen sheinen wie's himmelslicht.*' [Your eyes shine like the heavens.] After that this became her favorite expression whenever she wished to share in any of my childish aspirations and fancies. And, it was on these occasions that she always confided to me the secret knowledge which she possessed, namely the assurance that the time would come when I should read books and speak knowingly about important topics. I don't know precisely why this incident comes to mind just now unless it is my desire to tell you how difficult my real purposes were until you came to believe in them . . . I wanted you to know that there are hopes and stirrings of the heart which are prompted by your good self."[105]

Straight, who had long been uncertain about her own intellectual prowess, was both astonished and thrilled by Lindeman's proposed dedication: could it be that her contributions went beyond simply providing other people with funding, that the support she gave was emotional and intellectual as well as financial?[106] Nevertheless, it took her almost two weeks to reply. Confined to bed and enmeshed in one of her protracted "silences" with Leonard Elmhirst, Straight was feeling a despair whose cause she would not or could not reveal. When she finally wrote on Christmas Eve, her gratitude was so effusive that Lindeman might easily have mistaken it for something more intimate. "Your two letters were like the glimpse of a friendly ship on a rather solitary voyage across the Atlantic — my highest and gladdest gifts in many a month," Straight wrote. Digressing into a page or so of musings that she knew were "deliberately postponing the moment when I have to try to tell you what I think about the dedication," Dorothy finally took up the matter directly. "Your suggestion," she admitted, "completely took my breath away! You really gave me one of the great moments of my life! It never occurred to me that you could possibly think me of sufficient importance for a dedication — in fact I still feel so inadequate and unworthy that I can't bring myself to the point of feeling that it is at all right from your point of view — Of course for me it's just pure joy and gratitude to know that you could even have thought of it." But torn between "unworthiness and elation," Straight gave Lindeman neither a yes nor a no. Instead, she suggested that he seriously consider dedicating the book to someone more deserving, most notably Mary Follett, and proposed that they discuss the matter together. Her closing, however, was more auspicious: "Will you please not call me Mrs. Straight any more? And I want to call you something besides Mr. Lindeman! I feel much closer to you than those terms suggest."[107]

One of Lindeman's biographers, David Stewart, suggests that Lindeman's decision to end the joint project with Mary Follett was almost entirely a result of Follett's limitations as a colleague. "The exacting, sickly, maidenly, and (to judge from her correspondence with Lindeman) severely neurotic Mary Follett," Stewart writes, "did not always achieve good personal chemistry with the volatile, convivial, lusty, and often disorganized Eduard Lindeman." Furthermore, the "erratic" and "ethereal Miss Follett" required "personal and professional surroundings that were predictable, built upon ground that was solid — very solid. She never learned that a predictable, ordered world was not possible for friends or close associates of Eduard Lindeman." Stewart's characterization of Follett is based solely on the Follett-Lindeman correspondence and Lindeman's angry two-sentence description of Follett in the 1923 letter to Charles Shaw discussed earlier in this chapter.[108] Such a characterization is misleading, given what is now known about Follett's accomplishments in the complex arena of Boston politics and civic life as well as her success in maintaining important personal and professional relationships. Stewart's attempt to attribute the dissolution of the Follett-Lindeman partnership to a difficult Follett temperament simply is not credible.

It seems far more likely that Lindeman's decision to end the joint project was motivated by his determination to dedicate his book to Dorothy Straight. Follett, who once had been a major source of inspiration to Lindeman, now was an unwelcome intruder in his relationship with Straight and an obstacle to be overcome — Eduard's gift to Dorothy, after all, could be given only if his book was his own. When Follett refused to give her immediate assent to separating their endeavors, Lindeman was furious. Even the knowledge that

Follett's illness was causing her terrible suffering and anxiety did not dissuade him from pressing single-mindedly for an immediate termination of the project. The abruptness of Lindeman's abandonment of the project left Follett baffled and bristling with resentment. "Now you see that it is possible that by the time you come back from the West," she trenchantly remarked in her letter of Christmas Eve, "I may have had an operation & that I may be well, even tho. it is a serious one, or I may be out of the way entirely."[109]

At no time did Lindeman reveal the real reason underlying his decision, and this made the dispute exceedingly difficult for the two of them to resolve. A. D. Sheffield, who learned of Lindeman's decision while paying Follett a holiday visit, tried to intervene. "[Miss Follett] seems to be a little fluttered at the prospect of near publication of your book," he told Lindeman, "and seems anxious to have a talk that shall clarify the status of what she still thinks of as a joint enterprise. I tried to intimate that the exchange of manuscripts between you and her was sufficient to keep both apprised of the progress in your thinking, and would give opportunity for all the appropriate acknowledgements, but she seemed a little worried lest Mr. Croly should get the impression that her illness had made more of a break in your joint project than it really had."[110] Lindeman, buoyed by Dorothy Straight's Christmas Eve letter, stood firm in his desire for a complete separation: "I had to write a rather stiff letter to [Miss Follett] last week in order to make myself clear about the problem of credit. I do not expect the least credit for anything that I have contributed to her and it seemed to me that we ought to stop talking about 'my' and 'your.' All of this I had to say to her very frankly and I do hope that it did not hurt her too much."[111]

After receiving Lindeman's letter, Follett took a taxi to the Sheffields' Cambridge home to have another discussion with Sheffield about the "joint" enterprise. Following her visit, Sheffield approached Lindeman again, thinking it "important that we should all hit upon some arrangement that will leave her easy in mind before she goes to the hospital." Sheffield proposed two principles that might form the basis of a resolution: first, "the two books should contain in their respective prefaces the statement that they had originated in joint conference with some pooling of ideas and illustration"; and second, "the two books should be issued by the same publisher, so as to present the aspect of companion volumes on the same list, and . . . her book should be issued first."[112] This proposal evidently suited Lindeman's purposes. Within a few days Follett had a letter from Herbert Croly telling her that his Republic Publishing Company planned to publish Lindeman's book and asking if it might publish hers as well; this arrangement, he said, would allow the press "to push them as companion books." Discussing the pros and cons of the offer with Harry Overstreet, Follett was worried about the "cheap form" the book might take in the hands of an inexperienced press and for that reason was inclined to sign with her old publisher, Longmans; finally, however, she accepted Croly's offer.[113]

Once this decision was made, Lindeman immediately requested that the arrangements between them "in regard to the publishing of our two books" be made by Sheffield. Reluctant to reveal his yearning for Straight and perhaps also feeling guilty about the way he was treating Mary Follett, Lindeman no doubt found Sheffield a useful buffer. Follett assented to the arrangement and was pleased to learn that Lindeman "heartily agreed" that her book should come out first. But tired of the endless misunderstandings, she asked Lindeman to "kindly express this [priority of publication] in writing so that if I should be incapacitated the matter will be clear to others." She also asked him to make the publication dates definite so that she could be certain there was "time for the general public to become aware of the publication" of her book before his appeared. After concluding these arrangements, Follett ended this otherwise formal letter on a personal, conciliatory note, perhaps mindful that the outcome of her next hospital visit was at best uncertain: "As my family has a soft place in its heart for you, & as I have always felt affection for the Lindeman family as a whole, there is a bond between us all I think which will continue when the immediate work is finished."[114]

Struggling to take care of her mother's affairs while at the same time trying to put the finishing touches on the manuscript, Follett had delayed her return to the hospital for more than a month. "I have worked so hard for 6 weeks — almost literally all my waking time — that I am really dazed with it," Follett confessed to the Cabots in early February. But even with surgery looming ominously ahead, she would not willingly give up any part of the planning for her book — including decisions about "paper & type & margins."[115] Genuine consideration — playfully turning over and over even the most mundane matters so that she might examine them from several angles — simply gave her too much pleasure. Recalling this aspect of Follett's character, one friend could only marvel:

> If one took her some small problem of the running of one's office or the adjustment of some more or less difficult relationship, Mary would think about it for hours and set out the question in all its aspects and discuss each angle till we could both feel satisfied that we had at least done our best to find the right solution. Mary would apply the same methods to the choice of dress or of curtains or of wallpapers. She would bring a whole selection of pieces into my sitting room and spread them over tables and chairs till one could hardly move and far less find what one wanted — then the discussion would

begin. Differences between the pieces might only be some slight difference of shade or weight. And after going backwards and forwards, I would feel that I could no longer rivet my attention to the choice and suggest tossing up. Mary would squeal at the idea as frivolous and wasteful of the chance of considered choice. It was the actual process she enjoyed and I learned a great deal from her as to the value of considered choice.[116]

Once Follett felt ready to leave the manuscript in Isobel's hands, she entered Phillips House for four days of tests. When she received the results on February 10, 1924, she was jubilant. "I am so happy," she wrote excitedly to the Cabots. "Dr. Jones says no operation if Dr. Cabot agrees, & I am sure he will."[117] The new round of tests, like the first, showed no definite pathology. Follett's physicians found some evidence that the lower calyx of her right kidney looked as if a "rounded mass were pressing upon it," but Dr. Crabtree felt "quite certain that the mass is not a malignant growth." As a result, the doctors decided that the appropriate course of action was to keep her under observation, examining her every two months. "I can make no other diagnosis in Miss Follett's case than congenital cystic kidney," Dr. Jones wrote Richard Cabot, "and that diagnosis would of course fill all the requirements."[118] Follett found this diagnosis a welcome relief: she could expect continuing pain and a variety of other discomforts, but with the disease apparently confined to one kidney, her life was not threatened, and she would escape the dangers of surgery.

In this same early February letter reporting the good news about her health, Follett broached with the Cabots a subject she felt "a little diffident about." She wondered if they would allow her to dedicate *Creative Experience* to them. "I say I feel diffident. That is because I do not know how much you will like this book, but I am hoping you will like it. I think Mr. Croly thinks it an advance on The New State (Miss Briggs does) & you liked that a little . . . The reason that I wish to dedicate this book to you is because it has come from a deeper place than any work I have done hitherto, has reached down into the roots of my thinking & being, & therefore it seems appropriate to ask you for whom I care so much to accept it from me. Moreover, our talks together have not only fertilized my thought, but the more subtle, the more intangible, relation than the mere external discussion has strengthened me in more ways than intellectually." It was like Follett not to raise the matter of the dedication until she was certain she would live, perhaps fearful that her friends might give their consent merely out of pity or sympathy for her condition. Now this particular fear had been allayed, and she was free to look to the future. "One last thing must be said before I sleep tonight," she confided in closing. "I realize that Richard has not only saved me from the operation, (Dr. Jones would have performed it in Nov.) but that thereby he may have saved my life. How then, *avanti* — to make it worthwhile."[119]

Leaving the hospital, Follett took as her first task the resolution of all out-standing questions about the publication of the forthcoming books. Still un-certain as to what having "companion books" really meant and having no clarification from Lindeman about "priority of publication," Follett hoped that a meeting in New York might settle matters. Fearful that Lindeman had been offended by her request for a written agreement, she assured him that *"there cannot possibly be any disagreement between us.* For I am willing to assent to anything that seems right to you & Mr. Croly when we talk it over together . . . Please make Mr. C. understand this too. I have spoken of ap-pearance of books, type etc., as one always does, not that I am not willing to fall in with any group plan."[120] The next day, Follett tried in a somewhat different way to explain the nature of her concern: "I wish I could make you understand just what my puzzle has been . . . I don't think I am an obstinate person, I am perfectly willing, as a rule, to give in to others' judgment, but I just hate not to know where things stand. Mr. Henry S. Dennison is always reproving me for this thinking that things must be so definite, but I can't seem to contemplate them unless they are. After our conference I shall be perfectly satisfied, I know, for all I want is definiteness, not to insist on anything."[121]

Still hopeful that their impending conversations might make possible the continuation of some sort of working relationship, Follett asked if they might use some of her time in New York "to plan about the rest of the year." Perhaps they could get Lord Haldane and a few others from different fields "to con-sider our books together," getting from them "some estimate of the fundamen-tal idea back of your book & mine . . . In that way we could continue the joint enterprise."[122] No such plan emerged, but the New York meetings were pro-ductive in other ways. Follett conferred with Herbert Croly about the form her book might take under the auspices of his Republic Publishing Company, and they amicably agreed that Follett might be more comfortable with another publisher. Once this was all "arranged pleasantly with Mr. Croly," Follett con-tacted the New York representative of Longmans and found that they could have her book out by mid-April 1924. She immediately signed a contract.[123]

Follett and Lindeman also worked out some of their problems. They agreed to read each other's prefaces before submitting them to their respective pub-lishers in order to "prevent duplication" and "treat the joint nature of the enterprise in the same general way."[124] They also talked over some matters of content. Because Follett had failed to get her manuscript to Lindeman before she arrived in New York, his critique was less detailed than she would have liked; still, some suggestions seem to have been helpful. "My room was so gory last night I could hardly get into bed, for I had slaughtered 23 Gestalts," Mary jocularly remarked in a note to Eduard after one especially productive conversation. Since she had written this provocative comment on the back of a postcard, Follett appended a facetious disclaimer: "Dear me, I didn't think how this would sound. If Mrs. L. reads this & if she doesn't know what a G. is (I didn't a year ago), she may think I am staying at a low hotel. Please make the necessary explanations!"[125]

This note suggests that Lindeman had carefully critiqued aspects of Follett's manuscript, but he was much more guarded when it came to his own. Follett had come to New York prepared for a lengthy stay in the hope that the two of them might edit his manuscript together; but when she recognized that her help was not welcomed, Mary confined her critique to a quick read on the train on the way back to Boston.[126] Even after her return, Lindeman continued to maintain his distance, rejecting multiple overtures from Follett about ways they might use the summer to continue their collaboration.[127]

Lindeman's deliberate distancing of himself from Mary Follett took yet another form — this time involving their patrons, Croly and Straight. In 1922, when the project began, it was Follett who had used her experience and connections to convince Croly and Straight of Lindeman's potential; but by 1924 Lindeman felt certain that only he could be relied on to interpret accurately their patrons' concerns. Lindeman objected vigorously, for example, to Follett's suggestion that Dorothy Straight be acknowledged in each of their prefaces. Dorothy was much too self-effacing for this sort of tribute, he told Follett, and would be sure to disapprove.[128] This assertion, coming from Lindeman, seems at best disingenuous. Straight, after all, had been "thrilled" by his proposed dedication and eventually gave her consent.

Lindeman's conviction that his growing intimacy with Croly and Straight somehow authorized him to interpret their wishes surfaced in yet another way during the New York meetings. Follett's stipend for the project — $4,000 for salary and expenses beginning September 1922 — had been extended by Straight for a second year in January 1923; but once she was taken ill, Follett had written to Straight asking if the second year's payment might run over two years instead of one.[129] "That would make me feel that I need not work so many hours a day if I should find that it seemed best to have shorter working days," Mary explained in a letter from Kansas City. "If you should happen to see Dr. Cabot, you may hear that I am not going to live, but I am absolutely convinced that I am. But I do not want you this winter to send me my checks ahead, let me do the work first."[130] When Straight did not reply, probably because of her own illness, Follett was perplexed. She assumed all was well, but when February arrived and none of the second year's money had been paid, Follett decided that it was time to clear up the confusion.

When she mentioned the situation to Lindeman while in New York, he insisted that nothing should be done until Straight was well enough to be approached directly. When Follett rejected his advice and raised the matter in a letter to Straight's private secretary, Lindeman was furious. The prospect of being saddled with yet another year of Mary Follett just when he thought he was finally free to deal with Straight and Croly on his own was apparently more than Lindeman could bear. His written reprimand was both icy and patronizing. "When you mentioned your arrangement with Mrs. Straight to me, I thought I made it clear that this ought not to be taken up until Mrs. Straight had recovered . . . You will remember that in the early days of the undertaking neither Mrs. Straight nor Mr. Croly anticipated your participation on a paid basis. After considerable difficulty, this adjustment was made by both of them in terms of what they considered a changed situation . . . Your intervening illness, the fact that your book was written quite independently of my collected materials, and the fact that conditions necessitated a course of activity different from the original project—all of these facts must now be considered . . . the three of us [Croly, Bogue, Lindeman] agree in thinking that she considered her support for what you were doing ended with the single payment." Recognizing that Follett was more likely to be influenced by Herbert Croly's opinion than his own, Lindeman sought Croly's authorization. "If Mr. Croly disagrees with any portion of my interpretation," he said at one point in the letter, "he will add his own since I am sending this letter on to him for approval."[131] Croly apparently did not approve, for he seems to have kept Eduard's letter rather than, as Lindeman had hoped, forwarding it directly on to Mary. "I have rec'd no other letter from you than the special yesterday," Follett wrote on March 10 in response to Lindeman's news that he had been offered a position at the New York School of Social Work. "Was there one lost? You seem to refer to one."[132]

Although Lindeman was working feverishly both to distance himself from Follett and to oust her from the partnership with Croly and Straight, Follett doggedly worked to salvage something of their relationship. She crafted a letter responding to Lindeman's news about the proposed faculty position that was both congratulatory and encouraging. "Advance," she advised Lindeman, "always consists in recognizing your point of vantage, of leverage, the rock from wh. *you* can leap etc. At the S. of S.W. you will do so splendidly that you will get a reputation & that will lead to other things. At one of the large universities, you would have so much competition, so much rivalry & jealousy (the large universities are so *reeking* with that) that the way in which you are in advance of other people might not be acknowledged, but in a little while when you have made more of a reputation, you would be in a better position to hold your own against that."[133] She also apologized again for having requested before her hospitalization that Lindeman put in writing his assent to her having priority of publication. "I wrote it because I felt so in the dark about everything," she explained. "I wish you could understand this, that I am so made that I have to have something to clutch hold of, it doesn't matter so much whether it is favorable to myself or not, but I can't just wriggle along without knowing where I am." Now wishing that the letter had never been written, Follett pleaded: "don't we respect & esteem each other enough at bottom to be able to see each other make mistakes? Unless we do we cannot keep that respect for we shall both make mistakes. You told me once even that you felt affectionate regard for me. I want you to keep that. I think it far more important for our contribution to the world that we keep right through to the end of our enterprise everything that we felt for each other at the beginning, far more important than that we add 2 more books to the world."[134]

The publication later that year of Follett's *Creative Experience* and Lindeman's *Social Discovery* effectively marked the end of the Follett-Lindeman collaboration. Follett would go on to produce her widely acclaimed management lectures, while Lindeman would go on to a career as an educator, a prolific author and journalist, and a social activist. Lindeman's *Social Discovery* seemed to have little positive impact on his career, other than helping him acquire his teaching position at the New York School of Social Work. But in the late 1920s he would begin working in the emerging field of adult education and would eventually be recognized nationally and internationally as the "earliest major conceptualizer of the progressive-pragmatic tradition in American adult education." In social work, too, Lindeman would achieve distinction among his colleagues, being seen as one of only a few "who consciously emphasized and constantly reminded the profession of its philosophical base."[135]

Although their working relationship had been disrupted and their accomplishments tarnished by illnesses and emotional distress, the two principals succeeded in maintaining the "affectionate regard" that Follett so deeply valued. The prefaces to their 1924 books include generous acknowledgments of each other's contributions, and after Follett's death Lindeman would write a touching memoir of his former colleague, acknowledging "her great gift to me." He explained: "The important fact to be registered concerning my indebtedness to Mary Follett may be stated thus: She asked questions which led toward the future and hence revealed to me the prophetic nature of her thought; but she also pointed toward fundamental solutions, as distinguished from superficial opportunisms, and in this demonstrated her fine wisdom."[136]

19

Creative Experience

Longmans was expeditious in getting Follett's manuscript into print; by mid-April of 1924 she was sending copies to friends. A year after its publication, the philosopher Harry Overstreet found himself so impressed with *Creative Experience* that he reviewed it a second time. This book has "made a profound impression upon a number of readers," Overstreet observed, "profound in the sense that its ideas have become actively incorporated in their lives as functioning techniques. This, for the reviewer," he quipped, "is a rather rare experience."[1] The ideas expressed in *Creative Experience* continue to have an impact. Follett's process of integration, for example, forms the basis of what is now commonly referred to as a "win-win" approach to conflict resolution; and her distinction between "power-with" and "power-over" has been used by so many distinguished thinkers that it has become a part of our popular vocabulary.[2]

Follett opened *Creative Experience,* just as she had *The New State,* with a critique. She began by taking issue with her generation's veneration of expert fact-finding and judicial intervention as solutions to the problems of modern society.[3]

Follett's Critique of the Expert

The widespread clamor for the expert—which could be heard in different forms in the writings of Walter Lippmann, Herbert Croly, John Dewey, and others—seemed to Follett "a confession of our own weakness . . . acutely conscious of the mess we are in, we want someone to pull us out. What we really wish for is a 'beneficent' despot, but we are ashamed to call him that and so we say scientific investigator, social engineer, etc. Many of us are like the little girl who goes to her mother with her tangled knitting: she goes, often, not to learn to knit, but to be got out of a scrape."[4]

Follett was not suggesting that experts should never be used; her experience had convinced her of the need for accurate information. Yet we must remember, Follett insists, that we seek facts "not to do away with *difference* but to do away with *muddle* . . . What accurate information does is to clear the ground for genuine difference and therefore make possible, I do not say make sure, agreement . . . I wholly agree that the number of decisions people are willing to make daily without such [scientific] information is amazing, and yet I think that after we have obtained the greatest amount possible, there will still be difference, and that dealing with difference is the main part of the social process."[5]

With regard to the process by which "facts" are discovered, Follett's experience had shown her that fact-finding "bristles with difficulties." Many of our most serious social problems "defy the possibility of precise measurement." Even in those cases in which useful information can be gathered, "if it is partial, decisions based upon it will be disastrous." All too often, however, the information acquired by experts is only partial; the fact-finder is seriously hampered both by the briefness of the opportunity to observe a situation and by the distortions introduced by the observer's mere presence. Even if the expert somehow overcomes these difficulties and manages to capture the "whole situation with whatever sentiments, beliefs, ideals enter into it," this accomplishment is fleeting. A situation "changes faster than anyone can report on it." The process of expert fact-finding is further biased by the prejudices, interests, stereotypes, and moral codes of the investigators—as Lippmann's penetrating analysis in *Public Opinion* (1922) had made abundantly clear. Indeed, experts often are chosen for particular fact-finding tasks precisely because of their "known leanings." Follett was also mindful that the gathering of facts requires more than honesty and disinterestedness; accuracy often demands of the fact-finder "the greatest delicacy of perception, the ear to hear overtones, the sensitiveness to impressions as well as a certain imperviousness to impressions"—and these qualities often can be obtained only through the participation in the fact-finding process of a wide variety of people. Finally, Follett was convinced that "there is a time and place for fact-finding"; in particular, "there is possible a cooperative gathering of facts which is more useful to the resolution of conflict than for each side to get them separately and then try to integrate them, for when each side gets them separately there is a tendency for each to stick rigidly to its own particular facts." Follett knew well from her experience on minimum wage boards that even where cooperative investigations are undertaken, the facts still might be interpreted differently by each side, "but the initial difficulty would be avoided — we should at any rate be looking at the same facts."[6]

For many of Follett's contemporaries, the problems associated with the use of experts automatically ceased once the facts had been gathered; as they might have put it, "the expert gathers and the official interprets." Follett, however, challenged this claim. The expert interprets whenever he deliberately withholds facts or uses statistics to suit his own purposes, and he also interprets whenever he condenses or labels facts, since language is "overlaid with the ideas and emotions of the race." Then, too, the expert interprets whenever he presents what he has found; secure in the belief that he is "right," he all too often seeks "to stampede the general public into acceptance of his opinions."[7]

The expert's tendency toward manipulation was reinforced, Follett believed, by the widespread acceptance in America of the political doctrine known as "the consent of the governed." This view — which would "divide society on the one side into the expert and the governors basing their governing on his reports, and on the other the people consenting" — seemed to Follett "a disaster-courting procedure."[8] Among the many flaws in the theory of consent, Follett found most objectionable the assumption that the automatic result of scientific investigation is the overcoming of difference. "This view both fails to see the importance of diversity, and also ignores the fact that the accumulation of information does not overcome diversity . . . It is always the inexperienced man on the Board who brings in his 'facts' and expects that the *impasse* of the previous meeting will be removed. Can you not see him in your various memories, smiling round at his companions in this happy expectation? And can you not see that smile gradually fade as the expectation fails?" Yet another serious flaw mars the notion that consent could bridge the "gap" between the expert and the people: "before the expert has finished reporting and the administrative official deciding and the people 'willing,' the situation has changed."[9]

Rejecting the democratic elitism expressed in Walter Lippmann's *Public Opinion*, Follett insists that expertise must be understood and accepted "as expressing an attitude of mind which we can all acquire, rather than the collecting of information by a special caste." This change in attitude, she admits, will not make us professional experts, but "it will enable us to work with professional experts and to find our place in a society which needs the experience of all, to build up a society which shall embody the experience of all."[10]

The Law as Integrator of Interests

Just as Follett was skeptical of the expert as the "revealer of truth," she refused to accept the judge as the sole "guardian of truth."[11] Many of her contemporaries, having witnessed the injustices issuing from the nineteenth century's adherence to a laissez-faire economics, had entrusted to the legal order the guardianship of their "rights" or "interests" — particularly their "social" interests. Follett, however, was not so sanguine about using the courts in this way. "The social agency of the law is not something *outside* the democratic process, an apparatus of safeguards provided as a check upon misdirections of will. Still less can we think that there are patterns of what is socially valid which can be invoked from time to time to be superimposed upon the changing order in order to correct its aberrations. Law must be integral with the social order."[12] But despite these reservations, Follett acknowledges the valuable service provided by judges who are explicitly designing their decisions and opinions to *integrate* rather than simply *adjudicate* interests — for true social interests, she argues, emerge out of just such a process of integrating individual interests.

Dean Roscoe Pound of the Harvard Law School, whose acquaintance Follett made when she was writing *The New State*, was one of the champions of this trend in judicial thinking, and Follett made ample use of his legal writings in *Creative Experience*. Pound was urging justices to "seek and bring into use those modes of association which will reveal joint interests: those between employer and employee, landlord and tenant, master and servant. Law, he tells us, must find the essential nature of the relation." Pound's conception of social interests seemed to Follett "a more profound truth" than some of the more subjective or sentimental theories propounded by sociologists; nevertheless, she remained quite wary of the term. In her view, the concept of "social interests" had developed a number of negative connotations: the abandonment of the individual, a return to ungrounded abstractions and sentimental rhetoric, and a rationalization for the exercise of power by the governing class.[13] " 'Social interests' in some people's mouths (our worthiest and best!) give me nausea," Follett declared in one frank exchange with Pound.[14] But whatever reservations she had about using the term in her own work apparently were dispelled during a late February conversation with Pound. She rewrote the section on social interests and declared that social interests as described by Pound could be the stuff of individual and social progress, because by "integrating these interests you get the increment of the unifying."[15]

Despite the promise evident in legal writings such as Pound's, it seemed to Follett that jurists and economists remained too enamored of the notion of an "equilibrium" of interests, just as political scientists were still too enthralled with a "balance of power." By contrast, the more recent psychological literature seemed to contain "more than hints of a truth that may mean large changes for politics, economics and law," and Follett therefore devoted the next three chapters of her book to elucidating psychology's emerging "truth."[16] In the early 1920s, six systems of psychology were influencing the work of American theorists and researchers. Two of these systems, structuralism and associationism, were no longer predominant, but the analytical methodologies they had spawned lived on in functionalism and other newer systems. Behaviorism, introduced just before World War I, gained immediate distinction and was destined to dominate American psychology for more than fifty years. And two other systems, Gestalt psychology and psychoanalysis, were claiming increasing numbers of adherents. Follett, characteristically, did not ally herself with a single school but freely borrowed from the various systems those ideas that seemed most relevant to her concern with the constructive uses of conflict.

Given the plethora of psychological systems operative in the early 1920s and the intensity of the disagreements among their proponents about the domain and methods appropriate to psychological research, Follett's decision to make psychology the centerpiece of her argument about how to foster "creative" experience may have caused her more than a few anxious moments. Follett and many of her closest friends, most notably the Cabots, were inclined to consider "experience" in philosophical rather than psychological terms. But experience, though it had long been the ultimate subject matter of philosophy, had traditionally been a backward-looking concept. In a 1915 critique of philosophizing as a quest for certainty, for absolute knowledge and eternal truths, John Dewey charged that traditionally the "registration of what has taken place, reference to precedent, is believed to be the essence of experience. Empiricism is conceived of as tied up to what has been, or is, 'given.' " But Dewey challenged this traditional view, contending instead that "experience in its vital form is experimental, an effort to change the given; it is characterized by projection, by reaching forward into the unknown; connexion with a future is its salient trait."[17]

Follett's rejection of the traditional philosophical position regarding experience is evident even in the title of her book. Early in her writing, she was leaning toward using "The Lamp of Experience," a title drawn from Patrick Henry's "Give me liberty or give me death" speech; in the end she adopted the more explicitly dynamic and forward-looking title, *Creative Experience*.[18] Experiencing, for Follett, requires active participation in events or activities, always in an effort to create something new. In her preface, she argues that what is needed today "is a keen, analytical, objective study of human relations. We preach 'compromise' as the apex of the ethical life, we laud the 'balance of power' as our political and international faith . . . But compromise sacrifices the integrity of the individual, and balance of power merely rearranges what already exists; it produces no new values . . . By adherence to such a creed we bind ourselves to equivalents, we do not seek the plusvalents of experience. If experience is to be progressive," Follett insists, "another principle of human association must be found."

Ascertaining such a principle, however, would require a commitment to investigating actual experience, and doing so would require methods characteristic neither of philosophers nor of political theorists. "We need," Follett writes, "to study not the 'conception' of a general will but concrete joint activity. We should, without disregarding whatever light the past has thrown on these questions, now look at men in their daily occupations at factory or store, at town meeting or congress, and see what we can learn . . . We should take our language too from the concrete daily happenings; the words we now use have nearly always ethical connotations which prejudge, which merely in themselves attribute praise or blame to individuals or groups or state."[19]

But even this sort of enlightened observation would not be sufficient to the task. Social experiments must be undertaken to "find out what *may* be, the possibilities now open to us." Follett sees in particular a tremendous need for participant-observers: "those who will try experiment after experiment and note results, experiments in making human interplay productive — in industry and business, in legislative committees and administrative commissions, in trade unions and shop committees and joint boards of control, in athletic committees and college faculties, in our families, in parliamentary cabinets and international conferences." Only then will it be possible to learn "how men can interact and coact better" — not just to secure already-existing ends but to "understand and so broaden their ends."[20] The object of Follett's new book, then, is to urge that we "seek a way by which desires may interweave, that we seek a method by which the full integrity of the individual shall be one with social progress, that we try to make our daily experience yield for us larger and ever larger spiritual values."[21]

The Meaning of Experience in the Systems of the "New Psychology"

Follett was writing *Creative Experience* at a moment when the concept of experience was at the center of a struggle for control of the "new psychology." On one side of this struggle was John B. Watson (1878–1958), the highly regarded founder of the psychological system of behaviorism in the years before World War I. Structuralists such as Wilhelm Wundt (1832–1920) and Cornell University's Edward B. Titchner (1867–1927) had investigated individual experience by asking their subjects to reflect on elementary conscious experiences and classify them into a system of "*sensations* which seem to come to us from outside — colors, tones, elementary tastes and skin sensations — and *feelings* which seem to belong to ourselves." Watson, however, explicitly denied the existence of mind and consciousness. Recognizing "no dividing line between man and brute," Watson insisted that the only appropriate source of psychological data is behavior, whether verbal or nonverbal; and behavior, being "composed *entirely* of glandular *secretions* and muscular *movements* . . . is reducible ultimately to physiochemical processes." Watson furthermore argued for the existence of a strict cause and effect determinism in behavior, with every response having some kind of stimulus and every effective stimulus eliciting some sort of immediate response.[22]

The other contender in the struggle for preeminence in the "new psychology" was Gestalt theory, a system developing in Germany almost at the same moment as behaviorism was being introduced in America. Max Wertheimer (1880–1943) and his associates, Wolfgang Köhler (1887–1967) and Kurt Koffka (1886–1941), also objected to the artificiality of the analysis practiced by the older psychologies, particularly the structuralists' study of consciousness.[23] For example, structuralists had commonly treated the kind of "apparent movement" one sees in motion pictures "as the experience of a succession of states of rest." But the Gestaltists maintained that such an analysis captured nothing of the essential character of movement. The real subject matter of psychology must be found "at the level of experience itself" — in this case movement, not states of rest.[24] There was a wholeness in the Gestaltists' conception of experience that the older psychologies did not reflect. This contention — that wholes exist and "lose much of their identity and importance when they are analyzed into parts" — was anticipated by William James in his 1890 *Principles of Psychology,* a work to which Follett would often refer. James rejected the atomistic view of consciousness and chose, instead, to view it as a continuously flowing stream: "The traditional psychologist talks like one who would say a river consists of nothing but pailsful, spoonsful, quartpotsful, barrelsful, and other moulded forms of water. Even were the pails and the pots all actually standing in the stream, still between them the free water would continue to flow."[25]

In the 1920s, only Gestalt theory seemed capable of posing a genuine challenge to the preeminence of behaviorism in American psychology. It was the Gestaltists who argued that the machine model implicit in behaviorism as well as the traditional systems was wrong. "Relations among parts are conditioned by the properties of the parts, and are not empty hookups or stringlike connections such as are implied by use of the words 'plus' or 'and.' " Simple mental associations exist, the Gestaltists admitted, such as when one person remembers another's telephone number, but this form of relationship was atypical. "What usually happens . . . is a much more dynamic unfolding of events such that the nature of the things connected is at least in part affected by the connection and in turn affects the connection."[26]

Follett surely knew that the prominence she had given to the concept of experience in the title of her book would predispose some to welcome and others summarily to reject her analysis. The behaviorists, in their rejection of the relevance of consciousness, had either professed little interest in the concept of experience or objected vigorously to its study. On the other hand, the Gestaltists believed that the concept captured something essential to their work.[27] But believing that "the correlation of the results of entirely independent observation in different fields" might be valuable for all concerned, and appreciating the "experimental verification which psychology is bringing to certain philosophical conceptions," Follett characteristically immersed herself in a study of the various psychological systems and then forged ahead.[28]

Holt's Resolution of the Debate over the Appropriate Domain of Psychology

In her discussion of the contributions of recent psychological research, Follett referred to the work of functionalist, behaviorist, Gestaltist, and psychoanalytic theorists and acknowledged her indebtedness to such thinkers as William James, John B. Watson, Sigmund Freud, and the German Gestaltists; but it was the work of the Harvard neorealist philosopher and psychologist Edwin Bissell Holt (1873–1946) that provided the most immediate stimulus to her thinking.[29] Writing in the *Journal of Philosophy, Psychology and Scientific Methods* in 1915, Holt claimed to have worked out a resolution to the disciplinary debate over the appropriate domain of psychology — consciousness versus behavior. Holt agreed with the behaviorists that human psychology must follow the lead of animal psychology in studying behavior and, further, accepted the notion that behavior consists of reflex activities; nonetheless, he rejected the behaviorist claim that all human behavior can be reduced to reflex elements, conditioned reflexes, and simple neural processes. Instead, Holt saw behavior as existing in complex, *organized* forms that associationists and behaviorists, in their general failure to account for human purposes, had so far ignored.[30]

How could the behaviorists account for the purposiveness of human behavior without resorting to the sort of metaphysical "consciousness" characteristic of earlier psychological systems? According to Holt, the behaviorists must heed the functionalists' admonition that there is only one "pertinent, scientific" question, namely, "What is this organism doing?" By putting the question in this macro rather than molecular way, behaviorists would be constrained to "keep the man whole . . . and to study his movements until we have discovered *exactly what* he is doing, that is, until we have found that object, situation, process (or perhaps merely that relation) of which his behavior is a *constant function*." In accepting the functionalists' commitment to studying the "whole" person, it was also necessary, Holt argued, to examine the person's relation to the environment. Behavior, Holt insisted, differs from reflex action precisely because the organism is responding to something *outside* itself: "in order to understand what the organism is doing, you will just *miss* the essential point if you look inside the organism. For the organism, while a very interesting mechanism in itself, is one whose movements turn on objects outside of itself, much as the orbit of the earth turns upon the sun; and these external, and sometimes very distant, objects are as much *constituents* of the behavior process as is the organism which does the turning. It is this *pivotal outer object*, the object of specific response, which seems to me to have been overneglected."[31]

Holt was committed to studying observable behavior rather than introspecting a metaphysical consciousness, as was done in the more traditional systems of psychology. However, he "did not imply that human beings were not conscious" — merely that we could only observe behavior and that consciousness as a concept would be useful only if defined as a dimension of behavior. "Consciousness," Holt therefore asserted, "is not a substance but a relation — the relation between the living organism and the environment to which it specifically responds; of which its behavior is found to be this or that constant function; or, in other words, to which its purposes refer."[32]

Even more provocative than Holt's reconceptualization of the debate between behavior and consciousness was his effort in his 1915 book, *The Freudian Wish and Its Place in Ethics,* to join his ideas with those of Sigmund Freud. Defining the Freudian notion of "wish" as "a course of action which the living body executes or is prepared to execute with regard to some object or some fact of its environment," Holt drew one step closer to accounting for consciousness and human purpose in behavioral terms. "We have seen that the wish is purpose embodied in the mechanism of a living organism, that it is necessarily a wish about, or a purpose regarding, some feature of the environment; so that a total situation comprising *both organism and environment* is always involved. We have seen that will, thought, and the object of knowledge are all integral and inseparable parts of this total situation. Inseparable because, if organism and environment are sundered, the cognitive relation is dissolved, and merely matter remains; precisely as only water remains when a rainbow is pulled apart. Mind is a relation and not a substance."[33]

Holt's identification of the Freudian "wish" with his own notion of the "specific response relation" allowed him to use Freud's accounts of the suppression of wishes in dreams, humor, and slips of the tongue and pen to explain how various wishes (or specific responses) interact in human behavior. As Holt put it, the individual, living in a complex, precarious environment and suffering from lack of knowledge about how best to function in that environment, often seeks to cope by suppressing certain wishes. It is only by expanding individual experience and better utilizing it to integrate seemingly antagonistic wishes that the individual learns to respond harmoniously to its environment.[34] It is experience, Holt wrote, that allows us to go beyond the "anomalies, contradictions, perplexities" we are presented with in our first contact with environmental objects, to "discriminate further particulars within these objects" and thus makes possible "coherent, integrated conduct." Unlike suppression, this integrative way of meeting a dilemma "consists in a free play of *both* the involved sets of tendencies, whereby they *meet* each other, and a line of conduct emerges which is dictated by *both* sets of motives together, and which embodies all that was not downright antagonistic in the two. This sounds like compromise, whereas its mechanism is utterly different. And it were best called reconciliation or resolution."[35] Evidence of this sort of integration of wishes or specific responses seemed to Holt to provide further justification for rejecting the claim that behavior consists merely of simple reflex responses to immediate stimuli. Indeed, "any correlation between [behavior] and the stimuli which are immediately affecting the organism becomes increasingly remote, so that even in fairly simple cases it can no longer be demonstrated."[36]

Holt's theorizing provided the primary though scarcely the sole reference point in Follett's articulation of three principal contributions of recent psychological research: circular response, integrative behavior, and the total situation.[37]

Circular Response

Addressing first the notion of *circular response,* Follett writes that both the work of the Oxford physiologist Charles S. Sherrington and Edwin Holt's review of the reflex arc research have demonstrated that "when a muscle contracts, the sense organ in that muscle is stimulated so that there is an almost simultaneous afferent nerve impulse from the muscle back to the centre, and thus a circular reflex is established. Hence, the contraction of the muscle is only in a certain sense 'caused' by the stimulus; that very muscular activity is itself in part producing the stimulus which 'causes' the muscular activity." Follett has no intention of trying "to establish any exact parallel between the physiological circular reflex and circular response as seen by the students of social research," but she feels quite certain that a similar phenomenon is operating in human relations. "Through circular response, we are creating each other all the time . . . I never react to you but to you-plus-me; or to be more accurate, it is I-plus-you reacting to you-plus-me. 'I' can never influence 'you' because you have already influenced me; that is, in the very process of meeting, by the very process of meeting, we both become something different. It begins even before we meet, in the anticipation of meeting . . . On physiological, psychological and social levels the law holds good: response is always to a relating."[38]

Follett derives from this "law" three fundamental principles that must guide the "study of social situations: (1) that my response is not to a rigid, static environment, but to a changing environment; (2) to an environment which is changing because of the activity between it and me; (3) that function may be continuously modified by itself, that is, the activity of the boy going to school may change the activity of the boy going to school . . . functional relating has always a plus value."[39] Furthermore, we must change our whole notion of cause and effect in the study of social situations, for it is not the case that stimulus is cause and response the effect; these are merely "ways of describing certain moments in the situation when we look at those moments apart from the total process."[40] Thus, it is imperative that we "in the social sciences develop methods for watching varying activities in their relatings to other varying activities. We cannot watch the strikers and *then* the mill-owners. We cannot watch France and *then* Germany. We all know that the action of the mill-owners is changing daily the action of the strikers, that the action of the strikers is affecting daily that of the mill-owners; but beyond this is the more subtle point I am trying to emphasize here, that the activity between mill-owners and strikers is changing the activity of mill-owners, of strikers . . . The interweaving which is changing both factors and creating constantly new situations should be the study of the student of the social sciences."[41]

No doubt influenced by Holt's use of mathematics in *The Concept of Consciousness* (1914), Follett was intrigued by how the mathematical concept of "function" and, in particular, the language of calculus might be used to conceptualize the relating of changing phenomena, and thereby "open up whole reaches of thought for us."[42] Seeming to anticipate the contribution that analysis of sets of differential equations would make to modern multivariate analysis, Follett found the lexicon of differential equations personally "stimulating." At the same time, however, she recognized the difficulties that this complex, dynamic way of thinking could pose, noting that an unnamed professor of philosophy had told her that "it made him dizzy to talk with me because, he says, he wishes always to compare varying things with something stationary."[43] The discomfort of her fellow philosopher, however understandable, still struck Follett as odd, for she saw herself as merely articulating one of the oldest conceptions of philosophy — the unity of experience; all that is different is the use of new language drawn from different fields and different levels of research. If you wish, Follett tells us, you can tear experience to pieces "and find subject and object, stimulus and response, or — you can refuse to; you can claim the right to see it as a rational interplay of forces, as the functioning of a self-creating coherence."[44]

Integrative Behavior and the Total Situation

Turning to the concepts of *integrative behavior* and the *total situation*, Follett relies heavily on Holt's rejection of the claim of associationists and many behaviorists that behavior is governed solely by the immediate stimulus.[45] While this might be true of simple reflexes, Holt wrote, "the development from reflex action to highly organized behavior is one in which the correlation between stimulus and organism becomes less and less direct." Follett, too, had seen this recession of the immediate stimulus operating, in her case at the social level. "Both psychologist and sociologist," she tells us, "note that as the number of integral reflexes involved in behavior increases, the immediate stimulus recedes further and further from view as the significant factor. The stimulus becomes the total situation of which the total behavior is a function."[46] It is the task of the sociologist to consider in each particular case under investigation "how far the person or persons are acting from present stimuli and how far from action patterns already existing," the latter of course also being the product of integrations.[47]

Translating what she has learned from Holt to the level of social psychology, Follett outlines the major elements involved in creating the total, evolving situation: "1. Behavior is both internally and externally conditioned. 2. Behavior is a function of the interweaving between activity of organism and activity of environment, that is, response is to a relating. 3. By this interlocking activity individual and situation each is creating itself anew. 4. Thus relating themselves anew. 5. Thus giving us the evolving situation."[48]

Reconceptualizing the Concept of Purpose

Follett's rejection of the idea that behavior is governed solely by the immediate stimulus has important implications for the notion of purpose, a subject she had already addressed from a philosophical perspective in *The New State*. Many psychologists, when talking about purpose, use the expression "striving toward some goal," but their emphasis on goals, Follett insists, is misplaced. Perhaps thinking of her own lifelong striving for personal growth in social relations, she writes: "we can see in our own lives that the urge is always the lack; the goal changes as we try one means after another of meeting that lack."[49]

Two other mistakes in regard to purpose also seem to be made repeatedly: "we try to substitute an intellectualistic purpose for that involved in the situation, or, when the purpose appears from out [of] the activity, we think, by some strange mental legerdemain, that that was the purpose which had been actuating us all along." We also suffer, Follett writes, from our tendency to cling tenaciously to preconceived purposes even though it would be far more constructive to give them up. Using a story gleaned from her experiences in the woodlands and fields surrounding the house at Putney, Follett offers a moral for human relationships: "Last summer I noticed a strange plant in our pasture. I had no picture in my mind of what flower or fruit it would bear, but I . . . dug around it and opened the soil that the rain might fall on its roots, I cleared out the thistles with which it was entangled so that it might have room to spread, I cut down the undergrowth of small maples near so that it could get the sun. In other words, I simply freed it. Every friendship which is not treated in this way will surely suffer; no human relation should serve an anticipatory purpose. Every relation should be a freeing relation with the 'purpose' evolving. This is the truth underneath the admonition that we should not pray for specific things."[50]

Not only does Follett believe we should behave as though purpose is continually evolving; we are simply inaccurate if we assume anything else. Political leaders, for example, can no more "persuade" people to adopt purposes than the legal order can "assign" them; both purposes and ideals are found only "in the so-far integrated behavior of people." Similarly, in the business world, the decision of some firms to cooperate with each other rather than to compete "did not come about by emulating the bees and the beavers, as some of the biologists exhort us to do. One by one the integrations are made, as environment changes, and the behavior patterns constructed."[51]

The impetus of this dynamic, creative way of thinking, Follett insists, is desperately needed by politics, industry, and the law. "Our older social philosophy gave us the pernicious theories of the balance of power between nations, of adjustment between capital and labor. It gave us always equivalents; our more recent thinking shows us how to create plusvalents."[52]

Always searching out the implications of her thinking for practice in society, Follett examines two words that had come into common use in the law, economics, and sociology: *adjustment* and *verifying*. Spawned by the functionalists, these two terms had come to signify that the function of experience is to facilitate adjustment to the environment and to verify solutions to problem situations. Convinced that neither term adequately captured the "creative" function of experience so essential to constructive conflict, Follett devotes two chapters to a discussion of their limitations.

Limitations of "Adjustment"

Many discussions of adjustment to the environment, Follett writes, contain "on the one hand an implied rigidity of environment and on the other an environment which can and must be 'mastered' . . . Neither is true."[53] Wondering whether the popularity of the idea of conquering nature comes from "the urge to power," Follett bemoans our tendency to think of "our surroundings as 'adverse,'" to think that we have to wrest what we want from nature. For example, having read that the psychoanalyst Edward J. Kempf defined behavior as "wishes opposed by the resistance of the environment," Follett wishes to substitute "confronting the activity of the environment." This alternative has the virtue of not making an "anticipatory judgment; there may be opposition, there may be resistance, but this definition leaves it possible for us to wait until we find them. This would make a great change in the social sciences. Here we should have not necessarily the opposing, but the confronting, of interests. This confronting would make apparent many incompatibilities of interests, but does not judge the case beforehand as to what shall be done about it. Confront does not mean combat. In other words, it leaves the possibility of integrating as the method of the meeting of the difference."[54]

The common conception of adjustment, Follett continues, is deficient in numerous other ways. Not only is the environment more complex and dynamic than many conceptions of adjustment allow, but we forget that we respond to internal as well as external stimuli, and "that all stored-stimuli are themselves the result of previous responses, that every internal mechanism has incorporated environment." We must be concerned, therefore, not only with the present situation but with "how far the submerged experience of the past enters into the present." Watson and the other behaviorists, in defining behavior merely as "the integrated response of muscles and glands," seemed to Follett to fail to emphasize sufficiently the importance to behavior of the complex internal stimuli that have resulted from previous experience. And perhaps mindful of the profound impact that her own troubled childhood environment had on her sense of self, Follett charges that the Freudians, too, despite their apparent commitment to uncovering the dynamics by which the past acts on the present, have much to learn: "Properly on his guard against the rationalization of purpose in terms of overt consequence, [the Freudian] has not always thought sufficiently in terms of the *situation* of the past, but has often been more concerned with the *self* of the past. The importance which the *Gestalt* theory has given to the total situation raises the question whether there should not be some fresh scrutiny of Freudian conceptions about the way in which situations of the past enter as submerged experience into the situations of the present . . . The psychiatrist oversimplifies, therefore, when he is unduly occupied with the subjective aspects of the past."[55]

In sum, then, few who advocate "adjustment" seem to Follett to appreciate its dynamic, often "progressive" nature, to realize that "each response or 'functional adjustment' makes the organism capable of response to a more comprehensive environment." Nor do they sufficiently appreciate that organism and environment do not merely "act on" each other, or reciprocally relate, as the work of the biologists was making clear; the organism also responds to the relation between itself and the environment. "Any analysis of society which does not take into account that response is to a relating," Follett asserts, "gives us the determinism of the last century." The term *socialization,* for example, "which people speak of as a supreme virtue, is often a pure crowd idea, the crowd trying to preserve itself as it is. Harmony between the individual and the social order must mean changes in both individual and the social order, yet not arbitrary changes, but changes which will come about by a deeper understanding of that relation."[56]

Limitations of "Verifying"

Follett turns next to "verifying," a concept central to the pragmatism of James and Dewey. According to Dewey's formulation, human beings act primarily in accordance with established habits, or what we might today call attitudes, which have largely been determined by the environment. Periodically, however, individuals confront situations that are felt to be problematic, situations in which the habitual response does not seem suitable. To resolve this problem, the individual engages in a process of reflective thinking, the aim of which is to change the conditions in the cultural or physical environment that gave rise to the problem.

Verifying is the final stage of this process of reflective thinking. Confronted with a problem or difficulty, the individual first defines its parameters by using observation and analysis. Next, the individual creates hypotheses about possible solutions and imagines the consequences of their implementation. Finally, the individual seeks to verify these hypotheses, undertaking the additional observations or experiments that lead the individual to accept or reject a proposed solution.

Although Follett grants that "the main process of life is testing, verifying, comparing," she sees numerous errors in the pragmatists' idea of how this process works. Most important is what she calls the fallacy of preconceived purpose, for verification as it is usually described requires you to "decide on the purpose before you can decide on the validity of the verification." The separation of thinking and doing implied in this process seems to Follett a grave error, for it substitutes a linear fiction for the creative reality of circular response. "We do not think, and do, and think again, but the thinking is bound up in the doing . . . activity does not carry on the activity which produced it, it generates new energy."[57]

Follett also objects to the pragmatists' contention that hypotheses, which they consider merely principles with which to experiment, are simply discarded when rejected. Arguing from recent psychology, Follett contends that such hypotheses can never be fully discarded. "If we 'hold' a thought long enough to test it, it has become a part of the organism, of the internal mechanism. I am not saying that therefore we shall always have to 'hold' it, but only that something has happened, a very complex process has gone on, so that we can never discard that thought in the sense of things being for us as if we had never held it . . . In our own individual lives this sometimes seems one of the hardest laws to reconcile ourselves to, and yet it is the very heart of the truth in regard to individual as well as social progress, and I suppose the degree in which we accept it indicates in large part our capacity for growth."[58]

Finally, and perhaps most important in Follett's view, the pragmatists fail to remember in their formulation of verification that neither the things being compared nor the relation between them is fixed. "When we go to a conference," Follett reminds us, "we have to compare the idea we bring to it not with the idea we 'find' there, but with what is being developed there. The employer may meet his workmen expecting to find out what they have been thinking about things. He can never discover that! For as soon as he meets them, and partly by the very fact of his meeting them, a different situation has arisen. When you get to a situation, it becomes what it was plus you; you are responding to the situation plus yourself, that is, to the relation between it and yourself." In other words, not only does life never stop long enough for us to "test" it, but also we cannot get outside life to view it. "Not to understand this," Follett concludes, "is the onlooker fallacy: you cannot see experience without being a part of it."[59]

An Alternative to the Sterile Empiricism of the Pragmatists

Not only did "adjustment" and "verifying" fail to capture the creative nature of experience, but Follett also found stultifying the pragmatists' wholesale disparagement of the use of concepts. It was true that the pragmatists had performed a great service by attacking such universals as "the State" and "the Individual," but their once-admirable "diatribes against the conceptual" seemed to her to have degenerated into a sterile empiricism: "To test and discard, to test and verify? Life is not as simple as that, or as 'scientific' either. Life is an art. Life . . . is an endless interplay. And at this moment when we are urged so constantly to look at facts, the objective situation, the concrete circumstance, the actual event, it is especially necessary that we learn how to connect the conceptual and perceptual planes, how to let every fact contribute to those principles which by use again in the factual world become again transformed, and thus man grows — always through his activity."[60]

Echoes of the concern that Follett expressed in 1924 would resound fifty years later in the claims of critics that social science had come to overemphasize "empiricism at the expense of conceptualization or fact at the expense of ideas." Rom Harré and Paul F. Secord, for example, contended in *The Explanation of Social Behavior* (1972) that many social scientists "are acting as if observation and experiment *by themselves* can create a science." As they saw it, "This misplaced emphasis stems from an approach to science via logical positivism, with its stress on operational definition and its relegation of theory to a merely organizational role . . . This state of affairs obtains because psychologists, by and large, still believe that the way to clarify concepts is to invent experimental operations and to do experiments. They overlook the fact that such procedures, if they are to be used at all, have still to be linked up with social situations outside the laboratory, situations that are described by the subtle and enormously refined terms and concepts of ordinary language."[61]

Not once during her multifaceted examination of the deficiencies of pragmatism does Follett mention John Dewey by name. But her private correspondence leaves little doubt that Dewey was one of the primary targets of her critique. Writing to Viscount R. B. Haldane, the English statesman and philosopher who had written an introduction to the English edition of Follett's *New State* and critiqued *Creative Experience* before its publication, Follett makes clear her sentiments about Dewey. "Our young men have swallowed Dewey whole in the most deplorable way," an exasperated Follett confides. "In the first place he is not original (I have never got a single idea from Dewey) and in the second place he is — all that you have shown so well & so convincingly. I cannot understand his vogue in America." Grateful to find a critique of Dewey's *Human Nature and Conduct* (1922) prominently featured in Haldane's recently published book, *Human Experience* (1925), Follett is lavish in her praise. "It seems to me that this book is of greater value than any you have written. In this way that for many who still think in terms of idealism vs. realism, for those also who do not see Dewey's limitations, moreover for some of us who have been seeking out for something like this but have not been able to grasp it — you have done an inestimable service."[62]

At first glance, Follett's irritation with Dewey might seem curious, for they shared much intellectual ground. Each vigorously argued against the artificial dualism of self and other. Each firmly rejected absolutes in ethics, holding instead that values are relative to changing experience. Each argued against social control and governance by elites — instead believing fervently in participatory democracy as the ethical ideal toward which American society should strive. Each saw experience as profoundly creative, as directed toward the future rather than the past. Each saw education as a lever of social change. And each saw the scientific investigations of the emerging field of social psychology as holding great potential for the betterment of society. But despite this impressive list of shared commitments, Follett's letter to Haldane made it clear that John Dewey was not one of her intellectual heroes.[63]

Convinced that the rational problem-solving process central to pragmatism is too simplistic, too linear, and too detached from social relations to serve as a guide to truly "creative experiencing," Follett proposed an alternative.[64] Experience, she believed, becomes creative when differing interests meet and confront one another through a process of integration. This notion would become the core of her social philosophy.

The Virtues of Integration

As she begins her discussion of integrating, Follett acknowledges that we often feel admiration for those who hold steadfastly to a position, perhaps because they seem to display a kind of "moral self-preservation." Still, for her the real question is "Do we want to preserve that self or grow a bigger self? The progress of individual or race is by integration. The biological law is growth by the continuous integration of simple, specific responses; in the same way do we build up our characters by uniting diverse tendencies into new action patterns; social progress follows exactly the same law . . . We must guard against Mill's 'deep slumber of a decided opinion.' Our 'opponents' are our co-creators, for they have something to give which we have not. The basis of all coöperative activity is integrated diversity."[65]

Some of Follett's contemporaries believed that differences would be absorbed automatically if only opportunities were presented for increased cooperation and social contact. Follett is less sanguine. "When men come together to do something, the first thing that is obvious is their differences; the question then is what to do about it."[66] Others among her contemporaries who hoped to reconcile differences without domination had become avid advocates of compromise, saying that "it shows the humble heart." "What nonsense," Follett huffs. "In the first place it doesn't, as you will find if you watch compromise; in the second place, that kind of humility, if it existed, would not be worth much. Humility needs to be defined: it is merely never claiming any more than belongs to me in any way whatever; it rests on the ability to see clearly what does belong to me. Thus do we maintain our integrity."[67] Those who advocated compromise also seemed to Follett to be ignoring what the Freudians had revealed about the damaging effects of the suppression of desire: "for compromise is suppression, and as we have been shown that a suppressed impulse in the individual will be his undoing later, so we see again and again that what has been suppressed in the compromises of politics or labor disputes crops up anew to bring more disastrous results."[68]

Some who recognized the limitations of compromise continued nevertheless to promote it as a method of resolving conflict because, Follett suspected, they thought of individuals and their interests as static, incapable of change. "If the self with its purpose and its will is even for a moment a finished product," Follett admits, "then of course the only way to get a common will is through compromise. But the truth is that the self is always in flux, weaving itself and again weaving itself."[69] Indeed, it is "through an interpenetrating of understanding [that] the quality of one's own thinking is changed; we are sensitized to an appreciation of other values. By not interpenetrating, by simply lining up values and conceding some for the sake of getting the agreement necessary for action, our thinking stays just where is was. In integration all the overtones of value are utilized."[70]

Follett readily admits that not all differences can be integrated, but she feels certain that "there are fewer irreconcilable activities than we at present think, although it often takes ingenuity, a 'creative intelligence,' to find the integration."[71] Further, Follett had come to see that merely thinking about the problem was not always the best means to an integrative solution: "life processes integrate faster than our minds can integrate them." Her friend and colleague Alfred D. Sheffield was finding something similar in his studies of group discussion. Sheffield, Follett writes, had noted "how in controversy the real consensus takes place subterraneously in the motor [concrete behavioral] activity of the controversy, while the intellectual form of the controversy must proceed in terms of language and does not keep pace with the real integration."[72] Put simply, differences that conversations and discussions fail to resolve can sometimes be integrated through actual practice. Indeed, the research of the behaviorists had already persuaded Follett that "integration, the resolution of conflict, the harmonizing of difference, must take place on the motor level, not on the intellectual level . . . Genuine integration occurs in the sphere of activities, and not of ideas or wills. Hence the present aim of our international conferences is wrong; the aim should be not intellectual agreement alone, but to provide opportunities for actual agreement through the activities of the nations involved . . . Concepts can never be presented to me merely, they must be knitted into the structure of my being, and this can be done only through my own activity."[73]

The Method of Integration

Turning to the method of integration, Follett does not pretend to have fully worked out the process. This, she acknowledges, would require years of observation and analysis of industrial, international, and personal controversies — and much experimentation.[74] She does, however, introduce two key elements of that method in *Creative Experience*.

The first step in integration "is to break up wholes: to analyze, differentiate and discriminate."[75] In doing so, it is crucial that we carefully examine our symbols. "When you label a man a farmer or an artisan and then treat him as if his action tendencies were all farmer or artisan, you make a grave mistake." "Labor" and "capital," too, are imaginary wholes that must be broken up before capital and labor are able to cooperate.[76] Similarly, one must discover the meaning behind the demands that parties issue in the early stages of a conflict. Demands, Follett reminds us, never tell the whole story. Indeed, an integrative solution to conflict often can be found only if the parties are willing to probe painstakingly beneath the surface of each other's demands: "The behavioristic question, 'What is the individual really doing?' I have changed to, What does the individual really want? — the same question in another form . . . In all wage controversies this is important. We can say, at the very least, that the workman does not 'really want' wages above the point that will keep the factory open; that the employer does not 'really want' wages low enough seriously to impair the productive power of the workman. The first question is then always: What is the demand a symbol of?"[77]

Another common failure in analyzing conflict situations appears when parties to a conflict refuse to divide the matter before them into its various parts. Their failure to do so often means that "either the disputants are discussing a vague and non-existent whole, or else they are discussing different parts of the questions without knowing that they are doing so." It would be far more profitable, Follett had learned from her experience on minimum wage boards, if the disputants would "first agree to differentiate the question into its parts and then to take them up one by one," perhaps even voting as they went along.[78]

A second, equally important component of the method of integration introduced in *Creative Experience* involves what Follett calls the "revaluation" of interests. This occurs when "the confronting of diverse interests each claiming right of way leads us to evaluate our interests, and valuation often is evolved into revaluation."[79] Follett warns that revaluation does not occur "on the mere viewing of [competing] interests: it is more than a process of inspection, introspection or retrospection. The realizing of a second value involves activities which change my attitude towards the first value. The evaluation of my interest changes as I *do* things."[80]

Follett as yet had only an incomplete notion of the method of integration, but she felt certain, nevertheless, that "the psychology of integration gives us hints of a new conception of power."[81] It is to this new conception of power that she next turned and, in so doing, produced for students of organizations one of the seminal sections of *Creative Experience*.

Political scientists, economists, applied psychologists, and even educators seemed to Follett to be consumed with one of two goals with regard to power: they wish either to balance power or to gain power over others. Indeed, Follett tells us, "the paradox of American democracy has been that its slogan of equal opportunity has meant, often, equal opportunity to get power over your fellows."[82]

Power-With versus Power-Over

Follett did not oppose either the acquisition of power or its use. That "would be abolishing life itself." But the method of integration suggested a new way of thinking about power. "The power of the strong," she writes, "is not to be used to conquer the weaker: this means for the conquerors activity which is not legitimately based, which will therefore have disastrous consequences later; and for the conquered, repression."[83] Power-over, nevertheless, "is resorted to time without number," Follett tells us, "because people will not wait for the slower process of education. We can see this every day in the countless meetings held to persuade people of this or that. A man said to me, 'You are never going to get people to accept government ownership or free trade by your discussion meetings,' but I do not want people to accept government ownership or free trade — that is power-over. Yet is seems impossible to convince the 'reformers' of this. Many people, confident that their object is for the good of society, are willing to take measures to attain it which are essentially coercive."[84]

Deploring the coercive element of "power-over," Follett presents an alternative, using one of her simple but remarkably lucid illustrations to demonstrate how the integrating of desires can create "power-with." This passage from *Creative Experience* has become quite famous through its use (in a slightly modified version, without attribution) in Roger Fisher and William Ury's highly regarded book on negotiation, *Getting to Yes:* "In the library today, in one of the smaller rooms, someone wanted the window open, I wanted it shut. We opened the window in the next room where no one was sitting. This was not a compromise because there was no lopping off of desire; we both got what we really wanted. For I did not want a closed room, I simply did not want the north wind to blow directly on me; likewise the other occupant did not want that particular window open, he simply wanted more air in the room. Therefore, by the process I gave in the last chapter — breaking up wholes, finding out what we really wanted — an integration was possible without resorting to power. By reducing the area of irreconcilable controversy, you reduce the area of arbitrary power."[85] Although Follett writes here that "integration was possible without resorting to power," she might more properly have said that the integration of desires was accomplished without resorting to power-*over*. As early as her 1896 book on the Speakership, Follett had been a strong advocate of both the acquisition of power and its use. As Follett sees it, "the more power any one has the better, if we mean by power integrated control."[86]

In asserting to friends and colleagues that power-*with* was "what democracy should mean in politics or industry," Follett repeatedly found herself questioned about whether hers was a "conservative or a radical point of view." "It is both," Follett writes; "it is conservative because it is concerned with only *actual* power, and it takes time and education and training to develop that; it cannot be got by revolution, it involves a process and a slow process; it is concerned with neither granting power nor grabbing power but with evolving power. At the same time it is a radical view because opportunity must be given for this process."[87]

Power-With in a Participatory Democracy

Always concerned with the implications of her thinking for the creation of a truly democratic society, Follett next explored how her distinction between power-over and power-with might bear on the question of the appropriate role of the expert in a democracy. Many of her contemporaries, including Herbert Croly and Walter Lippmann, had urged the creation of governmental structures and processes in which policy experts would recommend and the people and their representatives would consent. Others, such as John Dewey, had sought to empower the average citizen, convinced that it was "not 'right' for the few to decide and the many to assent." But to Follett's way of thinking, this issue was not so much a moral question as a practical one. As she puts it, consent is not wrong; it is simply "an impossibility." The new psychological research had convinced her that "we cannot really carry out the will of another, for we can use only our own behavior patterns. If we consent to the will of the expert or administrative official, it is still the will of expert or official; the people's will can be found only in their motor mechanisms or habit systems."[88] This being true, efforts directed at perfecting mechanisms of voting and representation are sadly mistaken. Participation must "take place further back, in the activity from which the policies emerge."[89] "In the ballot-box," Follett writes, "there is no confronting difference, hence no possibility of integrating, hence no creating; self-government is a creative process and nothing else. Thus the suggestion box of the modern factory is not a democratic device although often so-called. Nor is a factory democratically organized when questions are put formally to a committee of workmen and a Yes or No vote taken. Democracy does not register various opinions; it is an attempt to create unity."[90]

Follett was not one to glorify "the people" or "public opinion," but in an era that venerated the supposed wisdom of experts, not even John Dewey could rival her faith in the potential of an active participant electorate. Our goal, Follett urged, should be "to maintain vigor and creativeness in the thinking of everybody, not merely of chosen spirits." Indeed, the "problem of democracy is how to make our daily life creative. People talk of the apathy of the average citizen, but there is really no such thing. Every man has *his* interest; at those points his attention can be enlisted. At those points he can be got to take an experimental attitude toward experience. The result will not be a mere satisfaction of wants — that alone would be a somewhat crude aim — but the emerging of ever finer and finer wants. The lamp of experience is both to illumine our way and to guide us further into new paths." "We want nothing from the people but their experience," Follett continues, "but emphatically we want that. Reason, wisdom, emerge from our daily activities . . . Public opinion must be built up from concrete existence, from the perceptual level."[91]

How might this best be done? Not by having impassioned speakers address large crowds in lecture halls. Experiments must be tried in more intimate and interactive venues. "I believe so wholly in decentralization," Follett writes, "that I dread to think we may lose its fruits unless we are basing that decentralization not on mere changes in structure but on vital modes of association . . . our hope for the future lies not in increasing institutions but in improving process."[92]

In particular, Follett encourages the development of "experience meetings," in which the subject under consideration would be presented "in such a way as to show clearly its relation to all our daily lives. This is important and usually neglected," Follett notes. "I have never heard anyone tell people the actual difference in their own lives a League of Nations might make." Each person attending such a meeting would be asked to search his or her own experience for anything that would "throw light on the question." This process might over time encourage us to "begin to observe and analyze our experience much more carefully than we do at present; it is almost wholly insignificant to us now as having social value." Perhaps this sort of careful examination would even encourage us to "take an experimental attitude toward our experience, and have many experiments to report with reasons for their success or failure, and suggestions as to what direction new experiments should take." Finally, Follett hopes that efforts would be made at such meetings "to see if we could unite our various experiences, one with the other and with the material provided by the expert. The material of the expert would always thus be thrown into the situation, not put up for acceptance or rejection."[93]

Follett recognized that many obstacles would have to be overcome in order to create true participation, whether in government, business, or voluntary associations. She encouraged her readers to experiment with less-hierarchical structures and to learn to revalue their own interests while confronting the interests of others. She urged executives of organizations to find better methods of presenting prospective policies so that others would not be forced to take "a for or against attitude." And she cautioned labor unions and cooperatives about the dangers of creating an executive body that acquired "a solidarity of its own" and drifted apart "from the rank and file which created it."[94]

The Value of Diversity

Follett concludes *Creative Experience* with some of her most stirring rhetoric. Mindful that "thinker after thinker is trying to find some way to get rid of conflict," she finds it deeply troubling that what "people often mean by

getting rid of conflict is getting rid of diversity." It is "of the utmost importance," Follett emphasizes, "that these should not be considered the same. We
may wish to abolish conflict but we cannot get rid of diversity. We must face
life as it is and understand that diversity is its most essential feature . . . fear of
difference is dread of life itself."[95]

What Follett tried to show in *Creative Experience* "is that the social process
may be conceived either as the opposing and battle of desires with the victory
of one over the other, or as the confronting and integrating of desires. The
former means non-freedom for both sides, the defeated bound to the victor,
the victor bound to the false situation thus created — both bound. The latter
means a freeing for both sides and increased total power or increased capacity
in the world . . . We seek a richly diversified experience where every difference
strengthens and reinforces the other. Through the interpenetrating of spirit
and spirit, differences are conserved, accentuated and reconciled in the greater
life which is the issue. Each remains forever himself that thereby the larger
activity may be enriched and in its refluence, reinforce him. The activity of co-
creating is the core of democracy, the essence of citizenship, the condition of
world-citizenship."[96]

The essence of experience then, as Follett sees it, is "reciprocal freeing."
"All human intercourse," she proclaims, "should be the evocation by each
from the other of new forms undreamed of before, and all intercourse that is
not evocation should be eschewed. Release, evocation — evocation by release,
release by evocation — this is the fundamental law of the universe. The test
of the validity of any social process is whether this is taking place — between
one and another, between capital and labor, between nation and nation . . . To
free the energies of the human spirit is the high potentiality of all human
association."[97]

"No reform will be successful," Follett warns, "which tries to circumvent
life instead of facing it. I believe in no happy (or unhappy) land where expert
or leader can overcome diversity. I believe in no shadow country where vicar-
ious experience can take the place of our own experience. I see no golden age
in the past or in the future, but I believe in the possibilities of human effort, of
disciplined effort, in truth in its Anglo-Saxon meaning (tryw) of faithfulness,
and in the essence of relation from the amoeba and its food to man and man,
as the release of energy, the evocation or the calling forth of new powers one
from the other."[98]

Creative Experience was widely reviewed in the academic and popular press,
and with one exception was received very favorably. Appraisals appeared in
the *New York Times,* the *New Republic,* and *The Nation,* as well as in disci-

plinary journals concerned with philosophy, psychology, sociology, political science, and social work.[99]

Each of the philosophers who reviewed the book (Hartly Burr Alexander, James H. Tufts, and Harry A. Overstreet) had previously reviewed *The New State* and seemed as favorably disposed toward this book as toward its predecessor. The philosophers were particularly taken with the practical significance of Follett's ideas. Tufts pronounced the process of seeking integrative resolutions of conflict a "genuine working tool instead of a museum specimen."[100]

Social scientists were even more enthusiastic in their praise for *Creative Experience*. Walter J. Shepard, writing in the *American Political Science Review*, called Follett's application of the principle of integrative behavior to political and social problems "illuminating."[101] The sociologist Charles A. Ellwood, who had "waited with eager anticipation for another book from [Follett's] pen," found *Creative Experience* fully up to the level of its predecessor, with every chapter containing "a vital contribution to social theory." This book, Ellwood continued, "again demonstrates that Miss Follett is easily the foremost woman thinker along social and political lines of our time, and perhaps one of the most philosophical thinkers in the field of social theory of all time — a fact which should be highly gratifying to all advocates of the emancipation and education of women as well as to all who are seeking to further the progress of the social sciences."[102] Robert W. Bruère, an industrial relations specialist and associate editor of *The Survey*, called the book "an exhilarating spiritual adventure, in which all of the problems that confront social workers and socially minded folk generally take on new significance. Here the individual, the group, the courts, the law, classes, nations, diverse desires, conflicting purposes cease to be discrete and irreconcilable entities and appear as living strands on the loom of time whose interweaving we can guide, whose pattern we can control."[103] Arthur E. Wood, the University of Michigan sociologist and 1925–27 president of the National Community Center Association, reviewed both *The New State* and *Creative Experience* in a 1926 issue of the *Journal of Social Forces*. "One gets the impression that here the material is amassed with not quite so sure a hand as in *The New State*," Wood wrote, "or, at least, that the drift of things is not always so clear. However, the major concepts are illuminating and suggestive, and they are, as in the former treatise, enriched with a wealth of concrete illustration." Wood found himself in agreement with other reviewers that the "genius of Miss Follett's work lies in her effective synthesis of theory and practice." Follett "combines a speculative mind with a social outlook and a knowledge of affairs. She sees politics as a matter of bread and jobs, and the development of collective sentiments. Her general trend is decidedly idealistic, yet she reveals a type of idealism that seems fully aware of the most stubborn facts. There is no exhortation in terms of vague principles, but rather a most painstaking analysis of means by which any principles worth holding may be had."[104] Follett's only real detractor among the social scientists was Russell Gordon Smith of Columbia University, an avowed disciple of the Social Darwinist sociologist William Graham Sumner.[105]

Two psychologists also reviewed Follett's book, and their evaluations are particularly noteworthy given Follett's use of psychological research as the foundation of *Creative Experience*. Mary Whiton Calkins, professor of philosophy and psychology at Wellesley College and president of the American Psychological Association (1905) and the American Philosophical Association (1918), pronounced herself "in eager agreement" with the "main teachings" of *Creative Experience*. Calkins' criticisms, however, reflect her deeply held conviction that the behaviorists had underestimated the importance of the conscious self in psychological research. It seemed to Calkins that Follett was "in danger of swallowing Holt's unjustified intolerance of the self which has the desires and the behaviorist's dogmatic refusal to deal with the psychic organism — doctrines which," she added, "are wholly incompatible with [Follett's] own position."[106]

Gordon Allport, then a young Harvard psychologist, also reviewed *Creative Experience*. He and Follett were acquainted, probably through Richard Cabot. Follett had credited Allport with having generously allowed her to "read his paper on Contemporary German Psychology in advance of its publication," and also with having corresponded with her about the research of the German Gestaltists.[107] Allport characterized *Creative Experience* as a "psychological sequel to *The New State*," seeing it as a work in which Follett further developed "her highly original thesis of creative group activity." Although Follett successfully "brings together with fine perception several lines of contemporary thought, including theories of jurisprudence, behaviorism, and *Gestalt* psychology, and causes them to converge upon the problem of human conflict," Allport was not convinced that integration was a widely applicable method of resolving conflict: "The chief criticism against this position is that it regards social behavior exclusively as a manifestation of circular response . . . Members of a group most certainly do interact upon one another; but they are also to a discouraging extent *influenced* by one another. The 'power-over' which Miss Follett abjures is an ineradicable fact . . . So fundamental is 'power-over' in fact that many writers consider the true function of the group to be fulfilled when the influence of the best equipped individuals has been extended over the group as a whole."[108]

Skeptical of the creative capabilities of individuals acting in groups, Allport summarized the extant body of experimental evidence. According to Allport, existing studies suggested that individuals "are more conservative in a group, their haste is greater, the quality of their opinions likely to be poorer, and rivalry (prejudicial to integration) is unwittingly aroused." Placing his faith in these early experimental results, Allport concluded that "it will be difficult indeed to find salvation in the 'intelligent interweaving' of interests, for as soon as a group is formed irrational and emotional factors tend to dominate behavior."[109] If Allport were able to revisit this judgment today, he probably would reach a different conclusion. With many decades of research on individual and group performance to inform us, it now seems clear that individuals sometimes perform better than groups, but also that groups sometimes perform better than individuals. Which is superior in a particular situation depends on a variety of factors, including the nature of the problem, the reward system in use, time constraints, and the knowledge and skillfulness of individual members.

Allport had one other complaint about *Creative Experience,* namely, that Follett saw social behavior as characterized *exclusively* by circular response. This seems a curious charge. Follett not only repeatedly acknowledged the presence of "domination" and "power-over" in social life; she also wrote her book specifically to propose a method that might effectively replace it. Later in his review, Allport himself suggested that his criticism might have been unfair. "Miss Follett through a failure to take account of the natural obstructions in the path of integration, seems (to the reviewer) to regard the solution of conflict as an easier task that it really is. On the other hand, a hundred books treat of the part played by suggestion, imitation, and traits of personality in social adjustments to one which gives adequate recognition to the circular response. For this reason Miss Follett's disproportionate emphasis may be readily forgiven. As a practical guide for those who are every day dealing with actual conflict the book will prove of inestimable value."[110] Concluding on this positive note, Allport expressed hope that Follett "will follow up her present significant contribution with additional studies in conflict. Particularly valuable would be a book of actual cases, recording instances of success and failure, with particular reference to the technique of modulating linear influences and achieving true integration."[111]

In fact Follett was seriously considering producing just this sort of book. "My next book is to be on Conflict," Follett wrote Harold Laski in April 1924. Confessing that she was "looking to take any step that would develop my thinking further," Follett wondered whether a trip to England to meet the guild socialists and some of the intellectuals from the Labor party would help her preparation. "I do not want to come," she told Laski, "unless there is a great deal there which I cannot get here."[112] Soon, however, the publication of *Creative Experience* would change her plans. According to her longtime Newnham friend Melian Stawell, Follett was "flooded with letters" from businessmen who asked "not only for public lectures but for private talks over their own problems."[113] She apparently found these conversations compelling, for by 1926 Follett had firmly decided to study business management. She explained her reasons in a lecture delivered in England. "Free to choose between different paths of study," Follett told her audience, "I have chosen this for a number of reasons."

> First of all, it is among business men (not all, but a few) that I find the greatest vitality of thinking to-day, and I like to do my thinking where it is most alive . . . Moreover, I find the thinking of business men to-day in line with the deepest and best thinking we have ever had. The last word in science — in biology — is the principle of unifying. The most profound philosophers have always give us unifying as the fundamental principle of life. And now business men are finding it is the way to run a successful business. Here the ideal and the practical have joined hands. That is why I am working at business management, because while I care for the ideal it is only because I want to help bring it into our everyday affairs . . .
>
> Another reason is because industry is the most important field of human activity, and management is the fundamental element in industry . . . whatever changes should come, whether industry is owned by individual capitalists, or by the state, or by the workers, it will always have to be managed. Management is a permanent function of business.
>
> The third reason why I am working at business management is because I believe in *control,* and so do our most progressive business men. I believe in the individual not trusting to fate or chance or inheritance or environment, but learning how to control his own life. And nowhere do I see such a complete acceptance of this as in . . . the thinking of the more progressive business men. They are taking the mysticism out of business.[114]

20

Professional Transition, Personal Tragedy

Mary Follett suffered yet another health-related crisis in the summer of 1924 following the publication of *Creative Experience,* but this time she felt so overwhelmed that she could no longer hide her fears and frustrations. She turned to the Cabots for solace, but later felt embarrassed about having imposed herself on them "in a rather weak moment." Writing to Richard and Ella in late July, Follett announced that she had had regained both her poise and a modicum of health after several weeks with Isobel at Overhills. "I am working, reading etc., staying out of doors a great deal & all the time letting this marvellous beauty, this *quiet* beauty & peace sink in & in." She also had been doing a great deal of thinking about spiritual healing. "I do believe in it," Follett declared. "I believe that we have access to certain sources of power. The Bible, the writings of many holy men & women, mean to me the teaching to live down in the deep wells of our being where we become so at one with God that his powers are ours, according to our capacity . . . Perhaps I shall never go far in the control of my body, but it seems to me I must begin to try to attain this control. Our impotence, I think, often comes from the fact that our spiritual energies are scattered & need to be mobilized. If we wait on God & gather the forces of our soul—have we yet tried that enough to know its potentialities?"[1]

Follett's renewed strength was attributable not only to her meditations on spiritual healing, but also to the growing intimacy of her relations with the Cabots. "I have felt the last year or two my debt to you two constantly increasing," Follett confided. "When one has really faced & recognized a human soul, one never gets away from the influence of that contact. If one leaves those inner places where such contact is possible, one hurries back, home-sick for that wh. has richer content because of those we have known there. I have you not by coming to Cambridge or Waltham but by dwelling in those places in which there is no barrier between one & another."[2]

Follett's painfully wrought spiritual convictions and the loving support she received from Isobel and the Cabots saved her from despair and gave her the courage she needed to continue to work. In August, Alfred and Ada Sheffield were overnight guests at Overhills and reported to Eduard Lindeman that Follett's health was "pretty dubious"; they feared she was "in for a serious operation." Nevertheless, Alfred noted, Mary "keeps plugging at work." Specifically, she was "giving some days" to a study of employee morale at Henry S. Dennison's paper products manufacturing firm.[3]

Follett had become acquainted with Henry Dennison as early as 1913 when he had served as the representative of the Boston Chamber of Commerce on the five-person Board of Directors of one of Follett's most notable civic projects, the Boston Placement Bureau. What began as a business relationship grew into a close family friendship. Dennison's daughters, who in the early 1920s were in their late teens and early twenties, remember Follett as a lively presence at the family dinner table, a charming yet scholarly woman with sparkling eyes, enthusiasm, and wit who took considerable interest in their own aspirations. One of the daughters also recalled a Sunday morning in the Dennison's kitchen, where her mother tried with only moderate success to teach her flustered and thoroughly undomestic friend to make scrambled eggs.[4]

It was obvious to Dennison's daughters that both of their parents had become Mary Follett's friends — but their father, they felt certain, was particularly fond of her. Nine years younger than Follett, Henry Dennison had amassed an impressive list of accomplishments, but he ached for intellectual companionship and genuine professional collaboration. As a young man, Dennison had been forced to rely on his uncle Charles for support and guidance; his father's alcoholism had created a family scandal that forced the senior Dennison from the company presidency when Henry was only fifteen. When Henry was thirty-five, his uncle died, leaving the young man for all practical purposes as the head of the firm; and a mere five years later, in 1917, Henry Dennison was officially named president. Feeling the burden of his family history and acutely conscious of his responsibilities, Dennison was determined to make a success of his tenure. It was in this context that Follett became Dennison's mentor: not only was he enthusiastic about her ideas, but he also welcomed her backing and was grateful for her responsiveness to his desires to improve his company.[5]

By the early 1920s Henry Dennison was a recognized innovator in employee relations. His service on Follett's Placement Bureau and his simultaneous membership on a Massachusetts governor's commission charged with alleviating unemployment had led Dennison to become deeply concerned with issues of worker security. Seeking to stabilize employment at his own firm, Dennison quickly moved to establish the country's first company-sponsored unemployment compensation fund. Yet another reform — an employees' works committee that advised management about labor policies — emerged from Dennison's service on a 1919 national industrial commission. Convinced that greater employee participation would increase company profits, Dennison persuaded the management group to establish a stock-dividend profit-sharing plan for nonmanagerial employees. Dennison's innovative concern with labor policies was further evident in activities outside the firm: for example, during his term as president of the Taylor Society, a professional association for those interested in scientific management, he supported the expansion of the society's concerns from production to personnel processes.[6]

Little is known about the particular Dennison project that had Mary Follett's attention in the fall of 1924. But John A. Garvey, the firm's employment manager, recalled having been asked by Dennison to brief Follett on a problem they were having: factory and office managers felt that their authority was being threatened by a recent board decision to adopt uniform policies for all personnel. Garvey expected Follett to be "one of the 'do-good' type that was so common in the field of personnel at that period . . . who thought that being 'nice' to men and women would solve all problems." He quickly discovered that she "was definitely not of that type nor did she feel that paternalism was the answer with the byproducts of bands and picnics, athletic teams and Christmas baskets. This came out strongly in further meetings I had with her," Garvey continued, "and my respect for her judgment grew and so did my liking for her."[7]

About this same time, a second business-related project claimed the attention of both Follett and Dennison. Each was invited by the Bureau of Personnel Administration to speak to a group of business executives in midtown Manhattan early in 1925, as a part of one of the nation's first executive development seminars. The founder of the bureau, Henry Metcalf, had been a professor of political science at Tufts University for nearly twenty years and during this time was active in Boston civic affairs. He most likely made Mary Follett's acquaintance while serving on the Executive Committee of the

Henry S. Dennison, 1922. Courtesy of the Harvard University Archives.

Vocation Bureau, the group whose vocational guidance activities were taken over and expanded within Follett's Placement Bureau.[8]

Before America's entry into World War I, Metcalf had conducted numerous labor surveys, and his growing reputation in this field led the War Industries Board to ask him to develop wartime employment management courses for shipyard and munitions plant managers. These experiences, in turn, became the basis for a textbook on personnel administration that Metcalf coauthored in 1920 with Ordway Tead. Great believers in the potential of scientific research, Metcalf and Tead optimistically predicted that a more scientific selection, placement, and training of personnel would lead to a time when "proper work habits could be formed and emotions controlled, and creative leadership could lead to reduced conflict and improved morale." Soon after the publication of his personnel textbook, Metcalf became the founding director of the Bureau of Personnel Administration, an organization designed to provide employment management consulting services and continuing education programs to firms throughout the eastern United States.[9]

The bureau's first "Evening Course for Executives," held in 1923–24 under the title "Linking Science and Industry," had proved sufficiently popular that a second was scheduled for the following year. The presenters for "The Scientific Foundations of Business Administration" included, in addition to Follett and Henry Dennison, Mary's longtime friend at the City College of New York, Harry Overstreet, and three others: Harlow S. Person, managing director of the Taylor Society and former dean of the Amos Tuck School of Administration and Finance at Dartmouth; Thomas Nixon Carver, the Social Darwinist economist from Harvard; and Otis W. Caldwell, a professor of education at Columbia University and former professor of botany at the University of Chicago.[10] The presenters almost certainly were paid an honorarium, but the amount is unknown.

Advertised as "especially designed for men and women who are engaged in industrial, commercial and governmental administrative work," almost all of the thirty or so participants in the Executive Conference Group were personnel managers, vice-presidents, or presidents of their firms; most or perhaps all were men. Individuals were charged $50 for the full complement of Friday-evening meetings, while corporations paid $200 for up to four representatives. An impressive array of firms was represented on the membership list: R. H. Macy, Metropolitan Life Insurance, Borden Farm Products, U.S. Rubber Company, General Motors Corporation, Standard Oil Company, Irving Bank–Columbia Trust Company, American Telephone & Telegraph, New York and Queens Electric Light and Power Company, and the New York Central Lines. At least at this stage, Metcalf seems not to have tried to attract labor leaders.[11]

Following the 1924–25 conference, Metcalf published the conference papers in a book that he described as "a serious attempt to analyze the philosophical, biological, economic, psychological foundations of business administration and its basic administrative principles; and to apply them to practical business affairs."[12] Henry Dennison's contribution to the volume was a discussion of the practical applications of each of the academic fields under consideration. Mary Follett's four lectures were concerned with the psychological foundations of business administration. Her lectures recapitulated concepts central to *Creative Experience* and, to a lesser extent, *The New State*, but this time in the context of business management. As a result, these particular lectures shed considerable light on Follett's assessment of the most widely known and influential management system of her day — "scientific management."

Developed in response to the inefficiencies and labor problems of the late nineteenth-century factory system, the early twentieth-century reforms in production, distribution, and personnel management that came to be called "scientific management" were conceived largely by engineers. The most prominent among them were Frederick W. Taylor, Harrington Emerson, Henry L. Gantt, and Morris L. Cooke; but nonengineers, such as Carl Barth and Frank and Lillian Gilbreth, also consulted with industrial firms that were seeking to reform their business methods and shop practices. Much has been written since 1980 analyzing the shades of difference in ideology and methods among the various contributors to scientific management — as well as evaluating the extent to which the consultants' actual practices corresponded to the principles they espoused.[13] But since Follett mentions none of the various efficiency advocates by name and probably had only a modicum of information about how well scientific management theory was being implemented in practice, her remarks are perhaps best considered in the context of the ideology articulated by the most notable of the reformers, Frederick W. Taylor (1856–1915).[14]

Taylor, born to a wealthy Philadelphia Quaker family, made the unusual choice of forgoing a classical education at Harvard in favor of a four-year apprenticeship as a metal patternmaker and machinist. It was during his apprenticeship that Taylor first experienced what he later called "bad industrial conditions" — the harassment and tyranny of the late nineteenth-century foreman and his "rule of thumb" style of supervision, the restriction of output by workers, and poor plant management. More of the same was waiting for Taylor in 1878 when, after completing his apprenticeship, he moved to Midvale Steel. Taylor began work as a common laborer but during the next six years rose rapidly through a series of positions, including gang boss of the machinists and supervisor of the machine shop, to become the plant's chief engineer. Early in this period he also received an engineering degree, largely by means of correspondence courses.

It was during Taylor's twelve years at Midvale that he developed many of the techniques commonly associated with scientific management. The focus of these production management and control techniques was the establishment by expert staff specialists of procedures and standards of performance based on the facts of the situation. Expert intervention, Taylor argued, was not just desirable, but essential: "[The] law is almost universal — not entirely so, but nearly so — that the man who is fit to work at any particular trade is unable to understand the science of that trade without the kindly help and cooperation of men of a totally different type of education, men whose education is not necessarily higher but of a different type from his own."[15] Taylor's experts engaged in a wide range of activities: they analyzed work processes around machines, identified and timed process components to discover how each task might be speeded up, improved machine design and layouts, standardized tools and materials, prescribed rest periods, and prepared daily written work orders for each job. To encourage individuals to surpass the prescribed standards and to penalize those who failed, they devised a differential piece-rate system; and they sought to select and train employees based on knowledge and skills relevant to their jobs.

Taylor's various production reforms greatly increased the pressure on managers to plan, organize, and supervise the work. This was as it should be, Taylor argued; employers had for too long put primarily on workers the burden of meeting production rates. To reduce the inefficiencies of the typical foreman, Taylor advocated replacing the first-line supervisor with a set of "functional foremen," some of whom would be responsible for planning aspects of an individual's work, others for supervising aspects of performance. He also gradually developed an entire crew of planning department officials and adapted the railroad accounting system to measure the cost savings derived from the various reforms.[16]

Scientific management was little known outside engineering and plant management circles until 1910. But when Gilbreth, Gantt, and Emerson testified before the Interstate Commerce Commission (ICC) in the highly publicized Eastern Rates hearings, the basic notions of scientific management began to reach a much wider audience. In the Eastern Rates case a group of trade associations, represented by Louis Brandeis, appeared before the ICC opposing the railroads' request for an increase in freight rates. Brandeis's strategy was to argue that a rate increase would be unnecessary if the railroads would cut costs by instituting a series of management reforms; the railroads, Brandeis boldly asserted, could save "a million dollars a day." Hoping to capture in another vivid phrase the essence of the reforms being recommended by Taylor's followers, Brandeis and his colleagues noted that Taylor had often used the word *scientific* to describe his methods; Taylorism thus became known as "scientific management."[17] The Brandeis characterization of scientific management, writes historian David Montgomery, "ran like a shock wave across the printing presses of America. It evoked an image of science in the service of the people, showing the way to hold down the cost of living while raising American wages under the guidance of modern management and experimental method. Only the reactionary railroads and unions opposed the public good. Even the interests of the railroad workers were best represented by enlightened management, not by their unions, which held back output and progress."[18]

Not surprisingly, a wave of efficiency experts emerged in the wake of the Eastern Rates case, promising employers "quick panaceas" for their labor troubles. Taylor was dismayed by this development, fearing that neither the consultants nor the employers appreciated the kind of "mental revolution" demanded by the adoption of scientific management.[19] Writing in *Principles of Scientific Management* (1911), Taylor contended that the "great revolution that takes place in the mental attitude of the two parties under scientific management is that both sides take their eyes off of the division of the surplus as the all-important matter, and together turn their attention toward increasing the size of the surplus until this surplus becomes so large that it is unnecessary to quarrel over how it shall be divided."[20]

Taylor fervently believed that adversarial relations between labor and capital would cease if sufficient wealth could be created by the intervention of a new managerial class — experts who would use science to create highly effective systems of production and distribution. The "core of Taylorism was clearly an explicit call for reconciliation between capital and labor, on the neutral ground of science and rationality," writes Judith A. Merkle in her study of the legacy of the international scientific management movement; furthermore, "the reconciliation, quite obviously, was to be made on the terms of neither party, but in terms of 'rationality' *as interpreted by Taylor himself.*"[21]

Thirty-five years would pass between the development of the basic elements of scientific management and the occasion of Mary Follett's lectures to the Bureau of Personnel Administration in January 1925. During the intervening years, a number of the more progressive managers had come to see scientific management, as Taylor himself had hoped, as advocating a scientific process rather than a set of specific techniques.[22] Some among the more progressive managers had even begun debating the efficacy of the "top-down," expert-driven character of scientific management. As early as 1917 Harlow S. Person, who would soon become managing director of the Taylor Society (1919–1933), had urged the membership of the society to acknowledge the significance of "three distinct angles of approach to the discussion of our problems; those of the manager, the workman, and the social scientist. It is my thesis that no one of these individuals sees the problems of scientific management with an eye which reveals the whole truth . . . that each is complementary to and essential to the other."[23]

The respondents to Person's paper included Henry C. Metcalf and Harvard Law School professor Felix Frankfurter. Metcalf expressed disappointment that the paper "offers no constructive machinery for putting the fundamental ideals it embodies into practice." Only a few years later, Metcalf would establish his Bureau of Personnel Administration with the specific intention of promulgating best-practice ideas among America's business managers. Frankfurter, on the other hand, had only praise for Person's remarks, characterizing the paper as an admirable "plea for an integration of the judgments of the manager, the workman and the social scientist."[24]

Mary Follett was surely well acquainted with this growing acknowledgment of the unique perspective of workers; she was an avid reader of the *Bulletin of the Taylor Society,* and her friend Henry Dennison served a term as the society's president in 1920.[25] But just as Follett, earlier in her career, had denied the claims of the good government associations that they were the ones who should govern Boston's immigrants "in their best interests," and later, in *Creative Experience,* had opposed her generation's eager reliance on the expert, she would express reservations about management experts in her upcoming lectures about scientific management. And she would do so in spite of the Taylor Society's newfound appreciation for the singular viewpoint of workers. The "joint responsibility of management and labour is an interpenetrating responsibility," Follett argued in one of her lectures, "and is utterly different from responsibility divided off into sections, management having some and labour some . . . This is the problem in business administration: how can a business be so organized that workers, managers, owners, feel a collective responsibility?"[26]

Mary Follett would use her lectures to the Executive Conference Group as a forum for engaging her audience in precisely this question: by what means could one move from an individual, functionalized responsibility for business management to a joint, interpenetrating responsibility?

Follett took up a portion of this question in the first of her four Friday-evening presentations to the Executive Conference Group. In so doing, she chose a topic that she believed would "go to the heart of personnel relations in industry." The country had just endured a decade rife with labor troubles. Between 1915 and 1920, jobs were readily available, and many workers willingly left their current places of employment in search of better work and higher wages. During this same period, writes historian David Montgomery, union membership almost doubled, and the unions went on strike "on a scale that dwarfed all previously recorded . . . strike activity." Even after a downturn in the economy, the strikes continued; in 1922 alone, more than a million and a half men and women went out on strike. Determined to retaliate, employers instituted lockouts and, wherever they could, rolled back union gains in wages, hours, and worker rights. Acutely conscious of the destructive nature of this sort of social discord, Mary Follett thought it imperative that business people find a "fruitful way of dealing with conflict."[27]

Making Conflict Constructive

In "Constructive Conflict," Follett exhorted her audience to refrain from automatically thinking that conflict is bad. "As conflict — difference — is here in the world, as we cannot avoid it, we should, I think, use it instead of condemning it, we should set it to work for us."[28] Follett believed that conflict could be made constructive and that joint, interpenetrating responsibilities could be created if ways were found to integrate differences rather than dealing with them through domination or compromise. She therefore reiterated in the context of modern business practice the method of integration that she had presented in *Creative Experience:* first uncovering together the real demands underlying the conflict; then bringing these real demands into the open; re-valuing desires by coming to a deeper understanding of all parties' demands; identifying the significant rather than dramatic features in the controversy; and breaking the demands of all parties into constituent parts so that each could be resolved, in turn.

Follett augmented this analysis with some new thinking about the importance of *anticipating* conflict. Such anticipation "does not mean necessarily the avoidance of conflict, but playing the game differently. That is, you integrate the different interests without making all the moves." Foresight of this sort, however, did not satisfy Follett. In anticipating conflict, she continued, it "is not enough to ask to what our employee or our business confrère or business competitor is responding, nor even to what he is likely to respond. We have to prepare the way for response, we have to try to build up in him a certain [constructive] attitude." Concerned as always with relations and convinced that "response is always to a relation," Follett stressed the necessity of attending to the circularity of behavior when dealing with conflict: "Employees do not respond only to their employers but to the relation between themselves and their employer. Trade unionism is responding not only to capitalism but to the relation between itself and capitalism."[29]

Another topic that Follett treated more comprehensively than in *Creative Experience* concerned the numerous *obstacles* to integration. It is unfortunate, Follett noted, that the matter in dispute all too often is "theorized over instead of being taken up as a proposed activity." Not only is purely intellectual agreement difficult to achieve; it never is sufficient to bring full integration. "I have been interested to watch how often disagreement disappears," Follett told her listeners, "when theorizing ends and the question is of some definite activity to be undertaken." Follett also had seen how obstacles to integration arise when the parties to a conflict are reckless in their use of language—projecting hostility toward one another or making negative judgments about one another's motives—and how conflicts are exacerbated when unscrupulous leaders emotionally manipulate their followers. Follett's own experience had taught her that integrating "requires a high order of intelligence, keen perception and discrimination, more than all, a brilliant inventiveness." It is far easier "for the trade union to fight than to suggest a better way of running the factory." Indeed, many people seem to prefer—even enjoy—domination. "Integration seems to many a tamer affair," Follett observed; "it leaves no 'thrills' of conquest."

Perhaps the greatest obstacle to integration was our lack of training for it. "Even if there were not the barriers of an unenlightened self interest, of prejudice, rigidity, dogmatism, routine, there would still be required training and practice for us to master the technique of integration. A friend of mine said to me, 'Openmindedness is the whole thing, isn't it?' No, it isn't, it needs just as great a respect for your own view as for that of others, and a firm upholding of it until you are convinced. Mushy people are no more good at this than stubborn people."

Concluding her discussion of constructive conflict, Follett offered her audience a test of good business administration: "is the organization such that both employers and employees, or co-managers, co-directors, are stimulated to a reciprocal activity which will give more than mere adjustment, more than an equilibrium?" Follett was convinced that our "outlook is narrowed, our activity is restricted, our chances of business success largely diminished when our thinking is constrained within the limits of what has been called an either-or situation." Imploring her listeners not "to be bullied by an 'either-or,'" Follett argued that there "is often the possibility of something better than either of two given alternatives. Every one of us interested in any form of constructive work is looking for the plus values of our activity."[30]

Creative Experience in the Workplace: Reflecting on the Giving of Orders

The second of Follett's lectures for the Executive Conference Group, "The Psychological Foundations: The Giving of Orders," occurred the following Friday evening. Follett's goal in this lecture was to demonstrate to her listeners what it would mean for them to take a "conscious and responsible" attitude toward their experience — to decide consciously on which principles they would act, to try experiments based on these principles, and to record and share results. Follett illustrated this process in terms of the experience of giving orders — for she was convinced that "more industrial trouble has been caused by the manner in which orders are given than in any other way." "What happens to a man, *in* a man," Follett asked, "when an order is given in a disagreeable manner by foreman, head of department, his immediate superior in store, bank or factory? The man addressed feels that his self-respect is attacked, that one of his most inner sanctuaries is invaded. He loses his temper or becomes sullen or is on the defensive; he begins thinking of his 'rights' — a fatal attitude for any of us. In the language we have been using, the wrong behavior pattern is aroused, the wrong motor-set [habit]; that is, he is now 'set' to act in a way which is not going to benefit the enterprise in which he is engaged."[31]

Recognizing that orders, nevertheless, have to be given, Follett urged her audience "to depersonalize the giving of orders, to unite all concerned in a study of the situation, to discover the law of the situation and obey that." It is in this context that Follett made one of her earliest explicit statements about the value of scientific management. One of scientific management's "largest contributions" is that "it tends to depersonalize orders. From one point of view, one might call the essence of scientific management the attempt to find the law of the situation. With scientific management the managers are as much under orders as the workers, for both obey the law of the situation." Follett at first called this process "depersonalizing" orders, but the term didn't satisfy her; in fact, the divorcing of persons and the situation seemed to her to do a great deal of harm: "We, persons, have relations with each other, but we should find them in and through the whole situation. We cannot have any sound relations with each other as long as we take them out of that setting which gives them their meaning and value . . . I have just said that scientific management depersonalizes; the deeper philosophy of scientific management shows us personal relations within the whole setting of that thing of which they are a part."[32]

Here, in the context of giving orders, Follett took up another aspect of the question about how one creates a joint, interpenetrating responsibility, and in so doing echoed ideas about authority, rights, participation, and consent first expressed in *The New State* and *Creative Experience*. Follett saw no necessary opposition between obedience to orders and freedom — as long as orders are "the composite conclusion of those who give and those who receive them" and express "the integration of the people concerned and the situation." Her long-standing concern with circular response and the evolving situation was also in evidence. "If the situation is never stationary, then the order should never be stationary." Indeed, the "situation is changing while orders are being carried out, because, by and through orders being carried out."[33] Orders, therefore, must somehow be made continually to integrate with this circular, evolving situation.

The Worker's Place in Unifying Business Organizations

Follett opened her third Friday-evening lecture, "The Psychological Foundations: Business as an Integrative Unity," by taking up the timely question of "the worker's place in industry." In the early 1920s, more than eight hundred employee representation plans had been formed nationwide — many of them thinly disguised efforts to thwart unionization during the labor unrest of the postwar period.[34] Mary Follett was one who saw through these manipulative schemes. "No gentlemanly name for fighting," she remarked, "will change the essential nature of the relation between capital and labor in those plants where 'sides' are sharply defined." It seemed to her that "the aim of employee representation should not be simply to transfer the antagonism of 'sides' to a different field, but to see how far sides — that is, controversial sides — can be done away with." Likewise, collective bargaining seemed to Follett only a "temporary expedient. It fixes the limits of wages, hours and conditions; it might be conceived perhaps as fixing certain limits to policies, but it does not create . . . I believe that something better will be found, is being found."[35]

What was that "something better"? "It seems to me," Follett continued, "that the first test of business administration, of industrial organization, should be whether you have a business with all its parts so coördinated, so moving together in their closely knit and adjusting activities, so linking, interlocking, interrelating, that they make a working *unit*, that is, not a congeries of separate pieces but what I have called a functional whole or integrative unit . . . this principle applies to the relation of men, the relation of services, the relation of departments, the last of which I have found one of the weakest points in the businesses which I have studied."[36]

Although Follett wished to do away with the "fight attitude" that all too often accompanies sides, she never sought to do away with sides themselves. There is "a sense in which sides are necessary to the richness of that unity which we are here considering," she explained, "essential even to its existence in any real sense . . . In a meeting of the superintendents of departments, each should consider not merely what is good for his department, but the good of the business as viewed from his department. Please notice the last phrase; I do not say that he should consider what is good for the whole business and end my sentence there, as is so often done. I say what is good for the whole *as seen from his department*. We do want sides in this sense."[37]

In her first lecture Follett had described how "fighting sides" might be replaced with "integrative sides." In this one Follett reiterated the basic elements of that integrative method, but she had a broader purpose in mind, namely, helping her audience understand the significance of business as an integrative unity. "We have been so delighted with what has sometimes been called the functional theory, that is, the division of work so that each can do what he is best fitted for, that we have tended to forget that our responsibility does not end with doing conscientiously and well our particular piece of the whole, but that we are also responsible for the whole. A business should be so organized," Follett proclaimed, "that all will feel this responsibility."[38]

Follett knew that her emphasis on collective responsibility sometimes led others to think that she did not believe in decentralization. Determined to correct this misapprehension, she took up the subject directly, echoing arguments she had made seven years earlier in *The New State*. "I know no one who believes more strongly in decentralization than I do, but I believe that collective responsibility and decentralized responsibility must go hand in hand; more than that, I think they are parts of the same thing . . . That centralization and decentralization are not opposed is, I believe, the central lesson for business administration to learn . . . I do not minimize the difficulties we shall meet. This is one of our gravest problems: how to foster local initiative and at the same time get the advantages of centralization."[39]

Follett saw evidence of movement toward the kind of integrative unity in business that she was advocating. For example, in job analysis — the most fundamental of the scientific management techniques — she saw an "excellent example of a very real appreciation of joint responsibility for technique in the large unanimity of opinion that job analysis should be a matter for experts, managers and workers together." This, of course, represented a marked change from the expert-driven character of job analysis under Taylorism. Follett was equally encouraged by another development. Convinced that "almost everyone has some managing ability," she applauded the suggestion, recently made in a "very valuable" paper read by Henry Dennison to the Taylor Society, that "the distinction between those who manage and those who are managed is somewhat fading."[40] Follett emphatically agreed. "Whenever labor uses its judgment in planning, that perhaps is managing. If the worker is given a task and allowed to decide how he will do it, that perhaps is managing. It would not be possible to carry on a business if the workers did not do some managing."[41]

Despite her appreciation for the managerial capability of the average worker,

Follett did not believe that every form of decision making could be termed managing. Convinced that responsibility is a necessary part of managing, she constructed a more limited definition: "I should say that when men are allowed to use their own judgment in regard to the manner of executing orders, *and accept the responsibility involved in that,* they are managing."[42]

Although Follett's lifelong appreciation of group organization had convinced her "that a form of departmental organization which includes the workers is the most effective method for unifying a business," joint departmental organization would put in place only one element of the interpenetrating responsibility Follett was seeking. In business, Follett acknowledged, "there really is not such a thing, strictly speaking, as a departmental problem," and few of the wide array of business relations had received even cursory study. She therefore urged careful investigation of all business relations, including the production and distribution functions; production and personnel managers; the workers, consumers, and investors associated with a single plant; a main firm and its branches; and the various firms that constitute a particular industry.[43]

Follett concluded her third lecture with a stirring expression of confidence in the capabilities of business people and also with an appeal to her audience's sense of social responsibility. "The business man has probably the opportunity today of making one of the largest contributions to society that has ever been made, a demonstration of the possibility of collective creativeness." Little in the field of politics was encouraging, Follett confessed, "but in the League of Nations, in the cooperatives, above all in business administration, we see an appreciation emerging, not in words but in deeds, of what collective creativeness might mean to the world . . . The world has long been fumbling for democracy, but has not yet grasped its essential and basic idea. Business and industrial organization is, I believe, on the verge of making large contributions to something far more important than democracy, democracy in its more superficial meaning—to the development of integrative unity." A feat this momentous, however, would not be easily accomplished. "Business cannot serve its maximum degree of usefulness to the community," Follett warned, "cannot perform the service which it has, tacitly, *bound* itself to perform, unless it seeks an enlarged understanding of the practical methods of unifying business organization."[44]

The Place of Power in Integrating Differences

Follett opened the last of her January 1925 lectures, "The Psychological Foundations: Power," by focusing on another of the pressing problems confronting the 1920s business manager: in dealing with differences between management and labor, when should the manager rely on scientific management methods and when on collective bargaining? Under scientific management, the work of those in the skilled trades had been subject to unprecedented scrutiny. Between 1910 and 1920 the number of supervisory employees in manufacturing, mining, and transportation increased by 66.3 percent; the number of wage earners in these fields, on the other hand, grew by a mere 27.7 percent. As a result, the typical production worker increasingly found himself "at the bottom level of a highly stratified organization" in which his "established routines of work, his cultural traditions of craftsmanship, his personal interrelations" were all "at the mercy of technical specialists." Often, the worker's only recourse was to join a union and fight for the right to bargain collectively over working conditions, wages, and hours.[45]

Mary Follett was well aware that a significant difference of opinion existed between employers and workers about how to determine the value of goods and services, wages and hours, and working conditions. "Most labor men tell us that value is, or should be, determined by collective bargaining," Follett noted. "Many business men say that value should be determined by scientific methods which will do away with collective bargaining."[46] In 1911 Frederick Taylor had predicted that "the great mental revolution" underlying the practice of scientific management would generate a surplus so large that it would be unnecessary for employers and employees "to quarrel over how it shall be divided." But fifteen years later, the happy era envisioned by Taylor had not yet arrived. Trade unionists, Follett told her listeners, "do not want to do away with, or even to narrow the field of, collective bargaining, they want to bargain over everything . . . If you tell them that industrial technique is a purely scientific matter, then they reply, 'It is never the question alone of the advantage of a new method; but of who is going to get the advantage? If the worker is to get his share that must be bargained for.' This is true," Follett admitted, "as far as it goes."[47]

The goal that Follett was seeking, however, was the "business as an integrative unity" that she had described so eloquently in her preceding lecture. As a result, she was less enamored with schemes seeking "equal power" for labor in the bargaining process than with those that would develop "a jointly developing power."[48] It was to a consideration of this jointly developing power that Follett devoted the remainder of her final January 1925 lecture for the Bureau of Personnel Administration.

Convinced that relatively little was known about power, Follett sought first to impress upon her audience the urgency of studying power. Detailed observations are necessary, Follett explained, if we are to understand "what gives one person influence over another: social position, professional standing, the special knowledge of the expert, wide experience, mere wealth, age, sex, certain personal characteristics, even physical strength." At the same time, however, she recognized that such studies would be of little value unless they were informed by carefully drawn distinctions among the terms power, control, and authority. Follett therefore suggested the following definitions: "Power might be defined as simply the ability to make things happen, to be a causal agent, to initiate change . . . Control might be defined as power exercised as means toward a specific end; authority, as vested control."[49] On the basis of these definitions, which are familiar to modern students of organization and management, Follett astutely argued that "the main problem of the workers is by no means how much control they can wrest from capital or management, often as we hear that stated; that would be a merely nominal authority and would slip quickly from their grasp. Their problem is how much power they can themselves grow. The matter of workers' control which is so often thought of as a matter of how much the managers will be willing to give up, is really as much a matter for the workers, how much they will be able to assume; where managers come in is that they should give the workers a chance to grow capacity or power for themselves."[50]

Distinguishing here, as she had in *Creative Experience,* between "power-with" and "power-over," Follett focused on how to reduce power-over. The most promising method involved the process of integration. "The integrating of desires," Follett told her listeners, "precludes the necessity of gaining power in order to satisfy desire." And the basis of such integration could be found in circular behavior: "If your business is so organized that you can influence a co-manager while he is influencing you, so organized that a workman has an opportunity of influencing you as you have of influencing him; if there is an interactive influence going on all the time between you, power-with may be built up. Throughout history we see that control brings disastrous consequences whenever it outruns integration."[51]

Power-over also could be reduced through the submission of all parties to the law of the situation. "If both sides obey the law of the situation," Follett explained, "no *person* has power over another. The present-day respect for facts, for scientific methods, is the first step in this method of seeking the law of the situation . . . bargaining becomes limited by the boundaries set by scientific methods of business administration; it is only possible within the area thus marked out." As Follett had seen in her minimum wage board experiences, "Facts, by reducing the area of irreconcilable controversy, reduce power-over."[52]

In seeking to reduce power-over, Follett's ultimate aim was not to do away with collective bargaining. Collective bargaining is at present necessary, Follett repeatedly reaffirmed, for without it "both wages and working conditions would fall below even minimum standards." But although we should accept collective bargaining "for the moment and surround it with the fairest conditions we are able to," we should also seek in our organizations to move "toward a functional unity which, if it does not abolish collective bargaining (it may not) still will give to it a different meaning from that which it has at present."[53]

Once all the conference papers had been delivered, Follett's friend Henry Dennison had the task of discussing the practical applications of the other speakers' ideas. Dennison readily admitted that he could "find nothing but agreement throughout the papers with Miss Follett . . . I glory in the frame of mind—what she herself calls the experimental frame of mind—all through, which to me is a delight. In so far as those of us who are in the midst of business administration can hold it, it constitutes a most hopeful factor."[54]

Dennison's eager appreciation of Follett's ideas also was evident when he specifically contrasted her views with those espoused by the Harvard economist Thomas Nixon Carver. A conservative Social Darwinist, Carver's presentations for the Executive Conference Group, Dennison said, presumed a society that is "relatively simple and orderly and . . . running right. It is a quieting view, leaving us in fact nothing to do about it but to follow our best interests, save and invest." But Dennison, seeing nothing in Carver's viewpoint that took account of the "aerial jumble of non-economic motives, enthusiasms, and obsessions which so greatly affect social dynamics," could not be satisfied with Carver. It was in Follett's work that Dennison found a compelling portrayal of the complexity of business relations. "Those of us who would rather pull our weight on the trace of progress, whether the old world budges a bit or not," Dennison declared, "will turn to Miss Follett with a gladder heart."[55]

Surely one of the attractions to Follett of giving the Bureau of Personnel Administration lectures was the opportunity it afforded her to earn some money. Since the death of Pauline Agassiz Shaw in 1917, neither Follett nor Briggs seems to have had a regular source of income. Although this was a periodic source of concern, the pair was hardly destitute. A frugal lifestyle, prudent savings, and astute investments in stocks and bonds would eventually produce a joint estate of nearly $70,000.[56]

In January 1925, however, Follett was sufficiently concerned about her financial situation that she spoke with Eduard Lindeman about the prospect of filling in for him for a semester at the New York School of Social Work. Lindeman, then a professor of social philosophy, was about to go abroad on a hastily conceived six-month leave of absence as a result of a recently diagnosed thyroid deficiency.[57] Writing to thank him for agreeing to recommend her, Follett made plain her motive: "I would not trouble you, but this is so exactly what I have been hoping for. I have got to earn some money, but I didn't want to take a whole position. And this would not only be short, but would involve no obligation for another year, for you will be back then. It would just enable me to earn some money that I need now." The financial pressure that Follett was feeling may have been exacerbated by the pending move of her ailing eighty-four-year-old mother from her home in Quincy to a nursing home in nearby Wollaston.[58]

In the end, nothing came of the potential vacancy at the School of Social Work, as the administrators there had already made other arrangements. But even if a deal had been made, Follett would have had to bow out of the engagement. During a trip to Washington, D.C., following her Bureau of Personnel Administration lectures, she again became seriously ill and was forced to cancel all her plans. This turn of events left Follett deeply discouraged. "I am up again today, but this has taught me a lesson," she confessed to Lindeman. "I cannot attempt any definite obligations of any duration. I must just work along as I can & do a little writing perhaps if I am able. And I must give up any hope of earning any money, I fear, except for a separate lecture or two, or conferences, if anyone should want me for those." Bearing in mind that Lindeman, too, was suffering with his thyroid condition, Follett wished him well and sent her "remembrances & warm regards" to his family: "I think often of Mrs. L., for I have suffered so much on Miss B.'s account, that she shd. have the anxiety & burden of my illness, that it makes me think very often of Mrs. L. & what she must be going through. Please tell her she has one extraordinarily understanding friend."[59]

Among the engagements that Follett had to forgo as a result of this most recent flare-up of her recurring illness was a visit to the School of Citizenship and Public Affairs (now known as the Maxwell School) at Syracuse University. The school, established in the fall of 1924 as an integral part of the College of Liberal Arts, sought to prepare undergraduate and graduate students for positions of leadership in public affairs, government, and civic research; this mission was to be fulfilled through an innovative program of active cooperation with a wide range of academic departments. To assist his faculty in their pioneering work, Dean William E. Mosher arranged a series of informal discussions with people interested in the new enterprise, including Dean Roscoe Pound, Mary Follett, and Alexander Meiklejohn, former Amherst College president and the newly appointed chairman of the University of Wisconsin's Experimental College.[60]

Before issuing an invitation to Follett, Mosher discussed the matter with

Henry Metcalf, an acquaintance from Mosher's days at New York's Bureau of Municipal Research. Soon thereafter Metcalf reported back to Mosher. "I have talked with Miss Follett about your work and am a bit surprised and delighted to find that she has no hesitation about addressing any sized audience that you place her before. I had not remembered that Miss Follett had done a great deal of teaching in former years. She tells me she would not hesitate to stand before 1000 people. She was very easy before our Group on Friday evening and although she had a terrible cold, I thought she did very well . . . I think you need have no concern in making a program for her that you would like to see put across, — whether a small, medium or a large group. Let me know your pleasure and I will take the matter up with her."[61]

As it turned out, Mosher was able to pursue the matter himself. A member of the 1924–25 Executive Conference Group, Mosher attended Follett's lecture in New York the following Friday evening, and the two of them quickly agreed that she would pay a visit to Syracuse. The schedule of events and subjects to be considered were worked out over the next several days in an exchange of correspondence shaped by Follett's questions and enlivened by her charm and wit: "I feel that I still don't know as much as I ought of what you want of me. First Dr. Metcalf put words in your mouth in his suggestion of Power as my subject, & then the next day I put words in your mouth, & I think it is time that I heard what *you* want!" Mosher responded to her detailed inquiries by proposing a two-part engagement involving about twenty members of the faculty and staff: an informal discussion in the afternoon, followed by an evening lecture with questions. The afternoon session was to be concerned with pedagogy — specifically the use of "the conference technique" in undergraduate classes and the use of "leadership" as opposed to "salemanship" by teachers; the evening lecture was to be on a subject of Follett's choice, though Mosher thought "the one on power sounded very good."[62]

Only a week after concluding these arrangements, Follett was forced by her relapse to postpone indefinitely the eagerly anticipated visit to Syracuse. Hearing the news, Mosher wrote a warm, understanding letter, expressing the hope that her meeting "is a privilege but temporarily deferred." Nevertheless, Follett was mortified. "I have been well enough for several days to write you," she confessed to Mosher in early February, "but haven't liked even to think of you! I feel so badly at having failed to keep my engagement & at having caused you the annoyance of upset arrangements. Your very kind letter eased the burden a little, at first, but then I thought, 'It is only his kindness, I did it just the same.'" Ending on a more hopeful note, Follett reiterated her desire to come to Syracuse as soon as she was able, for she saw Mosher's program as having "an opportunity to lead the way for all the universities." But "this time," Follett declared, "it *must be without any pay except expenses.* This I should insist on."[63]

A year earlier, Follett's health problems had been diagnosed as a congenital cystic kidney. Her doctors at Massachusetts General Hospital, convinced that there was no malignancy, had thought the best course of action was to keep her under close observation. This time, however, they decided to operate. On April 2, Dr. Daniel Fiske Jones of Massachusetts General Hospital performed a nephrectomy, the removal of Follett's right kidney. The pathologist's report revealed a large, 10.5 cm tumor. The diagnosis was "hypernephroma," now referred to as renal cell carcinoma.[64]

Follett almost certainly would have insisted on being told what the surgery had revealed, but it is harder to discern what prognosis the doctors might have offered her. The medical literature on hypernephroma published early in the 1900s documented the tendency of this type of tumor to grow very slowly; indeed, physicians reported cases of many patients whose histories could be traced for twenty years, one even as long as forty years. Unfortunately, hypernephroma was rarely diagnosed early; as a result, the tumors tended either to be inoperable or, when operable, to have developed metastases to one or more organs.[65]

After more than twenty years of agonizing over the source of her recurring pain and abdominal distress and enduring a series of misdiagnoses, Follett surely took some solace in having that mystery solved. But if Richard Cabot and Dr. Jones were forthcoming about the likelihood of metastases—and Cabot's custom had been to speak truthfully as well as compassionately to patients about their conditions—it would have taken considerable courage for Follett to face the future with optimism.[66] Only one letter has survived from the first month of Follett's recuperation, a loving letter to Ella Cabot written near the end of April, but Follett makes no mention of her prognosis there.[67] She may have decided to withhold her cancer diagnosis from colleagues and friends, and perhaps even from Isobel. Or, more likely, she confided in Isobel, who then put the "best face" on Mary's situation when talking about it with others. "You will be glad to learn that Miss Follett's very severe operation has resulted favorably," Alfred D. Sheffield wrote Eduard Lindeman in late April. "The latest word from Miss Briggs last Friday was that Miss Follett was still at the Massachusetts General Hospital [a period of more than three weeks], but was showing daily improvement, so that in the natural course she can be expected back at her studies and writing."[68]

Amazingly, only six weeks after her surgery, Follett sounded almost buoyant and was beginning to think about another project. "I am getting well fast," she reported to Richard Cabot in mid-May. "I am not a bit of an 'interesting invalid,' it quite embarrasses me to watch friends' faces fall when they see me! Having set their features for condolence. In fact, I am hoping to begin work as soon as we get to the country."[69] Follett and Briggs soon left for Vermont, and Mary happily spent much of her summer preparing two new lectures for the Bureau of Personnel Administration.

The bureau's 1925–26 lecture series was titled "Business Management as a Profession." Joining Follett, Henry Dennison, Harlow Person, and Harry Overstreet as presenters were nine others, including William E. Mosher, dean of the School of Citizenship and Public Affairs at Syracuse University, and Wallace B. Donham, dean of the Harvard Graduate School of Business Administration. The purpose of this new series of lectures was to "analyze the fundamentals of business administration and help develop the professional status of business management."[70]

Returning members of the Executive Conference Group no doubt welcomed the bureau's new program, for American businessmen early in the century were caricatured in the most unflattering terms. Businessmen, it was said, were motivated solely by greed, ruthless in their pursuit of profits, content with "making do" and "getting by" rather than really solving business problems, and satisfied with "hunches" and "rules of thumb" rather than relying on reasoning and education in making business decisions.[71] Recognizing that businessmen had been denied the social approbation reserved for professions such as medicine, law, and architecture, Follett organized her first lecture around the question: "How Must Business Management Develop in Order to Possess the Essentials of a Profession?" "The word 'profession' connotes for most people a foundation of *science* and a motive of *service*," Follett told her audience. "That is, a profession is said to rest on the basis of a proved body of knowledge, and such knowledge is supposed to be used in the service of others rather than merely for one's own purposes."[72] Follett took up these two issues in turn, devoting her October 29 lecture to a discussion of the extent to which business management rests on scientific foundations and her November 5 lecture to a discussion of service.

Service had long been seen as a secondary matter for businessmen: they were thought to earn money during the day and provide community service at night; or they were thought to devote their early and middle years to business and, after retirement, spend a portion of their earnings in service to the community. "The much more wholesome idea, which we have now," Follett told her audience, "is that our work itself is to be our greatest service to the community. A business man should think of his work as one of the necessary functions of society, aware that other people are also performing necessary functions, and that all together these make a sound, healthy, useful community. 'Function' is the best word because it implies not only that you are responsible for serving your community, but that you are partly responsible for there being any community to serve."[73]

What else is involved in developing business management as a profession? Love of the work and the satisfaction of work well done — and a willingness to join with others in associations where they might work together to develop business as a profession. "One of the aims of the professional man," Follett observed, "is not only to practise his profession, to apply his science, but to extend the knowledge upon which that profession is based . . . This is pioneer work and difficult, but it has always been pioneer work to which men have responded with courage and vigour."[74]

She left until last what she saw as the "chief function, the real service" of business: "to give an opportunity for individual development through the better organization of human relationships." This goal seemed to Follett to be every bit as noble as the aims of justice, health, and beauty touted by the more established professions of law, medicine, and architecture — and surely just as essential to the future of society.[75] It should be no surprise that the more progressive businessmen found her viewpoint inspirational.

One such admirer was the management consultant Lyndall F. Urwick, who would make Follett's acquaintance in 1926 while he was organizing secretary of Rowntree and Company in England. Urwick deeply appreciated Follett's contribution to the development of business as a profession. "One of the more valuable features of Mary Follett's philosophy," Urwick would later write in a 1935 paper for the *Bulletin of the Taylor Society,* "is that it . . . enables those whose lot is cast in business to see their work, not merely as a means of livelihood, not only as an honorable occupation with a large content of professional interest, but as a definite and vital contribution towards the building of that new social order which is the legitimate preoccupation of every thinking citizen of the times. It clarifies their position and puts them in touch with the most vivid intellectual and political movements of their place and period . . . They must be in accord not only with the interests of their stockholders, the desires of their consumers and the temper of their workers, but also with the deep flowing currents of opinion which are shaping the society of the future. It is because Mary Follett's philosophy of organization opens up the possibility of such an identification," Urwick proclaimed, "that it is the most important contribution to the business literature of our time."[76]

In early October 1925, while Follett was putting the finishing touches on her lectures for the Bureau of Personnel Administration, William Mosher wrote to inquire about whether she could reschedule for later that fall the visit to Syracuse she had previously postponed. Follett wanted to come, but she told Mosher she could not commit to a definite arrangement until the New York trip was over and she saw whether her body "takes kindly to trains, subways etc." She apparently responded well to the stresses of the New York trip, because she soon made a two-day visit to Mosher's School of Citizenship and Public Affairs. There she met in informal discussions with the faculty and staff and lectured on the subject of power as it related to the problems the interdisciplinary school was experiencing. The conversations seem to have provided a first-rate intellectual experience for all concerned: Follett discovered "many points of contact" between her thinking and what Mosher and his staff were doing, and the staff found her contributions so stimulating that Mosher invited her to return the following summer.[77]

Suddenly, however, everything changed. For nearly two decades, the primary medical concern in the Follett-Briggs household had been the state of Mary's health. This time, however, the person in pain was Isobel. Perhaps the pain was new, or perhaps she had been careful to hide her growing distress. In any case, Briggs's suffering now was intense. Seeking medical attention, Briggs and Follett went in late November or early December to Massachusetts General Hospital, where Isobel was seen by Dr. Theodore Badger. His examination almost certainly revealed the cause of her distress — a breast tumor. An advanced-stage malignant tumor that had developed metastases to the spine or the bones would have produced just the sort of agonizing pain that Briggs was experiencing.[78]

Follett immediately sought the advice of Richard Cabot. Although Cabot was no longer practicing medicine, Richard and Ella had become Mary Follett's close friends and confidants. Cabot first consulted with Dr. Badger and then confessed to Follett that "there seems nothing important or encouraging to say. Professionally we are stumped. It is humiliating but not at all unfamiliar & I doubt if from the point of view of diagnosis it would be any use to look further for light from others." Although he was not "sanguine" about the effects of any known treatment (x-ray, quartz light), he suggested that Follett urge Dr. Badger "to try anything that holds out any claim to help, with the exception of anything that seems obviously painful or harmful." Anticipating a difficult road ahead, he implored Mary to "draw upon your friends as one would upon a bank reserve. I want to be used by you as far as other ties permit."[79]

The end came swiftly. The week before Christmas would prove to be the last Follett really had with the woman she called her "beloved friend."[80] A few days after Christmas, Ella Cabot reached out to Mary, sending her a tender note: "I think of you, & I think of you, longing to be a little shelter to your anxious, lonely soul. Seeing dear Miss Briggs last autumn made me aware ever more of the tender strength of your relations together and of her responding and protecting care. It must be very hard not to be able to take away her pain."[81] Even as she was dying, Isobel, whose first concern had always been for Mary's welfare, urged her beloved to turn to the Cabots for comfort.[82] It proved to be wise counsel. On January 8, 1926, at age seventy-seven, Mary Follett's life partner of thirty years died.[83] Three days later, her body was cremated.

Without delay, Ella and Richard Cabot brought Mary to their Cambridge home and lavished on her three weeks of loving care.[84] Follett began her stay expecting it to be a mere "tiding-over," an exhibition of kindly concern that the Cabots would show to any number of acquaintances in a crisis. This misconception was typical of Mary. She had always had difficulty accepting the depth of her friends' affections. But by the end of her visit, Follett realized her error and confessed it to the Cabots: "after I had been with you for ten days or so, I became aware that what you were doing for me was far more than a 'tiding-over.' My imagination was rebuked, it had been too niggardly for what you have to give. I saw that the affection was to last, that I was to have it forever, that it was too real to be only for emergencies."[85]

The loving intimacy that Follett shared with the Cabots eased her distress and allowed her to pick up the threads of work she had cast aside when the seriousness of Briggs's illness had become evident. But even as Follett resumed her professional correspondence, she made no effort to hide her pain. "My friend died on January 8, and how I am to face life without her I can not see," Follett confided to William Mosher. "I wish you had known her and had realized what an unusual person she was, and then you would understand the terrible blow this is for me." Follett sent a similar letter to her colleague at City College of New York, Harry Overstreet. Follett wrote that she had begun an article about his latest book but put it aside when "the illness of Miss Briggs took such an acute form that all my time and thought had to be given to her. She died on January the 8th and I cannot tell you what this means to me. We had lived together for thirty years and I do not know how to face life without her."[86]

In early February the Cabots left Cambridge for a trip abroad, and their absence made it even more difficult for Follett to cope. "Three weeks tomorrow & I have not yet written you. But I have not been behaving very well," Follett confessed in a late February letter to her vacationing friends. "I ache to the roots of me. I want her, & I cannot seem to rise above it. But of course I am going to. I am so glad you are away! For I must face this fully."[87]

She did rise above it — at least well enough to complete preparation of the three papers she had promised to deliver in late April at the Bureau of Personnel Administration in New York. But emotionally, Mary continued to struggle. "There are some very different mes at present," Follett explained to the Cabots in early April. "There is the one I told you about last night — the one that seems on the verge of defeat. But there are others too, not so easily crushed." She continued: "My fear has been that I should break down, give in before I had learned the lesson of this experience. But if I can only keep on for a little while, I feel that I shall be stronger than I have been in the past. For this experience is revealing to me a weak side of myself, a side *far* weaker than I was aware of . . . This is my valley of darkness, my Gethsemane. If I can win through, it will be done, in a certain sense, once for all. Christ did not have to go into the tomb twice. Because he conquered. That is my Easter lesson." Christ, she believed, "conquered because he had victory *in his heart* all the time. Have I victory in my heart? That is my searching question. If I win through, it will be like putting on the armor which I need for the service I really do want to give." Determined to bear her grief and emerge victorious, Follett nevertheless poignantly admitted that "the only desire I am acutely conscious of at the moment is this longing to have Isobel again."[88]

21

*"You Have Been Extraordinarily
Helpful to Executives"*

More than twenty-five years earlier, Isobel Briggs had persuaded the thirty-year-old Mary Follett to abandon the solitude of Vermont in favor of a life of self-realization and service in Boston's immigrant neighborhoods. Now, engulfed in grief over Isobel's death, Follett again sought refuge in service. Committed to giving three spring lectures at the Bureau of Personnel Administration, she resolutely fulfilled her obligation. In these lectures and others that Follett would give from 1926 through 1928, she would apply the principles articulated in her earlier books and lectures to some of the pressing problems of business management. Taken together, these impressive lectures would mark Follett as one of the preeminent contributors to organizational and management thought.

The first of these talks, delivered on April 29, 1926, was titled "The Meaning of Responsibility in Business Management." Believing the topic she had been given was too broad, Follett narrowed the focus to the matter of "final" responsibility. By this, she meant something akin to what Sidney Webb, the English socialist, had called "ultimate authority" and what Oliver Sheldon, British author of *The Philosophy of Management* (1923), meant when he called "supreme control" and the final determination of policy two of the important functions of administration.[1] Conceptions such as these, despite their popularity with executives, seemed to Follett to be of little value to the future management of business organizations. Instead, Follett argued, the most fundamental idea in business organization was "function": "Research and scientific study determine function in scientifically managed plants. A man should have just as much, no more and no less, responsibility as goes with his function or his task. He should have just as much, no more and no less, authority as goes with his responsibility. Function, responsibility, and authority should be the three inseparables in business organization."[2]

Follett's Dynamic, Cumulative Conception of Authority and Responsibility

Since authority and responsibility are derived from function, it followed that their definitions should "have little to do with the hierarchy of position." A new way of thinking about authority was increasingly being accepted, Follett told her audience, in scientifically managed plants: "One of the differences between the old-time foreman and the present is that the former was thinking in terms of his authority; he thought he could not keep up his dignity before his men unless he had this thing which he called authority. Many foremen of today are learning to think in terms of responsibility for definite tasks or for a defined group of tasks."[3]

Follett's way of conceptualizing these terms had serious implications for the widely held notion that a company's president "*delegates* authority and responsibility." This expression, Follett argued, assumed that the "owner or chief executive has the 'right' to all the authority, but that it is useful to delegate some of it." But just as Follett had in *The New State* roundly critiqued the conception of "rights" traditionally found in political theory, here, too, she firmly rejected any abstract notion of rights. "I do not think that president or general manager should have any more authority," Follett declared, "than goes with *his* function."[4]

Not only was Follett convinced that authority and responsibility derive from function; she also was persuaded that "the essence of organization is the interweaving of function." As a result, authority and responsibility also must be seen as a matter of interweaving within a group process. "An order, a command, is a step in a process," Follett explained, "a moment in the movement of interweaving experience. We should guard against thinking this step a larger part of the whole process than it really is. There is all that leads to the order, all that comes afterwards . . . more than one man's experience has gone to the making of that moment."[5] The illusions of final determination, supreme control, and ultimate authority in administration must therefore give way — and be replaced in theory as well as practice by *cumulative* control and *cumu-*

lative responsibility. "That one person or board becomes the symbol of this cumulative responsibility," Follett concluded, "should not blind us to the truth of the matter."[6]

An extremely important consequence of Follett's dynamic, cumulative conception of authority and responsibility is that it "should greatly dignify the position of underexecutive and operator, for this conception makes each one's work tremendously important. If you see that your activity is, in its measure, contributing to authority, in the sense that is it part of the guiding will which runs the plant, it will add interest and dignity to the most commonplace life, will illumine the most routine duties."[7]

Given that the interweaving of functions is essential to the development of modern business organizations, why, Follett asked her audience, has coordination among functions been so difficult to achieve? Here, in the first of her analyses of the process of coordination, Follett posited several possible answers: first, coordination often is resisted by those whose major concern is having their individual contributions noticed; second, the necessity and advantages of coordination are not yet valued by managers, and often are pursued only when joint consultation is obviously required; third, the cross-relations required by coordination are blocked by the rigid hierarchies that characterize most business organizations; and, finally, coordination must begin much earlier in a decision process than is commonly recognized. "You cannot always bring together the *results* of departmental activities and expect to coordinate them. You have to have an organization which will permit an interweaving all along the line. Strand should weave with strand, and then we shall not have the clumsy task of trying to patch together finished webs."[8]

The Aim of Employee-Management Consultation Should Be to Increase the Power of All

In Follett's second lecture, on May 6, 1926, she took up the question "How Is the Employee Representation Movement Remolding the Accepted Type of Business Manager?" She had first broached the subject of employee representation plans in January 1925 in her lecture "Business as an Integrative Unity." There her focus had been on the *worker's* place in industry; here, her task was to sort out the implications of employee representation for *managers*.

Follett opened with a lengthy discussion of the utility of employee representation plans. Some commentators had argued for the plans because they seemed to recognize the "rights" of labor; others supported them because the plans offered a means of gaining employee consent to managerial initiatives. Follett, vigorously objecting to both of these ideas, echoed notions expressed years earlier in *The New State.* Not only had she long opposed any claims of abstract rights, but she also believed consent by voting was a thoroughly inadequate means of creating the collective will. "The vote is a deceptive business altogether," Follett proclaimed. She illustrated this point with a memorable analogy. "How often we used to see a tiny child driving with his father made happy by being allowed to hold the end of the reins. The vote makes many people happy in the same way; they think they are driving when they are not."[9]

Employee representation plans would be valuable, Follett argued, only if they were made an integral "part of a sound scheme of organization." And any such scheme had to take account of the interweaving responsibilities that Follett had seen in her studies of businesses. Thus, the form of employee representation plan envisioned by Follett would be based on function rather than on hierarchy or rank and, of necessity, would require "conference as its method."[10]

Much as she had done in her discussion of group process in *The New State,* Follett identified for her audience the attitudes and skills managers must have in order to consult meaningfully with their employees. Foremost among them is a "willingness to change the traditional fight attitude into a cooperative attitude." Indeed, Follett observed, it has been said that "one of the chief aims of employee representation is to secure a partnership spirit. But when this is said, the speaker is almost always thinking of a partnership spirit on the part of the workers. It is just as essential that the executives should have this spirit else they would be like the man who wrote to a Christian Scientist: 'There is disharmony between my wife and me. Will you please give my wife treatments?' "[11]

In creating a genuine partnership, the manager must first demonstrate both a willingness to "search for the real values involved on both sides, and the ability to bring about an interpenetration of these values." Second, the manager must fully acknowledge "that labor can make constructive contributions to management." And finally, the manager must come to "the realization that management is not a fixed quantity." Echoing ideas she had expressed years earlier about the Speaker's power in *The Speaker of the House of Representatives,* Follett continued: "When we used to talk of 'sharing' management, it was because we tended to think then of management as a fixed quantity. We thought that if some one was given a little, that amount had to be taken from some one else. But the fact is that the successful business is one which is always increasing management throughout the whole enterprise in the sense of developing initiative, invention. Any manager who is looking with farseeing eyes to the progress of his business wants not so much to locate authority as to increase capacity." Anticipating the central idea of our modern thinking about employee "empowerment," Follett added that the "aim of employee representation, because it should be the aim of every form of organization, should be not to share power but to increase power, to seek the methods by which power can be increased in all."[12]

Leadership, in Part, Can Be Learned

In her third lecture, given in May 1926, Follett took as her subject the "type of administrative leadership demanded by the present development of business management." This paper, developing notions of leadership first expressed in *The Speaker of the House of Representatives* and *The New State*, was the first of several papers on leadership that Follett would give over the next two years. Her expressed goal here was to "take the mysticism out of leadership." Oliver Sheldon had recently called leadership "an 'intangible capacity,'" Follett told her audience. "Someone else says it is 'beyond human calculation.' I think one of the hopes for the development of business management lies in the fact that leadership is capable of analysis, that it can, in part, be learned. That is my main thesis this evening."[13]

In her previous lectures Follett had argued that "a certain amount of management, of planning, even of leadership, belongs to all functions" and that it was the responsibility of the administrative head "to gather these up and make use of them."[14] As a consequence, the chief executive "should be the symbol of that functional unity, while his chief task should be to provide the conditions for a continuous and continually progressive unifying."[15] This conception of the chief executive's role, Follett said, "does away with the notion held by many that successful leadership depends chiefly on a compelling personality." Instead, "the type of administrative leader demanded by present-day thinking is not the man who wishes to do all the leading himself, but one who wishes to develop leadership all along the line; one who does not wish to do people's thinking for them, but to train them to think for themselves."[16] She continued: "Perhaps we cannot illustrate the president's position except by a three-dimension chart, with the president in the center . . . of a flow in and out. It is then as much his function to receive, from executives or workers, as to give out to them. He has not merely to give to others from those superqualities he alone possesses; he is all the time enriching himself by what he receives. He gives to each what he has received from all."[17] "Thus, you see," Follett said, carefully explicating the implications of her thinking, "I am not advocating a type of leadership which abandons to others, for some thoroughly mistaken notion of democracy, one iota of power. The great leader gathers power, and uses it as the energizing, the motor, force of a progressive enterprise."[18]

This conception of leadership — which drew on Follett's notions of cumulative authorities and cumulative responsibilities — makes "organizing ability the chief requirement of the administrative head." And central to this organizing ability is "the ability to see relationships — between facts, between functions."[19] Indeed, Follett explained, returning to a concept central to *Creative Experience,* the "chief mistake in thinking of leadership as resting wholly on personality lies in the fact that the administrative leader is not a leader of men only, but of something we are learning to call with Dr. [Elton] Mayo 'the total situation.'" Because the total situation includes "facts, present and potential, ideals, and men," executives must possess a high order of cognitive ability.[20]

Having argued in *Creative Experience* that the "total situation" is continually changing, Follett wisely stipulated here that executives seeking to exercise leadership also must be capable of carrying "the business forward, to look into the future and see what that will demand. This means," she continued, "he must have his ear to the ground, be alert to every symptom. He should have large vision, generous imagination, and the power of anticipatory judgment."[21]

Even before completing this series of lectures for the Bureau of Personnel Administration in May 1926, Mary Follett was arranging her next speaking engagement. She had been invited to return to the School for Citizenship and Public Affairs at Syracuse University for the July 1926 Summer Session for Social Science Teachers. There she would deliver two talks and join in informal conferences with ten or twelve staff members drawn from university social science faculties around the nation. Follett was intrigued by the prospect of this visit, because it afforded her an opportunity to discuss with Dean Mosher's staff a problem of common interest — building bridges between the increasingly fragmented social sciences.[22] This was a subject of immediate concern to Follett because she and Richard Cabot had been planning a Harvard graduate seminar on a similar topic. A few weeks before Follett left for Syracuse, Cabot wrote to her, responding to some of the ideas she had proposed for their 1926–27 seminar. "I consider it (the seminary) fully as much yours as mine now, though (as you are not yet officially appointed at Harvard)," Cabot ruefully observed, "it still has to be announced in my name."[23]

At Syracuse, the highlight of the school's summer session involved a series of evening lectures. Follett had been asked to inaugurate these lectures with "a discussion of the methods of teaching the social sciences and of the possibility and necessity of unifying the complex body of knowledge commonly spoken of as social science."[24] Her address was attended by more than a hundred students and faculty, including the eminent psychologist Floyd H. Allport, whose brother Gordon had helped Follett with her research on the German Gestaltists. "When I was in college," Follett told her listeners, "we discussed economic problems in the economics courses, psychological problems in the psychological courses, and the ethical problems in the ethics courses. The disadvantage in this method is that there isn't anything anywhere in the world such as an ethical problem; there isn't anything anywhere in the world such as a economic problem, nor is there anything anywhere such as a psychological problem. There are only human problems. If I say to a maid 'Hand me that book,' there you have a human problem with psychological, economic, and ethical aspects."[25]

If we were able to reach the goal of creating more progressive unifyings among the social sciences, Follett wondered aloud, what might be achieved? We almost certainly would enrich our understanding of human problems; and if we were to discuss problems from a number of disciplinary perspectives, we might eventually enable ourselves to discover principles that underlie the various social sciences. Cross-disciplinary investigations might also facilitate the development of more valuable pedagogies — ones in which students would learn "abstract conceptions by concrete manifestations," cooperate in assignments and experiments, and be taught "by situation rather than by subjects."[26]

Follett's topic was intriguing, but the actual lecture was not one of her finer moments. Her text was rambling, unfocused, and often difficult to follow. That Follett had any impact at all on this occasion, however, was truly remarkable. It had been barely more than a year since she had been diagnosed with cancer and six arduous months since she had lost her beloved Isobel. Mosher would later tell Follett that he heard "many reverberations" of her visit and assured her that "you scattered 'seminal thoughts' that are bound to grow as time goes on."[27]

Despite the uneven quality of Follett's Syracuse lecture, its content was notable in one respect. For the first time, Follett neatly summarized human behavior as a process comprised of three elements: interacting, unifying, and emerging.[28] She had little more to say about these three elements while at Syracuse, but they were a harbinger of the main intellectual contribution that she would make to the 1926–27 "Follett-Cabot Seminary."

Having used the occasion of her summer 1926 Syracuse lecture to begin thinking about her contributions to the upcoming Harvard seminar, Follett wrote Richard Cabot in mid-June and urged him to get the other faculty participants lined up and enlisted in the task of working out "cooperatively the fundamentals of the social sciences."[29] Cabot, however, urged caution. Aware of the sensitivities of his faculty colleagues, he believed it imperative that they move at a more deliberate pace. "Curiously enough, though I am one of the most impatient of mortals," Cabot wrote, "I think I shall be the drag, this time, on the speed of your aspirations. I know that I want to do all the things that you have in mind & do them 'immediately or sooner.' But I want still more to avoid giving offense to the other teachers. I mean to avoid making them think that I am trying to order them about & make them play my little game, or that I disregard the value of their intrenched ideas." Cabot playfully observed that "not one of them would be pleased with your simile of the orchestra and of RCC as its leader! . . . Affectionately your fellow conspirator."[30]

Less than a week after Mary returned from Syracuse, she embarked on a four-month stay in England. Surely one motivation for this trip, which required a week-long voyage at sea, was her longing to visit places she and Isobel had known and to spend time in the company of Briggs's relatives. She also would have eagerly anticipated a chance to relax and reminisce about Isobel with her old Newnham friend Melian Stawell, whose longtime intimate relationship with another ex-Newnhamite, Clara Reynolds, enabled her to appreciate the intensity of Mary's loss.[31]

There were other reasons, too, to look forward to a trip abroad. It would have been a fascinating time for someone with Mary Follett's interests to be in England: only two years earlier, the Labour party had been asked, for the first time in its history, to form a government. And although Labour's tenure was brief, a mere ten months, Labour's intellectuals were confident that the party would soon return to power — this time as the largest party in the House of Commons.[32]

The turbulent state of English industrial relations would also have been of interest to Follett. Worker militancy had begun to intensify in 1924 with strikes of engine drivers, dockers, and London tramwaymen. In 1926, coal miners went on strike and were supported for a time by workers in a number of other industries.[33] It was in mid-July, two months after the end of the nationwide strike, that Mary Follett arrived in England. But instead of immersing herself immediately in this complex labor-management crisis, Follett chose first to relax by the Cornish sea in Tintagel and then continue on to nearby Minehead in Somerset, where she visited with Isobel's relatives. Only after this interlude in the west of England did Follett travel north to Edinburgh, where, at the invitation of Lord Haldane, she stayed for two days in mid-August at Cloan, the Haldane family home in Scotland.

Follett's relationship with Haldane, the longtime Liberal philosopher-statesman, dated from the time he had offered to write an introduction to the English edition of *The New State*. Haldane had been driven from political office as lord chancellor in 1915 by charges that he was pro-German; but by 1924 he had fully resumed his political career, serving as lord chancellor in England's first Labour government. Early in 1924, shortly before he was named lord chancellor, Follett had asked Haldane to review the manuscript of *Creative Experience* and was stunned when he did so, even after assuming office. "What fun," Follett wrote, expressing her gratitude for his suggestions, "that you are *doing* some of the things I can only write about. You will now probably have many opportunities to recognize and work with functional wholes, that is, at one and the same time to reject abstract wholes, and also the conceptions of those who think atomism is going to save their hugged-to-their-hearts individualism. It is so wonderful that England just at this moment should have a philosopher at the helm."[34]

By the time Follett arrived in England, the Labour party and Haldane had been out of office for well over a year, replaced by the Conservatives. Follett, nonetheless, was still enthusiastic about meeting with Haldane. She had recently received a copy of the report of the Machinery of Government Committee that he had chaired and was anxious to talk over with him certain fundamental principles of organization. She also had read Haldane's *Human Experience* (1926), and she pronounced this book-length critique of some of John Dewey's ideas "of greater value" than any other book Haldane had written.[35]

As it turned out, the chance to converse at leisure with Haldane was not the only reason that Follett's visit to Cloan made her feel "spiritually at home there." One of the unexpected pleasures of her visit was the opportunity to make the acquaintance of Haldane's sister, Elizabeth Sanderson Haldane. The discussions that ensued between these women about vocational guidance and placement and the significance of group activity sparked a friendship that would be sustained by periodic correspondence.[36]

Perhaps at the suggestion of the Haldanes, Follett spent a few days at Aviemore, southeast of Inverness, before leaving for England, where she had been invited to lecture in early September at Rowntree & Company Ltd., a family-owned chocolate and confectionery manufacturing firm in York that had operated since the mid-1800s.[37] Follett had met the renowned chairman, B. Seebohm Rowntree (1871–1954), during his 1921 lecture tour in the United States.[38] At Rowntree & Company, Seebohm Rowntree had helped his father introduce a system of company pensions for workers (1906); and after the war, the younger Rowntree led in the establishment of a five-day working week (1919), the codification of factory work rules by a committee that included workers as well as managers (1921), and the institution of company-based unemployment insurance (1921) and profit-sharing systems (1923) for the company's rapidly growing workforce. Taken together, these initiatives earned for Seebohm Rowntree a national and international reputation as an enlightened employer.[39]

Rowntree was warmly received in the United States, where he already was well known for the advanced management methods described in his book *The Human Factor in Business* (1921). Rowntree's platform, reported in the *New York Evening Post,* called for wages that would allow workers to live in reasonable comfort, working hours that would allow time for recreation and self-expression, methods for alleviating unemployment and giving workers increased economic security, a share for workers in determining working conditions, and a share for workers in the "prosperity" of their industry.[40] Among the many men and women with whom Rowntree became acquainted during this visit were Dorothy Whitney Straight, in whose home he stayed while in New York, and Henry S. Dennison, who would eventually become his "dearest" friend.[41]

In early September 1926 Mary Follett lectured at Rowntree & Co. in York. No written records of her presentations have been found, but Follett reported to Richard Cabot that the "folks" at Rowntree "seemed to like my lectures." Indeed, for the first time since Isobel's death in January, Mary seemed positively ebullient. "I have simply heaps to tell you, too much to write. I am quite full & running over." A variety of stimulating social engagements had been planned for her in London, which she previewed for Cabot with her customary self-deprecating wit: "Tonight I dine with . . . Mr. John Lee, head of Telephone system of England & Sir Geoffrey Clarke, head of Cable Construction Co., who have both (poor, misguided things) expressed a wish to meet me! Lord & Lady Emmott have asked me to dine to meet Sir Arthur Steele-Maitland [*sic*], the Minister of Labor, & Sir Arthur Wilson. So the fraud goes on! All will be well if only you stay out of England until after [my departure on October]14th so that I shan't be exposed."[42] Follett apparently also met with Harold Laski, G. D. H. Cole, and R. H. Tawney—the trio of prominent Labour party intellectuals—but she found these encounters something of a disappointment because the intellectuals of the Labour party still saw "the whole labor question in the fight pattern" between management and labor. A few months later she would write to Elizabeth Haldane expressing her dissatisfaction with "even Tawney whom I like personally so much" and inquiring of the Haldanes whether her judgment of the group was "wholly wrong."[43]

At the end of September, Follett gave a lecture at the National Institute for

Industrial Psychology, a nonprofit organization devoted to industrial research, training, and testing. This appearance most likely had been arranged at the behest of either Seebohm Rowntree (who had served on the institute's Executive Committee since its founding) or Lord Haldane (an institute vice-president).[44] Follett's lecture, "The Basis of Control in Business Management," opened with a brief reprise of ideas she had expressed at the Bureau of Personnel Administration in New York, concerning ways to enhance the development of business management as a profession. Her primary goal, however, was to illustrate the variety of ways in which "psychology can help to give us scientific foundations for business management" — among them, the nature and timing of supervision; the process of giving orders; the effects that particular words and phrases have on people's attitudes and behavior; methods of crafting meaningful distinctions among power, authority, and influence; the process of representation in labor disputes; and the effective use of committees and conferences.[45] Given Follett's generous vision of the role that psychology might play in industry, her remarks, not surprisingly, were well received at the institute. A few months later in a note to Elizabeth Haldane, Mary jocularly reported that she and Dr. Charles Myers, the director, "seemed to get on very nicely together in spite of the prophecy to the contrary."[46]

Immediately after her presentation in London, Follett traveled to Oxford to speak at Balliol College on October 1 and 2 at the Twenty-third Lecture Conference for Works Directors, Managers, Foremen and Forewomen. This Rowntree-sponsored conference was an outgrowth of a 1918 meeting of Quaker employers who "pledged themselves to do everything within their power to develop and extend the sense of responsibility of employers to their workers, and urged that there should be a regular series of further conferences."[47] Seebohm Rowntree took up this challenge by instituting in 1919 a semiannual series of conferences aimed at reducing labor unrest through the reeducation of "tactless and unsympathetic foremen . . . in new ideas." One of the speakers at the first meeting, a son-in-law of the master of Balliol College at Oxford, was so enthusiastic that he persuaded his father-in-law to make the conferences a regular extracurricular activity at Balliol. Although business management as a profession was not held in particularly high esteem in England, once Rowntree had gained the personal endorsement of the master of Balliol, he was able for more than a decade to hold semiannual conferences at this 650-year-old bastion of higher learning for approximately forty firms representing "a fair cross-section of British industry."[48]

Lyndall Urwick, then a thirty-five-year-old executive at Rowntree & Co. Ltd., vividly recalled the autumn 1926 Oxford conference when he first met Mary Follett. Urwick had only recently been married and was eagerly

Mary P. Follett, ca. 1925. Lyndall Fownes Urwick Archive, Henley Management College, Henley-on-Thames.

anticipating a special weekend with his new wife when he was informed by Rowntree that Mary Follett would be speaking at Oxford. Not wanting to disappoint his boss, Urwick felt compelled to attend, but went "in no very good humour about the Conference." His mood was not improved when he heard Follett's singularly "academic" contributions to the informal discussion following the Friday-evening speaker's presentation. Nor did he find anything at all physically attractive in his first glimpse of this fifty-eight-year-old "gaunt Boston spinster lady." She was "no 'oil painting,'" Urwick later recalled, "and though she spent a great deal of money on her clothes, they were never completely successful. I can remember thinking 'What on earth is my dear, kind master, Seebohm, thinking about? He's ruined my lovely weekend, and for what? This woman and I can have nothing in common.'" At the end of the evening, however, Rowntree captured Urwick and introduced him to Mary Follett. It was then that the magic began. "In two minutes flat," Urwick remembered, "I was at her feet, and I stayed there as long as she lived."[49]

What caused such a dramatic reversal of opinion? Reconstructing the meeting more than forty years later, Urwick was surprised to find himself, "a man in his eightieth year, writing about [Mary Follett] as though she was a girl he had just fallen in love with." He explained: "Imagine yourself meeting complete strangers and, in two minutes' conversation, conveying to them a. That you were immensely interested in them as individual people, in their experience, their thoughts, everything about them, but b. That this interest, this curiosity were impersonal in the sense that you were *not* curious about them as individuals. You were identifying them from the first syllable that passed between you as part of that much greater whole — the human condition. Your petty experience *mattered* to her, not because she was inquisitive, or curious, but because *you were* important, *as part of that whole*. I doubt if she ever met anyone who was her intellectual superior," Urwick said in admiration, "just as I doubt if she ever met anyone without making them feel more important in themselves. Cleverness with no conceit, pity without patronage, sympathy with no superiority, interest without intrusion, it was a marvellous equipment."[50]

Urwick got his first opportunity to hear Follett lecture the day after their meeting. Follett's speech, "Some Methods of Executive Efficiency," was organized around two principles by now central to her thought: the law of the situation and integration. The core of the paper was based on the "Constructive Conflict" lecture she had given in 1925 to the Bureau of Personnel Administration, but she included elements of other lectures as well.[51] Perhaps the most striking element of this first Oxford lecture is that Follett chose this moment — in a distinguished academic setting reminiscent of Newnham, where she had first come to have a sense of her intellectual powers — to make a stirring testimonial about why she had chosen to study business management. It was in business, Follett unabashedly declared, rather than in government or philosophy that she found the "greatest vitality of thinking to-day." And she joyfully cast her lot with those involved in business management, because "while I care for the ideal, it is only because I want to help bring it into our everyday affairs."[52]

The following morning, Follett lectured on "The Illusion of Final Responsibility." Here, too, the ideas she expressed owed much to a lecture she had made at the Bureau of Personnel Administration. But Follett added a series of rich illustrations that typified how she could wrest, from the most seemingly insignificant experiences of daily life, instructive insights about both the functioning of organizations and her own thought process.[53]

Follett's Oxford lectures were attended by her old Newnham friend Melian Stawell, who was amazed that Follett captured this critical and exacting audience from her first sentence. "I felt a good deal of feminist pride," Stawell later recalled, "when I saw how she could handle them and still more patriotic pride when, ardent as in her youth, she let her enthusiasm for England overflow, 'O there's only the school-girl phrase for it,' she cried, 'I'm just crazy about you all in England.' "[54]

Follett returned home from England on October 23, a week later than originally planned, because of a change made by the steamship line. The delay was of some consequence, because it meant that she would miss the first two sessions of the Follett-Cabot Seminary, which had begun on October 4, 1926.[55]

This year-long graduate seminar, Social Ethics 20a, was an outgrowth of Follett's persistent desire to find corollaries among different academic disciplines. Richard Cabot shared this concern, but he also had a more personal agenda. Cabot hoped that the increasingly tenuous place of his Social Ethics Department in the curriculum might be strengthened if ways could be found "to break down departmental barriers so that social ethics could draw freely upon the resources of the other social sciences."[56] Thus, the Follett-Cabot Seminary was conceived by Cabot, at least in part, as an opportunity to entice the social science faculty into exploring the feasibility of interdisciplinary study and research under the guidance of the Department of Social Ethics. Because it was the faculty participants who were of prime concern to Cabot, he complained early on to Follett that "we have a lot of students (— too many)."[57]

Virtually every Harvard department concerned with the social sciences was represented, some by more than one person. Among those on the impressive roster of presenters were Dean Roscoe Pound (Law School); Dean Henry W.

Richard Clarke Cabot, ca. 1920. The Schlesinger Library, Radcliffe Institute, Harvard University.

Holmes (Graduate School of Education); Dean William W. Fenn (School of Theology); Earnest A. Hooten (Department of Anthropology), who specialized in criminal anthropology; and Arthur M. Schlesinger (History), newly appointed in 1924 and a proponent of the "New History," which advocated studying historical periods in terms of human activity as a whole rather than as a single part.[58] From the joint Department of Philosophy and Psychology, the presenters were William E. Hocking, Ralph B. Perry, and Alfred North White-head, the last having brought his studies of metaphysics to Harvard in 1924 after his retirement from the University of London. From the Department of Economics, three faculty contributed lectures: Allyn A. Young, who was conversant in statistics, mathematics, and philosophy as well as economics; Thomas N. Carver, the conservative Social Darwinist who had shared the platform in 1925 with Follett at the Bureau of Personnel Administration; and Edwin F. Gay, former dean of the Harvard Business School.[59] From the Department of Government, Arthur N. Holcombe made a presentation, and William Y. Elliott attended; both men had been instrumental in upgrading their department through the addition of courses in such subjects as political theory and municipal government.[60] Among those who participated in the postlecture discussions was Harold D. Lasswell, who in later years would pioneer American research in political psychology; Lasswell had just received his doctorate from the University of Chicago.[61]

There were two other distinguished participants in the 1926–27 seminar. Lawrence H. Henderson, a professor of biological chemistry at the Harvard Medical School and one of the most "original and distinguished biological chemists of his time," made an early presentation. Henderson had only recently read Vilfredo Pareto's *Traité de sociologie générale* (1917) and was much taken with Pareto's emphasis on "such matters as equilibrium, the social system, the mutual dependence of variables, and the problems of induction and abstraction." Over the next decade, Henderson's persistent explications of Pareto would make these ideas a part of the thinking of a generation of Harvard sociologists. In a more applied vein, Henderson also was interested in problems of worker fatigue and in 1926 had become director of the Rocke-feller Foundation–funded Laboratory of Industrial Physiology, established in the basement of the Business School.

In the adjoining office, charged with undertaking scientific studies of human relations in industry, was forty-six-year-old Elton Mayo, an Australian industrial psychologist and practitioner of psychiatry. Mayo had recently written a paper for the Taylor Society about the importance of the "total situation" in analyzing the psychological and performance problems of individual workers. And he would soon become involved in the industrial research project being pursued at the Hawthorne plant of the Western Electric Company in Chicago — one of the pioneering studies of the effects of human relations in industry. Mayo, who had just been appointed associate professor and head of the Industrial Research Department of the Business School, did not make a seminar presentation, but he did participate in some postpresentation discussions.[62]

The seminar had already met twice by the time Follett arrived home to find this breathless letter from Richard Cabot: "Bless you! Welcome home! We have been counting the days — there is so much work for you to do (& inspire) in relation to the Seminary, & if you get there Monday as I devoutly hope . . . you won't have missed much. It has all been religiously stenographed," Cabot continued, "but I don't think amounts to much yet. Whitehead was fine but hardly got round to our field in his exposition of metaphysics. Ford & I who preceded him were very tenuous & unsatisfactory. Hocking comes on Monday. I have asked each person who speaks to answer the questions & discuss the topics on the enclosed sheet. But Ford didn't & Whitehead said he couldn't!"[63] As it turned out, illness prevented Follett from attending Hocking's lecture on Monday, but she apparently did not miss much. "It was a most lamentable exhibition," Cabot groaned, "and contributed zero."[64]

Follett's first appearance at the seminar was on November 1, at the lecture by Lawrence J. Henderson. Three years earlier, when Follett was working on *Creative Experience,* Henderson had told her in his characteristically acerbic style, "You've got hold of the idea which a few of the greatest minds in the course of the last few thousand years have tried to say, but no one has said and I don't believe you will." Still, Follett thought he had seemed "immensely interested" in the idea, and she had been buoyed by their exchange.[65]

Follett participated in the conversation that followed Henderson's presentation, as she would in many of the seminar sessions during the next months. She certainly was not the dominant figure in these discussions, but she also showed no reluctance in intellectually engaging some of Harvard's best faculty — even Henderson himself, whose demeanor in conversation, one colleague quipped, was "feebly imitated by a piledriver."[66] Transcripts show Follett requesting clarifications, noting contradictions, contributing information gleaned from her own investigations, testing the validity of ideas by applying them to concrete situations, and positing possible convergences among various disciplinary lines of thought.

Follett's own lecture was scheduled for delivery in late December. By late November she had not yet begun to write it, but a visit to Ella Cabot roused her from her doldrums. "It really did help," she wrote appreciatively to her dear friend. "It wasn't just the pleasure of the actual hours with you . . . I feel sometimes such a lonely cat nowadays that I like to have the little feeling of belonging which you are so good as to let me have with you. I don't know anyone else with whom I could have it, because there is no one else I care enough for." At the same time, Mary was careful not to impose or to appear too needy: "I don't want you to think because I told you I was lonely that you must have me on your mind. I will promise to let you know when I need you. But I intend that those times shall be few, & I feel something inside which tells me that in the end I shall conquer . . . I began my paper for the Seminar & wrote half of it, an unusual rate of speed for me."[67]

It was important that Follett make rapid progress on her December seminar paper because she also had another professional obligation: on December 10 she was scheduled to be in New York to make a major presentation to an audience of 500 business people, consultants, and business professors at a meeting of the prestigious Taylor Society. Fortunately, the basic elements of this paper, "The Illusion of Final Authority," had been delivered twice before, first in April at the Bureau of Personnel Administration and then in October at the Rowntree Conference at Oxford. It was a judicious choice, for the material apparently was new to most in her audience and was extremely well received.

When Follett's paper was published in the *Bulletin of the Taylor Society,* the editor bemoaned the "misfortune that the article in cold print cannot re-produce the atmosphere of the session at which it was presented; the inter-ested, concentrated, tense attention with which it was received."[68] Further evidence of the largely favorable reception appears in the published remarks of the six session respondents. George G. Barber, chairman of the board of Con-tinental Baking Corporation in New York, testified that her ideas about meth-ods of coordination had been "of practical, *cumulative* value" in his own company: "She has helped us get our minds away from personalities and keep our thinking on the job. She has helped us define function more sharply. She has helped us appreciate the importance of conference, committees, good will and mutual understanding. I am sure that this process has helped us all to become more scientifically minded and increasingly to respect each other."

Even as Barber celebrated Follett's intellectual contributions to the func-tioning of his firm, he had some words of advice for her in her role as author: "her business philosophy would be wonderfully enhanced in acceptance by business executives and hence widened in service if it could be presented in more direct, simple language. The average business executive is not willing to take the time to stretch his mind on many of Miss Follett's most penetrat-ing sentences." Barber nevertheless concluded with a ringing affirmation: "I know no stronger appeal to the business executive than the fact that this new business philosophy gives the executive opportunities, influence, constructive power immeasurably greater than the old autocratic, individualist methods of management."[69]

Ten days after delivering her address in New York, Follett returned to the Harvard seminar and the philosophical musings of Harvard's social scientists. When she rose to give her lecture on December 20, she looked out onto an audience that included Whitehead, Henderson, Mayo, Ford, Cabot, and Lasswell. "Dr. Cabot has asked me for fundamentals," Follett began. "I think the most fundamental thought for the social sciences concerns the *nature of unities.*"[70] Two years earlier, in *Creative Experience,* Follett had explicated the three principal contributions of recent psychological research: circular response, integrative behavior, and the total situation. In this lecture she looked beyond psychology to research and theorizing in a wide range of physical and social science disciplines — always in a search for evidence of the organic whole as the unit of study. In presenting the findings of her investigations, Follett continually emphasized the importance of *relations* — "because while it is customary now to speak of 'the total situation,' that phrase means to many people merely that we must be sure to get all the [relevant] factors into our problem." Follett had in mind something more dynamic, namely, that "all these factors are influencing one another while they are making the total." As she saw it, "the reciprocal activity of the parts changes the parts while it is creating the unity. That," she added, "is the first point of this paper."[71]

Follett next turned to a discussion of "the nature of the interacting" that takes place in the total situation. "If we could discover that," Follett told her audience, "I think we should have arrived at something very fundamental." When two activities, A and B, interact by reciprocally influencing each other, the phenomenon is something like what the physiologists have called "circular response" — the second of the three concepts she had presented in *Creative Experience.* "In every situation our own activity is part of the cause of our activity. We respond to stimuli which we have helped to make." She offered an illustration: "When we read in books on business management . . . that general policy dictates departmental policy, our tendency may be to deny this and to say that departmental policies are contributing to general policy. But there is a deeper truth than either of these, and that is this something which I am trying to express tonight, that it is the same activity which is making the whole and parts simultaneously. We don't put parts together. We watch parts behaving together, and the way they behave together is the whole. I say parts, and people often speak of the factors or elements in a total, but when we use any of these words we must remember that we are talking of activities."[72]

Having described the kind of interacting that constitutes an organic unity, Follett turned to the evolving situation. Reciprocal relating, Follett asserted, is more than mere adjustment of one factor to another — something new is created. Or, as she had put it in her July lecture at Syracuse, every true social process "has three aspects: the interacting, the unifying, and the emerging." These are not linear stages; instead, "There is one simultaneous process and these three are aspects of that process." Follett emphasized that Professor

Whitehead, with his conception of an organism as a structure of activities that are continually evolving, had got "nearer the heart of the truth of this matter than anyone has yet."

The challenge for social scientists, as Follett saw it, was to seek to discover what forms of interacting and unifying opened the way for emerging — for the creation of the plus-values she had spoken about in *Creative Experience*. "Progress is through release and integration. A releases something in B, B releases something in A, and by the nature, *the essential nature* of the interacting, we have an integrating which is an emerging." Follett also emphasized the opposite: "when we do not have the reciprocal interacting, we do not get the emerging. For instance, when an arbitrator in a dispute says that one side is right and the other wrong, you have not the interacting which gives you a new situation which is a little in advance of the old situation. The job of the arbitrator . . . should be first to try to release the latent possibilities of value on both sides, understanding that such release involves new relatings, new integratings, or a new unity, a new situation." Follett concluded this first half of her presentation — which is laced throughout with telling illustrations from government, international relations, labor-management relations, economics, and social work — with an admonition: "We must learn how to make any human association most effective, most fruitful. The reciprocal influence, the interactive behavior, which involves a developing situation, is fundamental for politics, economics, jurisprudence, and ethics."[73]

In the remainder of her lecture, Follett sought to apply the "fundamentals" identified earlier to "some of the conceptions of the social sciences." She took up several concepts — freedom, loyalty, justice, responsibility, purpose — and also spoke briefly of the arts, education, and culture. Concluding her interdisciplinary survey, Follett left her distinguished audience with this plea: "What I am wishful for, what I hope this Seminar may lead to is that certain philosophers, biologists, psychologists, and social scientists should . . . join forces" to better understand this process of progressive unifyings."[74]

In the discussion that followed, several of the principals in the audience took turns connecting Follett's ideas to their own work. Henderson, who had a long-standing interest in the methodology of studying the relations among multiple, interdependent variables, pronounced himself largely in agreement with Follett. "So far as I understand the general position concerning the nature of organization, integration, and that kind of thing," Henderson began, "so far as I understand it I agree with it precisely and think that that type of consideration can be and should be applied in certainly all spheres of scientific study above the level of the lowest biological phenomena if not lower down." And even though Henderson balked at Follett's application of her social process to the concept of "*justice* or anything ethical," he could not "help thinking it might be possible in a field like this, by some kind of a quasi-mathematical analysis . . . to make the kind of survey of all the conceivable relationships between two things at a time, between three things at a time, between four things at a time, etc., and so to avoid that which I do object to about ethical and such considerations, namely, the subjective element in it."[75]

Elton Mayo acknowledged that he had not previously considered whether "this integrate unity is an important conception in comparing one scientific research or one part of human knowledge with another." On this question, Mayo graciously admitted, "I still feel that I am pursuing rather breathlessly Miss Follett."[76] Mayo continued: "I am afraid that in industrial investigation our only notion was to discover whether there was a possibility of stating some of the industrial disputes, in terms of the effects of fatigue . . . I suppose one might say that the idea, so far as we have an idea, in getting these very crude and elementary beginnings of an investigation is very much the idea that you have been expounding as a leading idea for social investigation." Mayo then challenged Follett by asking whether "empirical investigation is not more important really than the principle, because at the present time one cannot assume that interaction will lead to unification and emergence." That question led to the following exchange.

> FOLLETT: "I thought everything I said was in favor of empirical investigation."
> MAYO: "I understood you to imply that out of interaction emerged unification."
> FOLLETT: "I said it would be wise for us to learn the kind of interaction that does lead to it, that empirical investigations of social situations had led me to think that we could perhaps deal with a kind of interaction that might produce unification . . ."
> MAYO: " . . . I really feel that I have not considered at all the sort of problem you have stated tonight. I should like time."[77]

Several others also participated in this lively discussion, including Ford and even Whitehead, who expostulated on versions of the "one" and the "many." Harold Lasswell, after describing the kinds of problems currently of interest in the field of politics, remarked that "at the present time individuals who are dissatisfied with the historical type of politics are interested in Miss Follett because here is at least an effort to face these problems clearly and see what implications can be drawn from them."[78]

Follett did not let the evening end without returning to a earlier remark of Henderson's that had been bothering her. "I have only one sore point," Follett protested, "and that is Dr. Henderson's saying what he said about justice, because I don't think I am so bad." "You are no worse than anybody else," Henderson retorted. "I am denouncing the whole human race. I should like to ask Prof. Whitehead if he knows what justice is?" "No," was the professor's lighthearted reply, "but I trust Miss Follett and Plato together."[79]

With her Harvard seminar presentation successfully behind her, Follett finally was able to surrender to the sorrow that had been intensifying for weeks — for it was during the Christmas holidays a year ago that Isobel had become deathly ill. "I cannot bring myself to buy cards etc this Xmas," she explained in a note to Eva Whiting White, her former colleague in the Boston community centers movement, "as this is an inexpressibly sad time for me. This week last year was the last I really had with my beloved friend. The change came on Xmas Day. The memories are so poignant as to be almost unbearable." Follett spent Christmas Eve with a friend across the street and then Christmas dinner with the Dennisons in Framingham, but these holiday gatherings did little to raise her spirits.[80] On December 30 she wrote a revealing letter to Elizabeth Haldane and enclosed a gift of George Santayana's poems for Elizabeth's brother. "I have never thanked you for your letter — yet it has meant much to me, for I think it was good of you to accept me as a friend on such short probation. And I think I will say something more, for it has been very much in my thoughts and I feel sure you will be willing to let me say it."

> These days which I am passing through now are the hardest I have ever known, for these weeks a year ago were the last in which I had my beloved friend, and the loneliness is sharp and poignantly present. I miss her in two ways just because she was she, but also because she was a rare and noble soul, high-minded and single-minded to a degree which few people attain. What I wanted to say was that I feel a little less bereft at having that gone out of the world because in August I found these qualities in someone else. Please don't mind my saying this. We are so far apart and may never meet again so that it may never get expressed in any other way than in these words. I shall just carry the knowledge tucked away to warm me when life seems too sad.[81]

Less than a week after writing this letter, Follett gamely returned to the Harvard seminar — this time to lead a session intended primarily for the graduate students. On this occasion, Follett's motive was to implore the students to learn by watching and interpreting their own experience. " 'Experiment, record, pool.' We do not do any of those things enough."[82]

A lively discussion ensued, probably lasting nearly an hour. Two things are striking about this conversation. Most of the students were focused on the limitations rather than the possibilities of Follett's ideas. They seemed unwilling even to consider trying to put the ideas into action without perfect prior conceptualizing. Follett, by comparison, was remarkably pragmatic. "You just have to do the best you can," Follett replied to one student who had complained that it was not possible to look at all the factors in a situation. To another who was looking for explicit guidance on how to apply what they were being taught in the seminar, she answered that they were being asked "simply to see whether you could [apply these principles], whether it was possible. As we have to begin somewhere, take interacting, unifying, emerging." Finally, Follett became so exasperated with the students' timorousness about taking her ideas into the field to test their utility (as she herself had done in so many contexts) that she erupted: "I think what I rather object to is this, that I have not sat and read books on philosophy and decided that the deepest fundamental principles of the universe were three. I have simply for about 25 years been watching boards and groups and have decided from that watching on these principles on interacting, unifying, and emerging. And it seems to me that you are supposing that I begin the other way around. In my experience that is what happens when you have fruitful results. I am giving my experience. I am not giving philosophy out of a book."[83]

The Follett-Cabot Seminary continued through the spring of 1927, with Follett attending many of the sessions. Although the seminar failed in the sense that it was not instantly successful in enlisting Harvard's preeminent social scientists in developing new programs of cross-disciplinary theorizing and research, the seminar is widely believed to have had at least one immediate, salutary consequence. By a faculty vote in 1927, Harvard reorganized its academic requirements for an undergraduate degree in the social sciences. Social science students would now elect a joint concentration in sociology and social ethics administered by a special committee of faculty from several disciplines (history, government, economics, anthropology, philosophy, and psychology), most of whom had participated in the 1926–27 seminar. At least for a short time, therefore, the Follett-Cabot Seminary delayed at Harvard what one expert has described as the "fragmentation of the academic world into clusters of technique specialists, each playing a variation on the theme of objectivity."[84]

In March and April 1927, Follett returned to New York to give four papers at the Bureau of Personnel Administration in its 1926–27 lecture series, "The Psychological Foundations of Management."[85] Building on her Harvard seminar work, Follett's goal in her first lecture, "The Psychology of Control," was to propose four "fundamental principles of human relations": evoking (which she had newly added), interacting, unifying (or integrating), and emerging.[86] In three subsequent lectures she would test these fundamental principles against a set of specific relations familiar to her audience: the relations implicit in consent and participation, the relation of arbitrator and conciliator to the group, and the relation of leader and expert.[87]

The Fundamental Principles

Follett's presentation of the four fundamental principles repeated much of the paper she had just given in the Follett-Cabot Seminary, including its rather abstruse concepts. Follett was taking a risk, but she apparently believed that she could keep the attention of the practical business people in her audience by balancing the abstractions with a new set of pithy illustrations. Most of Follett's examples were drawn from accounts of current industrial practice, but others were taken from her own experience, including a detailed description of having her watch repaired in London's Bond Street.[88]

Progressive business people such as the ones Follett was addressing in this BPA audience were by now quite accustomed to talking among themselves about the importance of emphasizing functions over personalities and about how best to define functions in the workplace; but they would have been less familiar with the emphasis that Follett put on the *relating* of functions. In her discussion of "emerging," the third of her fundamental principles, Follett told her listeners that "functional relating has always a value beyond the mere addition of the part. A genuine interweaving or interpenetrating by changing both sides creates new situations. Recall what the president of the factory said in regard to the coordinating of his departments — that a genuine coordinating changed to some extent the two parts coordinated." Summing up her concerns, Follett used a phrase that had first appeared in her Follett-Cabot Seminary lecture: "Functional relating is the continuing process of self-creating coherence. Most of my philosophy," Follett proclaimed, "is contained in that sentence . . . If you have the right kind of functional relating, you will have a process which will create a unity which will lead to further unities — a self-creating progression."[89]

Participation as a Means of Evoking, Interacting, Integrating, and Emerging

In her next lecture, "The Psychology of Consent and Participation," Follett put her fundamental principles of human relations to their first test. Here, Follett made the argument (familiar to readers of *The New State* and *Creative Experience*) that "mere consent, bare consent" — including voting —

does not follow the principles of evoking, interacting, integrating, and emerging. Consent "gives us only the benefit of the ideas of those who put forward the propositions for consent; it does not give us what others may be capable of contributing."[90]

If we believe in contribution and active participation rather than in consent, how do we get effective participation? Follett identified three ways: "by an organization which provides for it, by a daily management which recognizes and acts on the principle of participation, and by a method of settling differences, or a method of dealing with the diverse contributions of men very different in temperament, training, and attainments."[91] Her focus in this lecture would be on the last — and, more specifically, on the process of integration as a way of dealing with differences.

Follett had lectured before on integrating differences as a means to securing the contribution of each individual and making conflict constructive. What was different on this occasion was her emphasis on *coordinating* contributions. Coordination, Follett argued, had become a particular concern of modern businesses, many of which had become massive enterprises. In large organizations such as these, it was increasingly necessary to "join the opinions" of such diverse parties as the foreman and the staff psychologist, the foreman and the staff member in charge of equipment maintenance, and the salesman and the staff member responsible for setting prices.

Coordination, Follett believed, required first a concerted effort to avoid either-or situations, because "it is the for-or-against attitude which makes conflict." She suggested an alternative approach: "Look for all the factors in the situation; guide your conference or committee so that two alternatives do not present themselves in the early stages of discussion; curb those who wish to vote the moment two clear-cut alternatives appear from out the discussion . . . If two are proposed prematurely, break them up, add others, and then the final alignment may be different from the first."[92]

Coordination also requires understanding; and understanding, in turn, is grounded in openness and explicitness. Openness is essential, "for you cannot integrate differences until you know what they are." And explicitness is necessary in order to "find out what we *really* want, ourselves and others, for you can seldom tell by the general phrases people use."[93] Perhaps the most important thing to remember about coordination, however, is that it must begin at the beginning rather than the end of the process. Follett's experience had taught her that "any contribution I may have to make to an undertaking may be correlated with the contributions of the others more successfully if the opportunity is given early in the undertaking."[94]

In sum, Follett was intent on working out a "system of decentralization combined with a satisfactory system of cross-functioning" that would make employee participation a continuous process in business management. She noted that in the past year, the president of the American Federation of Labor had on three separate occasions offered the services of the unions to help solve the problems of management, and that organizations as diverse as the Baltimore and Ohio Railroad and the American Telephone and Telegraph Company had successfully introduced joint manager-worker conferences. Although Follett felt confident that labor was already making constructive contributions to management in the United States and England, she urged the business leaders in her audience to be more forthcoming in acknowledging how much they need the workers' input: "Whenever the workmen are taken into counsel, I think it should be made clear to them that the aim is not merely industrial peace, to avoid strikes, nor to anticipate the union organizer, that is, to create some internal machinery which will make union affiliation seem unnecessary; that it is not merely to adjust petty grievances more expeditiously, nor is it merely a sop, or a way to get the managerial policy across, or even to provide a better field for collective bargaining, and certainly not a matter of altruism." Instead, the workers must come genuinely to feel that the consultations serve a larger purpose: they are being undertaken for the good of all "in order to get every bit of knowledge and experience the man in daily touch with the processes and details of the business has gained."[95]

The conception of participation that Follett proposed was clearly grounded in the fundamental principles of human relations with which she opened her first lecture: evoking, which is concerned with drawing out the capacities of all; interacting and integrating, which are achieved by means of coordinating; and finally emerging or creating something new, "which, translated as business progress, is the aim of organization engineering."[96]

Creating Integrations through Mediation rather than Arbitration

Follett took up another matter of immediate concern to business organizations when she applied her fundamental principles to "The Psychology of Conciliation and Arbitration," the title of her third lecture. Briefly reviewing legislation concerning the settlement of industrial disputes in the United States, Germany, the Netherlands, and England, Follett noted a trend away from arbitration toward conciliation or mediation. She heartily approved. "In pure arbitration the only task recognized is that of deciding *between,* not bringing the two parties *together.*" By contrast, a mediator "tries to energize the two parties to the controversy to reach their own decisions. Unless both sides are satisfied, the struggle will go on, underneath if not openly. We see again and again that unless an agreement is heartily ratified by both sides, it seldom lasts."[97]

Follett, of course, believed that the "most satisfactory way of settling disputes is to get as near an integration as possible." She abhorred settling for compromise, but she also recognized that integrating required special skills and a substantial commitment of time on the part of the conciliator or mediator. She explained that even before formal discussions begin, mediators frequently find it necessary to hold preliminary discussions with individual parties. And then, not only must the mediator "find" the integration, he also must find just the right moment to introduce it or, even better, help the parties to discover it themselves. Once the integration is found, the job is still not over, for mediators report that "their chief difficulty is in finding the solution which seems just to both sides and at the same time gives those representing the workers a chance to go back and make their constituents feel they have won something for them."[98]

Rethinking Leadership and the Role of the Executive

In Follett's final lecture for the 1927 Bureau of Personnel Administration meetings, titled "Leader and Expert," she applied her four fundamental principles to the process of leadership. She built on conceptions of "central administration leadership" that she had presented to another BPA audience the previous year, as well as on ideas expressed in her three books. But this time Follett opened with two provocative assertions: first, that leadership of various kinds may appear in many places throughout the organization; and, second, that the person acting as the true leader in a situation may not be the one "holding the highest official position." Furthermore, Follett told her audience of senior executives, we are "coming to regard the leader as the man who can energize his group, who knows how to encourage initiative, how to draw from all what each has to give . . . who knows how to relate these different wills so that they will have a driving force." Therefore, it no longer makes sense to equate the leader with the person who can secure mere "consent" through persuasion, or "assert his individual will and get others to follow him," or even behave with his group as "democrat." Moreover, the executive should not be concerned with checking or balancing leadership, but instead with encouraging the creation of "multiple" leaderships.[99]

Follett saw the value in multiple leaderships, but this did not mean that business executives should abdicate their own reasoned judgment to the burgeoning cadre of consulting engineers and other professional experts. Concerned since her days in the community centers of Boston with the proper role of the expert, Follett argued that ways must be found "by which the specialist's kind of knowledge and the executive's kind of knowledge can be joined."[100] To illustrate, she described an experience with an electrician who came to her wire her house: "I say that I want it done in a certain way. He says that there are mechanical difficulties about doing it in that way. I suggest another way. He says that the laws of the state in regard to fire safeguards do not permit that way. Then he tells me how he thinks it should be done. Do I accept his suggestions? No, because I have a very decided objection on account of esthetic reasons or reasons of convenience. We continue our discussion until we find a way which meets the mechanical difficulties and the laws of the state and at the same time satisfies me." Having noticed that we often manage to integrate with experts without being fully conscious that we are doing so, Follett observed that "we do not usually think of our relation with the expert as that of a fight. We *expect* to be able to unite a difference of opinion with the expert. We have gone to him for that purpose. We recognize that he has one kind of knowledge and we another."[101]

Having articulated how leadership was evolving, Follett turned to a problem raised for her five months earlier at a meeting of the Taylor Society. There some of the discussants had encouraged her to apply her conceptions of leadership to the functions of the chief executive. She had apparently taken this request seriously, for she devoted the remainder of her lecture to that topic.[102]

Convinced that functional unity is the "chief task of management," Follett maintained that the chief executive's main job is coordination. Not only must the executive prevent each department head from playing "a lone hand," but the executive must also see "that departmental or divisional policies do not get crystallized too quickly before it is discovered whether they are in accord with one another or with general policy." And when dissension occurs, as is bound to happen, the chief executive's job is to integrate differences rather than acting as "umpire or arbitrator." In doing so, Follett cautioned, the chief executive "has to weld together the functions of critic, judge, and active participator. In other words, if we say that he passes *on* a situation, we must remember that he is *in* that situation."[103]

Follett, of course, was aware that the chief executive could not integrate the parts of the business successfully unless the *purpose* of the firm had been developed in close consultation with those who would enact it. "The best leader," Follett noted, "does not ask people to serve him, but the common end." Having seen firsthand during her trip to England the power of Seebohm Rowntree's regular conversations with the Cocoa Works employees about their contributions to the firm, Follett exhorted her audience to attempt something similar. "I am convinced, and I cannot tell you how strongly I feel this, that one could get much larger output from the rank and file throughout a factory if they had some idea of what they were working for, of what it was all about . . . They need not feel, as most of them do now, that they are mere bits in a huge machine. Their individual worth, their own wills and aims, could, I am sure, be made to find a place in the purposes of the industry in which they are working."[104]

While helping others to understand, and perhaps even to create, their place in the purpose of the firm, the executive must never forget that "each unit has to be fitted into a whole which is constantly changing, that is, into an evolving whole." In business, Follett reminded her audience, "we are always passing from one significant moment to another significant moment, and the leader's task is preeminently to understand the *moment of passing*. This is why the leader's task is so difficult, why it requires great qualities." In her view, a business leader must possess "the most delicate and sensitive perceptions, imagination and insight, and at the same time courage and faith. A business man, the president of a large industry, once told me that I would not make a good business woman because I had not enough faith. He did not, of course, mean religious faith, he meant faith in my own purposes, that I wanted to safeguard myself too much, that I would trust only the present which I could see, not the future which I could not see. This was in regard to some committee work we were doing together. I thought then he was wrong, not about me necessarily, but about the course he wanted to take in the matter under discussion, but I have come to think he was right in the matter, as I have come to understand the fundamental principles underlying what he was saying." This sort of "insight into, and faith in, the future" Follett called "anticipation." And anticipation, as she saw it, meant "making" the next situation rather than just coping with what comes.[105]

In closing, Follett returned to the fundamental principles of human relations articulated in her first lecture: "namely, evoking, interacting, integrating, and emerging." Having established that the leader's task with regard to evoking is "to draw out from each his fullest possibilities," Follett was pleased to report that several speakers at a recent American Management Association meeting had maintained that *leader* and *teacher* were synonymous concepts. She applauded this as "a long step forward . . . The leader today of the best type does not want men who are subservient to him, those who render him a passive obedience. He is trying to develop men exactly the opposite of this, men themselves with mastery, and such men will give his own leadership worth and power." With regard to the second and third principles, interacting and integrating, Follett believed the "leader should be leader of a coherent group . . . of men who are finding their material welfare, their most effective expression, their spiritual satisfaction, through their relations to one another, through the functioning of the group to which they belong." As Follett saw it, the "great leader is he who is able to integrate the experience of all and use it for a common purpose."[106] Emerging, the fourth fundamental principle of organization, denoted for Follett "the evolving, the creating of new values, the forward movement." It was this possibility of emerging that really thrilled her. Follett believed that business people, by putting these four principles into action in the realm of commerce, were actually helping "to solve the problems of human relations, and that is certainly the greatest task man has been given on this planet."[107]

Having received numerous invitations to lecture to business and government leaders in the United States and the United Kingdom, Follett was clearly one of the most prominent among those advocating reform of traditional business practice. Businessmen were drawn to Follett because of the relevance of her ideas to their particular concerns. Nevertheless, it took a woman of uncommon personal qualities to command the attention of a largely male audience in the 1920s. Elizabeth Balch, a friend from Radcliffe days and the woman Follett would name as her literary executor, was well acquainted with Follett's charisma. Follett had "extraordinary charm," which she exerted as an adult "especially over young men," Balch observed. "Her play of humor, the quick turns of her illustration, of her wit, had quite extraordinary versatility and fascination. Her beautiful voice and hands are vivid memories to all who heard her."[108]

Despite the accolades and encouragement that Follett was receiving from many quarters, she revealed in a 1927 letter to Alice Brandeis, her old friend and former Otis Place neighbor, that Richard Cabot was not entirely pleased with the turn that her work had taken. Sending Brandeis a copy of the recently published paper on leadership she had delivered to the Taylor Society, Follett added, "It will show you the kind of thing I am doing. I hope you will read it, & if you do, please bear in mind while doing so that I have had many enthusiastic letters & messages in regard to that paper. If I can help a little in this direction, as these letters vigorously affirm, is it not right for me to go on with this work? This is not a rhetorical question. I should like your opinion because Dr. Cabot thinks I am all wrong. He wants me to write on philosophical questions, he is all the time at me about it . . . Several men have written me that this was one of the most helpful papers they had every heard. Another writes: 'You have been extraordinarily helpful to executives. As I go about in industrial establishments, I get the impression that no one has done so much to free their minds from rigid & sterile preconceptions & to infuse vitality into their thinking as you have done.' " Obviously anxious for ammunition to use against Cabot's arguments, Follett was hardly subtle in her effort to influence Brandeis's response: "I think I will mark the passages in the remarks of the man who opened the discussion, again not out of vanity but in order to help you make up your mind about my future. I shall underline twice where he says that my ideas are of practical value, because if they are, why shouldn't I keep on?"

Follett was scheduled to give a talk in Philadelphia, but she hoped, after her return in late June, to "come down [to the Brandeises' summer home south of Boston] for one day & talk the matter over with you & Mr. Brandeis." Such a visit, however, would serve more than a professional purpose for Mary, who was continuing to feel lost without Isobel. "I cannot tell you what a happiness it was to see you yesterday — a real happiness — I mean it very literally & fully. I am cheerful & I have work which interests me, but underneath is the gnawing loneliness for Isobel." Follett then confided: "To be with someone whom I truly care for, as I do for you, is now for me a rare & joyful occasion. All these new people who merely like what I write are not the same. Deep as are the intellectual sympathies between you & me, I believe that there is a deeper bond still, & that I value."[109]

In July Follett left the city for several weeks at Overhills, the summer home north of Putney, Vermont, that she and Isobel had enjoyed for thirty years. But now the place that had given them such pleasure was the focus of an excruciatingly difficult decision. Briggs had willed the property to Follett, and as a result she was now solely responsible for its taxes and maintenance, including an impending $1,500 bill for waterpipes. At the same time, Follett also bore sole financial responsibility for the rent on the Otis Place apartment in Boston and for the continuing care of her aged mother in Wollaston. These mounting financial burdens were made all the more difficult by Follett's determination neither to borrow money nor to dip into her investment capital.

Happily, a potential buyer for the Vermont property appeared, and Follett thought it might be wise to sell. Yet Richard and Ella Cabot, aware of what an extraordinary treasure that Overhills had been to Mary and Isobel, begged their friend to consider other alternatives. "Ella and I are quite clear that you must not sell Putney," Richard Cabot firmly announced. " 'All right' I hear you say 'but tell me how I can keep it.' " The Cabots offered three alternatives for her consideration: accepting a gift of $1,500, taking out a bank loan on which they would pay the interest, or selling them several pieces of her antique furniture. "In any case, dear Mary, you surely must not part with any organ of your life so essential as Putney," Richard cautioned. "Take the advice of your close friends and partners. Your ideals are ours and there is no good reason why we shouldn't be allowed to forward them . . . Listen! I'm knocking on your door as I did here a few weeks ago to wake you up out of a bad dream. And now please answer just as you did then after a minute: 'All right! All right!' and relieve now, as you did then, the mind of your affectionate friends."[110]

The Cabots followed this vivid appeal with yet another round of alternative proposals, but Follett had made up her mind. Always reluctant to depend too much on her friends, she was fearful of seeming too needy or demanding. And at this particular moment she may well have been reluctant to be financially beholden to Richard, given his insistence that she stop wasting her intellectual energy thinking about business management. Or perhaps it was simply too painful to contemplate being at Overhills without Isobel. On August 25, 1927, Mary reluctantly let go. She sold the land, the house, and the furniture — and kept only her tender memories.[111]

Throughout the summer and early fall of 1927, Follett continued to receive numerous requests for lectures. In June she spoke in Philadelphia at the request of Morris L. Cooke, then president of the Taylor Society. Cooke (who as a young engineer had been one of Frederick Taylor's most trusted associates) in later years had served as director of public works in Philadelphia and had become a close adviser to Samuel Gompers, president of the American Federation of Labor. Deeply committed to worker participation in industry and convinced that the collaboration of labor and management was essential to achieving the productivity and wage gains that would be of benefit to all, Cooke found much to admire in Follett's work.[112] Later in the summer, Follett received an invitation from a totally different quarter when the president of an association of deans of women's colleges begged Follett to speak on the relation of deans and student government councils at their spring convention in Boston; Follett declined, citing a lack of time.[113] And in November she repeated her paper "Leader and Expert" at the fall meeting of the Bureau of Personnel Administration in New York.

Also in November, Follett shared some of her recent BPA papers with her colleague Dean William Mosher at Syracuse University. He was highly enthusiastic. "I hope that you will let me know where they are to appear because you have expressed a number of things that I would like to quote in a manuscripts that I am now working with on personnel employment administration. This will indicate to you how heartily I approve of the ideas expressed." Mosher then offered a proposition: "I would like very much to have this point of view worked out for the teacher-student relationship and presented to our faculty members. All too many of them are entirely autocratic in handling their subjects. Do you think that you care to do this and present it sometime to our Faculty Club?"

Follett set the letter aside. She thought they could talk the proposal over when Mosher next came to Boston; but coming across the letter again in April, she finally replied. Enclosing a copy of her paper "Leader and Expert," Follett proposed that she first establish an appropriate conceptual foundation by speaking to the faculty about leadership and then, in a second lecture, take up the question of the teacher-student relation. Follett told Mosher that she had been dismayed by a recent address of President Ernest M. Hopkins at Dartmouth in which he discussed the role of higher education institutions in training students for leadership. Persuaded that he had made "the usual mistake of confusing leadership and aggressiveness," Follett was eager for a forum that would allow her to refute Hopkins' assertions. Mosher's interest was piqued by this formulation of her proposed visit, and he immediately replied, asking her "preferred rate" for her lectures.[114]

Caught up in the urgency, real or manufactured, of these various obligations, Follett made virtually no progress on her book on conflict. "Something which seems important is always happening to prevent," she complained to Alice Brandeis, and she cited new controversies concerning Boston's community centers and Vocational Guidance Department. "Yet it is difficult to know what is right, for almost every day people are asking me for more writing on human relations in industry, and asking in such a way that it seems as if I could help there more than in any other way—that that at the present moment is where the greatest need lies. So you see I am often perplexed and wish I could run in to No. 6 and get some wise advice."[115]

Though obviously ambivalent about the course her life had taken, Mary Follett kept her focus squarely on business organizations. In March 1928 she delivered yet another lecture for the Bureau of Personnel Administration. This speech, along with Follett's earlier lecture "Leader and Expert," would eventually be published by Henry C. Metcalf as a part of an edited collection on business leadership. The other contributors to this volume—professors, business managers, educational administrators, and consultants—were well acquainted with Follett's work, and most of them either made explicit, complimentary references to her ideas in their own essays or cited her books in their bibliographies.[116]

Follett's lecture, the third in her series of papers on leadership, was devoted to identifying "Some Discrepancies in Leadership Theory and Practice." It would be one of her most incisive and compelling lectures. She began by using profiles of figures from business, government, and politics to challenge the widely accepted notion that the leader is supposed to be "one who has a compelling personality, who wields a personal power, who constrains others to his will." Follett admitted that personal qualities play a large part in leadership, but suggested that too little importance has been given to the person's knowledge of the business at hand. "Take even Joan of Arc," Follett remarked in one of her typically unforgettable anecdotes; "her leadership was obviously and pre-eminently due to the ardour of her conviction and her power to make others share that conviction — yet we are told that no trained artillery captain could excel Joan of Arc in the placement of guns."[117]

Continuing her search for differences between leadership theory and practice, Follett turned to discrepancies she had uncovered in her investigations of business organizations. She began with a point made in more elaborate form in her 1925 paper "The Giving of Orders." The old theory of leadership, Follett argued, "envisaged the leader as one who could get orders obeyed — any order — while in the best modern practice the leader is the man who can show that the order is integral to the situation . . . The leader gets an order followed first, because *men do really want to do things in the right way* and he can show them that way, and secondly, because he too is obeying. Sincerity more than aggressiveness is a quality of leadership." Remarkably, she had observed this new practice not only in the behavior of managers, but also in the often-despised role of the foreman; the "test of a foreman now is not how good he is at bossing, but how little bossing he has to do because of the training of his men and the organization of their work."[118]

Follett next focused on the widely held notion that leadership is limited to an elite few. On the contrary, she told her listeners, it was increasingly accepted that many people have at least some capacity for leadership. Furthermore, firms were increasingly accepting responsibility for working out "a form of organization and methods of management which will make the most effective use of such leadership capacity." Likewise, it was coming to be recognized that "different situations require different kinds of knowledge, and the man possessing the knowledge demanded by a certain situation tends in the best managed businesses, and other things being equal, to become the leader at that moment."[119] And Follett had also noticed that leadership was increasingly demonstrated not by the person with the most senior position, but rather by the one "who can grasp the essentials of an experience and, as we say, see it whole . . . And the most successful leader of all is one who sees another picture not yet actualized."[120]

In the latter part of her lecture, Follett focused explicitly on the role of the chief executive, a subject that she had begun to explore in her earlier paper "Leader and Expert." Some people, Follett told her audience, think that the job of the executive is to make decisions for his subordinates, but she thought it essential that the executive instead "teach them how to handle their problems themselves, how to make their own decisions . . . If the best leader takes all the means in his power to develop leadership among his subordinates and gives them opportunity to exercise it, he has then, his supreme task, to unite all the different degrees and different types of leadership that come to the surface in the ramifications of a modern business . . . [The leader is] the one who knows how to relate the different wills in a group so that they will have driving force."[121]

To secure such an integration of wills, the members of the group must share in the leader's experience — and the leader must also share theirs. "This insight alone," Follett argued, "changes our whole conception of leadership. The leader knows that any lasting agreement among the members of the group can come only by their sharing each other's experience. He must see that his organization is such as to make this possible." And if one of the greatest aims of leadership is to successfully unite followers in a common purpose, the executive must see that this is "a common purpose not only in the sense of being shared by all, but it should be a purpose evolved by all the interweaving activities of the enterprise. The best type of leader does not seek *his* ends, but the ends disclosed by an evolving process in which each has his special part." In this effort to work out an ever-expanding common purpose, Follett saw potential in joint committees of managers and workers and in the expansion of "cross-relations between [functional] departments." Both practices contradicted the old authoritarian ideas about leadership.[122]

Having devoted considerable attention to the role of the chief executive, Follett next focused on those who are "the led in the leadership situation." Noting that H. G. Wells, in his most recent novel, was appealing for a broader base of leadership as a means to the regeneration of society, Follett heartily agreed. But she also thought it imperative that we recognize that those who are "led have not merely a passive part, they have not merely to follow and obey, they have to help keep the leader in control of the situation." No doubt remembering her experiences in the neighborhoods and the community centers of Boston, Follett reminded her audience that we need not think "that we are either leaders or — nothing of much importance." Everyone should be involved. "Part of the task of the leader is to make others participate in his leadership. The best leader knows how to make his followers actually feel power in themselves, not merely acknowledge his power. But if the followers must partake in leadership, it is also true that we must have followship on the part of leaders. There must be a partnership of following. The basis of industrial leadership is creating a partnership in a common task, a joint responsibility."[123] "One of the tragedies of history," Follett poignantly added in what was surely a reference to the resounding defeat of Wilson's postwar blueprint for peace, "is that Woodrow Wilson did not understand leadership."[124]

Follett concluded this lecture, as she often did, by inspiring her audience to action — in this particular case by explaining how effective leadership in business can serve a larger social purpose. When you exercise this new form of leadership, Follett told her audience, you are not only organizing forces currently at your command, but you also are drawing forth energies that have heretofore been untapped. It was William James, Follett continued, who showed us "that my capacities are related to the demands of the universe." Great leaders, Follett was convinced, "can show me this correspondence, can arouse my latent possibilities, can reveal to me new powers in myself, can quicken and give direction to some force within me." She concluded: "There is energy, passion, unawakened life in us — those who call it forth are our leaders."[125]

Throughout the remainder of the spring of 1928, Follett continued to respond selectively to requests for lectures and chose occasions that would give her further opportunities to expound upon the concept of leadership. In late April, for example, she reported to William E. Mosher that the paper on the teacher-student relation was almost finished; and they agreed, after some confusion, that she would come in the fall to Syracuse to deliver it as well as a lecture on leadership.[126]

Follett opened this paper, intended as it was for the faculty of the School of Citizenship and Public Affairs, by noting that she found most enjoyable her conversations with businessmen and teachers. "I should not have anticipated this juxtaposition," Follett confessed, "for one usually thinks of these two groups as rather far apart. But the reason is that both these groups are in a position to try out their ideas of human relations any day, and also both these groups are coming to have the experimental mind."[127]

Having begun her talk in a manner that almost certainly would have established a genuine, positive connection with her audience, Follett turned directly to the subject at hand: "what opportunities for leadership has the teacher and what is the nature of his leadership?" For Follett, the teacher's greatest service was to help the student "increase his freedom — his free range of activity and thought and his power of control . . . The teacher releases energy, frees potentialities, but within method, within the laws of group activity and group control." This could be accomplished, Follett believed, only by a teacher who was intimately acquainted with the ever-changing world that the student was being prepared to meet, who knew "the spirit of the age," and who communicated it effectively to others. Furthermore, the wise teacher, while seeking always to find productive continuities between the lessons of his own life and the aspirations of his students, must acknowledge that "our adventures are not to be theirs. A new voice speaks and they must hear it and enter their own kingdom and meet their own high adventures."[128]

Specifically, what are the methods a teacher can use to increase this sort of freedom in students? Follett's suggestions resonate with advice she had given previously to audiences seeking to elevate the practice of business management to the status of a profession. The function of the teacher, in Follett's view, was "to train the student to watch for meanings, to organize meanings, perhaps to create new meanings, and all with the aim of increasing his ability to live not only harmoniously but effectively with his fellows." This sort of instruction in human relations, Follett urged, must be taught to students not only directly through the particular academic subject under consideration, but also using more experimental and interactive means. She recommended using "outside group activities for our students to experiment with, observe and report on in class" as well as "activities devised for the classroom group" in which the "class itself may be made a training ground in joint thinking."[129] Such collaborative discussion and problem-solving, which Follett had been advocating since her days in the neighborhood centers of Boston, would require that teachers first learn what Follett called "a technique of classroom conference [discussion] . . . I think this because of my profound belief that man is not wilfully evil so much as deeply ignorant of *how* to live with his fellows . . . If we can teach this, our students will have learned something of far greater social value than merely a subject."[130]

Follett judged as mere sentimentality the notion that teachers "get more from their students than they give." But being ever mindful of the continually evolving, reciprocal relations involved in teaching and learning, she recognized that the process works best when teachers as well as students enjoy the experience. For Follett, one of the tests of any relationship, including the teacher-student relationship, was: "does it bring renewal, an increase of spiritual energy? Is it cumulative? Is there more substance in it as it continues? Is there an increment — an earned increment?"[131]

Follett concluded with a reminder that the teacher often plays a major role in inspiring and helping students choose their purpose in life — in showing them their "relation to the world's needs." She explained: "We hear often today the expression conscious control. Jurists, [such] as Roscoe Pound, economists, [such] as Maynard Keynes, use this phrase. From many quarters we hear expressed the profound belief of men that we can control our lives. I believe that this is the legacy which our generation can leave to the next. I believe the chief duty of the teacher to the student is to make him feel, to quote

[H. G.] Wells again, that we are filled with 'a mighty power . . . against which the forces of hell, of destruction, of caprice, of lawlessness, of the jungle, cannot prevail.'" Follett may well have been recalling her own brilliant mentors and teachers — Anna Boynton Thompson, Albert Bushnell Hart, and Henry Sidgwick — when she concluded, in a less rhetorical tone, that the master teacher can, above all, "show his student the relation of his own purpose to larger purposes, the relation of his daily acts to the community life, the relation of any part to as large a whole as the student is capable of understanding."[132]

During this period Follett wrote yet another paper about the concept of leadership. In "The Psychiatrist in Industry," Follett was openly critical of the psychiatrist who applied Freudian methods of analysis to industrial settings without appreciating that "many of the conceptions with which he is concerned have been changed of late years by the greatly enriched thinking of business men." Among the errors she specifically cited were the continuing tendency of psychiatrists to label leaders as having "superiority complexes," followers as being in need of a "father substitute," and subordinates as having a "natural" tendency to rebel. Follett was likewise critical of the tendency of psychiatrists to derive their analyses solely from the client's internal conflicts — and to fail to carefully investigate external influences on the individual and to appreciate the reciprocal influencing of one set of relations on the other. Despite these shortcomings, she was optimistic about the role that psychiatrists could play in understanding and creating better human relations in industry.[133]

In early May 1928, Morris L. Cooke, the Taylor Society president, and his wife, Eleanor, invited Follett to spend a memorable weekend with them, first at the Bach Festival in Bethlehem, Pennsylvania, and then at the Cookes' home, Playwicky, on the Delaware River in Bucks County.[134] Later that month Follett traveled to New Haven, Connecticut, to address a meeting of the American Association of Industrial Nurses. There she applied her notions about leadership to the various reciprocal relations of the industrial nurse with the workers, foremen, and upper management.[135]

Apparently invigorated rather than exhausted by this rush of activity, Follett felt well enough to set sail for Europe from New York City. She left on May 28, 1928, expecting to spend the summer as a private citizen investigating the functioning of the League of Nations in Switzerland. Established in 1920, this international peacekeeping body had come to include more than fifty countries, among them Great Britain, France, Italy, Japan, and Germany. The United States, however, had never joined, largely because isolationist forces in the Senate would not accept Article X of the League's Covenant requiring all members to protect the territorial independence of all other member nations.

Early in 1922, however, Charles Evans Hughes, the U.S. secretary of state in the Harding administration, began sending informal observers to League agencies and commissions, as a means of participating in the organization's humanitarian activities without antagonizing those opposed to formal membership. This low-profile policy developed so rapidly that by 1930 the United States had participated in "some forty League conferences and had five permanent representatives stationed at Geneva"; in addition, the United States was actively involved in the work of "the Reparations Commission, in the League Health Organization, and in the International Labor Organization."[136]

"I expect to learn much," Follett told William E. Mosher, writing to inform him about her impending trip. "I have not been to Geneva since the war & I thought it would be helpful to me to see all the 'integrations' (or lack of them!) there."[137] Her old Newnham friend Melian Stawell, who would later remember having "tried for years to rouse in [Follett] an active passion for the League," was very amused to receive a "real propagandist letter" from Mary in Geneva, telling her she "had no idea how impressive it was to see these men at their work. 'You really should come and see for yourself,' she wound up, 'and mind, I shouldn't have been nearly so impressed if they hadn't spoken to me quite frankly about the drawbacks and the difficulties and the dangers.'" Stawell fondly recalled that "what awakened May's [*sic*] keenest delight" was "the power of putting things through in spite of, no, that is too weak, *because of* difficulty and danger."[138]

22

"I Am Almost at the Same Moment Happy and Unhappy"

The exuberance with which Mary Follett began her League of Nations adventure in Geneva persisted through the better part of the summer. Writing to LeRoy Bowman, one of her former colleagues in the National Community Centers Association, Follett apologized profusely for failing to be a continuing participant in the community centers movement. "But the fact is," Mary told him, "that I am being increasingly asked for work in other directions, am made to feel that it is a matter of grave importance to one of the most pressing problems of the world, that of industrial relations, that those of us who have been especially interested in this matter of *relation,* should now work steadily together in applying certain principles of relation to industry. Here in Geneva this is carried further still & they wish me to apply these same ideas to international relations. I had no idea that anyone here had read my books, & am immensely surprised to find so many here who are interested in what I have tried to say about *the process of adjustment* & who beg me for further work in that direction. Of course I realize how little it is that I have to give, but I see where my work must lie no matter how tiny the contribution may be."[1]

Follett apparently communicated much the same sentiment to Ella Cabot. Ella, writing in early August to make arrangements for a late-summer rendezvous with Mary at the Hotel Grand Bellevue in Switzerland, exclaimed that "I am leaping with joy that you have found at Geneva what I felt 3 years ago was its almost inevitable *gift for you*. My mind was full of you there with all the issues of co-operation, leadership, conflict, use of power, skill in difficult situations writ large."[2]

In addition to her time at the League of Nations, Follett undoubtedly also visited the International Management Institute, an organization founded in 1927 with funding from American foundations to study and promote modern methods of management on an international scale. Follett's longtime friend Henry S. Dennison was the founding vice-chairman of the institute, and Lyndall F. Urwick, the young Rowntree manager who had been so impressed with her when they met in 1926, was the newly appointed director.[3] By late September Follett felt ready to speak about some of what she had seen and heard in Geneva, and did so at Oxford at the Twenty-seventh Lecture Conference for Works Directors, Managers, Foremen and Forewomen, sponsored by her friend Seebohm Rowntree. Follett's paper for the Rowntree conference was based on the leadership lecture she had recently given at the Bureau of Personnel Administration meeting in New York, but she had added several new illustrations of functional leadership drawn from her observations of the League's Assembly and the commissions.[4]

Although Follett's time in Geneva was intellectually stimulating, she was becoming increasingly frustrated by her lack of stamina. In her July letter to LeRoy Bowman, she confessed "with humiliation" that "I am a very slow person & can accomplish really very little in any one year. This you, with your greater capacity, will hardly be able to understand, but I assure you that it is an ever-present handicap with me. In order to be able to do the least bit in any one direction, I have to give up everything else. Do forgive me, Mr. Bowman . . . I can give you a convincing proof that I am really a pretty stupid person, for I am finding that it is taking me a long time to get & keep in mind all the facts in regard to the League wh. I need as a background for the studies I want to make here. You could probably do in 2 weeks what will take me 2 months."[5]

Two weeks before her Oxford lecture, Follett sounded similarly discouraged in a letter to Elizabeth Haldane expressing her sympathy about the death of her brother, Viscount Haldane. "I feel so deeply & truly your loss," Mary wrote. "I understand it through my own loss, that of the friend with whom I had lived so long, and which I cannot in the least recover from." Although Follett had found her visit to Geneva "an interesting & fruitful experience," she confessed to Haldane that it had also been "very tiring" and that "I should take the opportunity, if I had any extra time, not to see people but to rest, which I feel might be very beneficial before going home & beginning a strenuous winter."[6]

By early November Follett was back in Boston, having returned in time to cast a ballot in the 1928 presidential election, the third in which women were eligible to vote. Follett admired the skillfulness with which New York's progressive governor, Alfred E. Smith, was struggling to knit together the warring northern urban immigrant and more rural southern and western factions of the Democratic party through the various state political machines. But Follett's decision to vote for Herbert Hoover, which she publicly announced during her Oxford lecture, probably had little to do with the most common reasons for opposing Smith — his Catholicism, his opposition to prohibition, and his association with Tammany Hall politics.[7] Follett would probably have been disappointed with Smith's vigorous stand against prohibition, given her father's struggle with alcoholism and her own early activities in support of "alternatives to the saloon." But the other common reasons for opposing Smith would have carried little weight with her: Follett was not a religious bigot, and she certainly would not have been put off by Smith's lower-class ethnic origins. Even Smith's Tammany Hall political connections would not, in Follett's mind, automatically have disqualified him for higher office. Her years in Boston's Ward 18 had given her a complex view of local political machines — in particular, an appreciation of their ability to provide essential services to immigrants during an era when municipal governments could not. Follett's vote for Hoover, in other words, was not a mere reflexive vote against Smith; there was much for her to appreciate in Herbert Hoover.

For decades following the Great Depression, President Hoover was vilified by progressive historians as a stubborn "laissez-faire ideologue" whose failures had prevented Americans from extricating themselves from an economic nightmare. More recently, however, historians have come to see Hoover, despite the mistakes that he made in confronting the depression, as "a modernizer and rationalizer, seeking in particular to forge a new synthesis between managerial and libertarian values, to build modern institutions retaining traditional virtues, and to nurture more system-conscious forms of individualism and nationalism."[8] Hoover, who had built a reputation as an internationally successful mining engineer, became involved in public service in 1914 as director of Belgian relief operations and then as the wartime U.S. food administrator. As a result of these widely acclaimed humanitarian accomplishments, "the Great Engineer" was considered for a time by Democrats as well as Republicans as a possible candidate in the 1920 presidential election. According to Hoover's biographer, David Burner, "the roster of those who advanced his candidacy in 1919 and 1920 is thick with the names of reformers," among them Franklin Roosevelt, Herbert Croly, Jane Addams, Louis Brandeis, and Walter Lippmann.[9] With the election in 1920 of the Republican, Warren G. Harding, Hoover was appointed secretary of commerce, a position he retained through both the Harding and Coolidge administrations. Having wrested from Harding a promise of considerable autonomy, Hoover "turned Commerce from a themeless hodgepodge of bureaucratic leftovers (wags described its pre-Hoover responsibilities as 'turning out the lighthouses at night and putting the fish to bed') into a dynamic laboratory for his theory of a federal government eager to encourage private associations as the surest path to progress for all without domination by any — including Washington itself." In the process, Hoover came to be widely regarded as "the most important cabinet official of the decade."[10]

Mary Follett would have been especially taken with Hoover's desire to further develop at Commerce the idea of problem-solving through government-assisted voluntary cooperative associations — a strategy he had first tested in Belgium and honed in the Food Administration. Indeed, one of Hoover's major objectives at the Commerce Department was the "collectivizing of free individual initiative, a light but efficient ordering of the nation's private and local energies to national purposes."[11] Hoover's determined and dynamic search for a middle way between individualism and collectivism (of either the socialistic or monopolistic variety) was evident in a wide variety of department activities, causing the commerce secretary to be judged by one revisionist historian as "engrossed in the problems of stabilizing modern industrial society, involved in the effort to promote harmony between capital and labor, devoted to the task of fostering cooperative competition among businessmen, committed to the use of scientific techniques to solve national problems, and inclined to accept limited governmental responsibility in the struggle to manage the business cycle and eradicate poverty."[12] Sharing many of these values, Mary Follett would have found Hoover's election to the presidency in November 1928 an occasion for hopeful celebration.

Follett did not feel well the whole month after her return from Geneva, and on December 6 she again became "acutely ill." Three days later she was taken to Phillips House at Massachusetts General Hospital, where she remained for the next two months. In late November, just before Follett entered the hospital, William Mosher had written to see if she could come to Syracuse to give the lectures they had planned earlier in the spring, but near the end of December a nurse replied on Follett's behalf, ominously saying that she was "unable to attend to anything. Her recovery will probably be slow." Mosher immediately sent a note of encouragement, adding that he had spoken with some of Follett's admirers in Chicago. "I assured them that the writings were in a class with themselves but that you in person surpassed what you had written from the point of view of stimulus and inspiration."[13]

The immediate cause of Follett's distress apparently was shingles, a recurrence of the chicken-pox virus that follows the path of spinal nerves.[14] The resulting rash first blisters and then scabs before clearing up in a few weeks, but the skin is hypersensitive, and the post-herpetic neuralgia and long-term fatigue can be severe. Surviving a month in which, as Mary put it, she was "all the time either in *hideous* pain or under morphine," she was finally able at the end of January to write to Morris Cooke that "now I am slowly, oh so slowly, getting better. I don't know when I shall be back at Otis Place. In fact the doctors don't want me to go there but to go South when I am able to leave here, but I can hardly see myself going South alone, so I have no plans as yet."[15] She considered staying for a time in Milton, Massachusetts, with the Andrews sisters, friends from summers in Vermont; but Mary was anxious to be in her own home and returned to Otis Place in early February.[16] Three weeks later she still did not feel up to attending a concert with Ella Cabot. "I call it that I am getting on 'splendidly,' " she confessed, "only because I have accepted this snail's pace. I am improving but it is very slow. The back & ankle still pain me, sometimes rather badly. I go down the steps every day & walk 10 minutes in Brimmer St., with difficulty & with some help, but it requires such a great effort that I usually feel rather faint & exhausted at the end of that time."[17]

During this trying period, however, Follett had made some major decisions. With considerable help from Ella Cabot's personal secretary, she would pack up her things and leave Otis Place at the end of March so that she could rent her apartment until her lease expired in October. And, amazingly, if she felt up to it, she would sail for Europe on April 13, 1929.[18]

The occasion of this particular European venture was an invitation to visit from Dame Katharine Furse, whose acquaintance Follett had made while in Geneva the previous summer. The fifty-two-year-old Furse, who had just taken on responsibility for establishing the World Bureau of the World Association of Girl Guides and Girl Scouts, had been in Geneva in the summer of 1928 for the Assembly of the League of Nations. Furse's longtime colleague and friend Rachel Crowdy had an executive position in the League Secretariat. Invited by Crowdy to dine with the Cabots and Mary Follett, who were staying in the same hotel, Furse immediately found that this fifty-nine-year-old American "interested [her] immensely" and was someone she wished to know a lot better. "I never allowed convention to waste time," Furse later recalled, "if I want to know someone who was going to be known. Being a real Bostonian with Puritan traditions Mary would not have made such fast advances but she talked to me of her philosophy and I immediately ordered two of her books and became enthralled by them."[19] The discussions of psychology in *Creative Experience* particularly fascinated Furse, and she urged her youngest son's fiancée to read Follett's books despite their difficulty.[20]

Realizing that Follett would be in Geneva only through October, Furse urged her to return the following spring so that they might travel together in Italy and Switzerland and then spend the rest of the summer at Furse's home in London. Follett, however, was reluctant to commit herself, since she did not have the same immediate attraction to Katharine. Indeed, she found the Englishwoman's boldness and assertiveness more than a little unnerving. "K. wrote me every single day from the time I left her last October," Follett would eventually disclose in a letter to the Cabots, "expressing her love for me, her great love, her deep & lasting love, her wish to love & cherish me 'for such time as we may be allowed here on earth & possibly beyond,' of her longing to have me here again, begging me to let her come to America to take care of me when she heard I was ill. (I didn't want her & refused.)" It wasn't until nearly a year later, in August 1929, that Follett finally shared these intimacies with the Cabots, and even then she did so reluctantly. But back in the fall of 1928, when Furse was adamantly declaring her "deep & lasting love," all that Follett had told her friends was that Furse seemed immature.[21]

Despite her reservations about Furse, Follett finally decided to make the trip to Europe. There was little in Boston any longer to hold her. And she was lonely. She had exceptionally attentive friends, most notably Richard and Ella Cabot, but Mary longed for the daily warmth, affection, and intellectual stimulation that Isobel had brought to her life. She realized that she was taking something of a gamble, especially given the precarious nature of her health, by traveling abroad with someone she hardly knew; but after only a few weeks, Follett felt certain that she had made the right decision. She told Morris and Eleanor Cooke that she was thinking of staying with Furse in London for a year. And to the Cabots, she wrote a sort of retraction. "I think I ought to correct something I said to you," Follett began. "I said that in some ways Katharine was immature, but I made a mistake because she is so entirely different from anyone I have ever known. She is an absolutely fine, disciplined soul, made on a large scale, a sort of elemental force, & that last was what I mistook for immaturity in my own smallness & ignorance. Also it is true that her expression is not always equal to what is behind it. But she is a splendid creature whom you must know better some day."[22]

During their travels through Italy, Follett and Furse were joined by two of Katharine's friends, Walter and Florence Roch, who took them for a drive almost every day. Mary had to be lifted in and out of the car because of weakness in her right leg and ankle, perhaps resulting from a metastasis to her sciatic nerve. Nevertheless, Mary found the drives captivating. "Umbria in May is a dream of beauty," she cheerfully reported to the Cabots, "& we go to one hill town after another & I am loving it all."[23] After exploring Assisi, Mary and Katharine continued north to Lake Como, where the cliffs of the surrounding area were alive with rhododendrons, red lilies, and cascading wildflowers. Leaving Como, they began the journey to Switzerland, traveling first by train to Chiavenna and then by chartered car to the tiny village of Soglio, which was perched on a south-facing ledge high above the valley floor and commanded picturesque views of the Bregaglia Valley to the southwest. From Soglio they made their way through Sils Marie and the upper Engadine Valley, finally reaching the crisp air of the high mountains of Davos and Klosters, very near the Austrian border.

It was outside Davos, on their first walk beyond the village, that Follett rejoiced to find a tranquil stretch of meadow that she and Isobel had first come across years earlier when traveling to Davos to visit a sick friend.[24] Follett also was overjoyed to find the Alpine landscape rich in springtime wildflowers, and she longed to share the experience with Ella Cabot, an ardent and knowledgeable horticulturalist. "I can't ask Katharine to make you a list of the Engadine flowers," Follett explained, "for it would take her too long—fields, meadows & woods are full of flowers—hundreds of kinds. K. is a wonder about flowers —she knows every single one, has shown me 6 kinds of gentians etc. etc. She carries a heavy knapsack on our journeys in which she puts her 'pots.' Thus she can keep our rooms full of the Alpine flowers." Furse, who had lived in this upland village from the time she was two until she was married at age twenty-four, considered Davos her home and loved it passionately. "She thinks her beloved mountains have helped me," Follett wrote the Cabots. "However that may be, I *am* decidedly better lately. I am taking little walks & finding them not too much for me."[25]

Mary Follett's new friend, Katharine Symonds Furse, was born in Bristol in November 1875. She was the youngest daughter of John Addington Symonds, a distinguished poet and historian of the Italian Renaissance, and Janet Catherine North Symonds, whose passion for beauty was displayed in her flowers, gardens, watercolors, and other arts and crafts. When Katharine was only two years old, the family moved to Switzerland, where they hoped the mountain air of Davos would "cure" her father's tuberculosis.[26]

Life in the Symonds household, despite serious illnesses, was hardly somber or dull. All four daughters, but especially Katharine, relished outdoor adventures and winter sports. And their family life seemed quite "Bohemian" for the

Mary P. Follett (*right*) and Katharine Furse on vacation in Europe, ca. 1930. Lyndall Fownes Urwick Archive, Henley Management College, Henley-on-Thames.

time. Upon later reflection, Katharine recalled that people often used "the words 'peculiar' and 'original' and 'eccentric'" to describe their experiences with the Symondses. "Looking back," Katharine wrote in her memoir, *Hearts and Pomegranates*, "I realise what an unusual life I lived and with what individualists. Though consciously I may not have taken much interest in the brilliant conversation or in the literary achievements of my father, I felt his activity of mind, and was permeated by the whole atmosphere . . . The alert criticism of the Symonds family, and its unceasing analysis of people and their works, as well as of their motives, became a habit, so that I have viewed life and people ever since with the same sort of interest and questioning."[27]

There were "practically no taboos," and "conversation was very free" even in front of the children. Although her father's research on homosexuality was openly discussed within the family circle, Symonds felt, for the sake of his family, that his own homosexual relations with men could not be brought into the open. Perhaps as a result, he suffered periodic bouts of depression and would leave his family for months at a time, ostensibly to conduct his academic research. In later years, Katharine was haunted by the thought that the psychological strain of being forced to live this dual existence had sapped her father's strength, already weakened by tuberculosis, and had quickened his death in 1893 at age fifty-three.[28]

Katharine Furse would begin trying to "unravel the story of this side" of her father's life in 1929, less than a year after meeting Mary Follett.[29] Ten years later, discussing her father in her memoir, Katharine may have been thinking of herself as well as her father when she declared that "much has been discovered in the last half-century concerning the biological and psychological make-up of the individual, and it has become increasingly clear that clean-cut divisions of individuals into classes, such as healthy and unhealthy, moral and immoral, homosexual and heterosexual, are quite impossible — there are intermediate grades as varied as are the shades of colour."[30]

In 1899 Charles Wellington Furse, already a well-known painter at age thirty-one, came to Davos seeking relief from his tuberculosis. Katharine, who at twenty-three was earning a small income using her carpentry, carving, and inlay skills, was immediately drawn to Furse. The couple soon married and returned to England, where they began a period of intense activity. Charles painted numerous portraits, including *Diana of the Uplands* (Katharine was the model), which has hung since 1906 in the Tate Gallery in London.[31] Katharine quickly became pregnant with their first child.

"It was a breath-taking time," Katharine later wrote. "I had been accustomed, as a child, to hearing Father tell of the number of books he had published in a year, and here I was again with a man who was accomplishing herculean work . . . In my view it was a matter of his being conscious, just as J. A. S. was, that he had not long to live, and that he still had a great deal to express while on earth." In the autumn of 1904, just as Katharine had long feared, Charles developed a heavy cold and began hemorrhaging in his lungs. Katharine nursed him alone day and night "for what seemed like weeks," even though she was pregnant with their second child. On October 13 the couple's second son, John Paul, was born. Only three days later, Charles succumbed to his illness, leaving Katharine a twenty-nine-year-old widow with an infant and a three-year-old son.[32]

Yet she coped. Six weeks later, the author Virginia Stephens (Woolf), who had known all the Symonds girls since childhood, described the young widow to a friend: "[Katharine] is very sad and splendid, and strikes one at once as full of a grave kind of courage — a reasoned courage I mean, which will last her all through this terrible time I know, for however she takes it [Charles Furse's death], it *is* terrible, as one can see." Two years later, Stephens reported to another close friend that Katharine "makes herself go on, and never says a word about it, though every day is hard work, like some one cutting steps in the ice."[33]

In 1909 Furse made a decision that would profoundly affect the rest of her life: she joined one of the new Voluntary Aid Detachments attached to the Territorial Force, the British army reserve. Formed to provide medical assistance in time of war, the V.A.D.'s would grow to number 2,500 local units by the summer of 1914, two-thirds of the members being women and girls.[34] Placed in charge of establishing relief stations for wounded men in France, Furse was so successful that she was next asked to assume the position of commandant-in-chief of a newly formed V.A.D. department in the British Red Cross. Furse's distinguished wartime service was recognized in 1917 when she was one of five women chosen by His Majesty George V to receive the "honour of Dame Grand Cross of the British Empire." Within months of this honor, Furse took on another challenge as head of the new Women's Royal Naval Service, where she recruited, trained, and dispatched to service more than 7,000 women, who in turn freed men for service at sea.[35]

When the war finally ended, Furse readily admitted that she had suffered from the strain of years of having "to keep calm and to face with kindly equanimity the vicissitudes of public life under high pressure." Feeling the need for "recharging" and finding her "right level again after having served for four years as a bureaucratic figurehead," she entered psychotherapeutic analysis with Dr. Carl Jung in Zurich. Jung advised Furse against retreating to her childhood home in the mountains at Klosters. In his view, Furse later recalled, "it was the duty of a healthy woman to live among her own people down in the valleys, helping human beings to recover their sanity in the midst of all the damage and misery left by war."[36]

Returning to London, Furse resumed her professional career by joining the Girl Guides, an organization begun in 1910 in England by Robert Baden-Powell, the founder of the Boy Scouts. By 1929, when Mary Follett met her, Furse was helping to form the World Association of Girl Guides and Girl Scouts, an organization that under her leadership came to involve thirty-four countries. It was to this work on behalf of the World Association that she was returning when Follett and Furse left the Engadine for London on June 25. Furse had a speech to deliver in England on June 28 and, soon thereafter, a conference to run in Holland.[37]

Two months in Katharine Furse's company seems to have convinced Mary Follett that Furse had "taken her feeling of friendship for me not as an emotion, but just in that way, that she wanted to help me. She has been so simple about it," she wrote the Cabots. "That is what she is, utterly simple & straight

& true, really touchingly simple & fine & unself-seeking, & so conscientious about her work. I mean she gives herself so largely, as darling Ella does, when it is often not easy for her to do so."[38]

Furse gave of herself but got something in return, too. Enthralled by Follett's books, she took personal pleasure in being in daily contact with such an accomplished thinker. Mary Follett, Furse later recalled, was "one of the most remarkable human beings I have ever known and one of the best people to talk to. She had a fund of wisdom which seemed to be inexhaustible and she would give hours to thinking out whatever point caught her attention. If one took her some small problem of the running of one's office or the adjustment of some more or less difficult relationship, Mary would think about it for hours and set out the question in all its aspects and discuss each angle till we could both feel satisfied that we had at least done our best to find the right solution . . . I learned a great deal from her as to the value of considered choice."[39]

Furse, who was sometimes sensitive about her lack of formal education, also appreciated Follett's willingness to take her opinions seriously. Not having had the opportunity to learn how to engage in intellectual discussions and debates, Furse tended to falter when challenged. "I seem to grope," she would later confide to Ella Cabot; "can't marshal my facts & rapidly become discouraged." But this never happened to her when talking with Mary, Katharine continued, and it "was one of the things I loved her for. Her infinite patience & tolerance of my clumsy efforts to express myself & her expressed interest in my views. It was something almost new to me from some one with her intelligence."[40]

Follett's "constant search for inspiration from beauty" was another quality that Furse admired, particularly as it reminded her of her own mother. But although Follett "could look at a view for hours and watch a sunset with a concentration she could bring to bear on a problem," she seemed to Furse to know "practically nothing of the actual flowers or insects or birds which go to make nature in its more homely relationship to those of us who love her. Mary had not realized the possibility of having close relationship with God's small creatures themselves because her bringing up at home had not included such frivolous interests. And it was fun to watch the way in which, as a result of my own interests, she began to enjoy a flower or a bird for its own sake instead of as a contributing factor to a landscape or to the pleasure of watching a sunset." Near the end of her memoir, Furse quotes a portion of Follett's *Creative Experience* and then continues: "It is the sum total of one's experiences which counts as one looks back, and I feel more than ever that life has offered me wonderful chances through association with many of what Walt Whitman called 'the Great Companions.' "[41]

Furse's extensive experience — in building new organizations, in recruiting and developing the personnel who would staff them, and in building collaborative relations with such complex bureaucracies as the Red Cross and the Royal Navy — enabled her to appreciate the value of Follett's ideas. But that in itself would not explain why she invited Mary Follett to share her home. There were other, more personal reasons, too. Furse's Beaufort Street home was now nearly empty; her son Peter had recently married, and her son Paul, then in Africa, was to be married in October. The prospect of having the daily companionship and intimate friendship of someone as fascinating as Follett was exceedingly appealing to the gregarious Furse. Then, too, Furse likely would have felt challenged rather than put off by Follett's poor health. An experienced caretaker who had been trained in an assortment of nursing skills during her early years in the V.A.D., Furse felt confident that she could help Follett restore her health and resume her valuable work.

Furse naturally gravitated toward taking charge when a problem presented itself, and Follett's health would have been no exception. She immediately began a personal correspondence with Richard Cabot, exchanging information and consulting with him about Follett's symptoms. At first Mary didn't seem to mind — or at least she didn't specifically object. Indeed, she told Cabot that she was "very grateful to K. for giving me this chance for getting well & getting back to work again," and she appreciated his ready acknowledgment of Furse's good intentions: "I am so glad you wrote to her as you did . . . & I was pleased with the way you expressed yourself — 'essential service of friendship' — for she certainly deserves your happy expression. I remember sitting at the little table in Waltham one Sunday last Nov. & talking a good deal about K., & I am a little ashamed now that I was not big enough to appreciate sooner her bigness. She is wholly different from any one I have every known & I was judging her on that Sunday in a way I certainly shouldn't now. Every week I am with her, I feel her fineness more & more. She has *nothing* in her shop windows & it takes time to disclose the splendid things behind there. And she is *so* good to me. Thank you again for letting her see your appreciation of that."[42]

Despite Furse's ministrations, Follett's health improved only very slowly. By mid-July, Mary was walking better, even going up and down stairs. But she was exceptionally tired, finding it difficult even to read a newspaper article without effort. "Katharine is very busy," she wrote the Cabots, "so I just laze thro. the day by myself — write necessary letters, do a few errands etc. K's friends are very kind about taking me on lovely drives — that is a great pleasure. I have variety, pleasure & beauty, & at the same time plenty of time for rest & sleep. K. often has people to dine, but I go to bed just the same afterward."[43]

Richard Cabot's next letter was full of exhortations, urging Follett to begin to write—or at least to read and take notes. Her response to this particular letter, however, is chilling. "Yesterday I thought I should never work again," Mary confessed. "Now comes your letter & I hope it will make me do what I know I ought to do. But it is impossible for me to tell you how tired I am, for there are no other words."

> If I put my stockings on & then find there is a hole in then (as I did this morning) I almost cry because I have to change them, although it takes about a minute! And this is not like me. The chief reason I have been able to do whatever social work I have done is just because I have never minded difficulties. This is really true—with all my many faults & limitations. But now I am always wanting to cry. Things seem to go wrong altho. as a matter of fact I am having the easiest & pleasantest life possible. I am even cross to Katharine sometimes which I certainly don't what to be & she is a perfect angel to me. I really hurt her sometimes & then I feel so badly . . . My tongue I think I shall be able to curb in the future, but the tendency to cry & to "make mountains out of mole-hills" is there all the time. Perhaps confessing it like this to you will make me so ashamed of myself that I shall now do better.[44]

It was in the midst of this depression that Follett made the decision to stay with Furse for a year. Having sold Overhills and given up the lease on Otis Place, she was acutely conscious of having no obvious place to go. "I at present have no home," she wrote Richard. "Except that K. is making this seem like home to me. There are here the spiritual essentials of a home—a warm & I think deep affection, congenial tastes, & the help & stimulus one needs—no, perhaps not everyone, but I need stimulus." Follett acknowledged that Furse would often be away because of her work (indeed, she planned to be in the United States for three months in the winter) and that she would be alone in the house, except for the maids, for weeks and even months. Nevertheless, Mary was hopeful that Katharine would be able to provide her some small portion of the abundant encouragement, support, and loving consideration that Isobel had long given her.[45]

Within a few weeks, however, these hopes seemed shattered. At a dinner with the Baden-Powells, Follett thought Furse was "outrageously rude to 3 people" and afterwards took Katharine to task for her behavior. This event might soon have been forgotten except that Katharine, unbeknownst to Mary, immediately wrote Richard Cabot with details about what she saw as Mary's overreaction and appealed for his help. Incensed and hurt by Cabot's response and, more importantly, by the way Furse had used his comments against her, Follett fired back a reply.

She did not hide her distress from Cabot, but she nevertheless began her letter with an affirmation of qualities she appreciated in her longtime friend: "K. read me your letter & I felt really moved at your gift for human relationships, your directness & openness & honesty, & at your being willing to take the time & trouble to write it." But Follett had a list of grievances about his letter and began by focusing on some glaring inaccuracies: "Have I had nerve-storms . . . with the frequency your letter implies? Also, is the fact that I screamed once in the night at Waltham & once at Camb. [the Cabots' homes] (I do it once or twice a year on an average & have not done it for a year now) sufficient basis for you to write as you did of that?" Several times throughout her letter, Follett tried to get Cabot to consider how he might feel if *he* had been the subject of such a wholly critical and one-sided analysis. "Would it be fair for me to pick out your weaknesses (I think you have fewer than most people) & say nothing of your splendid strength of character?" Follett also was troubled by Cabot's failure to seek her version of what had transpired at the Baden-Powells. Suggesting another possible explanation for Furse's one-sided account of the evening, Follett added, "When one [Furse] doesn't like being blamed, it is too easy a way out to say that the one who blames [Follett] is in a pathological condition! Thus one saves one's face."

Further into her letter, Follett was even more forthcoming about her real concerns. "Richard, dear," she said at one point, "it always seemed to me so understanding of you & Ella that you shd. understand what Isobel's loss meant to me, shd. understand that we had not lived together for convenience or a superficial companionship, but that there was a deep bond between us, the breaking of which (as far as it is broken, not really) was a terrible grief to me." "Now," Follett pleaded, "a new friendship is opening to me . . . don't you think you might help me in it by finding something good to say about me instead of all this about defects & weaknesses?" Follett was particularly concerned about the negative impact that Richard's letter had had on Furse's estimation of her. "She has up to now," Mary wrote, "given me real love & devotion." But ever since Cabot's letter had arrived, "all these defects & weaknesses stand between us."

Since she was already "writing so frankly," Follett decided to seize this opportunity to let Richard know her reservations about his continuing correspondence with Furse. "You take the attitude that you are helping K. to take care of me. I have not," Follett declared, "given K. the right to take care of me. You, yes, you are sane & sensible & strong, & I am humbly & deeply grateful for your help, but K. is on the verge of a nervous break-down & is in no condition to observe accurately or to judge wisely. I shall take care of myself unless I break down & then I shd. go to a nursing home."[46]

Ella Cabot responded immediately to Follett's impassioned letter, trying her best to explain to her dear friend what her husband had done. "It is rather hard for you to understand Richard's letter without seeing Dame Katharine's to which it was an answer. She was anxious to have you see a doctor & asked him why not & he meant his answer I know to be purely the answer to a medical question, not in the least the description of a dear person whom he greatly admires — If he said too much or more than could be understood without a fuller picture forgive us — dear." She also assured Mary that her "friendship with Dame Katharine shall be by all in our power the stronger & clearer & deeper for anything I can do." A relieved Follett quickly responded in language reminiscent of *Creative Experience:* "I see clearly from your letter exactly what happened. Katharine, I can see, wrote to Richard, thinking of herself as a person taking care of me & wishing medical advice. Richard replied in the same spirit. Then the Katharine who received his answer was not the person taking care of me wishing medical advice! That is, not only that. She was now a new friend who did not know me very well hearing, what she thought, most adverse criticism of me from some one who did know me well. It is all in the past now — except what lessons we can get from it. If we can grow through experience, then there is all the more of me to love you with. I will try."[47]

Richard, unlike Ella, seems not to have responded quickly to Follett's original letter, and when he finally did, he offered a rather grudging apology. Having judged from Mary's subsequent letters that she and Furse had resolved matters between them, he seems a bit cavalier about the role his own misjudgments and carelessness had played in all this. "It assures me that Ella & I were right," Cabot told her, "in believing that your friendship with K. was too firmly rooted to be much hurt by any mistake of mine. She could never take her ideas of you at second hand; no good friend could. So that's all in the past now & we can start on towards the splendid future."[48]

By the end of 1929, Follett had made her decision: she would spend the rest of her life in England. Ella Cabot's sadness was palpable: "I seem to miss most your not coming back here at Waltham . . . My Saint Francis Cross spoke of you; the cleansing of dishes; the sun on the porch; the snow shoes you gave. We must face the fact that we shall meet at most once in two or three years & that writing is not the same, but friendship is steadfast." Ever gracious and always considerate of those who depended on her for support, Ella rose above her own disappointment. "I think it is wise and beautiful that you and Dame Katharine are to live on together — wise for the sake of intimate, stirring growing companionship & beautiful because it seems a new light shed on your way — a path so darkened by Miss Briggs' death. The capacity for strong & sustained friendships is one of the greatest gifts & you have it!"[49]

Although Ella Cabot spoke optimistically to Follett about the new living arrangement, friends in England who knew Furse were not so sure that she was temperamentally suited to live with anyone. They felt quite certain that this arrangement was bound to fail. According to Cicely (Polly) Furse, the wife of Katharine's younger son Paul, some of the people who had known Furse from her childhood knew how strong-willed and difficult she could be. Her children, too, knew all too well how challenging it was to deal with her. Furse gave little guidance but much criticism. Whenever her children did something she thought was wrong, she was right there to tell them about it, usually quite vociferously. To deal effectively with Furse's abrasiveness, Polly concluded, the only real option was to learn not to mind what she said.[50] This would prove to be impossible for Follett, who was in the uncomfortable position of being quite dependent on Furse while growing increasingly apprehensive about becoming a burden on her. Every hurtful remark seemed to Mary a sign that Katharine no longer wanted her.

Follett, of course, knew little or nothing at this stage of the friendship about Furse's obstinacy, temper, and sharp tongue. Instead, she attributed the few early difficulties they had experienced to the usual adjustments involved in a close relationship. Besides, there were plenty of happy moments to relish. Although Furse was no intellectual — she was more of a doer than a thinker and had had little formal education — she had brought joy, gaiety, and unabashed enthusiasm for living back into Follett's life. A trip that they took to Switzerland with Furse's son and daughter-in-law, Paul and Polly Furse, shortly after their 1929 wedding was filled with laughter, Polly remembered, as well as with debates and good conversation.[51]

Once Follett had finally decided to live with Furse, she seemed able to return slowly to work. She began by producing a review for *The Survey* of Ella Cabot's new book, *Temptations to Rightdoing,* based on Cabot's years of experience as an ethics lecturer in several Boston-area schools and colleges.[52] And Follett began reading again in earnest. She asked Morris Cooke to send her the new Taylor Society book on scientific management, and made several suggestions to Richard Cabot about books that he must find time to read.[53] Closer to home, she was helping Katharine plan the renovation of a house near the river at Five Cheyne Place in Chelsea to which they would soon move.

In April Follett met the Cabots for a few days in Paris. Richard used this opportunity to talk at length with Mary about her health, urging her to consult Sir Humphry Rolleston, a prominent British physician, about the fatigue and pain she was experiencing. Follett firmly refused. Katharine Furse would later conclude that Mary must have "suspected the cause of her suffering [metastases from her kidney cancer] and preferred not to have it diagnosed, and she fought valiantly against the effect of pain which must often have been almost unbearable."[54]

Despite her continuing pain and anxiety, Follett willed herself back into some semblance of a professional life. In May 1930 she made plans to visit Dorothy Whitney Straight Elmhirst and her husband, Leonard Elmhirst, who were developing a progressive school on an old estate in Devonshire. As it turned out, Dorothy would not be at Dartington Hall during their visit, having left to attend the funeral of Herbert Croly; but her husband was an amiable host. Before her departure, Dorothy Elmhirst asked Follett to speak to the staff and students at their regular Sunday-evening discussion on the small unit as the focus for social and political action. Follett agreed to speak and, she insisted, "to be spoken to!"[55] Follett and Furse (who also made the trip) had a wonderful time, but Mary was quickly fatigued and had a hard time concentrating. In a thank-you note to Leonard Elmhirst, she inserted this apology: "May I say a word about the question you asked on Leadership? Because my unresponsiveness was rather amusing in view of the fact that I have given a good deal of thought to that subject, & gave an hour's lecture on it at Oxford a year & a half ago! But I was so tired that my mind simply stopped working . . . I have not been well for over a year, & although I am much better, I still get tired at the end of the day. Do forgive me for my stupidity. Perhaps sometime in the future you will let me atone."[56]

In early September 1930, Follett and Furse decided to escape the heat of London and spend a few days with Katharine's friends on the Isle of Caldey, in south Wales. They also were fleeing the stress of the house renovations, which put yet another strain on their relationship. Follett felt guilty about the huge sums Furse was having to spend and, as a result, was determined to cover the expenses for her own bedroom and sitting room. In addition to paying for papering and painting, staining the floors, opening up a fireplace, having bookcases made, and replacing electrical wiring, Follett also had to buy furniture.

Ever frugal, Follett was reluctant to tap into the principal of her investments and decided to purchase only a secondhand desk and a bed until she was able to sell some of her furniture that was in storage in Boston.[57] When Ella Cabot learned about her friend's predicament, she again leaped to her aid. Cabot first volunteered to have Follett's furniture appraised and then told her to count on $500 for pieces she could use at their summer home in Maine. Ella's generosity was especially welcome, since she had reported in mid-September that "most folks are feeling rather poor or anxious about business, so it is hard to sell anything."[58] Although the stock market crash of September and October 1929 had so far had a greater impact on speculators than on average citizens, it was unsettling in its abruptness and magnitude. People were hoping that the reversal in the market was temporary, just another of the dips in the business cycle that Americans had grown accustomed to experiencing.[59]

Follett, like others of Cabot's friends, reacted cautiously to the decline in stock values. She decided to sell her share in the Boston Athenaeum, one of the nation's oldest and most distinguished private libraries, even though the librarian warned her that share price (about $750) was sure to be affected by the "present slump in the stock market." Informing Ella of the impending sale, Follett added, "Don't think for a moment that every further bond I break wh. ties me to Boston does not hurt. It does. Yet I still believe that I am right."[60]

Despite Follett's confidence in her decision to live with Katharine Furse, the transition to the new house proved to be more difficult than she had ever imagined, emotionally as well as financially. "As long as we were at Beaufort St.," Mary wrote Ella, "my point of view was that of a guest — it was all temporary. Whereas my *decision* was that it was to be permanent, the *feeling* still was of a temporary arrangement . . . The period of adjustment which I thought had been going on for months evidently only began really then. And I found it a very hard stage to go through. I feel sure now that it is going to be all right. So be happy about me. And after all, the difficulties of life are fun even if they make one wretched. It is fun to try to overcome them." Follett then displayed some of her old sense of humor. "But you won't understand this wholly," she added lightheartedly, "as you were not born with so much original sin as I was. I mean you won't understand how hard one has to work."[61]

Nearly three months later, in January 1931, little had changed in the Follett-Furse relationship. "I am at almost the same moment happy & unhappy," Mary told Ella. "It is a queer mixture. I should like to find a medium, that is, I should like to be less happy & less unhappy . . . I feel heavy all the time, as if there were weights on my mind & spirit. I crave & hunger for lightness & gaiety. I wish I could hear you & R. laugh." Struggling to understand Furse's moods and her "artistic temperament," Follett had picked up a copy of Horatio Brown's biography of Katharine's father. Although she was deeply moved by Symonds' struggles and developed genuine admiration for his endurance as well as his appreciation of beauty in art and nature, she learned little in her reading that would explain, much less justify, Katharine's behavior. It seemed to Mary, she wrote Ella, that people such as Katharine who claimed an artistic temperament "allow themselves to do just as they *damned* please. Now what K. pleases is usually very good, but when it isn't, she does it just the same & excuses everything with her 'artistic temperament.' "[62]

At least some of the difficulty between the two women arose from the way Furse's unpredictable nature and fierce need for independence conflicted with Mary Follett's own long-standing insecurities. Never having fully overcome the psychological damage of growing up with an indifferent and unsympathetic mother and an alcoholic father who in her earliest years had repeatedly abandoned his family, twenty-five-year-old Follett had been unbelievably fortunate to have had Isobel Briggs come into her life. The forty-five-year-old Briggs, having already completed her career as a headmistress, lovingly dedicated the rest of her life to Mary's happiness and to the furtherance of her work. Isobel had been utterly devoted to Mary, and Mary knew it.[63]

The situation with Katharine Furse could hardly have been more different. Constrained by her continuing poor health, Follett would find it difficult either to be in close contact with old friends or to make new ones. She was almost totally dependent on Furse and her friends for companionship—and thus often felt lonely. This situation was exacerbated by Furse's determination to keep her independence. As Katharine envisioned their lives together, she would continue her professional life and her relationships with her friends much as they had been before Mary arrived—and she expected Mary to do the same. Whereas Isobel would have devoted herself to helping Follett create the right conditions to begin working again, Katharine largely went about her own business. Follett found this combination of professed love and apparent indifference disconcerting. The notion developed in Mary's childhood—that she was loved for what she did rather than for who she was—echoed in her bemused plaint to Ella that "K. is so un-interested in my work that I often wonder why she likes me so much." After Follett's death, Furse reflected on their troubles in this period, telling Ella Cabot, "I realise more and more, of course, how much of our difficulty was due to my own lack of self control & to my selfishness. And to Mary's inexperience of the type of life she had come into with me. And to her puzzlement and anxiety. She hardly knew me. Why should she trust me? Is it any wonder that she got lost at times?"[64]

When spring arrived, Follett renewed her efforts to return to work and to friendships. Receiving a copy of Harry Overstreet's new book, *The Enduring Quest,* she devoured it in one sitting and immediately informed him that she wished to write a review. When this piece was published a year later in the *International Journal of Ethics,* Overstreet wrote to thank her for the "perfectly scrumptious review," saying that it "really puts the book in a better light than it was able to secure for itself."[65] Follett also found the energy to accompany Furse to Geneva for a meeting of her League Committee on Child Welfare. Follett tried to see her friend, Lyndall Urwick, the director of the International Management Institute in Geneva and Follett's admirer from her Rowntree lectures at Oxford. Unfortunately, Urwick was in America on business, but she stayed for several days with his wife, who invited "interesting people" to their home so they could meet and talk with Follett. And when Follett returned to London, she was gratified to learn that Morris and Eleanor Cooke were planning a visit to London in September, giving her the prospect of seeing another pair of dear friends.[66]

Follett's primary activity during this period, however, was the preparation of a new paper for the Bureau of Personnel Administration. She had agreed to speak in New York in April 1932, but, as it turned out, the 1931–32 meetings were canceled because corporations suffering from the Great Depression could not afford to send representatives.[67] Instead, the papers would be reproduced and distributed by the bureau.[68]

The meetings scheduled by the bureau on the topic "Economic and Social Planning" spoke to an increasing sense among many Americans that vigorous action must be taken if the country were to forestall a serious depression. In 1929 President Hoover had responded to the stock market crisis by calling together the nation's economic leaders and securing their voluntary cooperation in maintaining wages and expanding construction — policies that he hoped would provide the consumer purchasing power and business investment necessary to avoid a major depression. For a time it appeared that these policies had worked and the recession was coming to an end. Bank failures abated in the early part of 1931, while indices of employment, payrolls, and production steadied and even rallied slightly.[69]

Unfortunately, the historian Ellis Hawley writes, in a matter of months it became clear "that the downward cycle had not been checked, that construction was rapidly declining, layoffs continuing, markets shrinking, and wage cuts becoming increasingly frequent. Farm income . . . continued to decline. 'Sick' industries became 'sicker.' And in a contracting economy, where cooperative associationists behaved more and more like competitive individualists, the notion of a self-disciplined, coordinated business community, which could and would act in the 'public interest' as determined by scientific experts, was proving to be mostly an illusion."[70]

"It was primarily in this second period," writes the historian James T. Patterson, "from mid-1931 to March of 1933 that the stock market troubles were accompanied by an ever deepening economic depression."[71] By mid-1932, when Mary Follett completed her paper for the BPA conference, the country was undeniably in a serious depression. Between 1929 and 1932, the gross national product had dropped 30 percent, industrial production had dropped by almost 45 percent, and 85,000 businesses had failed. President Hoover and the Congress responded in the early part of 1932 by passing a series of measures, most notably the Reconstruction Finance Corporation, in an effort to pump governmental funds into private enterprise. But unemployment in the nonfarm labor force continued to grow, from an already sizable 15 percent at the end of 1930 to 25 percent at the end of 1931, eventually reaching a startling 40 percent (12 million workers) at the end of 1932.[72]

Numerous critics of the Hoover administration began to appear, many of them advocating hitherto-unprecedented forms of national planning. Among liberal intellectuals, Ellis Hawley writes, there was talk of "central planning boards, functional syndicates, massive welfare measures, and a 'democratic collectivism' that would 'administer' the economy in the national interest. Similarly, in farm and labor circles, there were calls for 'real' agricultural planning and stronger action to maintain labor's purchasing power. And from businessmen came a flood of proposals for government-sanctioned cartels. By late 1931 such groups as the National Civic Federation, the American Bar Association, the Chamber of Commerce, and a newly formed Congress of Industries were all pushing specific plans. Gerald Swope, the 'progressive' president of General Electric, had attracted wide attention with his vision of a planned order administered by compulsory trade associations, and in industry after industry, lesser figures had set forth their own schemes."[73]

It was in the midst of this ferment that Henry Metcalf developed the Bureau of Personnel Administration's 1931–32 lecture series on the subject of "Economic and Social Planning" for leaders in business, government, and labor. The topics were wide-ranging and included such subjects as "The Objectives of Socialized Capitalism," "Planning in the General Electric Company," "Trade Union Planning in the Electrical Industry," "International Planning," "Constitutional and Legal Problems Involved in Developing Collective Planning," "Company Plans and Community Needs," and "Group Thinking and Group Planning." The topic for Mary Follett's presentation was "Individualism in a Planned Society," and it was scheduled near the end of the eight-month series.[74]

By early 1932, as Mary Follett prepared her paper, President Hoover had already made numerous speeches resolutely opposing national planning. He had dismissed the plans proposed in 1931 by Gerald Swope and the Chamber of Commerce as "unconstitutional, regressive and monopolistic," and he had a similar reaction to proposals made in the following year that called for suspension of antitrust regulations or revival of the wartime Council of National Defense. According to historian Ellis Hawley, Hoover told leaders of the Chamber of Commerce that he was strongly opposed to " 'unconstitutional' attempts to smuggle 'fascism' through a 'back door.' "[75]

It was against the backdrop of this intense national debate that Mary Follett took up her topic of "Individualism and a Planned Society." Never one to dodge a difficult issue, she immediately made clear her position on the desirability of planning: "The economic interdependence of men is a fact which is to-day generally recognized. This recognition makes imperative, as the only alternative to our present chaos, collective planning on a national or even international scale." Acknowledging that many people were opposed to national planning, Follett speculated that their objections rested on a "fear of the word 'control,' on a fear that the rights of the individual are to be invaded." These fears, Follett continued, were readily understandable, because the schemes for national planning currently under consideration had used terms such as *force* and *coerce* over and over again. How could planning succeed without coercion?[76]

Follett believed that the kind of control she had seen being exercised in the best-managed industries, if used in national planning, could obviate concerns about coercion. In these more progressive firms, Follett wrote, "control is coming more and more to mean fact-control rather than man-control," and "central control is coming more and more to mean the correlation of many controls rather than a super-imposed control." These two principles — fact-control and collective control — should, as Follett saw it, "be the foundation of any scheme for national planning."[77]

"The imperative need of the moment is a search for the best methods of co-ordination, of adjustment. But the process of adjusting," Follett argued, "is not one which can be imposed from outside — it is essentially, basically, by its very nature, a process of auto-controlled activity. No one can issue a fiat by which I am adjusted, I can only be helped to adjust myself. National planning should be a scheme for the self-adjusting of our various and varying interests. It should plan for the self-co-ordinating of industries and for the self-co-ordinating of plants within an industry. Beyond this it should, I think, include union-management co-operation within each plant, thus giving the workers a share from the beginning."[78]

What Follett had in mind with regard to national planning could be accomplished neither by " 'regulation,' our nineteenth-century panacea, nor 'coercion,' the socialist remedy." Experience had taught her that no policy "will be whole-heartedly carried out, which is the same as saying that no policy will be wholly successful, unless it is the result of conference and agreement. I do not mean to say," Follett continued, "that policies decided on will not have to be binding on reluctant individuals, I mean only that the plan made should reduce as far as possible the coercive element." At the same time, however, she was convinced that national planning could not be merely an extension of the voluntarism practiced by the Hoover administration. "I do not believe that our thinking can any longer stay within the limits of large-scale voluntary collaboration (although that may well be the next step), but the best form of collective control remains to be discovered."[79]

The heart of her approach to collective planning — a term she preferred to *central planning* — was the concept of coordination, a notion that she had written a bit about in three previous Bureau of Personnel Administration lectures in 1926 and 1927.[80] In "Individualism in a Planned Society," she used the concept of coordination to explicate four fundamental principles of organization and suggested that they might be used to "test any schemes for national planning which may be proposed to us . . . to test whether such schemes threaten individual freedom."[81]

Follett had seen the first principle — "co-ordination by direct contact of the responsible people concerned" — in examples of the increasingly productive relations between heads of departments of industrial organizations. She also had found it central to the more effective forms of Allied wartime cooperation as they had been discussed in Sir Arthur Salter's book *Allied Shipping Control*. Indeed, it was from Salter that she took the term *direct contact*. Follett derived her second principle of organization — "co-ordination in the early stages" — from having seen in industry that agreements between departments were greatly facilitated when matters were discussed in the earliest stages of the process rather than after each department had developed its policy and practice.

Follett took as her third principle of coordination "the reciprocal relating of all the factors in a situation." This principle, Follett wrote, "shows us just what this process of co-ordination actually is . . . This sort of reciprocal relating, this interpenetration of every part by every other part, and again by every other part as it has been permeated by all, should be the goal of all attempts at co-ordination, a goal, of course, never wholly reached." Since the process of coordination is fundamentally one of interpenetration, Follett continued, "it is obvious that it cannot be enforced by an outside body. That is why I have very grave doubts whether 'central' planning, as at present conceived by many, will bring us any appreciable degree of co-ordination. I am not saying that a National Planning Board *ought not* to arrogate to itself the task of co-ordinating, I am saying that it *cannot,* because co-ordination is by its very nature a process of auto-governed activity."[82]

Summarizing her position as articulated in the first three principles — direct contact in the early stages by the concerned parties seeking to reciprocally relate all the factors in the situation — Follett saw these principles as having important implications for any viable process of national planning. "In our highly complex economic society," Follett wrote, "there are many points of control. The organized relating of these should constitute the central control. A co-ordinating process active throughout our whole economic society should *be* the control. A National Planning Board should express the reciprocal relating of the co-ordinating process, but if it tries to take the place of that process, it will be giving us the shadow for the substance. Any National Planning Board which proceeds from the top down is, I am sure, doomed to failure."[83]

Follett's fourth principle of organization involved "co-ordination as a continuing process." Such continuing activity, appropriately recorded and classified, would make it possible for planners to have ready access to past experience, a process that Follett had observed working well in the functioning of the Supreme Court as well as in the political section of the Secretariat of the League of Nations. Another advantage of continuous planning, Follett argued, was "that then the circle, or spiral, is not broken in the transition from planning to activity and from activity to further planning. A mistake we often tend to make is that the world stands still while we are going through the process of a given adjustment. And it doesn't." Continuous planning also would help avoid the fallacy that problems can be "solved" for all time. "When we think we have *solved* a problem, well, by the very process of solving, new elements or forces come into the situation and you have a new problem on your hands to be solved." Rather than be discouraged by this state of affairs, Follett implored her readers to see it as "our strength and our hope. We don't want any system that holds us enmeshed within itself."[84]

Writing at a time when there were few of the industrywide or national economic analyses that are readily available today, Follett reminded her readers that the "underpinning of these [four principles of organization] is information based on research. A National Planning Board should collect and publish data in respect to each industry — on raw materials, productive capacity, sales, prices, new capital investment and so on and so on. This information of itself would be a form of control, for there would be a tendency to act in accordance with information given if it were accepted as accurate. Moreover, we might even hope perhaps that each industry, basing its plans on the same information as all others, might tend to fit its activity into what might more or less automatically become a general scheme. Ignorance," Follett confidently asserted, "always binds. Knowledge always frees. Collective research must be the basis of all planning."[85]

In her usual nondogmatic fashion, Follett found many questions about national planning still unanswered and cautioned that she believed in national planning "*only* if we can to some extent solve these problems." She ended her paper with a list of eighteen issues requiring further study, among them the proper mixture of centralization and decentralization in planning, the relation of the functions of planning and administration, the relation of control to competition, the role of experts, and the effect of political logrolling on legislation about tariffs and credit.[86]

Despite the many issues yet to be addressed, Follett ended her paper full of optimism, urging her readers to action and appealing to "the socially constructive passion in every man." "Our highest virtues," she told them, "have been service and sacrifice. Are we not now thinking of these virtues somewhat differently? . . . Sacrifice sometimes seems too negative, dwells on what I give up. Service sometimes seems to emphasize the fact of service rather than the value of the service. Yet service and sacrifice are noble ideals. We cannot do without them. Let them, however, be the handmaids of the great purpose of our life, namely, our contribution to that new world we wish to see rise out of our present chaos, that age which shall bring us individual freedom through collective control."[87]

23

"Prepared to Go or Stay with Equal Graciousness"

In early October 1931, Mary Follett made her first trip back to America in nearly eighteen months. With the stock market crash of 1929 having turned into a severe depression, Follett was increasingly concerned about her finances. Hoping that she might be able to earn some money in the States, she wrote to William Mosher asking if he might want her to give a talk at Syracuse. Mosher sent his regrets, saying that the college had eliminated from its budget most of the funds for outside lecturers.[1]

Follett did accomplish some other objectives. She repeatedly visited the storage warehouse where her possessions had been kept, sorting through boxes of papers and other items and disposing of her furniture.[2] She also spent as much time as possible with the Cabots and particularly cherished each hour that she spent in Ella's company. "I did so enjoy my Thanksgiving with you," Mary wrote her old friend, " — the music, the fire, the nice people & my beloved Ella who has become far more precious to me during these last weeks even than she was before. You have been so dear to me, helped me through all my troubles, & you have been so sympathetic & so sweet & so *wise*. I shall leave America feeling that I had a rich addition to my life in my new appreciation of you . . . I am so truly touched by your patience with me, for I realize that I have been very trying to anyone's temper & yet you have been so patient with me through it all, so astonishingly patient."[3]

Mary P. Follett, ca. 1930. Lyndall Fownes Urwick Archive, Henley Management College, Henley-on-Thames.

Katharine Furse was in Boston with Follett for part of the time, taking this opportunity to meet some of Mary's friends and to do some business with Girl Scout organizations.[4] She also consulted Richard Cabot about her own health. Furse had been having worrisome symptoms of what she and Mary thought might be heart trouble, but Cabot was able to find nothing amiss in his examination.[5]

Follett and Furse returned to London in December, and by February 1932 a relieved Mary reported to Ella that "everything continues to go perfectly smoothly & happily here with none of the drawbacks of last winter. I am working every day & K. is sympathetic, & in every way." Follett had written a brief review of Henry Dennison's *Organizational Engineering* for the *International Journal of Ethics* and was hard at work on her paper for the Bureau of Personnel Administration.[6]

Follett also continued anxiously to puzzle over how the United States might extricate itself from what had by then become an international economic depression. Later in 1932, during the last months of Hoover's tenure as president, the banking structure in the United States would nearly collapse; and by the inauguration of Franklin D. Roosevelt on March 4, 1933, "banks were either closed or under severe restrictions in forty-seven states" in an effort by state governors to stem the tide of heavy withdrawals. Only two days into his presidency, Roosevelt responded to the wave of panic by declaring a bank holiday that closed all banks for a four-day period. Three days later, Congress met in a special session and passed the Emergency Banking Act, which started a transfusion of over a billion dollars from Hoover's Reconstruction Finance Corporation into the banking system and directed Treasury officials to assess the solvency of banks and supervise their reopening.[7]

"The times are terribly serious, are they not," said a gravely concerned Mary Follett in a March 1933 letter to Morris Cooke. Conscious that the financial crisis in America had exacerbated the pressure the United States government was placing on England and France to repay wartime loans, Follett sent Cooke an article by Sir Arthur Salter on "War Debts" that she hoped Cooke might pass along to the right people.[8] She sent the same article to Richard Cabot, but he responded that there was no possibility of getting people to think of the debt question just now because there were even larger issues demanding consideration. "I voted for Hoover & had no confidence in Roosevelt," Cabot admitted. "But his actions since election have been such as to meet his unparalleled opportunity magnificently . . . never in my lifetime nor I think in our history has a president had Congress & the country so united behind him." Recounting a long list of changes that had already taken place or were likely in the next few months in banking, interstate commerce, agriculture, and tariffs, Cabot acknowledged that he was "enthusiastic and deeply impressed by the magnificence of these attempts. Politics in the ordinary sense has ceased (for the time) to exist. We are making such an attempt to control our fortunes by reason & in harmony with world interests, as we have not made before in our history so far as I know . . . I haven't been so happy for years & years . . . Of course we are nearer socialism than ever before. The government is doing & proposing to do far more than it has so far in our history, but I don't regret it nor I believe will you."[9]

Despite Follett's uneasiness and concern about the global financial crisis, she found time for personal pleasures, among them reading some of the works of Virginia Woolf. She had very much liked *Mrs. Dalloway* (1925) and was about to begin *The Waves* (1931) when Richard Cabot wrote her a long letter lauding the book as "one of the most extraordinary pieces of work I ever read." But he also added a caveat. *The Waves* would not sell widely, Cabot thought, because most people would find it too difficult. Follett disagreed: "I think you are wrong about her not being widely appreciated. She is a tremendous lion in London, & almost all my friends in Am. like her books immensely." Realizing that the Cabots were planning another visit to London, Follett mentioned that Furse and Woolf were old friends and asked if they would like to meet her.[10] When Katharine invited Woolf to dinner, she accepted, although she had not seen Furse for many years and had considerable anxiety about renewing this acquaintance. When Furse opened the door, Woolf later recorded in her diary, all that she could think of was: "Where had the handsome Katharine gone: she who strode; had firm red cheeks; & was decisive, masterly, controlled even in the great trench [?] of her unhappiness? Heavens, what an injury life inflicts! To have replaced that dashing youth with this almost intolerable look of suffering: a grudging look; a scraped bare look; the ugly poor woman look ... She never relaxed. Never lost her look of suffering the whole evening. To harden to blunt to coarsen that is the worst damage age — & I daresay she's only 8 years older than I am — can inflict. Is this all Charles' death? Or what?" Pausing to reflect, the fifty-year-old Woolf then turned the spotlight on herself: "Was that contained in my dismay with Katharine — the sense I look like that too. Perhaps. Then Leonard [Woolf] came in, in his grey suit & blue tie, sunburnt; & I felt that we are still vigorous & young."[11]

Woolf's letters are replete with mockery of herself and others. According to Nigel Nicholson, the editor of her collected letters, Woolf was one to whom "every new acquaintance was slightly ridiculous . . . She liked and disliked exaggeratedly. Even affection was best expressed by ridicule." This trait is fully apparent in her unvarnished characterization of the new acquaintances she made at the Furse-Follett dinner party. "The talk spattered & sprinkled," Woolf wrote in her diary. "A dry precise old pepperbox called Cabot, professor of Harvard, his vague wife, Mary Follett, verbose, diffuse — that was the party & we sat & let the light turn grey & cold & all the cabinets grow dim — all very elderly & ugly."[12]

Despite Woolf's disparaging assessment, Mary Follett still had enough vitality in the fall of 1932 to begin preparing a series of five lectures for the London School of Economics (LSE), the institution founded in 1895 by the Fabian socialists Sidney and Beatrice Webb. Follett's friend, the management consultant Lyndall Urwick, had arranged for her to speak at the newly formed Department of Business Administration, which was seeking "fruitful cooperation between academic and business authorities" and making significant use of the case method in its forms of instruction.[13] Follett hoped that the LSE lectures, which she would deliver in January and February 1933, could later be expanded into a small book. Although the individual lectures contain little that was new in her thinking, taken together, they embody many of the essential elements of Follett's ideas about business organizations.[14]

Even as Follett was preparing her LSE lectures, she was in enough pain in her back and leg that she finally gave in to Katharine's pleadings and had X rays taken. Her doctor, perhaps much to everyone's surprise, reported that he saw no problems in the bone or lower part of the spine and surmised that she must be having a muscular problem from sitting so much.[15] Katharine also was not well. As early as August 1929, Follett had thought that Furse was on the verge of a nervous breakdown, and late in 1931 Richard Cabot had examined her, thinking she might have heart trouble. By late winter of 1932–33, Furse was suffering dangerous bouts of heart palpitations and a rapid pulse. The doctors told Follett that Furse's auricular fibrillation, myocarditis, and lung damage could be symptoms of life-threatening heart disease and that Furse would have to be exceptionally careful for the rest of her life. "I shouldn't suppose that (if she gets out of the woods that she is now in)," wrote Richard Cabot, "she could ever go back to her work, or go to Switzerland or do much of anything that she wants to do."[16] It was ironic. Follett had chosen to stay in London, at least in part, because Furse had promised to help her recover her health, but now it seemed that Katharine was becoming the invalid.

Follett's writing, which she had begun in earnest only within the past year, came to an abrupt halt with Furse's poor health. Follett also found it impossible to return to the United States in June when her mother died at the age of ninety-one. The doctors were afraid that Furse might have a heart attack, and she was displaying a constellation of other symptoms: depression, restlessness, anxiety, and, perhaps the worst, the disorientation and mental instability resulting from lack of sleep. To complicate matters further, Katharine was dealing with the aftereffects of shingles.[17] With Furse in no state of mind to advocate for herself, the stress of pushing the doctors to find the cause of her assortment of troubling symptoms fell to her son Paul, to Mary, and to Katharine's friends.[18] Rachel Crowdy, one of Furse's comrades from their days as V.A.D.'s, came to her side and stayed at Cheyne Place for five weeks. Everyone was distraught, the scene was chaotic, and there were heated disagreements about what should best be done for Katharine.

It wasn't until late May 1933, after months of distress and worry, that the doctors were able to report that "goiter poisoning" was the probable cause of Furse's symptoms. The appropriate course of action in such a case was to remove part of the thyroid surgically.[19] In late September, weeks after the surgery, the doctor reported to Follett that Furse was no longer suffering emotional volatility as a result of the toxic goiter. But in her behavior toward Mary, Katharine remained either scathing or indifferent. "For 2 weeks before she left the nursing home to go to the sea (Folkestone)," Follett told Richard Cabot, "K. saw all her friends, or even acquaintances, freely, but me she would see only once for 10 minutes, (sent word for me to come at 4.10 & leave at 4.20) & then only glared at me with a few perfunctory remarks." Hurt and bewildered, Follett was indignant as she recounted this episode to the Cabots, asserting that Katharine "probably wouldn't have been there to glare at me if it hadn't been for me. I think I can show you sometime that I in all human probability saved her life. Ingratitude, thy name is Katharine . . . I am very tired with it all & certainly thoroughly tired & sick of it all. It is childish. It is wholly unworthy. It is not the life I should be leading. Somehow, sometime I will extricate myself."

As the daughter of an alcoholic father, Mary Follett had come to abhor impulsiveness and unpredictability and had a dreadful fear of being abandoned. She was now living her worst nightmare. "I feel sure she thinks that if she wishes us to continue to live together, I shall too," Mary wrote Richard. "But [if we talk] I shall say that I can't run that risk of her turning against me at any moment. In the first place that is not friendship. In the second place, I must have some stability in my life. I can't live on a volcano."[20]

Follett was desperate to have a talk with Furse, to work out whether they were to continue to live together and, if so, on what basis. But Katharine, in her unstable state of mind, felt overwhelmed by what she saw as Mary's neediness and was equally determined to stay away. Several months later, Furse would succinctly describe the dilemma: "Mary longs to be loved," she told Ella Cabot, "and I am afraid of being loved too much."[21]

Instead of returning directly to Cheyne Place after leaving the nursing home, Furse went to Folkestone for three weeks and then on to the London flat of a friend; she let Follett know that she expected to be at home only a few days in October before heading to the country with friends and then sailing to Bermuda — not returning until January. Nowhere in Furse's recitation of her itinerary, a bewildered Follett complained to the Cabots, was there a "mention of me, of what my life is to be during those months or what arrangements are to be made about this house." Furse had virtually disappeared from Follett's life, and Mary didn't know why. Even worse, she felt that she had to act as if everything were all right. Every day, she told Richard and Ella, "I see her friends & have to pretend & pretend. They say, 'Why aren't you at F. with K.?', & I go on pretending. For I must protect her at present. I can't say that she doesn't want me & has told me so brutally, or things like that, until we have an open break. While we are friends I must be loyal to her."[22]

By this time, the Cabots were so concerned about Follett that they urged her to leave Katharine and return to Boston. They apparently even offered Mary a home with them, but she would not hear of it. "One of my strongest failings in regard to [my future]," she wrote Richard, "is that I must learn to be more independent. I care greatly for you & Ella, more than either of you has ever realized perhaps, & I should love above all things to be near you, but I don't want ever again to be so dependent on anyone as I must have allowed myself to become on K., else I should not feel this so much." Follett also felt strongly that she could not "just bolt." "K. & I entered on this together & it would seem seemly that we should end it together. I must wait until I can talk with her. Secondly, I am terribly tired, too tired to do anything at all. It is now 7 months since I have had this daily, this hourly, strain & it is beginning to tell on me. I couldn't leave Eng. for Am. while I am as tired as this."[23]

Follett was fortunate during this most difficult period to have as confidantes not only the Cabots but also her old friends of Thayer Academy days, Harriet Mixter and Sophie Valentine. She also had a few close friends in England, but it was difficult to see them, since they were spread around the country and Follett had a hard time getting around. She did, however, correspond with her old Newnham friend Melian Stawell, and Follett took the Cabots to Oxford to meet Stawell when they visited England in the summer of 1932.[24] Follett also was able to confide in Cicely (Polly) Furse, Katharine's daughter-in-law, although she never revealed anything to her about her own health problems. Polly had always been exceptionally fond of Follett. Mary seemed, Polly later recalled, to have a kind of aura about her and was exceptionally kind, pleasant, helpful, interested, and caring. Follett had not had much contact with Polly while she was traveling with her naval officer husband, but later, especially when the young wife enrolled in a drawing school in London, they talked and wrote more often to each other. Their last conversation was typical, Polly later recalled. She and Follett sat together on the couch, their hands clasped, and Polly listened quietly while Mary agonized over what she might have done to cause the troubles in her relationship with Katharine. Seeing Follett so desperately unhappy, both Polly and Paul were angry with Katharine, feeling quite certain that she, rather than Mary, was the cause of the trouble between them.[25] Polly comforted Mary, and, perhaps more importantly, she helped Follett keep her sanity by corroborating some of her views about Katharine and her behavior.

"I do not think K. has ever been 'normal,' whatever that may mean," Follett finally concluded in an October 1933 letter to Richard Cabot. "I think she is going to be far less so in the future, not so much from goiter poisoning as from an inheritance wh. she has not controlled. I think anyone who lives with her—maid or nurse or friend—will have a hard time. I should have been willing to take all that hardness if she had wanted me with her. There is nothing I would not have put up with if she had continued to want me. It is my idea of friendship." Follett continued to hope that she might be able to have a discussion with Furse about their arrangement, rather than making a unilateral decision to leave. But up to this point Furse had been so "intensely nervous" that Follett was afraid any such talk would make her hysterical. An opportunity presented itself, however, when Follett learned that Furse's plans had changed to include a two-week stay at Cheyne Place before she left for Bermuda on November 8.[26]

The weeks at home together turned out better than either of them had expected, and their talks led them to think that they might have another chance. At the end of October, Furse wrote a letter to Ella Cabot. "One of the reliefs of coming home," she told Ella, "was to find that Mary had told you of the hurts caused to her by my behavior. I got an absolute obsession about her — long before I finally fell ill with shingles etc. It became a nightmare which haunted me through the summer and of which I still have the vague fear, due to being nervy and psychologically sick still. One can try to control these things & to pretend that they do not exist but one can only get them cured by rest & fresh air and change. Which is why I am keeping to the plan of going to Helen [Storrow] in Bermuda next week. Dr. Cotton says that my illness & operation have been a great shock & that it will take time to recover which is probably true. I wish that I had not a sort of horror of this house and fear of being caught in it again."[27]

Furse expected that Follett would remain in London, paying "two or three visits to friends" and perhaps having an American friend join her for awhile until Furse returned from Bermuda at Christmastime.[28] But by late November, Mary Follett had left London for Boston. The stock market, which had stabilized briefly in mid-1931, had been undergoing a second decline, with the index of common stocks dropping to 6.9 points from 16 points between 1929 and 1932. Concerned about the toll that the depression was taking on her investments, Follett told friends that she was anxious to return to Boston to check on them. She also had responsibilities as the executor of her mother's will, tasks that so far she had tried to fulfill through her attorney.[29] And she had yet one other reason for going to Boston.

Furse's recent dreadful experience with a toxic goiter had made Follett anxious about her own enlarged goiter. The goiter had been evident for several years, and Follett's nephew George remembered his aunt complaining about discomfort around the throat and neck.[30] Follett had been told by her doctor in England that her condition could not be cured by medicine, but she decided to seek another opinion from Dr. Frank H. Lahey, whose Commonwealth Avenue clinic in Boston had become "a surgical 'court of last resort' for persons with thyroid and abdominal disease."[31] Lahey recommended surgery because the goiter was pressing on the windpipe, and Follett consented, scheduling the operation for December 16.[32] When she wrote to Furse in Bermuda that she was to have the surgery, Katharine volunteered to come, but Follett declined, reportedly telling her that no one would be able to give her a place to stay. Ella Cabot would later tell Katherine that she thought Follett's reasons were different. Realizing that Katharine was still recovering herself, Mary did not want "to take any risk of wearing on you."[33]

In the days before the surgery, Follett was in contact, personally or by letter, with several of her oldest friends, among them Richard and Ella Cabot, Ernest and Agnes Hocking, Mary Dennison, Harriet Mixter, and Mary and Sara Andrews.[34] Follett stayed with the Andrewses in Milton, south of Boston, the week before the surgery, and Sara Andrews later recalled that Follett "carried herself superbly, valiantly even sharing our interests, and the day I took her to the hospital she went with the same fine spirit."[35]

Before entering New England Deaconess Hospital in Boston on Wednesday, December 13, Follett wrote to several friends. Melian Stawell was the recipient of one of these "gallant" notes. Mary told her that "she fully expected to get through," Stawell recalled, " 'but if I don't I want you to know' — and then she went on with a line of love and friendship which I must be allowed to keep for myself."[36] Follett also sent a few words to Eva Whiting White, her old colleague from the community centers days, saying: "I think of you always with deep appreciation & much gratitude for all your kindness to me." Once in the hospital, she wrote to thank her beloved friend, Ella Cabot, who had sent her Christmas roses that had come up under the heavy snow. "Everything is all right, dearest Ella. I am not writing any letters, but I wanted you to know that one thing. I don't any longer feel as if I had a lot of troubles & trials, I feel only that I have had & am having & very likely may continue to have a lot of hurdles to jump & I feel equal to jumping them. And for your part in bringing me to this point I do thank you. You & Richard have been wonderful friends to me, helping me through everything . . . Bless you both. My love to you both, now & always. Your help to me during these last months makes an unbreakable bond between us, & I don't mean wholly a bond of gratitude. I mean that I am stronger for your help & so am more capable of loving you." Follett also wrote a letter to Furse, who was aboard ship en route to England from Bermuda. According to Katharine, Mary expressed a wish that the two of them try again. "Neither of us," Katharine later wrote to Ella, "likes the idea of anything but success in living our ideals of friendship."[37]

During Follett's three days in the hospital awaiting her surgery, Mary Dennison came for visits every day, and the two of them managed to have a "merry time" with "many little jokes and jests." Richard Cabot also was a comforting presence, volunteering to be in attendance at the surgery. "It would make just all the difference," Follett wrote. "I hadn't thought of anything so wonderful. But I had thought of this. Dr. Dan Jones said . . . something to the effect that he had heard I was worth saving (I suppose from you), that he had heard I was of some value to the community. Now I went to Dr. Lahey as an absolute stranger, & I have been thinking it would be nice if there were someone to let him know, not your kind estimate of my possible future use in the world, but just that I wasn't wholly a waif & a stray even if I hadn't a Boston address, that there were people who would be glad to hear of my recovery."[38]

Before the operation on Saturday, December 16, Richard Cabot was with her and found her "peaceful" and nearly falling asleep. The surgery was brief, taking only about thirty-five minutes, and Mary Dennison visited with Dr. Lahey after the operation. "He was perfectly satisfied with everything," she later recalled, "and showed me the four or five tumors he had uncovered from Mary's neck and chest. He said she should be up and about in three days and able to leave in six." At this point Dennison, having been reassured about her friend, cabled Furse to tell her that the operation was successful.[39] Even when Follett developed terrible pain in her back on Sunday, the doctors saw no relation to the surgery itself and were not anxious about the outcome.[40] But by Monday morning the situation was more ominous. Follett's pulse and respiration were weak, and Richard Cabot was sufficiently concerned that he telephoned her brother as well as her friends Mary and Sara Andrews.[41]

He then sent a radiogram to Furse aboard ship warning her that there had been complications. Katharine was flooded with guilt for not having come to Boston to be with Mary. "It is pretty difficult to face having left her," she admitted to Ella Cabot. "It seems so unnatural, not up to my standard of friendship. But you may think my standard is a pretty low one considering all the pain I have caused to Mary this year . . . It seems desperately hard that my illness should have undermined my character to such an extent — even temporarily . . . I do love Mary just as much as I ever have. The Mary of her Philosophy of life. And the Mary of meditation and of great ideals and of kindness & generosity. Had I only known the way to keep on this plane with her always. I am such a guttersnipe as I have always told her. But as is the way of a guttersnipe I stick to my friends through thick & thin when I see the way clear."[42]

By Monday afternoon the doctors had decided to give Follett morphine to relieve her pain, and as a result, when Richard Cabot came to see her, she was no longer suffering. She also gave no sign that she knew she was dying, telling her old friend "merely that she was 'glad to see him' but it was not a 'good time for conversation.'" Throughout the late afternoon and evening, Follett's pulse and respiration continued to worsen until, at 11:45 P.M. on December 18, 1933, she died. She was sixty-five years old. "I don't know how to begin to write to you," said the distraught Mary Dennison to Furse, "but will do the best I can. I am still so stunned that I can't believe that Mary has died and all I can say is 'It isn't so, it can't be so.' "[43]

An autopsy was performed, establishing without question the cause of the pain, weakness, and debilitating fatigue that Follett had been suffering during her years in England. Cabot reported the grim news to Furse. There were malignancies, he told her, "not only in the thyroid itself but also extensively in the pancreas, in one superadrenal gland, in the remaining kidney . . . and in one of the vertebrae just opposite the point where she had the terribly severe pain." Cabot added that Follett's "own life-long friend, Miss Briggs, died of malignant disease in the vertebrae and Mary well knew what a torture the last months of her life were. But this is only one of the kinds of pain Mary would have had to suffer if we had not made this blunder of operating on her thyroid and thereby ending her life."[44]

The surgery and anesthesia had placed additional stress on Follett's organs, including her remaining kidney, which no longer functioned well enough to dispel wastes from her body. The resulting toxic fluid overloaded and stressed her heart, which in turn led to the accumulation of fluid in her lungs and created vascular congestion throughout her body. Once this cycle had begun, there was little her doctors could do but sedate her and wait for the end. If Dr. Lahey had suspected there was cancer in other parts of her body, Richard Cabot was convinced that Lahey would have refused to operate. "The operation killed her," Cabot confessed to Furse. "Yet if it had not been done, she would have had a long struggle of mental and bodily anguish. All the medical part of it was a complete series of blunders, blunders in diagnosis, blunders in treatment, and yet the total result of all these mistakes was to save Mary from a terrible end and send her on her way to her next job after only one day's suffering. I should be very thankful if I could look forward to such an end myself." Furse quickly sent an appreciative message to Ella Cabot, saying, "I am very grateful to Richard for telling me what the autopsy showed. [Mary's] physical condition accounts for everything which has puzzled me in her, probably for what has been so unlike her at times. Poor Mary. She knew it herself. Could she only have said it outloud & shed the worries."[45]

A simple memorial service was held on December 21 in the Crematory Chapel at the Forest Hills Cemetery in Boston, with reading from the scriptures, a prayer, and a benediction. Sophie Valentine, Follett's friend from her days at Thayer Academy, described to Furse the "gray flower-covered casket in which lay that part of our friend which we saw with our eyes and touched with our hands. The day which had opened somberly had gone radiant at that hour and as the little chapel slowly filled with those who loved her and I had the sudden vision of her standing there by the flowers greeting us with that look and with the tender caressing voice we all remember and loved so well. Pain, weariness were hers no longer, only joy and confidence in the eternal love . . . If we could have spared her even the short period of suffering that she had, if we could have kept her longer here for our comfort and inspiration, we would have done so. We could do neither & with souls like hers (I have known one other) though we long for the inspiration of her actual presence, death cannot dim its light. It has moved farther away through the darkness but it keeps bright the path ahead. Knowing that she went to the hospital feeling that the chance of returning to us was strong, I am comforted. She was prepared to go or stay with equal graciousness."[46]

Henry and Mary Dennison carried Mary Follett's ashes to her beloved Overhills, the Vermont home she had shared with Isobel, and scattered them "on the hill behind her house where she used to love to go to watch the sunset."[47]

24

Afterword

Most people who happen upon Mary Follett's writings and lectures are amazed by her intellectual brilliance and the continuing relevance of her thought, but they also are puzzled by her relative obscurity. Why, they wonder, is Mary Follett not included in the pantheon of twentieth-century intellectuals?

Follett's gender surely is one answer. As a woman, Follett had only limited access to the research funds and other resources that would make possible an ongoing, systematic investigation of her ideas. She had no affiliation with a college or university, no graduate degree, and no eager graduate-student assistants and disciples to carry on her ideas. Furthermore, in her work she was forced to rely on informal methods of investigation in an era when the emerging social sciences anxiously sought academic legitimacy through disciplinary specialization, "objective" research techniques, and quantitative methods. Lacking these, Follett's work was quickly discarded by many as out of date. Lyndall Urwick once observed with dismay that "Americans love novelty and are too inclined to think that anything which is more than ten years old is out of date, even in the realm of ideas."[1]

In addition, Follett's ideas in the three decades following her death in 1933 found an inhospitable political climate. With the New Deal generating a variety of federal programs in response to the suffering caused by the Great Depression, it was easy for government leaders and academicians to ignore Follett's concerns with citizen empowerment and effective group participation. And captains of industry concerned with the mere survival of their firms were more likely to centralize control rather than to empower their workers. Later, in the 1940s and 1950s, when World War II seemed to demand "domination" and the Cold War a "balance of power," Americans found it difficult to heed Follett's admonition to value differences and seek integrative resolution of conflict.

Other factors have contributed to Mary Follett's relative obscurity. The difficulty of categorizing her ideas has been a vexing problem for historians of management and organizational theory. During the years in which Follett wrote and lectured — the period of scientific management and classical theory — most management theorists were concerned with efficiency and order. Follett shared these concerns, but she also was keenly interested in enhancing individual growth and development and fostering a capacity for organizational learning and change. As a result, historians of organizational and management theory have found it exceedingly difficult to place Follett's work in their schemas. Some writers treat her ideas as an unexplained exception to the classical era; others call her a harbinger, variously associating her work with human relations (1930s), group dynamics (1940s), and systems theory (1970s). Still others "solve" the problem of where to place Follett in the history of the field by simply leaving her out.

In the 1980s and 1990s, a plethora of popular management books was published in America, but Follett's name was rarely mentioned. Yet many of the notions promulgated during these two decades — collaborative leadership, win-win forms of conflict resolution, worker empowerment, self-managed teams, valuing inclusivity and diversity, continuous improvement, cross-functional coordination, and corporate social responsibility — were close analogues to ideas Follett had developed in the 1920s.

Although Mary Follett's name may be obscure, her ideas are not. They have been "rediscovered" in American organizational theory and management circles at least three times in the years since her death, and they are currently being studied and discussed in countries around the world. Furthermore, her work is now the subject of scholarly inquiry and application in fields as diverse as government, political theory, history, sociology, psychology, communication, women's studies, conflict resolution and negotiation, and social work.

This widespread engagement will surely continue because of the complexity and richness of Follett's thought and its striking relevance to our times. Indeed, Follett's challenge to us as citizens of democratic societies is yet unmet. "We seek a richly diversified experience," Follett wrote near the end of *Creative*

Experience, "where every difference strengthens and reinforces the other. Through the interprenetrating of spirit and spirit, differences are conserved, accentuated and reconciled in the greater life which is the issue. Each remains forever himself that thereby the larger activity may be enriched and in its refluence, reinforce him. The activity of co-creating is the core of democracy, the essence of citizenship, the condition of world-citizenship."[2]

Abbreviations

ABH	Albert Bushnell Hart
BESAGG	Boston Equal Suffrage Association for Good Government
BSC	Boston School Committee
EB	Elizabeth Balch
ECL	Eduard C. Lindeman
ECLP	Eduard C. Lindeman Papers, Rare Books and Manuscript Library, Columbia University
ELC	Ella Lyman Cabot
FFPAP	Fannie Fern Phillips Andrews Papers, SL
HAO	Harry A. Overstreet
KF	Katharine Furse
LFU	Lyndall F. Urwick
LFUA	Lyndall Fownes Urwick Archive, Henley Management College, Henley-on-Thames
MPF	Mary P. Follett
MWP	Maud Wood Park
MWPP	Maud Wood Park Papers, WRC
RA	Radcliffe Archives, Radcliffe Institute, Harvard University
RBHP	Viscount Richard B. Haldane Papers, NLS MS. 5916, f. 97, National Library of Scotland, Edinburgh

RCC	Richard C. Cabot
RCCP	Richard Clarke Cabot Papers, Harvard University Archives
SL	Schlesinger Library, Radcliffe Institute, Harvard University
USESP	United South End Settlements Papers, University of Minnesota Social Welfare History Archives, Minneapolis
WRC	Woman's Rights Collection, SL

Notes

For full citations of sources mentioned in the notes, see the Bibliography.

Chapter 1: Introduction

1. Kanter and Bennis quoted in Graham, *Mary Parker Follett: Prophet of Management,* xv, 178.

2. For evidence of continuing international interest in Follett: L. D. Parker, "Control in Organizational Life"; Graham, *Dynamic Managing—the Follett Way;* Miller and O'Leary, "Hierarchies and American Ideals, 1900–1940"; Enomoto and Mito, *Mary Parker Follett; Mary Parker Follett, L'esperienza creativa: leadership, partecipazione, tecniche del consenso nelle democrazie moderne,* trans. Barbara DeLuca (Rome: Ediesse, 1994); and Mousli, "Le management selon Mary Parker Follett."

3. Urwick, "Mary Follett," 18; idem, "The Problem of Organization," 163.

4. RCC, "Mary Parker Follett: An Appreciation," 80.

5. Woolf, *Diary,* 4: 112–13.

6. EB, Memoir of MPF, LFUA; KF, Memoir of MPF, LFUA.

7. Urwick, "The Problem of Organization," 163; KF, Memoir of MPF, LFUA.

8. MPF, *The New State,* 5, 8–9.

9. Barber, "Mary Parker Follett as Democratic Hero," xv; Mansbridge, "Mary Parker Follett: Feminist and Negotiator," xxvii.

10. MPF, *Creative Experience,* ix–x.

11. MPF, "The Giving of Orders," 32–33.

12. Ibid., 31.

Chapter 2: *A Childhood That Was Rarely Happy*

1. McCormick, "Ella Lyman Cabot,"156; MPF to ELC, Dec. 14 [15], 1933, RCCP.
2. For history of the Baxters, see the Quincy Historical Society and *Quincy Patriot*, Aug. 7, 14, 21, 28, and Sept. 3, 1880.
3. *Quincy Patriot*, Jan. 3, 1885.
4. Paul R. Lyons, *Quincy: A Pictorial History* (Norfolk, Mass.: Donning, 1983), 47.
5. *Quincy Patriot*, Aug. 5, 1865.
6. *Quincy Patriot*, Jan. 3, 1885.
7. The 1875 Massachusetts state census reported 239 blacksmiths in Quincy; the largest employment category was stonecutters, with 479 men.
8. C. F. Adams, *Three Episodes of Massachusetts History*, 962–63.
9. For records of the brothers' military service, see "Battery Muster Rolls," National Archives; *Massachusetts Soldiers, Sailors and Marines in the Civil War*, vol. 5 (Norwood, Mass.: Norwood Press, 1932); and Charles Allen Follett Papers, Quincy Historical Society, Quincy, Mass.
10. J. L. Parker, *Henry Wilson's Regiment*, 168; Dawles and Bowen, *Massachusetts in the War, 1861–1865*, 798.
11. Morison, *The Oxford History of the American People*, 655–56.
12. *Quincy Patriot*, Dec. 12, 1863, and April 29, 1871.
13. "Diary," Charles A. Follett Papers.
14. *Quincy Patriot*, Feb. 17, 1866; May 4, 1867; May 20, 1865.
15. *Quincy Patriot*, May 8, 1869.
16. Morison, *Oxford History of the American People*, 621, 624; Parker, *Henry Wilson's Regiment*, 170, 244. For Follett's comments on whiskey, see "Diary," June 7 and July 4, 1864, Charles A. Follett Papers.
17. "Henry Hardwick Faxon," *Quincy Patriot Souvenir Edition*, 1899, 22; Adams, *Three Episodes of Massachusetts History*, 978.
18. Although the origin of Follett's name is uncertain, she probably was named after her mother's younger sister, Mary, and her husband, J. Parker Hayward, from nearby Braintree. Annie Wood Follett may have been named in a similar way, after an older sister, Ann, and her husband, John Adams Wood.
19. *Quincy Patriot*, March 4, 1876. For a summary of studies of alcohol abuse in bereavement, see Marian Osterweis, Fredric Solomon, and Morris Green, eds., *Bereavement: Reactions, Consequences, and Care* (Washington, D.C.: National Academy Press, 1984), 40.
20. See Barbara Welter, "The Cult of True Womanhood, 1820–1860," *American Quarterly* 18 (1966): 159–62; and Gerda Lerner, "The Lady and the Mill Girl: Changes in the Status of Women in the Age of Jackson," *Midcontinent American Studies Journal* 10 (1969): 11–13.
21. It is difficult to be certain about the activities of Mary's father during the period 1870–1874 because of the existence of a second Charles A. Follett, who served as a U.S. Marine during the Civil War and again in 1866–70 and 1875–78. I believe that *Boston City Directory* entries for 1871, 1872, and 1874 refer to Mary's father. The other Follett consistently reported his occupation as "laborer," both in official enlistment records and

in Boston city directories of the 1880s and 1890s; however, none of the *Boston City Directory* entries for "Follett" in the period 1870–1874 concerns a "laborer." Also, the 1873 entry places Follett's home in Quincy.

22. In 1877 George Dexter Follett died in Somerville, probably in the McLean Asylum for the Insane. See Nina F. Little, *Early Years of the McLean Hospital* (Boston: Francis A. Countway Library of Medicine, 1972). Annie Wood Follett was born in March 1873.

23. Rosenberg, *The Cholera Years*, 151; MPF to ECL, Dec. 24, 1923, ECLP.

24. Rosenberg, *The Cholera Years*, 218. The cholera vibrio was not discovered until ten years after Annie's death. In the 1873 Mississippi River Valley epidemic, Quincy recorded few cholera deaths. For information about U.S. cholera epidemics, see "The Cholera Epidemic of 1873 in the United States," in *House Executive Document no. 95, Part A*, 43d Cong., 2d sess., Serial Set 1646 (Washington, D.C., 1875). For attitudes of Quincy citizens toward infectious diseases, see *Quincy Patriot:* "What Could We Have Done?" Nov. 16, 1878, and "Public Health," Sept. 24, 1887.

25. In George Follett's will, probated in Norfolk County (Mass.) in 1877, Charles received $400 (or $100 per year plus interest), a sum that paid less than two-thirds of the average annual expenses of a wage-earning family of four.

26. "Henry Hardwick Faxon," *Quincy Patriot Souvenir Edition*, 1899, 2.

27. *Quincy Patriot*, March 4, 1876.

Chapter 3: "An Eager, Fearless Mind"

1. Harriet French Mixter to KF, Sept. 3, 1924, LFUA; EB, Memoir of MPF, LFUA. Only Mixter had had personal contact with both Follett's father and mother; Balch was acquainted with Follett's mother.

2. The distance that ordinarily separated nineteenth-century girls from their fathers may have intensified their daughters' emotional attachments to them, even when the father's personal setbacks created family difficulties. See Hill, *Charlotte Perkins Gilman*, 31–32; Brady, *Ida Tarbell*, 21–23. For the reactions of children of alcoholics, see *Monitor on Psychology*, Nov. 1984, 21; and Judith S. Sexias and Geraldine Youcha, *Children of Alcoholism: A Survivor's Manual* (New York: Crown, 1985).

3. C. F. Adams, *Three Episodes of Massachusetts History*, 935–38; Katz, "The 'New Departure' in Quincy," 5–14; *Quincy Patriot*, Sept. 20, 1879; Feb. 22, 1873; Aug. 31, 1878. By 1878 the reformed "Quincy System" was a model for other cities and towns; but this was too late to influence Mary's choice of grammar school.

4. *Quincy Patriot*, Feb. 22, 1873; D. M. Wilson, *Three Hundred Years of Quincy*, 244–45; Holly, "The Academy Founded by John Adams," 1–2; *Quincy Patriot*, June 22 and July 13, 1872; author's correspondence (Aug. 22, 1983) with H. H. Holly of the Quincy Historical Society. In 1883 the Greenleaf Street School hired a college graduate to prepare students for college preparatory academies; the school eventually specialized in "fitting" students for Thayer Academy. Records of public school enrollment in this period no longer exist, but Mary's name does not appear in the newspaper's 1877–1880 lists of public grammar school graduates.

5. KF, Memoir of MPF, LFUA; Wakerman, *Father Loss*, 99, 110, 184, 198–99.

6. John Modell and Tamara K. Hareven, "Urbanization and the Malleable Household:

An Examination of Boarding and Lodging in American Families," *Journal of Marriage and the Family,* August 1973, 476–78.

7. Lizzie's mother was a Curtis, and her family had been in the Quincy boot and shoe industry almost from its inception; see *Quincy Daily Ledger,* Aug. 9, 1890; and *Quincy Patriot:* Feb. 9, Oct. 19, and Nov. 2, 1878; Nov. 27, 1880; May 12, 1883. This estimate of expenses, published in the *East Norfolk News,* Oct. 22, 1880, is confirmed in the 1875 Massachusetts Census. For wages see the Bureau of the Statistics of Labor (Massachusetts), 1873, table III. George Follett was named after his father's oldest brother, who had died only a few months earlier.

8. Photographs of the School Street houses are from the Quincy Public Library and the Quincy Historical Society. For architectural styles, see Foley, *The American House,* 28–29 and 96–145. Daniel Baxter's store, a temple-style Greek Revival structure fronting on School Street, was located between the McDonnell property and the Baxter house; two barns and a hay field were at the rear.

9. *Quincy Patriot,* Feb. 28 and March 7, 1885.

10. Wentworth, *The Thayer Academy,* 1–3. As a resident of Quincy, Mary did not have to pay the seventy-five-dollar-per-year tuition.

11. *The Catalogue of Thayer Academy,* 1880–81, 9–10; 1883–84, 9–10; Schwager, "'Harvard Women,'" 116–31. Even at the Harvard Annex, the Harvard Examination for Women was not formally used as the entrance examination until 1884.

12. *The Catalogue of Thayer Academy,* 1880–81, 7, 11; 1896–97, 32; *Braintree Observer,* July 3, 1880.

13. *Quincy Patriot,* Oct. 9, 1880; Thayer Academy Admissions Book, Thayer Academy Archives, Thayer Academy, Braintree, Mass. (hereafter TAA). Entries for other students admitted about that time show no evidence of nicknames.

14. Class rank books, 1880–1884, TAA.

15. EB, who met MPF at the Harvard Annex after Charles Follett had died, thought that he had been a clergyman — an indication of the aura of religiosity surrounding him in stories Follett must have told; see EB, Memoir of MPF, LFUA. Harriet French Mixter remembered Follett's mother as being much less religious than her husband and daughter; see Mixter to KF, July 4 and Sept. 3, 1934, LFUA. In the autumn after her graduation from Thayer Academy, Follett also was confirmed at Christ Church; records of the First Parish (Unitarian) Church and author's correspondence with H. Holly, Jan. 22, 1985.

16. Harriet French Mixter to KF, July 4, 1934, LFUA.

17. Mixter to KF, Sept. 3, 1934, LFUA; Wentworth, *The Thayer Academy,* 9–10.

18. Information on women teachers is from the author's private telephone conversation with Lillian Wentworth, July 8, 1985; Wentworth, *The Thayer Academy,* 10–11; Sprague, "In Memory of Anna Boynton Thompson," 16–17; "A Tribute to Anna Boynton Thompson," *Braintree Observer,* April 19, 1957.

19. Sprague, "In Memory of Anna Boynton Thompson," 16.

20. "Thayer Pays Glowing Tribute to Anna Boynton Thompson," *Quincy Patriot Ledger,* Jan. 31, 1929, 8; Anna Boynton Thompson to ABH [1889], Albert Bushnell Hart Papers, Harvard University Archives.

21. Sprague, "In Memory of Anna Boynton Thompson," 17; Lillian Wentworth, "Anna Boynton Thompson on Education," 1, TAA; "Thayer Pays Glowing Tribute to Anna Boynton Thompson," *Quincy Patriot Ledger,* Jan. 31, 1929, 8.

23. *Quincy Patriot,* June 11, 1881; June 9, 1883; June 30, 1883; June 27, 1884.

24. Unpublished excerpts from Anna Boynton Thompson's writings on education prepared by Lillian Wentworth, Anna Boynton Thompson Papers, SL; Wentworth, *The Thayer Academy,* 11; *Braintree Observer,* June 9, 1883, and June 27, 1884; "Founder's Day Programme," June 8, 1883, TAA.

25. Sir Paul Harvey, ed., *The Oxford Companion to English Literature,* 4th ed. (Oxford: Oxford University Press, 1967), 200; Follett, "Essay on Cowper," 7, 17, 10, 2–4, 13, 16, MPF Essays, SL. Since general course students read Milton and Wordsworth in their "junior middle" year, Follett most likely wrote the Cowper essay sometime after her second year. For reform activities of Thayer faculty, see Wentworth, *The Thayer Academy,* 9–11.

26. Follett, "Expectant Attention," 1–2, 15, MPF Essays, SL. See also William B. Carpenter, *Principles of Mental Physiology* (New York: D. Appleton, 1882), 148–71, 282–93, 386–95, 413–28, 626–35, 682–90; "Exercises of the Graduating Class," June 24, 1884, TAA. Much of the concluding section of MPF's essay has been lost.

27. Anna Boynton Thompson to Alice Mary Longfellow, June 12, 1891, Alice Mary Longfellow Papers, Longfellow National Historic Site, National Park Service, Cambridge, Mass. Since Thompson took her first classes at the Harvard Annex in 1884–85, it seems quite likely that she heard about the mind cure through Follett's graduation essay.

Chapter 4: "What Shall We Do with Our Girls?"

1. Anna Boynton Thompson to Alice Mary Longfellow, June 12, 1891, Alice Mary Longfellow Papers, Longfellow National Historic Site, National Park Service, Cambridge, Mass.

2. Barbara Sicherman, "The Uses of Diagnosis: Doctors, Patients, and Neurasthenia," *Journal of the History of Medicine and Allied Science* 32 (January 1977): 33–54; A. D. Wood, " 'The Fashionable Diseases' "; Drinka, *The Birth of Neurosis,* 184–209; Smith-Rosenberg, "The Hysterical Woman," 663–71; Hill, *Charlotte Perkins Gilman,* 148.

3. Strouse, *Alice James,* 244–48.

4. Anna Boynton Thompson to Alice Mary Longfellow, June 12, 1891, Longfellow Papers.

5. G. T. Parker, *Mind Cure in New England,* 13–14.

6. Gottschalk, *The Emergence of Christian Science in American Religious Life,* xxiii–xxiv.

7. Ibid., 120–23, 284–85; Parker, *Mind Cure in New England,* 8.

8. M. F. Moran, quoted in Gottschalk, *The Emergence of Christian Science,* 128; Cousins, *Anatomy of an Illness as Perceived by the Patient,* 39–40, 143–50.

9. Smith-Rosenberg, "The Hysterical Woman," 674–76; Drinka, *The Birth of Neurosis,* 202–3; MPF, "Expectant Attention," 1–2, MPF Essays, SL.

10. Parker, *Mind Cure in New England,* 72–3, 19.

11. Anna Boynton Thompson to Alice Mary Longfellow, undated [1888], Longfellow Papers.

12. For Charlotte Perkins Gilman's nearly disastrous experience with Mitchell's rest cure, see Hill, *Charlotte Perkins Gilman,* 148–49; and Parker, *Mind Cure in New England,* 87–94. For Jane Addams' experience see Davis, *American Heroine,* 27–29.

13. Anna Boynton Thompson to Alice Mary Longfellow, June 12, 1891, Longfellow Papers.

14. Wakerman, *Father Loss,* 174; *Quincy Patriot,* March 7, 1885, and June 26, 1886.

15. By Nov. 1887 Lizzie had received about $32,000; her disbursements from the estate eventually totaled slightly more than $42,000. For a discussion of the impact of the father's death on the daughter through the actions of the mother, see Wakerman, *Father Loss,* 167–79; Michael E. Lamb, "Paternal Influences and the Father's Role," *American Psychologist* 34 (1979): 940–41; Michael E. Lamb, M. T. Owen, and L. Chase-Lansdale, "The Father-Daughter Relationship: Past, Present, and Future," in Kopp and Kirkpatrick, *Becoming Female,* 102.

16. Wakerman, *Father Loss,* 37; Harriet French Mixter to KF, Sept. 3, 1934; EB, Memoir of MPF, both in LFUA.

17. Antler, " 'After College, What?' " 409–34.

18. KF, Memoir of MPF, LFUA.

19. A fine summary of the work of the society appears in Schwager, " 'Harvard Women,' " 35–61. For similar organizations, see Society to Encourage Studies at Home (SESH), *Memorial Volume,* 211–12; *Boston Herald,* June 9, 1878.

20. Ticknor enlisted several of her Boston and Cambridge friends in the project as unpaid "correspondents." Two of them, Alice Mary Longfellow and Elizabeth Cary Agassiz, were known to Anna Boynton Thompson through her studies at the Harvard Annex; SESH, *Memorial Volume,* 8–13, app. A. See also H. B. Adams, "The Society to Encourage Studies at Home," 3.

21. SESH, *Secretary's Report, 1883–84,* 9, Society to Encourage Studies at Home Papers, Rare Books Department, Boston Public Library (hereafter SESHP); SESH, *Memorial Volume,* 8; SESH, *Secretary's Report, 1880–81,* 8, SESHP.

22. Adams, "Society to Encourage Studies at Home," 3–4. As a member of the fledgling American Historical Association, Thompson might have been familiar with Adams' report; see American Historical Association, *Secretary's Report of the Proceedings at the Second Annual Meeting* (New York: G. P. Putnam's Sons, 1886), 44, 5–6, 73.

23. SESH, *Secretary's Report, 1880–81,* 8, SESHP; SESH, *Memorial Volume,* 100–101.

24. SESH, "Journal 1885–87," 18, 104, 202; SESH, "Journal 1888," both SESHP. During much of the history of the society, only one-sixth of the students were under age twenty. Follett, enrolling at seventeen, once again was something of a prodigy.

25. In 1884 the most popular branches of study were English literature and history; Adams, "Society to Encourage Studies at Home," 3–4. In 1884, 38 history correspondents were available for 129 students; SESH, *Secretary's Report, 1885–86,* 19, SESHP.

26. Adams, "Society to Encourage Studies at Home," 4; SESH, *Memorial Volume,* 28–29. Katharine Peabody Loring was most responsible for developing the history curriculum and recruiting the correspondents; Strouse, *Alice James,* 89, 190–93, 209–211.

27. SESH, *Secretary's Report, 1886–87,* 12, SESHP; SESH, *Memorial Volume,* 29. Loring became the head of the political economy section a few years after its inception, and new applications such as crime, punishment and reform, trade unions, and cooperation were added to the curriculum; SESH, *Memorial Volume,* 30.

28. SESH, *Catalog, June 1886,* 6–7, SESHP; SESH, *Secretary's Report, 1885–86,* 5, SESHP; Adams, "Society to Encourage Studies at Home," 4.

29. SESH, *Secretary's Report, 1881–82,* 16–17, SESHP.

30. Ibid., 6. For the ways that separate female institutions empowered women in the nineteenth century, see Freedman, "Separatism as Strategy."

Chapter 5: "Very Unusual Privileges"

1. Solomon, *In the Company of Educated Women,* 62–64. Even by 1900 the share was still less than 3 percent.

2. "Educating Women," *The Nation,* Feb. 8, 1883, 188–199.

3. Solomon, *In the Company,* 119–122.

4. Ibid., 56–57; RCC, "Medical History and Record of Mary Parker Follett, 1910–1933," RCCP.

5. Society to Encourage Studies at Home (SESH), *Memorial Volume,* 12–13; SESH, "Health Pamphlet," 15–16, Gutman Library, Harvard University.

6. Davis, *American Heroine,* 39; Heilbrun, *Reinventing Womanhood,* 30; Gwendolyn Wright, "On the Fringe of the Profession: Women in American Architecture," in *The Architect,* ed. Spiro Kostof (New York: Oxford University Press, 1977), 305–306.

7. Harriet French Mixter to KF, Sept. 3, 1934, LFUA; MPF, "Report of the East Boston Centre by Committee on Extended Use of School Buildings, 1911–12," 6–7.

8. MPF, "Report of the East Boston Centre," 6–7; Solomon, *In the Company,* 116.

9. Solomon, *In the Company,* 65–68.

10. Mixter to KF, Sept. 3, 1934, LFUA. Quincy newspapers regularly and sympathetically reported the activities of women's suffrage organizations, temperance organizations, and local charitable groups. Lizzie Follett was involved for a time with her husband in temperance work and had long-term involvement with the Circle of the Charitable Ten of the King's Daughters, a branch of a national nondenominational social and charitable group; and the Women's City Club of Quincy.

11. LFU, unpublished notes for a talk on Follett at University of New South Wales, Author's files—Fox. For comments on Mary's adolescent social life, see KF, Memoir of MPF, LFUA. For more on her appearance and dress, see KF to LFU, Aug. 13, 1940, LFUA; and interviews with Nancy Follett Alvord (May 13, 1982, Quincy, Mass.) and George D. Follett Jr. (June 16, 1982, Quincy, Mass.).

12. Solomon, *In the Company,* 65, 68. Mothers of this era often recognized that a college education might help to shield their daughters from future marital and economic difficulties; however, there is direct evidence of Lizzie Follett's contrary attitude.

13. "Reminiscences of K. G. Francke," Annie Ware Winsor Allen Papers, SC 35, RA (hereafter AWAP).

14. Horowitz, *Alma Mater,* 223–24; 96–7. For ideas motivating the founders of New England women's colleges, see Solomon, *In the Company;* and Schwager, " 'Harvard Women.' "

15. ABH to George H. Chase, Feb. 25, 1929; "Reminiscence of E. Folsom Hall," both in Anna Boynton Thompson Papers, SL.

16. Morison, *Three Centuries of Harvard,* 324, 335–36; Hugh Hawkins, *Pioneer: A History of Johns Hopkins University, 1874–1889* (Ithaca: Cornell University Press, 1960), 8–13.

17. For a discussion of the changes at Harvard in this period, see Frederick Rudolph,

The American College and University: A History (New York: Vintage, 1962), 287–94, 331–36; Brubacher and Rudy, *Higher Education in Transition,* 107–15, 184–95; and Morison, *Three Centuries of Harvard,* 323–64.

18. Horowitz, *Alma Mater,* 209 and 382; Solomon, *In the Company,* 122; "The Society for the Collegiate Instruction of Women," quoted in Horowitz, *Alma Mater,* 97. For the history of Girton College and Newnham College, see McWilliams-Tullberg, *Women at Cambridge,* chaps. 3–7.

19. Schwager, " 'Harvard Women,' "187, 211, 272–74. The standard compensation rate for faculty became about $500 per course.

20. "The Privilege of Being a Woman," *Boston Evening Transcript,* March 23, 1888.

21. "Reminiscences of Lucy Allen Paton, Class of 1892"; unnamed Reminiscences, 1890–96; "Reminiscence of Mosetta Isabel Stafford Vaughan, 1890–96," all AWAP.

22. "Reminiscences of Lucy Allen Paton, Class of 1892," AWAP; E. B. Pearson, "Harvard Annex Letter," 101.

23. Schwager, " 'Harvard Women,' " 213.

24. Pearson, "Harvard Annex Letter," 99; Kinney, "Women's Colleges — The Harvard Annex," 683.

25. Society for the Collegiate Instruction of Women (SCIW), *Annual Report, 1888–89,* 5; *Annual Report of Radcliffe College, 1897–98,* 12; "Statistics of Radcliffe College," all RA. In 1888, the year that Follett enrolled, almost three-quarters of the 115 Annex students were "specials"; the share declined to 50 percent in 1896 and to less than one-third by 1900.

26. Solomon, *In the Company,* 70–71; Association of Collegiate Alumnae, *A Preliminary Statistical Study of College Graduates* (Bryn Mawr, Pa., 1917), 172–73.

27. Morison, "A Memoir and Estimate of Albert Bushnell Hart," 32–33.

28. Ibid., 32, 40; Morison, *The Development of Harvard University,* 168–69.

29. Morison, "Memoir and Estimate of Hart," 33–36, 40–43.

30. Ibid., 36; ABH to Blanche H. Sprague, June 3, 1935, Thompson Papers. Hart saw Anna Boynton Thompson as "one of the first teachers of high school history to realize that history is founded on sources and that sources are the most interesting statement of history."

31. Wilson, *Three Hundred Years of Quincy,* 234–35; *Quincy Patriot,* April 2, 1881; Sept. 20, 1884; Oct. 2, 1886; Jan. 15, 1887. Inspired by Quincy's new school superintendent to experiment with individualized instruction and "hands-on learning," Follett redesigned the primary school curriculum. Her career flourished in Boston and Pennsylvania before she returned to Quincy to marry and resume teaching.

32. Solomon, *In the Company,* 70.

33. Anna Boynton Thompson to Blanche Hazard, Dec. 3, 1892, Thompson Papers. Blanche Hazard (Sprague) taught school and did not receive her Radcliffe degree until 1907. In 1913 she wrote and eventually published a master's thesis on the Massachusetts boot and shoe industry. In 1914 she became a member of the Home Economics faculty at Cornell, where she taught "Women in Industry," "History of Housekeeping," and "Woman and the State."

34. Thompson to Hazard, Aug. 24, 1894; June 25 and 27, 1893; and Aug.17, 1896, ibid.

35. Thompson to Hazard, June 27 and 25, 1893, ibid.

36. "Debating Club: Record of Meetings, 1885–88," RA; Pearson, "Harvard Annex Letter," 100–101; MPF, *The Speaker of the House of Representatives,* ix; "Reminiscence of Mosetta Isabel Stafford Vaughan, 1890–96," AWAP.

37. Grade Sheets, Registrar's Records, RGXII, Series 4, 1888–89, RA; SCIW, *Courses of Study for 1888–89: Tenth Year,* 7; SCIW, *Annual Report: Tenth Year,* 16, both RA. The course was taught by F. C. Hutchinson.

38. ABH, "Preparation for Citizenship," 636–37; Beulah Dix Flebbe to her cousin, Nov. 8, 1896, Beulah Dix Flebbe '97 Papers, RA.A F593, RA; Morison, "Albert Bushnell Hart (1889–1939)," 435.

39. Grade Sheets, 1888–89, RA. Follett completed the first half of History 9 with a makeup examination in 1894, when she decided to seek a degree. Hart then awarded her a grade of B for the full course; see Hart's note of Oct. 10, 1894, Grade Sheets, 1888–89; and Transcript, Registrar's Records, 1887–93, 122, RGXII, both RA.

40. SCIW, *Annual Report: Eleventh Year,* 27–8, RA; Morison, *The Development of Harvard University,* 160.

41. "Reminiscence of Mosetta Isabel Stafford Vaughan, 1890–96," AWAP; Morison, *Three Centuries of Harvard,* 351; Morison, *The Development of Harvard University,* 76–77; Barrett Wendell, "The Relations of Radcliffe College with Harvard," *Harvard Monthly,* October 1899, 6, 8.

42. SCIW, *Annual Report: Eleventh Year,* 21.

43. Ibid., 28–9.

44. Ibid., 7; Woodrow Wilson, quoted in Bragdon, *Woodrow Wilson: The Academic Years,* 143. Lucy Salmon's extremely unsatisfactory experience with Wilson while she was a graduate student at Bryn Mawr is described in Bragdon, 153–54.

45. "Reminiscence of Mosetta Isabel Stafford Vaughan, 1890–96," AWAP; Grade Sheets, 1888–89, RA.

46. SCIW, *Annual Report: Eleventh Year,* 29; *Boston Evening Transcript,* Jan. 27, 1891; Anna Boynton Thompson to Alice Mary Longfellow, June 12, 1891, Alice Mary Longfellow Papers, Longfellow National Historic Site, National Park Service, Cambridge, Mass.; KF, Memoir of MPF, LFUA.

Chapter 6: "The Great Milepost and Turning Point"

1. Harriet French Mixter to KF, Sept. 3, 1934, LFUA. Mixter thought Thompson did not finance Follett's year at Newnham; in that case Follett's mother probably paid her tuition and fees ($400–450 according to an Oct. 24, 1891, report by Martha Foote Crow to the Association of Collegiate Alumnae) and travel expenses; *Quincy Daily Ledger,* July 11 and Sept. 5, 1890.

2. Phillips, *A Newnham Anthology,* 33.

3. Strachey, *Millicent Garrett Fawcett,* 144–45.

4. Field, "Women at an English University," 291. Students from Follett's residence, Sidgwick Hall, were especially active in the club; see Newnham College Club, *Cambridge Letters,* 1891, 9; "Newnham College Report, December 1890," 4–5, 29, Newnham College Archives, Newnham College, Cambridge.

5. Field, "Women at an English University," 291; Clough, "The Making of Sidgwick Avenue," in Phillips, *A Newnham Anthology,* 29.

6. For more on Irish Home Rule and the Parnell divorce case, see J. L. Hammond, *Gladstone and the Irish Nation* (1938; reprint, London: Frank Cass, 1964), 622–97; Martin Pugh, *The Making of Modern British Politics, 1867–1939* (New York: St. Martin's, 1982), 38.

7. KF to Myra Curtis, Nov.14, 1951, LFUA.

8. McWilliams-Tullberg, *Women at Cambridge,* 43; Fawcett and Sidgwick, quoted in McWilliams-Tullberg, 56 and 57; Oldfield, *Spinsters of This Parish,* 31.

9. Alice Mary Longfellow to Edith Dana, Oct. 12, 1883, Alice Mary Longfellow Papers, Longfellow National Historic Site, National Park Service, Cambridge, Mass.; Field, "Women at an English University," 288–89.

10. Sidgwick, quoted in McWilliams-Tullberg, *Women at Cambridge,* 59; Field, "Women at an English University," 289–90, 293; Alice Mary Longfellow to Edith Dana, October 29, 1883, Longfellow Papers.

11. Oldfield, *Spinsters of This Parish,* 32; Field, "Women at an English University," 292.

12. Sheepshanks, quoted in Oldfield, *Spinsters of This Parish,* 33.

13. Newnham College Club, *Cambridge Letters,* 1891, 11, Newnham College Archives.

14. Mayor, Sheepshanks, and Edward Marsh, quoted in Oldfield, *Spinsters of This Parish,* 38, 33, and 41.

15. Stawell, "Mary Parker Follett," 40. Follett apparently made at least one other good friend at Newnham; see Margaret Tabor to Melian Stawell, undated [1935]; and Tabor to KF, Jan. 5, 1934, both LFUA.

16. Stawell was willing to talk about her childhood; see Oldfield, *Spinsters of This Parish,* 74, 165. Follett continued to see Stawell on trips to England; see EB, Memoir of MPF, LFUA.

17. "Diary of Alice Mary Longfellow," Oct. 11, 1883, Longfellow Papers.

18. "Newnham College Report, December 1890," 18–20.

19. Slee, "History as a Discipline," 152, 164, 154, 190.

20. Wormell, *Sir John Seeley and the Uses of History,* 41, 178.

21. Seeley, quoted in ibid., 43; Slee, "History as a Discipline," 159, 161.

22. Slee, "History as a Discipline," 195.

23. Creighton, quoted in ibid., 192; also 195.

24. Wormell, *Sir John Seeley,* 71; Slee, "History as a Discipline," 199.

25. Slee, "History as a Discipline," 200, 202.

26. Winsor, "With Bradford and Harvard," 68. The author of "An Annex Girl at Newnham," *Boston Evening Transcript,* Jan. 27, 1891, said that "Mr. Winsor doubtless refers to Miss Mary Parker Follett" and quoted ABH's assessment of Follett's work.

27. Alice Mary Longfellow to Edith L. Dana, Oct. 12, 1883, Longfellow Papers; Winsor, "With Bradford and Harvard," 67; Stawell, "Mary Parker Follett," 40.

28. KF, Memoir of MPF, LFUA; Blanshard, *Four Reasonable Men,* 196, 242, 226–27.

29. Blanshard, *Four Reasonable Men,* 196; Arthur Balfour, quoted in Hamilton, *Newnham,* 151–52, Newnham College Archives.

30. Blanshard, *Four Reasonable Men,* 237–38; Alice Mary Longfellow, "Diaries and Notebooks, Newnham 1883–84," Oct. 11, 1883, Longfellow Papers; M. A. Wilcox, quoted in Phillips, *A Newnham Anthology,* 13; James Bryce, quoted in Blanshard, *Four Reasonable Men,* 224.

31. Wilcox, quoted in Phillips, *A Newnham Anthology,* 13; Blanshard, *Four Reasonable Men,* 199.

32. Frederic W. Maitland, quoted in Blanshard, *Four Reasonable Men,* 232.

33. Longfellow, "Diaries and Notebooks, Newnham 1883–84," Nov. 6 and 8, 1883, Longfellow Papers.

34. KF, Memoir of MPF; EB, Memoir of MPF, both LFUA.

35. Hamilton, *Newnham,* 152–53.

36. MPF to Henry Sidgwick, Sept. 17, 1891, Henry Sidgwick Papers, Trinity College Archives, Cambridge University.

37. KF to Myra Curtis, Nov. 14, 1951; KF, Memoir of MPF, both LFUA.

38. *Quincy Daily Ledger,* July 7 and Sept. 14, 1891. Mrs. Follett accompanied Mary to Washington for the Dec. American Historical Association meeting; *Quincy Daily Ledger,* Dec. 26, 1891, and Jan. 8, 1892.

39. *Quincy Daily Ledger,* July 19, 1891. This article seemingly began the apparently erroneous claim that Mary studied in Paris.

40. MPF to Henry Sidgwick, Sept. 17, 1891, Sidgwick Papers; Hawkins, "Agassiz, Elizabeth Cabot Cary," in James, *Notable American Women,* 1: 22–23.

41. Maud Wood Park, "Pauline Agassiz Shaw," *Boston Transcript,* Feb. 6, 1941, 8; Massachusetts Board of Education, *Fifty-fifth Annual Report, 1890–1891,* 99–141. Among the better schools, Hopkinson's had 138 students and Thayer Academy had 125; all others were much smaller, and only Thayer was coeducational.

42. Names of enrollees were compiled from Radcliffe College admissions records, Harvard College classbooks, and student memoirs.

43. MPF to Henry Sidgwick, Sept. 17, 1891, Sidgwick Papers. For descriptions of the school, see Shurcliff, *Lively Days: Some Memoirs by Margaret Homer Shurcliff,* 7–9; and Morison, *One Boy's Boston,* 43–44. A carpentry shop, physics laboratory, and gymnasium were built in the Marlborough Street building. According to the Boston assessor, Shaw purchased the building next door in 1889 and used it as a school beginning in 1890.

44. In 1888 Shaw brought to Boston one of the prominent practitioners of sloyd. Gustav Larsson established a training school for teachers and spread the movement throughout Massachusetts; Marvin Lazerson, *Origins of the Urban School,* 102.

45. MPF to Henry Sidgwick, Sept. 17, 1891, Sidgwick Papers.

46. ABH, "How to Teach History in Secondary Schools," 91, 93–94, 97; Morison, "A Memoir and Estimate of Albert Bushnell Hart," 32–33.

47. ABH, "How to Teach History," 101, 107–08.

48. Committee of Seven, "The Study of History in Schools," 433. Among the ten conference members were ABH, Woodrow Wilson, and James Harvey Robinson.

49. Ibid., 441.

50. Ibid., 469, 438–39.

51. Hart took a personal active interest in the new field of civil government; Morison, "Memoir and Estimate of Hart," 43–44. For more on this controversy, see J. W. Burgess,

"Political Science and History," in *Annual Report of the American Historical Association for the Year 1896* (Washington, D.C.: Government Printing Office, 1897); Committee of Seven, "Study of History in Schools," 473. Within eight years, these and other recommendations of the Committee of Seven "became the accepted standard, greatly improving the position of history in the secondary schools"; John Hingham, *History: Professional Scholarship in America* (1965; reprint, Baltimore: Johns Hopkins University Press, 1983), 19–20.

52. MPF to Henry Sidgwick, Sept. 17, 1891, Sidgwick Papers; Eleanor Sidgwick, quoted in Blanshard, *Four Reasonable Men,* 231. Sidgwick had a long-standing interest in American political institutions and was deeply involved with James Bryce in the conceptualization of *The American Commonwealth;* see Eugene Ions, *James Bryce and American Democracy, 1870–1922* (London: Macmillan, 1968), 133–34.

53. There is considerable evidence that Follett taught at Shaw's School for more than one year: Margaret Nichols, who had Follett as a teacher, was in Europe during much of 1891–92; also, the Quincy city directories list Follett's occupation as "teacher" in 1893 and "teacher in Boston" in 1894; and the Radcliffe student directories give her address as 8 Marlborough in 1894 and 1895. Follett did not enroll in classes at the Annex during the 1892–93 and 1893–94 academic years; RA.

Chapter 7: The Speaker of the House of Representatives

1. MPF, *The Speaker of the House of Representatives,* ix.

2. Carol F. Baird, "Albert Bushnell Hart," in Buck, *Social Sciences at Harvard,* 150, 155; ABH, "Preparation for Citizenship," 634.

3. Morison, "Albert Bushnell Hart (1889–1939)," 436.

4. Davidson and Oleszek, *Congress against Itself,* 23; MPF, *Speaker,* 187.

5. Henry Cabot Lodge, "The Coming Congress," *North American Review* 149 (September 1889): 293.

6. ABH, "Preparation for Citizenship," 632–33.

7. John L. Thomas, "The Politics of Reform," in Bailyn et al., *The Great Republic,* 582.

8. David H. Donald, "National Problems," ibid., 516–38; Thomas, "Nationalizing the Republic," ibid., 542–95.

9. George Galloway, *The History of the United States House of Representatives* (New York: Thomas Y. Crowell, 1968), 239.

10. J. M. Burns, *The Workshop of Democracy,* 227.

11. Congressional Quarterly, *Origins and Development of Congress,* 2d ed. (Washington, D.C., 1982), 115–16.

12. Thomas, "The Politics of Reform," 575, 581.

13. For Reed's objections see MPF, *Speaker,* 210.

14. Bryce, *The American Commonwealth,* 1: 304.

15. Wilson, *Congressional Government,* 56, 206; MPF, *Speaker,* 246.

16. Wilson, *Congressional Government,* 84, 87–92; Bryce, *The American Commonwealth,* 1: 186, 304–05. For Wilson's 1891 views, see Woodrow Wilson to ABH, May 19, 1891, Ray Stannard Baker Papers, Library of Congress.

17. Wilson, *Cabinet Government in the United States,* 9.

18. Bragdon, *Woodrow Wilson: The Academic Years,* 61; Robert L. Peabody, "Afterword," in Wilson, *Congressional Government,* 226; ibid., 141–42.

19. Bragdon, *Woodrow Wilson: The Academic Years,* 61–62, 60; Wilson, *Congressional Government,* 87.

20. Wilson, quoted in Bragdon, *Woodrow Wilson: The Academic Years,* 62.

21. Ibid., 134.

22. Ibid., 136–38.

23. Ibid., 233–36.

24. Reed, "Obstruction in the National House," 427–28.

25. Davidson and Oleszek, *Congress against Itself,* 24–25; MPF, *Speaker,* 193.

26. Davidson and Oleszek, *Congress against Itself,* 24.

27. ABH, "The Speaker as Premier," *The Nation,* March 1891, 384–85.

28. Woodrow Wilson to ABH, May 19, 1891, Ray Stannard Baker Papers.

29. ABH to Herbert B. Adams, Nov. 12, 1891, Herbert Baxter Adams Papers, Johns Hopkins University; Herbert B. Adams to ABH, Nov. 19, 1891, American Historical Association Papers, Library of Congress. DuBois would become a prominent sociologist and one of the most influential African Americans of the early twentieth century.

30. The student remembered Follett as reading "her paper before a Committee of the House," but this is probably incorrect. See "Reminiscence of Mosetta Stafford Vaughan," Annie Ware Winsor Allen Papers, SC 35, RA.

31. For the *Boston Herald* editorial, see *Papers of the American Historical Association,* vol. 1 (New York: G. P. Putnam's Sons, 1886), 9. Thompson was a member of the American Historical Association by 1885; for a list of members, see ibid., 487–93.

32. For information about the 1890 and 1891 meetings, see *Papers of the American Historical Association,* vol. 5 (New York: G. P. Putnam's Sons, 1891).

33. "Power of the Speaker," *Washington Post,* Dec. 31, 1891; "In Session at the Capital," *New York Times,* Dec. 31, 1891. See also "Report of the Proceedings," in *Annual Report of the American Historical Association for 1891,* 5.

34. MPF, "Henry Clay as Speaker of the United States House of Representatives," 344. Clay was first elected Speaker in 1811.

35. Ibid., 346–47.

36. Ibid., 347; Davidson and Oleszek, *Congress against Itself,* 24; William A. Robinson, *Thomas B. Reed, Parliamentarian* (New York: Dodd, Mead, 1930), 99. Follett recognized the problems with Reed's style; see "Henry Clay," 347.

37. MPF, *Speaker,* 82; ABH, "Introduction," ibid., xiv.

38. MPF, "Henry Clay," 347.

39. Hart brought Follett's manuscript to the attention of Longmans, Green and continued to play a kind of intermediary role; see C. J. Mills to ABH: July 3, Oct. 4, Oct. 12, and Oct. 23, 1895; Feb. 27 and June 6, 1896, Albert Bushnell Hart Papers, Harvard University Archives. For more on the publication history of Follett's manuscript, see *Annual Report, Radcliffe College, 1895–96,* 9–10, RA; ABH to Anna Boynton Thompson, March 23, 1892, Anna Boynton Thompson Papers, SL; *Cambridge Chronicle,* Nov. 19, 1892. The contract and some information about copies sold still exist; Longmans, Green and Company Archives, University of Reading.

40. MPF, *Speaker,* vii.

41. Although the documents were available in Boston-area libraries, it was not always easy for a woman to gain access to them. The women of the Annex were rarely allowed into the Harvard College Library, but Hart interceded on Follett's behalf. Because Follett did not take examinations, there is no formal record of her studies at Newnham. Citations in *The Speaker* suggest that she read works central to the English Constitutional History portion of the historical Tripos exam; see *Cambridge University Calendar, 1893,* 12–22, Newnham College Archives, Newnham College, Cambridge.

42. Wormell, *Sir John Seeley and the Uses of History,* 150–51; Hart repeatedly advocated studying actual government; see, for example, ABH, "Preparation for Citizenship," 631.

43. MPF, *Speaker,* viii.

44. Bragdon, *Woodrow Wilson: The Academic Years,* 140; ABH, "Introduction," in MPF, *Speaker,* xiii, xvi.

45. MPF, *Speaker,* vii–viii; 94, 297.

46. EB, Memoir of MPF, LFUA. Henry Sidgwick was a close associate of numerous political figures, including James Bryce, who sought Sidgwick's advice in conceptualizing *The American Commonwealth*. Sidgwick's wife, Eleanor Balfour Sidgwick, was the niece of the Tory prime minister, and her brother was the chief secretary for Irish affairs. Newnham's political relations, however, were not restricted to the Conservative party. William Gladstone's daughter, Helen, was vice-principal and the head resident of Sidgwick Hall, Mary's home during her year at Newnham. See F. Smithhurst, collection of unused contributions for *A Newnham Anthology,* Newnham College Archives; "Reminiscence of M. A. Wilcox," in Phillips, *A Newnham Anthology,* 14–15, 39; "Diary of Alice Mary Longfellow," Oct. 11, 1883, Alice Mary Longfellow Papers, Longfellow National Historic Site, National Park Service, Cambridge, Mass. One of Follett's acquaintances, Philippa Fawcett, was the daughter of Millicent Garrett Fawcett, a major figure in the women's suffrage movement and an active supporter of radical reform legislation. Follett's closest friend at Newnham, Melian Stawell, also came from a political family. See Strachey, *Millicent Garrett Fawcett,* 95–99, 141; "Registrar of the Roll," Newnham College Archives.

47. Hofstadter, *The Progressive Historians,* 183.

48. M. White, *Pragmatism and the American Mind,* 48. Dewey was impatient with his fellow philosophers, finding them excessively preoccupied with formal logic and metaphysics and reluctant to examine the moral aspects of social systems or the moral ills of industrialism. Veblen attacked the abstract reasoning of the classical laissez-faire economists, judging as patently false their assumption that human behavior is governed by the single motive of acquiring and consuming wealth. By 1908 the revolt had been joined by two historians, Charles Beard and James Harvey Robinson. Beard objected to the tendency of his fellow historians to glorify heroic figures and institutional ideals rather than to analyze the workings of actual governmental systems.

49. M. White, *Social Thought in America,* 13.

50. Beard, quoted in White, *Pragmatism and the American Mind,* 66.

51. Baird, "Albert Bushnell Hart," 169.

52. Ashley, quoted in Robert L. Church, "The Economists Study Society," in Buck, *Social Sciences at Harvard,* 63. For more on Namier, see Henry R. Winkler, "Sir Lewis

Namier," *Journal of Modern History* 35 (March 1963): 1–19. For more on the one-dimensional thinking that came to characterize Beard's economic interpretations of American institutions, see Hofstadter, *The Progressive Historians,* 243–45, 462–63.

53. "The Speaker's Power," *New York Times,* July 19, 1896, 27; "The American Speakership," *The Times of London,* August 13, 1896, 10; Morse, "Review of *The Speaker of the House of Representatives,*" 313; Smith, "Review of *The Speaker of the House of Representatives,*" 332.

54. Wilson, *Congressional Government,* 83–84.

55. Grade Sheets, 1891–92, Registrar's Records, RGXII, Series 4, 1888–89; Society for the Collegiate Instruction of Women, *Annual Report, 1891–92,* 29, both RA.

56. MPF, *Speaker,* 17–19, 302–303.

57. Ibid., 25–26.

58. ABH, "Introduction," ibid., xvi; also MPF, *Speaker,* 26.

59. MPF, *Speaker,* 35–39.

60. Ibid., 120–21, 247.

61. Ibid., 308; "The Speaker of the House," *The Nation,* September 10, 1896, 200.

62. "The Speaker of the House," *The Nation,* 199; "The Speaker's Power."

63. ABH, "Introduction," in MPF, *Speaker,* xiii, xvi.

64. "The American Speakership," 13.

65. Roosevelt, "Thomas Brackett Reed and the Fifty-first Congress," 415–16, 418; idem, "Review of *The Speaker of the House of Representatives,*" 177–78.

66. MPF, *Speaker,* 317.

67. Bryce, "A Word as to the Speakership," 387–94.

68. MPF, *Speaker,* 310, 316–17. Wilson was also attracted to Mill's idea; *Congressional Government,* 90.

69. "The Speaker's Power"; "The Speaker of the House," *The Nation,* 200.

70. MPF, *Speaker,* 318. In her own hometown of Quincy, Follett had seen how government by town meeting had broken down and been replaced in 1885 by a strong mayoral system. For more on the Quincy reforms, see *Quincy Patriot,* Nov. 14, 1885, and Nov. 19, 1887; C. F. Adams, *Three Episodes in Massachusetts History,* 1002–3; and MPF, *Speaker,* 313–14.

71. White, *Social Thought in America,* 18. Follett introduced a note of realism into considerations of the Constitution without deprecating (as Charles Beard would) the intentions of the nation's founders; see Hofstadter, *The Progressive Historians,* 243–44.

72. Simkhovitch, *Neighborhood,* 44–46. Simkhovitch, who founded the Greenwich House settlement in New York City at the turn of the century, was one of Ashley's graduate students in 1892; see Carroll Smith-Rosenberg, "Simkhovitch, Mary Kingsbury," in Sicherman and Green, *Notable American Women,* 649.

73. MPF, *Speaker,* 315, 318. A 1990 analysis of the Speakership outlines Follett's call for centralization of power but does not mention her call for greater accountability; Peters, *The American Speakership,* 2.

74. MPF, *Speaker,* 308. For the Cannon era, see Davidson and Oleszek, *Congress against Itself,* 25–32.

75. For ways in which publicity resulting from open legislative hearings and public service commission investigations had helped to promote responsible action on behalf of

the public in Massachusetts, see Abrams, *Conservatism in a Progressive Era*, 3–10. MPF, *The Speaker*, 308–09.

76. "The Speaker of the House," *The Nation*, 198–99.

77. Follett's position as an outsider helped her avoid the unfortunate tendency of the antiformalists to rely exclusively on empirical methods. See Stephen Jay Gould, *The Panda's Thumb* (New York: W. W. Norton, 1992), 59–68.

78. Follett's conviction about the appropriateness of employing deductive as well as inductive forms of reasoning was surely influenced by her studies with Henry Sidgwick; see Kloppenberg, *Uncertain Victory*, 61.

79. Davidson and Oleszek, *Congress against Itself*, 286.

80. Wilson, *Congressional Government*, 60.

81. MPF, *Speaker*, 222. For Follett's notion of the "illusion of final authority," see *Dynamic Administration*, ed. Metcalf and Urwick, 117–131.

82. MPF, *Speaker*, 171–73. For evidence of the House members' responsiveness to Clay, see MPF, "Henry Clay," 347.

83. *Dynamic Administration*, 29–35; MPF, *Speaker*, 305–06.

84. MPF, *Speaker*, 308.

Chapter 8: "To I. L. B."

1. Alice W. Shurcliff, ed., *Lively Days: Some Memoirs by Margaret Homer Shurcliff* (Taipei: Literary House, 1965), 9.

2. Alice M. Gordon, "The After-Careers of University-Educated Women," *Nineteenth Century* 37 (1895): 955–56; Mary Van Kleeck, "A Census of College Women," *Journal of the Association of Collegiate Alumnae* 11 (May 1918): 557–60; Vicinus, *Independent Women*, 177.

3. Harriet French Mixter to KF, Sept. 3, 1934, LFUA. Harriet French studied at the Annex for only two years (1888–89 and 1892–93) before marrying (Radcliffe Archives and Thayer Academy Archives). Among Follett's new Annex friends were Ada Eliot (Sheffield), innovator in social work case management and the sister of T. S. Eliot; Eda Woolson (Hurlbut), whose husband became the dean of Harvard College (1902–1916); and Christina Hopkinson (Baker), in later years acting dean of Radcliffe College and wife of George P. Baker, who developed the study of drama at Harvard College. See EB, Memoir of MPF, LFUA.

4. Barbara Miller Solomon, "Balch, Emily Greene," in Sicherman and Green, *Notable American Women*, 41–45; EB, Memoir of MPF, LFUA. For more on the Balch family, see Randall, *Improper Bostonian;* and Warner, *Province of Reason*, 90–92.

5. Grade Sheets, Registrar's Records, RGXII, Series 4, 1891–92, RA; EB, Memoir of MPF, LFUA.

6. EB, Memoir of MPF, LFUA.

7. Jenni Calder, *Women and Marriage in Victorian Fiction* (New York: Oxford University Press, 1976), 170. For more on Meredith, see Calder, 171–94.

8. Heilbrun, *Reinventing Womanhood*, 124, 92.

9. Harriet French Mixter to KF, Sept. 3, 1934; EB, Memoir of MPF, both LFUA.

10. MPF, *The New State*, 208.

11. "Headmaster's Daybook," Jan. 6 and March 29, 1893; Feb. 9, May 22, and June 22, 1894, Thayer Academy Archives, Thayer Academy, Braintree, Mass.; Mixter to KF, Sept. 3, 1934, LFUA.

12. Transcript, Registrar's Records, RGXII, RA; Horowitz, *Alma Mater*, 237–38; Solomon, *Higher Education for Women*, 55.

13. Marlborough Street was no longer used as a school in 1893; see Boston Assessor's Records, Boston City Archives, Hyde Park, Mass. Shaw's children had graduated, and she began to close the school.

14. Records of births and deaths at the General Register Office, London; U.K. Census records for 1851 and 1861, Great Yarmouth, Norfolk. Isobel was named Isabella Louisa; at some point Briggs began to use either Isobel or Isabel.

15. The older daughters left home in this period, presumably to marry; see the will of Isobel Briggs, Suffolk County, Boston. William Briggs's third wife is named in the 1861 Great Yarmouth census.

16. Vicinus, *Independent Women*, 22–26. Isobel's younger sister became a governess in Germany; see the will of Alice Bertha Briggs, probated March 6, 1913, Somerset House, London.

17. Nonita Glenday and Mary Price, *Reluctant Revolutionaries: A Century of Headmistresses, 1874–1974* (London: Pitman, 1975), 3–4. One of the best schools for girls was the North London Collegiate School, which provided almost one-third of the candidates taking the 1863 experimental local examinations. The North London Collegiate School has no records of students attending for the first twenty years of its existence. The Chantry School and Sydenham College, both of which sent candidates to the 1863 examination, are no longer in existence.

18. *Boston Evening Transcript*, Jan. 9, 1926. The obituary was probably written by MPF, who would have been well informed about Briggs's educational background. Isobel was fifteen years old at the time of the 1863 local examination experiment. She apparently did not attend the Cambridge or Oxford women's colleges, probably because they were established too late.

19. Vicinus, *Independent Women*, 26.

20. Briggs's estate left about 4,000 pounds. The estate was probably divided among the three sons, Isobel, and Alice Bertha; this left Isobel a substantial amount of money. See the will of William Briggs, 1864, Somerset House, London.

21. Vicinus, *Independent Women*, 26. The records of the Association of Headmistresses, an organization founded in 1874 that Briggs would probably have joined had she been a headmistress, do not list Briggs as a member.

22. *Yarmouth Independent*, Jan. 23, 1864. Briggs was an active Wesleyan Methodist.

23. Winnifred Mercier, quoted in Vicinus, *Independent Women*, 205–06. For the reforms begun after 1870, see Joyce Senders Pederson, "Schoolmistresses and Headmistresses: Elites and Education in Nineteenth-Century England." *Journal of British Studies* 15 (1975): 135–62.

24. Obituary of Isobel L. Briggs, *Boston Evening Transcript*, Jan. 9, 1926.

25. Shurcliff, *Lively Days*, 9; the student was the same Margaret Nichols who found the regimentation of Follett's classroom distressing.

26. Interview with George D. Follett Jr., June 16, 1982, Quincy, Mass. Eva Whiting

White described Mary as "a masculine type, tall and angular"; notes of interview with Eva Whiting White, Oct. 18, 1967, author's files–Fox.

27. Obituary of Isobel L. Briggs, *Boston Evening Transcript,* Jan. 9, 1926; MPF to Henry Sidgwick, Sept. 17, 1891, Henry Sidgwick Papers, Trinity College Archives, Cambridge University. Follett is most likely writing about Briggs; Anna Boynton Thompson was already acquainted with political philosophy.

28. EB, Memoir of MPF, LFUA.

29. See the Thompson-Longfellow correspondence, especially June 12 and July 18, 1891, Alice Mary Longfellow Papers, Longfellow National Historic Site, National Park Service, Cambridge, Mass.; see also Oct. 25 and Nov. 2 [1894] about Thompson's desire to dedicate her book on Fichte to Alice Mary Longfellow, Anna Boynton Thompson Papers, SL.

30. EB, Addendum to Memoir of MPF, LFUA.

31. Ibid.; Vicinus, "Distance and Desire," 611; Faderman, *Surpassing the Love of Men,* 226.

32. MPF, *Speaker.* Briggs witnessed Follett's signature on her Longmans contract; Longmans, Green and Company Archives, University of Reading.

33. Putney Historical Society; Edith DeWolfe et al., eds., *The History of Putney, Vermont, 1753–1953* (Putney, Vt.: Fortnightly Club, 1953), 161.

34. School Tax Rolls, Harrietstown Township, New York (1899); Maitland DeSormo, *Summers on the Saranacs* (Saranac Lake, N.Y.: Adirondack Yesteryears, 1980), 60–61.

35. EB, Memoir of MPF, LFUA.

36. Vicinus, *Independent Women,* 35; Smith-Rosenberg, *Disorderly Conduct,* 256–57.

37. During the years 1894–97, Briggs is listed in the Boston City Directory at Eight Marlborough. For the years 1894 and 1895, Follett is listed in the Boston directory and the Radcliffe student directory as being at Eight Marlborough Street; she is not mentioned in either directory for 1896; in 1897 the Boston directory lists her at 44 Worcester Street. The Quincy directories report her as boarding with her mother in 1896 and 1897, but they also reported this, erroneously it seems, for the years 1894 and 1895. By 1896 her mother and brother were living at Linden Place, having moved out of the big School Street house sometime after Mary's return from Newnham.

38. This late nineteenth-century transformation in society's views about intimacy between women has been used to explain differences between Willa Cather and Sarah Orne Jewett; see O'Brien, " 'The Thing Not Named,' " 585.

39. Smith-Rosenberg, "The Female World of Love and Ritual," 9, 14–16.

40. Solomon, *In the Company of Educated Women,* 98; Smith-Rosenberg, "The Female World of Love and Ritual," 19.

41. Nancy F. Cott, "Passionlessness: An Interpretation of Victorian Sexual Ideology, 1790–1850," in *A Heritage of Her Own,* ed. Nancy F. Cott and Elizabeth H. Pleck (New York: Simon and Schuster, 1979), 175.

42. Smith-Rosenberg, "The Female World," 27, 20–21.

43. F. M. Wilson, quoted in Phillips, *A Newnham Anthology,* 69; Oldfield, *Spinsters of This Parish,* 33–34, 297. Melian Stawell was admired by many young women, including Mary Sheepshanks, who called Stawell her "special flame." Stawell eventually settled

down with one of her Newnham classmates, Clare Reynolds, who survived her by only a few months.

44. Smith-Rosenberg, "The Female World," 27; Solomon, *In the Company,* 99.

45. Blackwell, quoted in Nancy Sahli, "Smashing: Women's Relationships before the Fall," *Chrysalis,* summer 1979, 20, 22.

46. Vicinus, "Distance and Desire," 602; Solomon, *In the Company,* 100; Smith-Rosenberg, *Disorderly Conduct,* 253.

47. Faderman, *Surpassing the Love of Men,* 227.

48. For more on women as social outsiders, see Vicinus, " 'One Life to Stand beside Me,' " 608; Smith-Rosenberg, *Disorderly Conduct,* 257.

49. O'Brien, " 'The Thing Not Named,' " 585.

50. Ibid., 584. For more on the medical literature of this period and early charges of lesbianism, see Smith-Rosenberg, *Disorderly Conduct,* 272–82.

51. Vicinus, "Distance and Desire," 604; Thompson, *The Unity of Fichte's Doctrine of Knowledge,* iv, vii. Concerning the dedication, also see Anna Boynton Thompson to Alice Mary Longfellow, Oct. 25 [1894], and Longfellow to Thompson, Nov. 2 [1894], Thompson Papers.

52. EB, Memoir of MPF, LFUA. For a discussion of the complexity of relationships between women of substantially different ages, see Vicinus, "Distance and Desire," 610–17.

53. Grade Sheets, 1895–96; *Annual Report, Radcliffe College, 1895–96,* 32; *1896–97,* 38, all RA.

54. Turgot, *Reflections on the Formation and the Distribution of Riches,* x–xii; William James Ashley to Thomas J. Kiernan, July 28, 1896, Record of Applications for Library Privileges, Harvard University Archives.

55. Grade Sheets, 1894–96; *Annual Report, Radcliffe College, 1891–92,* 13; *1894–95,* 35–36; *1895–96,* 32, all RA.

56. Turgot, *Reflections,* v–xiii; Ashley used third-person pronouns to describe the work of the translator and editor and did not "sign" the introductory essay as his own; Anne Ashley, *William James Ashley* (London: P. S. King, 1932), 52, 64.

57. "The Speaker's Power," *New York Times,* July 19, 1896, 27; Stawell, "Mary Parker Follett," 40.

58. Only records of English sales of Follett's book have been located; Longmans Archives. The book was reprinted four times in the United States during Follett's lifetime: 1902, 1904, 1909, and 1924. Bragdon, *Woodrow Wilson: The Academic Years,* 134–35; and Robert L. Peabody, "Afterword," in Wilson, *Congressional Government,* 216.

59. For more on the sacrifices made by the women receiving a doctor of philosophy degree from an American college or university before 1924, see Hutchinson, "Women and the Ph.D.," 20.

60. President Eliot essentially forced Ashley, an inductive economist, onto a more theoretical economics faculty. He hoped this would foster curricular change, but between 1893 and 1897 the department refused even to offer American economic history. After nine years of battles, Ashley left for the University of Birmingham. See Robert L. Church, "The Economists Study Harvard," in Buck, *Social Sciences at Harvard,* 61–76.

61. Jane Knowles, "Radcliffe Graduate School, 1879–1902," 3, RA.

62. The Ph.D. that Thompson received in 1900 was an honorary degree from Tufts; Tufts University Archives.

63. Hutchinson, "Women and the Ph.D.," 20; Walter Crosby Eells, "Earned Doctorates for Women in the Nineteenth Century," *Bulletin of the American Association of University Professors* 42 (winter 1956): 648–51. For new scholarship about early women historians, see Jacqueline Goggin, "Challenging Sexual Discrimination in the Historical Profession: Women Historians and the American Historical Association, 1890–1940," *American Historical Review* 97 (June 1992): 769–802.

64. Morison, "A Memoir and Estimate of Albert Bushnell Hart," 41. Thompson was vice-president the first year; Hart was president the next. See New England History Teachers' Association, *Report of the First Annual Meeting and Register* (Boston, 1897), 5–7, 47–51; *Report of the Annual Meetings, 1898, and Register* (Boston, 1898), 30.

65. Transcript, Registrar's Records, RGXII, RA. Follett was eventually named to Phi Beta Kappa when Radcliffe was awarded a chapter in 1914; see PBK-Iota Chapter of Mass. Directory, RA.

66. Vicinus, *Independent Women,* 40; idem, " 'One Life to Stand beside Me,' " 608.

67. Sicherman, *Alice Hamilton,* 1, 135–36.

68. MPF, *Speaker,* ix; MPF to Henry Sidgwick, Sept. 17, 1891, Sidgwick Papers.

69. Vicinus, " 'One Life to Stand beside Me,' " 607–08; MPF, *The New State,* 194.

Chapter 9: Self-Realization and Service

1. *Boston City Directory,* 1897, 1898; and Boston Assessor's Records, 1898, Boston City Archives, Hyde Park, Mass. MPF's address was 44 Worcester Street.

2. For the living arrangements of "New Women," see Vicinus, *Independent Women,* 36–40. Wages for office work ranged from $500 to $1,500; given her education, MPF's salary was probably quite high. See Grace H. Dodge et al., *What Women Can Earn: Occupations of Women and Their Compensation* (New York: Frederick A. Stokes, 1899), 141–75. When a teacher, MPF might have earned about $1,300 for the school year; schools comparable to Mrs. Shaw's paid their women teachers about $170 per month in 1891. See Massachusetts Board of Education, *Fifty-fifth Annual Report,* 112–167.

3. Seilhamer, *Leslie's History of the Republican Party,* 2: 80.

4. *National Cyclopaedia of American Biography,* 33: 180. Wardwell and McCall had entered the Massachusetts House together as "freshman" representatives in 1887. When MPF worked for Wardwell, McCall's office was next door. See *Boston City Directory,* 1897, 1898.

5. For fourteen years McCall served on the Ways and Means Committee of the U.S. House; in 1915 he was elected governor of Massachusetts and served three terms. McCall's books include a biography of Thomas B. Reed. See *National Cyclopaedia of American Biography,* 20: 303–4; Charles E. Hurd, ed., *Representative Citizens of the Commonwealth of Massachusetts* (Boston: New England Historical Society, 1902), 259–63; Seilhamer, *Leslie's History of the Republican Party,* 2: 419.

6. Morison, "A Memoir and Estimate of Albert Bushnell Hart," 47–48.

7. *Quincy Patriot,* Nov. 29, 1884.

8. Thomas C. Quinn, ed., *Massachusetts of Today: A Memorial of the State Issued for the World's Columbian Exhibition* (Boston: Columbia, 1892), 397; Edwin M. Bacon, *Men of Progress* (Boston: New England Magazine, 1896), 269–70; idem, *The Book of Boston* (Boston: Book of Boston, 1916), 413; *National Cyclopaedia of American Biography*, 33: 180; and Seilhamer, *Leslie's History of the Republican Party*, 2: 79–80.

9. *New York Times*, July 1, 1890.

10. Abrams, *Conservatism in a Progressive Era*, 64; Paper, *Brandeis*, 56.

11. Abrams, *Conservatism in a Progressive Era*, 54, 15.

12. Paper, *Brandeis*, 56.

13. *New York Times*, Feb. 27, Nov. 25 and 26, Dec. 10, 1896.

14. Melvin I. Urofsky and David W. Levy, eds., *Letters of Louis D. Brandeis*, vol. 1. (Albany: State University of New York Press, 1971), 128; Paper, *Brandeis*, 57.

15. *New York Times*, March 7 and June 11, 1897.

16. Melvin I. Urofsky, *Louis D. Brandeis and the Progressive Tradition* (Boston: Little, Brown, 1981), 23; Alpheus T. Mason, *Brandeis: A Free Man's Life* (1946; reprint, New York: Viking, 1956), 108, 109; Abrams, *Conservatism in a Progressive Era*, 54. For Brandeis's argument, see Paper, *Brandeis*, 58.

17. Evidence from city directories indicates that MPF probably left her job between July 1898 and June 1899.

18. For evidence of their friendship beginning early in 1900, see MPF to Alice Goldmark Brandeis, Sept. 4, 1918, Louis D. Brandeis Collection, Brandeis University Library.

19. Paper, *Brandeis*, 58. Neither MPF's manuscripts nor friends' memoirs explicitly mention her work for Wardwell.

20. For a discussion of "weak-party, issue-focused" politics, see Rodgers, "In Search of Progressivism," 114–17.

21. MPF to Henry Sidgwick, Sept. 17, 1891, Henry Sidgwick Papers, Trinity College Archives, Cambridge University; Stawell, "Mary Parker Follett," 41.

22. Longfellow was probably known to MPF and Briggs through his association with Shaw's brother-in-law and his work at Harvard and Radcliffe; see Bainbridge Bunting, *Harvard: An Architectural History*, ed. Margaret Henderson Floyd (Cambridge: Harvard University Press, 1985), 123–24, 130–40, 297 n. 29, 303 n. 9. For more on Longfellow's work, see Margaret Henderson Floyd, *Architecture after Richardson: Regionalism before Modernism — Longfellow, Alden, and Harlow in Boston and Pittsburgh* (Chicago: University of Chicago Press, 1994).

23. MPF to ELC and RCC, July 28, 1924, RCCP; EB, Addendum to Memoir of MPF, LFUA; Records of the Putney Historical Society, Putney, Vt.; interview with Cary Carpender (June 1982, Putney, Vt.), then the owner. In 1900 an icehouse was added, and running water was piped in beginning in 1913; electricity was added after MPF sold the house and property.

24. In 1900 Windham County had a population of 64 "Negroes," only .3 percent of the 26,660 people residing in the county; U.S. Census records for Putney, Vt., 1900; EB, Memoir of MPF and Addendum to Memoir of MPF, LFUA.

25. Robert N. Bellah et al., *Habits of the Heart* (1985; reprint, New York: Harper and Row, 1986), 66, 120–21; Alexis de Tocqueville, *Democracy in America*, ed. J. P. Mayer (Garden City, N.Y.: Anchor, 1969), 601, 592.

26. Thomas G. Bergin, *A Diversity of Dante* (New Brunswick, N.J.: Rutgers University Press, 1969), 76–77.

27. Dante Alighieri, *The Paradiso*, trans. John Ciardi (New York: New American Library, 1970), 48.

28. MPF to ELC and RCC, July 28, 1924, RCCP.

29. Anna Boynton Thompson usually "spoke her mind" — and not only with her students. "How can you write a life of Anna B. Thompson," ABH once remarked, "and leave out an account of her interview with the Pope; and her 'Oh, I asked if he did not think religion was too formal.' "; ABH to Blanch Hazard Sprague, June 3, 1935, Anna Boynton Thompson Papers, SL.

30. Thompson, "How to Study History," 170–71, 177.

31. Richter, *The Politics of Conscience*, 25; Copleston, *A History of Philosophy*, 8: 147.

32. Merkle, "Integrative Management," 8–11.

33. For more on Green's influence, see "A Mid-Victorian Style of Politics," in Richter, *The Politics of Conscience*, 292–343; also John Passmore, *A Hundred Years of Philosophy*, 2d ed. (1966; reprint, Harmondsworth: Penguin, 1984), 56.

34. Henry Scott Holland, quoted in Richter, *The Politics of Conscience*, 35. Green's idealist philosophy had its greatest influence in the years between 1890 and 1914; see Richter, 293.

35. Ibid., 114, 115, 104, 106.

36. Ibid., 108–09, 134–35.

37. Ibid., 36, 19. According to Richter, "the most prominent spokesmen for British Idealism [Green, F. H. Bradley, and Bernard Bosanquet] were all sons of Evangelical clergymen within the Church of England."

38. Ibid., 120–21. Sidgwick refused to accept either laissez-faire individualism or socialism as a form of political organization; see Blanshard, *Four Reasonable Men*, 235.

39. Kuklick, *The Rise of American Philosophy*, 215.

40. When Sprague asked eighty-year-old ABH to recall his impressions of Anna Boynton Thompson, ABH said: "Miss Thompson could have written a history and I think it was a distinct misfortune that she tangled herself up with Greek philosophy. It is perfectly clear from your manuscripts that Josiah Royce did not know what she was talking about and that she did not know what he was talking about"; ABH to Blanche Hazard Sprague, June 3, 1935, Thompson Papers. Indeed, Thompson seems to have been drawn to philosophical speculation more by Fichte than by Royce. See especially two letters to Alice Mary Longfellow concerning Fichte (Oct. 22, 1892, and undated) and two concerning Royce (June 12 and July 18, 1891), Alice Mary Longfellow Papers, Longfellow National Historic Site, National Park Service, Cambridge, Mass. MPF's friend Harriet French took Royce's "Cosmology" class; Grade Sheets, Registrar's Records, RGXII, Series 4, 1892–93, RA.

41. Kuklick, *The Rise of American Philosophy*, 142. MPF used the phrase "by wireless" in her introductory remarks in *The New State*, 12. She referred to her "German philosophy of long ago" in a letter to RCC, April 14, 1930, RCCP.

42. Kuklick, *The Rise of American Philosophy*, 215, 177, 259, 294–95. The paper that Royce gave was "The Principle of Individuation." See Clendenning, *The Life and Thought of Josiah Royce*, 232.

43. Ralph H. Gabriel, *The Course of American Democratic Thought: An Intellectual History since 1815,* 2d ed. (New York: Ronald, 1956), 307–13; Bellah et al., *Habits of the Heart,* 30–31, 335.

44. Gabriel, *Course of American Democratic Thought,* 308; Clendenning, *Life and Thought of Royce,* 274; Copleston, *A History of Philosophy,* 8: 279.

45. Copleston, *A History of Philosophy,* 8: 278–79.

46. Clendenning, *Life and Thought of Royce,* 275; Copleston, *A History of Philosophy,* 8: 282–83.

47. Stawell, "Mary Parker Follett," 40–41.

48. Conway, "Women Reformers and American Culture," 171.

49. Oldfield, *Spinsters of This Parish,* 49; Vicinus, *Independent Women,* 215–18.

50. Vicinus, *Independent Women,* 221.

51. Newnham College Club, *Cambridge Letters,* 21, 10–11, Newnham College Archives, Newnham College, Cambridge.

52. Davis, *Spearheads for Reform,* 12.

53. Ibid., 15–16.

54. Link and McCormick, *Progressivism,* 12; for more about the settlement residents, see Davis, *Spearheads for Reform,* 33–39.

55. Solomon, *In the Company of Educated Women,* 110; Conway, "Women Reformers and American Culture," 172–73.

56. Conway, "Women Reformers and American Culture," 173; EB, Addendum to Memoir of MPF, LFUA; Sicherman, *Alice Hamilton,* 136.

57. Vicinus, *Independent Women,* 215–16.

58. Conway, "Women Reformers and American Culture," 174.

59. *Boston City Directory,* July 1901. Since MPF and Briggs are not listed in the July 1900 directory, they probably returned from Putney in the fall of 1900.

60. For the intimacy of Briggs's relationship with Shaw, see Isobel L. Briggs to Mary Hutcheson Page, Feb. 25, 1917, Page Scrapbook, WRC.

61. Andover House, the first settlement house in Boston, was opened in the South End in 1891. In Dec. 1892 Denison House, a residence for women, was opened.

62. Geoffrey T. Blodgett, "Shaw, Pauline Agassiz," in James, *Notable American Women,* 3: 278–80; Pierce, "Pauline Agassiz Shaw," 20, SL.

63. James T. Mulroy to EB, March 24, 1935, LFUA. In May 1906 Roxbury House, another area settlement, joined Children's House, and the new organization was incorporated as Roxbury Neighborhood House. See Roxbury Neighborhood House, *Report of the Board of Managers: May 1, 1906–April 30, 1907* (Boston, 1907), 4–6; idem, *Annual Report for the Year Ending October 1, 1908* (Boston, 1908), 5.

64. According to Theodore Glynn, the debating club met at a "clubroom" on Albany Street; Children's House, and later Roxbury Neighborhood House, was located at 858 Albany Street after 1895. See *Boston Sunday Post,* Aug. 27, 1922, 41; and Roxbury Neighborhood House, *Annual Report for . . . 1908,* 4. Not until 1907 did the director report that "the time is ripe for starting a men's club"; Roxbury Neighborhood House, *Report . . . 1906–1907,* 11.

65. William I. Cole, *Motives and Results of the Social Settlement Movement: Notes on Exhibit at Social Museum at Harvard University* (Cambridge: Department of Social Ethics, Harvard University, 1908), 25–26.

66. Stawell, "Mary Parker Follett," 44.

67. It is difficult to establish the exact time when MPF began her work in Roxbury. According to Mulroy, MPF began her debating club in 1900; James T. Mulroy to EB, March 24, 1935, LFUA. According to the 1900 U.S. Census, MPF and Briggs were living in Putney on June 13, 1900; they do not reappear in the *Boston City Directory* until 1901.

68. Shirley A. Hickson, "Albert Bushnell Hart," in *Dictionary of Literary Biography*, vol. 17 (Detroit: Gale Research, 1983), 200–201; Carol F. Baird, "Albert Bushnell Hart," in Buck, *Social Sciences at Harvard*, 145.

69. Elshtain, *Public Man, Private Woman*, 14.

70. Bragdon, *Woodrow Wilson*, 26. Henry Adams, *The Education of Henry Adams: An Autobiography* (1918; reprint, Boston: Houghton Mifflin, 1961), 24, 32. James Curley was one of several Irish politicians who trained in public speaking at the Staley School of Speech; see Zolot, "James Michael Curley," 232.

71. The nucleus of the club was a group of Dearborn School graduates who were members of a local baseball team. Charles A. King, headmaster of the school, probably helped MPF interest them in the debating club. See James T. Mulroy to EB, March 24, 1935, LFUA; and *Boston Sunday Post*, Aug. 27, 1922, 41.

72. Mulroy to EB, March 24, 1935, LFUA.

73. For more on Glynn's reminiscences about the debating club, see *Boston Sunday Post*, Aug. 27, 1922, 41.

74. Solomon, *Ancestors and Immigrants*, 95; Hickson, "Albert Bushnell Hart," 199; Morison, "Memoir and Estimate of Hart," 51. One measure of the depth of ABH's conviction is the vigor with which he publicly opposed the imperialist policies advocated by Theodore Roosevelt; as Hart saw it, the acquisition of colonies contradicted the basic spirit of American democracy. See Baird, "Albert Bushnell Hart," 143–44.

75. ABH, *National Ideals Historically Traced, 1607–1907* (New York: Harper, 1907), 44, 46.

76. Baird, "Albert Bushnell Hart," 145.

77. *Pauline Agassiz Shaw*, 78; Woods and Kennedy, *Handbook of Settlements*, 108; Blodgett, "Pauline Agassiz Shaw," 279.

78. EB says that Robert Bruere was one of MPF's helpers, but the evidence suggests that it was Henry Bruere.

79. At the time that he was contacted by Shaw, Bruere was directing boys' clubs at Denison House and giving "little talks" on "Early American Patriots." See Henry Bruere, Part I, 11–14, Henry Bruere Interview, Columbia Oral History Project, Rare Books and Manuscript Library, Columbia University; *Who Was Who*, 3: 114.

80. Bruere left Roxbury in 1903 to work with Stanley McCormick in Chicago; Henry Bruere, Part I, 14–15, Henry Bruere Interview. MPF apparently began the Highland Union in 1902; see James T. Mulroy to EB, March 24, 1935, LFUA; and *The Highland Union, 1902–03*.

81. Although Quincy had a local suffrage organization, MPF's mother seems not to have participated; nor did she register to vote in school committee elections.

82. MWP, "Supplementary Notes: How I Came to Start my Work for Woman Suffrage," 3, box 24, Mary Earheart Dillon Collection, SL. MWP was named to replace Alice Stone Blackwell as chairman of the board of the Massachusetts Women Suffrage

Association and then became the first executive director of BESAGG. See MWP, "Mary Hutcheson Page: Supplementary Notes," reel 15, frames 54–55, National American Woman Suffrage Association Papers, Library of Congress.

83. Strom, "Leadership and Tactics in the American Woman Suffrage Movement," 299, 303. For more on the vote, see James J. Kenneally, "Woman Suffrage and the Massachusetts 'Referendum' of 1895," *The Historian* 30 (August 1968): 630.

84. MWP, "BESAGG: 1901–1907, Introductory Note," box 53, folder 706, MWWP; for a brief biography of Page, see Strom, "Leadership and Tactics," 301–02.

85. Strom, "Park, Maud May Wood," in Sicherman and Green, *Notable American Women*, 520.

86. Pauline Agassiz Shaw to RCC, undated [early 1901], Ella Lyman Cabot Papers, SL. Shaw, like many other women of this era, suffered repeated bouts of depression early in her life. For more on her health, see Shaw to her Uncle William [Gardiner?], June 2, 1870, folder 48, Gardiner Family Papers, SL; A. Alexandra Pierce, "Pauline Agassiz Shaw: A Memorial Essay," 9–31, SL; Louise Hall Tharp, *Adventurous Alliance*, 278–79.

87. MWP, "Boston Equal Suffrage Association, Excerpts from 'First Report,' 1901–1903," box 53, folder 716, MWWP.

88. *Woman's Journal,* Feb. 1, 1902, 34.

89. On the differences between the "justice" arguments of the early suffragists and the later "expediency" arguments, see Aileen S. Kraditor, *The Ideas of the Woman Suffrage Movement, 1890–1920* (Garden City, N.Y.: Doubleday/Anchor, 1971), 43–74; on the grounding of both positions in nineteenth-century liberalism, see Elshtain, *Public Man, Private Woman,* 228–39.

90. MWP, "Boston Equal Suffrage Association, Excerpts from 'First Report,' " box 53, folder 716, MWWP; on MPF as one of the founders of the BESAGG, see MWP, "BESAGG: 1901–1907, Introductory Note," box 53, folder 706, MWWP.

91. Stawell, "Mary Parker Follett," 41.

Chapter 10: Ward 17

1. Allswang, *Bosses, Machines, and Urban Voters,* 8–19.

2. Ibid., 13, 20.

3. ABH, *Actual Government,* 213–14.

4. Ibid., 204–05; Carol F. Baird, "Albert Bushnell Hart," in Buck, *Social Sciences at Harvard,* 145.

5. ABH, *Actual Government,* 100.

6. Baird, "Albert Bushnell Hart," 144; ABH, *Actual Government,* 101–02.

7. Baird, "Albert Bushnell Hart," 145, 151.

8. MPF, *The New State,* 106, 224, 167.

9. Ibid., 166–67, 227.

10. Ibid., 165–66, 227.

11. Ibid., 166.

12. Ibid., 221–22.

13. Allswang, *Bosses, Machines, and Urban Voters,* 25; James T. Mulroy to EB, March 24, 1935, LFUA.

14. See Woods and Kennedy, *The Zone of Emergence*.

15. Warner, *Streetcar Suburbs*, 66; Woods and Kennedy, *The Zone of Emergence*, 142. In this census, one was considered "foreign-born" if born of foreign parents, even while in the United States.

16. Woods and Kennedy, *The Zone of Emergence*, 138; Warner, *Streetcar Suburbs*, 88.

17. Woods and Kennedy, *The Zone of Emergence*, 136–37.

18. Ibid., 135–37, 140–41.

19. James T. Mulroy to EB, March 24, 1935, LFUA; *The Highland Union*, 1902–03, 3; *Bromley's Atlas* (Boston: City of Boston, 1899); *National Cyclopaedia of American Biography*, 20: 121; boxes 1, 7, and 8 and Pauline Agassiz Shaw Correspondence, Nichols-Shurtleff Family Papers, SL. Shaw probably provided the early funding for union activities.

20. *Bromley's Atlas; Boston Globe*, March 17, 1987; EB, Addendum to Memoir of MPF, LFUA.

21. For more on the Hull House Men's Association and the Seventeenth Ward Civic Federation, see Davis, *Spearheads for Reform*, 151–69.

22. *The Highland Union*, 1902–03, 3; EB, Addendum to Memoir of MPF, LFUA.

23. Woolston became a sociologist at the University of Washington.

24. Boston Equal Suffrage Association, *Annual Report, 1901–03*, MWPP. See also Woolston's recollections of 1902, Howard Woolston Papers, University of Washington.

25. Robert C. Brooks, "Business Men in Civic Service: The Merchants' Municipal Committee of Boston," *Municipal Affairs* 1 (September 1897): 494; *Bromley's Atlas; Boston Equal Suffrage Association, Annual Report, 1901–03*. Shaw had close connections with the kindergarten movement in Boston.

26. Woolston apparently worked for Follett both on this project and on the Highland Union; Boston Equal Suffrage Association, *Annual Report, 1901–03;* and 1902 Woolston Papers.

27. James T. Mulroy to EB, March 24, 1935, LFUA.

28. Ibid.; *The Highland Union*, 1902–03, 3. Union courses included mechanical drawing and applied mathematics, physiology, physical culture, and dancing. Mulroy graduated from Boston College (1902) and took graduate courses at Harvard.

29. Robert L. Church, "The Economists Study Society," in Buck, *Social Sciences at Harvard*, 65; Warner, *Province of Reason*, 98.

30. *Boston Globe*, Oct. 1, 1925. Glynn's likely birthdate was Nov. 8, 1881, not 1885.

31. *Boston Sunday Post*, Aug. 27, 1922, 41; James T. Mulroy to EB, March 24, 1935, LFUA.

32. *The Highland Union*, 1902–03, 3.

33. *Boston Sunday Post*, Aug. 27, 1922, 41; EB, Addendum to Memoir of MPF, LFUA. The 1902 Union membership list includes J. Curley and F. Curley; *The Highland Union*, 1902–03.

34. *Boston Sunday Post*, Aug. 27, 1922. The production probably occurred in 1902, and certainly before 1906, when Glynn married. Glynn said that he met his future wife during rehearsals.

35. Curley, *I'd Do It Again*, 40, 46. For more on Curley, see Jack Beatty, *The Rascal*

King: The Life and Times of James Michael Curley (Reading, Mass.: Addison-Wesley, 1992).

36. For more on Maguire's strategy and tactics, see John T. Galvin, "Patrick J. Maguire: Boston's Last Democratic Boss," *New England Quarterly,* September 1982, 392–415.

37. Geoffrey T. Blodgett argues that Boston politics had been "fundamentally transformed" by the 1890s with the disappearance of Irish-Yankee cooperation; "Yankee Leadership in a Divided City," 373. Others argue that considerable cooperation existed through 1905, the year of Mayor Collins' death.

38. Trout, "Curley of Boston," 170; see also Galvin, "Patrick J. Maguire," 392.

39. Blodgett, *The Gentle Reformers,* 241.

40. Blodgett, "Yankee Leadership in a Divided City," 387.

41. Blodgett, *The Gentle Reformers,* 243; Quincy, "The Development of American Cities," 536; Blodgett, "Yankee Leadership in a Divided City," 388.

42. Quincy, "The Development of American Cities," 537.

43. Ibid., 529. For more on the corruption and elitism involved in Quincy's actual style of governing, see David A. Shannon, ed., *Beatrice Webb's American Diary, 1898* (Madison: University of Wisconsin Press, 1963), 75–78.

44. MPF, *The New State,* 103, 156, 222, 342. Even with regard to alcohol, Follett's committee focused on alternatives rather than restrictions.

45. The five prominent figures were Patrick J. Kennedy in East Boston and John F. Fitzgerald in the North End (the grandfathers of the future president), Joseph Corbett in Charlestown, Martin Lomasney in Boston's West End, and "Smiling Jim" Donovan in the South End.

46. Zolot, "The Issue of Good Government and James Michael Curley," 61–62; Curley, *I'd Do It Again,* 47.

47. *Boston Globe,* Nov. 16, 1899.

48. Zolot, "The Issue of Good Government," 32–33, 167–69; Abrams, *Conservatism in a Progressive Era,* 97; Board of Election Commissioners, *Report,* 1902, 15. Zolot's ward election results seem incorrect; see *Boston Herald* and *Boston Evening Transcript,* Nov. 20, 1902.

49. William P. Grady, a Tammany man who won one of the other council seats, was also a member of the Highland Union.

50. *Boston Sunday Post,* Aug. 27, 1922, 41; *Boston Herald,* Nov. 16, 1902.

51. Report written by L. Minot, Dec. 14, 1909 and Printed Report on Curley for 1903; Curley File, Good Government Association Papers, Massachusetts Historical Society (hereafter GGAP). For information on the Luce Act, see Zolot, "The Issue of Good Government," 68–69.

52. *Boston Post,* Nov. 16, 20, 23, and Dec. 6, 1903; Zolot, "The Issue of Good Government," 170.

53. Board of Election Commissioners, *Report,* 1903, 119, 135; *The Highland Union,* 1902–03, 11–14.

54. Trout, "Curley of Boston," 178; letter to the editor, *Boston Post,* Nov. 23, 1903, Curley file, GGAP.

55. *The Twentieth Century Club of Boston, 1894–1904* (Boston: Davis, 1904), 4–5,

31–32. A Dec. 1903 survey revealed that almost three-quarters of members were social workers, educators, or clergymen.

56. "Calls Curley a Leader," undated newsclipping, probably from *Boston Sunday Post;* a subsequent clipping, "Dr. Pritchett on Municipal Reform," softens Pritchett's defense of Curley; Curley file, GGAP.

57. *Boston Post,* Dec. 6, 1903.

58. Curley, *I'd Do It Again,* 58; Abrams, *Conservatism in a Progressive Era,* 97–103.

59. Zolot, "The Issue of Good Government," 173; Trout, "Curley of Boston," 176–77.

60. Trout, "Curley of Boston," 177.

61. Peter K. Eisinger, "Ethnic Political Transition in Boston, 1884–1933," *Political Science Quarterly* 93 (summer 1978): 223, 220, 228; Trout, "Curley of Boston," 170.

62. MPF, "Report of the Committee on Substitutes for the Saloon," in BESAGG, *First Annual Report, 1901–03* (Boston: Garden, 1903), 23. "The work . . . has been in charge of a subcommittee consisting of the Chairman of the general committee [Follett], Miss Briggs as Secretary and Treasurer, Mrs. Quincy Shaw, and Mr. Cole."

63. EB, Addendum to Memoir of MPF, LFUA; James T. Mulroy to EB, March 24, 1935, LFUA.

64. Interview with Mulroy's son, Dr. Richard Mulroy, October 26, 1983, Wellesley Hills, Mass. John died of his tuberculosis two years after starting his new job; one of the girls also died from tuberculosis or appendicitis. This story illustrates how a larger-than-life figure such as Curley is seen as responsible for things in which he played little part. If Mulroy's father died when James was twelve, the date was 1893, well before Curley's first election to office; also, Curley did not head McCarthy's ward committee until 1900, two years before Mulroy graduated.

65. According to ABH, any investigation had to uncover "the actual source of the authority exercised by a government . . . the real propelling force of the population that makes an enforceable decision"; ABH, quoted in Morison, "A Memoir and Estimate of Albert Bushnell Hart," 45.

66. Trout, "Curley of Boston," 182.

67. Follett never mentions Curley by name in her books or lectures. In a 1928 lecture, she says: "For several years I was doing a piece of work which brought me into close connection with a Tammany organization. I knew the head of the organization, the ward boss, and several of his lieutenants . . . The boss . . . was an adept in organization, in using the power of his henchmen and in focusing it, in turning it toward certain ends." See *Dynamic Administration,* ed. Metcalf and Urwick, 284.

68. *National Union Catalog,* 176: 664.

69. Allswang, *Bosses, Machines, and Urban Voters,* 24–26.

70. MPF, *The New State,* 231, 223.

71. Allswang, *Bosses, Machines, and Urban Voters,* 27–28.

72. MPF, *The New State,* 222–23.

73. Allswang argues that when the political scientists had anything at all to offer by way of reform, they tended to argue for reform "from above"; *Bosses, Machines, and Urban Voters,* 20–29.

74. MPF, *The New State,* 202, 6, 167–68, 168–69.

75. Ibid., 167.

Chapter 11: Substitutes for Saloon, Schools, and Suffrage

1. Paul C. Conley and Andrew Sorenson, *The Staggering Steeple: The Story of Alcoholism and the Churches* (Philadelphia: Pilgrim, 1971), 50–52, 61; MPF, "Report of the Committee on Substitutes for the Saloon,"17.

2. Raymond Calkins, *Substitutes for the Saloon* (Boston: Houghton, Mifflin, 1901), iii–xiii; Charles Dudley Warner, "Editor's Study," *Harper's Magazine*, February 1897, 483–84.

3. Calkins, *Substitutes for the Saloon*, 2, 9.

4. Cole and Durland, "Report on Substitutes for the Saloon in Boston," in Calkins, *Substitutes for the Saloon*, 321–23; also see Francis G. Peabody, "Substitutes for the Saloon," *The Forum*, July 1896, 598, 603; and "Refreshment," 7–9, box 7, USESP.

5. The employment agency function once served by saloons had largely been discontinued, apparently because employers wanted a more reliable grade of worker. See Cole and Durland, "Report on Substitutes," 337.

6. Roy Rosenzweig, *Eight Hours for What We Will: Workers and Leisure in an Industrial City, 1870–1920* (Cambridge: Cambridge University Press, 1983), 58, 63.

7. MPF, "Report of the Committee on Substitutes" (1901–03), 17; Worrell, *The Women's Municipal League of Boston,* 208; MPF, "The Social Centre and the Democratic Ideal," 5.

8. James T. Mulroy to EB, March 24, 1935, LFUA; MPF, "Report of the Committee on Substitutes" (1901–03), 19.

9. MPF, "Report of the Committee on Substitutes" (1901–03), 17–18.

10. Follett does not name the league in the BESAGG report, but Mulroy does so in his 1935 reminiscences; Mulroy to EB, March 24, 1935, LFUA.

11. Lazerson, *Origins of the Urban School*, 120–21, 136–37.

12. Ibid., 97–99.

13. Seaver, quoted in ibid., 105; Woods, quoted in ibid., 99.

14. Ibid., 120–21, 112.

15. "Community Work in Boston," *Community Center,* June 1917, 22–23. MPF, "Report of the Committee on Substitutes" (1901–1903), 19–20. Shaw regularly urged her friend Richard Cabot to use his influence to oppose use of tobacco and alcohol; see Pauline Agassiz Shaw to RCC, June 24, 1899, RCCP; and Shaw to Cabot, undated [1901], Ella Lyman Cabot Papers, SL.

16. MPF, "Report of the Committee on Substitutes" (1901–03), 18.

17. H. G. Pearson, *Son of New England,* 31–32, 36–42, 44.

18. Storrow, quoted in ibid., 46.

19. BSC, *Proceedings,* Feb. 11, 1902, 66–67. All BSC documents may be found in the BSC Papers at the Boston Public Library.

20. Lazerson, *Origins of the Urban School*, 224–26.

21. BSC, *Proceedings,* Feb. 11, 1902, 67.

22. Storrow, quoted in BSC, *Proceedings,* March 11, 1902, 114.

23. BSC, *Proceedings,* Oct. 28, 1902, 415–16; Boston School Document (BSD) No. 15, 1902, 21; MPF, "Report of the Committee on Substitutes" (1901–1903), 18; see also James T. Mulroy to EB, March 24, 1935, LFUA.

24. BSC, *Proceedings,* March 11, 1902, 114; MPF, "Report of the Committee on Substitutes" (1901–03), 19–20.

25. BSD No. 15, 1902, 24–25; *Report of the Committee on the Extended Use of School Buildings,* BSD No. 9, 1903, 3–4.

26. Ibid., 9; Pearson, *Son of New England,* 48–49; Lazerson, *Origins of the Urban School,* 227–28.

27. Lazerson, *Origins of the Urban School,* 211, 214, 216.

28. *Report of the Committee on the Extended Use,* BSD No. 9, 1903, 11–12.

29. MPF, "Report of the Committee on Substitutes" (1901–03), 22–23.

30. RCC, "Medical History and Record of Mary Parker Follett, 1910–1933," RCCP; Vogel, *The Invention of the Modern Hospital,* 61–62.

31. "Maurice Howe Richardson," in *National Cyclopaedia of American Biography,* 18: 426; Hyman Morrison, "Reginald Heber Fitz," *Bulletin of the History of Medicine* 10 (1941): 259; Fitz, quoted in Morrison, "The Chapter on Appendicitis in a Biography of Reginald Heber Fitz," *Bulletin of the History of Medicine* 20 (1946): 267–68.

32. RCC, "Medical History and Record of Follett"; Shorter, *Bedside Manners,* 153.

33. MPF, "Report of the Committee on Substitutes" (1903–05), 23; RCC, "Medical History and Record of Follett."

34. George Follett's son was born on Jan. 2, 1904, six months after the wedding date; thus a pregnancy may have influenced his decision to marry and caused some additional family turmoil. See Records of Births, Deaths, and Marriages, Office of the City Clerk, Quincy, Mass.

35. Interviews with George D. Follett Jr. (June 16, 1982, Quincy, Mass.) and Nancy Follett Alvord (May 13, 1982, Quincy, Mass.).

36. Lazerson, *Origins of the Urban School,* 227.

37. BSC, *Proceedings,* Oct. 11, 1904, 401–02.

38. For an analysis of Duff's actions as a member of the committee, see Kaufman, "Boston Women and City School Politics," 332–80.

39. Pearson, *Son of New England,* 49; Burns, "The Irony of Progressive Reform," 140–41.

40. Duff may have wished to register personal displeasure with Storrow for helping to scuttle her 1902 legislative proposal to grant four-year degrees in Boston's Normal School. See Burns, "The Irony of Progressive Reform," 142–43; Kaufman, "Boston Women and City School Politics," 360–64.

41. BSD No. 13, 1904, 46–47.

42. Ibid., 52, 55, 60; Filene, "Salespeoples Classes in School Centers," Edward A. Filene Papers, Credit Union National Association, Madison, Wis..

43. BSC, *Proceedings,* March 22, 1911, 130; for information on Dierkes, see Kaufman, "Boston Women and City School Politics," 366–69.

44. BSD No. 13, 1904, 62; Burns, "The Irony of Progressive Reform," 140; Lazerson, *Origins of the Urban School,* 228; Kaufman, "Boston Women and City School Politics," 375.

45. BSD No. 7, 1905, 49, 51–52; Burns, "The Irony of Progressive Reform," 143; Lazerson, *Origins of the Urban School,* 228; Pearson, *Son of New England,* 49–54.

46. MPF, "Report of the Committee on Substitutes" (1901–03), 19–20; MPF, "Report of the Committee on Substitutes" (1903–05), 22–23; James T. Mulroy to EB, March 24, 1935, LFUA; "Community Work in Boston," *Community Center,* June 1917, 22–23.

47. MPF, "Report of the Committee on Substitutes" (1903–05), 23–24.

48. Ibid.; MPF, "Report of the Union Committee," 20; "Harvard College Class of 1891 Fiftieth Anniversary Report," 440–41, Harvard University Archives. Woodworth's investigation is mentioned in other publications, but an actual published report has not been located.

49. A few elective courses were available for day and evening high schools. See BSD, Nos. 4 and 13, 1906.

50. BSD, No. 13, 1907; "Minutes of the Annual Meeting of the BESAGG," March 24, 1908, FFPAP; BSC, *Proceedings,* Sept. 23 and Dec. 16, 1907; *A Civic Reader for New Americans,* 5–6.

51. MWP, "Notes for Annual Report of the Secretary, 1905–06," box 53, folder 715, MWWP; for a record of Follett's attendance, see the seating plan for the April 28, 1905, dinner, box 201, Charles J. Bonaparte Papers, Library of Congress. For more on how the Union Committee did its work, see MPF, "Report of the Union Committee," 20–21.

52. Frank Mann Stewart, *A Half-Century of Municipal Reform: The History of the National Municipal League* (1950; reprint, Westport, Conn.: Greenwood, 1972), 38–43; National Municipal League, "Clippings Sheet," no. 4, March 24, 1906, Bonaparte Papers. ABH was involved in many National Municipal League investigations and served as an officer or an Executive Board member; see Stewart, 29; and box 201, Bonaparte Papers.

53. Corman, "The School City," 281. For more, see *National Cyclopaedia of American Biography,* 4: 90–91; and Slicer, "The School City as a Form of Student Government," 285.

54. MPF, "Report of the Union Committee," 21–22. The 1903 National Municipal League Committee reached a similar conclusion; see National Municipal League, "Clippings Sheet," no. 4, March 24, 1906, Bonaparte Papers.

55. Corman, "The School City," 282; BESAGG, "Executive Board Minutes," March 2, 1909, and April 13, 1910, FFPAP.

56. MPF, "Report of the Union Committee,"22–23; City History Club of Boston (hereafter CHC), *Annual Report for 1906,* 8, 17; BESAGG, "Minutes of the Annual Meeting," March 24, 1908, box 15, folder 225, FFPAP; South End Social Union, "Minutes of the Executive Committee," May 15, 1906, box 5, USESP. The BESAGG voted on March 18, 1908, to "approve Miss Follett's judgment that this work ought not to be turned over entirely to the Good Government Association." See also BESAGG, "Minutes of the Executive Board," May 11 and Dec. 2, 1908, FFPAP.

57. *National Cyclopaedia of American Biography,* 15: 367; and "The Vocation Bureau," box 87, folder 1, North Bennett Street Industrial School Papers, SL.

58. CHC, *Annual Report for 1908,* 3, 5, 10; Solomon, *Ancestors and Immigrants,* 104, 122–23, 136–37.

59. CHC, *Annual Report for 1906,* 11.

60. Ibid., 17; and CHC, *A Brief Report of the Work for 1910,* 4, box 15, folder 229,

FFPAP. Allen reported that "thirty-five to forty per cent. [of Club members] are Jews, about the same number Irish-American. The rest are divided among various nationalities with American and Italian leading"; CHC, *Annual Report for 1908,* 21.

61. CHC, *Brief Report of Work for 1910,* 1–3.

62. "Plans for Junior City Councils," attachment to South End Social Union, "Minutes of the Executive Committee," May 15, 1906, box 5, USESP.

63. CHC, *Brief Report of Work for 1910,* 4.

64. Frederick J. Allen, "The City History Club of Boston," *National Municipal Review,* 1913, 708–09.

65. For Shaw's BESAGG contributions (1907–1913), see MWP to Quincy Adams Shaw and attachment, May 1, 1913, box 5, Shaw Folder, MWPP.

66. MWP to Pauline Agassiz Shaw, Dec. 22, 1907, box 7, BESAGG Folder, MWPP. Another attack may have occurred early in 1906; see references to Follett in South End Social Union, "Minutes of the Executive Committee," box 5, USESP.

67. Pauline Agassiz Shaw to MWP, April 10, 1907, box 7, BESAGG Folder; Biographical sketch, box 17; MWP to Shaw, May 21, 1908, box 5, Shaw Folder, all MWPP.

68. Strom, "Leadership and Tactics in the American Woman Suffrage Movement," 308.

69. Pauline Agassiz Shaw to MWP, Oct. 22, 1908, Shaw Folder, MWWP.

70. Ibid.; MWP to Robert Hunter, Nov. 13, 1908, box 2, MWPP.

71. Susan W. Fitzgerald to Fannie Fern Andrews, Nov. 13, 1908; BESAGG, "Minutes of the Executive Board," Nov. 21, 1908, box 15, folder 205, FFPAP.

72. BESAGG, "Minutes of the Executive Board," Nov. 21, 1908.

73. BESAGG, "Minutes of the Plan of Work Committee," Jan. 29, 1909, box 15, folder 205, FFPAP. The committee apparently included the BESAGG officers (Ames, Fitzgerald, Williams) and two other members of the Executive Board (Page and Follett).

74. BESAGG, "Minutes of the Executive Board," Dec. 2, 1908, box 15, folder 205, FFPAP.

75. Ibid.

76. For example, see BESAGG, "Minutes of the Executive Board," Jan. 25, 1909; and "Minutes of the Committee on Plan of Work," Jan. 29, 1909, both box 15, folder 205, FFPAP; also Mary Hutcheson Page to MWP, March 3, 1909, box 5, Page Folder, MWPP.

77. Strom, "Leadership and Tactics," 304; MWP to Mary Hutcheson Page, Nov. 25, 1907, box 5, Page Folder, MWPP.

78. Page to MWP, March 3, 1909, box 5, Page Folder, MWPP.

79. Strom, "Leadership and Tactics," 306; Page to MWP, April 11, 1909, box 5, Page Folder, MWPP.

80. For the BESAGG's new tactics, see Strom, "Leadership and Tactics," 306–11.

81. Undated newspaper clipping in Page Scrapbook, vol. 23a, WRC.

82. BESAGG, "Minutes of the Executive Board," undated [Nov. 1909?], box 15, folder 205, FFPAP; Mary Hutcheson Page to MWP, Dec. 12, 1909, box 5, Page Folder, MWPP.

83. Page to MWP, March 3, 1909, box 5, Page Folder, MWPP; MWP, "Mary Hutcheson Page: Supplementary Notes," reel 15, frames 54–55, National American Woman Suffrage Association Papers, Library of Congress.

84. Page to MWP, Dec. 12, 1909, box 5, Page Folder, MWPP.

85. Page to MWP, March 3, 1909, box 5, Page Folder, MWPP. For Page's persuasive powers, see MWP, "Mary Hutcheson Page: Supplementary Notes," reel 15, frames 54–55, National American Woman Suffrage Association Papers; and Carrie Chapman Catt to Mary Hutcheson Page, Aug. 12 [1905], Page Scrapbook, vol. 23a, WRC.

86. BESAGG, "Minutes of the Executive Board," March 9 and April 7, 1909, box 15, folder 205, FFPAP.

87. Page to MWP, March 3, 1909, and June 15, 1910, box 5, Page Folder, MWPP.

88. Page to MWP, May 1, 1910, box 5, Page Folder, MWPP.

89. Page to MWP, Dec. 12, 1909, box 5, Page Folder, MWPP. See also BESAGG, "Minutes of the Executive Board," undated [Nov. 1909?], box 15, folder 205, FFPAP.

90. Page to MWP, Dec. 12, 1909, box 5, Page Folder, MWPP.

91. Page to MWP, March 23, 1910, box 5, Page Folder, MWPP.

92. MWP, "Notes for Annual Report of the Secretary, 1905–06," box 53, folder 715, MWWP. MWP became the first president of the League of Women Voters. See Strom, "Park, Maud May Wood," in James, *Notable American Women,* 520.

93. Page to MWP, May 1, 1910, box 5, Page Folder, MWPP.

94. Page to MWP, June 15, 1910, box 5, Page Folder, MWPP.

95. BESAGG, "Minutes of the Executive Board," Sept. 14, 1910, box 15, folder 205, FFPAP; see "Minutes of the Executive Board" for the years following 1910, ibid.

96. BESAGG, *Sixth Report, Oct. 1910–Oct. 1912* (Boston: Libbie, 1912), 17. The *Boston Evening Transcript* reported that MWP, who introduced Pankhurst, also presided, but the BESAGG's own account is probably more accurate.

97. Flyer from Bay State Campaign Finance Committee, June 18, 1914, box 53, folder 714, WRC. Follett's name appears among the honorary vice-presidents on Oct. 1, 1916; Pauline Agassiz Shaw to BESAGG members, Page Scrapbook, vol. 23a, WRC.

98. MPF, *The New State,* 171, 157.

99. Ibid., 189–90.

Chapter 12: Private Funds for Public Purposes

1. *Boston Globe,* Jan. 16, 1909.

2. For Follett on coordination, see *Dynamic Administration,* ed. Metcalf and Urwick, 262–70.

3. *An Account of the Women's Municipal League of Boston,* 1–4. This approach was quite different from that of the Good Government Association, a group of largely Republican men who sought to expose and eliminate corruption among the city's immigrant politicians. See Burns, "The Irony of Progressive Reform," 147.

4. *Boston Globe,* Jan. 16, 1909; Worrell, *The Women's Municipal League of Boston,* 189.

5. *Account of Women's Municipal League,* 2, 6–7; Worrell, *Women's Municipal League of Boston,* 188.

6. Here, too, the experience of the Good Government Association was probably instructive. The association, by failing to produce either widespread support for reform or a popular political leader, was becoming "increasingly irrelevant to the politics of the city."

See Burns, "The Irony of Progressive Reform," 146–47; Goodwin, *The Fitzgeralds and the Kennedys,* 107–09.

7. *Account of Women's Municipal League,* 7–8.

8. Ibid., 4–5.

9. Kaufman, "Boston Women and School City Politics," 70–72, 99–100, 129–33, 238–39.

10. Ibid., 93, 248–49; K. Gerald Marsden, "Philanthropy and the Boston Playground Movement, 1885–1907," *Social Science Review* 35 (March 1961): 49–56; Boston School Document (BSD) No. 15, 1900, 3–6; BSD No. 13, 1900, 3; Massachusetts Civic League, *Annual Report,* 1900, 13; 1901, 33; 1902, 54–55.

11. "Résumé of ELC," box 1, folder 1, Ella Lyman Cabot Papers, SL; ELC, Massachusetts Civic League, *Annual Report,* 1902, 54.

12. "Candidates of the Public School Association, 1904"; "Résumé of ELC"; McCormick, "Ella Lyman Cabot," 156; ELC, "Journal/Diary for 1892–93," Nov. 21, 1893, Ella Lyman Cabot Papers.

13. Paper, *Brandeis,* 84, 209. Paper asserts that Alice Brandeis "could not keep up with it all," but she was active in social and civic work. By 1915 Brandeis was a BESAGG vice-president; see box 15, folder 226, FFPAP.

14. *Account of Women's Municipal League,* 36.

15. *National Cyclopaedia of American Biography,* 29: 103; Cornelius Dalton, John Wirkkala, and Anne Thomas, *Leading the Way: A History of the Massachusetts General Court, 1629–1980* (Boston: Office of the Secretary of State, 1984), 421; Strum, *Louis D. Brandeis,* 67.

16. *Account of Women's Municipal League,* 8; Worrell, *Women's Municipal League of Boston,* 188. The following year Pauline Agassiz Shaw was named the league's honorary vice-president.

17. Katherine Bowlker, "Mrs. Quincy A. Shaw," *Bulletin: The Women's Municipal League,* Jan. 1917, 8. During 1911–13 Shaw gave $2,000 to the committee's work. For other major donors, see *Bulletin: The Women's Municipal League of Boston,* March–April 1912, 40, 56; May 1913, 56.

18. MPF, "Report on Schoolhouses as Social Centres,"14–15.

19. *Christian Science Monitor,* Feb. 15, 1909.

20. MPF, "Report on Schoolhouses,"15; MPF, "Report of the Department of Civic Training, 1909," 28–29; MPF to ECL, Sunday, 3 P.M. [probably early 1923], ECLP.

21. ELC, "Report of the Department of Education," in *Account of Women's Municipal League,* 12–13; Tyack, *The One Best System,* 133.

22. *National Cyclopaedia of American Biography,* 16: 269–70; Fannie Fern Andrews to Robert Treat Paine Jr., Jan. 1, 1908 [1909], box 161, FFPAP. Munroe had worked in 1897 to create administrative reform in the Boston public schools.

23. Fannie Fern Andrews to Robert Treat Paine Jr., Jan. 1, 1908 [1909], box 161, FFPAP.

24. Kuehl, "Andrews, Fannie Fern," in James, *Notable American Women,* 1: 46; *Christian Science Monitor,* Nov. 26, 1910; Lazerson, *Origins of the Urban School,* 228; Boston Home and School Association, *Report for December 1907–June 1909,* 14, box 161, FFPAP.

25. Excerpts of Pauline Agassiz Shaw to Fannie Fern Andrews, March 19 and April 15, 1908, enclosed in Secretary to Mrs. Andrews to Edward P. Shute, June 14, 1918, box 161, FFPAP.

26. Lazerson, *Origins of the Urban School,* 228; BSC, *Proceedings,* Feb. 11, 1902, 67.

27. Fannie Fern Andrews to Robert Treat Paine Jr., Jan. 1, 1908 [1909], box 161, FFPAP; Boston Home and School Association, *Report for December 1907–June 1909,* 19, box 161, FFPAP; *Christian Science Monitor,* Feb. 16, 1909.

28. *Christian Science Monitor,* Feb. 17, 1909.

29. ELC, "Report of the Department of Education," in *Account of Women's Municipal League,* 12–13; *Boston Herald,* Feb. 18, 1909. The ten cosponsors were the Women's Municipal League of Boston, the Women's Educational and Industrial Union, the Women's Education Association, the BESAGG, the New England Women's Club, the Massachusetts Civic League, the Home and School Association, the Women's Trade Union League, the Consumers' League, and the Massachusetts Association of Women Workers.

30. For New York school reformers' use of media, see Tyack, *The One Best System,* 132–33.

31. Fannie Fern Andrews to Robert T. Paine Jr., Jan. 21, 1909, box 161, FFPAP; Boston Home and School Association, *Report for December 1907–June 1909,* 7, box 161, FFPAP. For biographical descriptions of the members, see *Who Was Who,* 2: 17, 31 and 3: 230; Dalton, Wirkkala, and Thomas, *Leading the Way,* 422; "Class of 1885, Report VII, 1910," 58, Harvard University Archives; Massachusetts Civic League, *Annual Report for . . . 1911,* 2; BESAGG, *Fifth Report, October 1908–October 1910* (Boston: Libbie, 1910); *National Cyclopaedia of American Biography,* 32: 411–12; Woods and Kennedy, *Handbook of Settlements,* 117–20; Boston Social Union, "Minutes for Nov. 16 [1909]," box 4, USESP.

32. MPF, "Report of the Department of Civic Training, 1909," 29; Fannie Fern Andrews to Robert T. Paine Jr., March 9, 1909; Boston Home and School Association, *Report for December 1907–June 1909,* 18, both box 161, FFPAP.

33. Burns, "The Irony of Progressive Reform," 151.

34. Ibid., 152; *Boston Herald,* March 11, 1909.

35. Burns, "The Irony of Progressive Reform,"152.

36. Goodwin, *The Fitzgeralds and the Kennedys,* 190–96; Burns, "The Irony of Progressive Reform," 133, 152–58.

37. Ibid., 158–59.

38. Follett discusses the role of the expert in *The New State,* 175, 180, 234–40; *Creative Experience,* 2–30; *Dynamic Administration,* 212–34.

39. All five members had Public School Association and Republican party endorsements. Ellis, Brock, and Lee also had the Democratic endorsement. See Board of Election Commissioners, *Annual Report* (1906–1910); *Who's Who in New England* (1916), 161, 371, 660, 712, 948.

40. Eva Whiting White, "Mary Parker Follett: Tribute Read at the 25th Anniversary for the Boston School Centres, Oct. 16, 1937," Eva Whiting White Papers, SL; notes of interview with Eva Whiting White, Oct. 18, 1967 (Author's Files — Fox).

41. MPF, "Further Uses for School Buildings," 6–7. The *Boston Common* reported

that Follett had secured this agreement on Feb. 10, 1910, but there was no official meeting of the School Committee on that date; see Crawford, "Schools as Social Centers," 4–5.

42. BSC, *Proceedings,* Feb. 21, 1910, 19.

43. *Acts and Resolves Passed by the General Court* (Boston, 1909), chap. 120, 82; MPF, "Further Use for School Buildings," 6–7.

44. *Boston Globe,* Feb. 9, 1910.

45. *Boston Globe,* Dec. 17, 1909.

46. Robert T. Paine Jr. to Mayor John F. Fitzgerald, March 4, 1910, box 161, FFPAP; also see Paine to John W. DeBruyn, March 7, 1910, ibid.

47. Boston city directories, 1908–1910; Records of the Boston City Assessor.

48. EB, Memoir of MPF, LFUA; interviews with George D. Follett Jr. (June 16, 1982, Quincy, Mass.) and Nancy Follett Alvord (May 13, 1982, Quincy, Mass.).

49. RCC, "Medical History and Record of Mary Parker Follett, 1910–1933," RCCP. These symptoms might have been caused by low blood pressure, low potassium, fever, infection, migraine, or seizure.

50. MPF, "Report of the Department of Civic Training, 1909," 28. Follett apparently withdrew, because her name is not included on either National Municipal League civic education committee; see Sheppard, "Municipal Civics in Elementary and High Schools"; Nov. 15–18, 1909, conference program in *National Municipal League Proceedings,* 11; "Civics in the Public Schools," in *National Municipal League Clipping Sheet,* 6th ser., no. 3 (Oct. 30, 1911), box 201, Charles J. Bonaparte Papers.

51. RCC, "Medical History and Record of Follett." Some complications also involved her family.

52. E. F. Mason to Fannie Fern Andrews, May 14, 1910; Andrews to Miss Mason, June 8, 1910, both box 15, folder 229, FFPAP.

53. ELC, "Annual Report of Department of Education," 18.

54. Boston Social Union, "Report of the Athletic Committee with the Executive Committee," Oct. 11 [1910], box 4, USESP.

55. RCC, "Medical History and Record of Follett." Follett last visited Fitz in March 1909.

56. Thomas Franklin Williams, "Cabot, Peabody, and the Care of the Patient," *Bulletin of the History of Medicine* 24 (1950): 465–69; Chester R. Burns, "Richard Clarke Cabot (1868–1939) and Reformation in Medical Ethics," *Bulletin of the History of Medicine* 51 (1977): 358–59, 365–67; RCC, "A Study of Mistaken Diagnoses," *Journal of the American Medical Association,* October 15, 1910, 1343.

57. RCC, "One Hundred Christian Science Cures," *McClure's Magazine,* Aug. 1908, 476; RCC, "Medical History and Record of Follett."

58. RCC, "The Use of Truth and Falsehood in Medicine," 248–56.

59. RCC, "Medical History and Record of Follett." Cabot noted that there was a slight murmur in the systolic and pulmonic arteries but that Follett's heart and lungs seemed normal. There is no blood pressure notation, even though physicians at Massachusetts General Hospital were measuring the blood pressure of every entering patient by 1912. The record does not mention X rays; this technology was in an early stage of development. Cabot found Follett's urine "o.k," but he knew that organic problems often went

undetected; see RCC, "The Limitations of Urinary Diagnosis," *Johns Hopkins Hospital Bulletin* 158 (May 1904): 174–77.

60. RCC, *Physical Diagnosis,* 109; Stanley J. Reiser, *Medicine and the Reign of Technology* (Cambridge: Cambridge University Press, 1978), 106; McGrew, *Encyclopedia of Medical History,* 304–05; P. D. White, "Richard Clarke Cabot," 1050.

61. RCC, "Medical History and Record of Follett."

62. Ibid.; Walton, Beeson, and Scott, *The Oxford Companion to Medicine,* 2: 1276.

63. RCC, *Physical Diagnosis,* 378–86; *Good Housekeeping Family Health and Medical Guide* (New York: Hearst, 1980), 339–40.

64. Shorter, *Bedside Manners,* 144; RCC, "Medical History and Record of Follett."

65. Ibid. For 1930s investigations of the relationship between colon distress and psychological symptoms, see Shorter, *Bedside Manners,* 147.

66. RCC, "Mind Cure: Its Service to the Community," *Colorado Medicine* 5 (Jan. 1907): 5, 9–10.

67. RCC, *Psychotherapy and Its Relation to Religion,* 28, 43.

68. In a 1906 address Cabot spoke knowledgeably of the work of Pierre Janet, Paul DuBois, and Sigmund Freud. Cabot called psychotherapeutic methods "solid science" and added that "we have been verifying its results at the Massachusetts General Hospital"; "Mind Cure," 8–10.

69. RCC, *Psychotherapy,* 20–23. DuBois's treatment plan required the physician to engage the patient in a kind of rational discussion or "moral therapy." Cabot probably was amenable to this, but he probably discarded massages and "overfeeding." See Shorter, *Bedside Manners,* 167.

70. RCC, *Psychotherapy,* 47–48.

71. Interview with George D. Follett Jr. Later Follett would demonstrate comparable interest in her young niece, Nancy, an aspiring musician. Through MPF, Nancy received a cello from Pauline Agassiz Shaw, played recitals at the Andrews sisters' home, and went to symphony concerts with the Cabots; interview with Nancy Follett Alvord.

72. Boston Social Union, "Minutes for Nov. 10, 1910," box 4, USESP. Follett met with the School Committee secretary on Nov. 5 and five days later attended a meeting of the Boston Social Union; MPF to BSC, Nov. 7, 1910, Boston School Committee Papers, Rare Books Department, Boston Public Library (hereafter BSC Papers).

73. The process of resolving the dispute is discussed in BSC, *Proceedings,* Nov. 22, 1910, 185; Dec. 5, 1910, 195; Dec. 28, 1910, 209; Jan. 2, 1911, 213; Oct. 2, 1911, 128.

74. ELC, "Report of the Department of Education," 23–25.

75. MPF, "Further Use for School Buildings," 6–7.

76. Brooks originally asked Boston-1915 to assist boys and girls in selecting high schools. Edward Filene, whose brother was a major contributor to the Vocation Bureau, suggested that the bureau draw up a plan. See Brewer, *A History of Vocational Guidance,* 57–69.

77. Mary A. Gilson, who became a prominent figure in personnel administration, was one of the first vocational counselors appointed in the Trade School for Girls; ibid., 77.

78. Bloomfield did not directly succeed Parsons; ibid., 69.

79. Ginn, "Mary Parker Follett," in Worrell, *Women's Municipal League of Boston,* 207–08; MPF, "The Placement Bureau," 13–14.

80. E. F. Mason to Fannie Fern Andrews, May 14, 1910, box 15, folder 229, FFPAP.

81. Follett described her Roxbury League as being particularly interested in "the influence the politicians had on the boys of the neighbourhood . . . [and] in the manner in which the politicians could get positions for boys at any time in large corporations, such as the elevated Railway." See South End Social Union, "Executive Committee Minutes for Jan. 3, 1906," box 5, USESP.

82. Keyssar, *Out of Work,* 256–62.

83. Fannie Fern Andrews to Robert T. Paine Jr., April 23, 1910, box 161, FFPAP.

84. Andrews to Paine, April 23, May 5 and May 16, 1910, box 161, FFPAP; Andrews to Miss Mason, June 8, 1910, box 15, folder 229, FFPAP; Andrews, "The Further Use of School Buildings"; *Christian Science Monitor,* Nov. 26, 1910.

85. Andrews, "Further Use of School Buildings," 116; BSC, *Proceedings,* June 20, 1910, 125.

86. For some information about how this citywide plan was prepared, see Fannie Fern Andrews to Robert T. Paine Jr., April 23, May 5 and May 16, 1910, box 161, FFPAP.

87. ELC, "Report of the Department of Education," 23–25. The director was Lilian V. Robinson; see committees in *Bulletin: The Women's Municipal League of Boston,* June 1910.

88. MPF, "Report of the Committee on Extended Use," 18–20.

89. The petition was filed by Warren F. Spaulding, secretary of the Massachusetts Prisons Association; see *New Boston,* Oct. 1911, 214; *Boston Home and School News-Letter,* March 1, 1911, 1; *Christian Science Monitor,* March 7, 1911; *Acts and Resolves Passed by the General Court* (Boston, 1911), 355; Eva Whiting White, "Mary Parker Follett," Eva Whiting White Papers.

90. *Boston Home and School News-Letter,* March 1, 1911, 1.

91. For the evolution of one organization's position on extended use, see *United Improvement Association Bulletin,* Nov. 1910, 4; March–April 1911, 5; June 1911, 7; Nov. 1911, 4, 12–13; Dec. 1911, 9. For references to the support of other organizations, see James P. Munroe to David A. Ellis, May 23, 1911, BSC Papers; *New Boston,* June 1911, 42.

92. ELC, "Annual Report of Department of Education," 18.

93. "The Significance of Boston-1915," *New Boston,* Nov. 1910, 299–300.

94. H. W. Poor, "Shows Gain Made by 'Boston-1915' Though Plan Dies," *Chicago Tribune,* May 11, 1913; Edward A. Filene to Garrett Droppers, Feb. 13, 1912, Edward A. Filene Papers, Credit Union National Association, Madison, Wis.; "Report on Boston-1915," 25–29, ibid. The causes of Boston-1915's demise included the massive size of the enterprise, inadequate funds and publicity, an uninterested business community, quarrels among religious leaders, and a failure to follow through on commitments.

95. Kellogg, "Boston's Level Best," 387; Poor, "Shows Gain"; "Draft of First Annual Report of Boston, 1915," 2, Filene Papers. Woods was the president of the Boston Social Union, a citywide settlement federation; Follett was elected vice-president in 1911. See "Minutes of the Boston Social Union for Nov. 14, 1911," box 4, USESP.

96. Kellogg, "Boston's Level Best," 396.

97. MPF, *The New State,* 192–93. Follett participated in the Boston-1915 Committee on Construction and Location of Schoolhouses. See "What Boston-1915 Is Doing," *New*

Boston, June 1910, 57; C. Bertrand Thompson, "How Boston-1915 Works," *New Boston,* Nov. 1910, 306; "Report on Boston-1915," appended section on conference and committees, 7, Filene Papers.

98. *Christian Science Monitor,* March 6, 1911; see also Andrews, "Schoolhouses as Neighborhood Centers," 490.

99. James P. Munroe to John F. Fitzgerald, March 25, 1911, BSC Papers.

Chapter 13: *"My Beloved Centres"*

1. Brandeis, "Mary Parker Follett," 1, VI.7, Louis D. Brandeis Collection, Brandeis University Library; Eva Whiting White, "Mary Parker Follett," Eva Whiting White Papers, SL. See also James T. Mulroy to EB, June 24, 1935, LFUA.

2. MPF, "Social Ethics Seminary, January 3, 1927," box 62, RCCP. For charges of naiveté, see Quandt, *From the Small Town to the Great Community,* 42–45; and Henry S. Kariel, *The Decline of American Pluralism* (Stanford: Stanford University Press, 1961), 158–60.

3. A popular strategy for coping with such restrictions was to include among an organization's officers a sympathetic "token man" (Samuel Eliot in the Society to Encourage Studies at Home and Arthur Gilman in the Society for the Collegiate Instruction of Women); see SESH, *Memorial Volume,* 13; Horowitz, *Alma Mater,* 100.

4. ABH, *Records of the Class of 1880 — Report X,* 35, Harvard University Archives.

5. Zolot, "The Issue of Good Government," 127–28. For details, see *Boston Globe,* March 18, 1910; Boston City Council, *Proceedings,* Feb. 6, 1911, 3.

6. *New Boston,* June 1911, 42; "Report on Boston-1915," app., 8, Edward A. Filene Papers, Credit Union National Association, Madison, Wis. There reportedly was so much public support that the mayor took the "further use" issue to the BSC.

7. BSC, *Proceedings,* June 5, 1911, 81. For the committee's concerns, see James P. Munroe to David A. Ellis, May 23, 1911, BSC Papers, Rare Books Department, Boston Public Library; *Journal of the House of Representatives of the Commonwealth of Massachusetts,* 1357, 1438–39; see also *Journal of the Senate of the Commonwealth of Massachusetts* (Boston: Wright and Potter, 1911), 1268–69; *Boston Globe* and *Christian Science Monitor,* June 5, 1911.

8. MPF, "Evening Recreation Centers," 389–90. One hundred thirty-nine people were registered for the conference; J. Clements Boyers, "Recreation Institute for the New England States," *The Playground,* April 1912, 10.

9. The first attempt had been made a few months earlier; see James P. Munroe to John F. Fitzgerald, March 25, 1911, BSC Papers.

10. Boston City Council, *Proceedings,* June 13, 1911, 210.

11. John F. Fitzgerald to Boston City Council, June 12, 1911, in ibid.

12. *Boston Globe,* June 14, 1911.

13. *Boston Herald,* Feb. 18, 1912. For the expanded published version of Follett's speech see MPF, "Report of the East Boston Centre," 5–12.

14. MPF, "Evening Recreation Centers," 388–89.

15. *New Boston,* Aug. 1911, 123.

16. Boston City Council, *Proceedings,* Sept. 9, 1911, 335.

17. *Boston Herald,* Oct. 9, 1911.

18. Boston City Council, *Proceedings,* Oct. 9, 1911, 371–72.

19. Richard had seen how the Rochester newspapers opposed Ward's social center idea once the political bosses and certain private interests felt threatened by the civic clubs. Richard resigned and became editor of *Boston Common; Christian Science Monitor,* Oct. 10, 1911; MPF, "Report of the East Boston Centre," 12; Ward, *The Social Center,* 195–96; Livy S. Richard, "School Centers as 'Melting Pots,'" *New Boston,* April 1911, 530.

20. John C. Merrill and Harold A. Fisher, *The World's Great Dailies: Profiles of Fifty Newspapers* (New York: Hastings House, 1980), 96; *Christian Science Monitor,* Oct. 14, 1911.

21. Boston City Council, *Proceedings,* Oct. 30, 1911, 411–12.

22. "The Further Use of School Buildings," *New Boston,* Nov. 1911, 224.

23. *Christian Science Monitor,* Oct. 24, 1911; Crawford, "Schools as Social Centers," 4; "Fifteen Years of the Ford Hall Forum," 4, Filene Papers.

24. Crawford, "Schools as Social Centers," 5.

25. ELC, "Annual Report of Department of Education," 28. For a description of East Boston, see Woods and Kennedy, *The Zone of Emergence,* 187–219.

26. R. E. Hawley, "Director's Report," 13; *Boston Globe,* Oct. 23 and 27, 1911. The morning after the center opened, the *Boston Globe* reported that "60 girls who work every day formed classes in novelty sewing, plain sewing, homemaking club, literary club, dramatic club and game club. Tonight the girls will have the opportunity of forming into folk dancing clubs, gymnastic clubs, practice basket-ball, club swinging and engage in marches and games. Tomorrow night will be devoted entirely to music." About 80 boys appeared, joining a "junior city council, printing class, debating and public speaking classes, a class in clay modeling and a dramatic club." The boys also could also "form a band, orchestra and drum corps . . . [and] engage in gymnastics, practice basket-ball and dancing." A program of vocational guidance and placement was also included.

27. MPF, "Evening Recreation Centers," 392.

28. MPF, "Report of the East Boston Centre," 8.

29. Ibid., 5, 8–9.

30. Crawford, "Schools as Social Centers," 5; MPF, "Report of the East Boston Centre," 10.

31. MPF, "Evening Recreation Centers," 387.

32. MPF, "Report of the East Boston Centre," 9–10; MPF, "Evening Recreation Centers," 387. Follett envisioned a further step in which "the different School Centres in different parts of the city find that they can, through chosen delegates, combine for a common end."

33. Reese, *Power and the Promise of School Reform,* 191; Gleuck, "The Community Use of Schools," 49; John Collier, "Proceedings of the National Community Center Conference," typescript, 391, LeRoy Bowman Papers, Rare Books and Manuscript Library, Columbia University; Fisher, "Community Organizing and Citizen Participation," 476.

34. *Boston Evening Transcript* and *Boston Herald,* Feb. 18, 1909.

35. Edward J. Ward, quoted in Gleuck, "The Community Use of Schools," 52.

36. Ibid., 54; Fisher, "Community Organizing and Citizen Participation," 478.

37. Crawford, "Schools as Social Centers," 4.

38. MPF, "Report of the East Boston Centre," 6; MPF, "Evening Recreation Centers," 388. No list of conference participants has been located.

39. MPF, "Further Uses of School Buildings," 6. See remarks of Ralph Hawley in Frank Dazey, "The Social Centre Experiment in South Boston," typescript, 7, Guttman Library, Harvard University.

40. MPF, "Evening Recreation Centers," 392.

41. Fitzgerald reiterated his support for extended use in his 1912 Boston City Council address; Boston City Council, *Proceedings,* Feb. 5, 1912, 3. *Boston Herald,* Feb. 10, 1912.

42. Massachusetts Civic League, *Annual Report for . . . 1912,* 5; United Improvement Association *Bulletin,* March 1912, 8; Boston Chamber of Commerce, *Annual Report,* 1912, 8, 14, 52; "Recreation Centers," *The Playground,* April 1912, 16–17. The man who introduced the bill, Courteney Crocker, had been a lawyer for Burdett and Wardwell (1905–1910) before forming his own firm; *Who's Who in New England* (1916), 288.

43. Boston Social Union, "Minutes of the Executive Committee," March 21, 1912, and "Minutes for April 9, 1912," box 4, USESP.

44. Suggested sites were East Boston, Charlestown, South Boston, Roxbury, and the West End.

45. MPF to Chairman of the BSC, March 15, 1912, BSC Papers. Follett's Women's Municipal League committee consisted of Mrs. Richard Cabot, Mrs. Robert Treat Paine II, Mrs. T. J. Bowlker, Mrs. Louis Brandeis, Miss Lillian Robinson, Mrs. John Lindsley, and Mr. Arthur Woodworth.

46. BSC, *Proceedings,* March 22, 1912, 39; *Boston Herald,* March 23, 1912; *Boston Globe,* March 24, 1912.

47. BSC, *Proceedings,* April 1, 1912, 45. Follett worked effectively with Brooks but probably did not agree with his management style; see *Boston Evening Transcript,* March 23, 1912.

48. BSC, *Proceedings,* April 15, 1912, 73; April 22, 1912, 78; May 6, 1912, 92. The principles underlying the East Boston center (linking recreation and education, training in social relationships and self-government, breaking down prejudices of race, class, and religion, and fostering responsibility through charging dues) were successfully transferred to South Boston; Dazey, "The School Centre Experiment in South Boston," 1, 8–11, 14, 18, 20.

49. BSC, *Proceedings,* Dec. 5, 1910, 176; Brewer, *A History of Vocational Guidance,* 70–73, 77.

50. Brewer, *A History of Vocational Guidance,* 72. Mary Hutcheson Page suggested replacing Bloomfield on the BESAGG Board: he had difficulty "following through," never came to meetings, and "was always better at a promise than a fulfillment"; Page to MWP, March 23, 1910, box 5, Page Folder, MWPP.

51. Brewer, *A History of Vocational Guidance,* 78. One writer erroneously credits Bloomfield with having "added placement and follow-up to Parsons' method"; Edmund C. Lynch, *Meyer Bloomfield and Employment Management* (Austin: Bureau of Business Research, University of Texas, 1970), 11. Another omits Follett's contributions to the development of vocational guidance in Boston; Sanford M. Jacoby, *Employing Bureaucracy: Managers, Unions, and the Transformation of Work in American Industry* (New York: Columbia University Press, 1985), 73–88.

52. MPF, "The Placement Bureau," 8–9.

53. BSC, *Proceedings,* April 22, 1912, 75.

54. MPF, "The Placement Bureau," 11.

55. Rogers, "The Placement Bureau," 20. Rogers reported that "145 children, 97 employers and 64 placements in 43 establishments were registered."

56. MPF, "The Placement Bureau," 11, 15–16. For one discussion of reciprocal relating, see *Dynamic Administration,* ed. Fox and Urwick, 159–63.

57. One study investigated job opportunities for "the negro boy"; see MPF, "The Placement Bureau," 12.

58. MPF, "Committee on Extended Use" (1913), 9. Seventy-two students participated from Harvard, Radcliffe, and Wellesley. Many Wellesley students were enrolled in Emily Greene Balch's economics courses; see "Committee on Opportunities for Vocational Training," *Bulletin: The Women's Municipal League of Boston,* Jan. 1913, 11.

59. "Committee on Opportunities for Vocational Training," *Bulletin: The Women's Municipal League of Boston,* May 1913, 15.

60. MPF, "Committee on Extended Use" (1913) 9; MPF, "Committee on Extended Use" (1914), 22–24.

61. Brewer, *A History of Vocational Guidance,* 80–84.

62. MPF, "Committee on Extended Use" (1914), 22–24; BSC, *Proceedings,* May 5, 1913, 62.

63. "Committee on Industrial Conditions," *Bulletin: The Women's Municipal League of Boston,* May 1915, 58–59. As the Follett-Dennison collaboration began, the Chamber of Commerce brokered a trip for chamber representatives and others to Madison, Wisconsin, to investigate the work of the University Extension Department; see Boston Chamber of Commerce, *Fifth Annual Report,* 1913, 57.

64. MPF, "The Boston Placement Bureau" (1915), 18–19; BSC, *Proceedings,* June 12, 1914, 126; and Nov. 16, 1914, 195; Franklin P. Dyer to BSC, June 12, 1914, BSC Papers; Brewer, *A History of Vocational Guidance,* 83–84.

65. MPF, "Committee on Extended Use" (April 1914), 24. For others sharing Follett's views, see W. Stanwood Field, "The Continuation School Law," in Massacusetts Civic League, *Annual Report for the Year Ending October 31, 1913* (Boston: A. T. Bliss, n.d.), 24–25.

66. Mary B. Gilson, *What's Past Is Prologue: Reflections on My Industrial Experience* (New York: Harper, 1940), 46–50.

67. Rogers, "The Placement Bureau," 25, 32. Follett's accomplishments can be contrasted with Bloomfield's dreams; see Lazerson, *Origins of the Urban School,* 194–97.

68. MPF, "The Boston Placement Bureau" (1915), 27–28; Rogers, "The Placement Bureau," 23, 26.

69. MPF, "Committee on the Extended Use" (1914), 22; for illustrations of profitable interventions, see MPF, "The Boston Placement Bureau" (1915), 15–17.

70. MPF, "The Boston Placement Bureau" (1915), 25–27.

71. The bureau's services were publicized in the chamber's newsletter; Boston Chamber of Commerce, *Fifth Annual Report,* 1913, 56.

72. MPF, "The Boston Placement Bureau" (1915), 14–15; MPF, "Boston Placement Bureau" (1916), 10–11. As of Nov. 1915, the bureau had made 2,330 placements.

73. MPF, "The Boston Placement Bureau" (1915), 25–26.

74. MPF, "Committee on the Extended Use" (1914), 28; *Christian Science Monitor,* May 26, 1914. The bureau sent a "representative" (probably Follett or Ginn) to testify at hearings by the U.S. Commission on Industrial Relations on employment offices and unemployment.

75. MPF, "The Placement Bureau," 8; MPF, "The Boston Placement Bureau" (1915), 17–18.

76. MPF, "Boston Placement Bureau" (1916), 10–11; Field, "The Continuation School Law," 24–25.

77. The 1918 committee included Henry B. Sawyer (Stone and Webster), Edith M. Howes, Bernard Rothwell, Henry S. Dennison, and Follett; see BSC, *Proceedings,* Jan. 24, 1918, 253.

78. Susan J. Ginn to Patrick T. Campbell, Dec. 21, 1933, LFUA; Susan J. Ginn, "Mary Parker Follett," in Worrell, *The Women's Municipal League of Boston,* 207–08; Susan J. Ginn to Ada L. Comstock, May 25, 1934, Ada Louise Comstock Records of the President, RA.

79. MPF to ELC, June 29, 1917, RCCP. Follett hints that Alice G. Brandeis may have been less enthusiastic about the Placement Bureau than about the centers; MPF, "Boston Placement Bureau" (1917), 10; BSC, *Proceedings,* June 28, 1917, 125.

80. MPF to ELC, June 29, 1917, RCCP. Follett's affection for the centers is illustrated in her delight that "one club offered to make my Easter hat!" See MPF, "Midnight Oil in the Schools."

81. For Dyer's favorable views on the use of schools for civic discussion, see Ward, *The Social Center,* 175.

82. BSC, *Proceedings,* May 19, 1913, 74; June 23, 1913, 107; April 3, 1916, 50; Keyssar, *Out of Work,* 272–73.

83. For Curley's motivation, see Goodwin, *The Fitzgeralds and the Kennedys,* 242–52; Zolot, "James Michael Curley," 314–23.

84. Zolot, "James Michael Curley," 346, 367–78.

85. MPF, "Midnight Oil in the Schools." Average combined weekly attendance was "about 7000," and average attendance at Saturday evening lectures was 435 (this compared with 179 in New York).

86. *Boston Globe,* April 2, 1914 (evening ed.); *Boston American,* April 3 and 4, 1914.

87. MPF, "Midnight Oil in the Schools"; see also BSC, *Proceedings,* May 25, 1914, 87; Ralph E. Hawley to Franklin P. Dyer, May 25, 1914, BSC Papers; *Christian Science Monitor,* May 25, 1914.

88. For the series of events concerning Hawley's departure, see BSC, *Proceedings,* April 22, 1912, 75; May 5, 1913, 59; June 2, 1913, 87; *Boston Journal* and *Boston Globe,* June 24, 1913; BSC, *Proceedings,* June 27, 1913, 115; May 25, 1914, 87; Ralph E. Hawley to Franklin P. Dyer, May 25, 1914, BSC Papers; *Boston Globe,* May 26, 1914; *Christian Science Monitor,* May 25, 1914.

89. *Christian Science Monitor,* May 25, 1914; White Papers; notes of Elliot Fox's interview with Eva Whiting White, Oct. 18, 1967, author's files.

90. *Boston Globe, Boston Herald,* and *Christian Science Monitor,* May 26, 1914; BSC, *Proceedings,* June 1, 1914, 91. Corcoran later voted against White's $3,420 salary. The

Finance Commission may have been asked to comment on the appropriateness of White's salary; see remarks attributed to the 1914 "Finance Committee," Eva Whiting White Papers.

91. MPF to Eva Whiting White, undated [late Dec. 1914?], Eva Whiting White Papers.

92. *Boston Evening Transcript,* Oct. 16, 1915.

93. Follett was a member of Alice G. Brandeis's Women's Municipal League committee that surveyed school center facilities throughout the United States and made recommendations (accepted by the superintendent of schools and the director of school centers) concerning schoolhouse construction and equipment. See Alice G. Brandeis, "School-House Construction and Equipment in Their Relation to School Centres," supplement to *Bulletin: The Women's Municipal League of Boston,* April 1915, 1–17; idem, "Sub-Committee on School-House Construction and Equipment in Relation to School Centres," ibid., May 1915, 28–29.

94. Boston Social Union, "Minutes for Dec. 8, 1915," and "Minutes for Jan. 31, 1916," box 4, USESP; *Journal of the House of Representatives of the Commonwealth of Massachusetts,* 48; Massachusetts Civic League, *Annual Report for . . . 1916,* 5.

95. *Acts and Resolves Passed by the General Court* (1916), 60.

96. BSC, *Proceedings,* June 11, 1914, 105, 108.

97. Kaufman, "Boston Women and School City Politics," 294–98.

98. Managers received $8.00 per day, assistant managers $3.50 to $4.50 per day. Most managers could serve no more than 95 days over the term. In the 1915–16 budget; only Follett's protégé James T. Mulroy (manager of the Roxbury Center) was granted an additional 55 days of service. BSC, *Proceedings,* Oct. 5, 1914, 162; Nov. 2, 1914, 185; Nov. 16, 1914, 194; Jan. 25, 1915, 241–42; Oct. 4, 1915, 131, 134.

99. BSC, *Proceedings,* April 3, 1916, 50; *East Boston Free Press,* May 6, 1916.

100. *Christian Science Monitor,* May 16, 1916; BSC, *Proceedings,* May 15, 1916, 80.

101. For more on community support, see *Christian Science Monitor,* May 16, 1916.

102. *Boston Herald, Christian Science Monitor,* and *Boston Globe,* May 16, 1916.

103. Managers were shifted from daily to hourly rates; BSC, *Proceedings,* June 5, 1916, 102. Eight school centers opened in Oct. for 1916–17; BSC, *Proceedings,* Oct. 16, 1916, 144, 147.

104. Finance Commission of the City of Boston, *Report on the Boston School Department* (Boston: City of Boston , 1916), 3–4, 36; *Report of a Study of Certain Phases of the Public School System of Boston, Mass.,* City Document 87–1916 (Boston, 1916), 66–68. Studies of three centers were made by Harvard professor James Ford's students during 1922–23. The report on the Dorchester center is condensed in Gleuck, "The Community Use of Schools," 1049–84. During 1923–24, eleven centers were operating with 183 paid workers and a budget (from public funds, contributions, fees) of $40,000; see Gleuck, 629–30.

105. Dazey, "The School Centre Experiment in South Boston," 4.

Chapter 14: Community Centers

1. Gleuck, "The Community Use of Schools," 82. For the "western" movement, see Reese, *Power and the Promise of School Reform,* 197–208.

2. Rowland Haynes to HSB [Howard S. Braucher], Oct. 30, 1911, box 29, National Recreation Association Papers, University of Minnesota Social Welfare History Archives; Gale, "If You Know People, Things Look Different," 49.

3. Wilson, "The Social Center," 5, 7, 10–13. Excerpts appear in *American City,* Nov. 1911.

4. Conference program and Rowland Haynes to HSB [Howard S. Braucher], Oct. 30, 1911. For more on the Vandergrift-Kirk faction, see George B. Ford, "Madison Conference on Social Centers," *The Survey,* November 18, 1911, 1229–30.

5. Reese, *Power and the Promise of School Reform,* 196; J. E. Boell to Lloyd D. Somers, July 20, 1965, and attached excerpts from 1910–1915 Board of Regents records, Ward Correspondence, Extension Division, University of Wisconsin Archives.

6. Baldwin and Beard, "Social Center Conference," 142–43; see also Gale, "If You Know People," 49; Rowland Haynes to HSB [Howard S. Braucher], Oct. 30, 1911.

7. Thomas, "Nationalizing the Republic," 552; E. W. Hawley, *The Great War and the Search for a Modern Order,* 9–10; McCraw, *Prophets of Regulation,* 108–112; Levy, *Herbert Croly of the New Republic,* 112–13.

8. MPF, "The Social Centre and the Democratic Ideal," 3.

9. Ibid., 2–3.

10. MPF, "The Social Centre and the Democratic Ideal," 3, 11, 12, 1, 12. See also Wilson, "The Social Center," 13.

11. MPF, "The Social Centre and the Democratic Ideal," 8–9.

12. Ibid., 14, 10–11.

13. Ellen Paine Huling, "Ford Hall — an Experiment in Cooperation," *New Boston,* May 1911, 18–19; George W. Coleman, ed., *Democracy in the Making: Ford Hall and the Open Forum Movement* (Boston: Little, Brown, 1915), 43–49.

14. MPF, "The Social Centre," 14. In the question-answer period, Follett made clear that upper-class people should receive this training too; see *Ford Hall Folks,* Dec. 21, 1913, 2, Ford Hall Forum Collection.

15. MPF, "Evening Centers — Aims and Duties of Managers and Leaders Therein," 16–17.

16. Ibid., 9, 13.

17. Ibid., 7; MPF, "The Social Centre," 9.

18. MPF, "Evening Centers," 11, 17–19.

19. Ibid., 5, 6, 11.

20. Ibid., 3.

21. MPF, "Committee on Extended Use of School Buildings" (1913), 10; Boston Social Union, "Minutes for Feb. 11, 1913," box 4, USESP. On the founding of the school, see clippings from the *Boston Globe,* March 2, 1904, and *Boston Evening Transcript,* May 10, 1905, in Jeffrey Brackett's biographical file, Harvard University Archives; Mark, *Delayed by Fire,* 121–24.

22. "Course in Neighborhood and Community Work," School of Social Work, Academic Programs, box 2, folder 7, Simmons College Archives; "Neighborhood and Community Work," ibid., folder 2. Also see Boston Social Union, "Minutes for June 10, 1913," box 4, USESP; *Bulletin,* School for Social Workers, 1912–13, 18–19.

23. MPF, "Committee on Extended Use" (1913), 10, 13.

24. MPF, "The Social Centre," 14–15.

25. MPF, "The Aims of Adult Recreation," 261–68; Charles F. Weller, "Notes from the Recreation Congress at Richmond," *The Playground,* July 1913, 142.

26. The participants included: Albert J. Kennedy, Robert A. Woods, Meyer Bloomfield, Vida Scudder, Helena S. Dudley, and Eva Whiting White from Boston and Lillian Wald (president of the National Federation of Settlements), Mary K. Simkhovitch, Mary Dreier Robbins, and John Lovejoy Elliott from New York. "Inter-City Settlement Conference," box 1, Robert A. Woods Papers, Houghton Library, Harvard University; *Ford Hall Folks,* Dec. 21, 1913, 1–2; Sidney Dillick, *Community Organization for Neighborhood Development—Past and Present* (New York: Woman's Press and William Morrow, 1953), 56–57.

27. Gale, "If You Know People," 49; Baldwin and Beard, "Social Center Conference," 142–43. Brandeis, who would soon become Wilson's senior adviser, was named a vice-president. Twenty-four honorary vice-presidents included Governor Woodrow Wilson, Supreme Court Justice Charles E. Hughes, Senator Robert LaFollette, William Allen White, Jane Addams, and Mary E. McDowell.

28. Fisher, "Community Organizing and Citizen Participation," 477–82.

29. "Call for a National Conference on Community Centers and Related Problems," People's Institute Papers, New York Public Library.

30. Assessor's Office, City of Quincy, 1891–1933. Mrs. Follett was reportedly good with numbers until well into her eighties; interview with George D. Follett Jr., June 16, 1982, Quincy, Mass.

31. Charles A. Beard, "A Declaration of Independence for the Public Forum," *Community Center,* March 17, 1917, 10.

32. Beard, quoted in Richard Hofstadter and Wilson Smith, eds., *American Higher Education: A Documentary History,* vol. 2 (Chicago: University of Chicago Press, 1961), 883–84, 887–92; Collier, "Definitions and Debates of the Community Center Conference," 573.

33. For speeches favoring self-support, see Luther H. Gulick, "Freedom through Self-Support," *Community Center,* Feb. 3, 1917, 13; and James Ford, "The Cooperative Principle and the Community Center," *Community Center,* Feb. 3 and 24, 1917.

34. "The National Conference on Community Centers and Related Problems: Summary of the Tentative Findings of Special Committees," 4–6, box 46, LeRoy Bowman Papers, Rare Books and Manuscript Library, Columbia University.

35. Boston Social Union, "Minutes for March 12, 1912," box 4, USESP; see also R. E. Hawley, "Director's Report," 22–23; *Acts and Resolves Passed by the General Court* (1916), 60.

36. Kenneth R. Philip, "John Collier and the American Indian, 1920–1945," in *Essays on Radicalism in Contemporary America,* ed. Leon B. Blair (Austin: University of Texas Press, 1972), 65; Collier, *From Every Zenith,* 84, 106.

37. *Community Center,* Oct. 1917, 8; *Who Was Who,* 2: 556; J. E. Boell to Lloyd D. Somers, July 20, 1965, and excerpts from 1910–1915 Board of Regents records, Ward Correspondence, Extension Division, University of Wisconsin Archives.

38. Fisher, "Community Organizing and Citizen Participation," 481; "National Gatherings," box 46, Bowman Papers; *New York Times,* April 21, 1916.

39. *New York Times,* April 22, 1916; "The First National Conference on Community

Centers," *National Municipal Review,* July 1916, 496–98; "How Grown-Ups Act in School," *The Survey,* May 6, 1916, 170.

40. Collier, *From Every Zenith,* 83; Collier, "Definitions and Debates," 573; "Proceedings of the National Community Center Conference," 355, box 46, Bowman Papers.

41. Mabel Dodge Luhan, *Movers and Shakers* (1963; reprint, Albuquerque: University of New Mexico Press, 1985), 323.

42. "Report of Mr. Melville, District Representative, The Bureau of Civic and Social Center Development," 2; and "Report from the Secretary of the Lecture Department upon Mr. Ward's Work," 2, both University Extension, University of Wisconsin Archives; Frederick M. Rosentreter, *The Boundaries of the Campus: A History of the University of Wisconsin Extension Division, 1885–1945* (Madison: University of Wisconsin Press, 1957), 56–59.

43. MPF to ELC, July 22, 1917, RCCP.

44. MPF to RCC, Aug. 14, 1923, RCCP; *Dictionary of American Biography* (New York: C. Scribner's Sons, 1958–1964), s.v. William P. Graves. For more on Corey Hill Hospital, see Vogel, *The Invention of the Modern Hospital,* 92–94, 103–04.

45. Cameron, *Kidney Disease,* 78–80, 87–88; William P. Graves, *Gynecology* (Philadelphia: W. B. Saunders, 1916).

46. EB to George W. Coleman, Wed., Rec'd 10/18/16, Correspondence "B," Ford Hall Forum Collection. Further evidence of MPF's recovery is in a letter asking Roosevelt to participate in a community centers conference; see MPF to Theodore Roosevelt, Jan. 9, 1917; Roosevelt to MPF, Jan. 15, 1917, Theodore Roosevelt Papers, Library of Congress.

47. "National Gatherings," box 46, Bowman Papers.

48. "Proceedings of the National Community Center Conference," 343–44, 353–54, 356, box 46, Bowman Papers.

49. Ibid., 362, 371.

50. Ibid., 377–80, 389.

51. Ibid., 390–91.

52. Ibid., 394; Collier, *From Every Zenith,* 83. Collier said that the New York "experience and philosophy" of centers as confederations of groups was "spelled out at book length by Mary Follette [*sic*] of Boston."

53. "Proceedings of the National Community Center Conference," 398–404. Simkhovitch asked the Executive Committee to consult with the National Federation of Settlements, an organization with a plan in place.

54. Ibid., 409; "Brief Outline of Organization Reported for Adoption," *Community Center,* June 1917, 13–14.

55. *Community Center,* June 1917, 22.

56. "Proceedings of the National Community Center Conference," 464, 466.

57. See MPF, *The New State,* 229–31; and *Creative Experience,* 175–76.

58. MPF, "Constructive Conflict," in *Dynamic Administration,* ed. Fox and Urwick, 16.

Chapter 15: The War Years

1. Isobel L. Briggs to Mary Hutcheson Page, Sunday [postmark Feb. 25, 1917], Page Scrapbook, WRC.

2. Pauline Agassiz Shaw to "My dear children," Nov. 30, 1916, box 12, MWPP; administration of Pauline Agassiz Shaw will, Probate Court, Suffolk County, Mass.

3. Follett contributed $1,400 (1917) and $700 (1918), and Briggs gave $400; R. P. Brandish to E. L. Burchard, Feb. 8, 1921, box 46, LeRoy Bowman Papers, Rare Books and Manuscript Library, Columbia University. The $1,400 figure may have included contributions from others in Boston; see E. L. Burchard, "Community Center Support in Defending Democracy and for Social Reconstruction," 6, box 46, Bowman Papers; also MPF to ELC, July 22, 1917, Ella Lyman Cabot Papers, SL.

4. According to Follett, Alice G. Brandeis, ELC, and Arthur Woodworth encouraged her; MPF, *The New State*, 15. Stawell says that *The New State* was written at a time when MPF "had to undergo a severe operation." Perhaps Stawell confused *The New State* with *Creative Experience* (1924), which was completed under the threat of impending surgery. Stawell, "Mary Parker Follett," 41.

5. EB, Memoir of MPF, LFUA.

6. Notes from Elliot M. Fox interview with Eva Whiting White, Oct. 18, 1967, author's files; EB, Addendum to Memoir of MPF, LFUA.

7. Follett was appointed a member of BSC's Advisory Committee on Extended Use along with Lillian Robinson and Clifford Warren, the attorney who would write Follett's will; the next year, Alice G. Brandeis and ELC also were appointed. BSC, *Proceedings*, Dec. 6, 1917, 220; Oct. 21, 1918, 188.

8. Interviews with George D. Follett Jr. (June 16, 1982, Quincy, Mass.) and Nancy Follett Alvord (May 13, 1982, Quincy, Mass.).

9. Keyssar, *Out of Work*, 288.

10. Records of Quincy City Assessor, 1917–1921; Appraisal of the Estate of Elizabeth Follett, Oct. 30, 1933, Probate Court, Norfolk County, Mass. Principal and interest charges accrued against George's portion of his mother's estate.

11. BSC, *Proceedings*, June 26, 1918, 128, 131; Edward L. Burchard to Alice G. Brandeis, undated [July 1918], box 46, Bowman Papers; notes from Fox interview with Eva Whiting White, Oct. 18, 1967.

12. MPF to ELC, July 22, 1917, Ella Lyman Cabot Papers.

13. Mary Hutcheson Page to Fannie Fern Andrews, Jan. 7, 1915, box 15, folder 226; Elizabeth Tilton to Andrews, undated [Jan. 1915], box 31, folder 368, both FFPAP.

14. For the Washington rally, see *The Survey*, Jan. 23, 1915, 433–34; and C. Roland Marchand, *The American Peace Movement and Social Reform, 1898–1918* (Princeton: Princeton University Press, 1972), 186–205.

15. *Boston Globe*, Jan. 15, 1915; *The Survey*, Dec. 5, 1914, 230.

16. "Boston Members" (Massachusetts Branch of the Woman's Peace Party), box 31, folder 368, FFPAP. Elizabeth Glendower Evans, Follett's neighbor, was the party's national organizer; see *The Survey*, Feb. 20, 1915, 549.

17. For the damage done to Addams' reputation, see Davis, *American Heroine*, 212–47; and Mary Louise Degen, *A History of the Woman's Peace Party* (New York: Garland, 1972), 198–202. The Massachusetts branch repeatedly issued statements correcting misinterpretations of its principles; see documents in box 31, folder 368, FFPAP.

18. MPF, *The New State*, 356.

19. Following closely on the sinking of the *Housatonic* and publication of the "Zim-

merman Telegram," eighty-seven Boston social workers sent a supportive telegram to President Wilson; see *The Survey,* March 10, 1917, 659. It is not known whether Follett signed the telegram; names of professional colleagues appearing on the partial published list include Meyer Bloomfield, Jeffrey Brackett, RCC, Ada E. Sheffield, and Robert A. Woods.

20. *Community Center,* June 1917, 8; Burchard, "Community Center Support in Defending Democracy," 6, box 46, Bowman Papers.

21. *Community Center,* Aug. 1917, 10; MPF to ELC, July 22, 1917, Ella Lyman Cabot Papers. The National Community Centers Association opened school centers for Red Cross chapters; *Community Center,* June 1917, 9; and July 1917, 7.

22. For the National Community Centers Association's relationship with Food Administration, see "The National Community Centers Association," 2, box 46, Bowman Papers. For examples of food conservation publicity and local activities, see *Community Center,* July 1917, 4–6, 10–12; July–Aug. 1917, 2, 5–6; Aug. 1917, 10.

23. Gary Dean Best, *The Politics of American Individualism: Herbert Hoover in Transition, 1918–1921* (Westport, Conn.: Greenwood, 1975), 8–10; Burchard, "The Part and Place of the National Community Center Association in War Service through Food Conservation," 2, box 46, Bowman Papers.

24. Fisher incorrectly suggests that all community centers required persons using them to sign the food conservation pledge. He cites a single newspaper article concerning plans for newly established community councils in New York City. See Roger Fisher, *Let the People Decide: Neighborhood Organizing in America* (Boston: Twayne, 1984), 19; "Community Centre as a War Council," *New York Times,* Oct. 13, 1918, sec. 4, 8.

25. Burchard, "The Part and Place of the National Community Center Association in War Service through Food Conservation," 1–3; *Community Center,* July 1917, 10.

26. MPF to ELC, July 22, 1917, Ella Lyman Cabot Papers.

27. *Community Center,* July–Aug. 1917, 46. The council (secretaries of war, the Navy, the interior, agriculture, commerce, and labor) was advised by a commission whose members had special expertise or represented important segments of society.

28. Waldo G. Leland and Newton D. Mereness, *Introduction to the American Official Sources for the Economic and Social History of the World War* (New Haven: Yale University Press, 1926), 317, 319.

29. Ibid., 319–21; Wil A. Linkugel and Kim Giffin, "The Distinguished War Service of Dr. Anna Howard Shaw," *Pennsylvania History,* October 1961, 374–76, 382–83. The National Community Centers Association apparently worked through the state councils rather than the state divisions of the Woman's Committee.

30. E. L. Burchard, "The Reasons Why a Propaganda to Educators Is a Necessary War Measure, Part I," 4; idem, "Ways and Means for a Propaganda to Educators to Enlist Their Support for Community Councils of Defense," 8, both box 46, Bowman Papers.

31. Davis, *Spearheads for Reform,* 227.

32. Burchard, "Community Center Support in Defending Democracy," 1, box 46, Bowman Papers; *New York Times,* March 8, 1918, 4. For information about school centers and the Council of National Defense, see Gleuck, "The Community Use of Schools," 92–101.

33. Wilson, quoted in MPF, *The New State,* 247. For Wilson's support for community

councils, see *New York Times,* July 24, 1918, 13; Aug. 13, 1918, 6; also reprints of letters from Wilson in *The Survey,* Aug. 31, 1918, 605. For the impact of Wilson's support, see E. L. Burchard, "Community Councils and Community Centers," *Proceedings of the National Conference of Social Work* (1918), 470–72.

34. Burchard, "Community Center Support in Defending Democracy," 1, box 46, Bowman Papers.

35. Burchard, "Ways and Means for a Propaganda," 1, ibid.; Burchard, "The Reasons Why a Propaganda to Educators, Part II," 6–7, ibid.

36. Follett's sensitivity to the importance of the masters is evident in all her Boston school center activities.

37. *Community Center,* July–Aug. 1917, 46. The National Education Association did not yet have much political influence. It was seen as an organization that issued bulletins, passed resolutions on proposals such as federal aid for education, and generated basic educational statistics. See Edgar B. Wesley, *NEA: The First Hundred Years* (New York: Harper, 1957), 244–47, 288.

38. Burchard, "The Reasons Why a Propaganda to Educators, Part II," 8, box 46, Bowman Papers. Alice G. Brandeis apparently was instrumental in putting the National Community Centers Association in touch with the National Education Association; Edward L. Burchard to James Ford, May 11, 1919, Correspondence: Com–E, Folder: Community Councils, James Ford Papers, Harvard University Archives.

39. Wesley, *National Education Association,* 377.

40. Follett was to have an active role at the Pittsburgh conference. She was to copreside at a session on "the community councils at the school centers," make opening remarks at the General Assembly of the National Community Center Conference, and preside at a general session on "the varied arms of the community center service"; *Community Center,* March–April, 1919, 19–20. Follett did not attend, probably because of ill health. See Edward L. Burchard to MPF, July 15, 1918, and Burchard to Alice G. Brandeis, [July 1915], both box 46, Bowman Papers.

41. Frederick Lewis Allen, "The Forty-eight Defenders," *Century Illustrated Magazine,* December 1917, 261–66.

42. Follett and Burchard were an exception to the argument that "experts" naively expected to have a significant impact on social and economic policy; see McClymer, *War and Welfare,* 158–75. For the top-down character of the Council of National Defense, see Mattson, *Creating a Democratic Public.*

43. Burchard, "The Reasons Why a Propaganda to Educators, Part II," 11, box 46, Bowman Papers.

44. MPF, *The New State,* 248.

45. Follett mentions writing in a room where the thermometer was at 42 degrees in Feb. 1918; MPF, *The New State,* 124; and Pearson, *Son of New England,* 223.

46. MPF to HAO, April 5 and May 8, 1918, Harry A. Overstreet Papers, Lilly Library, Indiana University; HAO to Elliot M. Fox, Aug. 27, 1967, author's files. For his writing on vocational representation, see Harry A. Overstreet, "The Government of Tomorrow," *The Forum,* July 1915, 6–17.

47. The manuscript was read "in full or in part" by Harvard philosophy professor W. Ernest Hocking and her friend of Thayer Academy days, Harriet French Mixter; MPF, *The New State,* 15.

48. ABH to Roscoe Pound, April 26, 1918, folder 222: 19, Roscoe Pound Papers, Harvard Law School Archives.

49. MPF to Pound, June 21, 1918, Pound Papers; Kramnick and Sheerman, *Harold Laski*, 86–88, 99–100.

50. MPF to Pound, June 28 and July 21, 1918; Secretary to Dean Pound to MPF, July 30, 1918; Pound to MPF, Aug. 14, 1918, Pound Papers. Follett's *New State* contract and related correspondence were lost when the Longmans building was destroyed; Dr. J. A. Edwards to author, Nov. 24, 1983, author's files.

51. MPF, *The New State*, 3.

Chapter 16: The New State

1. MPF to Alice G. Brandeis, Sept. 4, 1918, Louis D. Brandeis Collection, Brandeis University Library.

2. MPF, *The New State*, 5, 8–9.

3. Barber, "Mary Parker Follett as Democratic Hero," xv; Mansbridge, "Mary Parker Follett: Feminist and Negotiator," xxvii.

4. See on this issue Mattson, "Reading Follett: An Introduction to *The New State*," li–lii.

5. McDougall is mentioned by name in Follett's "Introduction," as are the titles of Wallas's books; MPF, *The New State*, 14.

6. Ibid., 12–13, 14; Stawell, "Mary Parker Follett," 41–42. Follett's decision to emphasize the principles underlying the movement meant that much of the discussion of the centers themselves was "pressed into the appendix."

7. Follett herself sensed that there might be some difficulties with the text, warning readers that "a certain amount of repetition has seemed necessary in order to look at the same idea from a number of angles and to make different applications of the same principle"; see *The New State*, 14.

8. Ibid., 3, 9; Horwitz, "John Dewey," in *History of Political Philosophy*, ed. Leo Strauss and Joseph Cropsey, 3d ed. (Chicago: University of Chicago Press, 1987), 860; Laski, *Studies in the Problem of Sovereignty*, 1–25.

9. MPF, *The New State*, 9, 11.

10. Ibid., 22.

11. Ibid., 24.

12. Ibid., 25, 33.

13. Ibid., 26, 28.

14. Ibid., 26–27. For Ross's favorable evaluation of compromise, see *Social Psychology*, 338–45.

15. Kuklick, *The Rise of American Philosophy*, 428. Follett mentions in her "Introduction" that she had consulted Harvard philosopher W. Ernest Hocking, who in 1916 argued that Holt's reasoning was identical to that of Royce and Palmer; see Hocking, "The Holt-Freudian Ethics and the Ethics of Royce," *Philosophical Review* 25 (May 1916): 479–506.

16. MPF, *The New State*, 40.

17. Ibid., 27–30.

18. Ibid., 52, 54–55. Believing that "education above and beyond everything is to teach

[young people] to create life for themselves," Follett echoes Dewey when she says that "education should be largely the training in making choices."

19. Ibid., 55–57.

20. Ibid., 57–58.

21. Ibid., 58–59; Levy, *Herbert Croly of the New Republic*, 125–27.

22. MPF, *The New State*, 33. On this point, see Moscovici, "Social Influence and Conformity," 352.

23. Cooley, *Social Organization*, 151, 149.

24. MPF, *The New State*, 33, 88, 153. For more on Le Bon, see Gordon W. Allport, "The Historical Background of Social Psychology," in *The Handbook of Social Psychology*, ed. Gardner Lindzey and Elliot Aronson, 3d ed. (New York: Random House, 1985), 14, 22–23; Karpf, *American Social Psychology*, 134–43; Barnes, *Introduction to the History of Sociology*, 481–92. Graham Wallas deplored ambiguity in the use of collective terms; see *The Great Society*, 133–34.

25. MPF, *The New State*, 87, 85–86.

26. Ibid., 30–32.

27. Ibid., 91. Social theorists such as Cooley and Wallas thought too much emphasis was being placed on analyzing the crowd, but crowd psychology proved to be a remarkably popular and resilient concept. See Graham Wallas, *Human Nature in Politics* (1908; reprint, Lincoln: University of Nebraska Press, 1962), 76; idem, *The Great Society*, 132–33; Cooley, *Social Organization*, 151–55.

28. Moscovici, "Social Influence and Conformity," 347; Allport, "Historical Background of Social Psychology," 15, 23; Ross, *Social Psychology*, 11–13. For more on Tarde's theory, see Karpf, *American Social Psychology*, 93–95, 101–03; Allport, "Historical Background of Social Psychology," 14; Barnes, *Introduction to the History of Sociology*, 476–78. For more on important aspects of Ross's theory, see Karpf, *American Social Psychology*, 308–18; Thomas Bender, *Community and Social Change in America* (1978; reprint, Baltimore: Johns Hopkins University Press, 1982), 35; Price, "Community and Control," 1664–65; Ross, quoted in Edgar F. Borgatta and Henry J. Meyer, eds., *Social Control and the Foundations of Sociology* (Boston: Beacon, 1959), 179–81; Ross, *Social Psychology*, 57. For more on Giddings' theory, see Franklin H. Giddings, *The Principles of Sociology*, 3d ed. (1896; reprint, New York: Macmillan, 1928), 15–20, 109–14, 150–51; Karpf, *American Social Psychology*, 246–47; Allport, "Historical Background of Social Psychology," 11; Sills, *International Encyclopedia of the Social Sciences*, 6: 176; Franklin H. Giddings, *The Responsible State* (Boston: Houghton Mifflin, 1918), 19–25; idem, *Democracy and Empire* (New York: Macmillan, 1900), 213–14; Harry Elmer Barnes, *Sociology and Political Theory* (New York: Alfred A. Knopf, 1924), 198.

29. Tarde's theory provided the foundation for the work of such American scholars as Boris Sidis, James Mark Baldwin, Charles Horton Cooley, and George Herbert Mead. Ross's *Social Psychology* (1908) "brought to a climax this whole vigorous movement," and Ross became one of the Progressive Era's most influential social theorists. See Wiener, *Between Two Worlds*, 73; Ross, *Social Psychology*, 1–3; Allport, "Historical Background of Social Psychology," 15, 23; Kuklick, *Josiah Royce*, 86–93; Marshall J. Cohen, *Charles Horton Cooley and the Social Self in American Thought* (New York: Garland, 1982), 117–24, 129–30.

30. MPF, *The New State*, 38. In a footnote on 39, Follett offers "a list of words which can be used to describe the genuine social process and a list which gives exactly the wrong idea of it." Follett was not alone in her criticisms; see John Dewey, "The Need for Social Psychology," *Psychological Review* 24 (May 1917): 267–69. Follett thought that books such as McDougall's *Introduction to Social Psychology* (1908) might help people learn to free the channels of "the fundamental instincts of man" so that they "shall not be dammed but flow forth in normal fashion, for normal man is constructive." But she thought McDougall's work had important deficiencies — particularly in its acceptance of imitation as central to social life. See MPF, *The New State*, 14.

31. MPF, *The New State*, 33–34, 29; Giddings, *The Principles of Sociology*, 134.

32. MPF, *The New State*, 29. Follett objects to the idea proposed by Tarde and accepted by Giddings that the social process is an individually based version of a Hegelian logical dialectic.

33. Ibid., 44. These ideas were found in the work of numerous social theorists; see Allport, "Historical Background of Social Psychology," 10–12; Sills, *International Encyclopedia of the Social Sciences*, 15: 441–46.

34. MPF, *The New State*, 44. Follett apparently objects to views espoused in Kropotkin's *Mutual Aid* (1902). Nor does she believe that an "instinct" to help exists and that sympathy is the result of the helping. Instead, "the feeling and the activity are involved one in the other."

35. Ibid., 46–47. It is through the group that "you find the details, the filling-out of Kant's universal law. Kant's categorical imperative is general, is empty; it is only a blank check. But through the group we learn the content of universal law."

36. Ibid., 47, 80; also see Wren, *The Evolution of Management Thought*, 158–59. Some of the kind of confusion to which Follett refers can be found in Croly, *The Promise of American Life*, 417–18.

37. MPF, *The New State*, 82–83.

38. Ibid., 60.

39. Ibid., 19, 34, 75.

40. Cooley, *Social Organization*, 5. There is reason to doubt Mead's influence on Follett. Karpf writes that "Mead's influence . . . has been exerted chiefly by way of the classroom and only secondarily by way of his published writings," which are "fragmentary . . . involved and obscure, hence limited in their appeal." Mead's collected writings, furthermore, were not published until 1934. See Karpf, *American Social Psychology*, 318; Mead, "Social Psychology, Behaviorism, and the Concept of the Gesture," 430.

41. Somjee, *The Political Theory of John Dewey*, 112–13; Kloppenberg, *Uncertain Victory*, 97; Dewey, "The Need for Social Psychology," 267–68. For a discussion of the differences between Follett and Dewey on social mind, see Hoopes, *Community Denied*, 152–53.

42. MPF, *The New State*, 82.

43. Ibid., 77.

44. Ibid., 75–77. For more on Cooley and Dewey, see Charles H. Cooley, *Social Process* (1918; reprint, Carbondale: Southern Illinois University Press, 1966), 26–28; Somjee, *The Political Theory of John Dewey*, 81–82.

45. MPF, *The New State*, 34 n. 1, 37, 38, 41, 39.

46. Ibid., 35.

47. Ibid., 36, 38.

48. Ibid., 95–96. For more on Kropotkin's *Mutual Aid,* see Sills, *International Encyclopedia of the Social Sciences,* 8: 463–65; and Allport, "Historical Background of Social Psychology," 12.

49. MPF, *The New State,* 97.

50. Quandt, *From the Small Town to the Great Community,* 44; MPF, *The New State,* 357, 103.

51. MPF, *The New State,* 97, 63, 97–98.

52. Ibid., 98–100. In *From the Small Town,* Quandt writes (45): " 'The unified . . . community is the bored community,' a social scientist wrote recently. Mary Follett would not have agreed." Follett would indeed have objected, but not because of boredom. For Follett, a true community is never "unified"; it is always becoming.

53. Wiener, *Between Two Worlds,* 81–84; Karpf, *American Social Psychology,* 201–04. For more on Wallas' objections to Tarde and Le Bon, see Terence H. Qualter, *Graham Wallas and the Great Society* (London: Macmillan, 1980), 120.

54. MPF, *The New State,* 8, 73–74. For more on Wallas, see Wallas, *The Great Society,* 137–38; Wiener, *Between Two Worlds,* 150–54.

55. MPF, *The New State,* 106. Follett discusses new forms of association, 105–21.

56. Ibid., 122, 125; Maine, quoted in Sills, *International Encyclopedia of the Social Sciences,* 9: 530.

57. MPF, *The New State,* 126–28, 130–31. Although Follett makes no explicit reference to the writings of Florence Kelley in regard to this notion of the community as the basis of law, she knew of Kelley's work through citations in Pound's *Harvard Law Review* articles.

58. MPF, *The New State,* 48, 137.

59. W. L. Reese, *Dictionary of Philosophy and Religion,* (Atlantic Highlands, N.J.: Humanities, 1980), 380.

60. Sills, *International Encyclopedia of the Social Sciences,* 11: 86; Paul Edwards, ed., *The Encyclopedia of Philosophy,* vol. 6 (New York: Macmillan and Free Press, 1967), 382; Greengarten, *Thomas Hill Green,* 56–61.

61. Follett mentions Green by name in *The New State,* 163, 172, 267.

62. Ibid., 137. A series of U.S. Supreme Court cases (1959–1962) considered whether constitutional rights, especially those guaranteed by the First Amendment, should be interpreted by the courts as "absolute." According to the prevailing view, usually associated with Justice Frankfurter, "there are no absolute rights, even in the First Amendment, and when the interest protected by a constitutional right conflicts with a weightier interest in public safety or public order, the courts must permit infringement of the right." See Joel Feinberg, *Social Philosophy* (Englewood Cliffs, N.J.: Prentice-Hall, 1973), 79–80.

63. MPF, *The New State,* 69.

64. Ibid., 70. This disparaging reference was probably not directed at John Dewey. His idea of "freedom as choice" is considerably more complex and has much in common with Follett's idea of freedom; see Alfonso J. Damico, *Individuality and Community: The Social and Political Thought of John Dewey* (Gainesville: University of Florida Press, 1978), 81–92.

65. MPF, *The New State*, 138, 71. Follett obviously cannot be classified with the many suffragists who based their arguments on traditional liberal political principles. See Alison Jaggar, *Feminist Politics and Human Nature* (Totowa, N.J.: Rowman and Allanheld, 1983), 35–48; Jean Bethke Elshtain, *Meditations on Modern Political Thought: Masculine/Feminine Themes from Luther to Arendt* (New York: Praeger, 1986), 61–68; idem, *Public Man, Private Woman*, 228–39.

66. MPF, *The New State*, 70, 69.

67. Ibid., 71–72.

68. Greengarten, *Thomas Hill Green*, 99–100.

69. Kloppenberg, *Uncertain Victory*, 395–97; see in this regard Follett's comment about Green and Bosanquet in *The New State*, 267.

70. MPF, *The New State*, 138–39; Follett says more on this point in her discussion of pluralism, 266–67.

71. Quandt, *From the Small Town*, 42; Stever, "Mary Parker Follett and the Quest for Pragmatic Administration," 171–75.

72. MPF, *The New State*, 70.

73. Ibid., 139–40. A similar though considerably more detailed critique of the "equal rights" doctrine was put forward in Croly, *The Promise of American Life*, 179–85. For Croly's view of the relationship between justice and individual liberty, see Kloppenberg, *Uncertain Victory*, 400.

74. MPF, *The New State*, 139. Follett's difficulty in finding language to express the dynamic quality of her vision is evident in the phrase "his place in the whole," 65.

75. Ibid., 139. For a modern discussion of human rights and social justice that raise concerns similar to those discussed by Follett (albeit without reference to the group process), see Feinberg, *Social Philosophy*, 93–94, 117–19. For a modern critique of the liberal conception of equality, see Jaggar, *Feminist Politics and Human Nature*, 46–47.

76. MPF, *The New State*, 143–44, 145–46, 147.

77. Ibid., 160.

78. Ibid., 171, 172. Follett offers a brief history of the growth of democracy. She begins with the assertion that historically "a marked increase in the appreciation of social values has gone hand in hand with a growing recognition of the individual." She then cites the individualistic emphasis of the Reformation; the subsequent effort to join these "isolated" individuals through social contract theory; the entrenchment of individual rights in the work of Bentham, Spencer, and Mill; the emergence of a theory of the state in Green's work, which called for "man to get his rights and his liberty from membership in society"; and, finally, state sponsorship of social legislation. Follett reiterates her view that theory and practice react on each other. When she turns her attention to the growth of democracy in America, Follett repeats ideas from her book on the Speakership and then adds her evaluation of "good government" reforms, often finding them seriously flawed; ibid., 164–70.

79. Ibid., 195–97.

80. Ibid., 199–200, 201.

81. Ibid., 208–09, 209–10, 211–12.

82. Ibid., 228.

83. Ibid., 229–30.

84. Ibid., 230–31.

85. Ibid., 232–33.

86. Ibid., 237–38.

87. Ibid., 249, 253.

88. Ibid., 245. Also see E. W. Hawley, *The Great War and the Search for a Modern Order*, 23, 94–5.

89. MPF, *The New State*, 258, 320.

90. Sills, *International Encyclopedia of the Social Sciences*, 12: 164–67. Pluralism took many forms, including industrial democracy, economic federalism, occupational representation, functional corporatism, and guild socialism.

91. MPF, *The New State*, 263, 315. Follett's reference is to Laski's *Studies in the Problem of Sovereignty*, especially 14–17.

92. MPF, *The New State*, 316–17.

93. Ibid., 264, 266. For an illustration of the denial of the collective, see Laski, *Studies in the Problem of Sovereignty*, 10–11.

94. MPF, *The New State*, 266–67. Follett believed that T. H. Green and Bernard Bosanquet "in measure more or less full taught the true Hegelian doctrine." For a typical pluralist interpretation of Hegel, see Laski, *Studies in the Problem of Sovereignty*, 6–7.

95. See William James Ashley, *An Introduction to English Economic History and Theory* (1888) and *The End of the Middle Ages* (1893). Follett took Ashley's "Medieval Economic History of Europe" at Radcliffe in 1895–96. For more on Ashley, see Robert L. Church, "The Economists Study Harvard," in Buck, *Social Sciences at Harvard*, 73–74; Warren J. Samuels, "Ashley's and Taussig's Lectures on the History of Economic Thought at Harvard, 1896–97," *History of Political Economy* 9 (1977): 385–88, 390–91; Anne Ashley, *William James Ashley* (London: P. S. King, 1932), 65–67.

96. Follett says: "This is exactly the tendency we must avoid in any plan for the direct representation of industrial workers in the state"; *The New State*, 267–69. For more on the futility of separating economics and politics, see 261, n. 1.

97. Ibid., 269, 324–25. Certain unexamined assumptions are specified by Kariel; see Sills, *International Encyclopedia of the Social Sciences*, 12: 164–67.

98. MPF, *The New State*, 283–84, 286. Follett provides a lengthy critique of Duguit, whose "so-called 'objective' theory of *le droit*" forms the basis of the guild socialists' idea of sovereignty; see 273–82. Roscoe Pound agreed with Follett that Duguit was inadequate; see Roscoe Pound to MPF, Aug. 14, 1918, Roscoe Pound Papers, Harvard Law School Archives.

99. MPF, *The New State*, 322–23; Croly, *The Promise of American Life*, 169–71.

100. MPF, *The New State*, 306, 322, 307.

101. Ibid., 327. Guild socialism was centered on the sovereignty of workers' guilds, but on some matters agreements would have to involve multiple guilds and other societal groups. Follett's critique seems to have been directed at the system proposed in Cole's *Self-Government in Industry* (1917). For more on early stages of guild socialism, see G. D. H. Cole, *Self-Government in Industry*, 5th ed. (London: G. Bell and Sons, 1920), 1–23, 136–42, 147–48; A. W. Wright, *G. D. H. Cole and Socialist Democracy* (Oxford: Oxford University Press, 1979), 13–101; L. P. Carpenter, *G. D. H. Cole: An Intellectual Biography* (Cambridge: Cambridge University Press, 1973), 46–111; Sills, *International Encyclopedia of the Social Sciences*, 14: 516. Syndicalism, the other major form of plural-

ism, appeared in the United States only among the western Industrial Workers of the World. Follett considers that the "best part of syndicalism is its recognition that every department of our life must be controlled by those who know most about that department, by those who have most to do with that department"; 328.

102. MPF, *The New State,* 308. Follett notes another underlying problem: "it is often assumed that because the occupational group is composed of men of similar interests we shall have agreement in the occupational group. What we must do is to get behind these electoral methods to some fundamental method which shall *produce* agreement"; 309.

103. For Laski's views on federalism, see *Studies in the Problem of Sovereignty,* 267–75. Follett summarizes her view as follows: "(1) Sovereignty, we have seen, is the power generated within the group—dependent on the principle of interpenetration. (2) Man joins many groups—in order to express his multiple nature. These two principles give us federalism"; *The New State,* 296.

104. MPF, *The New State,* 288–89, 291–92.

105. Ibid., 290, 278, 290. Follett recognized that vocational schemes excluded many, including women. She insists that "in any proper system of occupational representation every one should be included—vocational representation should not be trade representation"; 261, n. 1.

106. Ibid., 297, 299.

107. Ibid., 292, 295.

108. Ibid., 303, 302.

109. Kloppenberg, *Uncertain Victory,* 413, 193–94; MPF, *The New State,* 99.

110. Kloppenberg, *Uncertain Victory,* 4.

111. MPF, *The New State,* 286, 333–34, 340. The ordering of relations involved in the morality of the state begins for Follett with her consciousness of the interdependence of family members. See in this connection Jaggar, *Feminist Politics and Human Nature,* 46.

112. MPF, *The New State,* 344–45, 347.

113. Ibid., 353.

114. Ibid., 348.

115. Ibid., 342–43.

116. MPF to Alice G. Brandeis, Sept. 4, 1918, Brandeis Collection; MPF, *The New State,* 6, 23.

117. MPF, *The New State,* 103, 312.

118. Ibid., 190–91.

119. Ibid., 191, 359, 3, 100.

120. Ibid., 337–38, 241–42.

121. Ibid., 360.

122. Ibid., 30, n. 1.

123. MPF to Alice G. Brandeis, Sept. 4, 1918, Brandeis Collection.

Chapter 17: An Integrative Group Process

1. Alexander, "Review of *The New State,*" 579–81.

2. MPF to HAO, Sept. 22, 1919, Harry A. Overstreet Papers, Lilly Library, Indiana University.

3. Bosanquet, "Review of *The New State,*" 370. Bosanquet later called *The New State*

"the most sane and brilliant of recent works on political theory" and acknowledged the "debt which I owe to its author." See Bernard Bosanquet, *The Philosophical Theory of the State,* 3d ed. (London: Macmillan, 1920), xiii, liv–lv, lxii. He claimed that Follett might owe some of her thinking about neighborhood groups to his book (xvii), but Follett's conception grew quite directly from her experience.

4. Tufts, "Review of *The New State,*" 374, 376–77; MPF to HAO, Jan. 31, 1920, with postscript of Feb. 2, 1920, Overstreet Papers; HAO, "Review of *The Problem of Administrative Areas* and *The New State,*" 814; HAO, "Review of *The New State,*" 582, 584.

5. MPF to Alice G. Brandeis, Sept. 4, 1918, Louis D. Brandeis Collection, Brandeis University Library. MPF mentions Toronto, but Laski lectured at McGill in Montreal (1914–1916) before coming to Harvard. See Kramnick and Sheerman, *Harold Laski,* 80, 97.

6. H. J. L. [Harold Laski], "Review of *The New State,*" 61–62; Herbert A. Deane, *The Political Ideas of Harold J. Laski* (New York: Columbia University Press, 1955), 85, 56; MPF, *The New State,* 55, 268, 261.

7. Ford, "Review of *The New State,*" 494–95. An anonymous reviewer for the *Boston Evening Transcript* also took issue with Follett's rhetoric; H. S. K., "Review of *The New State,*" 7. Howard Lee McBain, a Columbia University professor of constitutional law, also disliked Follett's vivid rhetoric but admitted that she "knows her Hegel, her Duguit, her James, her Roscoe Pound, her Harold Laski. She knows her particularism, her syndicalism, her guild socialism, her dualism, her pluralism"; "Review of *The New State,*" 169–70.

8. "Review of *The New State,*" *The Nation,* 96–97.

9. "What Is Democracy?" *Times Literary Supplement,* 353; MPF to HAO, Sept. 22, 1919, Overstreet Papers. A few months later Follett said: "Laski *now* does nothing but flatter me, at least in private, I don't know what he says in public"; MPF to HAO, Jan. 31, 1920, with Feb. 2 postscript, Overstreet Papers.

10. Barnes, *Introduction to the History of Sociology,* 864.

11. Ellwood, "Review of *The New State,*" 97–99.

12. Quandt's interpretation of the significance of the neighborhood group in Follett's work is deficient. First, by ignoring Follett's discussion of pluralism, the possible place of functional groups in political life, and her later discussions of groups in business organizations, Quandt suggests that the neighborhood group played a more central role in Follett's thought than was actually the case; second, by emphasizing the spatial characteristics of the neighborhood group (small, intimate, "face-to-face") rather than the dynamic characteristics (interpenetrating, bringing out, and unifying differences), Quandt does not reflect Follett's sophisticated appreciation of the training and practice required to create groups of genuine value, whether in the neighborhood or elsewhere. See Quandt, *From the Small Town to the Great Community,* 42, 45.

13. Cooley, *Social Organization,* 23–50; MPF, *The New State,* 323–24.

14. Ellwood, "Review of *The New State,*" 98.

15. Barnes, *Introduction to the History of Sociology,* 864–65.

16. Bailey, "'Orange' Journalism," 227, 235; Robert K. Murray, *Red Scare: A Study in National Hysteria, 1919–1920* (1955; reprint, New York: McGraw-Hill, 1964), 177.

17. Dorothy M. Brown, *Setting a Course: American Women in the 1920s* (Boston:

Twayne, 1987), 3, 5; Dallek, "Modernizing the Republic," in Bailyn et al., *The Great Republic,* 701–04.

18. Collier, *From Every Zenith,* 115–19.

19. "Unifying Neighborhoods," *New York Times,* May 9, 1920, sec. 7, 16. For more on the Cincinnati group, see Roger Fisher, *Let the People Decide: Neighborhood Organizing in America* (Boston: Twayne, 1984), 20–27.

20. MPF to Alice G. Brandeis, Sept. 4, 1918, Brandeis Collection; "New Developments," *Community Center,* July–Aug. 1918, 54. A committee that included MPF was appointed to work on this problem.

21. "Community Council in After-War Work," *New York Times,* Jan. 24, 1919, 8; "Community Councils Get Results," *Community Center,* Jan.–March 1919, 63; *New York Times,* Dec. 15, 1918, sec. 2, 5. The War Camp Community Service operated in 600 communities, the Red Cross Home Service section in 10,000. See McClymer, *War and Welfare,* 180–81; "Plan a Health Campaign," *New York Times,* Jan. 31, 1919, 10. Women's groups hoped to turn the work of their state divisions over to permanent local community councils; Emily N. Blair, *The Woman's Committee, United States Council of National Defense: An Interpretive Report* (Washington, D.C.: Government Printing Office, 1920), 136, 140.

22. "National Overhead for Community Centers," *Community Center,* Jan.–March 1919, 64; McClymer, *War and Welfare,* 177–79; Blair, *The Woman's Committee,* 133.

23. "War Funds Discontinued," *New York Times,* Feb. 22, 1919, 3; "Republicans Waver on Big Money Bills," *New York Times,* March 1, 1919, 3; "Congress Ends," *New York Times,* March 5, 1919, 1, 3. Wilson declined to use emergency funds to continue the agencies; McClymer, *War and Welfare,* 177–78; "Employment Work Curtailed," *The Survey,* 1919, 894.

24. Blair, *The Woman's Committee,* 134–35.

25. *Community Center,* July–Sept. 1920, 86; Perry, "The Future of 'The Community Center'" and "Minutes of the Executive Committee," March 2, 1921, both box 46, LeRoy Bowman Papers, Rare Books and Manuscript Library, Columbia University.

26. For cooperating organizations, see letterhead printed July 1, 1920, box 46, Bowman Papers. The National Community Centers Association had had formal committees of cooperation with the National Education Association, the National University Extension Association, the American Red Cross, and the American Country Life Association.

27. ECL, "Community Can Utilize Class Conflict," box 6, Wilbur Phillips Papers, University of Minnesota Social Welfare History Archives. Lindeman made this case again in "Next Steps in Community Center Movement," *Community Center,* Nov.–Dec. 1921, 42. In Oct. 1920 another cooperative meeting was held involving about eighty national social work organizations; *Community Center,* July–Sept. 1920, 86. The U.S. Bureau of Education had tried to coordinate the movement, but many saw these activities as riddled with "institutional selfishness"; Perry, "The Washington Conference," *Community Center,* March–April 1921, 15.

28. *Community Center,* Sept.–Oct. 1922, 81. The secretary was LeRoy Bowman of Columbia University; Edward Burchard of American Red Cross was treasurer. The Executive Committee included ABG, ECL, and James T. Mulroy; see "Officers of the National Community Centers Association, 1922–1923," box 46, Bowman Papers. For

more on the transformation of the National Community Centers Association to a professional association and the demise of the national movement, see Mattson, *Creating a Democratic Public.*

29. *Community Center,* Jan. 1920, 67; "Tentative Plan for Reorganization of the National Community Center Association," Feb. 21, 1920, and "Minutes of Meeting of Executive Committee of Council," Feb. 27, 1920, both box 46, Bowman Papers; also letterhead printed July 1, 1920, ibid.

30. "Minutes of Annual Business Meeting and Election," March 2, 1921, and "Minutes of the Executive Committee," March 2, 1921, both box 46, Bowman Papers. Several of Follett's associates remained active: Alice G. Brandeis was president in 1920–21 and served on the Executive Committee for years; James T. Mulroy was elected to the Executive Committee in 1921–22 and served for years, as did ECL.

31. MPF, "The Teacher Student Relation," in *Dynamic Administration,* ed. Fox and Urwick, 309.

32. ECL, *Social Discovery,* v–vi. See also Stuart I. Rochester, *American Liberal Disillusionment* (University Park: Pennsylvania State University Press, 1977), 88–104; McClymer, *War and Welfare,* 183.

33. *Radcliffe Quarterly,* Sept. 1919, 136–37; Mark, *Delayed by Fire,* 122–23.

34. MPF, *Creative Experience,* 105–07, 165–66. Sheffield makes explicit reference to Follett in "Three Interviews and the Changing Situation," 699.

35. From 1913 to 1920 the Department of Social Ethics had no tenured faculty. President Lowell split the department along two lines: instruction intended to stimulate undergraduates' thinking on ethical problems and professional instruction under the auspices of the Divinity School. For the former, Lowell sought "a man . . . who would, by his personality, attainments and reputation, impress the students to an unusual degree." The man appointed was RCC. See David B. Potts, "Social Ethics at Harvard," in Buck, *Social Sciences at Harvard,* 119–23.

36. Roy Lubove, *The Professional Altruist: The Emergence of Social Work as a Career, 1880–1930* (Cambridge: Harvard University Press, 1965), 23–35.

37. *Radcliffe Quarterly,* March 1920, 63; RCC to Ruth Morgan, Oct. 21 [1921], HUG4255.10, Correspondence Box 10, RCCP; *Radcliffe College Catalogue, 1921–22,* 72; MPF to HAO, Sept. 22, 1919, Overstreet Papers. At Harvard only a few women had been employed in any instructional capacity, and most of them were graduate assistants. See "Instructors' Salary Ledgers, 1896–1943", RA.

38. Lippmann to MPF, Sept. 9, 1919, box 9, folder 403, Walter Lippmann Papers, Manuscripts and Archives, Yale University; MPF, *Creative Experience,* 180. According to Follett, academic friends showed less interest in conducting group studies than did businessmen (some of whom wished to manipulate their workers).

39. Wiener, *Between Two Worlds,* 173–74.

40. MPF to HAO, Sept. 22, 1919, Overstreet Papers. For the sociological context of concern about loss of community, see Thomas Bender, *Community and Social Change in America* (1978; reprint, Baltimore: Johns Hopkins University Press, 1982).

41. Urban, "The Nature of Community," 547–48.

42. MPF to HAO, Sept. 22, Nov. 8, and Oct. 31, 1919, Overstreet Papers.

43. Urban, "The Nature of Community," 551–52, 556; Harold J. Laski, "The Pluralistic State," *Philosophical Review* 28 (November 1919): 565, 568; M. R. Cohen, "Com-

munal Ghosts and Other Perils in Social Philosophy," 687–88; James H. Tufts, "The Community and Economic Groups," *Philosophical Review* 28 (November 1919): 594–97.

44. MPF, "Abstract of 'Community as a Process,'" 715; see Holt's margin note on typescript (17) of "Community as a Process," LFUA.

45. MPF, "Community as a Process," 576; MPF, "Abstract of 'Community as a Process,'" 715.

46. MPF, "Community as a Process," 577–78.

47. Ibid., 582.

48. J. E. Creighton to W. Ernest Hocking, Jan. 2, 1919 (letter copied during author's review of Hocking Papers when they were with the family; not now found in W. Ernest Hocking Papers, Houghton Library, Harvard University); Parkhurst, "The Nineteenth Annual Meeting of the American Philosophical Association," 94–96. On the question of whether she was "an Hegelian," see MPF to HAO, Sept. 22, 1919, Overstreet Papers.

49. Urban, "The Nature of Community," 560; MPF, "The Nature of Community," 2, LFUA.

50. Cohen, "Communal Ghosts," 676–77; MPF, "The Nature of Community," 1, LFUA. Follett's difficulty perceiving the problems some had with her rhetoric is apparent in MPF to Lippmann, Dec. 23, 1919, Lippmann Papers.

51. Cohen, "Communal Ghosts," 677.

52. Ibid., 689–90; MPF, "The Nature of Community," 2, 10–11, LFUA. Parkhurst reported that in the discussion Follett was "unable to give a satisfactory solution in terms of interpenetration of the problem regarding the proper choice of a school by two parents of opposite opinion"; Parkhurst, "The Nineteenth Annual Meeting," 96–97. Follett apparently did not forget this failure; she takes up this problem (162) in *Creative Experience* as well as another question raised at "a philosophical conference" (169).

53. MPF to HAO, Jan. 31, 1920, with postscript of Feb. 2, 1920, Overstreet Papers. In addition to her letter from Haldane, Follett says that "another Englishman asks me to come to England because of so much interest there in my book and perhaps I could help in the general situation!!!!" Longmans issued a new printing of *The New State* in Jan. 1920 and reprinted it another three times before 1926; see *National Union Catalog*, 176: 664.

54. Stephen E. Koss, *Lord Haldane: Scapegoat for Liberalism* (New York: Columbia University Press, 1969), 214–15. For Haldane's involvement in postwar education matters, see Eric Ashby and Mary Anderson, *Portrait of Haldane* (Hamden, Conn.: Archon, 1974), 150–54, 173–74.

55. Ashby and Anderson, *Portrait of Haldane,* 165; for Haldane and adult education, see ibid., 110, 129–30, 154–57, 163–68.

56. Ibid., 157; Haldane, "Introduction," in MPF, *The New State* (1920), xiv.

57. MPF to HAO, Jan. 31, 1920, with Feb. 2 postscript, Overstreet Papers; *New York Times,* July 22, 1943.

58. Haldane, "Introduction," vi–xiii, xix–xx, xxv.

59. MPF to HAO, Jan. 31, 1920, with Feb. 2 postscript, Overstreet Papers.

60. Susan Ware, *Partner and I: Molly Dewson, Feminism, and New Deal Politics* (New Haven: Yale University Press, 1987), 44–47; Commonwealth of Massachusetts, *Acts and Resolves of 1912,* chap. 706, 780.

61. Ethel M. Johnson, "Fifteen Years of Minimum Wage," 1476, Ethel McLean John-

son Papers, SL; Commonwealth of Mass., *Acts and Resolves of 1912,* chap. 706, 781; Patterson, "Mary Dewson and the American Minimum Wage Movement," 142–43.

62. MPF, "Community as a Process," 586; "Stenographic Typescript of the Hearing of . . . Confectionery Wage Board," Sept. 24, 1921, 5–8, author's files.

63. Commonwealth of Massachusetts, *Acts and Resolves of 1912,* chap. 706, 781; *Acts and Resolves of 1919,* 83–84; *General Laws of 1921,* chap. 262, sec. 25, 2683; MPF to Alice G. Brandeis, June 9, 1927, IV.150, Brandeis Collection. MPF knew the chairman of the first wage board, Robert G. Valentine, an early management consultant and the husband of Sophie French Valentine, MPF's girlhood friend. Valentine died in 1916. In Aug. 1921, when MPF was appointed to her second wage board, Sophie Valentine's sister (Harriet Mixter) and MPF were among "authorized candidates" for public representatives; see "Minutes of the Minimum Wage Commission," Aug. 23, 1921, Massachusetts Department of Labor and Industries, Boston; and Elliot M. Fox, "Minimum Wage Boards, Massachusetts, 1920–21," author's files–Fox.

64. *Report of the Division of Minimum Wage,* 1920, 17.

65. Fox, "Minimum Wage Boards, Massachusetts, 1920–21," 1–2.

66. *Report of the Division of Minimum Wage,* 1921, 11–12.

67. Fox, "Minimum Wage Boards, Massachusetts, 1920–21," 2.

68. MPF, *Creative Experience,* 13.

69. Ibid., 166–67.

70. Ibid., 15.

71. Fox, "Minimum Wage Boards, Massachusetts, 1920–21," 2.

72. MPF, *Creative Experience,* 57. Fox summarizes Follett's comments at the June 1 meeting; see Fox, "Minimum Wage Boards, Massachusetts, 1920–21," 2.

73. *Report of the Division of Minimum Wage,* 1921, 11–12. For details on Follett's participation, see Fox, "Minimum Wage Boards, Massachusetts, 1920–21."

74. *Report of the Division of Minimum Wage,* 1921, 11–12. Follett's remarks at a Sept. 24 hearing before the Minimum Wage Commission suggest a continually changing situation; see "Stenographic Typescript of the Hearing . . . of Confectionery Wage Board," Sept. 24, 1921, 5–8, author's files. For compliance data, see "Enforcement of Minimum Wage Decrees in Massachusetts, 1921," Massachusetts State Archives, Boston.

75. Evans resigned from the Brush Wage Board, and Follett was appointed in her stead on Dec. 14, 1921; Fox, "Minimum Wage Boards, Massachusetts, 1920–21," 3.

76. MPF, *Creative Experience,* 14.

77. Ibid., 209–10.

78. Ibid., 233–34.

79. *Report of the Division of Minimum Wage,* 1922, 5, 9; 1923, 3.

Chapter 18: "Too Good a Joke for the World"

1. MPF to ECL, Jan. 11, 1923, ECLP.

2. ECL, "Community Can Utilize Class Conflict," box 6, Wilbur Phillips Papers, University of Minnesota Social Welfare History Archives; "Minutes of Annual Business Meeting and Election," March 2, 1921, and "Minutes of the Executive Committee," March 2, 1921, both box 46, LeRoy Bowman Papers, Rare Books and Manuscript Library, Columbia University.

3. Stewart, *Adult Learning in America,* 15–19.

4. Ibid., 30–40.

5. Ibid., 33.

6. Ibid., 39. One of Lindeman's daughters argues persuasively against Stewart's interpretation of these controversies; Betty L. Leonard to author, Oct. 13 and Nov. 3, 1990, author's files.

7. Leonard, *Friendly Rebel,* 35.

8. Follett refers to the North Carolina trip in MPF to ECL, Jan. 5 and Jan. 25, 1923, ECLP. ECL's article, "Steps in the Process of Community Action," *Community Center,* April–May 1921, 1–2, may have introduced MPF to his book.

9. ECL, *The Community,* 173–76.

10. Ibid., 134–35; typescript of "Lecture by Professor Lindeman" in Social Ethics 29, April 7, 1922; Corresp. 1907–1922, Folder: 1922, James Ford Papers, Harvard University Archives. Lindeman saw greater virtue in "compromise" than did Follett; see ECL, *The Community,* 135–37.

11. ECL, *The Community,* 136.

12. Stewart, *Adult Learning,* 33–35.

13. MPF to ECL, Dec. 19, 1922, ECLP. Follett apparently visited ECL a month after his Harvard lecture.

14. Konopka, *Eduard C. Lindeman and Social Work Philosophy,* 32. Konopka's account of the beginning of the Follett-Lindeman partnership agrees with Follett's; see MPF to ECL, Jan. 5, 1923, ECLP. In a 1934 testimonial written after Follett's death, ECL offered a revision, saying that Herbert Croly brought them together; ECL, "Mary Parker Follett," 86. Lindeman had come to revere Croly as a "father figure"; see Stewart, *Adult Learning,* 42; Betty Lindeman Leonard to author, May 15 and Aug. 1, 1982, and Nov. 3, 1990, author's files; ECL to Dorothy Straight Elmhirst, May 18, 1930, Betty Lindeman Leonard Papers, University of Minnesota Social Welfare History Archives (hereafter BLLP).

15. Levy, *Herbert Croly of the New Republic,* 206–07; Young, *The Elmhirsts,* 41,56.

16. MPF, *Creative Experience,* xix. For Follett's view of Croly, see MPF to Lippmann, Dec. 23, 1919, Walter Lippmann Papers, Manuscripts and Archives, Yale University; MPF to HAO, Jan. 6, 1924, Harry A. Overstreet Papers, Lilly Library, Indiana University.

17. Levy, *Herbert Croly,* 244–51, 264–70.

18. Ibid., 270–71; Peter M. Rutkoff and William B. Scott, *New School: A History of the New School for Social Research* (New York: Free Press, 1986), 21–23, 27–31.

19. MPF to ECL, Dec. 19, 1922, ECLP. Follett discussed the proposed collaboration with HAO and then arranged a meeting with Croly, most likely through HAO.

20. Dorothy Whitney Straight, "Calendar," Aug. 26, 1921, Dorothy Whitney Straight Elmhirst Papers, Dartington Hall Trust, Totnes, Devon (hereafter Elmhirst Papers); Dorothy Whitney Straight to Leonard Elmhirst, Aug. 27, 1921, reel 1, Dorothy Whitney Straight Elmhirst Papers, Cornell University Libraries (hereafter DSEP).

21. Young, *The Elmhirsts,* 72; Dorothy Whitney Straight to Leonard Elmhirst, Oct. 3, 1921, reel 1, DSEP.

22. Young, *The Elmhirsts,* 45, 55, 73; Straight to Elmhirst, Sept. 19, 1921, and April 15, 1922, reel 1, DSEP; see newspaper articles on reel 13, DSEP.

23. Straight to Elmhirst, Sept. 27, 1921, reel 1, DSEP.

24. Dorothy Whitney Straight, quoted in Young, *The Elmhirsts,* 74.

25. Konopka, *Eduard C. Lindeman,* 32; see also ECL to Dorothy Whitney Straight, July 19, 1922, General Corresp. 7, Elmhirst Papers. Straight would give Lindeman an additional year of $250 a month for half-time plus expenses; see HC to Straight, June 23, 1924, reel 15, no. 3725, DSEP; and Stewart, *Adult Learning,* 48–49, 63.

26. MPF to ECL, April 25, 1923, ECLP.

27. ECL, *Social Discovery,* vi; ECL to Dorothy Whitney Straight, July 19, 1922.

28. *Harvard College Class Books,* Class of 1896, "25th Annual Report" (1921), 518, and "50th Annual Report" (1946), 368–69; *Who Was Who,* 4: 854; "Alfred D. Sheffield," *Wellesley Magazine,* June 1940, 381–84, Wellesley College Archives; Alfred D. Sheffield, *Joining in Public Discussion* (New York: George H. Doran, 1922), ix–xv.

29. MPF to ECL, Dec. 29, 1922, ECLP.

30. ECL to Charles Shaw, quoted in Betty Lindeman Leonard to author, May 15, 1982, author's files; ECL, "Mary Parker Follett," 86–87.

31. MPF gave a draft of her work to HAO and was appalled when he later presented important elements of it as his own; see MPF to ECL, Dec. 19, 1922, ECLP; HAO, "Reason and the 'Fight Image,'" 94–95.

32. MPF to [ECL], undated [mid-1922?] and Dec. 19, 1922, ECLP; Levy, *Herbert Croly,* 199. An Oct. 1922 meeting is mentioned in MPF to ECL, Sept. 25, 1923, ECLP.

33. ECL to MPF, Dec. 10, 1922; MPF to ECL, Dec. 19, 1922, ECLP.

34. MPF to ECL, Dec. 19 and 29, 1922, both ECLP.

35. MPF to ECL, Jan. 5 and 6, 1923, ECLP.

36. Straight, "Calendar," Dec. 6, 1922, Elmhirst Papers.

37. Janet G. Woititz, *Adult Children of Alcoholics* (Pompano Beach, Fla.: Health Communications, 1983), 41, 44.

38. ECL's daughter says Lindeman lived with Baldwin from 1928 to 1935; Betty Lindeman Leonard to author, Oct. 13, 1990, author's files. For more on the Baldwin period, see Leonard, *Friendly Rebel,* 3–4, 51–53, 87–89.

39. Stewart, *Adult Learning,* 59–61. Also see Leonard, *Friendly Rebel,* 51, 92–93.

40. Dorothy Whitney Straight to ECL, Sept. 15 [1927], ECLP.

41. MPF to ECL, Sunday, 3 P.M. [Jan. 7, 1923], ECLP.

42. MPF to ECL, Jan. 11, 1923, ECLP.

43. MPF to Hazel Lindeman, Jan. 20, 1923; MPF to ECL, Jan. 22, 1923, both ECLP; Straight, "Calendar," Jan. 19, 1923, Elmhirst Papers.

44. ECL to Carl [Charles Shaw], undated [Jan. or early Feb. 1923?], BLLP.

45. MPF to ECL, Jan. 24, 1923, ECLP.

46. Alfred D. Sheffield to ECL, Dec. 31, 1923, ECLP. ECL expressed reservations, saying in Jan. it might be better to publish in a single large volume; by April he had changed his mind. Follett did not seem unduly perturbed by his vacillations; MPF to ECL, April 4 and 6, 1923, ECLP.

47. HAO may have spoken to Dorothy Whitney Straight on Follett's behalf; Straight, "Calendar," Feb. 13, 1923, Elmhirst Papers.

48. MPF to ECL, April 4, 1923, ECLP.

49. Ibid. A good illustration of their working style is in MPF to ECL, April 6, 1923; and ECL to MPF, Monday morning [April 9, 1923], both ECLP.

50. ECL to MPF, Monday morning [April 9, 1923], ECLP.

51. MPF to ECL, April 4, 1923, ECLP.

52. MPF to ECL, April 22, 1923; MPF to Hazel Lindeman, April 22, 1923, both ECLP.

53. MPF to ECL, April 25, 1923, ECLP.

54. MPF to ECL, May 5, 1923, ECLP.

55. RCC, "Medical History and Record of Mary Parker Follett, 1910–1933," RCCP.

56. *National Cyclopaedia of American Biography,* 46: 98–99; 28: 31.

57. RCC, "Medical History and Record of Follett"; MPF to RCC, Aug. 14, 1923, RCCP.

58. William R. Fair, "Urologic Emergencies," in *Cancer: Principle and Practices of Oncology,* ed.Vincent T. Devita Jr., Samuel Hellman, and Steven A. Rosenberg, 2d ed. (Philadelphia: J. Lippincott, 1985), 1894–95; Cameron, *Kidney Disease,* 78–80, 87–88; W. F. Braasch, "Clinical Data on Malignant Renal Tumors," *Journal of the American Medical Association,* Jan. 25, 1913, 274–78; Creevy, "Confusing Clinical Manifestations of Malignant Renal Neoplasms," 895–96, 913–14.

59. MPF to RCC, Aug. 14, 1923, RCCP.

60. Isobel L. Briggs to Alfred D. Sheffield, July 28, 1923, ECLP.

61. RCC, "Medical History and Record of Follett."

62. Isobel L. Briggs to Sheffield, July 28, 1923, ECLP.

63. James, *Notable American Women,* 1: 617–19.

64. Freeman, *The Story of Unity,* 126, 130.

65. Ibid., 194–95.

66. Ibid., 104–05.

67. Braden, *Spirits in Rebellion,* 260.

68. Ibid., 239.

69. Freeman, *The Story of Unity,* 173.

70. MPF to RCC, Aug. 14, 1923, RCCP.

71. Braden, *Spirits in Rebellion,* 45–46; 401–04. RCC was involved with the Emmanuel Movement from the beginning; see John Gardner Greene, "The Emmanuel Movement: 1906–1929," *New England Quarterly,* September 1934, 501–02, 512–13, 519–20.

72. Gottschalk, *The Emergence of Christian Science in American Religious Life,* 100, 119.

73. Ibid., 122–24; Braden, *Spirits in Rebellion,* 18–19; Parker, *Mind Cure in New England,* 4–5; Freeman, *The Story of Unity,* 190–93.

74. RCC, "Medical History and Record of Follett."

75. MPF to RCC, Aug. 14, 1923, RCCP.

76. Follett indicated in her Aug. 14 letter that she had not received a letter that Richard mentioned having sent—perhaps RCC to MPF, July 8, 1923, RCCP. Receiving no reply, RCC wrote again, this time to Isobel L. Briggs; this letter has not survived; see ELC to MPF, Aug. 26 [1923], Ella Lyman Cabot Papers, SL.

77. Alfred D. Sheffield to ECL, June 22 [1923], box 2, Sheffield Folder, ECLP; Lindeman replied in ECL to Sheffield, June 28, 1923, ibid.

78. Isobel L. Briggs to ECL, June 30 [1923], ECLP.

79. Isobel L. Briggs to ECL, Aug. 27 [1923], ECLP; for further evidence of the fondness between ECL and Briggs, see MPF to ECL, Dec. 2, 1923; Briggs to ECL, Christmas Day [1923]; MPF to ECL, Feb. 5, 1924; MPF to ECL, Jan. 17, 1925, all ECLP. For more on Follett's suffering in early Aug., see Briggs to ECL, Aug. 13, 1923, ECLP; and RCC, "Medical History and Record of Follett."

80. Stewart, *Adult Learning*, 50.

81. MPF to ECL, Sept. 25, 1923, ECLP.

82. Ibid. Lawrence J. Henderson (1878–1942), a Harvard professor of biological chemistry, had published two books: *The Fitness of the Environment* (1913) and *The Order of Nature* (1917).

83. MPF to ECL, Nov. 7, 1923, ECLP; Roscoe Pound to MPF, Nov. 12, 1923, Roscoe Pound Papers, Harvard Law School Archives.

84. MPF to ECL, Nov. 19 and Dec. 24, 1923, ECLP.

85. RCC, "Medical History and Record of Follett"; MPF to ECL, Dec. 2, 1923, ECLP.

86. Vogel, *The Invention of the Modern Hospital*, 106–15.

87. Cameron, *Kidney Disease*, 22–23; Dr. H. H. Crabtree, "Report of Cystoscopy," and Dr. G. W. Holmes, "Examination of the Genito-urinary Tract," in RCC, "Medical History and Record of Follett."

88. Cameron, *Kidney Disease*, 22–23; McGrew, *Encyclopedia of Medical History*, 304–05.

89. MPF to ECL, Dec. 24, 1923, ECLP.

90. MPF to ECL, Dec. 12, 1923, ECLP.

91. MPF to ECL, Dec. 24, 1923, ECLP.

92. MPF to ECL, Xmas Day [1923], ECLP.

93. MPF to Dorothy Whitney Straight, Sept. 25, 1923, ECLP.

94. MPF to ECL, Dec. 12, 1923, ECLP.

95. See, for example, Alfred D. Sheffield to ECL, Dec. 27, 1923, box 2, Sheffield Folder, ECLP.

96. Isobel L. Briggs to ECL, Christmas Day [1923], ECLP. Follett also made a plea; MPF to ECL, Xmas Day [1923], ibid.

97. One of ECL's biographers believes that ECL was in love with Dorothy Whitney Straight; Stewart, *Adult Learning*, 69, 75–76. Lindeman's daughter sees Straight as an important "mother figure" for Lindeman; letters to the author, Aug. 1, 1982, and Oct. 13, 1990. See also Leonard, *Friendly Rebel*, 56, 80–81.

98. Young, *The Elmhirsts*, 41, 74–75, 197.

99. Ibid., 61.

100. Ibid., 76, 81, 84–85, 94.

101. ECL to Dorothy Whitney Straight, Aug. 9, 1924, BLLP.

102. ECL to Dorothy Straight Elmhirst and Leonard Elmhirst, April 9, 1925, BLLP; for more on ECL's perception of Dorothy Whitney Straight's feelings for him and ECL's jealousy, see Wyatt [Rawson] to ECL, July 1927, box 2, Elmhirst Folder, ECLP.

103. Dorothy Whitney Straight to ECL, Sept. 23 [1923], ECLP.

104. ECL to Straight, Dec. 14, 1923, BLLP; Straight, "Calendar," Sept. 26, 1923, Elmhirst Papers; Young, *The Elmhirsts*, 87.

105. ECL to Straight, undated [around Christmas 1923], BLLP. ECL apparently had a number of relationships with women, particularly in the 1920s and early 1930s; Leonard, *Friendly Rebel,* 3–4, 51–52. See also Wyatt [Rawson] to ECL, July 1927, box 2, Elmhirst Folder, ECLP.

106. Dorothy Whitney Straight to Leonard Elmhirst, Oct. 24, 1921, reel 1, DSEP. One aspect of this continuing struggle is discussed in Straight to Elmhirst, Aug. 9, 1924, reel 2, DSEP.

107. Dorothy Whitney Straight to ECL, Christmas night [1923], ECLP.

108. ECL to Carl [Charles Shaw], undated [Jan. or early Feb. 1923?], BLLP.

109. MPF to ECL, Dec. 24, 1923, ECLP.

110. Alfred D. Sheffield to ECL, Dec. 27, 1923, box 2, Sheffield Folder, ECLP.

111. Sheffield to ECL, Dec. 29, 1923, ibid.

112. Sheffield to ECL, Dec. 31, 1923, ibid. Stewart says that Follett was unfairly concerned that Lindeman would co-opt her ideas, but this concern seems reasonable, given ECL's impulsive decision to leave the venture and HAO's unauthorized publication of MPF's "evolving situation" idea; *Adult Learning,* 147.

113. MPF to HAO, Jan. 6, 1924, Overstreet Papers; see also Sheffield to ECL, Feb. 5, 1924, box 2, Sheffield Folder, ECLP.

114. MPF to ECL, Feb. 5, 1924, ECLP.

115. MPF to RCC and ELC, Feb. 4, 1924, RCCP.

116. KF, Memoir of MPF, LFUA.

117. MPF to RCC and ELC, Feb. 10, 1924, RCCP.

118. Daniel F. Jones to RCC, Feb. 12, 1924, appended to RCC, "Medical History and Record of Follett."

119. MPF to RCC and ELC, Feb. 10, 1924, RCCP.

120. MPF to ECL, Wednesday night, Feb. 13 [1924], ECLP.

121. MPF to ECL, Feb. 14, 1924, ECLP.

122. Ibid.

123. MPF to ECL, Feb. 14 [24?], 1924, ECLP; MPF to RCC and ELC, March 1, 1924, RCCP.

124. MPF to ECL, Feb. 26 and March 10, 1924; ECL to MPF, March 3, 1924, all ECLP.

125. MPF to ECL, March 7 and Feb. 21, 1924, ECLP.

126. MPF to ECL, Feb. 26 and March 7, 1924, ECLP. She cautions him that definitions are "not ultimates but working tools" and suggests that his conception of "interest" is out-of-date.

127. ECL to MPF, March 3, 1924, ECLP; MPF to ECL, March 17, 1924, ECLP; ECL to MPF, March 31, 1924, ECLP.

128. MPF to ECL, Feb. 14 [24?], 1924, ECLP. Finding ECL's contention hard to believe, Follett consulted with Croly's wife and found that she agreed with ECL.

129. MPF to ECL, Nov. 7, 1923, ECLP.

130. MPF to Dorothy Whitney Straight, Sept. 25, 1923, ECLP. Early in 1923, before his feelings for Straight blossomed, ECL himself was having trouble getting paid and was not at all protective of Straight; MPF to ECL, April 25, 1923, ECLP.

131. ECL to MPF, March 6, 1924, ECLP.

132. MPF to ECL, March 10, 1924, ECLP.

133. MPF to ECL, March 10, 1924, ECLP.

134. MPF to ECL, March 7, 1924, ECLP.

135. Stewart, *Adult Learning,* 225; Konopka, *Eduard C. Lindeman,* 11–13. Lindeman's biographers mention only one review of *Social Discovery;* see Stewart, *Adult Learning,* 88.

136. ECL, "Mary Parker Follett," 86–87.

Chapter 19: Creative Experience

1. HAO, "Review of *Creative Experience,*" 498.

2. Those using the power-over, power-with distinction include Dorothy Emmett, the first woman president of the British Aristotelian Society, and Hannah Arendt; Mansbridge, "Mary Parker Follet: Feminist and Negotiator," xviii–xxii.

3. The seminal work on "the expert" in the Progressive Era is Robert H. Wiebe, *The Search for Order: 1877–1920* (New York: Hill and Wang, 1967); a bibliography on "reforming professionals" is available in Link and McCormick, *Progressivism,* 135–37. Also see Kloppenberg, *Uncertain Victory,* 383–94; and Westbrook, *John Dewey and American Democracy,* 300–18.

4. MPF, *Creative Experience,* 29–30.

5. Ibid., 6–7.

6. Ibid., 8–9,11,13,15–16.

7. Ibid., 10, 16–17, 21, 27.

8. Ibid., 5.

9. Ibid., 5–6, 28.

10. Ibid., 29–30; Walter Lippmann, *Public Opinion* (New York: Harcourt, Brace, 1922), 250–51.

11. MPF, *Creative Experience,* 31.

12. Ibid., 52.

13. Ibid., 47, 49–50.

14. MPF to Roscoe Pound, March 8, 1924, box 63, folder 19, Roscoe Pound Papers, Harvard Law School Archives.

15. MPF, *Creative Experience,* 46–47, 49–50; also see MPF to Pound, Feb. 14 and 19, 1924, box 63, folder19, Pound Papers.

16. MPF, *Creative Experience,* 53.

17. John Dewey, "The Need for a Recovery of Philosophy," in Stuhr, *Classical American Philosophy,* 339.

18. MPF to ECL, April 4, 1923, ECLP; see also MPF, *Creative Experience,* 230. For the way Henry used the term, see Robert D. Meade, *Patrick Henry* (Philadelphia: J. B. Lippincott, 1969), 32–35.

19. MPF, *Creative Experience,* x.

20. Ibid., xi–xii.

21. Ibid., xiv.

22. Woodworth and Sheehan, *Contemporary Schools of Psychology,* 38–42, 112–13, 117, 127–28; Marx and Cronan-Hillix, *Systems and Theories in Psychology,* 145, 155–

57. Watson's first book brought him sufficient renown that in 1915 he was elected president of the American Psychological Association.

23. Marx and Cronan-Hillix, *Systems and Theories,* 189–90.

24. Sills, *International Encyclopedia of the Social Sciences,* 8: 436.

25. William James, quoted in Marx and Cronan-Hillix, *Systems and Theories,* 195.

26. Michael Wertheimer, *A Brief History of Psychology,* rev. ed. (New York: Holt, Rinehart and Winston, 1979), 136–37.

27. Marx and Cronan-Hillix, *Systems and Theories,* 205.

28. MPF, *Creative Experience,* xvii; see also MPF to RCC and ELC, Feb. 10, 1924, RCCP. Follett's decision to focus on experience also risked criticism from those in the newly emerging field of social psychology. Despite her understanding that one must be careful of "substituting for observation of social relations facile and interesting analogies from psychological studies of the individual," much of the research she relied on was derived from studies of individuals.

29. Marx and Cronan-Hillix, *Systems and Theories,* 168. Follett referred to Holt's *The Concept of Consciousness* (completed in 1908 but not published until 1914); "The Place of Illusory Experience in a Realistic World," in Edwin W. Holt et al., *The New Realism* (New York: Macmillan, 1912); and *The Freudian Wish and Its Place in Ethics* (1915). Follett also made use of Holt's 1917 lectures, using students' notes (54, n. 1). By 1919 Follett and Holt were acquainted; see his margin notes on the draft of her *Philosophical Review* article, LFUA.

30. Holt, "Response and Cognition," 368–69; Kuklick, *The Rise of American Philosophy,* 424–27; Woodworth and Sheehan, *Contemporary Schools,* 129–30. Holt's position with regard to purpose was further developed by Edward C. Tolman (1886–1961), who became an important cognitive theorist; see Woodworth and Sheehan, 133–41, 214.

31. Holt, *The Freudian Wish,* 55. American functionalists were concerned with understanding how both behavior and mental activities (conscious and unconscious alike) are used by the organism in adapting to the demands of its environment. Functionalism developed into a school with the work of the University of Chicago psychologists John Dewey (1859–1952) and James Angell (1869–1949). See Woodworth and Sheehan, *Contemporary Schools,* 28–31; Merle Curti, *Human Nature in American Thought* (Madison: University of Wisconsin Press, 1980), 202–03; Marx and Cronan-Hillix, *Systems and Theories,* 107, 115–17, 127, 131–34.

32. Holt, *The Freudian Wish,* 96–97.

33. Ibid., 99.

34. Ibid., 56–57, 60; Kuklick, *The Rise of American Philosophy,* 427.

35. Holt, *The Freudian Wish,* 122, 128–29.

36. Holt, "Response and Cognition," 370, 372.

37. Follett wrote that "Holt goes on calling himself a realist and does not quite like my making his psychology prove idealism"; MPF to Haldane, March 10, 1924, RBHP.

38. MPF, *Creative Experience,* 58–59, 61–63. Follett draws her understanding of circular response from Holt's writings and the research of the Dutch physiologist S. T. Bok. She does not mention Dewey's classic paper "The Reflex Arc Concept in Psychology" (1896).

39. MPF, *Creative Experience,* 73.

40. Ibid., 61. It also changes our notion of stimulus and response and of subject and object; 60.

41. Ibid., 68–69.

42. Ibid., 64; for other comments on calculus, see 63–64, 67–68, 72.

43. Ibid., 69.

44. Ibid., 74–75.

45. Associationists, such as Columbia psychologist Edward Thorndike (1874–1949), focused on the postulate that complex ideas of consciousness emerge from the "linking" or "building up" of simpler ideas known directly by the senses. See Woodworth and Sheehan, *Contemporary Schools,* 59; Marx and Cronan-Hillix, *Systems and Theories,* 40.

46. Holt, quoted in MPF, *Creative Experience,* 78–79, n. 2; MPF, *Creative Experience,* 78–79. See Follett's comments (89) on this phenomenon in modern theater.

47. Ibid., 67.

48. Ibid., 89.

49. Ibid., 81.

50. Ibid., 82–83. The notion that knowledge is an activity, "a process which involves knower and known but which never looks from the windows of either," is apparent, Follett notes (88–89), in the work of modern playwrights.

51. Ibid., 84, 86.

52. Ibid., 75.

53. Ibid., 117–19.

54. Ibid., 119–120.

55. Ibid., 153–54.

56. Ibid., 121–22, 124, 128. Some writers, Follett notes (126), "write of individual and environment as if the individual were always man, and the environment were always 'nature,' whatever than may mean." But the work of Le Dantec, the biological sociologist, shows that "we decide which is the individual and that then all the rest is environment."

57. Ibid., 137.

58. Ibid., 138–39.

59. Ibid., 133–34.

60. Ibid., 141. Follett credits (152) Lippmann for seeing that "concepts should rest on facts."

61. Rom Harré and Paul F. Secord, *The Explanation of Social Behaviour* (Oxford: Blackwell, 1972), 36, 54.

62. MPF to Haldane, July 24, 1926, RBHP. Follett registers another complaint about Dewey in MPF, "The Psychology of Control," 162–63.

63. For a recent work examining differences between Follett and Dewey, see Hoopes, *Community Denied,* 152–53, 156–57. For some relevant works on Dewey, see Ross, *The Origins of American Social Science,* 162–71; Kloppenberg, *Uncertain Victory,* 86–87, 131–34, 139–44, 344–48, 358–59, 376–78, 383–94; Westbrook, *John Dewey and American Democracy;* Alan Ryan, *John Dewey and the High Tide of American Liberalism* (New York: W. W. Norton, 1995), 228–36; John J. Stuhr, "John Dewey," in Stuhr, *Classical American Philosophy,* 328.

64. A clue as to one source of irritation about Dewey's thought appears in RCC to MPF, [1926?], RCCP.

65. MPF, *Creative Experience,* 173–74.

66. Ibid., 164.

67. Ibid., 156–57.

68. Ibid., 164.

69. Ibid., 164.

70. Ibid., 163.

71. Ibid., 163.

72. Ibid., 176.

73. Ibid., 150–51.

74. Ibid., 177–78.

75. Ibid., 165.

76. Ibid., 167–68.

77. Ibid., 168–69.

78. Ibid., 166–67.

79. Ibid., 171.

80. Ibid., 172.

81. Ibid., 179.

82. Ibid., 180.

83. Ibid., 189.

84. Ibid., 190–91.

85. Ibid., 184–85: also see Roger Fisher and William Ury, *Getting to Yes: Negotiating Agreement without Giving In* (New York: Penguin, 1983), 41.

86. MPF, *Creative Experience,* 189.

87. Ibid., 187–88.

88. Ibid., 198–99.

89. Ibid., 198.

90. Ibid., 209.

91. Ibid., 211, 230, 216.

92. Ibid., 229. Much was being learned about the relation of the expert to democracy from the Cincinnati Social Unit and the southern cooperative movement; see 212–13.

93. Ibid., 212–13.

94. Ibid., 217.

95. Ibid., 300–01.

96. Ibid., 301–02.

97. Ibid., 303.

98. Ibid., 303.

99. In addition to the reviews discussed here, one has not been located; MPF refers to Keyserling's review in a letter to William E. Mosher, April 14, 1926, William E. Mosher Papers, Syracuse University Archives.

100. Tufts, "Review of *Creative Experience*," 190.

101. Shepard, "Review of *Creative Experience*," 618.

102. Ellwood, "Review of *Creative Experience*," 223–24.

103. Bruère, "Partners in Creation," 102. Jane Addams also comments favorably on

Creative Experience, especially the process of integration; *The Second Twenty Years at Hull-House* (New York: Macmillan, 1930), 202–03.

104. A. E. Wood, "The Social Philosophy of Mary P. Follett," 764, 768.

105. Smith, "Review of *Creative Experience*," 540–42.

106. Calkins, "Review of *Creative Experience*," 510; Virginia Onderdonk, "Mary Whiton Calkins," in James, *Notable American Women,* 1: 278–79; Laurel Furumoto, "Mary Whiton Calkins (1863–1930): Fourteenth President of the American Psychological Association," *Journal of the History of the Behavioral Sciences* 15 (1979): 353–54.

107. MPF, *Creative Experience,* 92, n. 1.

108. Allport, "Review of *Creative Experience*," 427, 426.

109. Ibid.

110. Ibid., 428.

111. Ibid.

112. MPF to Laski, April 17, 1924, Harold D. Laski Papers, Department of Special Collections, Syracuse University Library.

113. Stawell, "Mary Parker Follett," 43.

114. MPF, "Some Methods of Executive Efficiency," 75.

Chapter 20: Professional Transition, Personal Tragedy

1. MPF to RCC and ELC, July 28, 1924, RCCP. Follett discusses a "spiritual exercise" in a letter to W. Ernest Hocking, April 19, 1924, W. Ernest Hocking Papers, Houghton Library, Harvard University.

2. MPF to RCC and ELC, July 28, 1924, RCCP.

3. Alfred D. Sheffield to ECL, Sept. 6, 1924, box 2, Sheffield Folder, ECLP.

4. Interview with Elizabeth Dennison Dunker, June 28, 1982, Cambridge, Mass.; Helen Dennison Blustin to author, July 1, 1982, both in author's files.

5. Interview with Elizabeth Dennison Dunker; Helen Dennison Blustin to author, July 1, 1982; Dennison, *Henry S. Dennison,* 9–13; McQuaid, "Henry S. Dennison and the 'Science' of Industrial Reform," 80.

6. Wren, *The Evolution of Management Thought,* 176–77; Dennison, *Henry S. Dennison,* 14–16; McQuaid, "Henry S. Dennison," 82, 86–87; Dennison, "Practical Applications of Scientific Principles to Business Management: The Economist," 275–76. The stock was issued without voting powers at the request of the committee, whose members preferred to participate through the works committee.

7. John A. Garvey to Elliot M. Fox, Oct. 1, 1967, author's files; partially quoted in Fox, "The Dynamics of Constructive Change," 161. Another Dennison manager recalls Follett visiting the firm in the late 1920s; John W. Riegel to Elliot M. Fox, April 30 and Sept. 27, 1967, author's files.

8. *The Vocation Bureau, 1909,* box 87, series IIBii, folder 1, North Bennett Street Industrial School Papers, SL. While Metcalf was on the Executive Committee, Follett was on the Advisory Committee.

9. Wren, *The Evolution,* 162; see also William E. Mosher to James Pass, Jan. 16, 1926, box 66, William E. Mosher Papers, Syracuse University Archives; Henry C. Metcalf and Lyndall Urwick, "Introduction," in *Dynamic Administration,* ed. Metcalf and Urwick, 26.

10. *Who Was Who,* 2: 57; *National Cyclopaedia of American Biography,* 45: 222–23.

11. Brochure of the Bureau of Personnel Administration Conference, "Scientific Foundations of Business Administration"; Metcalf to William E. Mosher, Oct. 8, 1924, both in box 1 of the National Institute of Public Administration papers, Metcalf 1921–23, William E. Mosher Papers, Syracuse University Archives.

12. Metcalf, *Scientific Foundations of Business Administration,* 11.

13. For more on scientific management, see Merkle, *Management and Ideology;* Nelson, *Frederick W. Taylor and the Rise of Scientific Management;* Wren, *The Evolution;* Montgomery, *The Fall of the House of Labor;* Harry Braverman, *Labor and Monopoly Capital* (New York: Monthly Review, 1974).

14. Issues of the *Bulletin of the Taylor Society,* which Follett apparently read, carried some surveys of the success of scientific management; see the Feb. and April issues, 1924.

15. Taylor, quoted in Montgomery, *The Fall of the House of Labor,* 251.

16. Wren, *The Evolution,* 106–07; Nelson, *Frederick W. Taylor,* 26, 34–35, 85.

17. Merkle, *Management and Ideology,* 59.

18. Montgomery, *The Fall of the House of Labor,* 246–47.

19. Wren, *The Evolution,* 127.

20. Taylor, quoted in ibid., 128.

21. Merkle, *Management and Ideology,* 15. Montgomery reaches similar conclusions in *The Fall of the House of Labor,* 252–54.

22. See Person, "The Opportunities and Obligations of the Taylor Society," 3–4, and "What Is the Taylor Society?" 225. For the status of scientific management in 1928, see Person, "Scientific Management."

23. Person, "The Manager, the Workman, and the Social Scientist" (Feb. 1917), 2.

24. Metcalf, in Person, "The Manager" (Dec. 1917), 1; Frankfurter, in ibid., 6.

25. MPF, "The Psychological Foundations: Business as an Integrative Unity," 162, 168; Person, "What Is the Taylor Society?" 228.

26. MPF, "The Psychological Foundations: Business as an Integrative Unity," 156, 158.

27. MPF, "The Psychological Foundations: Constructive Conflict," 114; Montgomery, *The Fall of the House of Labor,* 332, 407.

28. MPF, "The Psychological Foundations: Constructive Conflict," 114.

29. MPF, "The Psychological Foundations: Constructive Conflict," 125–27.

30. Ibid., 127–31.

31. MPF, "The Psychological Foundations: The Giving of Orders," 138.

32. Ibid., 139–40.

33. Ibid., 145–46.

34. Wren, *The Evolution,* 176–77.

35. MPF, "The Psychological Foundations: Business as an Integrative Unity," 151.

36. Ibid., 150.

37. Ibid., 152.

38. Ibid., 152, 158; Follett reiterates (153–54) the basic elements of the integrative method.

39. Ibid., 157.

40. Ibid., 156, 161–62. The Dennison paper was "Who Can Hire Management?"

41. MPF, "The Psychological Foundations: Business as an Integrative Unity," 162–63.

42. Ibid., 165.

43. Ibid., 159, 166; Follett discusses (166–67, 169) the wide array of business relations deserving study.

44. Ibid., 170.

45. Roethlisberger and Dickson, quoted in Montgomery, *The Fall of the House of Labor,* 216. A similar argument is made in Braverman, *Labor and Monopoly Capital,* 135–37.

46. MPF, "The Psychological Foundations: Power," 187.

47. Taylor, quoted in Wren, *The Evolution,* 128; MPF, "The Psychological Foundations: Power," 187–88.

48. MPF, "The Psychological Foundations: Power," 189.

49. Ibid., 174–75. Follett's definitions of power, control, and authority are explicitly used in Arnold S. Tannenbaum, *Social Psychology of Organizations* (Belmont, Calif.: Wadsworth, 1966), 85, n. 1, and are similar to those used in Jeffrey Pfeffer, *Managing with Power* (Boston: Harvard Business School Press, 1992), 30, 130.

50. MPF, "The Psychological Foundations: Power," 183. For a modern explication of this idea, see Whetten and Cameron, *Developing Management Skills,* 380.

51. MPF, "The Psychological Foundations: Power," 179–80. Follett believed (177) that much of applied psychology had power-over as its aim.

52. Ibid., 180.

53. Ibid., 189.

54. Henry S. Dennison, "Practical Applications of Scientific Principles to Business Management: Psychologist and Industrial Engineer," in Metcalf, *Scientific Foundations,* 279.

55. Dennison, "Practical Applications of Scientific Principles: The Economist," 274. For more on Carver, see Buck, *Social Sciences at Harvard,* 79–80.

56. Inventory and appraisal of assets of the estate of MPF, Probate Court, Suffolk County, Boston, June 10, 1936.

57. Leonard, *Friendly Rebel,* 60–62, 68. Lindeman was devastated by the news of Dorothy Whitney Straight's marriage to Leonard Elmhirst.

58. MPF to ECL, Jan. 17, 1925, ECLP. On Mrs. Follett's health, see MPF to RCC, July 18, 1929, RCCP. At the time of her death in June 1933 after a "long illness," Elizabeth Follett's home was valued at $9,600; she left bonds, stocks, and mortgages worth $24,000. See *Quincy Directory,* 1924, 1926; obituary in *Quincy Patriot Ledger,* June 30, 1933; estate of Elizabeth C. Follett, Probate Court, Norfolk County, Dedham, Mass., Nov. 23, 1936.

59. MPF to ECL, Jan. 30, 1925, ECLP.

60. William E. Mosher, "School of Citizenship and Public Affairs," *Alumni News of Syracuse University,* Nov. 1925, 8–9, Mosher Papers; Dr. Frederick C. Mosher, "The Maxwell School: Some Recollections and Reflections," enclosed with Dwight Waldo to Elliot M. Fox, Aug. 12, 1968, author's files; Mosher to Roscoe Pound, Feb. 16, 1925, box 66, P Misc 1924–26, Mosher Papers.

61. Metcalf to Mosher, Jan. 5, 1925, Mosher Papers.

62. MPF to Mosher, Jan. 17, 1925; Mosher to MPF, Jan. 20, 1925, ibid.

63. Mosher to MPF, Jan. 28, 1925; MPF to Mosher, Feb. 4, 1925, ibid.

64. *National Cyclopaedia of American Biography,* 28: 31; H. F. Hartweel to Dr. Jones, April 2, 1925, in RCC, "Medical History and Record of Mary Parker Follett, 1910–1933," RCCP; Cameron, *Kidney Disease,* 87–88; Anderson, *Mosby's Medical Dictionary,* 1349. There is no evidence that the surgeons looked beyond the kidney for metastases.

65. A 1913 Mayo Clinic study reported postnephrectomy survival rates of 27 percent for three years and 10 percent for five years; a 1935 study of hypernephroma detailed common metastases; W. F. Braasch, "Clinical Data on Malignant Renal Tumors," *Journal of the American Medical Association,* Jan. 25, 1913, 278; Creevy, "Confusing Clinical Manifestations of Malignant Renal Neoplasms," 895–97.

66. RCC had a deeply held commitment to truthtelling with his patients; see RCC, "The Use of Truth and Falsehood in Medicine," in *Richard Cabot on Practice, Training, and the Doctor-Patient Relationship,* ed. John Stoeckle and Lawrence A. May (Oceanside, N.Y.: Dabor Science, 1977), 249–52, 262–63.

67. MPF to ELC, April 29, 1925, RCCP.

68. Alfred D. Sheffield to ECL, April 28, 1925, box 2, Sheffield Folder, ECLP.

69. MPF to RCC, May 16, 1925, RCCP. The spark for some of this energy came from a letter she had just received from Elliott Dunlap Smith, a Harvard Law School graduate who was working as a division manager at Dennison Manufacturing.

70. Metcalf, "Introduction," in *Business Management as a Profession,* 3.

71. For this unflattering portrayal of businessmen, see MPF, "How Must Business Management Develop in Order to Possess the Essentials of a Profession?" 75–76; and MPF, "How Must Business Management Develop in Order to Become a Profession?" 99–100.

72. MPF, "How Must Business Management Develop in Order to Possess the Essentials of a Profession?" 73.

73. MPF, "How Must Business Management Develop in Order to Become a Profession?" 89–90.

74. Ibid., 90–91, 94–95.

75. Ibid., 97–98.

76. Urwick, "The Problem of Organization: A Study of the Work of Mary Parker Follett," 166. Urwick served as director of the International Management Institute in Geneva (1928–1933) and later as chairman of Urwick, Orr and Partners, Ltd.

77. William E. Mosher to MPF, Oct. 6, 1925; MPF to Mosher, Oct. 10, 1925; Mosher to MPF, Dec. 4, 1925; MPF to Mosher, Jan. 28, 1926, all Mosher Papers.

78. *Who Was Who,* 7: 23. Isobel L. Briggs's death was caused by breast cancer and cancer of the spine; "Copy of Record of Death for Isobel L. Briggs," Division of Vital Statistics, Commonwealth of Massachusetts.

79. RCC to MPF, undated [Dec. 1925?], RCCP.

80. MPF to Eva W. White, Dec. 23, 1926, Eva Whiting White Papers, SL.

81. ELC to MPF, Dec. 29 [1925], Ella Lyman Cabot Papers, SL.

82. ELC to MPF, undated [Jan. 11, 1926?], ibid.

83. According to Isobel L. Briggs's birth certificate, she was born Nov. 22, 1848; General Register Office, London. Therefore, her death certificate incorrectly gives her age as 75 rather than 77.

84. MPF to HAO, Jan. 28, 1926, Harry A. Overstreet Papers, Lilly Library, Indiana University.

85. MPF to ELC and RCC, Jan. 28, 1926, RCCP.

86. MPF to William E. Mosher, Jan. 28, 1926, Mosher Papers; MPF to HAO, Jan. 28, 1926, Overstreet Papers.

87. MPF to ELC and RCC, Feb. 25, 1926, RCCP.

88. MPF to ELC and RCC, April 3, 1926, RCCP.

Chapter 21: "Extraordinarily Helpful to Executives"

1. MPF, "The Meaning of Responsibility in Business Management," 318.

2. Ibid., 319.

3. Ibid.

4. Ibid., 320–21.

5. Ibid., 321–22.

6. Ibid., 327.

7. Ibid., 324.

8. Ibid., 330–31.

9. MPF, "How Is the Employee Representation Movement Remolding the Accepted Type of Business Manager?" 343; for her discussion of the utility of employee representation plans, see 339–44.

10. Ibid., 345–46.

11. Ibid., 348.

12. Ibid., 352–53. For more on empowerment, see Whetten and Cameron, *Developing Management Skills*, 379–81.

13. MPF, "What Type of Central Administrative Leadership Is Essential to Business Management as Defined in this Course?" 355.

14. Ibid., 356.

15. Ibid., 359.

16. Ibid., 360.

17. Ibid., 362.

18. Ibid., 364.

19. Ibid., 364.

20. Ibid., 363–64. Follett does not cite her reference to Mayo, but she probably read "The Basis of Industrial Psychology."

21. MPF, "What Type of Central Administrative Leadership?" 365.

22. William E. Mosher to MPF, April 13 and May 11, 1926; MPF to Mosher, April 14, 1926, all William E. Mosher Papers, Syracuse University Archives.

23. RCC to MPF, June 14 [1926], RCCP.

24. "Special Summer Session in the Social Sciences for Secondary School Teachers," Bulletin of Syracuse University School of Citizenship, Maxwell School, General Information, box 1, Bulletins 1922–36, Syracuse University Archives.

25. MPF, "The Essential Unity of the Social Sciences," 1, transcription of lecture and an informal discussion, box 94: 1926 Summer Session Integration Seminar, Mosher Papers.

26. Ibid., 2.

27. William E. Mosher to MPF, July 7, 1926, Mosher Papers. Another lecture on ways that teachers might use the experiences of their students in classroom instruction, "The Place of Student Experiences in Educational Progress," has not been found. There is a reference to it in *Syracuse Post-Standard,* July 2, 1926, 7.

28. MPF, "The Essential Unity of the Social Sciences," 8. Follett also sent an outline of a problem-solving process to one of the Syracuse faculty; see MPF, "Twelve Steps," enclosure with William E. Mosher to MPF, July 7, 1926, Mosher Papers.

29. RCC, "Social Ethics 20a — Oct. 4, 1926," box 62, RCCP.

30. RCC to MPF, June 14 [1926] and July 9 [1926], RCCP.

31. "Register of Roll," Newnham College, 8, 98; Sybil Oldfield, *Spinsters of This Parish,* 33, 297. Stawell had lectured in classics at Newnham for more than a decade and published numerous books and articles.

32. A. J. P. Taylor, *English History, 1914–1945* (New York: Oxford University Press, 1965), 208–10.

33. Ibid., 213, 238–44; James Hinton, *Labour and Socialism: A History of the British Labour Movement, 1867–1974* (Amherst: University of Massachusetts Press, 1983), 131–40.

34. MPF to Lord Haldane, March 10, 1924, RBHP.

35. MPF to Lord Haldane, July 24, 1926, RBHP.

36. Anne Crawford et al., *The Europa Biographical Dictionary of British Women* (London: Europa, 1983), 184; MPF to Elizabeth Sanderson Haldane, Dec. 30, 1926, RBHP.

37. Ibid.; MPF to RCC, Sept. 16, 1926, RCCP; Briggs, *Social Thought and Social Action,* 4.

38. Fox, "The Dynamics of Constructive Change," 164–65.

39. Briggs, *Social Thought and Social Action,* 100–01, 234, 237, 239.

40. Ibid., 175, 167.

41. Ibid., 168, 170, 178.

42. MPF to RCC, Sept. 16, 1926, RCCP. John Lee (1867–1928) spoke at the fall 1926 Rowntree Oxford Conference. Lord Alfred Emmott (1858–1926) was one of the leading men of the Lancashire cotton industry. Sir Arthur Steel-Maitland (1876–1935) became minister of labor in 1924 and was in office during the 1926 General Strike.

43. MPF to Elizabeth Sanderson Haldane, July 24, 1926; MPF, "Social Ethics Seminary, Monday, Dec. 20th, 1926," 15, box 62, RCCP.

44. Briggs, *Social Thought and Social Action,* 231. In a noteworthy industrial experiment, Rowntree established a Psychological Department at his company in 1922; see Briggs, 235; Charles Myers, "The Late Lord Haldane," *Occupational Psychology* 4 (October 1928): 191–92. Elizabeth Sanderson Haldane also was associated with the institute, having arranged for financial support as one of the trustees of the Carnegie United Kingdom Trust.

45. MPF, "The Basis of Control in Business Management," 239, 241.

46. MPF to Elizabeth Sanderson Haldane, Dec. 30, 1926, RBHP.

47. Briggs, *Social Thought and Social Action,* 268.

48. Ibid., 270. Briggs reports conference attendance for each year. He says that there were no conferences in 1926, but Follett's correspondence indicates that there was a fall

conference in 1926. In addition, there are dated printed copies of the papers given at Balliol, LFUA. The master at Balliol was Arthur Lionel Smith; see John Jones, *Balliol College* (Oxford: Oxford University Press, 1988), 259.

49. Lyndall Urwick to Avrum I. Cohen, Aug. 5, 1970, in Cohen, "Mary Parker Follett," 177–78. Urwick gave a somewhat less polished account of this meeting in LFU, "Notes for a 'Talk' on Mary Parker Follett at the University of N.S.W. [New South Wales]," a, author's files.

50. LFU to Avrum I. Cohen, Aug. 5, 1970, in Cohen, "Mary Parker Follett," 179.

51. The lectures included those on the giving of orders, leadership, and business management as a profession.

52. MPF, "Some Methods of Executive Efficiency," 75.

53. MPF, "The Illusion of Final Responsibility," 28–30.

54. Stawell, "Mary Parker Follett," 43.

55. MPF to RCC, Sept. 16, 1926, RCCP.

56. Robert L. Church, "The Economists Study Society," in Buck, *Social Sciences at Harvard,* 89–90; David B. Potts, "Social Ethics at Harvard, 1881–1931," ibid., 123.

57. RCC to MPF, Friday [Oct. 22, 1926], RCCP.

58. Ephraim Emerton, "History," in Morison, *The Development of Harvard University,* 170, 177.

59. Frank W. Taussig, "Economics," in ibid., 191–92; Church, "The Economists Study Society," 79–81, 89–90.

60. ABH, "Government," in ibid., 184–85.

61. RCC, "Social Ethics 20a, Oct. 4, 1926," box 62, RCCP.

62. George C. Homans, "L. J. Henderson," in Sills, *International Encyclopedia of the Social Sciences,* 6: 350–51; Homans, *Coming to My Senses,* 104–05; Trahair, *The Humanist Temper,* 197–204, 213; Wren, *The Evolution of Management Thought,* 241; RCC to MPF, July 9 [1926], RCCP. Follett refers to Mayo's use of the "total situation" concept in a May 1926 Bureau of Personnel Administration (BPA) lecture; see MPF, "What Type of Central Administrative Leadership?" 364.

63. RCC to MPF, Friday [Oct. 22, 1926], RCCP.

64. RCC to MPF, Friday [last week in Oct. 1926], RCCP.

65. MPF to ECL, Sept. 25, 1923, ECLP.

66. Homans, *Coming to My Senses,* 90.

67. MPF to ELC, Nov. 28, 1926, Ella Lyman Cabot Papers, SL.

68. "Comment," *Bulletin of the Taylor Society* 11 (Dec. 1926): 241.

69. "Discussion," ibid., 250–51.

70. MPF, "Social Ethics Seminary, Monday, Dec. 20th, 1926," 1, box 62, RCCP.

71. Ibid., 7; Mayo, "The Basis of Industrial Psychology," 1.

72. MPF, "Social Ethics Seminary, Dec. 20th, 1926," 7–9.

73. Ibid., 10–12, 14.

74. Ibid., 20–21.

75. Lawrence J. Henderson, typescript of discussion in ibid., a–b.

76. Elton Mayo, typescript of discussion in ibid., f–g.

77. Elton Mayo and MPF, typescript of discussion in ibid., h.

78. Harold D. Lasswell, typescript of discussion in ibid., j.

79. Lawrence J. Henderson, Alfred N. Whitehead, and MPF, typescript of discussion in ibid., l.

80. MPF to Eva Whiting White, Dec. 23, 1926, Eva Whiting White Papers, SL; MPF to ELC, Dec. 22, 1926, Ella Lyman Cabot Papers.

81. MPF to Elizabeth Sanderson Haldane, Dec. 30, 1926, RBHP.

82. MPF, "Social Ethics Seminary, Monday, January 3, 1927," 7, box 62, RCCP.

83. Ibid., c, h–i, m–n.

84. In 1930 Pitrim Sorokin was brought to Harvard from the University of Minnesota as professor of sociology and chairman of the combined concentration; a promoter of sociology as a distinct social science with its own methods and functions, Sorokin convinced the administration to eliminate the Department of Social Ethics and include its courses in a new Department of Sociology. See Potts, "Social Ethics at Harvard, 1881–1931," 120–24; James Ford, "Social Ethics," in Morison, *The Development of Harvard University*, 227–28. Neither of the historical accounts of the 1926–27 Social Ethics 20a seminar mentions Follett's contributions to its conceptualization and implementation.

85. *Who Was Who*, 2: 597; 3: 76. The opening lecture was given by Henry S. Dennison, the concluding lecture by HAO. Other presenters were Elton Mayo, with whom Follett had just interacted at the Follett-Cabot Seminary at Harvard; Harlow S. Person, managing director of the Taylor Society; Dr. Clarence S. Yoakum, professor of psychology, University of Michigan; Dr. Walter V. Bingham, head of the Personnel Research Federation (a group that encouraged scientific research on personnel problems and published a personnel journal); and John A. Garvey, employment manager at Dennison Manufacturing Company. References to Bingham may be found in Trahair, *The Humanist Temper*, 237. Mayo makes no reference to Follett or her work in his two Bureau of Personnel Administration lectures.

86. Follett thought "The Psychology of Control" a "very poor title"; MPF to William E. Mosher, Nov. 26, 1927, Mosher Papers. RCC sought unsuccessfully to get MPF to change her list of principles to "understanding, evoking, integrating of purpose, and improving of purpose"; RCC, "Social Ethics Seminary, Monday, February 7, 1927," 1, box 62, RCCP. But Follett continued to use her original terminology in the March BPA lecture. She first mentions "evoking" in *Creative Experience* (303); uses the terms *reciprocal interacting, unifying,* and *emerging* in her Syracuse speech; and uses these terms in various forms, along with *integrating,* in her BPA lectures.

87. MPF, "The Psychology of Consent and Participation," 183.

88. MPF, "The Psychology of Control," 178–79. The manuscript of this lecture includes an initialed margin note in Follett's handwriting that says "title not chosen by me"; LFUA.

89. Ibid., 173.

90. MPF, "The Psychology of Consent and Participation," 183.

91. Ibid., 186.

92. Ibid., 193.

93. Ibid., 194–95.

94. Ibid., 196.

95. Ibid., 196–97, 200.

96. Ibid., 202.

97. MPF, "The Psychology of Conciliation and Arbitration," 209.

98. Ibid., 213–14.

99. MPF, "Leader and Expert," 220–24.

100. Ibid., 229.

101. Ibid., 229–30.

102. Ibid., 236. She explicitly sets aside the chief executive's policymaking role as too large a task for this lecture.

103. Ibid., 233–34.

104. Ibid., 234–36. For reference to Rowntree's address to his workers, see MPF, "Some Discrepancies in Leadership Theory and Practice," 252.

105. MPF, "Leader and Expert," 236–37.

106. Ibid., 240–41.

107. Ibid., 243.

108. EB, Addendum to Memoir of MPF, LFUA.

109. MPF to Alice G. Brandeis, June 9, 1927, IV.150, Louis D. Brandeis Collection, Brandeis University Library.

110. RCC to MPF, Aug. 3, 1927; RCC and ELC to MPF, Monday [Aug. 8, 1927?], RCCP.

111. Elaine Dixon (Curator, Putney Historical Society) to author, March 30, 1985.

112. Wren, *The Evolution,* 153–55. Morris Llewellyn Cooke to MPF, June 22, 1927, box 101, Morris Llewellyn Cooke Papers, Franklin D. Roosevelt Library, Hyde Park, N.Y.; MPF to Alice G. Brandeis, June 9, 1927, IV.150, Brandeis Collection. Neither the group addressed nor the topic of the lecture has been determined.

113. MPF to William E. Mosher, April 2, 1928, Mosher Papers.

114. Mosher to MPF, Dec. 10, 1927, and April 4, 1928; MPF to Mosher, April 2, 1928, all Mosher Papers.

115. MPF to Alice G. Brandeis, March 22, 1928, IV.151, Brandeis Collection.

116. Those who had papers in this edited collection were William E. Mosher, dean of the School of Citizenship and Public Affairs; William R. Gray, dean of the Tuck School of Administration and Finance, Dartmouth; C. S. Yoakum, dean of Northwestern University; Walter V. Bingham, director, Personnel Research Federation; Morris Llewellyn Cooke, president, Taylor Society; Harlow S. Person, managing director, Taylor Society; Henry C. Metcalf, director, BPA; Charles R. Mann, director, American Council on Education; Ordway Tead, editor, Harper Brothers; Robert B. Wolf, president, Pulp Bleaching Corporation; Otto S. Beyer, consulting engineer; Elliott Dunlap Smith, professor, Department of Industrial Engineering, Yale University; HAO, professor of philosophy, City College of New York; Thomas V. Smith, professor of philosophy, University of Chicago; Harrison S. Elliott, professor of practical theology, Union Theological Seminary; W. S. Cowley, assistant professor of psychology, Ohio State University; Alfred D. Sheffield, associate professor of rhetoric and composition, Wellesley College; and four others.

117. MPF, "Some Discrepancies in Leadership Theory and Practice," 206, 208.

118. Ibid., 211–12, 210.

119. Ibid., 213.

120. Ibid., 215.

121. Ibid., 218.

122. Ibid., 220, 223, 221.

123. Ibid., 224–26. The H. G. Wells novel quoted was *Meanwhile;* MPF, "Leadership," in *Proceedings of the Twenty-seventh Lecture Conference,* 23.

124. MPF, "Some Discrepancies in Leadership Theory and Practice," 226. Elsewhere Follett says: "Woodrow Wilson's ideal of world unity was, I believe, directly in harmony with the spirit of twentieth-century development. Nevertheless he failed because he could not make America see this"; MPF, "The Teacher-Student Relation," 307.

125. MPF, "Some Discrepancies in Leadership Theory and Practice," 228.

126. MPF to William E. Mosher, April 21, 1928; Mosher to MPF, May 5 and May 9, 1928, all Mosher Papers. Because of Follett's ill health, this paper was not presented.

127. MPF, "The Teacher-Student Relation," 303.

128. Ibid., 304–05, 308.

129. Ibid., 312–14.

130. Ibid., 315–16.

131. Ibid., 322–23.

132. Ibid., 324–25.

133. MPF, "The Psychiatrist in Industry," 294, 297–98, 302. The content of this paper suggests that it was written during the same period as Follett's papers on leadership. The intended audience is unknown.

134. Morris Llewellyn Cooke to MPF, May 5, 1928, May 3, 1929, and March 12, 1930; MPF to Cooke, Feb. 19, 1930, all box 101, Cooke Papers.

135. MPF, "The Opportunities for Leadership for the Nurse in Industry," 292. For more on the nurses' association and the places in which this paper was published, see Fox, "The Dynamics of Constructive Change," 166.

136. Link and Catton, *American Epoch,* 352–53.

137. MPF to William E. Mosher, April 21, 1928, Mosher Papers.

138. Stawell, "Mary Parker Follett," 43–44.

Chapter 22: "Almost at the Same Moment Happy and Unhappy"

1. MPF to LB, July 26, 1928, V.33, Louis D. Brandeis Collection, Brandeis University Library.

2. ELC to MPF, Aug. 4 [1928], Ella Lyman Cabot Papers, SL.

3. "The International Management Institute," 1, box 21, folder 3, Roscoe Pound Papers, Harvard Law School Archives; Dennison, *Henry S. Dennison,* 17.

4. Follett offers several examples of functional leadership; see MPF, "Leadership," 22–23.

5. MPF to LeRoy Bowman, July 26, 1928, V.33, Brandeis Collection.

6. MPF to Elizabeth Sanderson Haldane, Sept. 10, 1928, RBHP.

7. MPF, "Leadership," 21.

8. E. W. Hawley, *Herbert Hoover as Secretary of Commerce,* 11.

9. Burner, *Herbert Hoover,* 152–53. Jane Addams voted for Hoover in 1928 and 1932. She approved "his stand for collective bargaining, his ingenious plan of farm cooperatives, his 'war' against poverty, his relief work, his promise to enforce prohibition without federal gunmen"; ibid., 207.

10. Richard Norton Smith, *An Uncommon Man: The Triumph of Herbert Hoover* (New York: Simon and Schuster, 1984), 98; Bailyn et al., *The Great Republic,* 709. Dennison agreed to serve as a member of Hoover's successful Unemployment Commission of 1921 as well as the 1928 Committee on Recent Economic Changes; see Burner, *Herbert Hoover,* 164–66; McQuaid, "Henry S. Dennison and the 'Science' of Industrial Reform," 87.

11. Burner, *Herbert Hoover,* 160.

12. Melvyn Leffler, quoted in Hawley, *Hoover as Secretary of Commerce,* 10.

13. William E. Mosher to MPF, Nov. 28, 1928, and Jan. 2, 1929; Marian Hamlin to Mosher, Dec. 27, 1928, all William E. Mosher Papers, Syracuse University Archives.

14. RCC to MPF, July 8, 1929, RCCP; Anderson, *Mosby's Medical Dictionary,* 735.

15. MPF to Morris Llewellyn Cooke, Jan. 25, 1929, Morris Llewellyn Cooke Papers, Franklin D. Roosevelt Library, Hyde Park, N.Y.

16. MPF to ELC, Feb. 7, 1929, Ella Lyman Cabot Papers; RCC to MPF, July 8, 1929, RCCP.

17. MPF to ELC, Feb. 25, 1929, Ella Lyman Cabot Papers.

18. Ibid.; MPF to RCC and ELC, May 12, 1929, RCCP. It was announced in a brochure for the Bureau of Personnel Administration that Follett would give a lecture on March 21, 1929, on "Freedom" as a part of the series "Fundamental Objectives of Business Management"; she did not deliver this lecture. See Bureau of Personnel Administration (BPA), "Brochure — Seventh Series: Oct. 25, 1928 to April 18, 1929," box 8, folder 16, Pound Papers.

19. KF, Memoir of MPF, LFUA; "Dame Rachel Crowdy," in *The Dictionary of National Biography, 1961–70,* ed. E. T. Williams and C. S. Nicholls (Oxford: Oxford University Press, 1981), 250–51.

20. Notes of interview with Cicely (Polly) Furse, May 20, 1984, Smarden, Kent. For Katharine's long-standing interest in psychology, see KF, *Hearts and Pomegranates* (London: Peter Davies, 1940), 175, 392–93.

21. MPF to RCC, Aug. 24, 1929; MPF to RCC and ELC, May 12, 1929, both RCCP.

22. MPF to RCC, July 18, 1929, RCCP; MPF to Morris Llewellyn Cooke, May 21, 1929, Cooke Papers; MPF to RCC and ELC, May 12, 1929, RCCP.

23. MPF to RCC and ELC, May 12, 1929, RCCP; on the Rochs, see also MPF to Cooke, May 21, 1929, Cooke Papers.

24. KF, Memoir of MPF, LFUA.

25. MPF to ELC, June 20, 1929, RCCP.

26. KF, *Hearts and Pomegranates,* 80–85, 11, 26–28. One of Furse's older sisters would die of tuberculosis when Katharine was twelve.

27. Ibid., 42–43, 35–38.

28. Ibid., 99, 102–03, 82, 86–88. Katharine's mother, who herself had a "highly-strung nervous nature," faced nearly two decades of pressures and anxieties, culminating in 1892 in "a form of nervous breakdown" that lasted for nearly two years; see Phyllis Grosskurth, ed., *The Memoirs of John Addington Symonds* (Chicago: University of Chicago Press, 1984), 159, 213, 261.

29. KF, *Hearts and Pomegranates,* 106–07, 95–97. Furse sought access to her father's papers, including (unsuccessfully until 1949) the unexpurgated version of his unpub-

lished memoirs then controlled by the London Library. She also sought out Dr. Havelock Ellis, author of *Sexual Inversion* and one of her father's colleagues, "for elucidation of various puzzles." For more on Katharine's views of her father and homosexuality, see Louise A. DeSalvo, "Virginia Woolf and Katharine Furse: An Unpublished Correspondence," *Tulsa Studies in Women's Literature* 9 (fall 1990): 201–30.

30. KF, *Hearts and Pomegranates,* 101.

31. Ibid., 183–84, 187, 205–07, 215.

32. Ibid., 225–28.

33. Woolf, *Letters,* 1: 162–63, 272; KF, *Hearts and Pomegranates,* 125–26.

34. KF, *Hearts and Pomegranates,* 290. Katharine decided in the winter of 1912–13 to move to London to live with the four Crowdy sisters, colleagues she had met during her V.A.D. work.

35. Ibid., 291, 310–11, 325, 336, 356–57, 360–68.

36. Ibid., 392.

37. Ibid., 596, 589; MPF to ELC, June 20, 1929, RCCP.

38. MPF to RCC, July 14, 1929, RCCP.

39. KF, Memoir of MPF, LFUA.

40. KF to ELC, May 6, 1934, RCCP.

41. KF, Memoir of MPF, LFUA; KF, *Hearts and Pomegranates,* 591.

42. RCC to MPF, July 8, 1929; MPF to RCC, July 18, 1929, RCCP.

43. MPF to RCC, July 18, 1929, RCCP.

44. RCC to MPF, July 8, 1929; MPF to RCC, July 18, 1929, RCCP.

45. MPF to RCC, July 18, 1929, RCCP.

46. MPF to RCC, Aug. 24, 1929, RCCP.

47. ELC to MPF, Sept. 16 [1929], Ella Lyman Cabot Papers; MPF to ELC, Oct. 3, 1929, RCCP.

48. RCC to MPF, Sept. 30, 1929, RCCP.

49. RCC to MPF, Jan. 27, 1930, RCCP; ELC to MPF, Feb. 1 [1930], Ella Lyman Cabot Papers.

50. Notes of interview with Cicely (Polly) Furse. Katharine also describes her own willfulness and temper; KF, *Hearts and Pomegranates,* 4, 7, 85, 362.

51. Notes of interview with Cicely (Polly) Furse.

52. MPF, "Review of *Temptations to Rightdoing* by ELC." See also ELC to MPF, Feb. 1 [1930], Ella Lyman Cabot Papers.

53. MPF to Morris Llewellyn Cooke, Feb. 19, 1930, Cooke Papers; RCC to MPF, March 4, 1930; MPF to RCC, April 4 and April 30, 1930, all RCCP.

54. Walton, Beeson, and Scott, *The Oxford Companion to Medicine,* 2: 1279; MPF to RCC, May 4, 1930, RCCP; KF, Memoir of MPF, LFUA.

55. MPF to Dorothy Straight Elmhirst, May 8, 1930; Dorothy Straight Elmhirst to MPF, May 10 and May 22, 1930, Dorothy Whitney Straight Elmhirst Papers, Cornell University Libraries (hereafter DSEP); http://www.dartington.u-net.com/history.html.

56. MPF to Leonard Elmhirst, June 13, 1930, DSEP.

57. MPF to ELC, Sept. 1, 1930, RCCP.

58. ELC to MPF, May 14, 1930, and Sept. 17 [1930], Ella Lyman Cabot Papers; MPF to ELC, Sept. 1, 1930, RCCP.

59. Patterson, *America in the Twentieth Century,* 198; Rice and Krout, *United States History from 1865,* 225.

60. Charles Knowles Bolton to MPF, Oct. 29, 1930, Correspondence files, Boston Athenaeum; MPF to ELC, Feb. 28, 1931, RCCP.

61. MPF to ELC, Nov. 9, 1930, RCCP.

62. MPF to ELC, Jan. 28, 1931, RCCP.

63. EB, Memoir of MPF, LFUA.

64. MPF to ELC, Jan. 28, 1931; KF to ELC, May 3, 1934, both Ella Lyman Cabot Papers.

65. MPF to HAO, March 19, 1931; HAO to MPF, April 23, 1932, Harry A. Overstreet Papers, Lilly Library, Indiana University; MPF, "Review of *The Enduring Quest* by HAO."

66. MPF to RCC, April 17, 1931, RCCP; Morris Llewellyn Cooke to MPF, June 2 and Sept. 29, 1931, Cooke Papers.

67. BPA, "Brochure — Economic and Social Planning, Tenth Series on Business Management as a Profession: Sept. 15, 1931 to April 21, 1932," box 8, folder 17, Pound Papers.

68. Henry C. Metcalf to Roscoe Pound, Oct. 30, 1931, ibid.; MPF to HAO, March 30, 1932; HAO to MPF, April 23, 1932, both Overstreet Papers.

69. E. W. Hawley, *Herbert Hoover and the Crisis of American Capitalism,* 21; Link and Catton, *American Epoch,* 379. For more on the optimism of 1929 and 1930, see Burner, *Herbert Hoover,* 250.

70. Hawley, *Herbert Hoover,* 1–2.

71. Patterson, *America in the Twentieth Century,* 198.

72. Rice and Krout, *United States History from 1865,* 225–26.

73. Hawley, *Herbert Hoover,* 22.

74. For the speakers, who included Norman Thomas (Socialist candidate for president in 1932), see BPA, "Brochure — Economic and Social Planning, Sept. 15, 1931 to April 21, 1932," box 8, folder 17, Pound Papers.

75. Hawley, *Herbert Hoover,* 24.

76. MPF, "Individualism in a Planned Society," 260.

77. Ibid., 260–61.

78. Ibid., 261–62.

79. Ibid., 278–79.

80. For other references to coordination see MPF, "The Meaning of Responsibility in Business Management," "The Psychology of Consent and Participation," and "Leader and Expert."

81. MPF, "Individualism in a Planned Society," 262.

82. Ibid., 264–65.

83. Ibid., 268.

84. Ibid., 268–69.

85. Ibid., 270.

86. Ibid., 276–78.

87. Ibid., 279.

Chapter 23: "Prepared to Go or Stay"

1. MPF to William E. Mosher, Aug. 31, 1931; Mosher to MPF, Sept. 10, 1931, both William E. Mosher Papers, Syracuse University Archives.

2. MPF to Gordon Allport, Oct. 26, 1932, Corresp. 1930–45, box D, folder F: 1930–38, Gordon Allport Papers, Harvard University Archives.

3. MPF to ELC, Nov. 29, 1931, RCCP.

4. KF to Morris Llewellyn Cooke, Oct. 30, 1931, Morris Llewellyn Cooke Papers, Franklin D. Roosevelt Library, Hyde Park, N.Y.; MPF to ELC, Feb. 26 and Sept. 7, 1932, RCCP.

5. ELC to MPF, May 3, 1933, Ella Lyman Cabot Papers, SL.

6. MPF to ELC, Feb. 7, 1932, RCCP; MPF, "Review of *Organizational Engineering*"; MPF to ELC, Aug. 19, 1931, Ella Lyman Cabot Papers.

7. Link and Catton, *American Epoch*, 391–92, 394; Bailyn et al., *The Great Republic*, 734–35.

8. MPF to Morris Llewellyn Cooke, March 10, 1933, Cooke Papers; Patterson, *America in the Twentieth Century*, 208.

9. RCC to MPF, undated [March 1933?], RCCP.

10. RCC to MPF, March 20, 1932; MPF to RCC, March 31, 1932, both RCCP.

11. Woolf, *Letters*, 5: 73; idem, *Diary*, 4: 112–13.

12. Woolf, *Letters*, 1: xiv; idem, *Diary*, 4: 113.

13. LFU, "Preface," in MPF, *Freedom and Coordination*, vii; LFU, unpublished lecture at University of New South Wales, March 10, 1933, b, author's files; "Director's Report," *Calendar for 1932–33*, 12, London School of Economics Archives.

14. MPF to Gordon Allport, Nov. 21, 1932, Corresp. 1930–45, box D — Frank, folder F: 1930–38, Allport Papers. Four of the papers repeat, albeit with new illustrations, lectures already given: "Basis of Order Giving" (similar to "Giving of Orders," 1925, Bureau of Personnel Administration; BPA); "Basis of Authority" (built on "Illusion of Final Authority," 1926, Taylor Society); "Business Leadership" (built on "Leader and Expert," 1927; and "Some Discrepancies in Leadership Theory and Practice," 1928, both BPA); "Basic Principles of Organization" (parallels "Individualism in a Planned Society," 1932, BPA). Follett's other LSE lecture, "Coordination," had been covered in previous BPA papers: "The Meaning of Responsibility in Business Management," "The Psychology of Consent and Participation," "Leader and Expert," and "Individualism in a Planned Society."

15. F. A. Phillipps to MPF, Nov. 24, 1932, in RCC, "Medical History and Record of Mary Parker Follett, 1910–1933"; KF to ELC, Dec. 19, 1933, RCCP.

16. Stawell, "Mary Parker Follett," 44; ELC to MPF, April 24 and May 3, 1933, Ella Lyman Cabot Papers; RCC to MPF, May 18, 1933, RCCP; R. I. S. Bayliss, *Thyroid Disease: The Facts* (Oxford: Oxford University Press, 1982), 36–42.

17. KF to ELC, Oct. 31, 1933, Ella Lyman Cabot Papers.

18. RCC to MPF, May 18, 1933; MPF to RCC, Sept. 29, 1933, both RCCP.

19. KF, Memoir of MPF, LFUA.

20. MPF to RCC, Sept. 29, 1933, RCCP.

21. KF to ELC, Dec. 19, 1933, RCCP.

22. MPF to RCC, Sept. 29, 1933, RCCP.

23. MPF to RCC, Sept. 29 and Oct. 5, 1933, RCCP.

24. Sophie Valentine to KF, Dec. 27, 1934; Harriet French Mixter to KF, March 4, 1934; F. M. Stawell to KF, Feb. 11, 1935, all LFUA.

25. Notes of interview with Cicely (Polly) Furse, May 20, 1984, Smarden, Kent.

26. MPF to RCC, Oct. 5, 1933, RCCP.

27. KF to ELC, Oct. 31, 1933, Ella Lyman Cabot Papers; KF to ELC, Dec. 20, 1933, RCCP.

28. KF to ELC, Oct. 31, 1933.

29. Patterson, *America in the Twentieth Century,* 198; Stawell, "Mary Parker Follett," 44. Follett had $12,000 in stocks and $37,000 in bonds, including AT&T, American Can, N.E. Power Association, Eastman Kodak, du Pont, Standard Oil, Union Pacific Railroad; Probate of Will of Mary Parker Follett, June 10, 1936, Norfolk County, Mass.

30. Interview with George D. Follett Jr., June 16, 1982, Quincy, Mass.

31. Martin Kaufman, Stuart Galishoff, and Todd L. Savitt, eds., *Dictionary of American Medical Biography,* vol. 1 (Westport, Conn.: Greenwood, 1984), 430–31.

32. ELC to KF, Dec. 19, 1933, LFUA.

33. KF to MPF, Dec. 19, 1933, Ella Lyman Cabot Papers; ELC to KF, Jan. 8, 1934, LFUA; see also KF to ELC, Jan. 19, 1934, Ella Lyman Cabot Papers.

34. MPF to ELC, undated [Dec. 3, 1933], RCCP.

35. Sara Andrews to KF, Dec. 28, 1933, LFUA.

36. Stawell, "Mary Parker Follett," 44.

37. MPF to Eva Whiting White, Dec. 15, 1933, Eva Whiting White Papers, SL; MPF to ELC, Dec. [15], 1933, RCCP; KF to ELC, Dec. 19, 1933, Ella Lyman Cabot Papers.

38. Mary Dennison to KF, Dec. 19, 1933, LFUA; MPF to RCC, Dec. 8, 1933, RCCP.

39. ELC to KF, Dec. 19, 1933, LFUA; Mary Dennison to KF, Dec. 19, 1933, LFUA.

40. ELC to KF, Dec. 19, 1933, LFUA.

41. Sara Andrews to KF, Dec. 28, 1933, LFUA.

42. KF to ELC, Dec. 19, 1933, Ella Lyman Cabot Papers.

43. ELC to KF, Dec. 19, 1933; Mary Dennison to KF, Dec. 19, 1933, both LFUA.

44. RCC to KF, Dec. 21, 1933, LFUA.

45. Ibid.; KF to ELC, Dec. 20, 1933, RCCP.

46. Sophie Valentine to KF, Dec. 26, 1933, LFUA.

47. Mary Dennison to KF, Dec. 21, 1933, both LFUA.

Chapter 24: Afterword

1. LFU, "Notes for a 'Talk' on Mary Parker Follett at the University of N.S.W. [New South Wales]," b, author's files.

2. MPF, *Creative Experience,* 302.

Bibliography

Manuscript and Archival Collections

UNITED STATES

Boston City Archives, Archives and Records Management Division, City Clerk's Office, Hyde Park, Mass.
Boston Public Library, Rare Books Department
• Boston School Committee Papers
• Ford Hall Forum Collection
• Society to Encourage Studies at Home Papers
Brandeis University Library
• Louis D. Brandeis Collection
Columbia University, Rare Books and Manuscript Library
• LeRoy Bowman Papers
• Henry Bruere Interview, Columbia Oral History Project
• Eduard C. Lindeman Papers
Cornell University Libraries, Division of Rare and Manuscript Collections
• Dorothy Whitney Straight Elmhirst Papers
Credit Union National Association, Madison, Wis.
• Edward A. Filene Papers
Harvard Law School Archives
• Roscoe Pound Papers

Harvard University, Houghton Library
  •W. Ernest Hocking Papers
  •Robert A. Woods Papers
Harvard Univerity, Radcliffe Institute, Radcliffe Archives
  •Annie Ware Winsor Allen Papers, SC 35
  •Ada Louise Comstock Records of the President
  •Beulah Dix Flebbe '97 Papers, RA.A F593
  •Grade Sheets, Registrar's Records, RGXII, Series 4
  •Transcripts, Registrar's Records, RGXII, Series 1
Harvard University, Radcliffe Institute, Schlesinger Library
  •Fannie Fern Phillips Andrews Papers
  •Ella Lyman Cabot Papers
  •Mary Earhart Dillon Collection
  •Mary Parker Follett Essays
  •Gardiner Family Papers
  •Ethel McLean Johnson Papers
  •Nichols-Shurtleff Family Papers
  •North Bennett Street Industrial School Papers
  •Maud Wood Park Papers, Woman's Rights Collection
  •Anna Boynton Thompson Papers
  •Eva Whiting White Papers
Harvard University Archives
  •Gordon Allport Papers
  •Richard Clarke Cabot Papers
  •James Ford Papers
  •Albert Bushnell Hart Papers
Indiana University, Lilly Library
  •Harry A. Overstreet Papers
Johns Hopkins University
  •Herbert Baxter Adams Papers
Library of Congress, Washington, D.C.
  •American Historical Association Papers
  •Ray Stannard Baker Papers
  •Charles J. Bonaparte Papers
  •National American Woman Suffrage Association Papers
  •Maud Wood Park Papers
  •Theodore Roosevelt Papers
Massachusetts Historical Society, Boston
  •Good Government Association Papers
National Archives, Washington, D.C.
National Park Service, Longfellow National Historic Site, Cambridge, Mass.
  •Alice Mary Longfellow Papers
New York Public Library
  •People's Institute Papers
Quincy Historical Society, Quincy, Mass.
  •Charles Allen Follett Papers

Franklin D. Roosevelt Library, Hyde Park, N.Y.
  • Morris Llewellyn Cooke Papers
Simmons College Archives
Syracuse University Archives
  • William E. Mosher Papers
Syracuse University Library, Department of Special Collections
  • Harold Laski Papers
Thayer Academy Archives, Braintree, Mass.
  • Anna Boynton Thompson Papers
Tufts University Archives
University of Minnesota Social Welfare History Archives
  • Betty Lindeman Leonard Papers
  • National Recreation Association Papers
  • Wilbur Phillips Papers
  • United South End Settlements Papers
University of Washington
  • Howard Woolston Papers
University of Wisconsin Archives
Wellesley College Archives
Yale University, Manuscripts and Archives
  • Walter Lippmann Papers

UNITED KINGDOM

Principal and Fellows, Newnham College, Cambridge
  • Newnham College Archives
Dartington Hall Trust, Totnes, Devon
  • Dorothy Whitney Straight Elmhirst Papers
Henley Management College, Henley-on-Thames
  • Lyndall Fownes Urwick Archive
London School of Economics Archives
Master and Fellows of Trinity College Cambridge
  • Henry Sidgwick Papers
National Library of Scotland, Edinburgh
  • Viscount Richard B. Haldane Papers, NLS MS. 5916, folio 97
University of Reading
  • Longmans, Green and Company Archives

Complete Works of Mary P. Follett

PUBLISHED WORKS

"Abstract of 'Community as a Process.'" *Journal of Philosophy, Psychology and Scientific Methods* 16 (December 1919): 715–17.
"The Aims of Adult Recreation." Excerpt of a paper read at the seventh annual meeting of the Playground and Recreation Association of America, Richmond, Va., May 7, 1913. *The Playground*, October 1913, 261–68.

"The Basis of Authority." Paper presented in January 1933 at Department of Business Administration, London School of Economics. Published in *Freedom and Co-ordination,* 34–46.

"The Basis of Control in Business Management." Paper presented on September 30, 1926, at National Institute of Industrial Psychology, London. Published in *Journal of the National Institute of Industrial Psychology* 3 (January 1927): 233–41.

"The Boston Placement Bureau." *Bulletin: The Women's Municipal League of Boston,* May 1915, 14–28.

"Boston Placement Bureau." *Bulletin: The Women's Municipal League of Boston,* March 1916, 10–11.

"Boston Placement Bureau." *Bulletin: The Women's Municipal League of Boston,* May 1917, 10.

"Committee on Extended Use of School Buildings." *Bulletin: The Women's Municipal League of Boston,* May 1913, 8–13.

"Committee on Extended Use of School Buildings." *Bulletin: The Women's Municipal League of Boston,* April 1914, 14–29.

"Community as a Process." *Philosophical Review* 28 (November 1919): 576–88.

"Co-ordination." Paper presented in January 1933 at Department of Business Administration, London School of Economics. Published in *Freedom and Co-ordination,* 61–76.

Creative Experience. New York: Longmans, Green, 1924.

Dynamic Administration: The Collected Papers of Mary Parker Follett, ed. Henry C. Metcalf and Lyndall Urwick. New York: Harper and Brothers, 1940.

Dynamic Administration: The Collected Papers of Mary Parker Follett, Elliot M. Fox and Lyndall Urwick. 2d ed. New York: Hippocrene, 1977.

"The Essentials of Leadership." Paper presented in January 1933 at Department of Business Administration, London School of Economics. Published in *Freedom and Co-ordination,* 47–60.

"Evening Centers—Aims and Duties of Managers and Leaders Therein." Paper presented at a meeting of the Evening Centers of the Public School System of the City of Boston, January 28, 1913. Boston: City of Boston Printing Department, 1913.

"Evening Recreation Centers." Paper presented at New England Institute of the Playground and Recreation Association of America, Brookline, Mass., February 17, 1912. Published in *The Playground,* January 1913, 384–400.

Freedom and Co-ordination: Lectures in Business Organisation by Mary Parker Follett, ed. Lyndall Urwick. London: Management Publications Trust, 1949.

"Further Uses for School Buildings." *Bulletin: The Women's Municipal League of Boston,* March 1910, 6–7.

"The Giving of Orders." Paper presented in January 1933 at Department of Business Administration, London School of Economics. Published in *Freedom and Co-ordination,* 16–33.

"Henry Clay, the First Political Speaker of the House." Paper presented at the annual meeting of the American Historical Association, Washington, D.C., December 30, 1891. Published as "Henry Clay as Speaker of the United States House of Representatives." In *Annual Report of the American Historical Association for 1891.* Washington, D.C.: Government Printing Office, 1892, 257–65. Also published as "Henry Clay as Speaker of the House." *New England Magazine* 6 (May 1892): 344–48.

"How Is the Employee Representation Movement Remoulding the Accepted Type of Business Manager?" Paper presented on May 6, 1926, at Bureau of Personnel Administration, New York. Published in Metcalf, *Business Management as a Profession,* 339–54.

"How Must Business Management Develop in Order to Become a Profession?" Paper presented on November 5, 1925, at Bureau of Personnel Administration, New York. Published in Metcalf, *Business Management as a Profession,* 88–102.

"How Must Business Management Develop in Order to Possess the Essentials of a Profession?" Paper presented on October 29, 1925, at Bureau of Personnel Administration, New York. Published in Metcalf, *Business Management as a Profession,* 73–87.

"The Illusion of Final Authority." Paper presented on December 10, 1926, at the Taylor Society, New York. *Bulletin of the Taylor Society* 11 (December 1926): 243–50. Also in *Freedom and Co-ordination,* 1–15.

"The Illusion of Final Responsibility." Paper presented on October 2, 1926, at Rowntree Lecture Conference, Oxford. Published in *Proceedings of the Twenty-third Lecture Conference for Works Directors, Managers, Foremen and Forewomen, Balliol College, Oxford (Sept. 30–Oct. 4, 1926).* York: Yorkshire Printing Works, n.d., 24–30.

"Individualism in a Planned Society." Paper prepared for presentation on April 14, 1932, at Bureau of Personnel Administration, New York; meetings were canceled. Published in *Dynamic Administration,* 295–314.

"Leader and Expert." Paper presented in April 1927 and again in November 1927 at Bureau of Personnel Administration, New York. Published in Metcalf, *Psychological Foundations of Business Administration,* 220–43. Also in *Business Leadership,* ed. Henry C. Metcalf. London: Pitman, 1931, 55–77.

"Leadership." Paper presented on September 28, 1928, at Rowntree Lecture Conference, Oxford. Published in *Proceedings of the Twenty-seventh Lecture Conference for Works Directors, Managers, Foremen and Forewomen, Balliol College, Oxford (September 27–30, 1928).* York: Yorkshire Printing Works, n.d., 17–24.

"The Meaning of Responsibility in Business Management." Paper presented on April 29, 1926, at Bureau of Personnel Administration, New York. Published in Metcalf, *Business Management as a Profession,* 318–38.

"Midnight Oil in the Schools." *Boston Evening Transcript,* April 1, 1914, 20.

The New State: Group Organization, the Solution of Popular Government. New York: Longmans, Green, 1918. An English edition in 1920 contained an introduction by Richard B. Haldane. Reprint, University Park: Pennsylvania State University Press, 1998, with introductory essays by Benjamin R. Barber, Jane Mansbridge, and Kevin Mattson.

"The Opportunities for Leadership for the Nurse in Industry." Paper presented on May 25, 1928, at twelfth annual conference of American Association of Industrial Nurses, New Haven. Published in *Nursing Mirror and Midwives' Journal,* April 1, 1944, 7–8; and April 8, 1944, 25–26.

"The Placement Bureau." *Bulletin: The Women's Municipal League of Boston,* December 1912, 7–18.

"The Process of Control." Paper presented in January 1933 at Department of Business Administration, London School of Economics. Published in *Papers on the Science of Administration,* ed. Luther Gulick and Lyndall Urwick. New York: Columbia University Press, 1937. Also in *Freedom and Co-ordination,* 77–89.

"The Psychiatrist in Industry." Place and time of delivery unknown. Published in *Dynamic Administration,* 2d ed., 294–302.

"The Psychological Foundations: Business as an Integrative Unity." Paper presented in January 1925 at Bureau of Personnel Administration, New York. Published in Metcalf, *Scientific Foundations of Business Administration,* 150–70.

"The Psychological Foundations: Constructive Conflict." Paper presented in January 1925 at Bureau of Personnel Administration, New York. Published in Metcalf, *Scientific Foundations of Business Administration,* 114–31.

"The Psychological Foundations: The Giving of Orders." Paper presented in January 1925 at Bureau of Personnel Administration, New York. Published in Metcalf, *Scientific Foundations of Business Administration,* 132–49.

"The Psychological Foundations: Power." Paper presented in January 1925 at Bureau of Personnel Administration, New York. Published in Metcalf, *Scientific Foundations of Business Administration,* 171–90.

"The Psychology of Conciliation and Arbitration." Paper presented in March 1927 at Bureau of Personnel Administration, New York. Published in Metcalf, *Psychological Foundations of Business Administration,* 203–19.

"The Psychology of Consent and Participation." Paper presented in March 1927 at Bureau of Personnel Administration, New York. Published in Metcalf, *Psychological Foundations of Business Administration,* 183–202.

"The Psychology of Control." Paper presented in March 1927 at Bureau of Personnel Administration, New York. Published in Metcalf, *Psychological Foundations of Business Administration,* 156–82.

"Report of the Committee on Extended Use of School Buildings." *Bulletin: The Women's Municipal League of Boston,* March 1911, 18–20.

"Report of the Committee on Substitutes for the Saloon." In *First Report of the Boston Equal Suffrage Association for Good Government, 1901–1903,* 17–23. Box 53, folder 716, WRC.

"Report of the Committee on Substitutes for the Saloon." In *Second Biennial Report of the Boston Equal Suffrage Association, 1903–05,* 22–24. Box 53, folder 716, WRC.

"Report of the Department of Civic Training, 1909." In *Fifth Report of the Boston Equal Suffrage Association for Good Government, Oct. 1908–Oct. 1910,* 28–29. Box 53, folder 716, WRC.

"Report of the East Boston Centre by Committee on Extended Use of School Buildings, 1911–1912." *Bulletin: The Women's Municipal League of Boston,* May 1912, 5–12.

"Report of the Union Committee." In *Third Biennial Report of the Boston Equal Suffrage Association for Good Government, 1905–07,* 20–23. Box 53, folder 716, WRC.

"Report on Schoolhouses as Social Centres." In *An Account of the Women's Municipal League of Boston as Given in the First Public Meeting, January 20, 1909.* Boston: Southgate, 1909, 14–16.

"Review of *The Enduring Quest* by H. A. Overstreet." *International Journal of Ethics* 42 (1932): 217–20.

"Review of *Organizational Engineering* by Henry Dennison." *International Journal of Ethics* 42 (1932): 375–77.

"Review of *Temptations to Rightdoing* by Ella Lyman Cabot." *The Survey,* February 15, 1930, 598.

"Some Discrepancies in Leadership Theory and Practice." Paper presented on March 8, 1928, at Bureau of Personnel Administration, New York. Published in *Business Leadership,* ed. Henry C. Metcalf. London: Pitman, 1931, 206–29.

"Some Methods of Executive Efficiency." Paper presented on October 1, 1926, at Rowntree Lecture Conference, Oxford. Published in *Proceedings of the Twenty-third Lecture Conference for Works Directors, Managers, Foremen and Forewomen, Balliol College, Oxford (Sept. 30–Oct. 4, 1926).* York: Yorkshire Printing Works, 1926, 72–76.

The Speaker of the House of Representatives. New York: Longmans, Green, 1896.

"The Teacher-Student Relation." Paper prepared in April 1928 for School for Citizenship and Public Affairs, Syracuse University. Not delivered. Published in *Dynamic Administration,* 2d ed., 303–25.

"What Type of Central Administrative Leadership Is Essential to Business Management as Defined in this Course?" Paper presented in May 1926 at Bureau of Personnel Administration, New York. Published in Metcalf, *Business Management as a Profession,* 355–69.

"Will Mayor Curley 'Economize' on the School Committee's Plan to Let Adults Use School Property at Night?" *Boston Evening Transcript,* April 1, 1914, 20.

Coauthored with Alice G. Brandeis, Ella Lyman Cabot, William B. Coffin, and Arthur V. Woodworth. "Schoolhouse Construction and Equipment in Their Relation to School Centres." Supplement to *Bulletin: The Women's Municipal League of Boston,* April 1915, 17pp.

UNPUBLISHED WORKS

"Essay on Cowper." Paper written ca. 1882 at Thayer Academy. Mary P. Follett Essays, SL.

"The Essential Unity of the Social Sciences" (with subsequent discussion). Paper presented on July 1, 1926, at School for Citizenship and Public Affairs, Syracuse University. Box 94, WEMP.

"Expectant Attention." Paper presented on June 24, 1884, at graduation exercises of Thayer Academy. Mary Parker Follett Essays, Schlesinger Library, Radcliffe Institute, Harvard University.

"The Nature of Community." Paper presented on December 31, 1919, at nineteenth annual meeting of American Philosophical Association, Cornell University. LFUA.

"The Social Centre and the Democratic Ideal." Paper presented on December 14, 1913, at Ford Hall Forum, Boston. LFUA.

"Social Ethics Seminary, Monday, Dec. 20th, 1926." Paper presented at 1926–27 Social Ethics Seminary (Social Ethics 20a), Harvard University. Box 62, RCCP.

"Social Ethics Seminary, Monday, January 3, 1927." Paper presented at 1926–27 Social Ethics Seminary (Social Ethics 20a), Harvard University. Box 62, RCCP.

"The Student as an Educator." Paper presented on June 8, 1883, at Founder's Day, Thayer Academy. The manuscript has not been located, but the speech is mentioned in the *Braintree Observer,* June 9, 1883.

"Twelve Steps." Problem analysis rubric prepared for William E. Mosher, School for Citizenship, Syracuse University; returned in Mosher to MPF, July 7, 1926. Box 94, WEMP.

Untitled draft paper on fundamental principles of organization. LFUA.

Reviews of Books by Follett

CREATIVE EXPERIENCE

Alexander, H. B. "The Newer State." *New York Evening Post Literary Review,* August 30, 1924, 6.

Allport, Gordon W. "Review of *Creative Experience.*" *Journal of Abnormal and Social Psychology* 19 (1924): 426–28.

Bruère, Robert W. "Partners in Creation." *The Survey,* October 15, 1924, 100, 102.

Calkins, Mary Whiton. "Review of *Creative Experience.*" *Philosophical Review* 33 (1923): 505–10.

Ellwood, C. A. "Review of *Creative Experience.*" *American Journal of Sociology* 30 (September 1924): 223–24.

E. N. "Review of *Creative Experience.*" *Boston Evening Transcript,* May 21, 1924, 5.

Lind, John E. "Facts Are Only Facts after All." *New York Times,* June 8, 1924, 11.

Overstreet, Harry A. "Review of *Creative Experience.*" *Journal of Philosophy* 22 (August 13, 1925): 498–501.

———. "Review of *Creative Experience.*" *New Republic,* July 16, 1924, 214–15.

"Review of *Creative Experience.*" *Times Literary Supplement,* July 10, 1924, 439.

Sheffield, Alfred D. "Problems of Society." *The Nation,* June 18, 1924, 713–14.

Shepard, Walter James. "Review of *Creative Experience.*" *American Political Science Review* 18 (August 1924): 617–19.

Smith, Russell Gordon. "Review of *Creative Experience.*" *Journal of Social Forces* 3 (March 1925): 540–42.

Tufts, James H. "Review of *Creative Experience.*" *International Journal of Ethics* 35 (January 1925): 189–90.

Wood, Arthur Evans. "The Social Philosophy of Mary P. Follett." *Journal of Social Forces* 4 (1926): 759–69.

THE NEW STATE

Alexander, H. B. "Review of *The New State.*" *Journal of Philosophy, Psychology and Scientific Methods* 16 (October 1919): 577–81.

Bailey, Thomas Pearce. " 'Orange' Journalism." *Sewanee Review* 27 (1919): 227–38.

Bosanquet, Bernard. "Review of *The New State.*" *Mind* (July 1919): 370–71.

Cunningham, G. Watts. "Review of *The New State.*" *Philosophical Review* 28 (1919): 325–26.

Ellwood, Charles A. "Review of *The New State*." *American Journal of Sociology* 25 (July 1919): 97–99.

Ford, Henry Jones. "Review of *The New State*." *American Political Science Review* 13 (August 1919): 494–95.

Hartman, Edward J. *Springfield Republican*, May 25, 1919, 17.

H. S. K. [Henry S. Kariel]. "Review of *The New State*." *Boston Evening Transcript*, December 31, 1918, 7.

H. J. L. [Harold J. Laski]. "Review of *The New State*." *New Republic*, February 8, 1919, 61–62.

McBain, Howard Lee. "Review of *The New State*." *Political Science Quarterly* 34, no. 1 (1919): 167–70.

Overstreet, H. A. "Review of *The New State*." *Journal of Philosophy* 16 (October 1919): 582–85.

———. "Review of *The Problem of Administrative Areas* and *The New State*." *The Survey*, March 1, 1919, 813–14.

"Political Regrouping." *New York Evening Post*, March 1, 1919, 6.

"Review of *The New State*." *The Nation*, January 18, 1919, 96–97.

"Review of *The New State*." *Springfield Republican*, March 31, 1919, 6.

"Review of *The New State*." *Times Literary Supplement*, April 24, 1919, 227.

Tufts, James H. "Review of *The New State*." *International Journal of Ethics* 29 (April 1919): 374–77.

"What Is Democracy?" *Times Literary Supplement*, July 3, 1919, 353–54.

Yarros, Victor S. "Reforming the Modern State." *Open Court* 35 (July 1921): 430–37.

THE SPEAKER OF THE HOUSE OF REPRESENTATIVES

Adams, John Quincy. "Review of *The Speaker of the House of Representatives*." *Annals of the American Academy of Political and Social Science* 9 (May 1897): 434–35.

"The American Speakership." *The Times of London*, August 13, 1896, 10.

Morse, Anson D. "Review of *The Speaker of the House of Representatives*." *Political Science Quarterly* 12 (June 1897): 309–14.

Roosevelt, Theodore. "Review of *The Speaker of the House of Representatives*." *American Historical Review* 2 (October 1896): 176–78.

Smith, C. H. "Review of *The Speaker of the House of Representatives*." *Yale Review* (November 1896), 332–33.

"The Speaker." *The Critic*, October 3, 1896, 200.

"The Speaker — American and English." *The Spectator* 77 (September 5, 1896): 296–97.

"The Speaker of the House." *The Nation*, September 10, 1896, 198–200.

"The Speaker's Power." *New York Times*, July 19, 1896, 27.

Selected Secondary Sources

Abrams, Richard M. *Conservatism in a Progressive Era: Massachusetts Politics, 1900–1912*. Cambridge: Harvard University Press, 1964.

An Account of the Women's Municipal League of Boston. Boston: Southgate Press–T. W. Ripley, 1909.

Adams, Charles F. *Three Episodes of Massachusetts History.* 3 vols. 1892; reprint, New York: Russell and Russell, 1965.

Adams, Herbert B. "The Society to Encourage Studies at Home." *The Independent,* September 17, 1885, 3–4.

Allswang, John M. *Bosses, Machines, and Urban Voters.* 1977; reprint, Baltimore: Johns Hopkins University Press, 1986.

Anderson, Kenneth N., ed. *Mosby's Medical Dictionary.* 4th ed. St. Louis: Mosby, 1994.

Andrews, Fannie Fern. "The Further Use of School Buildings." *New Boston,* July 1910, 115–20.

———. "Schoolhouses as Neighborhood Centers." *New Boston,* March 1911, 490–92.

Antler, Joyce. " 'After College, What?': New Graduates and the Family Claim." *American Quarterly* 32 (fall 1980): 409–34.

Baldwin, Roger N., and Charles Beard. "Social Center Conference." *National Municipal Review,* January 1912, 142–43.

Bailyn, Bernard, et al. *The Great Republic.* Vol. 2. 3d ed. Lexington, Mass.: D. C. Heath, 1985.

Barber, Benjamin R. "Mary Parker Follett as Democratic Hero." In Follett, *The New State.* 1998.

Barnes, Harry Elmer. *An Introduction to the History of Sociology.* Chicago: University of Chicago Press, 1948.

Blanshard, Brand. *Four Reasonable Men: Marcus Aurelius, John Stuart Mill, Ernest Renan, Henry Sidgwick.* Middletown: Wesleyan University Press, 1984.

Blodgett, Geoffrey T. *The Gentle Reformers: Massachusetts Democrats in the Cleveland Era.* Cambridge: Harvard University Press, 1966.

———. "Yankee Leadership in a Divided City: Boston, 1860–1910." *Journal of Urban History* 8 (August 1982): 371–96.

Board of Election Commissioners. *Report.* Boston, 1902–1914.

Braden, Charles S. *Spirits in Rebellion: The Rise and Development of New Thought.* Dallas: Southern Methodist University Press, 1963.

Brady, Kathleen. *Ida Tarbell.* New York: Seaview/Putnam, 1984.

Bragdon, Henry W. *Woodrow Wilson: The Academic Years.* Cambridge: Harvard University Press, 1967.

Brewer, John. *A History of Vocational Guidance.* New York: Harper, 1942.

Briggs, Asa. *Social Thought and Social Action: A Study of the Work of Seebohm Rowntree.* Westport, Conn.: Greenwood, 1974.

Brubacher, John S., and Willis Rudy. *Higher Education in Transition: A History of American Colleges and Universities, 1636–1956.* New York: Harper and Row, 1958.

Bryce, James. *The American Commonwealth.* 3 vols. 1888; reprint, New York: AMS, 1973.

———. "A Word as to the Speakership." *North American Review* 150 (October 1890): 385–98.

Buck, Paul, ed. *Social Sciences at Harvard, 1860–1920.* Cambridge: Harvard University Press, 1965.

Burner, David. *Herbert Hoover.* New York: Alfred A. Knopf, 1979.

Burns, Constance K. "The Irony of Progressive Reform." In *Boston, 1700–1980: The*

Evolution of Urban Politics, ed. Ronald P. Formisano and Constance K. Burns. Westport, Conn.: Greenwood, 1984.

Burns, James M. *The Workshop of Democracy.* New York: Alfred A. Knopf, 1985.

Cabot, Ella Lyman. "Annual Report of the Department of Education." *Bulletin: The Women's Municipal League of Boston,* June 1910, 17–19.

Cabot, Richard C. "Mary Parker Follett: An Appreciation." *Radcliffe Quarterly,* April 1934, 80–82.

———. *Physical Diagnosis.* 4th ed. New York: William Wood, 1910.

———. *Psychotherapy and Its Relation to Religion.* Boston: Emmanuel Church, 1908.

Cameron, Stewart. *Kidney Disease: The Facts.* Oxford: Oxford University Press, 1981.

City History Club of Boston. *Annual Reports.* Boston, 1906–1910.

Clendenning, John. *The Life and Thought of Josiah Royce.* Madison: University of Wisconsin Press, 1985.

Cohen, Avrum I. "Mary Parker Follett: Spokesman for Democracy, Philosopher for Social Group Work, 1918–1933." D.S.W. diss., Tulane University, 1971.

Cohen, Morris R. "Communal Ghosts and Other Perils in Social Philosophy." *Journal of Philosophy, Psychology and Scientific Methods* 16 (December 1919): 673–90.

Collier, John. "Definitions and Debates of the Community Center Conference." *American City* 14 (June 1916): 572–74.

———. *From Every Zenith: A Memoir and Some Essays on Life and Thought.* Denver: Sage, 1963.

The Committee of Seven. "The Study of History in Schools." In *Annual Report of the American Historical Association for the Year 1898.* Washington, D.C.: Government Printing Office, 1899.

Conway, Jill K. "Women Reformers and American Culture, 1870–1930." *Journal of Social History* 5 (1971–72): 164–77.

Cooley, Charles H. *Social Organization.* 1909; reprint, New York: Schocken, 1963.

Copleston, Frederick. *A History of Philosophy.* Vol. 8, Part II: *Modern Philosophy: Bentham to Russell.* 1967; reprint, Garden City, N.Y.: Image, 1985.

Corman, Oliver P. "The School City: An Inquiry into Its Success and Value." In *Proceedings of the New York Conference for Good City Government and the Eleventh Annual Meeting of the National Municipal League,* ed. Clinton R. Woodruff. Philadelphia: National Municipal League, 1905: 280–89.

Cousins, Norman. *Anatomy of an Illness as Perceived by the Patient.* 1979; reprint, New York: Bantam, 1981.

Crawford, Mary C. "Schools as Social Centers." *Boston Common,* December 2, 1911, 4–5.

Creevy, C. D. "Confusing Clinical Manifestations of Malignant Renal Neoplasms." *Archives of Internal Medicine,* 1935, 895–916.

Croly, Herbert. *The Promise of American Life.* 1909; reprint, Cambridge: Harvard University Press, 1965.

Curley, James Michael. *I'd Do It Again: A Record of All My Uproarious Years.* Englewood Cliffs, N.J.: Prentice-Hall, 1957.

Davidson, Roger G., and Walter J. Oleszek. *Congress against Itself.* Bloomington: Indiana University Press, 1977.

Davis, Allen F. *American Heroine: The Life and Legend of Jane Addams.* New York: Oxford University Press, 1973.

———. *Spearheads for Reform: The Social Settlements and the Progressive Movement, 1890–1914.* 1967; reprint, New Brunswick: Rutgers University Press, 1984.

Dawles, Henry L., and James L. Bowen. *Massachusetts in the War, 1861–1865.* Springfield, Mass.: Clark W. Bryan, 1889.

Dennison, Henry S. "Practical Applications of Scientific Principles to Business Management: The Economist." In Metcalf, *Scientific Foundations of Business Administration.*

Dennison, James T. *Henry S. Dennison (1877–1952): New England Industrialist Who Served America.* New York: Newcomen Society in North America, 1955.

Drinka, George F. *The Birth of Neurosis: Myth, Malady, and the Victorians.* New York: Simon and Schuster, 1984.

Elshtain, Jean Bethke. *Public Man, Private Woman: Women in Social and Political Thought.* Princeton: Princeton University Press, 1981.

Enomoto, Tokiho, and Tadashi Mito. *Mary Parker Follett.* Tokyo: Dobunken, n.d.

Faderman, Lillian. *Surpassing the Love of Men: Romantic Friendship and Love between Women from the Renaissance to the Present.* New York: William Morrow, 1981.

Field, Eleanor. "Women at an English University." *Century Illustrated Monthly Magazine,* May 1891, 287–94.

Fisher, Roger. "Community Organizing and Citizen Participation: The Efforts of the People's Institute in New York City, 1910–1920." *Social Service Review* 51 (September 1977): 474–90.

Foley, Mary Mix. *The American House.* New York: Harper and Row, 1980.

Fox, Elliot M. "The Dynamics of Constructive Change in the Thought of Mary Parker Follett." Ph.D. diss., Columbia University, 1970.

Freedman, Estelle. "Separatism as Strategy: Female Institution Building and American Feminism." *Feminist Studies* 5 (fall 1979): 512–29.

Freeman, James Dillett. *The Story of Unity.* Rev. ed. Unity Village, Mo.: Unity Books, 1978.

Furse, Dame Katharine. *Hearts and Pomegranates.* London: Peter Davies, 1940.

Gale, Zona. "If You Know People, Things Look Different." *Common Good,* January 1912, 48–50.

Gleuck, Eleanor T. "The Community Use of Schools: A Nation-Wide Study of School Centers." Ed.D. diss., Harvard University, 1925. Published as *The Community Use of Schools.* Baltimore: Williams, 1927.

Goodwin, Doris Kearns. *The Fitzgeralds and the Kennedys: An American Saga.* New York: Simon and Schuster, 1987.

Gottschalk, Stephan. *The Emergence of Christian Science in American Religious Life.* Berkeley: University of California Press, 1973.

Graham, Pauline. *Dynamic Managing—the Follett Way.* London: Professional Publishing and British Institute of Management, 1987.

———. *Mary Parker Follett: Prophet of Management.* Cambridge: Harvard Business School Press, 1995.

Greengarten, I. M. *Thomas Hill Green and the Development of Liberal-Democratic Thought.* Toronto: University of Toronto Press, 1981.

Hamilton, M. A. *Newnham: An Informal Biography.* London: Faber and Faber, 1936.

Hart, Albert Bushnell. *Actual Government: As Applied under American Conditions.* New York: Longmans, Green, 1903.

——. "How to Teach History in Secondary Schools." 1887. Reprinted in *Studies in American Education,* ed. A. B. Hart. New York: Longmans, Green, 1895.

——. "Preparation for Citizenship." *Education* 8 (June 1888): 630–38.

Hawley, Ellis W. *Herbert Hoover and the Crisis of American Capitalism.* Cambridge: Schenkman, 1973.

Hawley, Ellis W., ed. *Herbert Hoover as Secretary of Commerce: Studies in New Era Thought and Practice.* Iowa City: University of Iowa Press, 1981.

——. *The Great War and the Search for a Modern Order: A History of the American People and Their Institutions, 1917–1933.* New York: St. Martin's, 1979.

——. "Herbert Hoover, the Commerce Secretariat, and the Vision of an 'Associative State,' 1921–1928." *Journal of American History* 61 (1974): 116–40.

Hawley, Ralph E. "Director's Report." *Bulletin: The Women's Municipal League of Boston,* May 1912, 13–24.

Heilbrun, Carolyn G. *Reinventing Womanhood.* New York: W. W. Norton, 1979.

The Highland Union, 1902–03. Boston: Wm. B. Libby, n.d.

Hill, Mary A. *Charlotte Perkins Gilman: The Making of a Radical Feminist, 1860–1896.* Philadelphia: Temple University Press, 1980.

Hofstadter, Richard. *The Progressive Historians: Turner, Beard, Parrington.* 1968; reprint. Chicago: University of Chicago Press, 1979.

Holly, Hobart. "The Academy Founded by John Adams." *Quincy History,* winter 1984, 1–6.

Holt, Edwin B. *The Freudian Wish and Its Place in Ethics.* New York: Holt, 1915.

——. "Response and Cognition." *Journal of Philosophy, Psychology and Scientific Methods* 12 (July 8, 1915): 365–73 and (July 22, 1915): 393–409.

Homans, George C. *Coming to My Senses: The Autobiography of a Sociologist.* New Brunswick, N.J.: Transaction, 1984.

Homer, Joan Sandra. "Leadership and Organizational Communication: Mary Parker Follett's Contribution to the Understanding of Leadership Development." M.A. thesis, Simon Fraser University, 1978.

Hoopes, James. *Community Denied: The Wrong Turn of Pragmatic Liberalism.* Ithaca: Cornell University Press, 1998.

Horowitz, Helen L. *Alma Mater: Design and Experience in the Women's Colleges from Their Nineteenth-Century Beginnings to the 1930s.* New York: Alfred A. Knopf, 1984.

Hutchinson, Emilie J. "Women and the Ph.D." *Journal of the American Association of University Women* 22 (October 1928): 19–22.

James, Edward T., ed. *Notable American Women, 1607–1950: A Biographical Dictionary.* 3 vols. Cambridge: Harvard University Press, 1971.

Journal of the House of Representatives of the Commonwealth of Massachusetts. Boston: Wright and Potter, 1911.

Karpf, Fay Berger. *American Social Psychology.* 1932; reprint, Dubuque: Brown Reprints, 1971.

Katz, Michael B. "The 'New Departure' in Quincy, 1873–1881: The Nature of Nineteenth-Century Educational Reform." *New England Quarterly,* March 1967, 3–30.

Kaufman, Polly Welts. "Boston Women and School City Politics, 1872–1905: Nurturers and Protectors in Public Education." Ed.D. diss., Boston University, 1978.

Kellogg, Paul U. "Boston's Level Best." *The Survey,* June 5, 1909, 382–96.

Keyssar, Alexander. *Out of Work: The First Century of Unemployment in Massachusetts.* Cambridge: Cambridge University Press, 1986.

Kinney, M. K. "Women's Colleges — The Harvard Annex." *Harper's Bazaar,* October 13, 1888, 683–84.

Kloppenberg, James T. *Uncertain Victory: Social Democracy and Progressivism in European and American Thought, 1870–1920.* New York: Oxford University Press, 1986.

Konopka, Gisela. *Eduard C. Lindeman and Social Work Philosophy.* Minneapolis: University of Minnesota Press, 1958.

Kopp, Claire B., and Martha Kirkpatrick., eds. *Becoming Female: Perspectives on Development.* New York: Plenum, 1979.

Kramnick, Isaac, and Barry Sheerman. *Harold Laski: A Life on the Left.* New York: Allen Lane Penguin Press, 1993.

Kuklick, Bruce. *Josiah Royce.* Indianapolis: Bobbs-Merrill, 1972.

——. *The Rise of American Philosophy: Cambridge, Massachusetts, 1860–1930.* New Haven: Yale University Press, 1977.

Laski, Harold J. *Studies in the Problem of Sovereignty.* New Haven: Yale University Press, 1917.

Lazerson, Marvin. *The Origins of the Urban School: Public Education in Massachusetts, 1870–1915.* Cambridge: Harvard University Press, 1971.

Leonard, Elizabeth Lindeman. *Friendly Rebel: A Personal and Social History of Eduard C. Lindeman.* Adamant, Vt.: Adamant Press, 1991.

Levy, David W. *Herbert Croly of the New Republic.* Princeton: Princeton University Press, 1985.

Lindeman, Eduard C. *The Community: An Introduction to the Study of Community Leadership and Organization.* New York: Association Press, 1921.

——. "Mary Parker Follett." *The Survey,* February 1934, 86–87.

——. *Social Discovery: An Approach to the Functional Study of Groups.* New York: Republic, 1924.

Link, Arthur S., and William B. Catton. *American Epoch: A History of the United States since the 1890s.* New York: Alfred A. Knopf, 1963.

Link, Arthur S., and Richard L. McCormick. *Progressivism.* Arlington Heights, Ill.: Harlan Davidson, 1983.

Mansbridge, Jane. "Mary Parker Follett: Feminist and Negotiator." In Follett, *The New State.* 1998.

Mark, Kenneth L. *Delayed by Fire: Being the Early History of Simmons College.* Concord, N.H.: Rumford, 1945.

Marx, Melvin H., and William A. Cronan-Hillix. *Systems and Theories in Psychology.* 4th ed. New York: McGraw-Hill, 1987.

Massachusetts Board of Education. *Fifty-fifth Annual Report, 1890–1891.* Public Document No. 2. Boston, 1892.

Massachusetts Civic League. *Annual Report.* 1900–1903. Cambridge: Co-operative Press, 1900–1903.

———. *Annual Report for the Year Ending November 30, 1903.* Boston: George H. Ellis, 1904.

———. *Annual Report for the Year Ending October 31, 1911.* Boston: A. T. Bliss, 1911.

———. *Annual Report for Year Ending October 31, 1912.* Boston: A. T. Bliss, 1912.

———. *Annual Report for the Year Ending October 31, 1916.* N.p., n.d.

Mattson, Kevin. *Creating a Democratic Public: The Struggle for Urban Participatory Democracy during the Progressive Era.* University Park: Pennsylvania State University Press, 1998.

———. "Reading Follett: An Introduction to *The New State.*" In Follett, *The New State.* 1998.

Mayo, Elton. "The Basis of Industrial Psychology." *Bulletin of the Taylor Society* 9 (December 1924): 249–59.

McClymer, John F. *War and Welfare: Social Engineering in America, 1890–1925.* Westport, Conn.: Greenwood, 1980.

McCormick, Ada Pierce. "Ella Lyman Cabot." *Radcliffe Quarterly,* July 1935, 156–62.

McCraw, Thomas K. *Prophets of Regulation.* Cambridge: Harvard University Press, 1984.

McDougall, William. *An Introduction to Social Psychology.* 10th ed. 1908; reprint, Boston: John Luce, 1916.

McGrew, Roderick E. *Encyclopedia of Medical History.* New York: McGraw-Hill, 1985.

McQuaid, Kim. "Henry S. Dennison and the 'Science' of Industrial Reform, 1900–1950." *American Journal of Economics and Sociology* 36 (January 1977): 79–98.

McWilliams-Tullberg, Rita. *Women at Cambridge.* London: Victor Gollancz, 1975.

Mead, George Herbert. "Social Psychology, Behaviorism, and the Concept of the Gesture." In *Classical American Philosophy: Essential Readings and Interpretive Essays,* ed. John J. Stuhr. New York: Oxford University Press, 1987.

Merkle, Judith A. "Integrative Management: Applied Neo-Hegelianism in the Writings of Mary Parker Follett." Paper presented at the 45th annual conference of the American Society for Public Administration, Denver, April 1984.

———. *Management and Ideology.* Berkeley: University of California Press, 1980.

Metcalf, Henry C., ed. *Business Management as a Profession.* New York: A. W. Shaw, 1927.

———. *Scientific Foundations of Business Administration.* Baltimore: Williams and Wilkins, 1926.

Miller, Peter, and Ted O'Leary. "Hierarchies and American Ideals, 1900–1940." *Academy of Management Review* 14 (April 1989): 250–65.

Mills, Roger Q. "Mr. Speaker." *North American Review* 154 (January 1892): 1–9.

Montgomery, David. *The Fall of the House of Labor.* Cambridge: Cambridge University Press, 1987.

Morison, Samuel E. "Albert Bushnell Hart (1889–1939)." *Massachusetts Historical Society Proceedings* 66 (October 1936–May 1942): 434–38.

———. *The Development of Harvard University, 1868–1929.* Cambridge: Harvard University Press, 1930.

———. "Edward Channing." *Massachusetts Historical Society Proceedings* 64 (October 1930–June 1932): 250–84.

———. "A Memoir and Estimate of Albert Bushnell Hart." *Massachusetts Historical Society Proceedings* 66 (March 1965): 28–52.

———. *One Boy's Boston, 1887–1901.* 1962; reprint, Boston: Northeastern University Press, 1985.

———. *Three Centuries of Harvard, 1636–1936.* Cambridge: Harvard University Press, 1946.

———, ed. *The Oxford History of the American People.* New York: Oxford University Press, 1965.

Moscovici, Serge. "Social Influence and Conformity." In *Handbook of Social Psychology,* ed. Gardner Lindzey and Eliot Aronson. 3d ed. New York: Random House, 1985.

Mousli, Marc. "Le management selon Mary Parker Follett: Soixante-dix ans d'avance (à ce jour . . .)." *Futuribles* 209 (mai 1996): 69–74.

The National Cyclopaedia of American Biography. 50 vols. Ann Arbor: University Microfilms, 1967.

National Union Catalog, Pre-1956 Imprints. London: Mansell, 1968–1981.

Nelson, Daniel. *Frederick W. Taylor and the Rise of Scientific Management.* Madison: University of Wisconsin Press, 1980.

O'Brien, Sharon. " 'The Thing Not Named': Willa Cather as a Lesbian Writer." *Signs,* summer 1984, 576–99.

Oldfield, Sybil. *Spinsters of This Parish: The Life and Times of F. M. Mayor and Mary Sheepshanks.* London: Virago, 1984.

Overstreet, Harry A. "Reason and the 'Fight Image.' " *New Republic,* December 20, 1922, 94–95.

Paper, Lewis J. *Brandeis.* Englewood Cliffs, N.J.: Prentice-Hall, 1983.

Parker, Gail T. *Mind Cure in New England: From the Civil War to World War I.* Hanover, N.H.: University Press of New England, 1973.

Parker, John Lord. *Henry Wilson's Regiment: History of the Twenty-second Massachusetts Infantry, the Second Company Sharpshooters, and the Third Light Battery in the War of the Rebellion.* Boston: Regimental Association, 1887.

Parker, L. D. "Control in Organizational Life: The Contribution of Mary Parker Follett." *Academy of Management Review* 9 (October 1984): 736–45.

Parkhurst, Helen Huss. "The Nineteenth Annual Meeting of the American Philosophical Association." *Journal of Philosophy, Psychology and Scientific Methods* 17 (January 1920): 94–101.

Patterson, James T. *America in the Twentieth Century: Part One.* New York: Harcourt Brace Jovanovich, 1976.

———. "Mary Dewson and the American Minimum Wage Movement." *Labor History* 5 (spring 1964): 134–52.

Pauline Agassiz Shaw: Tributes Paid to Her Memory at the Memorial Service April 8, 1917. Boston: Privately printed, 1917.

Pearson, Eleanor B. "Harvard Annex Letter." *Wellesley Prelude* 1 (November 2, 1889): 99–101.

Pearson, Henry G. *Son of New England: James Jackson Storrow.* Boston: Thomas Todd, 1932.

Perry, Clarence A. "Ten Years of the Community Center Movement." *Community Center* 3 (September–October 1921): 34, 35, 40.

Person, Harlow S. "The Manager, the Workman, and the Social Scientist." *Bulletin of the Taylor Society* 3 (February 1917): 1–7.

———. "The Manager, the Workman, and the Social Scientist." Discussion. *Bulletin of the Taylor Society* 3 (December 1917): 1–18.

———. "The Opportunities and Obligations of the Taylor Society." *Bulletin of the Taylor Society* 4 (February 1919): 1–7.

———. "Scientific Management." *Bulletin of the Taylor Society* 13 (October 1928): 199–205.

———. "What Is the Taylor Society?" *Bulletin of the Taylor Society* 7 (December 1922): 225–28.

Peters, Ronald M., Jr. *The American Speakership: The Office in Historical Perspective.* Baltimore: Johns Hopkins University Press, 1990.

Phillips, Ann. *A Newnham Anthology.* Cambridge: Cambridge University Press, 1979.

Price, David E. "Community and Control: Critical Democratic Theory in the Progressive Period." *American Political Science Review* 68 (December 1974): 1663–78.

Quandt, Jean B. *From the Small Town to the Great Community: The Social Thought of Progressive Intellectuals.* New Brunswick: Rutgers University Press, 1970.

Quincy, Josiah. "The Development of American Cities." *The Arena* 17 (March 1897): 529–37.

Randall, Mercedes. *Improper Bostonian: Emily Greene Balch.* New York: Twayne, 1964.

Reed, Thomas B. "Obstructions in the National House." *North American Review* 149 (October 1889): 421–28.

Reese, William J. *Power and the Promise of School Reform: Grass-Roots Movements during the Progressive Era.* Boston: Routledge and Kegan Paul, 1986.

Report of the Division of Minimum Wage: Reprint from the Annual Report of the Department of Labor and Industries for the Year Ending November 30. 1920–1923. Boston: Wright and Potter, 1921–1924.

Rice, Arnold S., and John A. Krout. *United States History from 1865.* 20th ed. New York: Harper Perennial, 1991.

Richter, Melvin. *The Politics of Conscience: T. H. Green and His Age.* 1964; reprint, Lanham, Md.: University Press of America, 1983.

Rodgers, Daniel T. "In Search of Progressivism." *Reviews in American History* 10 (December 1982): 113–32.

Rogers, Helen W. "The Placement Bureau." *Bulletin: The Women's Municipal League of Boston,* December 1912, 18–37.

Roosevelt, Theodore. "Thomas Brackett Reed and the Fifty-first Congress." *The Forum* 20 (December 1895): 410–18.

Rose, Phyllis. *Writing of Women: Essays in a Renaissance.* Middletown: Wesleyan University Press, 1985.

Rosenberg, Charles E. *The Cholera Years: The U.S. in 1832, 1849, and 1866.* Chicago: University of Chicago Press, 1962.

Ross, Dorothy. *The Origins of American Social Science.* Cambridge: Cambridge University Press, 1991.

Ross, Edward A. *Social Psychology.* New York: Macmillan, 1911.

Schwager, Sally. " 'Harvard Women': A History of the Founding of Radcliffe College." Ed.D. diss., Harvard University, 1982.

Seilhamer, George O. *Leslie's History of the Republican Party.* 2 vols. New York: Judge, 1898.

Sheffield, Ada E. "Three Interviews and the Changing Situation." *Journal of Social Forces* 2 (September 1924): 692–97.

Sheppard, James J. "Municipal Civics in Elementary and High Schools." In *Proceedings of the Conference for Good City Government and Annual Meeting of the National Municipal League.* Philadelphia: National Municipal League, 1909: 366–79.

Shorter, Edward. *Bedside Manners: The Troubled History of Doctors and Patients.* New York: Simon and Schuster, 1985.

Sicherman, Barbara. *Alice Hamilton: A Life in Letters.* Cambridge: Harvard University Press, 1984.

Sicherman, Barbara, and Carol Hurd Green, eds. *Notable American Women: The Modern Period.* Cambridge: Harvard University Press, 1980.

Sills, David L., ed. *International Encyclopedia of the Social Sciences.* 18 vols. New York: Macmillan, 1968.

Simkhovitch, Mary Kingsbury. *Neighborhood: My Story of Greenwich House.* New York: W. W. Norton, 1938.

Slee, Peter R. H. "History as a Discipline in the Universities of Oxford and Cambridge, 1848–1914." Ph.D. diss., Emmanuel College, Cambridge University, 1983.

Slicer, Thomas R. "The School City as a Form of Government." In *Proceedings of the Chicago Conference for Good City Government and the Tenth Annual Meeting of the National Municipal League,* ed. Clinton R. Woodruff. Philadelphia: National Municipal League, 1904: 283–93.

Smith-Rosenberg, Carroll. *Disorderly Conduct: Visions of Gender in Victorian America.* New York: Alfred A. Knopf, 1985.

———. "The Female World of Love and Ritual: Relations between Women in Nineteenth-Century America." *Signs,* autumn 1975, 1–29.

———. "The Hysterical Woman: Sex Roles and Role Conflict in Nineteenth-Century America." *Social Research* 39 (winter 1972): 652–78.

Society to Encourage Studies at Home. *Memorial Volume.* Cambridge, Mass.: Riverside, 1897.

Solomon, Barbara M. *Ancestors and Immigrants: A Changing New England Tradition.* 1956; reprint, Chicago: University of Chicago Press, 1972.

———. *In the Company of Educated Women.* New Haven: Yale University Press, 1985.

Somjee, A. H. *The Political Theory of John Dewey.* New York: Teachers College Press, 1968.

Sprague, Blanche H. "In Memory of Anna Boynton Thompson." *Thayer Academy Alumni Bulletin, 75th Anniversary Memorial Edition,* 1952: 16–17.

Stawell, F. Melian. "Mary Parker Follett." *Newnham College Roll Letter,* January 1935, 39–44.

Stever, James. "Mary Parker Follett and the Quest for Pragmatic Administration." *Administration and Society* 18 (August 1986): 159–77.

Stewart, David W. *Adult Learning in America: Eduard Lindeman and His Agenda for Lifelong Education.* Malabar, Fla.: R. E. Krieger, 1987.

Strachey, Ray. *Millicent Garrett Fawcett.* London: John Murray, 1931.

Strom, Sharon Hartman. "Leadership and Tactics in the American Woman Suffrage Movement: A New Perspective from Massachusetts." *Journal of American History* 62 (September 1975): 296–315.

Strouse, Jean. *Alice James: A Biography.* 1980; reprint, New York: Bantam, 1982.

Stuhr, John J., ed. *Classical American Philosophy: Essential Readings and Interpretive Essays.* New York: Oxford University Press, 1987.

Tharp, Louise Hall. *Adventurous Alliance: The Story of the Agassiz Family of Boston.* Boston: Little, Brown, 1959.

Thomas, John L. "Nationalizing the Republic, 1877–1920." In Bailyn et al., *The Great Republic,* 542–695.

Thompson, Anna Boynton. "How to Study History." *Educational Review* 17 (1899): 169–77.

———. *The Unity of Fichte's Doctrine of Knowledge.* Boston: Ginn, 1895.

Tonn, Joan C. "Follett's Forgotten Book: The Speaker of the House of Representatives." Paper presented at the annual meeting of the Academy of Management, Boston, August 1984.

———. "Mary Parker Follett." In *American National Biography,* ed. John A. Garraty and Mark C. Carnes. 24 vols. New York: Oxford University Press, 1999: 8: 174–77.

———. "Follett's Challenge for Us All." *Organization* 3 (February 1996): 167–74.

Trahair, Richard C. S. *The Humanist Temper: The Life and Work of Elton Mayo.* New Brunswick, N.J.: Transaction, 1984.

Trout, Charles W. "Curley of Boston: The Search for Irish Legitimacy." In *Boston, 1700–1980: The Evolution of Urban Politics,* ed. Ronald P. Formisano and Constance K. Burns. Westport, Conn.: Greenwood, 1984.

Turgot, A. R. J. *Reflections on the Formation and the Distribution of Riches,* ed. William James Ashley. New York: Macmillan, 1898.

Tyack, David B. *The One Best System: A History of American Urban Education.* Cambridge: Harvard University Press, 1974.

Urban, Wilbur. "The Nature of Community." *Philosophical Review* 28 (November 1919): 547–61.

Urwick, Lyndall F. "Mary Follett: A Philosophy of Management." *Industry Illustrated,* May 1934, 18–20.

———. "The Problem of Organization: A Study of the Work of Mary Parker Follett." *Bulletin of the Taylor Society and of the Society of Industrial Engineers as Members of Federated Management Societies* 1(July 1935): 163–69.

Vicinus, Martha. "Distance and Desire: English Boarding School Friendships." *Signs,* summer 1984, 600–22.

———. *Independent Women: Work and Community for Single Women, 1850–1920.* Chicago: University of Chicago Press, 1985.

——. " 'One Life to Stand beside Me': Emotional Conflicts in First-Generation College Women in England." *Feminist Studies* 8 (fall 1982): 602–28.

Vogel, Morris. J. *The Invention of the Modern Hospital: Boston, 1870–1930.* Chicago: University of Chicago Press, 1980.

Wakerman, Elyce. *Father Loss.* Garden City, N.Y.: Doubleday, 1984.

Wallas, Graham. *The Great Society.* New York: Macmillan, 1914.

Walton, John, Paul Beeson, and Sir Ronald Scott, eds., *The Oxford Companion to Medicine.* Vol. 2. Oxford: Oxford University Press, 1986.

Ward, Edward J. *The Social Center.* New York: Appleton, 1913.

Warner, Sam Bass. *Province of Reason.* Cambridge: Harvard University Press, 1984.

——. *Streetcar Suburbs: The Process of Growth in Boston (1870–1900).* 2d ed. Cambridge: Harvard University Press, 1978.

Wentworth, Lillian. *The Thayer Academy, One Hundred Years, 1877–1977.* Braintree, Mass.: Thayer Academy, 1977.

Westbrook, Robert B. *John Dewey and American Democracy.* Ithaca: Cornell University Press, 1991.

Whetten, David A., and Kim S. Cameron. *Developing Management Skills.* 4th ed. Reading, Mass.: Addison-Wesley, 1998.

White, Morton. *Pragmatism and the American Mind.* New York: Oxford University Press, 1973.

——. *Social Thought in America.* Boston: Beacon, 1957.

White, Paul Dudley. "Richard Clarke Cabot." *New England Journal of Medicine* 220 (June 22, 1939): 1049–52.

Wiener, Martin J. *Between Two Worlds: The Political Thought of Graham Wallas.* Oxford: Clarendon Press, 1971.

Wilson, D. M. *Three Hundred Years of Quincy.* Quincy, Mass.: City Government, 1926.

Wilson, Woodrow. *Cabinet Government in the United States.* 1879; reprint, Stamford, Conn.: Overbrook, 1947.

——. *Congressional Government.* 1885; reprint, Baltimore: Johns Hopkins University Press, 1981.

——. "The Social Center: A Means of Common Understanding." *Bulletin of the University of Wisconsin,* Serial No. 470, General Series No. 306 (December 1911): 3–15.

Winsor, Justin. "With Bradford and Harvard." *The Nation,* January 22, 1891, 67–68.

Wood, Ann Douglas. " 'The Fashionable Diseases': Women's Complaints and Their Treatment in Nineteenth-Century America." *Journal of Interdisciplinary History* 4 (summer 1973): 25–52.

Wood, Arthur Evans. "The Social Philosophy of Mary P. Follett." *Social Forces* 4 (June 1926): 759–69.

Woods, Robert A., and Albert J. Kennedy. *Handbook of Settlements.* Philadelphia: Russell Sage Foundation, 1911.

——. *The Zone of Emergence: Observations of the Lower Middle and Upper Working Class Communities of Boston, 1904–1914,* ed. Sam Bass Warner Jr. 2d ed. Cambridge: Massachusetts Institute of Technology Press, 1962.

Woodworth, Robert S., and Mary R. Sheehan. *Contemporary Schools of Psychology.* 3d ed. New York: Ronald, 1964.

Woolf, Virginia. *Letters of Virginia Woolf,* ed. Nigel Nicholson. Vol. 1: *1888–1912.* Vol. 5: *1932–35.* New York: Harcourt Brace Jovanovich, 1975.

——. *Diary of Virginia Woolf,* ed. Anne O. Bell. Vol. 4. New York: Harcourt Brace Jovanovich, 1982.

Wormell, Deborah. *Sir John Seeley and the Uses of History.* Cambridge: Cambridge University Press, 1980.

Worrell, Dorothy. *The Women's Municipal League of Boston: A History of Thirty-five Years of Civic Endeavor.* Boston: Women's Municipal League Committees, 1943.

Wren, Daniel A. *The Evolution of Management Thought.* 4th ed. New York: John Wiley and Sons, 1994.

Young, Michael. *The Elmhirsts of Dartington.* London: Routledge and Kegan Paul, 1982.

Zolot, Herbert Marshall. "The Issue of Good Government and James Michael Curley: Curley and the Boston Scene from 1897–1918." Ph.D. diss., State University of New York at Stony Brook, 1975.

Index

Page numbers in italics refer to illustrations.

about democracy and, 287–89; neighborhood groups and, 289–92, 320–21; pluralism and, 292–98; uncertainty in group creation and, 298–301; Massachusetts Minimum Wage Commission and, 325–27

Interacting, 437, 440, 443–44

Interest groups: Follett's experience with lobbying and, 115–16; pluralism and, 296–97

Interests: law as integrator of, 363–65; "equilibrium" of, 364; "revaluation" of, 380. *See also* Integration of differences

Intergroup relations: coordination of, 182; neighborhood groups and, 292. *See also* Women's Municipal League

International Management Institute, 455, 472

International relations. *See* League of Nations; World War I, peace negotiations

Interpenetration: vs. imitation, 274–75; sovereignty and, 296–97; community as process and, 319. *See also* Integrative group process

Interview methodology: Speakership investigation and, 81–82; Ward 17 and, 136–37

Interweaving of function, 416–17

James, William, 121, 270, 293, 298, 299, 366–67, 450

Job analysis, 402

Johns Hopkins University, 109

Jones, Daniel Fiske, 340–41, 355, 409, 487

Joslin, Elliott, 340–41

Jung, Carl, 463

Junior city councils, 169–71

Justice, 434, 435–36. *See also* Law

Kant, Immanuel, 549n.35

Kanter, Rosabeth Moss, 1

Karpf, Fay Berger, 549n.40

Kaufman, Polly Welts, 165

Kelley, Florence, 323, 550n.57

Kempf, Edward J., 373

Kennedy, Albert J., 138, 542n.26

Kennedy, Patrick J., 523n.45

Keynes, John Maynard, 61, 451

Keyssar, Alexander, 199–200

King, Charles F., 156

Kloppenberg, James T., 298–99

Koffka, Kurt, 366

Köhler, Wolfgang, 366

Konopka, Gisela, 331

Kropotkin, Petr, 280, 549n.34

Kuklick, Bruce, 120

Labor-management relations: postwar labor unrest and, 397–98, 401; collective bargaining and, 401, 405–6; collective responsibility and, 401–3; scientific management and, 401–3, 404; in England, 422, 425, 427–28; concept of participation and, 439–40; mediation and, 440–41, 448–50. *See also* Employee representation

LaFollette, Robert, 542n.27

Lahey, Frank H., 486, 488, 489

Lane, Franklin K., 311

Language, use of, 399

Larsson, Gustav, 507n.44

Laski, Harold J., 317, 387–88; Follett's *The New State* and, 263–64, 293, 305–7, 308

Lasswell, Harold D., 430, 435

Law: modern theory of, 282–83; as integrator of interests, 363–64

Law of the situation: Speakership and, 92; business management and, 400, 405. *See also* Total situation concept

Lazerson, Marvin, 157

Leadership: democracy and, 135–36; in social centers, 240–43; training and, 242–43, 314; of NCCA, 247–48, 249–50; integrative group process and, 290–91; qualities needed for good, 418–19, 420, 447–48; throughout the organization, 419, 441–44, 448–50;